MW00636192

Prepare for your future!
Studying management will help you build life-long skills for college and career.

Jumpstart Your Future

As you prepare for college and career, the skills you gain from studying this text will help jumpstart your future. *Principles of Management* is a contemporary text that presents management concepts that are vitally important for success in today's workplace.

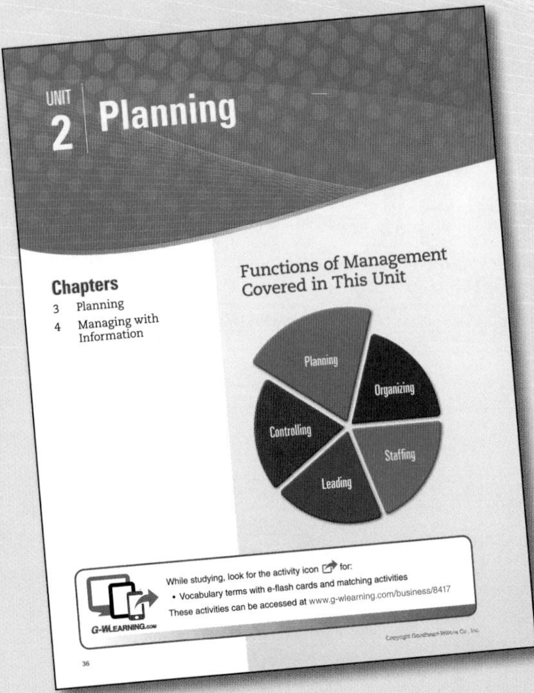

UNIT 2 Planning

Chapters

3 Planning

4 Managing with Information

Functions of Management Covered in This Unit

While studying, look for the activity icon for:

- Vocabulary terms with e-flash cards and matching activities

These activities can be accessed at www.g-wlearning.com/business/8417

G-WLEARNING.com

Copyright Goodheart-Willcox Co., Inc.

36

Content is presented in an easy-to-comprehend and relevant format. Topics are arranged in a logical progression. Learning the functions of management is one of the main goals of the text. Each unit focuses on a function of management, providing full coverage before progressing to the next one. Effective managers master the five basic functions of management: planning, organizing, staffing, leading, and controlling.

Each unit opener identifies the specific **function of management** that will be covered. This approach to learning helps you:

- focus on one function at a time to comprehend it in its entirety;
- learn basics about management to build mastery; and
- grasp each function of management by the conclusion of the text.

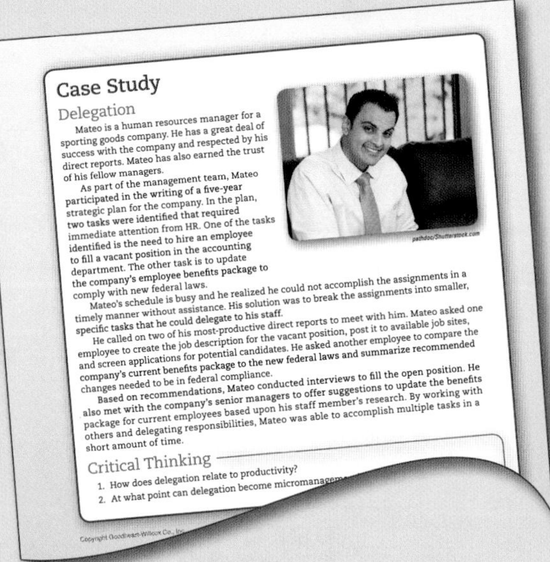

Case Study

Delegation

Mateo is a human resources manager for a sporting goods company. He has a great deal of success with the company and respected by his direct reports. Mateo has also earned the trust of his fellow managers.

As part of the management team, Mateo participated in the writing of a five-year strategic plan for the company. In the plan, two tasks were identified that required immediate attention from HR. One of the tasks identified is the need to hire an employee to fill a vacant position in the accounting department. The other task is to update the company's employee benefits package to comply with new federal laws.

Mateo's schedule is busy and he realized he could not accomplish the assignments in a timely manner without assistance. His solution was to break the assignments into smaller, specific tasks that he could delegate to his staff.

He called on two of his most-productive direct reports to meet with him. Mateo asked one employee to create the job description for the vacant position, post it to available job sites, and screen applications for potential candidates. He asked another employee to compare the company's current benefits package to the new federal laws and summarize recommended changes needed to be in federal compliance.

Based on recommendations, Mateo conducted interviews to fill the open position. He also met with the company's senior managers to offer suggestions to update the benefits package for current employees based upon his staff member's research. By working with others and delegating responsibilities, Mateo was able to accomplish multiple tasks in a short amount of time.

pathdoc/Shutterstock.com

Critical Thinking

1. How does delegation relate to productivity?
2. At what point can delegation become micromanagem

Copyright Goodheart-Willcox Co., Inc.

Did you ever wonder what it is like to be a manager in the business world? Managers assume a lot of responsibility. Practical activities relate everyday learning to enable you to experience real-life scenarios.

A **case study** in the unit opener presents a management situation that challenges you to answer thought-provoking questions about real-world situations. These cases will help you understand the connection between management theory and application.

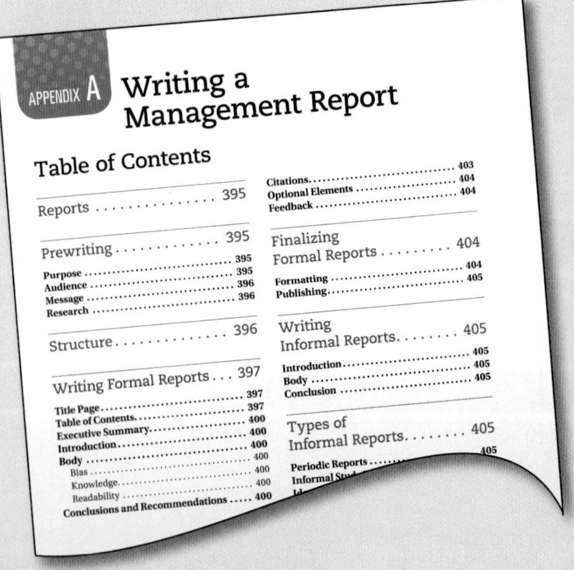

APPENDIX A Writing a Management Report

Table of Contents

How are your writing skills? An important skill for managers to learn and develop is writing. There are many types of reports written that represent the organization and its mission. Learning to write a report for management is a necessity.

The **Writing a Management Report** appendix delivers detailed information needed to create professional-looking reports. The content provides guidance to write management reports needed for business.

Maximize the Impact

It is all about getting ready for college and career. College and career readiness activities address literacy skills to help prepare you for the real world.

- English/Language Arts standards for reading, writing, speaking, and listening are incorporated in **Reading Prep** activities, as well as in end-of-chapter applications. These activities provide ways for you to demonstrate the literacy and career readiness skills you have mastered.
- **Exploring Careers** features present information about potential career opportunities in the Business, Management, & Administration career cluster. By studying these features, you can investigate career possibilities for your future.
- **Portfolio Development** activities provide guidance to create a personal portfolio for use when exploring volunteer, education and training, and career opportunities.

College and Career Readiness

Reading Prep
Before reading, turn to the opening pages of this unit and read the chapter titles. By previewing the chapter titles, you can prepare for the topics presented in the unit. What do the titles reveal about what you will be learning?

Exploring Careers

Business Management & Administration

Chief Executive Officer

In most businesses, the chief executive officer (CEO) is the person in charge. They hold the highest position within an organization and often have the most authority. CEOs are responsible for creating strategies and policies for a business as a whole. They collaborate with and direct the work of other top executives, such as chief financial officers. Their main responsibility is providing the overall direction of an organization established by a company's board of directors.

Typical job titles for this position include *chief executive, managing director, executive director,* and *president*. Examples of tasks that chief executive officers perform include

- managing and analyzing company operations;
- appointing department heads and managers;
- working closely with the board of directors; and
- formulating and implementing policies.

A chief executive officer position requires a bachelor degree; however, a postgraduate degree may be required. CEOs must have effective leadership and communication skills as well as strong decision-making and problem-solving skills. In addition, they should have a considerable amount of previous managerial experience.

College and Career Readiness

Portfolio Development

Writing Samples. As you collect academic samples to include in your portfolio, you may want to emphasize samples of your best writing. Writing skills are necessary for success in every part of life including academics and career. Regardless of occupation, industry, or position, at some point, every job will require written communication. Even jobs that are not done on a computer require writing skills. For example, an automotive mechanic or welder will undoubtedly have to write or summarize the scope of work for a given job. It is important to demonstrate your ability to communicate ideas and information through the written word.

As you review documents, collect those that highlight your writing skills. Select items you have written, such as essays, stories, or poems. Each person is different in terms of writing styles. Some can be as unique as a fingerprint. Focus on selecting items that not only positively demonstrate your writing abilities but also provide a glimpse of your signature writing style.

1. Select writing examples that demonstrate your writing style. Be critical and choose your best creative writing sample, an article you have written for the school newspaper, or other documents of which you are proud.
2. For each document, attach a note that (1) describes what the sample is and (2) states why it is included in your portfolio. For example, a note on an article you ...
3. Update your master portfolio spreadsh...

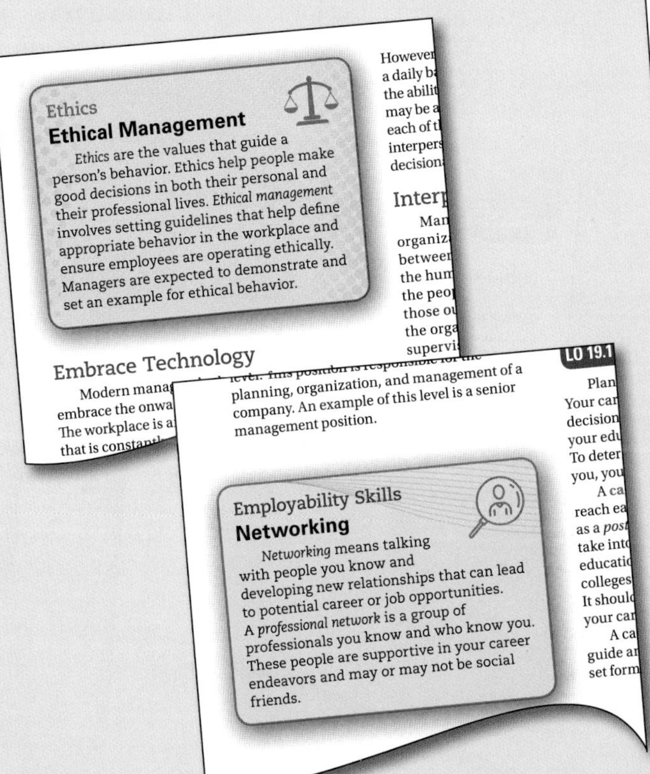

Ethics

Ethical Management

Ethics are the values that guide a person's behavior. Ethics help people make good decisions in both their personal and their professional lives. *Ethical management* involves setting guidelines that help define appropriate behavior in the workplace and ensure employees are operating ethically. Managers are expected to demonstrate and set an example for ethical behavior.

Embrace Technology

Employability Skills

Networking

Networking means talking with people you know and developing new relationships that can lead to potential career or job opportunities. A *professional network* is a group of professionals you know and who know you. These people are supportive in your career endeavors and may or may not be social friends.

Practical information helps you prepare for your future. Special features add realism and interest to enhance learning.

- **Ethics** offers insight into ethical issues with which you will be confronted in the workplace as well as tips on how to make ethical decisions.
- **Employability Skills** features review essential soft skills needed for success in the workplace.

Amplify Your Learning

Content is presented in an easy-to-comprehend and relevant format. Practical activities relate everyday learning to enable you to experience real-life situations and challenges.

- The **Essential Question** at the beginning of each section will engage you as you uncover the important points presented in the content.
- A **You Do the Math** activity in each chapter focuses on skills that are important to your understanding of math for business. You will be provided an opportunity to apply math concepts in the context of business applications.

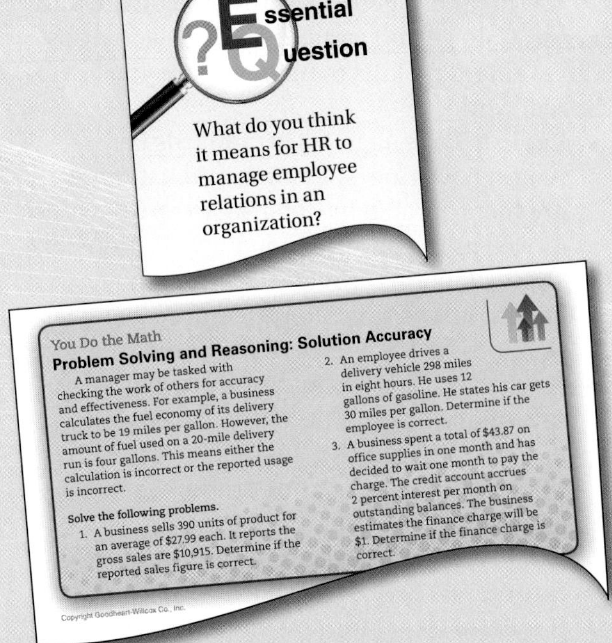

Essential Question

What do you think it means for HR to manage employee relations in an organization?

You Do the Math

Problem Solving and Reasoning: Solution Accuracy

A manager may be tasked with checking the work of others for accuracy and effectiveness. For example, a business calculates the fuel economy of its delivery truck to be 19 miles per gallon. However, the amount of fuel used on a 20-mile delivery run is four gallons. This means either the calculation is incorrect or the reported usage is incorrect.

Solve the following problems.

1. A business sells 390 units of product for an average of $27.99 each. It reports the gross sales are $10,915. Determine if the reported sales figure is correct.
2. An employee drives a delivery vehicle 298 miles in eight hours. He uses 12 gallons of gasoline. He states his car gets 30 miles per gallon. Determine if the employee is correct.
3. A business spent a total of $43.87 on office supplies in one month and has decided to wait one month to pay the charge. The credit account accrues 2 percent interest per month on outstanding balances. The business estimates the finance charge will be $1. Determine if the finance charge is correct.

Copyright Goodheart-Willcox Co., Inc.

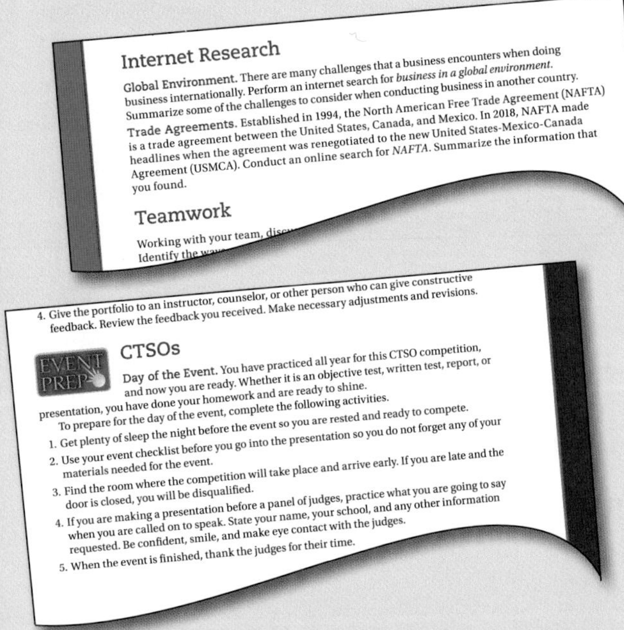

Internet Research

Global Environment. There are many challenges that a business encounters when doing business internationally. Perform an internet search for *business in a global environment*. Summarize some of the challenges to consider when conducting business in another country.

Trade Agreements. Established in 1994, the North American Free Trade Agreement (NAFTA) is a trade agreement between the United States, Canada, and Mexico. In 2018, NAFTA made headlines when the agreement was renegotiated to the new United States-Mexico-Canada Agreement (USMCA). Conduct an online search for *NAFTA*. Summarize the information that you found.

Teamwork

Working with your team,

4. Give the portfolio to an instructor, counselor, or other person who can give constructive feedback. Review the feedback you received. Make necessary adjustments and revisions.

EVENT PREP

CTSOs

Day of the Event. You have practiced all year for this CTSO competition, and now you are ready. Whether it is an objective test, written test, report, or presentation, you have done your homework and are ready to shine.

To prepare for the day of the event, complete the following activities.

1. Get plenty of sleep the night before the event so you are rested and ready to compete.
2. Use your event checklist before you go into the presentation so you do not forget any of your materials needed for the event.
3. Find the room where the competition will take place and arrive early. If you are late and the door is closed, you will be disqualified.
4. If you are making a presentation before a panel of judges, practice what you are going to say when you are called on to speak. State your name, your school, and any other information requested. Be confident, smile, and make eye contact with the judges.
5. When the event is finished, thank the judges for their time.

- Research skills are critical for college and career. **Internet Research** activities at the end of each chapter provide opportunities to put them to work.
- **Event Prep** presents information to use when preparing for competitive activities in career and technical student organization (CTSO) competitions.

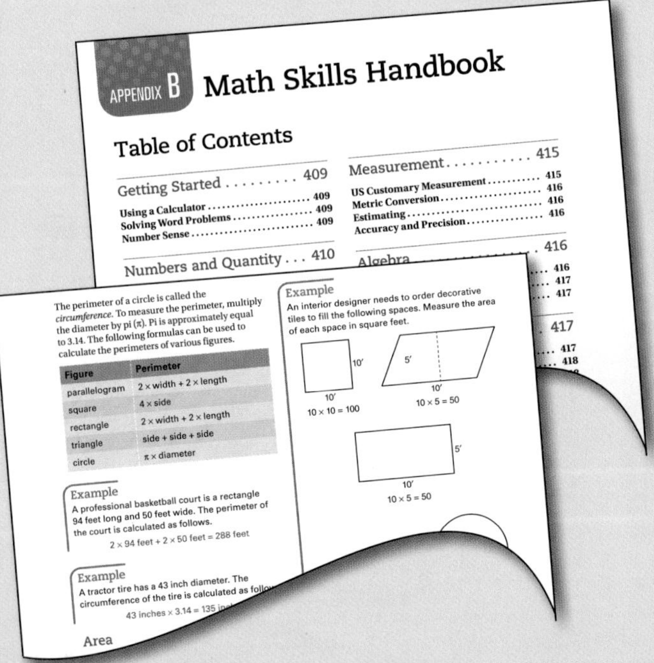

APPENDIX B Math Skills Handbook

Table of Contents

The perimeter of a circle is called the *circumference*. To measure the perimeter, multiply the diameter by pi (π). Pi is approximately equal to 3.14. The following formulas can be used to calculate the perimeters of various figures.

Figure	Perimeter
parallelogram	2 × width + 2 × length
square	4 × side
rectangle	2 × width + 2 × length
triangle	side + side + side
circle	π × diameter

Example

A professional basketball court is a rectangle 94 feet long and 50 feet wide. The perimeter of the court is calculated as follows.

2 × 94 feet + 2 × 50 feet = 288 feet

Example

A tractor tire has a 43 inch diameter. The circumference of the tire is calculated as follows.

43 inches × 3.14 = 135 in

Area

Example

An interior designer needs to order decorative tiles to fill the following spaces. Measure the area of each space in square feet.

- A **Math Skills Handbook** appendix provides you with a quick reference for basic math functions. This helpful information will help clarify business math that is presented in the chapters.

Assess Your Progress

It is important to assess what you learn as you progress through the textbook. Multiple opportunities are provided to confirm learning as you explore the content. *Formative assessment* includes the following:

- **Check Your Understanding** questions at the end of each section of the chapter provide an opportunity to review what you have learned before moving on to additional content.
- **Build Your Vocabulary** activities review the key terms presented in each section. By completing these activities, you will be able to demonstrate your understanding of management terms.

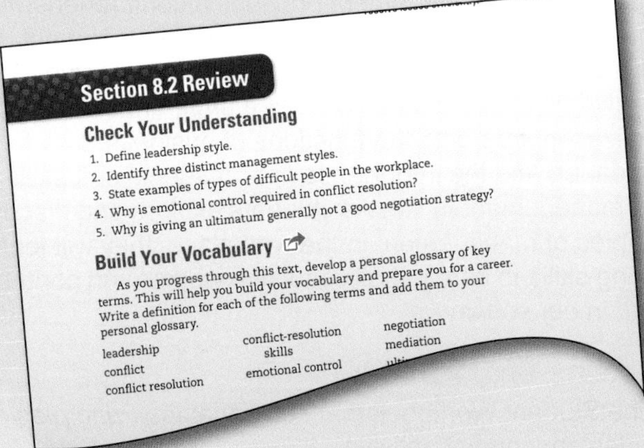

Section 8.2 Review

Check Your Understanding

1. Define leadership style.
2. Identify three distinct management styles.
3. State examples of types of difficult people in the workplace.
4. Why is emotional control required in conflict resolution?
5. Why is giving an ultimatum generally not a good negotiation strategy?

Build Your Vocabulary

As you progress through this text, develop a personal glossary of key terms. This will help you build your vocabulary and prepare you for a career. Write a definition for each of the following terms and add them to your personal glossary.

leadership
conflict
conflict resolution
conflict-resolution skills
emotional control
negotiation
mediation

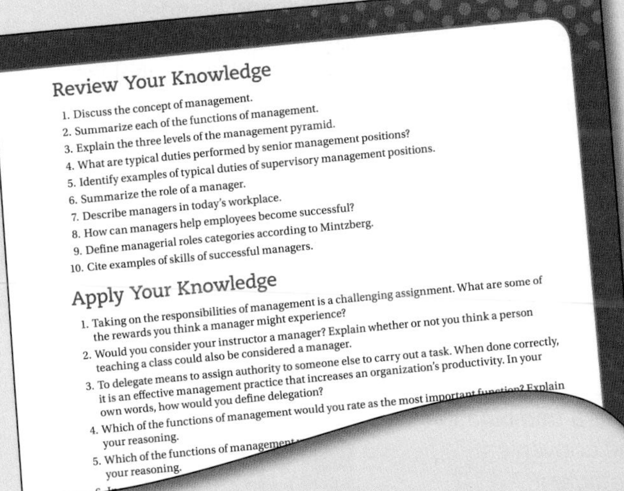

Review Your Knowledge

1. Discuss the concept of management.
2. Summarize each of the functions of management.
3. Explain the three levels of the management pyramid.
4. What are typical duties performed by senior management positions?
5. Identify examples of typical duties of supervisory management positions.
6. Summarize the role of a manager.
7. Describe managers in today's workplace.
8. How can managers help employees become successful?
9. Define managerial roles categories according to Mintzberg.
10. Cite examples of skills of successful managers.

Apply Your Knowledge

1. Taking on the responsibilities of management is a challenging assignment. What are some of the rewards you think a manager might experience?
2. Would you consider your instructor a manager? Explain whether or not you think a person teaching a class could also be considered a manager.
3. To delegate means to assign authority to someone else to carry out a task. When done correctly, it is an effective management practice that increases an organization's productivity. In your own words, how would you define delegation?
4. Which of the functions of management would you rate as the most important function? Explain your reasoning.
5. Which of the functions of management... your reasoning.

- **Review Your Knowledge** activities cover the basic concepts presented in the chapter so you can evaluate your understanding of the material.
- **Apply Your Knowledge** activities challenge you to relate what you learned in the chapter with your own ideas, experiences, and goals.
- **Communication Skills** activities provide ways for you to demonstrate the literacy and career readiness skills you have mastered.
- **Teamwork** activities encourage a collaborative experience to help you learn how to interact with other students in a productive manner.

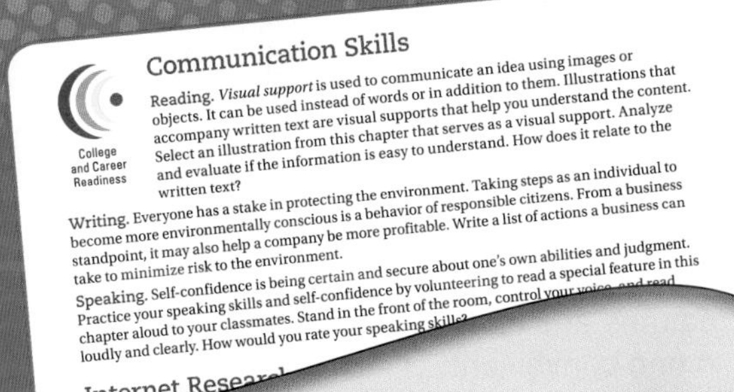

Communication Skills

College and Career Readiness

Reading. *Visual support* is used to communicate an idea using images or objects. It can be used instead of words or in addition to them. Illustrations that accompany written text are visual supports that help you understand the content. Select an illustration from this chapter that serves as a visual support. Analyze and evaluate if the information is easy to understand. How does it relate to the written text?

Writing. Everyone has a stake in protecting the environment. Taking steps as an individual to become more environmentally conscious is a behavior of responsible citizens. From a business standpoint, it may also help a company be more profitable. Write a list of actions a business can take to minimize risk to the environment.

Speaking. Self-confidence is being certain and secure about one's own abilities and judgment. Practice your speaking skills and self-confidence by volunteering to read a special feature in this chapter aloud to your classmates. Stand in the front of the room, control your voice, and read loudly and clearly. How would you rate your speaking skills?

Internet Resea...

in all areas of business. They help guide both managers and employees to make correct decisions for a company. Search for *ethical workplace behavior.* Explain in your own words what it means to behave ethically in the workplace.

Contemporary Ethics Cases. Research a contemporary case of a business dealing with a violation of ethics or social responsibility. Begin by searching for *business ethics violation* plus the current year, or a similar phrase. Summarize the situation and explain why it is an issue of ethics or social responsibility and explain what you think the best solution would be.

Teamwork

Working with your team, create chart to use as a visual aid to explain the advantages and disadvantages of types of organizational structures. Create a four-column chart and label each of the columns *Line, Line-and-Staff, Matrix,* and *Team.* List the advantages and disadvantages of each organizational structure in the appropriate column. Then, use this chart as a visual aid to explain each type of organizational structure to the class.

90

TOOLS FOR STUDENT AND INSTRUCTOR SUCCESS

Student Tools

Student Text

Principles of Management provides a comprehensive framework to learn about the functions of management. By studying this text, students learn about the responsibilities and rewards of being a manager in a profit or not-for-profit organization. Learning the functions of business, how to be a leader, and the importance of managerial soft skills bring management to life. As students explore and discover principles of management in the workplace, they will learn life-long skills to become a productive worker and contributing citizen in our society.

Student Workbook

The Student Workbook that accompanies *Principles of Management* reinforces the concepts in the text and provides enrichment activities.

Online Learning Suite

The Online Learning Suite provides the foundation of instruction and learning for digital and blended classrooms. An easy-to-manage shared classroom subscription makes it a hassle-free solution for both students and instructors. An online student text and workbook, along with rich supplemental content, brings digital learning to the classroom. All instructional materials are found on a convenient online bookshelf and accessible at home, at school, or on the go.

G-W Companion Website

The G-W Learning companion website is a study reference that contains e-flash cards and vocabulary exercises. The companion website is accessible from any digital device.

Online Learning Suite/Student Text Bundle

Looking for a blended solution? Goodheart-Willcox offers the Online Learning Suite bundled with the printed text in one easy-to-access package. Students have the flexibility to use the printed text, the Online Learning Suite, or a combination of both components to meet their individual learning styles. The convenient packaging makes managing and accessing content easy and efficient.

Instructor Tools

LMS Integration

Integrate Goodheart-Willcox content within your Learning Management System for a seamless user experience for both you and your students. LMS-ready content in Common Cartridge format facilitates single sign-on integration and gives you control of student enrollment and data. With a Common Cartridge integration, you can access the LMS features and tools you are accustomed to using and G-W course resources in one convenient location—your LMS.

To provide a complete learning package for you and your students, G-W Common Cartridge includes the Online Learning Suite and Online Instructor Resources. When you incorporate G-W content into your courses via Common Cartridge, you have the flexibility to customize and structure the content to meet the educational needs of your students. You may also choose to add your own content to the course.

QTI® question banks are available within the Online Instructor Resources for import into your LMS. These prebuilt assessments help you measure student knowledge and track results in your LMS gradebook. Questions and tests can be customized to meet your assessment needs.

Online Instructor Resources (OIR)

Online Instructor Resources provide all the support needed to make preparation and classroom instruction easier than ever. Available in one location, the OIR includes Instructor Resources, Instructor's Presentations for PowerPoint®, and Assessment Software with Question Banks. The OIR is available as a subscription and can be accessed at school, at home, or on the go.

Instructor Resources One resource provides instructors with time-saving preparation tools such as answer keys, chapter outlines, editable lesson plans, and other teaching aids.

Instructor's Presentations for PowerPoint® These fully customizable presentations for PowerPoint® provide a useful teaching tool for presenting concepts introduced in the text. Richly illustrated slides help you teach and visually reinforce the key concepts from each chapter.

Assessment Software with Question Banks Administer and manage assessments to meet your classroom needs. The question banks that accompany this textbook include hundreds of matching, true/false, completion, multiple choice, and short answer questions to assess student knowledge of the content in each chapter. Using the assessment software simplifies the process of creating, managing, administering, and grading tests. You can have the software generate a test for you with randomly selected questions. You may also choose specific questions from the question banks and, if you wish, add your own questions to create customized tests to meet your classroom needs.

G-W Integrated Learning Solution

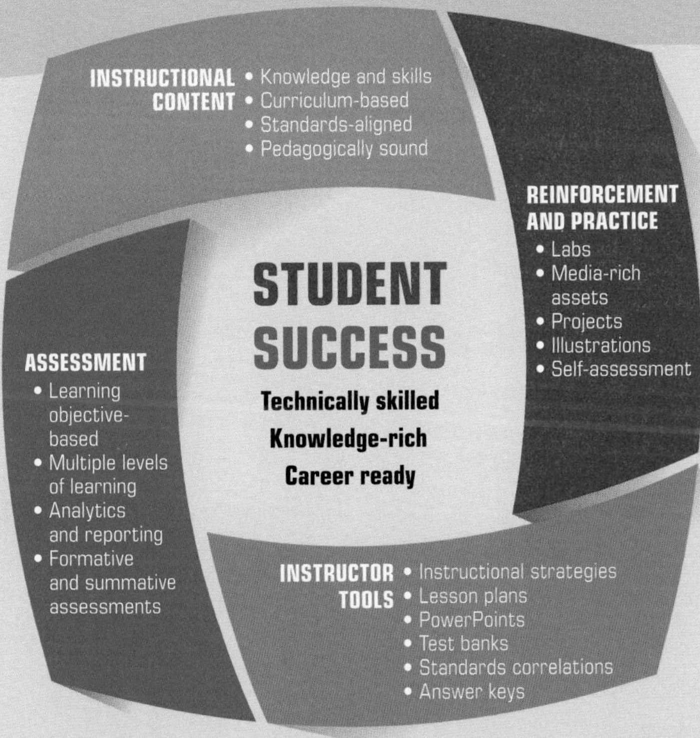

The G-W Integrated Learning Solution offers easy-to-use resources that help students and instructors achieve success.

- **EXPERT AUTHORS**
- **TRUSTED REVIEWERS**
- **100 YEARS OF EXPERIENCE**

EMPLOYABILITY SKILLS · TECHNICAL SKILLS · ACADEMIC KNOWLEDGE · INDUSTRY RECOGNIZED STANDARDS

Principles of Management

Robert L. Dansby, PhD

Chairperson of the Division of Business and Social Sciences
Instructor of Business
Chattahoochee Valley Community College
Phenix City, Alabama

Karel Sovak, PhD

Associate Professor
Gary Tharaldson School of Business
The University of Mary Grosse
Bismarck, North Dakota

Publisher
The Goodheart-Willcox Company, Inc.
Tinley Park, Illinois
www.g-w.com

Manufactured in the United States of America.

ISBN 978-1-63563-841-7

1 2 3 4 5 6 7 8 9 – 20 – 24 23 22 21 20 19

Cover/interior background image: fuart/Shutterstock.com
Cover image: ImageFlow/Shutterstock.com
Image p. v: Daniel M Ernst/Shutterstock.com
Employability Skills icon: VikiVector/Shutterstock.com

Introduction

Principles of Management presents a comprehensive framework to learn about the functions of management. By studying this text, you will learn about the responsibilities and rewards of being a manager for a profit or a not-for-profit organization. Learning the functions of management, how to be a strategic manager, and the importance of managerial soft skills bring management to life. As you explore and discover principles of management in the workplace, you will learn life-long skills to become a productive worker and contributing citizen in our society.

Principles of Management provides an opportunity for you to learn about the functions of management as well as develop leadership skills. As you explore and discover principles of management in the workplace, you will learn life-long skills that will follow you wherever your future career may lead.

About the Authors

Robert (Bob) Dansby is an instructor of accounting, business, and personal finance at Chattahoochee Valley Community College in Alabama, where he also serves as Chairperson of the Division of Business and Social Sciences. In addition, Bob is a small business, tax, and personal finance consultant. He is the author of numerous textbooks and workbooks in the areas of accounting, cost accounting, managerial accounting, business math, and personal finance. He has also written several articles for professional journals, served a five-year term as editor of the Georgia Business Education Association Journal, and has given more than 30 presentations at national and regional business education and accounting conferences. Bob holds a PhD in business education from Southern Illinois University at Carbondale.

Karel Sovak is an Associate Professor and program director for marketing, management, the Emerging Leaders Academy and Internships/Cooperatives at the University of Mary in Bismarck, North Dakota. Additionally, Karel is engaged in strategic planning and governance assistance for not-for-profit organizations. Karel is also involved in the Bismarck entrepreneurial ecosystem as chair of the ecosystem building committee for 1MCND. Karel is also an editor for Bismarck Magazine and River and Ranch publications in his community. He holds a PhD in Applied Management and Decision Sciences from Walden University.

Contributors

Goodheart-Willcox Publisher would like to thank the following professionals who contributed to the development of *Principles of Management*.

Jason Barth
Executive Vice President, CTO
Town and Country Financial Corporation
Springfield, Illinois

Cory Brace
Business Education Teacher
Long County High School
Ludowici, Georgia

Kimberly Evans
Business Administration/Management Teacher
James Madison High School
Dallas, Texas

Doug Garfinkel
Business Education Instructor
North Shore Hebrew Academy High School
Great Neck, New York

Veronica Robinson
Business Educator/Department Chair
North Mesquite High School
Mesquite, Texas

Sharon Row
Business, Marketing, and Computer Science Teacher
Merrillville High School
Merrillville, Indiana

Reviewers

Goodheart-Willcox Publisher would also like to thank the following instructors and professionals who reviewed selected chapters and provided input for the development of *Principles of Management*.

Melissa Bashore
Business Management Educator
Brentwood High School
Brentwood, Tennessee

Susan Beckenham
Technology Focus Program Director
Providence High School
Burbank, California

Moses Best
Marketing Teacher
Southern High School
Durham, North Carolina

Donna Guillot
Business and Computer Science Department Coordinator
Killingly High School
Dayville, Connecticut

Bob Kingston
Industry Development Specialist—CTE Business Programs and District-Wide NOCTI Coordinator
School District of Philadelphia
Office of Career and Technical Education
Philadelphia, Pennsylvania

LaQuanda Leary
Business Education Teacher
John A. Holmes High School
Edenton, North Carolina

Matt Mercy
Marketing Teacher
Ravenwood High School
Brentwood, Tennessee

Dr. Ron Pardee
Distinguished Professor
Business Administration and Management
Riverside City College
Riverside, California

Kathy Purviance-Snow
Business Education Teacher
Snohomish High School
Snohomish, Washington

Mark Ringenberg
Business and Computer Teacher
Culver Community High School
Culver, Indiana

Anna Swango
Entrepreneurship Teacher, FBLA Advisor
Lithia Springs High School
Lithia Springs, Georgia

Kevin Smith
Business and Technology Education Teacher
Henry Clay High School
Lexington, Kentucky

Le-An Thomason
Business Technology Instructor
Polk County High School
Benton, Tennessee

Angela Williams
Career Development Facilitator
Beaufort County School District
Hilton Head, South Carolina

Charisse Woodward
Business Information Technology Teacher
Sherando High School
Stephens City, Virginia

Precision Exams Certification

Goodheart-Willcox is pleased to partner with Precision Exams by correlating *Principles of Management* to the Standards, Objectives, and Indicators for Precision Exams Business Management exam. Precision Exams were created in concert with industry and subject matter experts to match real-world job skills and marketplace demands. Students who pass the exam and performance portion of the exam can earn a Career Skills Certification™. To see how *Principles of Management* correlates to the Precision Exam Standards, please visit www.g-w.com/principles-management-2020 and click on the Correlations tab. For more information on Precision Exams, please visit www.precisionexams.com.

Brief Contents

Contents

Features

Case Study

Exploring Careers

Employability Skills

Ethics

You Do the Math

UNIT 1 Introduction to Management

Chapters

Functions of Management Covered in This Unit

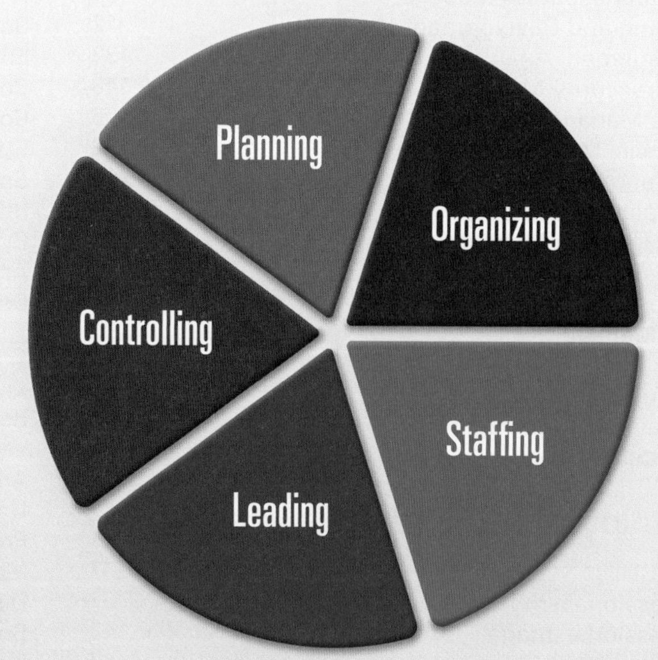

While studying, look for the activity icon for:

- Vocabulary terms with e-flash cards and matching activities

These activities can be accessed at www.g-wlearning.com/business/8417

Case Study

Interpersonal Skills

michaeljung/Shutterstock.com

As part of his yearly performance review, Terrance was promoted to a management position at the company for which he works. He received the promotion largely due to his lengthy tenure with the organization.

Terrance knows the company's products and markets exceptionally well. However, his interpersonal skills are lacking. Terrance often finds himself alienating his direct reports due to an inappropriate comment or a poor attempt at humor. Recently, he traveled with a sales representative to a meeting with one of the company's largest clients. The contract between the client and the company was scheduled for renewal, and the sales representative was looking forward to a profitable new contract.

During the meeting, Terrance reverted to poor behavior. When the client commented about disliking the amount of risk that she was absorbing in the contract, Terrance inadvertently made an inappropriate comment. The client was visibly upset by the remark, but Terrance did not seem to notice.

When the meeting concluded and Terrance left the conference room, the sales representative stayed behind to apologize to the client. The client confirmed she was upset by Terrance's comment but would continue to conduct business with the company provided she does not have to communicate with Terrance again.

The company learned a valuable lesson about the importance of interpersonal skills for a manager. An employee who knows products and markets does not necessarily mean the employee is a good management candidate for an organization. Managers must be well-rounded and possess people skills as well as technical skills. An employee lacking interpersonal skills can cost a business future revenue.

Critical Thinking

1. What are examples of interpersonal skills that every manager should possess?
2. Why is it important to have qualified people in management positions?

CHAPTER 1

Management

Sections

Reading Prep

The opening pages of a textbook generally provide a preview of the text and how the material is presented. Before reading this chapter, review the introductory material that appears before Chapter 1. How can this material help you understand how to use this text?

Exploring Careers

Chief Executive Officer

In most businesses, the chief executive officer (CEO) is the person in charge. They hold the highest position within an organization and often have the most authority. CEOs are responsible for creating strategies and policies for a business as a whole. They collaborate with and direct the work of other top executives, such as chief financial officers. Their main responsibility is providing the overall direction of an organization established by a company's board of directors.

Typical job titles for this position include *chief executive*, *managing director*, *executive director*, and *president*. Examples of tasks that chief executive officers perform include:

- managing and analyzing company operations;
- appointing department heads and managers;
- working closely with the board of directors; and
- formulating and implementing policies.

A chief executive officer position requires a bachelor degree; however, a postgraduate degree may be required. CEOs must have effective leadership and communication skills as well as strong decision-making and problem-solving skills. In addition, they should have a considerable amount of previous managerial experience.

wavebreakmedia/Shutterstock.com

Section 1.1 Management Responsibilities

What do you think of when you hear the word *management*?

Learning Objectives

LO 1.1-1 Define the term *management*.

LO 1.1-2 Summarize the functions of management.

LO 1.1-3 Identify three levels of management.

Key Terms 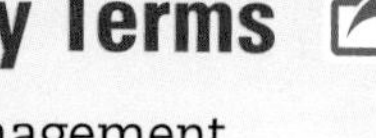

management	delegate	staffing
organization	authority	leading
resource	micromanagement	controlling
efficiency	planning	senior management
effectiveness	plan	middle management
productivity	organizing	supervisory management

LO 1.1-1 Management Overview

Management is a term that is used frequently in the workplace and has different meanings to different people. For some people, it might mean someone with authority who tells others what to do, whereas others look at management as a person who coaches employees to be successful.

Management is the process of controlling and making decisions about an organization, as well as overseeing others to ensure activities are performed efficiently and effectively. Management is the way work is accomplished in an organization through the efforts of other people.

An **organization** is a body of people that come together for a specific purpose. Your school, Netflix, and Old Navy are examples of organizations. They each have a group of people who have come together in a structured manner to accomplish a purpose.

Resources

To be effective, an organization must have a management team that understands how to allocate resources in a way that enables its goals to be met. A **resource** is a supply of money, labor, materials, and other items that a person or organization can draw from in order to meet needs. *Organizational resources* include capital resources, raw materials, human resources, monetary resources, and informational technology, as illustrated in Figure 1-1.

- *Capital resources* are tangible items needed to operate an organization. They include items such as equipment, computers, and buildings.
- *Raw materials* are natural or man-made materials that become part of a manufactured product. Raw materials include wood, minerals, metal, plastic, and other substances.
- *Human resources* are the employees of an organization. Many organizations view employees as their most valuable resource. It is people who have knowledge and ideas needed to perform tasks and expand operations.

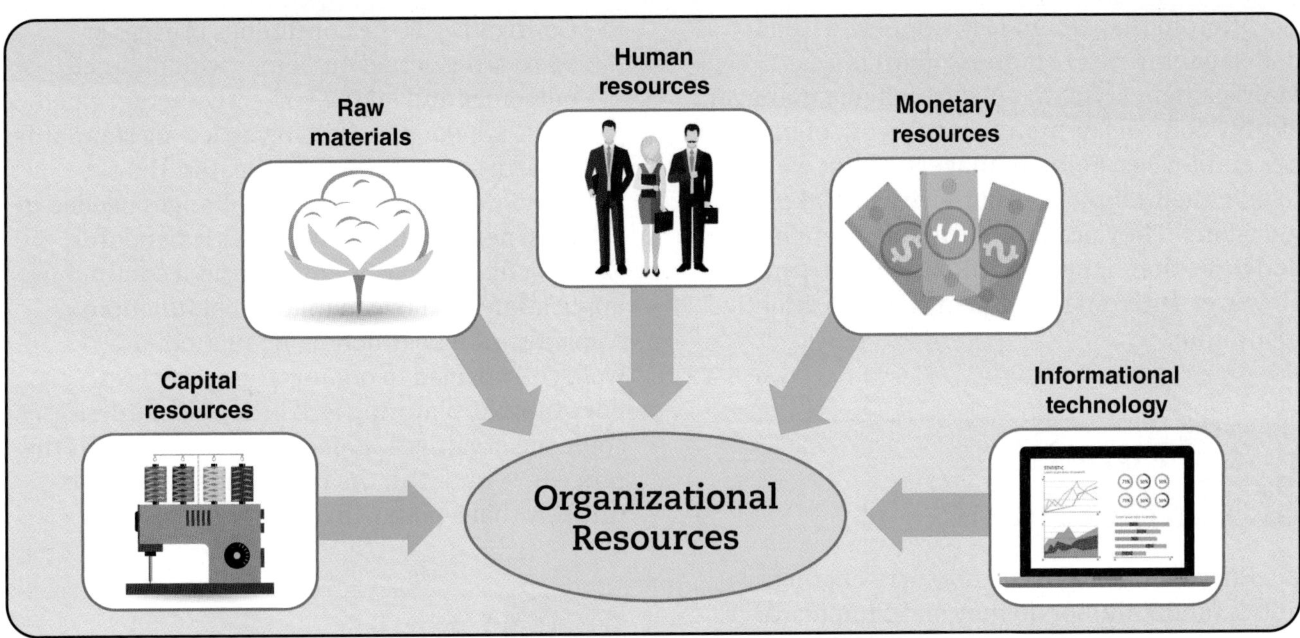

[Credits for Shutterstock images from left to right] Macrovector/Shutterstock.com; Macrovector/Shutterstock.com; Macrovector/Shutterstock.com; Lucia Fox/Shutterstock.com; Voin_Sveta/Shutterstock.com; Goodheart-Willcox Publisher

Figure 1-1 Organizational resources include capital resources, raw materials, human resources, monetary resources, and informational technology.

- *Monetary resources* are the funds needed to start, operate, and expand an organization. These resources include money on hand and in reserves in financial institutions, investments by owners, and various forms of credit.
- *Informational technology* is the use of computers for storing, sending, and retrieving information. It is a critical resource needed for efficiency and accuracy in an organization.

Delegation

Management oversees employees to ensure work is completed efficiently and effectively. **Efficiency** means to use resources to get a job done with minimal waste of time and effort. **Effectiveness** means the intended goals or objectives are achieved. When management is efficient and effective, productivity increases. **Productivity** is a measure of output accomplished by an employee in a specific amount of time.

Efficient management is not, however, the manager completing all the work without delegating some responsibilities to employees. Effective managers accomplish work through delegation of tasks to employees. To **delegate** means to assign authority to someone else to carry out a task. **Authority** is power to carry out a task and make decisions.

Delegation, when done correctly, is an effective practice. When employees are trained and competent to make specific decisions, a manager's time can be spent managing rather than performing tasks that can be completed by an employee.

Employability Skills
Soft Skills

Soft skills are the skills used to communicate and work well with others. They are considered essential employability skills, which are skills that help an individual find a job, perform well in the workplace, and gain success in a job or career. Soft skills are also known as people skills or interpersonal skills.

Micromanagement is the opposite of delegation. **Micromanagement** is a management style that occurs when a manager closely controls or monitors the work of his or her employees. Some managers do not want to give their employees authority to make decisions. They prefer to be hands-on in all the activities that happen within the department. However, micromanagement is not an effective technique.

LO 1.1-2 Functions of Management

Effective managers do not carry out their duties randomly, nor do they make impulsive decisions. Instead, they master the five basic functions of management: planning, organizing, staffing, leading, and controlling, as shown in Figure 1-2.

- **Planning** is the process of setting goals and objectives and deciding how to accomplish them. Managers set goals then develop strategies to achieve them. A **plan** is an outline of the actions needed to accomplish a goal.
- **Organizing** is the coordination of activities and resources needed to accomplish a plan. The organizing function asks, "what will be done, who will do it, and when?"
- **Staffing** is the process of recruiting, hiring, training, evaluating, and compensating employees. An organization is only as good as the people who operate it.
- **Leading** is the process of influencing others to work toward the attainment of common goals. To accomplish goals, managers need to do more than just plan, organize, and staff. They must also lead.
- **Controlling** is the continuous process of comparing actual outcomes with planned outcomes and taking corrective action when goals are not met. It involves setting standards, measuring performances against the standards, and making the changes needed to keep performances in line with standards.

Effective management requires a continuous application of all five management functions. Applying a single function, no matter how well, will not lead to organizational success. For example, planning is of little value unless someone organizes, staffs, leads, and controls the process. Without all the functions applied, it is unlikely that a plan will meet its goals.

LO 1.1-3 Levels of Management

Most organizations have various levels of management. These levels are the *management pyramid*, which includes senior management, middle management, and supervisory management, as illustrated in Figure 1-3. In most organizations, the largest number of managers is in the supervisory management level, with fewer in middle management, and the fewest in senior management. When ranked, this order resembles a pyramid.

Senior Management

Senior management, also called *top management*, is the highest level of management in an organization. Examples of senior-management titles are *chief executive officer (CEO)*, *board chairperson*, and *vice president*. An example of a senior manager is CEO Mark Parker at Nike.

Functions of Management				
Planning	**Organizing**	**Staffing**	**Leading**	**Controlling**
• Identify mission • Create goals and objectives • Strategize • Make decisions	• Design • Coordinate • Form structure • Utilize resources	• Recruit • Hire • Train • Evaluate • Compensate	• Lead • Team build • Communicate • Motivate	• Analyze • Evaluate • Measure • Adjust

Goodheart-Willcox Publisher

Figure 1-2 There are five basic functions of management.

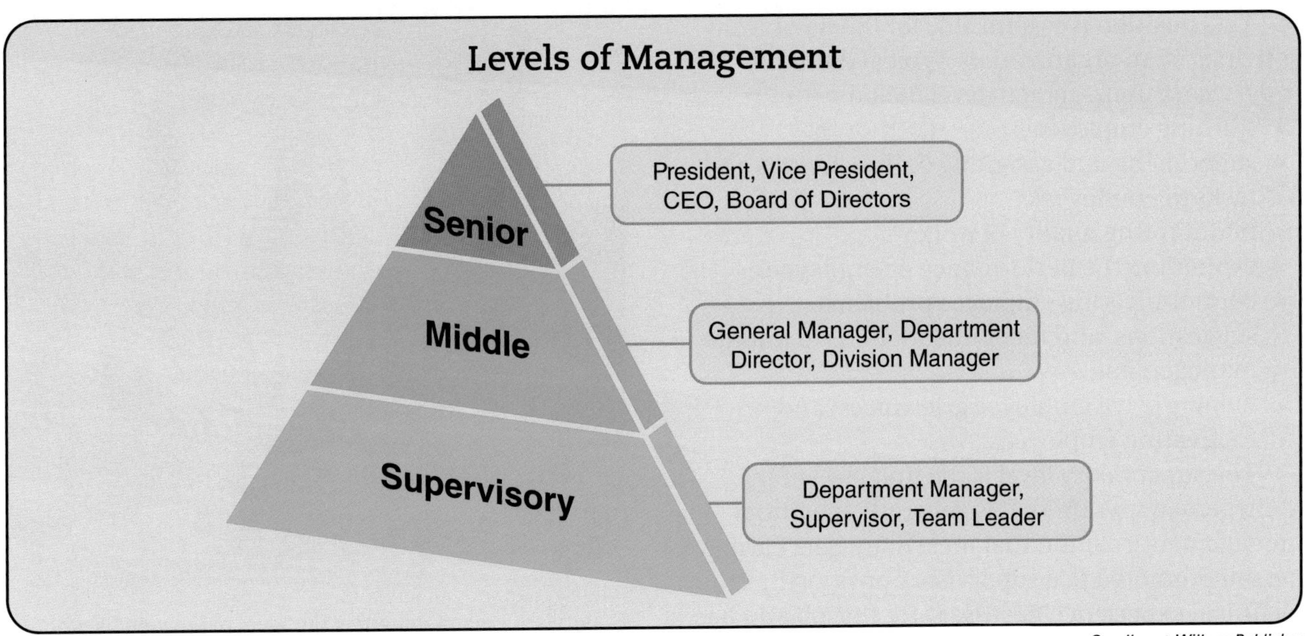

Goodheart-Willcox Publisher

Figure 1-3 The management pyramid ranks the three levels of management in an organization.

Senior management does not focus on the day-to-day activities of a business. Instead, people in these positions work with others in senior management, as well as middle management, to oversee the operation of the business. This level of management spends an equal amount of time on all five functions of management. Typical duties of senior management include:

- developing major goals and broad policies;
- preparing strategic plans;
- controlling and coordinating the activities of all departments;
- providing guidance, motivation, and direction; and
- taking responsibility for the performance of the entire business.

This level of management consists of people with a high level of expertise and experience. These professionals often have worked their way through lower-level management positions to achieve promotions to higher levels. They may be individuals who spent their entire careers with a company or were recruited from another organization.

Middle Management

Middle management is the level of management between the senior level and supervisory level. This level of management spends a great amount of time in one division of a specified area of operations for an organization. Examples of middle-management titles are *general manager* and *sales manager*.

Middle management reports to senior management and spends much of its time implementing the vision of the organization. People in middle management do not supervise day-to-day activities, but lead the organization and work with supervisory managers who report to them. Typical duties of middle management include:

- executing plans developed by senior management;
- conveying policies of senior management to supervisory management;
- participating in hiring and training supervisory management;
- evaluating the performance of supervisory management;
- inspiring and leading supervisory management; and
- managing activities of assigned divisions.

Middle managers are professionals who are generally promoted from a supervisory level. These managers exhibit an ability to manage and possess the technical knowledge necessary to perform the job.

Supervisory Management

Supervisory management is the level of individuals who coordinate and supervise the activities and duties of employees. It is also known as *first-line management*. They focus on monitoring and directing employees. Examples of supervisory-management titles include *supervisor* and *shift manager*. They report to middle management.

This position is responsible for the day-to-day activities in an organization. Typical duties of supervisory management level include:

- training employees;
- supervising and assigning daily activities and tasks to employees;
- maintaining quality of work;
- evaluating the performance of employees;
- communicating employee problems, suggestions, and recommendations to middle management;
- helping solve employee grievances; and
- motivating employees.

The supervisory level is the first level of the management pyramid. It is generally the initial management position that most managers earn. A person promoted to a supervisory position has the technical experience necessary for the job and has earned respect as a person who can direct others to accomplish tasks.

Monkey Business Images/Shutterstock.com

Supervisory management is the level of individuals who coordinate and supervise the activities and duties of employees. **Identify someone you know who is in a supervisory position. What responsibilities does he or she have in the position?**

Section 1.1 Review

Check Your Understanding

1. Cite examples of organizational resources.
2. List the five basic functions of management.
3. Define the *management pyramid*.
4. State examples of senior management titles.
5. List examples of middle management duties.

Build Your Vocabulary

As you progress through this text, develop a personal glossary of key terms. This will help you build your vocabulary and prepare you for a career. Write a definition for each of the following terms and add them to your personal glossary.

management
organization
resource
efficiency
effectiveness
productivity
delegate
authority
micromanagement
planning
plan
organizing
staffing
leading
controlling
senior management
middle management
supervisory management

Section 1.2 Managers Defined

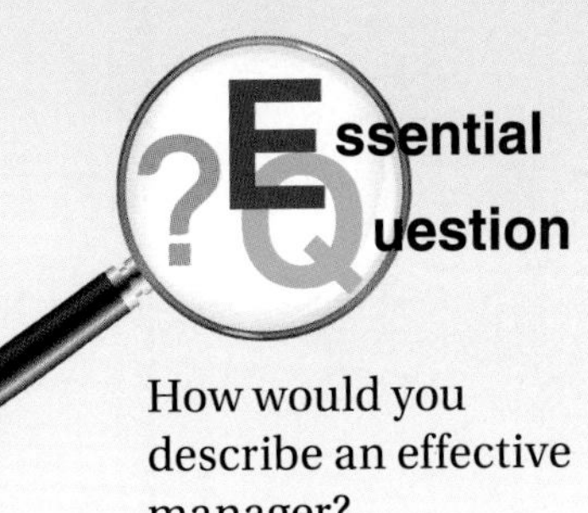

How would you describe an effective manager?

Learning Objectives

LO 1.2-1 Discuss the term *manager.*

LO 1.2-2 Describe managers in today's workplace.

LO 1.2-3 Identify managerial roles according to Mintzberg.

LO 1.2-4 Cite examples of skills of successful managers.

Key Terms

- manager
- direct report
- for-profit business
- not-for-profit organization
- glass ceiling
- diversity
- managerial role
- conceptual skills
- interpersonal skills
- soft skills
- communication
- technical skills
- hard skills

LO 1.2-1 Who Is a Manager?

A **manager** is a person who directs and oversees the work of others in order to achieve the goals of an organization. Employees who report to a manager are called direct reports. A **direct report** is an employee who reports directly to one manager.

Being a manager is not always an easy job. In a typical workday, a manager may hire a new employee, attend meetings, make a presentation for clients, and settle an argument between two workers. A manager receives praise when things go well and gets blame when things are not successful.

A manager works for an organization. An organization can be for-profit or not-for-profit. A **for-profit business** is an organization that generates revenue with the objective of earning a profit for its owners. One of its sole purposes is to be productive and generate profit for its owners. Google, Apple, and Walmart are examples of for-profit businesses. A **not-for-profit organization** is an organization that exists to serve some public purpose. It is also known as a *nonprofit organization* or a *nonprofit*. Goodwill, the American Heart Association, and the Humane Society are examples. Government groups, on all levels, are also considered not-for-profit organizations.

The duties of managers tend to be quite different from the duties of employees. Managers typically supervise others, assign tasks, and oversee workflow, while employees are more involved in specific tasks. A large part of what a manager does for an organization involves strategically dividing work to be accomplished into manageable tasks and assigning employees to perform those tasks. Managers act as communicators between their teams and senior management. They make certain that the goals of the organization established by senior management are conveyed to employees on their teams.

LO 1.2-2 Today's Managers

In earlier times, a manager was called "the boss." Managers were typically white males who controlled everything that happened at work. Few women or individuals of ethnicity were in management positions.

The stereotype of the 1950s of white male boss is gone, and the glass ceiling is gradually being eliminated. The **glass ceiling** is the invisible barrier that prevents a group of people from job advancement. Equal opportunities for management positions are now possible for all genders, abilities, and race.

You Do the Math
Numeric Reasoning: Real Numbers

Real numbers are all whole and fractional or decimal numbers on a continuous number line. *Whole numbers* are numbers with no fractional or decimal portion. *Decimals* are numbers with digits to the right of the decimal point.

Real numbers can be positive or negative. To add a positive number, move to the right on the number line. To subtract a positive number, move to the left on the number line. To add a negative number, move to the left on the number line. To subtract a negative number, move to the right on the number line.

Solve the following problems.

1. 73 + –8 – 12 =
2. 5.87 + 4.956 + 2.011 + 4 =
3. 34 + 9 – 127 + 783 =
4. 112.058 + –93.237 =
5. 987 + 705 + 827 + 4 =

Managers in today's workplace are in tune to business and understand what customers need as well as what their employees need. They earn the trust of those around them, listen to others, and realize the importance of team building. Managers today are forward thinking and work to improve the organization as a whole by focusing on 21st century issues, such as the value of employees, importance of diversity, and the use of technology.

Value Employees

Effective managers help employees become successful by providing support, guidance, and feedback. They remove obstacles so that individuals can perform their jobs and feel good about what they are doing. Rather than telling an employee what to do, they provide coaching on ways to perform a task and find solutions that work. The result is successful employees who are well trained and competent. They feel appreciated and tend to be more loyal, reliable, and hard working.

Respect Diversity

Diversity means having representatives from different backgrounds, cultures, or demographics in a group. Diversity includes age, race, nationality, gender, mental ability, physical ability, and other qualities that make an individual unique.

Successful managers realize that a diverse workforce has many advantages. Diversity can help organizations be more creative, be receptive to customer needs, and find new ways to complete tasks. Diverse employees can help a company create goods and services that may be new in the marketplace. New ways of thinking and looking at business are benefits of hiring people with varied backgrounds and experiences. Diversity also increases the pool of qualified potential job candidates, which can result in a more effective workforce.

Gorodenkoff/Shutterstock.com

Managers in today's workforce must be competent in the use and application of technology. **What advantages does a manager have in an organization by staying up-to-date with technology used in the workplace?**

Ethics

Ethical Management

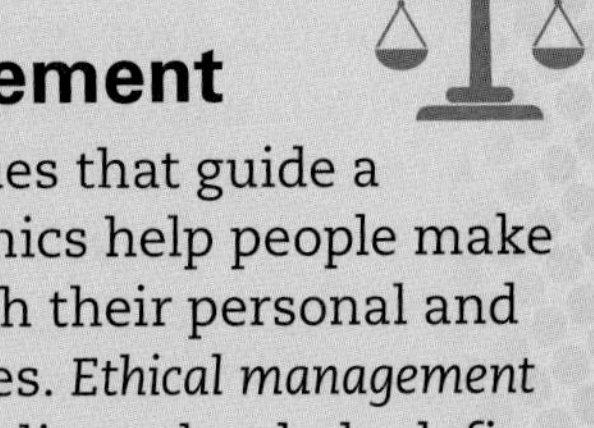

Ethics are the values that guide a person's behavior. Ethics help people make good decisions in both their personal and their professional lives. *Ethical management* involves setting guidelines that help define appropriate behavior in the workplace and ensure employees are operating ethically. Managers are expected to demonstrate and set an example for ethical behavior.

Embrace Technology

Modern managers look to the future and embrace the onward march of technology. The workplace is an ever-evolving environment that is constantly changing how tasks are accomplished. Managers in today's workforce must be competent in the use and application of technology. Team members might work remotely, and clients and vendors may be in locations across the world. This necessitates that the activities of an organization be conducted in person as well as through social media and other communication outlets. Managers are also responsible for guiding the company to make decisions on selecting and implementing new technology that helps increase efficiency in the operation of the organization.

LO 1.2-3 Managerial Roles

Managerial roles are the actions and behaviors that managers are expected to perform in an organization. Because there are many types of organizations with many different types of management, it is difficult to identify the precise role of a manager. However, all management duties focus on a core of responsibilities. According to management expert and university professor Henry Mintzberg, managers spend most of their time performing 10 specific roles, as illustrated in Figure 1-4.

Most managers do not consistently perform each of Mintzberg's 10 roles on a daily or even monthly basis, nor do all roles apply equally to all situations. However, all managers assume some of the roles on a daily basis. As a result, a mastery of all roles and the ability to apply them to any situation or issue that may be at hand is necessary. Mintzberg classified each of these roles into three main categories: interpersonal roles, informational roles, and decisional roles.

Interpersonal Roles

Managers play an interpersonal role in the organization. *Interpersonal* means relationships between people. An *interpersonal role* involves the human interaction that happens between the people within the organization as well as those outside of the organization. People in the organization are employees, peers, and supervisors. People outside the organization are customers and other organizations. Interpersonal roles include figurehead, leader, and liaison.

Informational Roles

Managers also play informational roles in an organization. *Information* means knowledge. An *informational role* involves collecting, receiving, and conveying information. It is the

Goodheart-Willcox Publisher

Figure 1-4 According to management expert and university professor Henry Mintzberg, managers spend most of their time performing 10 specific roles.

role in which a manager must generate and share knowledge to achieve organizational goals. The informational roles are disseminator, monitor, and spokesperson.

Decisional Roles

The third category of managerial roles is a decisional role. A *decisional role* involves the process of deciding or resolving questions or situations. Decisional roles include entrepreneur, disturbance-handler, negotiator, and resource-allocator.

LO 1.2-4 Skills of Successful Managers

To be successful, managers need a variety of skills. As illustrated in Figure 1-5, key managerial competencies required include conceptual, interpersonal, and technical skills.

Conceptual Skills

Conceptual skills involve the ability to formulate new ideas and think in abstract terms. Conceptual skills enable a person to think creatively, solve problems, and understand how programs and ideas interrelate. Conceptual skills involve applying critical-thinking, problem-solving, and decision-making skills.

Individuals with conceptual skills are able to think creatively and chart specific courses of action to solve problems. Conceptual skills also involve the ability to "think outside the box" and examine how ideas are interrelated.

Interpersonal Skills

Managers must interact with employees, peers, clients, and superiors. **Interpersonal skills**, also called *human skills*, are the skills that enable a person to work effectively with others. **Soft skills** are skills used to help an individual find a job, perform in the workplace, and gain success in a job or career. Examples of soft skills include listening skills, positive attitude, and emotional intelligence. These skills involve knowing how to interact with others in a manner that makes it conducive for everyone to be successful in their responsibilities. This in turn allows positive, effective workplace relationships to develop.

Interpersonal skills also include the ability to communicate. **Communication** is the sending and receiving of messages that convey information, ideas, feelings, and beliefs. *Communication skills* involve the ability to speak, write, and listen effectively. They also involve

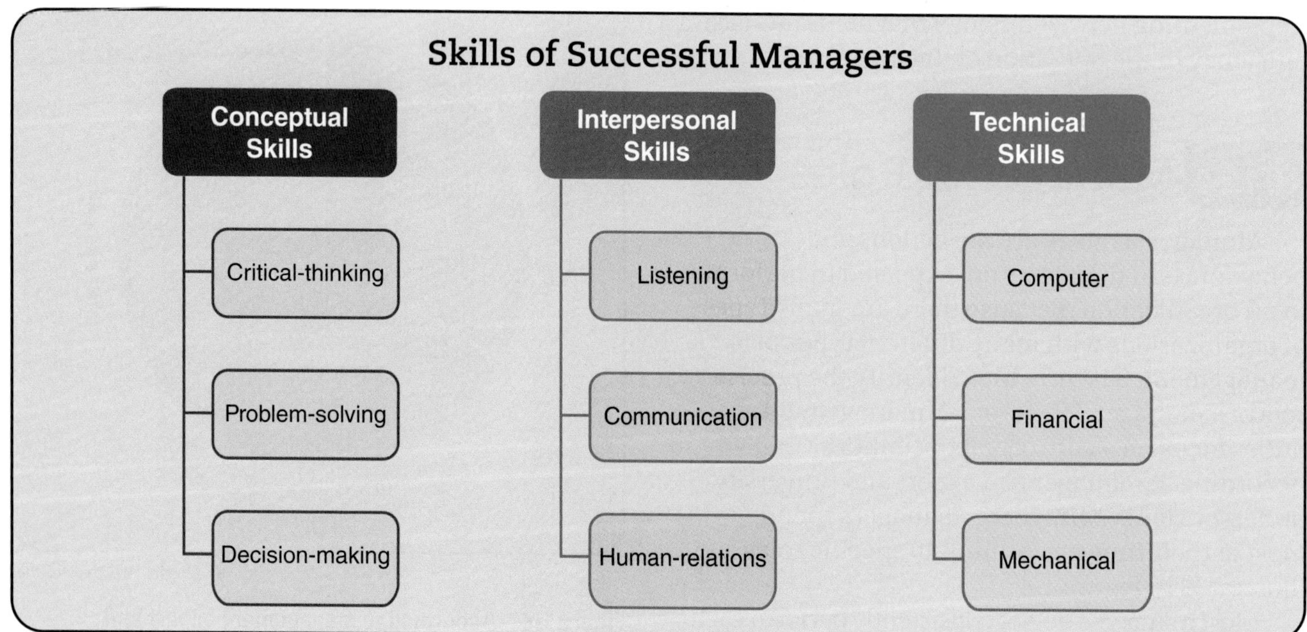

Goodheart-Willcox Publisher

Figure 1-5 Key managerial competencies include conceptual, interpersonal, and technical skills.

the ability to understand and interpret verbal and nonverbal communication. Nonverbal communication consists of facial expressions, eye movement, and body movement. Communication skills affect a manager's ability to understand others, establish positive relationships, and perform in most situations.

Technical Skills

Technical skills are specific skills managers need to perform duties related to their area of management. They include the specific training and education required for an industry and are considered as hard skills. **Hard skills** are critical skills necessary to perform the required work-related tasks of a position. They are teachable, clearly defined, and can be measured. Examples of hard skills, also called *job-specific skills*, include the ability to perform and direct others to perform activities, such as accounting tasks, repairing a computer, and changing the brakes on a car.

BaanTaksinStudio/Shutterstock.com

Technical skills are specific skills managers need to perform duties related to their area of management. **Why do you think technical skills are important for the workplace?**

Section 1.2 Review

Check Your Understanding

1. What is the difference between a for-profit business and a not-for-profit organization?
2. Cite 21st century issues that are the focus of today's managers.
3. List Mintzberg's three categories of managerial roles.
4. State examples of key managerial competencies required for successful managers.
5. Why are communication skills important for managers?

Build Your Vocabulary

As you progress through this text, develop a personal glossary of key terms. This will help you build your vocabulary and prepare you for a career. Write a definition for each of the following terms and add them to your personal glossary.

manager
direct report
for-profit business
not-for-profit organization
glass ceiling
diversity
managerial role
conceptual skills
interpersonal skills
soft skills
communication
technical skills
hard skills

Chapter 1 Review and Assessment

Chapter Summary

Section 1.1 Management Responsibilities

LO 1.1-1 **Define the term *management.***
Management is the process of controlling and making decisions about an organization, as well as overseeing others to ensure activities are performed efficiently and effectively. It is the way work is accomplished in an organization through the efforts of other people.

LO 1.1-2 **Summarize the functions of management.**
Planning is the process of setting goals and objectives and deciding how to accomplish them. Organizing is the coordination of activities and resources needed to accomplish a plan. Staffing is the process of recruiting, hiring, training, evaluating, and compensating employees. Leading is the process of influencing others to work toward the attainment of common goals. Controlling is the continuous process of comparing actual outcomes with planned outcomes and taking corrective action when goals are not met.

LO 1.1-3 **Identify three levels of management.**
Three levels of management include senior management, middle management, and supervisory management. These levels are described as the management pyramid.

Section 1.2 Managers Defined

LO 1.2-1 **Discuss the term *manager.***
A manager is a person who directs and oversees the work of others in order to achieve the goals of an organization. Managers supervise others, assign tasks, and oversee workflow. They also act as communicators between their teams and senior management.

LO 1.2-2 **Describe managers in today's workplace.**
Managers in today's workplace are in tune to business and understand what customers need as well as what their employees need. They are forward thinking and work to improve the organization as a whole by focusing on 21st century issues, such as the value of employees, importance of diversity, and the use of technology.

LO 1.2-3 **Identify managerial roles according to Mintzberg.**
Mintzberg classified 10 specific managerial roles into three main categories: interpersonal roles, informational roles, and decisional roles.

LO 1.2-4 **Cite examples of skills of successful managers.**
Key managerial skills include conceptual, interpersonal, and technical skills.

Review Your Knowledge

1. Discuss the concept of management.
2. Explain each of the functions of management.
3. Explain the three levels of the management pyramid.
4. What are typical duties performed by senior management positions?
5. Identify examples of typical duties of supervisory management positions.
6. Discuss the concept of a manager.
7. Describe managers in today's workplace.
8. How can managers help employees become successful?
9. Define managerial roles categories according to Mintzberg.
10. Cite examples of skills of successful managers.

Apply Your Knowledge

1. Taking on the responsibilities of management is a challenging assignment. What are some of the rewards you think a manager might experience?
2. Would you consider your instructor a manager? Explain whether or not you think a person teaching a class could also be considered a manager.
3. To delegate means to assign authority to someone else to carry out a task. When done correctly, it is an effective management practice that increases an organization's productivity. In your own words, how would you define delegation?
4. Which of the functions of management would you rate as the most important function? Explain your reasoning.
5. Which of the functions of management would you rate as the least important function? Explain your reasoning.
6. In your own words, describe an ideal manager candidate for today's workplace.
7. Many students have part time jobs while earning an education. Other students may volunteer their time to an organization. These jobs and volunteer work can offer career experience that will be valuable in the future. Summarize what you have learned at a part-time job or at a volunteer event that would help prepare you for a future position as a manager in a business.
8. According to Mintzberg, managers perform 10 specific roles. However, not all the roles apply to all situations or are used on a daily basis. Select three roles that you believe a manager should perform the majority of the time. Explain your choices.
9. Think of someone you know who is a manager, leader, or supervisor. What skills does that person have that are important in the role?
10. Now that you have read the introduction to management chapter, why do you think studying management will be helpful in your career?

College and Career Readiness

Communication Skills

Reading. *Sight words* are those words you recognize just by seeing them. They are words that appear on almost every page of text. Examples of sight words are *the, he,* and *me.* Identify ten sight words in this chapter.

Writing. *Note taking* is the process of writing key information from a lecture, text, or other source on paper or a digital device. Taking notes can help you recall information, and the notes can serve as a resource when studying. Reread this chapter and take notes on the content. When you come to the end of a section, write a brief summary in your own words. To summarize, identify the most important ideas in the material and retell them in your own words. Be selective about what you include in your notes.

Listening. *Hearing* is a physical process. *Listening* combines hearing with evaluation. Listen carefully to your instructor as a lesson is presented. Pay attention to the sounds and patterns of the words used. How would you rate your listening skills?

Internet Research

Functions of Management. Successful managers master the functions of management. Perform an Internet search for *functions of management.* Write several paragraphs explaining ways a manager could learn how to apply these functions and increase efficiency and productivity.

21st Century Manager. *Research* is investigating or studying information in order to reach a new conclusion. Research starts with asking a question, then seeking information to find the answer. Managers today are forward thinking. They work to improve the organization as a whole by focusing on 21st century issues. Conduct a search for *21st century manager.* Use the information you find to write a profile of a 21st century manager.

Teamwork

A *team* is a group of two or more people working together to achieve a common goal. Working with your team, discuss the concept of the glass ceiling in the workplace. Summarize each person's opinion on the glass ceiling. Discuss if the glass ceiling still is an artificial barrier that keeps employees from being promoted, earning raises, or kept from career opportunities.

College and Career Readiness

Portfolio Development

Overview. When applying for a job, a volunteer position, or entry into an educational institution, one way to demonstrate your qualifications is to present a portfolio to the interviewer. A *portfolio* is a selection of related materials that you collect and organize to demonstrate your job qualifications, skills, and talents. For example, a certification showing you have completed Microsoft Office Specialist training could help you get into an IT program. A portfolio is a *dynamic document,* which means it should be reviewed and updated regularly.

Visual artists and communication professionals have historically presented portfolios of their creative work when seeking jobs or admission to educational institutions. However, portfolios are now used in many professions. It is helpful to research and identify which type is appropriate for the industry in which you are interested in working after your educational career has ended.

Commonly used formats for a portfolio are print and electronic. A *print portfolio* is a hard-copy version that can be carried to an interview. It can be presented in a three-ring binder with divider tabs or any other method that works for you. An *electronic portfolio* is a digital version of a print portfolio. It can be saved to cloud-based storage services, flash drives, or CDs. There are many creative ways to present an electronic portfolio. The method you choose should allow the viewer to navigate and find items easily. It is beneficial to have both types when applying to a school or for employment.

1. Research *Types of Portfolios* and select the one that is most appropriate for you and your career goals.
2. Consider and plan for the technology that might be needed for creating and scanning documents for an electronic portfolio. You may need access to desktop-publishing software, scanners, cameras, and other digital equipment or software.

CTSOs

Student Organizations. Career and technical student organizations (CTSOs) are national student organizations with local school chapters that are related to career and technical education (CTE) courses. There is a variety of organizations from which to select, depending on the goals of your educational program. CTSOs are a valuable asset to any educational program. These organizations support student learning and enable the application of learned skills in real-world situations.

Competitive events sponsored by CTSOs recognize outstanding student performance. Competing in various events enables students to show mastery of specific content. These events also measure the use of decision-making, problem-solving, and leadership skills. Competitive events may be written, oral, or a combination of both.

To prepare for any competitive event, complete the following activities.

1. Go to the website of your organization to find specific information for the events. Visit the site often as information changes quickly. If the organization has an app, download it to your digital device.
2. Read all the organization's guidelines closely. These rules and regulations must be strictly followed or you can be disqualified from competing.
3. Communication plays a role in all the competitive events, so read which communication skills are covered in the event you select. Research and preparation are important keys to a successful competition.
4. Select one or two events that are of interest to you. Print the information for the events and discuss your interest with your instructor.

CHAPTER 2

History of Management

Sections

Reading Prep

A table of contents is a list of each section in a book and the page where it can be found. Before reading this chapter, review the table of contents for this text. Trace the content from simple to complex ideas. What does this tell you about what you will be learning?

Exploring Careers

Chief Financial Officer

The chief financial officer (CFO) is an upper level management position who reports directly to the CEO. CFOs are responsible for managing many aspects of the financial operations of an organization, such as financial planning, recordkeeping, and reporting. CFOs work with executive-level managers, such as CEO and COO, to develop strategic plans. They help create and track budgets, objectives, and financial goals for each department and the business as a whole. They also assess financial opportunities and risks presented to them by middle and supervisory managers.

Typical job titles for this position include *director of finance* or *vice president of finance*. Examples of tasks that chief financial officers perform include:

- reporting financial results to the board of directors and senior managers;
- ensuring that the company complies with all accounting requirements;
- managing financial risks; and
- developing and implementing best practices for the finances of a company.

Most CFO positions require a bachelor or master degree and a Certified Public Accountant (CPA) credential. CFOs should have relevant experience in the field of finance, financial management, and accounting. The ability to be analytical, detail-oriented, and a strong leader are also important skills for CFOs.

pxl.store/Shutterstock.com

Section 2.1

Early Management

How has the history of management shaped the job of a manager in the workplace today?

Learning Objectives

LO 2.1-1 Summarize the evolution of management.

LO 2.1-2 Define *management theory*.

LO 2.1-3 Discuss three branches of classical management.

LO 2.1-4 Explain behavioral management.

Key Terms 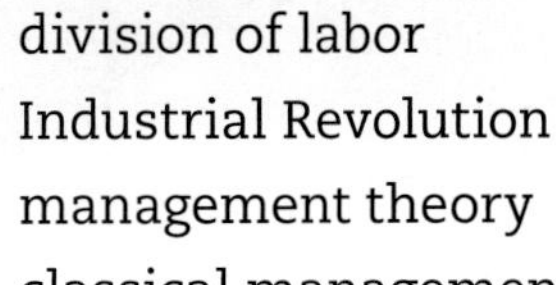

division of labor
Industrial Revolution
management theory
classical management
scientific management
administrative management
bureaucratic management
hierarchy
behavioral management

LO 2.1-1 Evolution of Management

To appreciate the importance of management in today's workplace, it is helpful to study the history and evolution of management through the ages. Management has a long history and has evolved over thousands of years.

The practice of management can be traced back to many different cultures. Ancient Babylonian, Chinese, and Egyptian civilizations created complex economies, farmed expansive tracts of land, paved extensive networks of roads, and built monuments and structures that still stand today. These accomplishments could not have been possible without management. A manager was needed to oversee tasks, provide direction, and organize efforts to the individuals and groups performing the work.

An example of evidence of early management is the Egyptian pyramids that are still standing today. It took thousands of people to build these structures. To be successful and complete the pyramids, someone had to plan, organize, staff, lead, and control the building process. These people were the managers of the time.

Early managers relied on experience, intuition, and drive to accomplish their end goals. The objective was to complete a job as quickly as possible, regardless of any consequences for the workers. The focus was on task completion with little regard for the health, safety, and well-being of individual workers.

Eighteenth Century

The pyramids are just one example of early management. As civilization advanced through the ages, the importance of organizations to accomplish workplace goals was realized. The study of management as we know it today is a result of events in the 18th, 19th, and 20th centuries, as illustrated in the timeline in Figure 2-1.

A particular historic event in the evolution of management was the introduction of the concept of division of labor in the 18th century. **Division of labor** is the specialization of individuals who perform specific tasks. It is also called *job-specialization*. In division of labor, jobs are broken down into smaller and repetitive tasks that are assigned to specific individuals. This enables workers to become efficient at their assigned roles. In turn, this leads to increased productivity and profits for an organization.

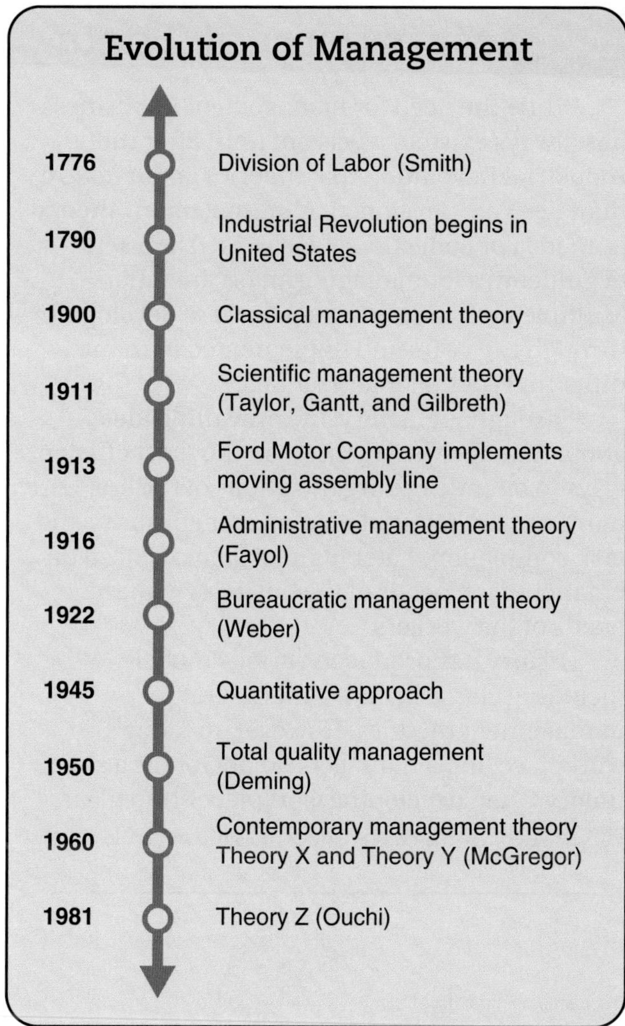

Goodheart-Willcox Publisher

Figure 2-1 The study of management as we know it today is a result of events in the 18th, 19th, and 20th centuries.

The Scottish economist and philosopher Adam Smith was a proponent of the division of labor concept. In 1776, Smith authored *The Wealth of Nations* in which he discussed the economic benefits an organization and society would gain from a division of labor among its workers.

Nineteenth Century

Another important event that contributed to the study of management was the Industrial Revolution that occurred in the United States during the late 18th and early 19th centuries. The **Industrial Revolution** was a time in history when machines replaced human and animal power.

As the nation moved from an agricultural society to an industrial society, the factory system began to appear in the 1800s. Machines were invented that increased productivity exponentially and mass-produced items at high rates. However, the factory system brought challenges in scheduling manufacturing operations, acquiring and managing materials, and meeting production deadlines. In addition, trained employees were needed and worker productivity was an issue.

These challenges created the need for a new rank of employee, the *professional manager.* A professional manager was tasked with the growing need for planning, organizing, staffing, leading, and controlling a business. It was this person's job to manage raw materials, assign tasks, direct activities, and keep the factories operating efficiently.

The Industrial Revolution was a turning point in history. It started in Western Europe and soon spread to the United States and the rest of the world. It changed the way that goods were produced, especially in industries like textiles, mining, and farming. The focus was to manufacture large quantities of products in order to make more money.

The Industrial Revolution created many new industries and led to a higher standard of living for many individuals, as well as the growth of cities and urban areas. It also created a need to address the complex economic and social issues that arose during this time, such as employees working long hours in unsafe conditions.

WitR/Shutterstock.com

An example of evidence of early management is the Egyptian pyramids that are still standing today. **What other examples of early management can you identify?**

Steve Mann/Shutterstock.com

The Industrial Revolution was a time in history when machines replaced human and animal power. **In your own words, how do you believe the Industrial Revolution affected modern management?**

Twentieth Century

The beginning of the 20th century saw the start of a new type of revolution. Henry Ford was an American automotive manufacturer who made his first car in 1896. Cars of that time were complicated and expensive. Only the wealthy could afford to own one. However, Ford dedicated himself to the production of an efficient and affordable automobile. In 1903, he established the Ford Motor Company. One month later, the company sold its first car.

In 1908, Ford introduced the Model T. A few years later, in 1913, the company implemented the world's first moving assembly line. It was an innovation that transformed the automobile industry and, eventually, the entire manufacturing industry.

However, the assembly line was not popular among all workers. No longer did craftsmen assemble an entire car. Instead, a division of labor meant that workers continually performed a single task as cars moved down the assembly line. The result was worker boredom and high employee turnover. *Turnover* refers to the rate employees quit or otherwise leave a company. Turnover requires replacements have to be hired and trained.

To reduce turnover, Ford shortened the workday from nine hours to eight hours. The shorter workday allowed for three eight-hour work shifts in a day and a 40-hour workweek, which became the standard in the United States. He also raised worker pay to $5 a day, which was about twice as much as what most factory workers earned at the time.

LO 2.1-2 Management Theory

While the need for management in business has always existed, it was not until after the Industrial Revolution that theories about *how* to manage were developed. A **management theory** is an idea or collection of ideas used as a set of guidelines for managing an organization. Multiple management theories were developed through the years and implemented in many different types of organizations.

Throughout history, the prevailing ideas about management focused on the most efficient ways to operate the organizations of the era. Early management focused on manager authority and task completion. Later management focused on balancing the needs of the business with the needs of the workers.

History has produced various models, including classical and contemporary management theories. However, in today's workplace, most managers do not follow a single theory when developing workplace strategies.

Uncle Leo/Shutterstock.com

Henry Ford was an American automotive manufacturer who implemented the world's first assembly line, which transformed the automobile industry. **What do you know about the history of Henry Ford and the assembly line?**

You Do the Math

Algebraic Reasoning: Variable Expression

Letters that stand in place of unknown numbers are called *variables*. When a variable appears with numbers and signs for adding, subtracting, multiplying, or dividing, the expression is called a *variable expression*. For example, "x + 5" is a variable expression.

Solve the following problems.

1. An office manager budgets $25 a week for office refreshments. Sometimes, the amount spent is less than $25. Write a variable expression to calculate the amount of remaining money after a given week.
2. An office manager orders $350 worth of office supplies from a single supplier each month. Payment for the order is a single payment or is sometimes divided into equal smaller payments. Write a variable expression to calculate equal payment amounts for the office equipment order.

Instead, they commonly use a combination of ideas that best suit the workplace, work environment, and nature of the workforce for their specific organization.

LO 2.1-3 Classical Management

Classical management is a theory that focuses on organizing work with the goal of increasing worker productivity. It rose to popularity in the late 1890s and early 1900s, especially in factories as it emphasized repetitive work tasks that are common in factory and assembly-line work. The theory evolved in the quest to establish "one best way" to complete a task.

The classical management theory, also called the *classical perspective of management* and the *classical approach to management*, consists of three branches. These branches are scientific, administrative, and bureaucratic management.

Scientific Management

Scientific management is a classical management theory that uses science to study worker productivity and workflow. Frederick Winslow Taylor, Henry Gantt, and Frank and Lillian Gilbreth contributed to the scientific management theory.

In the late 1800s, Frederick Winslow Taylor, an American mechanical engineer, conducted scientific studies in the workplace to evaluate performance efficiencies. He used a scientific approach to analyze work tasks and workflow to reveal a single "best way" to accomplish the work. Taylor believed that workers were inefficient in their habits and productivity could be improved by making four simple adjustments to how work was managed. Through his studies, he established Four Principles of Scientific Management, also called *Taylorism*. In 1911, he explained his theory of scientific management in his book *Principles of Scientific Management*. These principles are explained in Figure 2-2.

Taylor's Principles of Scientific Management

- Use a scientific method to determine the most efficient way to perform and replace "rule of thumb" or habitual approaches
- Match workers to jobs and tasks based on their capabilities, interests, and levels of motivation. Train, teach, and develop workers to reach maximum efficiency
- Monitor employee performance and provide supervision to ensure the employees are working efficiently
- Divide the work between managers and workers so that each can spend their time efficiently on the job

Goodheart-Willcox Publisher

Figure 2-2 Frederick Winslow Taylor, an American engineer, established Four Principles of Scientific Management, also called *Taylorism*.

Henry Gantt, an American mechanical engineer and management consultant, also contributed to the scientific theory of management. Gantt's idea was to create a tool managers could use to measure the progress of a project. In 1910, he created a graph that visually represented each task and how to schedule it for maximum efficiency. The graphs were used to analyze a project, track its progress, and determine time needed for its completion. Gantt named the tool *Gantt charts* and they are still in use today.

Frank and Lillian Gilbreth were American engineers and consultants. They built on the principles of scientific management by conducting time and motion studies. The goal of their study was to identify and analyze individual body movements used during work to eliminate inefficiencies.

While parts of the scientific theory of management are still in use today, the theory is criticized for overlooking basic human traits. The application of science does not take into account human creativity, employee morale, or job satisfaction.

Administrative Management

Administrative management is a classical management theory that focuses on the organization as a whole and identifies effective ways to organize and manage a business. An important contributor to this theory was Henri Fayol, a French mining engineer. He believed that analyzing the management of a business was the best way to identify issues and increase efficiency. Fayol identified the functions of management as *planning, organizing, commanding, coordinating*, and *controlling*. These functions are still recognized today.

Fayol also developed 14 general *principles of management*, as shown in Figure 2-3. For Fayol, management was separate from other business functions, such as accounting or production. Management was also a strategy that could be applied in all aspects of business. In 1916, he published a book called *General and Industrial Management* that outlined his principles of management and his research.

Fayol's 14 Principles of Management	
Division of Work	Specialization increases efficiency and productivity
Authority and Responsibility	A manager has authority to direct others as well as take responsibility for actions
Discipline	A manager requires respect and obedience from employees
Unity of Command	Only one supervisor should direct an employee
Unity of Direction	A business should have one overall company plan that is followed
Subordination of Individual Interest to General Interest	Employee interests are subordinate to those of the business
Remuneration of Personnel	Salaries must be fair to the employees and the organization
Centralization	A single authority within an organization is required in order to utilize employees in the most efficient manner
Scalar Chain	A chain of command should extend from the highest level to the lowest level
Order	The right employees and materials are necessary to be functional
Equity	Employees should be treated fairly and equally
Stability of Personnel	Productivity requires a stable personnel
Initiative	Initiative is needed at all levels for employees
Esprit de Corps (Team Spirit)	Teamwork is necessary for success

Goodheart-Willcox Publisher

Figure 2-3 French mining engineer Henri Fayol developed 14 general principles of management.

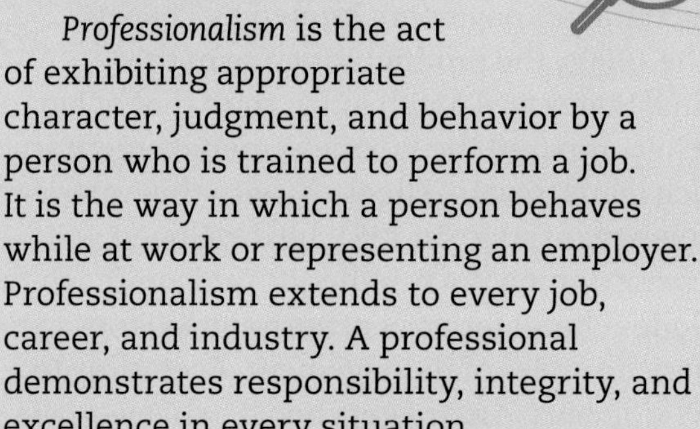

Employability Skills

Professionalism

Professionalism is the act of exhibiting appropriate character, judgment, and behavior by a person who is trained to perform a job. It is the way in which a person behaves while at work or representing an employer. Professionalism extends to every job, career, and industry. A professional demonstrates responsibility, integrity, and excellence in every situation.

Bureaucratic Management

Bureaucratic management is a classical management theory that is an approach based on precisely defined procedures and a clearly defined order of command. Max Weber, a German sociologist, was a contributor to this theory. Weber believed an organization should be structured as a hierarchy with rules that manage the organization and its members. A **hierarchy** is a system in which people, items, or issues are ranked in order of importance.

According to Weber, a hierarchy forces an organization to operate in a rational manner instead of following the whims and emotions of individuals. He believed that the defined structure of a bureaucracy helped make decision-making effective, controlled resources, protected workers, and accomplished organizational goals efficiently. *Weber's Six Principles of Bureaucratic Management* are explained in Figure 2-4.

The term "bureaucracy" is a common term used in today's workplace. Essentially, *bureaucracy* means that important decisions are made at the top of the organization. Weber's approach faces criticisms since it can take a long time for decisions to be made and all the power is given to the top levels of management. The formality and paperwork required for decision-making in this type of management can waste time, money, and effort.

LO 2.1-4 Behavioral Management

The classical management theory focused on the organization and increasing worker productivity, with little concern for worker satisfaction. As the study of management continued into the 20th century, management experts started to recognize the importance of worker satisfaction on workplace productivity and organizational improvement. The result was the emergence of the behavioral management theory.

Behavioral management is a theory that focuses on improving the organization through understanding employee motivation and behavior. It is also called *human relations management.*

Theory X and Theory Y

Every manager is different in his or her approach and style of leadership. To identify how managers view employees, American social psychologist Douglas McGregor developed two theories: Theory X and Theory Y. He described these theories in his 1960 book *The Human Side of Enterprise.*

Weber's Six Principles of Bureaucratic Management	
Division of Labor	Labor is divided into areas of specialization, and there is a balance between power and responsibility
Hierarchy	A clear chain of command is established to allow instructions and information to flow effectively from top to bottom
Framework of Rules	A written set of rules and operating procedures is necessary in a business
Impersonal	Rules and regulations are applied equally to employees
Formal Selection	The selection and promotion of workers is based on qualifications, skills, and experience, not on individual personalities or personal relationships
Career Orientation	Career building is desirable

Goodheart-Willcox Publisher

Figure 2-4 Max Weber, a German sociologist, developed *Weber's Six Principles of Bureaucratic Management.*

Theory X managers believe that employees dislike work and need close supervision in order to finish their tasks. As a result, Theory X managers maintain total control over the duties of employees.

Theory Y managers believe that employees like to work and do not need close supervision to accomplish their tasks. According to this theory, workers have potential and are capable of self-direction.

An important aspect of McGregor's idea is that of the *self-fulfilling prophecy*. He believed that managers create an environment in which employees behave to meet the manager's expectations. If a manager operates on the basis that people need supervision in order to stay on task, employees will act accordingly and require supervision. Alternatively, if the manager believes that employees will stay on task even without observation, they will respond and work without supervision.

Theory Z

The research of American Professor William Ouchi added another component to behavioral management known as Theory Z. In the 1980s, the productivity rate in the United States was much lower than that of Japan. Ouchi compared the Japanese management style, which leans toward Theory Y, with the American management style. In 1981, he developed *Theory Z*, which is a middle-ground approach that includes characteristics of both the Japanese and American styles of management. According to Ouchi, Theory Z managers believe that workers are motivated to work and can make sound decisions. This type of manager is more likely to act as a coach and let workers make most of the decisions.

Section 2.1 Review

Check Your Understanding

1. Explain the tasks of a professional manager in the 19th century.
2. What contributions did Henry Ford make to the 20th century?
3. Identify people who contributed to scientific management.
4. Cite the contributions of Henri Fayol to administrative management.
5. Explain Max Weber's theory on bureaucratic management.

Build Your Vocabulary

As you progress through this text, develop a personal glossary of key terms. This will help you build your vocabulary and prepare you for a career. Write a definition for each of the following terms and add them to your personal glossary.

division of labor
Industrial Revolution
management theory
classical management
scientific management
administrative management
bureaucratic management
hierarchy
behavioral management

Section 2.2

Trends in Management

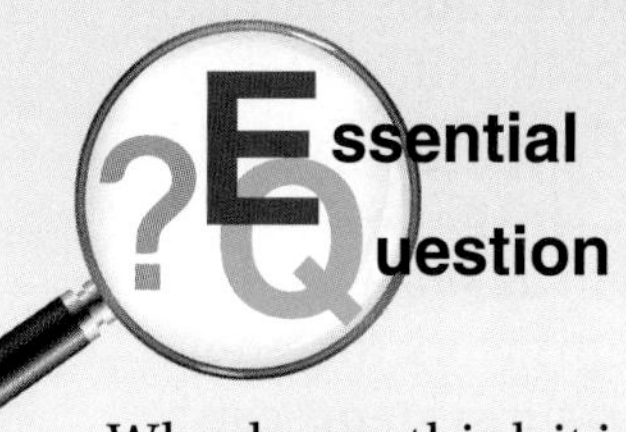

Why do you think it is important for a high school student to study management?

Learning Objectives

LO 2.2-1 Explain the quantitative approach to management.

LO 2.2-2 Summarize contemporary management theory.

LO 2.2-3 Define *evidence-based management.*

Key Terms 

quantitative approach	contingency approach
total quality management (TQM)	evidence-based management

LO 2.2-1 Quantitative Approach

The **quantitative approach** is a management theory that uses measurable techniques to improve decision-making in an organization. It is sometimes referred to as *management science.* The quantitative approach involves using statistical analysis, computer simulations, informational models, and other research-based methods for management decisions.

The origins of this theory of management can be traced back to the mathematic and scientific research conducted during World War II in the 1940s. Following the end of the war, much of the research was applied to business operations. The quantitative approach management theory gained popularity in the late 20th century in the form of total quality management.

Total quality management (TQM) is a management philosophy in which the success of an organization is directly related to customer satisfaction. TQM uses quantitative techniques to improve decision-making. The goal of TQM is to have all members of an organization committed to enhancing processes, improving quality of products, and reducing waste. TQM integrates customer satisfaction into every part of business operation. The key principles of TQM are shown in Figure 2-5.

With the expansion of production in the second half of the 20th century, the quality of goods produced in factories was slipping drastically. This became a drain on resources for companies because it cost time and money to fix the errors. Many companies hired quality-control managers to inspect products and ensure that production standards were met.

Key Principles of TQM

- Customer-focused
- Employee involvement
- Process-centered
- System integration
- Strategic and systematic approaches
- Continual improvement
- Fact-based decision-making
- Communications focused

Goodheart-Willcox Publisher

Figure 2-5 Total quality management (TQM) is a management philosophy in which the success of an organization is directly related to customer satisfaction.

An important contributor to TQM was Dr. W. Edwards Deming, an American engineer and inventor. After World War II, Japanese companies were producing subpar products. To address this issue, the Japanese Union of Scientists and Engineers hired Deming to train their engineers in quality control. This greatly improved the products made by Japanese factories to the point that, by the 1970s, Western countries were basing their own measures of quality management on the Japanese system.

LO 2.2-2 Contemporary Management Theory

Most of the early approaches to management theory focused on issues *inside* an organization. Starting in the 1960s, management researchers began recognizing and studying factors *outside* the organization that could affect organizational performance. Contemporary theories consider factors outside the boundaries of the organization, such as environmental resources or government regulations. Examples are the systems theory and contingency approach.

Systems Theory

The systems theory looks at an organization as a system that is open or closed. A *system* is a set of interrelated parts that function as a whole unit to accomplish a common goal. Systems can be either open or closed. An *open system* interacts with the environment around it. In contrast, a *closed system* does not interact with the environment around it.

One way to understand the difference between an open system and a closed system is to visualize a glass jar with a lid. Without the lid, the jar is an open system. It can interact with air or any liquid or solid placed in the jar for storage. On the other hand, when the jar is closed with a lid, it is a closed system that only interacts with what is already inside.

In an open system, the organization takes *inputs* from outside its environment and processes them into outputs. *Outputs* are goods or services that are then distributed into the environment. Figure 2-6 illustrates an example of inputs and outputs for a commercial bakery.

The open-systems theory contributes to an understanding of management because managers must coordinate work activities in different parts of the organization to ensure that all parts are working together as intended. The parts of the organizations can be referred to as *subsystems*. *Synergy* occurs when subsystems work together as intended. Working together, subsystems can produce the desired outcome more efficiently than working separately. The systems approach is one of the dominant management theories today.

Contingency Approach

As management research continued into the middle of the 20th century, researchers realized that management ideas and practices are not universal or are equally applied to all situations. This raised the question of what a manager should do if established management principles do not apply, or do not fully apply, to all situations. The answer depends on the particular situation or problem at hand.

The **contingency approach** is a theory that suggests the appropriate style of management depends on the situation. In other words, there is no single best way to handle all situations or problems encountered in an organization. Instead, managers need to be flexible and adapt management practices to changing circumstances.

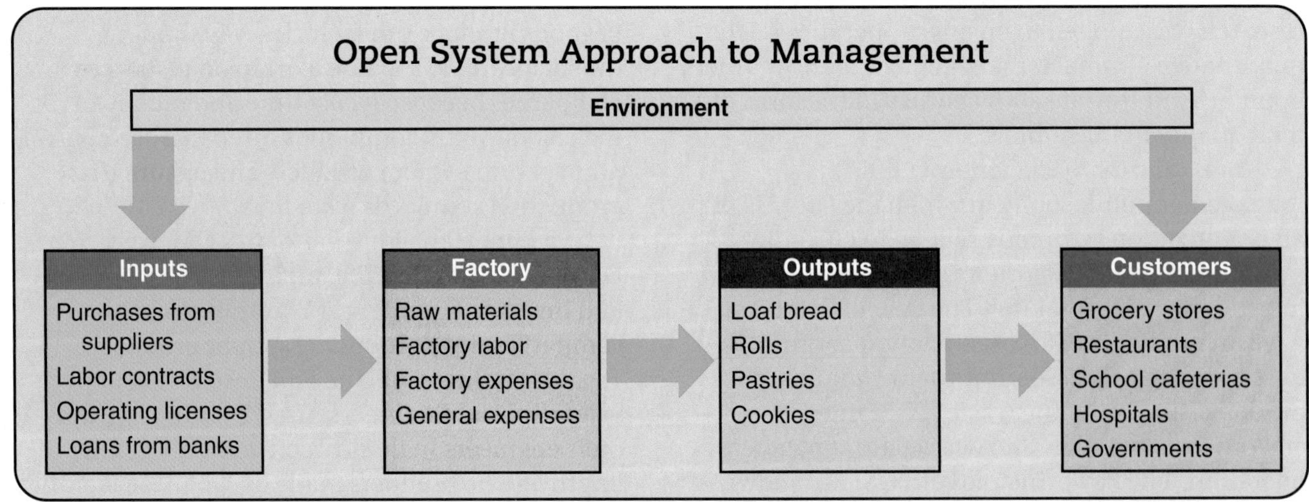

Goodheart-Willcox Publisher

Figure 2-6 In an open system, the organization takes *inputs* from outside its environment and processes them into outputs.

Advocates of the contingency approach believe that no two situations are identical. Therefore, managers should be adaptable and flexible in their approaches to problem solving.

LO 2.2-3 Evidence-Based Management

Evidence-based management is an emerging management theory in which decisions are based on a combination of critical thinking and the best-available evidence. *Evidence* refers to facts and information related to a particular issue or problem. Sources of evidence can be research outside the organization, internal documents, past experiences, government reports, and professional consultants.

The application of evidence-based management centers around five steps.

1. Translate a problem or issue into an answerable question.
2. Gather the best evidence available related to the problem or issue.
3. Carefully judge the trustworthiness and relevance of the evidence.
4. Incorporate the evidence into the decision-making process.
5. Evaluate the outcomes of decisions put into practice.

Evidence-based management helps managers use critical-thinking skills to evaluate the validity and reliability of the evidence used for important decisions.

Ethics

Taking Credit

Managers are responsible for people who report to them, while often reporting to bosses of their own. It may be tempting for a manager to pass off the work of direct reports as his or her own work. To do so is dishonest and unethical and can be grounds for dismissal.

Section 2.2 Review

Check Your Understanding

1. Provide examples of methods used to make management decisions when the quantitative approach is used.
2. What is the goal of TQM?
3. Name two examples of contemporary management theory.
4. What is the difference between an open system and a closed system?
5. List five steps of evidence-based management.

Build Your Vocabulary

As you progress through this text, develop a personal glossary of key terms. This will help you build your vocabulary and prepare you for a career. Write a definition for each of the following terms and add them to your personal glossary.

quantitative approach	contingency approach
total quality management (TQM)	evidence-based management

Chapter 2 Review and Assessment

Chapter Summary

Section 2.1 Early Management

LO 2.1-1 **Summarize the evolution of management.**
In the 18th century, the concept of division of labor was introduced. This enabled workers to become effective in a specific role, which increased productivity and profits for an organization. In the late 18th to early 19th centuries, the Industrial Revolution saw a change of human and animal power being replaced by machines. This change led to the creation of the professional manager. In the beginning of the 20th century, Henry Ford implemented the world's first moving assembly line. This transformed the automobile industry and, eventually, the entire manufacturing industry. Ford also shortened the workday and increased employee pay to reduce employee turnover.

LO 2.1-2 **Define *management theory*.**
Management theory is an idea or collection of ideas used as a set of guidelines for managing an organization. Management has historically focused on the most efficient ways to operate the organizations of an era. In today's workplace, most managers use a combination of ideas.

LO 2.1-3 **Discuss three branches of classical management theory.**
Three branches of classical management are scientific management, administrative management, and bureaucratic management. Scientific management uses science to study worker productivity and workflow. Administrative management focuses on the organization as a whole and identifies effective ways to organize and manage a business. Bureaucratic management is an approach based on precisely defined procedures and a clearly defined order of command.

LO 2.1-4 **Explain behavioral management theory.**
Behavioral management is a theory that focuses on improving the organization through understanding employee motivation and behavior. Examples of this theory are Theory X, Theory Y, and Theory Z.

Section 2.2 Trends in Management

LO 2.2-1 **Explain the quantitative approach to management.**
The quantitative approach is a management theory that uses measurable techniques to improve decision-making in an organization. It involves using statistical analysis, computer simulations, informational models, and other research-based methods for management decisions.

LO 2.2-2 **Summarize contemporary management theory.**
Contemporary theories consider factors outside the boundaries of the organization. Examples are the systems theory and contingency approach.

LO 2.2-3 **Define *evidence-based management*.**
Evidence-based management is an emerging management approach in which decisions are based on a combination of critical thinking and the best-available evidence. This theory helps managers use critical-thinking skills to evaluate the validity and reliability of the evidence used for important decisions.

Review Your Knowledge

1. Summarize examples of historical events that led to the development of management theory.
2. Explain management theory.
3. Identify and explain three branches of classical management theory.
4. Explain behavioral management theory.
5. Compare and contrast Theory X, Theory Y, and Theory Z.
6. Explain the quantitative approach to management.
7. Summarize contemporary management theory.
8. How does the open-systems theory contribute to understanding management?
9. What is the belief of the advocates of the contingency approach?
10. Summarize evidence-based management.

Apply Your Knowledge

1. Explain how you think the functions of planning, organizing, staffing, leading, and controlling might have applied in the ancient world.
2. Henry Ford made important contributions to our society. What kind of workplace do you think he created for his company?
3. Attempt to find the one best way to do a task with which you are familiar, such as setting the table for dinner. Begin by performing the task once and timing yourself. Then, perform the task again to see if you can reduce your time. Experiment with other ways to increase your efficiency in performing this task. Then, write a one- to two-paragraph summary of your experiment.
4. A 1900s Austrian-born American management consultant named Peter Drucker is quoted as saying, "What's measured improves." What do you think Drucker's quote means? Explain how you think this applies to management.
5. One of Taylor's principles of management is to replace "rule of thumb" or habitual approaches to a task with efficient and precise ways of doing the task. How can relying on a rule of thumb or habit lead to inefficiencies?
6. Fayol identified 14 principles of management, which are described in Figure 2-3. Select one of these principles of management and describe how it is applied in your school by the school administration.
7. Taylor, Fayol, and Weber each identified division of labor as an important component of organizational efficiency. Three different researchers studying three different management theories arrived at the same conclusion. What do you think this says about the value of division of labor?
8. Do you think you would work better under a manager who applies Theory X or Theory Y? Explain your answer with support drawn from your personal experiences.
9. Why do you think it is important to study the history of management?
10. In your own words, summarize what you learned from this chapter.

Communication Skills

Speaking. Effective speaking requires individuals to use correct pronunciation. This is especially true when using words you learned recently because you may be less familiar with how the word is pronounced. Identify three key terms you learned in this chapter. Practice pronouncing them by saying them aloud to yourself until you can pronounce each one correctly.

Reading. *Imagery* is descriptive language describing how something looks, feels, smells, sounds, or tastes. Using the information in this chapter, find an example of how the author uses imagery to describe a concept. What mental picture did you create? Note the page number and paragraph where you found the example. Why do you think this is a good example?

Writing. Standard English means that word choices, sentence structures, paragraphs, and the narrative follow standard conventions used by those who speak English. Well-written paragraphs are usually the product of editing. *Editing* means to rewrite sentences and paragraphs to improve their content and organization. Using Standard English, write several paragraphs to describe your reasons for taking this class. Edit and revise your work until the ideas are refined and clear to the reader.

Internet Research

Adam Smith. Background research is often needed to broaden your understanding of a topic. Conduct background research about the role of Adam Smith's writing in popularizing division of labor in the 18th century. To do this, enter *Adam Smith's Wealth of Nations* into a search engine. Note any important information, as well as the source you used. How does the background information help your understanding of Adam Smith?

Therbligs. Frank and Lillian Gilbreth conducted time and motion studies to identify how a worker could be more efficient in his or her tasks. They coined the word *Therblig* (a modification of *Gilbreth* spelled backward) to identify individual body movements needed to complete a task. Conduct an Internet search for *Therblig* and read about the different types. Then, identify how many Therbligs it takes to complete a simple task, such as opening a door.

Teamwork

Teamwork is the cooperative efforts by individual team members to achieve a goal. Working as a team, review the different trends in management discussed in this chapter. Create a chart that lists each trend and the important factors for each. Based on this information, what new management trends does your team predict might evolve in this century?

Portfolio Development

Objective. Before you begin collecting information, it is beneficial to write an objective for your portfolio. An *objective* is one or two complete sentences that state what you want to accomplish. Your objective will help keep you on track as you build your portfolio.

First, focus on your short-term and long-term goals. A *short-term goal* is a goal you would like to achieve in the next one to two years. A *long-term goal* is a goal you wish to accomplish in the next five to ten years. Your objective should be written in a way that allows you to achieve these goals. For example, if your short-term goal is to get accepted to a university within a year, but your long-term goal is to work in a field closely related to your career interests, your objective could be: "I will gain acceptance to one of my top-choice universities within a year and will be working in my desired field within five years." By focusing on your goals, you will be able to write a descriptive objective for your portfolio.

When writing your objective, include enough details so you can easily judge when it is accomplished. Consider this objective: "I will try to get into college." This is too general. A better, more detailed objective might read: "I will get accepted into the undergraduate program at one of my top-three colleges of choice." Creating a clear objective is a good starting point when beginning to work on your portfolio.

1. Using word-processing software, create a document with the heading "Portfolio Objective." Then create two subheadings, one that says "Short-Term Goals" and another that says "Long-Term Goals." List your goals under their respective heading. These are the goals on which you should focus when writing your objective.
2. Next, write your portfolio objective based on those goals. Keep in mind that this objective will likely change as your ideas and goals evolve during the portfolio creation process.
3. Save this document as PORTFOLIO_OBJECTIVE with your last name, for example PORTFOLIO_OBJECTIVE_SMITH, or use a different naming convention that is suitable for the management system you put into place in Lesson 1. Remember to back up your documents on a flash drive.
4. Place this document as the first page of your portfolio to guide you as you build it. This is your working document, so remember to remove it when you organize the final product.

CTSOs

Performance. Some competitive events for CTSOs have a performance component. Performance events provide an opportunity to demonstrate verbal communication skills, as well as decision-making and problem-solving abilities.

Depending on the organization, this event can be for individual participation or a team. The activity could potentially be a presentation, role-play, or decision-making scenario for which the participants provide a solution and present to the judges.

To prepare for the performance component of a presentation, complete the following activities.

1. On the website of your CTSO, locate a rubric or scoring sheet for the event.
2. Confirm if visual aids may be used in the presentation and the amount of setup time permitted.
3. Review the rules to confirm the type of activity and if questions will be asked or if a case or situation will be defended.
4. Make notes on index cards about important points to remember. Use these notes to study. You may also be able to use these notes during the event.
5. Practice the performance. You should introduce yourself, review the topic to be presented, defend the topic, and conclude with a summary.
6. After the practice performance is complete, ask for feedback from your instructor. You may also consider having a student audience listen and give feedback.

UNIT 2

Planning

Chapters

Functions of Management Covered in This Unit

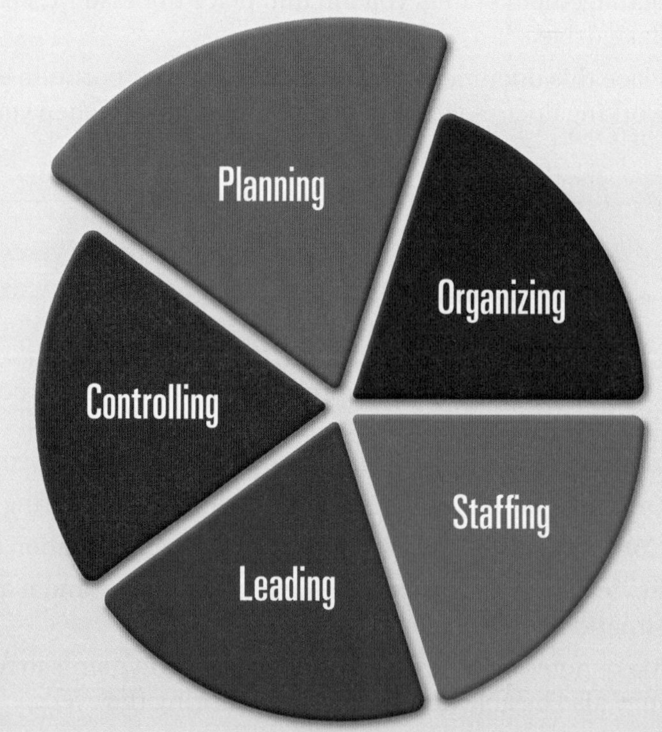

While studying, look for the activity icon for:

- Vocabulary terms with e-flash cards and matching activities

These activities can be accessed at www.g-wlearning.com/business/8417

Case Study

Persistence

StockLite/Shutterstock.com

Mollie is a product manager at a company that manufactures educational toys and games. She has a degree in marketing and product development.

Mollie's current project is a game that helps young children develop their counting and alphabet skills. The game will be a joint venture with an established children's television show and will feature characters from the show.

The company often themes their products around current trends and fads in an effort to cultivate interest. To facilitate this goal, they regularly perform market research to determine how well a product will sell before moving forward with the manufacturing process. During her review of the market research report, Mollie noted it was based on secondary research that was outdated by nearly five years. She asked the marketing team to conduct new research, but the request was declined. It was the team's opinion that market trends have not changed enough in five years to warrant conducting new research. Mollie persisted on acquiring current data, and the marketing team eventually agreed to perform new research.

The new research revealed that one of the actors on the show was arrested by local authorities. Such information would be harmful to a partnership for a new product. Mollie promptly cancelled the licensing contract with the television show.

Persistence is an interpersonal skill that can help a manager reach an appropriate decision. Knowing when to take a stand on an issue or when to let an issue go is sometimes the product of experience in a position.

Critical Thinking

1. To what degree should a product manager be persistent when requesting services of another team in the organization?
2. Why is persistence an important interpersonal skill for a manager to possess?

CHAPTER 3

Planning

Sections

3.1 Planning Basics

3.2 Developing Plans

Reading Prep

Before reading, turn to the opening pages of this unit and read the chapter titles. By previewing the titles, you can prepare for the topics presented in the unit. What do the titles reveal about what you will be learning?

Exploring Careers

Chief Operating Officer

The chief operating officer (COO) is an upper level management position who reports directly to the CEO. The overall function of a COO is to handle the daily operation of the company. Chief operating officers are responsible for helping an organization produce high-quality goods or services to increase profits and decrease production costs. COOs play a major role in the planning function to envision, establish, and meet long-term and short-term goals.

Typical job titles for this position include *operations director* and *director of operations*. Examples of tasks chief operating officers perform include:

- developing the organization's strategy and mission statement and sharing it with his or her direct reports;
- prioritizing customer, employee, and organizational requirements;
- monitoring and maintaining staffing, levels, and other expectations to fulfill organizational requirements; and
- driving performance measures for the operations of the organization.

Chief operating officer positions require a bachelor degree in business administration or a related field. Most companies also prefer COOs to have a master of business administration as well as prior work experience. COOs need to be organized, motivated, and possess strong communication and decision-making skills.

wavebreakmedia/Shutterstock.com

Section 3.1 Planning Basics

Why is planning necessary for an organization?

Learning Objectives

LO 3.1-1 Summarize the planning function of management.
LO 3.1-2 Discuss establishing goals.
LO 3.1-3 Identify types of plans written by management.
LO 3.1-4 Explain market research used for planning.
LO 3.1-5 Cite examples of data analysis used for planning purposes.

Key Terms

goal
SMART goal
strategic plan
tactical plan
operational plan
contingency plan
market research
primary research
secondary research
competition
competitive analysis
revenue
Management Information System (MIS)
sales forecast

LO 3.1-1 Planning Function

Planning is the process of setting goals and objectives and deciding how to accomplish them. It is referenced as the primary function of management because it forms the foundation for all other management functions. Planning requires that managers understand the challenges a business faces and know how to apply the decision-making process. Some benefits of planning include the following.

- **Planning results in more effective resource allocation.** Proper planning enables managers to allocate resources to activities and projects where they are needed. This, in turn, reduces waste and inefficiency and contributes to the overall success of the organization.
- **Planning provides direction.** Planning focuses the attention of managers and non-management employees on achieving specific results. It provides a blueprint for what the organization wishes to accomplish so that activities and resources can then be directed and coordinated to reach end goals.
- **Planning helps manage change.** Change occurs frequently in today's technological work environment and diverse workforce. Computer software updates, changes in payroll laws, and changes in labor laws are some of the factors that challenge organizations on a regular basis. Anticipating and planning for change puts an organization in a position to deal with events before they actually occur.
- **Planning establishes the basis for executing the other management functions.** After planning for an organization is in place, management can proceed to organizing, staffing, leading, and controlling.

Planning is an ongoing process that involves continuous effort. Without planning, an organization would not be successful.

LO 3.1-2 Establishing Goals

Well-executed planning includes the establishment of goals. A **goal** is something to be achieved in a specified timeframe. Goals are the desired outcomes or targets that an organization is striving to accomplish. They are the first step in planning and serve as guidelines for the decisions and actions of managers. Plans can then be developed to work toward the completion of those goals.

Goals may be short term or long term. A *short-term goal* is something the organization wishes to accomplish in a short time period, usually less than a year. An example of a short-term goal is a plan to increase the advertising budget for the next three months. Short-term goals are the steps necessary to achieve long-term goals.

A *long-term goal* is something an organization hopes to accomplish in a timeframe that exceeds one year. Long-term goals are broader than short-term goals and usually focus on the organization as a whole. Examples include developing a new product line, expanding business operations into another country, and paying off company debt.

For a goal to be effective, it should be a SMART goal. A **SMART goal** is one that is specific, measurable, attainable, realistic, and timely, as shown in Figure 3-1.

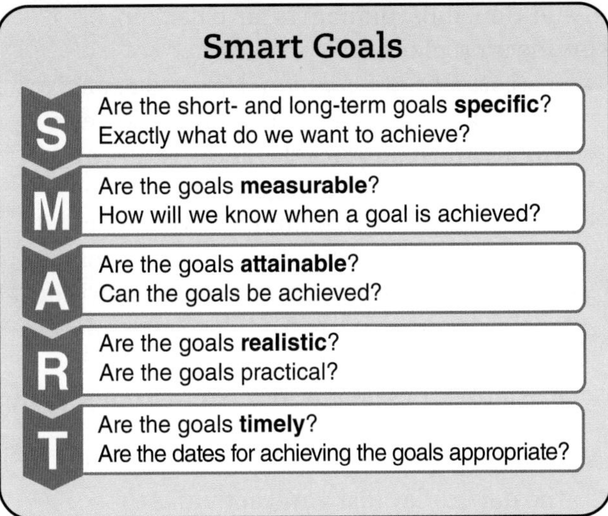

Goodheart-Willcox Publisher

Figure 3-1 A SMART goal is one that is specific, measurable, attainable, realistic, and timely.

- **Specific.** A goal should be specific and straightforward. "Our company will increase sales by five percent" is a specific goal.
- **Measurable.** Progress toward a goal should be measurable. "We will measure progress by using five percent increase as a benchmark."
- **Attainable.** A goal needs to be attainable. "Based on historical performance, five percent increase can be accomplished if we hire two additional salespeople."
- **Realistic.** A goal must be realistic. "It is realistic to increase sales by five percent by the end of the year based on our five-year history of four percent increase per year."
- **Timely.** A goal should be accomplished by a definite date. "Our company will increase sales by five percent by the end of the fiscal year."

The purpose of a goal is to reach a desired outcome and establish direction. By setting SMART goals, managers can plan ways to meet them.

LO 3.1-3 Types of Plans

Organizations depend on management to create and execute plans for the organization. A *plan* is an outline of actions needed to accomplish a goal. Three types of plans typically created include a strategic plan, tactical plan, and operational plan, as summarized in Figure 3-2.

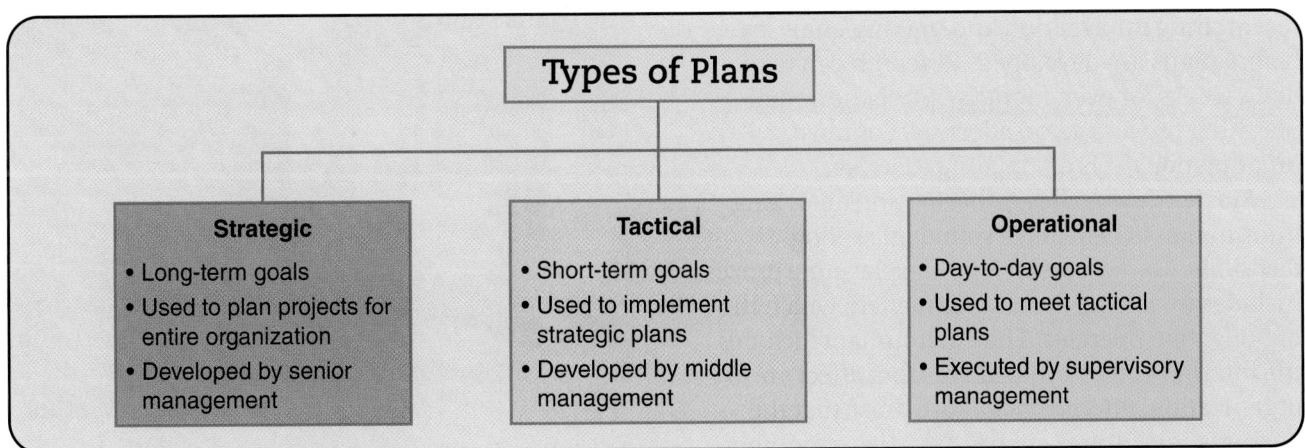

Goodheart-Willcox Publisher

Figure 3-2 Three types of plans that managers typically create include strategic, tactical, and operational plans.

In addition, most managers have backup, or contingency, plans.

- A **strategic plan** is a plan designed to achieve the long-term goals of an organization as a whole. The plan projects for the future and is written by senior management.
- A **tactical plan** is a plan that involves activities needed to implement strategic plans defined by senior management. It includes short-term goals of the company. Middle level managers are typically responsible for writing and executing these plans for their divisions in the organization.
- An **operational plan** is a plan that defines the day-to-day tasks and activities that employees must perform to meet company goals. Operational plans are usually written for a quarter and then a year. They are used by supervisory management to define job responsibilities outlined in the tactical plans.

Most managers also write a contingency plan. A **contingency plan** is a backup plan that outlines alternative courses of action to take if other plans prove unproductive or circumstances beyond control change. Management considers operating problems that can result from factors such as employee labor strikes, material shortages, or political instability. In addition, natural disasters, such as storms, floods, and fire, can affect the operation of a business. Good management requires "keeping all options open," and this is when contingency plans come into play.

LO 3.1-4 Research

Planning for an organization does not take place overnight. There is much time spent on researching information and making analyses before plans are developed. Research can take days, weeks, or even months before the actual planning process gets underway. For most organizations, it is an ongoing exercise.

Market research is gathering and analyzing information to help make sound marketing decisions. Market research for the planning process includes reviewing the environment in which the organization operates. The environment includes the internal and external factors that affect an organization. *Internal factors* are those that the business can control, such as facilities or number of employees. *External factors* are those that an organization cannot control, such as the economy and the competition. Information gathered from research helps managers plan what to produce, how to produce, and for whom to produce in the planning process. There are two types of research used to gather information for planning purposes: primary and secondary research.

Primary Research

Primary research is first-hand research conducted by a researcher. The researcher can be someone within the organization, such as a marketing manager. Gaining customer feedback and product research through surveys, focus groups, and case studies are examples of primary research tools. Online survey tools, such as Survey Monkey, are a good way to capture customer information.

Some organizations prefer to hire an outside agency, such as Nielsen, to provide market research. Both options are reliable ways to obtain firsthand information about internal and external factors that affect planning.

Secondary Research

Secondary research is data already collected and recorded by someone else. This is research that someone else has already gathered, but others can use it. Using the Internet to gather industry sales information and statistics about similar organizations is an example. Government sources, industry data, and academic data are examples of research that is already completed and available for use.

ESB Professional/Shutterstock.com

Market research is gathering and analyzing information to help make sound marketing decisions. **Why do you think organizations spend money on market research?**

LO 3.1-5 Data Analysis

The planning process requires market research data and analyzing company sales history data. By analyzing information, an organization can more accurately identify customers, forecast sales, and better plan which products to develop. Two important analyses that help businesses make decisions include market analysis and sales analysis.

Market Analysis

Market analysis is the process of gathering and analyzing information about markets, customers, industry trends, new technology, and competing businesses to help plan the future for an organization. The information gained from market research is used to define target markets, learn about the needs and wants of consumers, and understand what motivates people to buy. A *consumer* is a customer who buys a product for personal use.

Research helps identify the competition, learn about new business opportunities, and answer many other important business questions. Information provided by marketing research is also called *market intelligence* because it helps a business gain a competitive edge.

Understanding the competition is part of a market analysis. **Competition** is two or more businesses attempting to attract the same customers. In order for a company to achieve its sales goals, it may need to take business away from the competition.

> **Employability Skills**
> **Professional Image**
> An *image* is the perception others have of a person based on that person's dress, behavior, and speech. It is what people remember about a person from business, professional, and even social interactions. A *professional image* is the image projected by an individual in the professional world. A positive professional image projects honesty, skill, courtesy, and respect for others. Cultivating a professional image can pave the way for a successful career.

A **competitive analysis** is a tool used to compare the strengths and weaknesses of a business with those of competing businesses. Strengths are factors that give a company a competitive advantage. A *competitive advantage* of a product or business is offering better value, features, or service than the competition. Weaknesses are the factors that put a company in jeopardy compared to the competition.

In a competitive analysis, competitors are evaluated on facts such as physical locations, product lines, pricing, and market share. From this information, it can be determined how the company will compete with other companies to gain its share of sales in the market. An example of a competitive analysis is shown in Figure 3-3.

Competitive Analysis				
Variables	**Your Company**	**Competing Company A**	**Competing Company B**	**Competing Company C**
Physical Location	Yes	Yes	No	No
Product Lines	5	3	6	8
Designers	Well-known	High-end	Knockoff	Knockoff and Well-known
Pricing	\$28–\$50	\$40–\$100	\$30–\$60	\$20–\$80
Special Order	No	No	Yes	Yes
Continental US Shipping	\$0	\$4–\$6	\$5 flat fee	\$2.99–\$4.99
Market Share	7.5%	8.3%	10%	9.1%

Goodheart-Willcox Publisher

Figure 3-3 A competitive analysis is a tool used to compare the strengths and weaknesses of a business with those of competing businesses.

Learning about the competition includes estimating the portion of the market that each competitor holds. *Market size* is the total sales per year for a specific product held by all the competing businesses. *Market share* is the percentage of total sales in a market held by one business. *Market potential* is the maximum number of customers and amount of sales that can be generated from a specific segment in a defined timeframe.

Sales Analysis

Revenue is the money that a business makes from the goods and services it sells. Revenue is also called *income* or *sales*. A *sales analysis* shows whether sales are increasing or decreasing in an organization and helps determine future sales goals. Before sales goals are created, the sales history for the company must be analyzed.

Sales history is stored in the management information system of the company and is usually updated every day. A **Management Information System (MIS)** is an integrated system of computer hardware and software that gathers information and presents it in a manner to be used in the decision-making process. MIS is discussed in depth in Chapter 4.

Based on current and historical information, managers can plan and forecast sales for coming years. By evaluating past performance, future performance can be projected. **Sales forecast**, or *projections*, is a prediction of future sales based on past sales and a market analysis for a specific time period. The sales and executive teams create these forecasts. Sales forecasts are typically made for a minimum of one year to three to five years in the future.

The best opportunities are reviewed for making new and repeat sales. Opportunities to take business away from the competitors, expand into new geographic areas, and other potential sales sources are also identified.

Section 3.1 Review

Check Your Understanding

1. Identify examples of benefits that can result from the planning process.
2. Cite elements of a SMART goal.
3. List examples of types of plans written by management.
4. State the difference between internal and external factors that affect an organization.
5. What is a competitive advantage?

Build Your Vocabulary

As you progress through this text, develop a personal glossary of key terms. This will help you build your vocabulary and prepare you for a career. Write a definition for each of the following terms and add them to your personal glossary.

goal
SMART goal
strategic plan
tactical plan
operational plan
contingency plan
market research
primary research
secondary research
competition
competitive analysis
revenue
Management Information System (MIS)
sales forecast

Section 3.2 Developing Plans

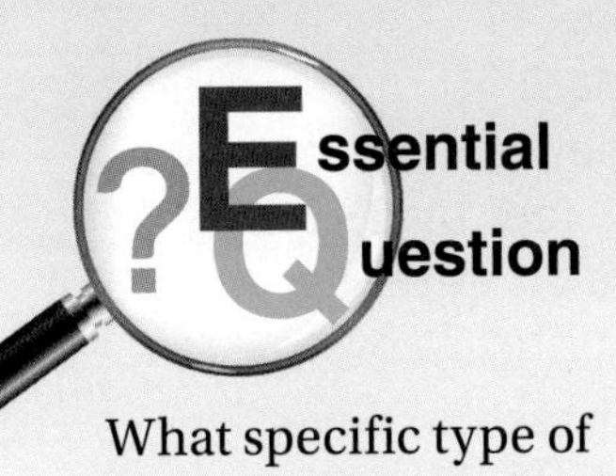

What specific type of planning do you think should take place in an organization?

Learning Objectives

LO 3.2-1 Summarize the strategic planning process.

LO 3.2-2 Explain the role of tactical plans in an organization.

LO 3.2-3 Describe two types of operational plans.

Key Terms

strategic planning process
business plan
mission statement
vision statement
planning tool
SWOT analysis
PEST analysis
tactic
budget
schedule
policy
procedure

LO 3.2-1 Strategic Plannning Process

Organizations typically perform various types of planning carried out by each level of management, starting with strategic planning by senior management. A *strategic plan* is designed to achieve the long-term goals of an organization as a whole. It is used to communicate to employees and owners where the organization is today, where it is going in the future, and how it will get there. It is a road map to the future of the organization. The plan projects two years, four years, or more for the future of an organization. Senior management is responsible for creating and putting the strategic plan in action.

The **strategic planning process** involves setting goals and allocating the resources necessary to achieve them. The process helps an organization look to the future and plan how to get there. As shown in Figure 3-4, the steps involved in strategic planning include:

- review organizational mission and vision statements;
- establish organizational goals;
- conduct situation analysis including internal and external analyses; and
- formulate the strategic plan.

Strategic planning, even though executed by senior management, draws on information provided by other levels of management and employees in the organization.

Review Organizational Mission and Vision Statements

The strategic planning process begins with a review of the mission statement found in the business plan of the organization.

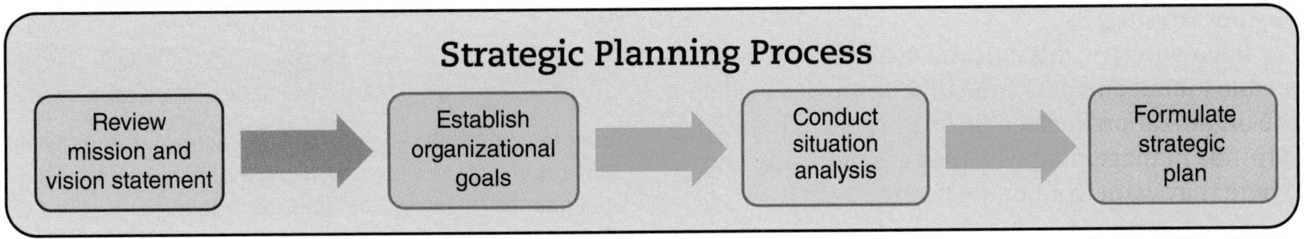

Goodheart-Willcox Publisher

Figure 3-4 The strategic planning process involves setting goals and allocating resources necessary to achieve them.

You Do the Math

Geometric Reasoning: Area

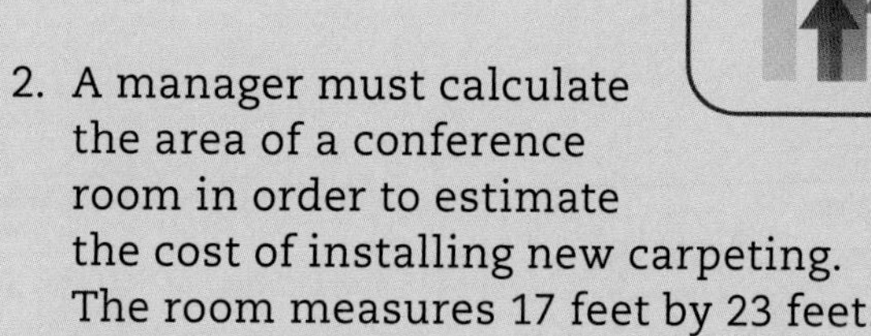

The area of a two-dimensional shape considers measurements of its perimeter. The area of a rectangle, for example, is calculated by multiplying the length of two sides that meet at a right angle. The area of a circle is calculated by multiplying the constant *pi* (3.14) by the radius of the circle squared.

Solve the following problems.

1. A facilities manager must calculate the area of a parking lot in order to estimate the cost of repaving it. The parking lot measures 75 feet by 125 feet. What is the area of the parking lot?
2. A manager must calculate the area of a conference room in order to estimate the cost of installing new carpeting. The room measures 17 feet by 23 feet. What is the area of the conference room?
3. Plywood must be purchased to cover a space that is 12 feet by 25 feet. One sheet of plywood is 4 feet by 8 feet. How many sheets of plywood must be purchased? Round up to the nearest whole sheet.

A **business plan** is a written document that describes a business, how it operates, and how it makes a profit. It defines the organization, its use of capital resources, and serves as a blueprint for operation and managerial success. It is typically written when the business is started and is updated each year. The business plan usually covers one year of operation.

In the business plan is the **mission statement**, which is the organization's message to customers about why the business exists. It describes the business, identifies the customers, and shows how the business adds value. Microsoft's corporate mission statement is "to empower every person and every organization on the planet to achieve more."

Management also reviews the vision statement in the business plan. A **vision statement** is what the business aspires to accomplish. The vision statement is like looking into a crystal ball and seeing the future of the company. Google's vision statement is "to provide access to the world's information in one click." A good vision statement should inspire employees and help drive the business to success.

Reviewing the mission and vision statements enable management to prioritize strategies to keep the organization focused on its purpose. This step reminds management why they are planning and where they want to go in the future.

Establish Organizational Goals

During the strategic planning process, managers set high-level goals for the whole organization to reach. Some examples include company acquisitions, facilities, and other plans to grow or otherwise position the business. Each year, senior management sets goals generally for one to five years to accomplish what the owners expect from operations. Owners expect challenging but reasonable goals that can be met.

wavebreakmedia/Shutterstock.com

A strategic plan is designed to achieve the long-term goals of an organization. **Why is it necessary for a business to look into the future and set long-term goals?**

After those goals are established, an analysis is completed to evaluate how a plan can be created to produce the expected results.

Conduct a Situation Analysis

After the organizational goals are established, a situation analysis is conducted. A *situation analysis* is a review of the internal and external factors that affects a business. Internal and external analyses provide a snapshot of the environment in which the business has been operating in over a given period, usually 12 to 16 months. It identifies factors of which an organization must be aware while working toward its goals.

To assist in this activity, planning tools are used. A **planning tool** is an instrument or document that guides a plan into action. Two common planning tools are SWOT and PEST analyses.

SWOT Analysis

A SWOT analysis is a planning tool used in the strategic process. A **SWOT analysis** is the identification of an organization's strengths, weaknesses, opportunities, and threats. It helps identify both internal and external factors that can affect success. A SWOT analysis includes four items as follows.

- *Strengths* are internal factors that give a company a competitive advantage. What is the business doing that is helping the company generate profits?
- *Weaknesses* are internal factors that place a company at a disadvantage relative to competitors. What are areas in which the organization needs to improve?
- *Opportunities* refer to favorable external conditions or trends that provide a company opportunity to generate profits. What opportunities can the company take advantage of that they may have missed in the past?
- *Threats* are external factors, such as the competition or economy that can potentially jeopardize a company's growth or ability to generate profits. Understanding the threats can help management refocus strategies.

For example, a SWOT analysis looks at whether the business offers a wider variety, better prices, or better sizing than the competition. A SWOT analysis is presented in a format similar to the one shown in Figure 3-5.

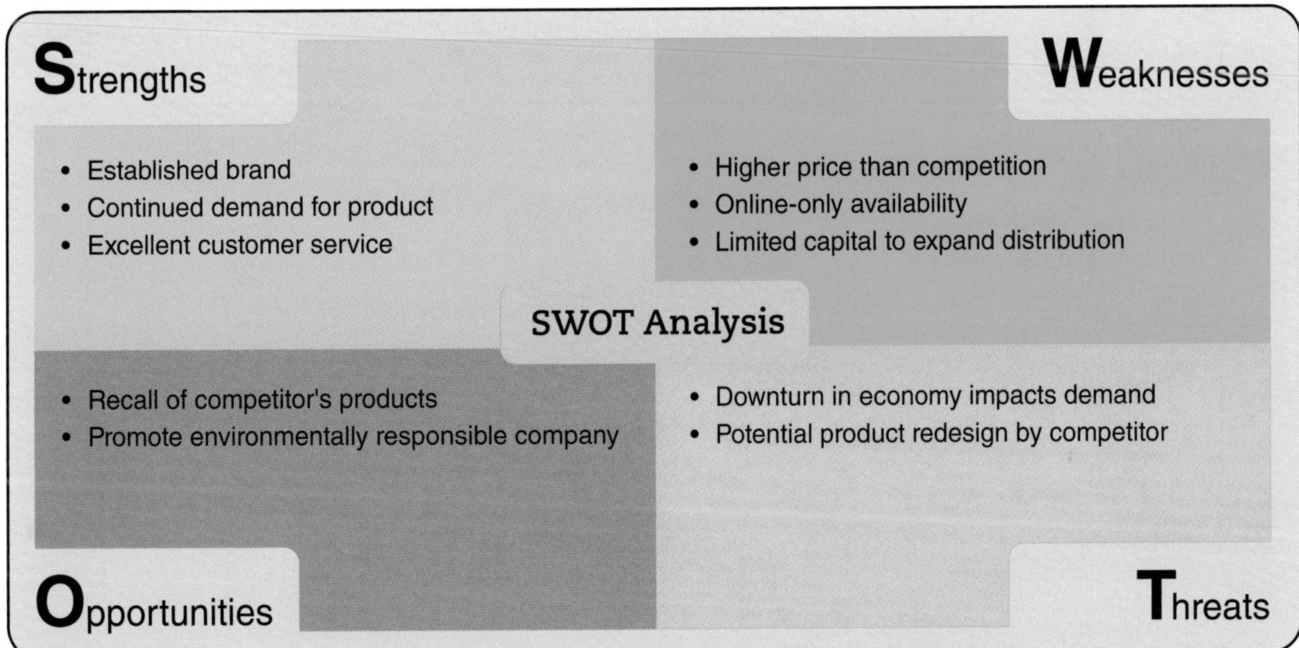

Goodheart-Willcox Publisher

Figure 3-5 A SWOT is a planning tool used to compare the strengths, weaknesses, opportunities, and threats of a business with those of competing businesses.

PEST Analysis

A **PEST analysis** is an evaluation of the political, economic, social, and technological factors in a certain market or geographic region that may affect the success of a business. A PEST analysis evaluates external factors that include four items as follows.

- *Political factors* affect the stability of the government and the success of the businesses that operate within it.
- *Economic factors* affect the ability of consumers to purchase products, as well as the costs of doing business.
- *Social factors* are cultural aspects within a business environment and personal characteristics of its customers, such as age, gender, income, ethnicity, education level, occupation, marital status, and family size.
- *Technological factors* affect the ease with which a business can operate within a market or region, as well as the level of productivity possible once the business is in operation.

A PEST analysis is an example of an environmental analysis, also called *environmental scan*. An environmental scan examines external factors that are beyond the control of a business and can affect its success. A PEST analysis can be presented in a format similar to the one in Figure 3-6.

Formulate the Strategic Plan

The result of the strategic planning process is to formulate a strategic plan. It involves *organizational strategy* which is identifying who is responsible for strategies, a timeframe for action, and resources needed. Specific details are put in writing to reflect the way in which the entire organization will implement the plan.

Using the strategic plan as the basis, individual tactical and operational plans are created. The plans are communicated to the organization so that employees understand the goals of the company and how to accomplish those goals.

LO 3.2-2 Tactical Plans

A *tactical plan* involves activities needed to implement strategic plans defined by senior management. A **tactic** is the strategy or action planned to reach the end goal. It is short term and usually covers a year or less.

Tactical plans define how an organization will use its resources to accomplish specific goals related to strategic plans. The plan outlines precise details on how to accomplish specific goals, work that will be done, who will do it, and what resources will be used. These plans are updated often as operating conditions change.

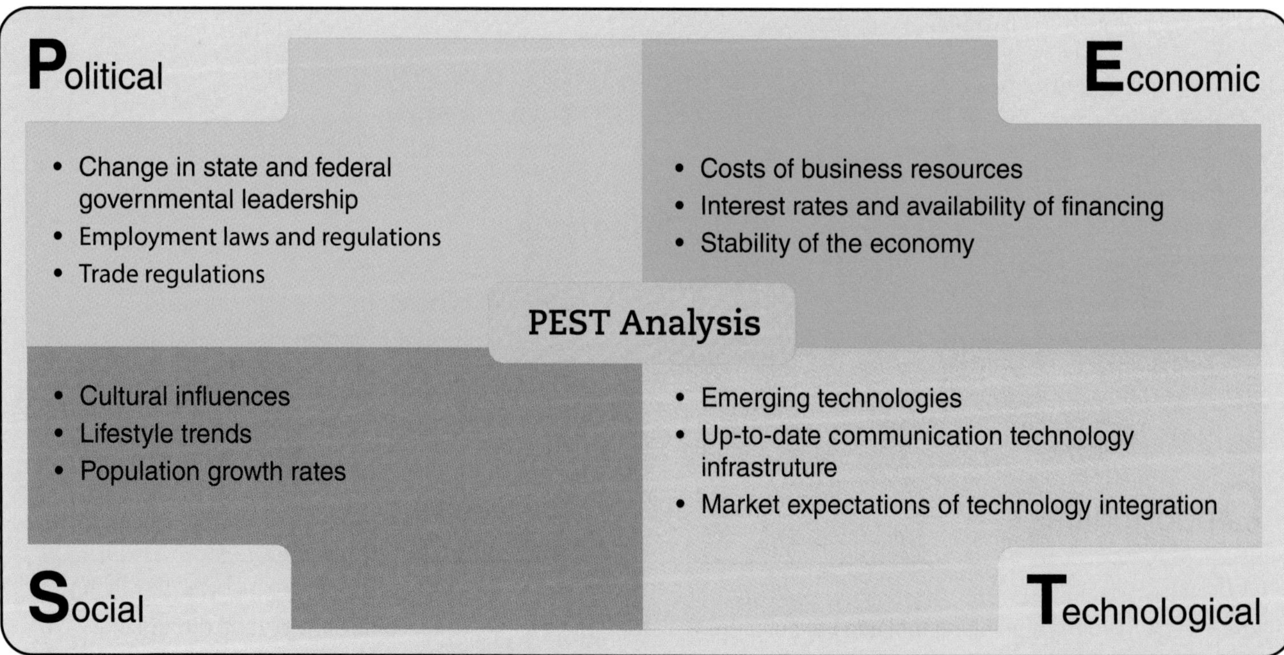

Goodheart-Willcox Publisher

Figure 3-6 A PEST analysis is an evaluation of the political, economic, social, and technological factors in a certain market or geographic region that may affect the success of a business.

Middle management is typically responsible for translating the strategic plan into tactical plans and guiding the execution of them in their divisions of the organization.

In large organizations, tactical plans are written for each specific functional area. Examples are human resources, financial management, sales and marketing, and production. Depending on the size of the company, the names of the groups may differ. Each functional area of a business creates its own tactical plan that outlines how it will meet its goals as defined by the strategic plan. Examples of tactical plans for individual areas are as follows.

- A tactical plan for *human resources* may focus on hiring and training employees, performance evaluations, governmental regulations, benefits, and all activities that relate to human resources.
- A tactical plan for *financial management* may be to manage the financial resources of a business including making decisions related to accounting, budgeting, and risk management.
- A tactical plan for *sales and marketing* may describe marketing or sales goals for the company and explain how they will be achieved. The plan might also include strategies for new product development.
- A tactical plan for *production* may focus on the activities needed to produce goods and services for the business, including how to convert raw materials and labor into a finished product in an efficient manner.

Tactical plans explain how the strategic plan is going to be accomplished and specific actions that need to take place. They can overlap with operational plans, which are even more detailed than tactical plans.

LO 3.2-3 Operational Plans

An *operational plan* defines the day-to-day tasks and activities that employees must perform to meet company goals to execute the tactical plan. Like all goals, these goals are specific and measureable. An example of a goal is *200 units* to be produced *per day*. Operational goals ask the following questions.

- Where are we now?
- Where do we want to be?
- How do we get there?

elwynn/Shutterstock.com

An operational plan defines the day-to-day tasks and activities that employees must perform to meet company goals to execute the tactical plan. **What do you believe would happen if a business did not create an operational plan?**

Operational plans usually cover one year or less. Supervisory management uses these plans to define how they will meet job responsibilities in the tactical plans that were conveyed to them by middle management. Depending on the organization, operational plans can be single-use or ongoing.

Single-Use Plan

A single-use plan is created for a specific purpose, such as sales. A sales plan is typically relevant for one year only. An example of a single-use plan is a budget. A **budget** is a financial plan that reflects anticipated revenue in numerical terms and shows how it will be allocated in the operation of the business. Budgets are usually created for each department in an organization and then rolled into one master company budget. Without a budget, a manager would not know how much money was available for operating his or her department. The goal is to stay within a budget during the timeframe for which it is projected.

Ongoing Plans

An ongoing plan is created once and updated as needed. This type of plan generally affects the daily operations to help guide a business to operate smoothly. These plans are also called *standing plans*. Examples of these plans include schedules, policies, and procedures.

Ethics

Accountability

Accountability is a person being responsible for his or her own activities and behavior. An ethical person accepts responsibility for his or her mistakes, whether large or small. Making a mistake is not unethical. However, not taking responsibility for an error or trying to cover it up is unethical.

Schedules

A **schedule** is a plan that identifies time and resources needed to complete tasks and activities. It is a tool used to allocate resources. Schedules are necessary to ensure deadlines are met and plans are executed in a timely manner. For example, a Gantt chart can be used to schedule completion dates for a project. A *Gantt chart* is a type of bar chart used to show when a task is supposed to be completed and compares it to the actual progress of the task. An example of a Gantt chart is shown in Figure 3-7.

In addition, schedules ensure the appropriate human resources are available as needed. Too many employees on the payroll will decrease profitability. Too few can put the organization at risk if there are not enough employees to create products to meet customer needs. Scheduling is especially important for managers who oversee day-to-day operations.

There are many software programs available for use that can increase efficiency of the scheduling process. Most management information systems have a program in which the manager is able to create a master schedule and then push the schedule electronically to employees. All workers see the same schedule at the same time. Changes can then be made and approved through the software, which eliminates the need for paper schedules.

Policies

A **policy** is a set of rules and regulations that guide the decision-making process. Policies support the mission and goals of an organization and define how to handle situations. Upper management typically creates policies that apply mostly to operational routines, recurring situations, or issues. For example, policies for customer service address issues such as how to

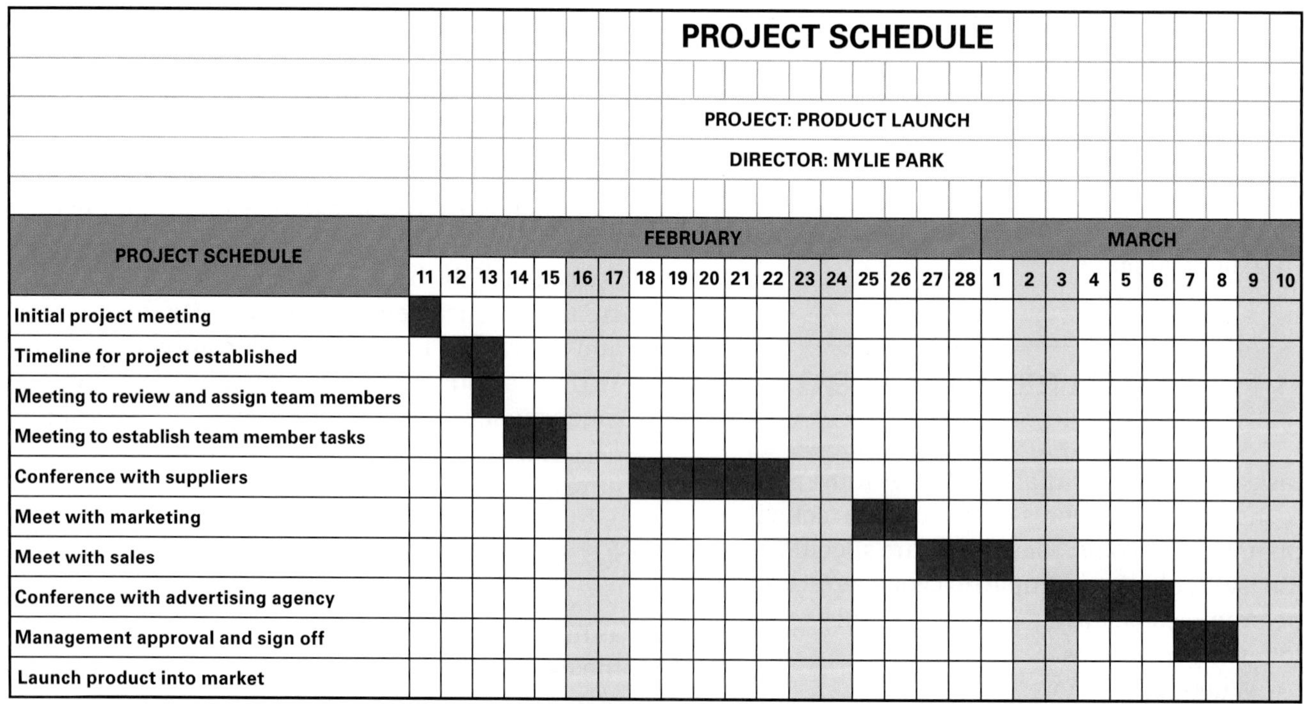

Goodheart-Willcox Publisher

Figure 3-7 A Gantt chart is a type of bar chart used to show when a task is supposed to be completed and compares it to the actual progress of the task.

handle a return. Macy's return policy for online purchases states, "If you're not completely happy with your macys.com purchase, ship it back to us for free!* It's easy."

Human resources policies that affect how employees request vacation days, hiring processes, and termination practices are established. Accounting departments may set policies on how to file an expense report or how reimbursement forms are completed. Once established, policies enable middle or supervisory management to resolve issues on their own without the need to consult other levels of management.

Procedures

A **procedure** is a description of how to complete a task and how a policy will be applied. Each procedure should outline:

- steps needed to complete a task;
- resources, forms, or documents needed to complete the task; and
- department or person responsible for completing the task.

Procedures improve efficiency and save money because they take the guesswork out of what needs to occur. For example, Figure 3-8 illustrates the procedure for returned merchandise by customer service in a department store.

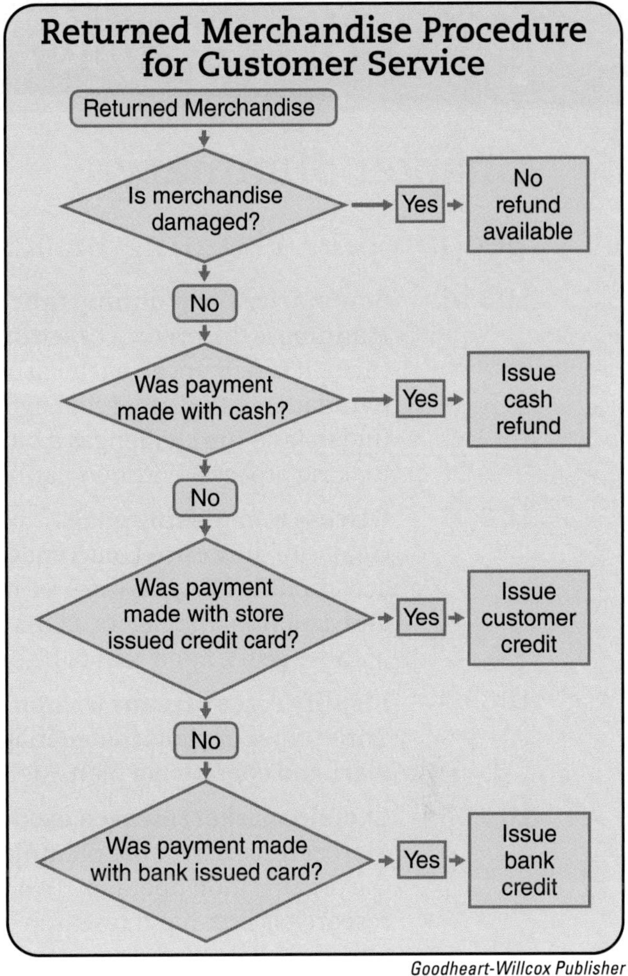

Figure 3-8 A procedure is a description of how to complete a task and how a policy will be applied.

Section 3.2 Review

Check Your Understanding

1. Identify the steps in the strategic planning process.
2. Define a situation analysis.
3. List examples of functional areas that might be in a large organization.
4. What is an example of a single-use plan?
5. Identify examples of ongoing plans.

Build Your Vocabulary

As you progress through this text, develop a personal glossary of key terms. This will help you build your vocabulary and prepare you for a career. Write a definition for each of the following terms and add them to your personal glossary.

strategic planning process	planning tool	budget
business plan	SWOT analysis	schedule
mission statement	PEST analysis	policy
vision statement	tactic	procedure

Chapter 3 Review and Assessment

Chapter Summary

Section 3.1 Planning Basics

LO 3.1-1 **Summarize the planning function of management.**
Planning is the process of setting goals and objectives and deciding how to accomplish them. It is referenced as the primary function of management because it forms the foundation for all other management functions. Planning requires that managers understand the challenges a business faces and know how to apply the decision-making process. Without planning, an organization would not be successful.

LO 3.1-2 **Discuss establishing goals.**
Goals are the desired outcomes or targets that an organization is striving to accomplish. They are the first step in planning and serve as guidelines for the decisions and actions of managers. Plans can then be developed to work toward the completion of those goals. For a goal to be effective, it should be a SMART goal.

LO 3.1-3 **Identify types of plans written by management.**
Three types of plans that managers typically create include a strategic plan, tactical plan, and operational plan. Most managers also have a contingency, or backup, plan.

LO 3.1-4 **Explain market research used for planning.**
Market research for the planning process includes reviewing the environment in which the organization operates. Two types of research are primary and secondary. Primary research is first-hand research conducted by a researcher. Secondary research is data already collected and recorded by someone else.

LO 3.1-5 **Cite examples of data analysis used for planning purposes.**
Two important analyses that help businesses make decisions during the planning process include market analysis and sales analysis.

Section 3.2 Developing Plans

LO 3.2-1 **Summarize the strategic planning process.**
The strategic planning process involves setting goals and allocating the resources necessary to achieve them. The process helps an organization look to the future and plan how to get there. The steps involved include review organizational mission and vision statements, establish organizational goals, conduct a situation analysis, and formulate a strategic plan.

LO 3.2-2 **Explain the role of tactical plans in an organization.**
Tactical plans define how an organization will use its resources to accomplish specific goals related to strategic plans. The plan outlines precise details on how to accomplish specific goals, work that will be done, who will do it, and what resources will be used.

LO 3.2-3 **Describe two types of operational plans.**
Operational plans can be single-use or ongoing. A single-use plan is created for a specific purpose, such as sales. An ongoing plan is created once and updated as needed. Examples include schedules, policies, and procedures.

Review Your Knowledge

1. Summarize the planning function of management.
2. Describe the process of establishing goals.
3. Explain each type of plan written by management.
4. Discuss research used during management planning.
5. Briefly explain two examples of data analysis used for planning purposes.
6. Summarize the strategic planning process.
7. What is the role of mission statements and vision statements in a business plan?
8. Explain the role of tactical plans in an organization.
9. What questions do operational goals ask?
10. Describe two types of operational plans.

Apply Your Knowledge

1. Planning provides obvious advantages for an organization. In your own words, explain the necessity of proper planning for an organization.
2. Using the SMART-goal format, write one short-term goal and one long-term goal for a business that provides accounting services.
3. Create a Venn diagram that compares and contrasts strategic, tactical, and operational plans. In each circle, list characteristics that are unique to one type of plan. Then, list qualities shared between the plans where the circles overlap. What do they have in common?
4. Businesses need contingency plans to prepare for the unknown. Without a backup plan, an organization could collapse if an unexpected event happens. Assume you are a manager for a manufacturing company. Identify an example of a circumstance that is beyond your control. How could you prepare for this circumstance with a contingency plan?
5. One component of a market analysis is the competitive analysis. Within the competitive analysis, businesses determine their competitive advantage. Choose a company or product that you consider a favorite. Determine three competitive advantages for that company or product.
6. A business plan is needed for managerial success and managing capital resources. Discuss why you think this statement is true.
7. A PEST analysis evaluates the political, economic, social, and technological factors that may affect the success of a business. Explain why you think it is important to examine each of these factors when making plans for a business.
8. Select a project you need to complete during the school year. Using Figure 3-7 as an example, create a Gantt chart to schedule the completion of this project. Along the Y-axis of the chart, list each task that must be completed. Then, project how long it will take you to complete each task along the X-axis of the chart.
9. Create a flowchart that could be used to guide an employee of a car-rental company who must decide whether to implement a refund policy.
10. Write a procedure to describe the steps required to complete a task with which you are familiar, such as how to apply for a job or how to change a tire. Include steps needed to complete the task; any resources, forms, or other documents needed; and any other person or organization who must be involved in order for the task to be completed.

Communication Skills

Speaking. *Circumlocution* is the use of many words to convey an idea when fewer would do. It can be used to communicate an idea when the exact word is not known. For example, suppose you do not know the word "democracy." Instead, you say, "the form of government in which each person has a say." Use circumlocution to describe to a classmate how to establish goals without using the word "goal." Was your classmate able to determine your meaning?

Listening. *Informative listening* is the process of listening to gain specific information or instructions from the speaker. Ask a classmate to give you directions to the school cafeteria. Take notes as the directions are given. If necessary, ask the speaker to slow down or repeat a point. Summarize your notes and retell the directions to your classmate to confirm your understanding of them. Follow the directions as they were given. Did you arrive at the cafeteria?

Reading. A *sentence* is a group of words that expresses a complete thought. In the English language, a complete sentence has a subject and a predicate. The *subject* is the person speaking or the person, place, or thing a sentence describes. The *predicate* describes the action or state of being for the subject. Select three sentences in this chapter. Identify the subject and predicate in each. Exchange your sentences with a partner to check each other's work.

Internet Research

Planning Function. Planning involves setting goals and objectives and deciding how to accomplish them. Conduct a search for *planning function of management.* What information did you learn about the planning function that was not discussed in this chapter? Write a summary of the new information you learned.

Contingency Plan. A contingency plan is a backup plan that outlines alternative courses of action to take if other plans prove unproductive or circumstances beyond control change. Conduct a search for *contingency planning.* Summarize the information you found.

Strategic Planning Process. A *graphic organizer* is a visual tool used to express concepts or ideas and observe the relationship between them. Examples include a concept map, Venn diagram, or a flowchart. Using the Internet, conduct secondary research for the *strategic planning process.* Use a graphic organizer of your choice to display information about the process.

Teamwork

Collaboration skills are skills that enable individuals to work with others to achieve a common goal. Working with your team, create a tool that could be used for primary research. Select one format such as a survey, focus group, case study, or another of your choice that is appropriate. Next, create and distribute the final product to your classmates for feedback.

Portfolio Development

File Structure. After you have chosen either a print or electronic portfolio type, determine a strategy for storing and organizing the materials. Think of this step in portfolio creation as building a pool of documents from which you can add to your portfolio. The file structure is similar for both hard-copy and electronic portfolios.

First, you need a place to store each item. Hard-copy documents can be stored in folders or in a three-ring binder. For digital files, ask your instructor about the best place to save your documents. This could be on the school's network or a flash drive of your own.

Next, decide how to organize related files into categories and subcategories. The names for folders and files should be descriptive but not too long. For example, you may label a folder *Certificates* with one subfolder named *Community Service Certificates* and a second subfolder that says *School Certificates*. Appropriate certificates would be saved in their respective subfolder.

1. Decide on the file structure for your documents.
2. Create folders and subfolders on the school's network drive or flash drive on which you will save your files.

CTSOs

Objective Test. Some competitive events for CTSOs require that entrants complete an objective component of the event. This event will typically be an objective test that includes terminology and concepts related to a selected subject area. Participants are usually allowed one hour to complete the objective test component of the event.

To prepare for an objective test, complete the following activities.

1. Read the guidelines provided by your organization.
2. Visit the website of the organization and look for objective tests that were used in previous years. Many organizations post these tests for students to use as practice for future competitions.
3. Look for the evaluation criteria or rubric for the event. This will help you determine what the judge will be looking for in your presentation.
4. Create flash cards for each vocabulary term with its definition on the other side. Ask a friend to use these cards to review with you.
5. Ask your instructor to give you practice tests for this chapter of the text that would prepare you for the subject area of the event. It is important that you are familiar with answering multiple choice and true/false questions. Have someone time you as you take a practice test.

CHAPTER 4

Managing with Information

Sections

4.1 Information Technology

4.2 Systematic Decision-Making Process

Reading Prep

Before reading this chapter, preview the content by examining its headings, key terms, and illustrations. Write three to four sentences on what you think this chapter will cover.

Exploring Careers

Computer and Information Systems Manager

Business Management & Administration

Computer and information systems managers determine the information technology goals of an organization. They are responsible for implementing computer systems to meet organizational needs. These managers are responsible for planning, coordinating, and directing computer-related activities in an organization.

Typical job titles for this position include *information technology (IT) manager* or *IT project manager*. Examples of tasks computer and information systems managers perform include:

- planning and directing the tasks of the IT department;
- identifying new technology and upgrades for organization's computer systems;
- working with senior managers to assess the cost and benefits of possible upgrades;
- negotiating with vendors to get the highest level of service; and
- directing installation and maintenance of computer hardware and software.

Computer and information systems manager positions require a bachelor degree in a computer or information science related field. Many organizations also require a master degree. The position also requires prior work experience in an information technology job or related field. Common skills that computer and information system managers have include analytical, decision-making, planning, organizational, and technology skills.

jijomathaidesigners/Shutterstock.com

Section 4.1 Information Technology

What comes to mind when hearing the term *management information system*?

Learning Objectives

LO 4.1-1 Summarize management information for planning purposes.

LO 4.1-2 Identify examples of budgets used in the budgeting process.

Key Terms

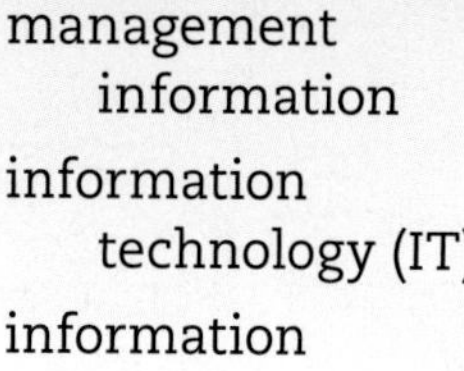

management information
information technology (IT)
information technology (IT) control
technology infrastructure
data mining
data processing
table
graph
chart
flowchart
illustration
operating budget
income statement
sales budget
quantitative
qualitative

LO 4.1-1 Management Information for Planning Purposes

Planning is about decision-making. In order to make sound decisions and reduce risk, information must be available to the management team. Gathering data and sharing information is an important component of the planning process.

Management information is data used for *strategic purposes. Data* are the pieces of information gathered through research. Management information is the basis for all planning in an organization. It provides historical data, current data, and the basis for forecasting future data for planning purposes.

Technology enables an organization to constantly research, gather, and update data from external and internal sources and put it into information systems. *External information* originates from research that includes observing the competition, evaluating economic conditions, and analyzing various other sources outside the company. *Internal information* originates from within an organization as business occurs. This is the strategic information that various departments, such as accounting or sales, enter on a regular basis.

An important consideration about information is that it must be collected from reputable sources. In addition, data must be protected and used for the good of the organization.

Information technology (IT) is the use of computers for storing, sending, and retrieving information. **Information technology (IT) control** is the procedures an organization follows to ensure information technology is used as intended, data is accurate, and information is in legal compliance. An information-technology system must control the confidentiality, honesty, and availability of data and the overall management of information technology.

Technology infrastructure is the hardware, software, and related equipment used to support IT. Most organizations use a management information system that facilities IT and its procedures. A *Management Information System (MIS)* is an integrated system of computer hardware and software that gathers information and presents it in a manner to be used in the decision-making process. It is an organized system of gathering, sorting, analyzing, evaluating, distributing, and storing information for the organization. A MIS is the technology infrastructure that supports data that flows, its storage, and its analyzation.

SeventyFour/Shutterstock.com

A technology system provides intelligence so planning can happen, decisions can be made, and problems can be resolved. **What types of technology systems are used in your school?**

A technology system provides intelligence so planning can happen, decisions can be made, and problems can be solved. Similar to other planning tools, output from an information system is used in all functions of management. It is of special importance in the controlling function when company performance is evaluated. The tasks a MIS must be able to perform are capture data; store, update, and process data; and present data.

Capture Data

Each department in an organization is responsible for tracking its success. Based on business needs, some departments have their own independent software programs used specifically for their purposes. Examples are a(n):

- accounting-information system (AIS) that reflects all financial aspects of the business;
- operations-information system that tracks production of products and inventory;
- sales-management information system that tracks sales and customer data;
- marketing-information system (MkIS) that manages all aspects of marketing and advertising; and
- human-resources-management system (HRMS) that includes information pertaining to employees, payroll, and benefits.

Most organizations have a MIS that feeds information from various department software programs into one system so data can be centrally housed and extracted. Organizations sometimes say that the various software programs "talk" to each other. This enables a user to generate reports that draw from all aspects of the company.

The important takeaway is that all data must be complete and accommodate the needs of an entire company. Information not in the system cannot be used.

Store, Update, and Process Data

After data is entered into a MIS, it must be stored for safekeeping. Some organizations store information on the server at the business location with a backup server off-site. The *cloud* is a common choice for an off-site secure method to store information.

Information for decision-making purposes is constantly updated. If it is not current, it will be useless. Each individual department typically updates their own system regularly, sometimes daily or multiple times within a day. This ensures information is up to "real time." The information is then available in a central location in the company's MIS and can be accessed by those who have permission to do so.

Without a central repository, each department maintains departmental spreadsheets and databases. The only way to share the information is to create reports and distribute them to management. This is inefficient since each department plays an integrated role in the overall success of the organization. With a MIS, information can be independently retrieved by every department in the organization and reports generated.

Through data mining, information is extracted from a MIS and presented in various formats for use in the decision-making process. **Data mining** is searching through large amounts of digital data to find useful patterns or trends.

Data processing is the process of transforming information into usable form. For data to be of value, it must be able to be processed. Most information in a MIS is number based, so the system must be able to process the data into a usable form.

Present Data

For most managers, an important part of a MIS is the reports generated to make decisions. Information is required in all aspects of business. For example, the sales team enters information that includes customer contact information. The accounting department enters units sold and sales dollars earned. When a report is needed to review revenue, an on-demand report is generated

Stephen Coburn/Shutterstock.com

Sometimes reports include visuals to display important points of information in a graphic format. **In what ways do you think visuals help a reader understand information?**

that includes information that was entered by both the sales and accounting departments. The output is a report that management can use for effective decision-making.

Extracted information is presented in various formats. The format chosen will depend on the type of information presented and the needs of those receiving the information. *Reports* are one method of presenting information.

Sometimes reports include visuals to display important points of information in a graphic format. Examples of visuals are a table, graph, chart, and illustration.

- A **table** is a visual that displays information in columns and rows and often used to compare data.
- A **graph** depicts information using lines, bars, or other symbols. Examples are circle graphs, line graphs, bar graphs, and infographics (information graphics). A bar graph is illustrated in Figure 4-1.
- A **chart** shows a process or hierarchy. An example is a **flowchart**, which depicts steps in a process.
- An **illustration** includes maps, drawings, and photographs. Illustrations add interest and provide a realistic view of the information.

LO 4.1-2 Budgets

Budgets are examples of reports for which information is extracted from the systems of an organization. A *budget* is a financial plan that reflects anticipated revenue in numerical terms and shows how it will be allocated in the operation of the business. It is a tool for allocating resources.

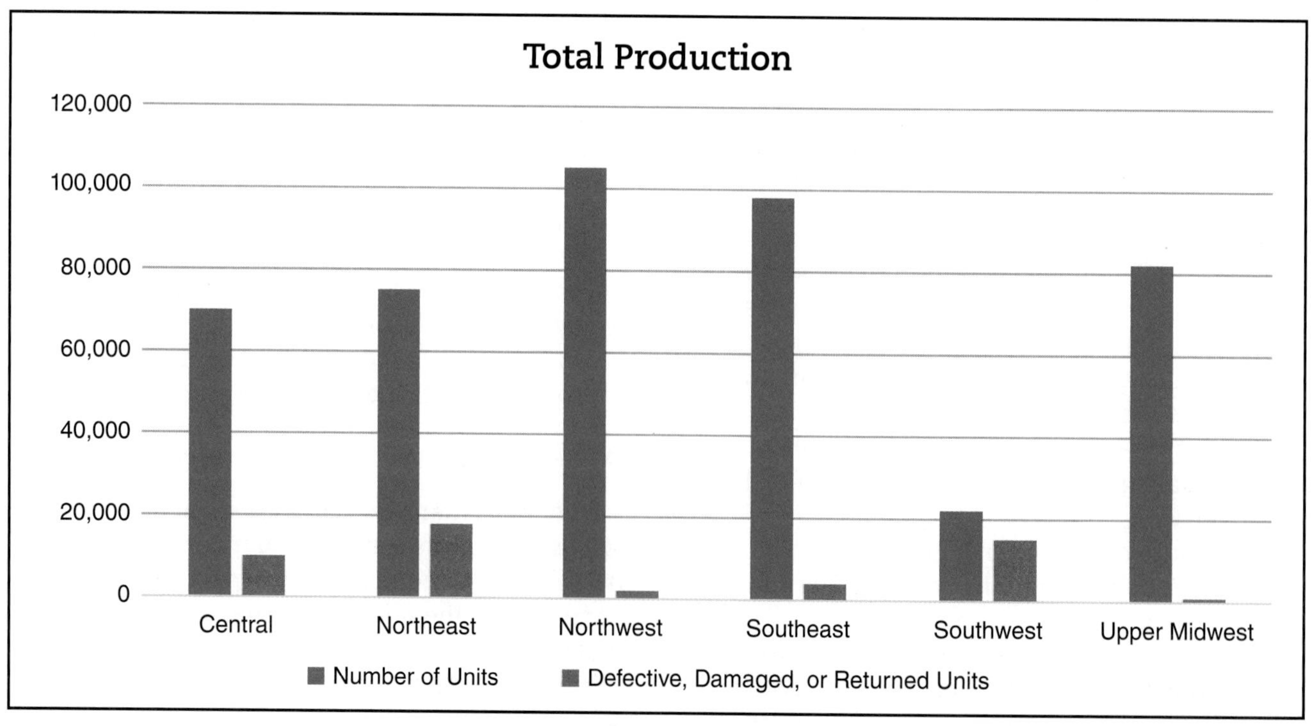

Goodheart-Willcox Publisher

Figure 4-1 A graph depicts information using lines, bars, or other symbols.

Budgets are typically created for a quarter and then for the year. Generally, each department creates a budget that becomes part of the company master budget.

Budgeting is a projection used to plan financial strategies. Some managers call it an *educated guess*. It is a forecast that helps management meet objectives and plan for growth. Eventually, budgets are reviewed during the control function and compared to actual financial statements. *Financial statements* are financial reports that summarize accounting data for the business. By comparing budgets to actual financial statements, managers can determine the accuracy of their estimates in relation to actual numbers. Examples of important budgets created in the planning process are an operating budget and a sales budget.

Operating Budget

An **operating budget** is a projection of the sales revenue that will be earned and the expenses that will be incurred during a future period of time. It is a master budget that combines information from departmental budgets, as shown in Figure 4-2. An operating budget typically contains the following sections.

- **Sales figure.** This projection is from the sales budget.
- **Cost of goods sold.** This number is a projection of the cost of goods to be sold to customers. If the company produces goods to sell, the cost of goods sold budget will include the labor, materials, and other costs of producing the goods.
- **Operating expenses.** Each department forecasts the expenses needed to operate. This includes salaries and other expenses needed for operation.

An operating budget uses the same accounts as an income statement. An **income statement** is a financial statement that reports the revenue and expenses of a business for a specific timeframe and shows a net income or net loss. The operating budget is compared to the income statement at the end of the quarter and year. This enables managers to evaluate the accuracy of their forecasts when compared to actual performance numbers. The process of comparing the operating budget to the income statement is a part of the controlling function of management.

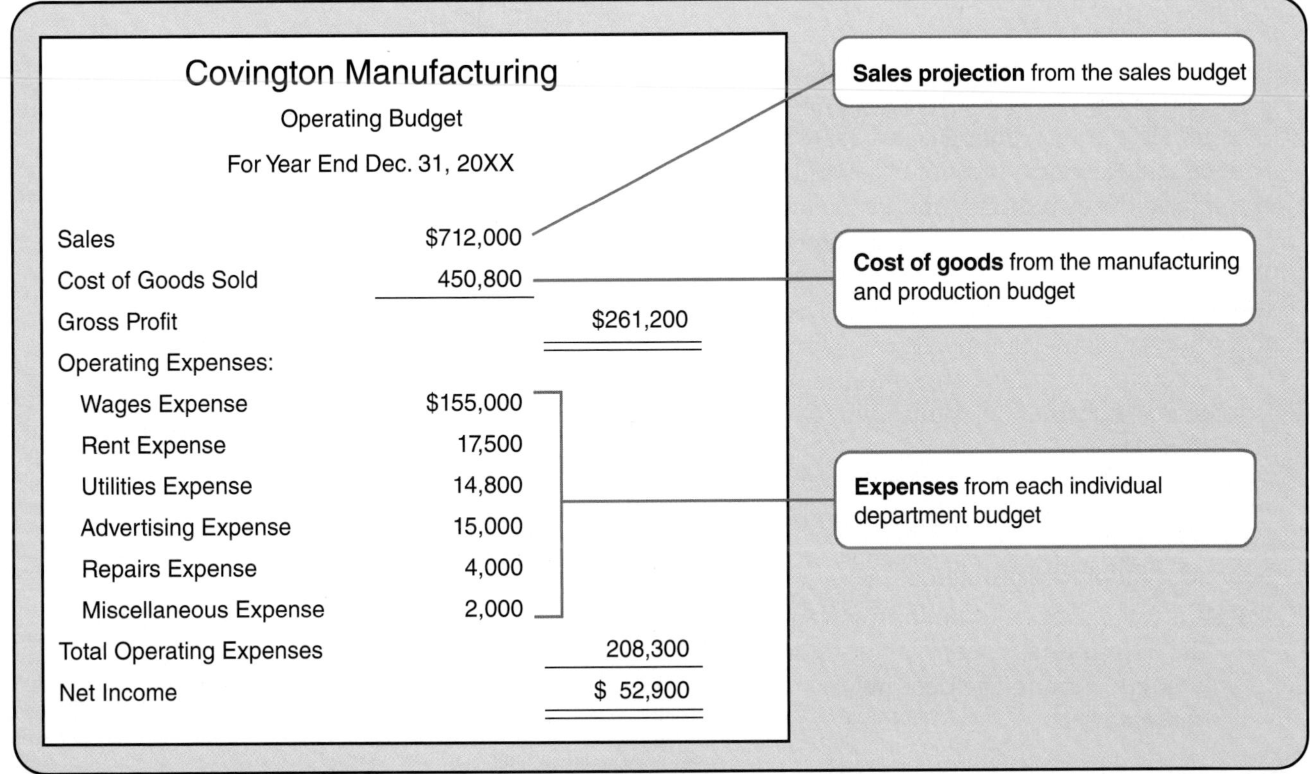

Covington Manufacturing
Operating Budget
For Year End Dec. 31, 20XX

Sales	$712,000	
Cost of Goods Sold	450,800	
Gross Profit		$261,200
Operating Expenses:		
Wages Expense	$155,000	
Rent Expense	17,500	
Utilities Expense	14,800	
Advertising Expense	15,000	
Repairs Expense	4,000	
Miscellaneous Expense	2,000	
Total Operating Expenses		208,300
Net Income		$ 52,900

Goodheart-Willcox Publisher

Figure 4-2 An operating budget is a projection of the sales revenue that will be earned and the expenses that will be incurred during a future period of time.

Sales Budget

An important source of information for an operating budget is the sales budget. A **sales budget** is a projection of sales in both units and dollars. Sales are also called revenue. *Revenue* is the money that a business makes for selling goods or services. A *sales forecast* is a prediction of future sales based on past sales and a market analysis for a specific time period. Sales information is extracted from the MIS of the organization. Historical sales figures are evaluated, marketing successes and failures are reviewed, and external and internal factors are considered. *External factors* are those things that are beyond company control, such as the economy or political events. *Internal factors* are events that occur within the organization, such as changes in the distribution channel or labor problems that influence sales.

By evaluating past performance, future performance can be predicted. A sales forecast helps define actions the sales and marketing team will take to meet those revenue goals. The formula for a *sales forecast* is as follows.

previous-year sales dollars + forecasted sales-increase dollars = forecasted sales-dollar goal

In the following example, the sales forecast for the year is $600,000 based on the previous year's sales dollars of $500,000 and an expected $100,000 increase sales goal.

$500,000 + $100,000 = $600,000

Sales forecasts may be **quantitative**, which means based on facts and figures. Quantitative data includes past sales history, market share, and the disposable income of the target market. One way to complete a quantitative sales forecast is to use the previous sales dollar amount and add a sales-increase factor. A *sales-increase factor* is the percentage of expected increase in sales. Many companies set sales goals based on a percentage of increase from the previous year.

You Do the Math

Measurement Reasoning: Unit Conversion

Various systems of measurement are used throughout the world. The United States uses a system called the US Customary System that consists of feet, pounds, and degrees Fahrenheit. However, most of the world uses a variation of the metric system called the *Système International d'Unités (SI)*, or International System of Units. The SI system consists of meters, grams, and degrees Celsius. The following are some common conversions.

- To convert degrees Fahrenheit to degrees Celsius, subtract 32, multiply by 5, and divide by 9.
- One inch is equal to 25.4 millimeters.
- One pound is equal to 0.45 kilograms.

Solve the following problems.

1. If a carton ready for shipping weighs 18.7 kilograms, how many pounds does it weigh? Round the decimal to the nearest tenth.
2. A sales manager must ship a temperature-sensitive good to a country that uses the metric system. The product cannot be exposed to temperatures below 0 degrees Fahrenheit. She must place a label on the package indicating this temperature in degrees Celsius. What temperature must be written on the label? Round the decimal to the nearest tenth.
3. A production manager must order lengths of specialized steel rods from a company in Germany. He needs the rods to measure 0.3 feet long. However, the rods must be ordered in increments of 10 millimeters. What length of rod must be ordered?

The formula for *forecasted sales dollar increase* is as follows.

previous-year sales dollars × sales-increase factor percentage = forecasted sales-increase dollars

For example, perhaps a company had a sales goal of a 20-percent increase in sales from year one to year two. If year-one sales were $500,000, the expected amount of sales increase is $100,000.

$500,000 × 20% = $100,000

Sales forecasts may also be **qualitative**, which means based on judgment. Qualitative sales forecasts are most often used when a new business is opening or a new product is being introduced. In order to remain profitable, it is important for a company to constantly monitor its sales forecasts and make changes as necessary.

Rawpixel.com/Shutterstock.com

By evaluating past performance, future performance can be predicted. **What does this phrase mean to you?**

Section 4.1 Review

Check Your Understanding

1. Describe basic technology infrastructure used by businesses.
2. What tasks must a MIS be able to perform?
3. List examples of visuals that can be used to present data.
4. How can an income statement aid in making financial plans for an organization?
5. State the formula for a sales forecast.

Build Your Vocabulary

As you progress through this text, develop a personal glossary of key terms. This will help you build your vocabulary and prepare you for a career. Write a definition for each of the following terms and add them to your personal glossary.

management information
information technology (IT)
information technology (IT) control
technology infrastructure
data mining
data processing
table
graph
chart
flowchart
illustration
operating budget
income statement
sales budget
quantitative
qualitative

Section 4.2

Systematic Decision-Making Process

What are examples of situations in which a manager might apply the systematic decision-making process?

Learning Objectives

LO 4.2-1 Discuss accounting information for managers.

LO 4.2-2 List the steps of the systematic decision-making process.

LO 4.2-3 Cite examples of decision-making tools.

Key Terms 

accounting	marginal benefit	trade-off
jargon	marginal cost	opportunity cost
decision-making	law of diminishing marginal utility	value
cost-benefit analysis		

LO 4.2-1 Accounting Information

Not every manager in an organization will have an accounting degree, or even have taken an accounting class. However, every manager must be responsible and understand how to make financial decisions that help keep a company profitable. Financial decisions can be as basic as how much money to spend on supplies. Alternatively, decisions can be more complex and costly, such as buying new equipment or hiring additional employees. Without accounting information, wise decision-making and planning are not possible.

Accounting is a system of recording business transactions and analyzing, verifying, and reporting results. Under the supervision of the financial manager, company accountants analyze and record all financial activities. The final output is financial statements and reports used by all levels of management to make decisions for the organization. Without accounting information, managers would not be able to make decisions that would meet the goals of profitability.

Business professionals need a basic knowledge of accounting jargon. **Jargon** is the language specific to a line of work or area of expertise. By understanding basic accounting terms, managers can learn how to use accounting information provided to them. A list of basic jargon used in reports and operations of the business is shown in Figure 4-3.

Ethics

Cyberethics

Cyberethics is the study of ethics in using computers and computer networks and the resulting effect on people, organizations, and society. An example of a cyberethics violation is using an employer's information technology system to gain restricted or confidential information about the company. Misuse of a company's technology is unethical and potentially illegal.

Accounting Jargon	
Jargon Term	**Definition**
Assets	Property or items of value owned by a business
Audit	Review of the financial statements of a business and the accounting practices that were used to produce them
Balance Sheet	Financial statement that reports the assets, liabilities, and owner's equity of an organization
Capital	Money and other assets owned by a business and used to produce goods and services
Cash Flow Statement	Financial statement that reports how cash moves into and out of a business
Expenses	Cost involved in operating a business
Fiscal Period	Period of time for which a business summarizes accounting information and prepares financial statements
Generally Accepted Accounting Principles (GAAP)	Rules, standards, and practices that a business follows to record and report financial information
Income Statement	Financial statement that reports the revenue and expenses of a business for a specific time period and shows a net income or net loss; also called profit and loss (P & L) statement
Liabilities	Business debts, or what a business owes
Owner's Equity Statement	Financial statement that summarizes changes in the owner's equity during a fiscal period
Revenue	Money that a business earns for the goods and services it sells; also called income
Sales	Revenue earned from selling goods or services
Working Capital	Difference between current assets and current liabilities

Goodheart-Willcox Publisher

Figure 4-3 Through the understanding of basic accounting terms, managers can learn how to use accounting information provided to them.

LO 4.2-2 Systematic Decision-Making

Everyone in an organization makes decisions each day. Employees decide which task to do first, how to interact with customers, and solutions to everyday challenges. Managers, by nature of their job, make decisions that directly influence employees as well as the success of an organization.

All workers can benefit by using a decision-making process. **Decision-making** is a process of choosing a course of action after evaluating available information and weighing the costs and benefits of alternative actions and their consequences. The process provides a structured way to find answers to problems, save time when looking for a solution, and can actually save money for an organization.

An example of application of the decision-making process is demonstrated during the planning process. Managers establish goals, project performance, and outline how success can be achieved. Decisions that affect the entire organization cannot be met without systematically reviewing the facts and potential outcomes of their actions. A rational, systematic decision-making process can help managers arrive at the best course of action during and after the planning process. It involves five steps, as shown in Figure 4-4.

1. **Define the decision to be made.** A clear idea of the issue must be formulated in order to find the best approach. If a problem is too broad, managers will not be able to accurately address the issue and find a solution.
2. **Gather information.** Once the issue has been defined, information must be gathered in order to make a sound decision.
3. **Choose the best alternative.** After considering all potential solutions, one that best fits the situation can be selected. It may be a single alternative or some combination of alternatives.
4. **Act on the decision.** Once a solution is narrowed down, action can be taken. Implementation can then occur.
5. **Evaluate the solution or decision.** Evaluation is an ongoing process. As a plan is implemented, the solution is evaluated and confirmed if it is working or if a new course of action should be taken.

There are times when the result of the decision-making process is not what was expected or achieved. When this happens, a contingency plan must be in place. A *contingency plan* is a backup plan that outlines alternative courses of action to take if other plans prove unproductive or circumstances beyond control change. Under Armour®, Target, and Instagram have detailed specific contingency plans to keep their businesses operating.

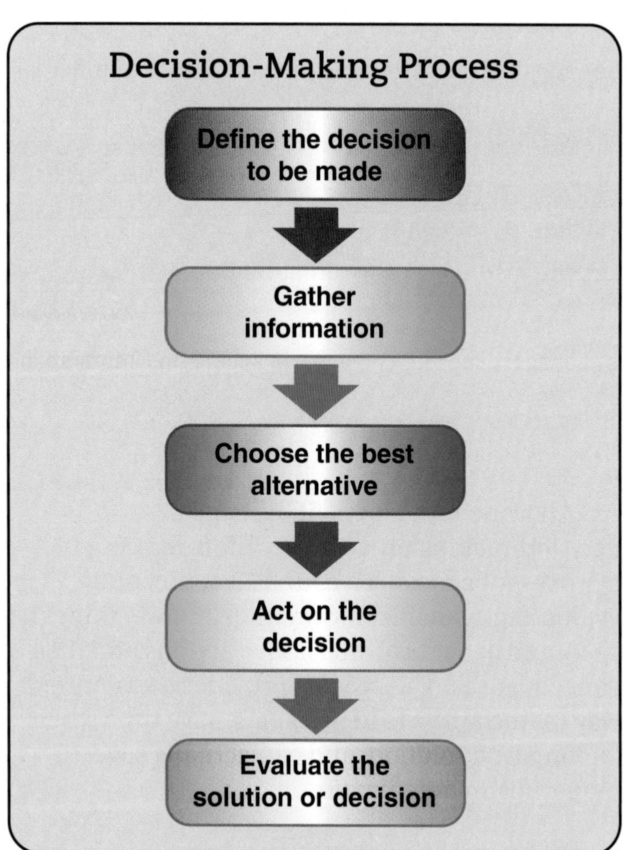

Goodheart-Willcox Publisher

Figure 4-4 Decision-making is a process of choosing a course of action after evaluating available information and weighing the costs and benefits of alternative actions and their consequences.

LO 4.2-3 Decision-Making Tools

SWOT and PEST analyses are important decision-making tools used by management. Other examples of tools used in the decision-making process include cost-benefit analysis, marginal analysis, and trade-off and opportunity costs.

Cost-Benefit Analysis

Cost-benefit analysis is a method of weighing the costs against the benefits of an action, a purchase, or a financial decision. It shows that it is in the interest of a business to take an action or make a purchase only if the benefits are at least as great as the costs.

Marginal Analysis

Marginal analysis is also a powerful decision-making tool. It measures the added benefit versus the added cost of one more unit of a product. The change in total benefit of using one additional unit is the **marginal benefit**. Marginal benefit measures the potential gains of producing more products because the profit margin is higher. The change in total cost of using one additional unit is the **marginal cost**.

Employability Skills
Netiquette

Netiquette is etiquette used when communicating electronically. It is also known as *digital etiquette*. Netiquette includes accepted social and professional guidelines for Internet-based communication. These guidelines apply to e-mails, social networking, and other contact with customers and peers via the Internet. Netiquette dictates proper usage of Standard English, grammar, and professionalism when communicating. It also involved avoiding spamming other people. *Spamming* is intentionally sending numerous, unwanted e-mails or social media messages.

The economic **law of diminishing marginal utility** states that the marginal benefit of using each additional unit of an item tends to decrease as the quantity used increases. For example, if you eat an apple, you experience satisfaction, or utility. If you eat a second apple, the satisfaction gained is less than from the first apple. If you eat a third apple, it becomes even less.

The law of marginal utility is particularly useful in business when measuring the cost of increasing production. By using marginal analysis, businesses can determine the correct number of workers needed to maximize their profits.

Trade-Offs and Opportunity Costs

All choices involve trade-offs and opportunity costs. A **trade-off** is the choice that is given up when the business makes one choice over another. For example, if the budget allocated $10,000 for new equipment but management wants to spend $15,000, trade-offs will have to be made. A budget has a limited amount of money for spending, so less can be spent on another item.

When a trade-off occurs, an opportunity cost is created. **Opportunity cost** is the value of the option that was given up. **Value** is the relative worth of something. If a company buys a forklift for the same amount of money necessary to buy a delivery truck, the opportunity cost is the delivery truck. The asset not purchased is the opportunity cost that was made as a result of the decision on what to buy.

Section 4.2 Review

Check Your Understanding

1. Why is it helpful for managers to understand basic accounting terms?
2. Briefly describe the decision-making process.
3. What type of plan is put in place if the result of the decision-making process was not expected or accomplished?
4. List examples of decision-making process tools.
5. What does a cost-benefit analysis show?

Build Your Vocabulary

As you progress through this text, develop a personal glossary of key terms. This will help you build your vocabulary and prepare you for a career. Write a definition for each of the following terms and add them to your personal glossary.

accounting	marginal benefit	trade-off
jargon	marginal cost	opportunity cost
decision-making	law of diminishing marginal utility	value
cost-benefit analysis		

Chapter 4 Review and Assessment

Chapter Summary

Section 4.1 Information Technology

LO 4.1-1 **Summarize management information for planning purposes.**
Management information is data used for strategic purposes. Data are the pieces of information gathered through research. Management information is the basis for all planning in an organization. It provides historical data, current data, and the basis for forecasting future data for planning purposes.

LO 4.1-2 **Identify examples of budgets used in the budgeting process.**
Budgeting is a projection used to plan financial strategies. Examples of important budgets created in the planning process are an operating budget and a sales budget.

Section 4.2 Systematic Decision-Making Process

LO 4.2-1 **Discuss accounting information for managers.**
Every manager must be responsible and understand how to make financial decisions that help keep a company profitable. In order to understand financial reports created by company accountants, business professionals need a basic knowledge of accounting jargon. By understanding basic accounting terms, managers can learn how to use accounting information provided to them.

LO 4.2-2 **List the steps of the systematic decision-making process.**
The five steps of the systematic decision-making process are define the decision to be made, gather information, choose the best alternative, act on the decision, and evaluate the solution or decision.

LO 4.2-3 **Cite examples of decision-making tools.**
SWOT and PEST analyses are important decision-making tools used by management. Additional examples include cost-benefit analysis, marginal analysis, and trade-off and opportunity costs.

Review Your Knowledge

1. What is the difference between external information and internal information?
2. Explain the role of a Management Information System (MIS) in planning.
3. What are examples of independent software programs used by businesses to capture data?
4. Why is data processing important?
5. Summarize examples of types of budgets used in the budgeting process.
6. What information is typically included in an operating budget?
7. Discuss accounting information for managers.
8. Identify and explain the steps of the decision-making process.
9. Discuss examples of decision-making tools.
10. How is the law of diminishing marginal utility useful in business?

Apply Your Knowledge

1. Gathering and sharing information is an important component of management planning. Explain why you think it is often the responsibility of a manager to gather information and share it with others in the organization.
2. Planning is about decision-making. In order to make sound decisions and reduce risk, information must be available to the management team. Define the strategic importance of having information available to management when making plans for an organization.
3. Departments usually create their own budgets that are combined to create a company master budget. Why would departments create a budget rather than assign this task to the accountant or the accounting department for the business?
4. Controlling compares actual outcomes with planned outcomes and takes appropriate actions when goals are not achieved. If you were a manager, outline the steps you would take when comparing a budget to an actual income statement.
5. How does evaluating past performances of a business help a company predict future performances?
6. Quantitative data is based on facts and figures, while qualitative data is based on judgment. Explain when each type of data is appropriate to use in the planning process.
7. Most companies have an accountant who is charge of finances. Why would it matter whether a manager is able to understand accounting jargon? Why should a manager be responsible for accounting information?
8. Identify a problem or situation in your school for which a solution must be found. Using a graphic organizer, write how each step of the decision-making process could be applied to arrive at a solution.
9. Cost-benefit analysis weighs the costs against the benefits of an action. Assume you are the manager of a manufacturing plant. Currently, there are two shifts of employees who operate the plant from 8:00 a.m. to midnight. Senior management has asked you to give your opinion on whether a third shift of workers should be added to expand production to 24-hours a day. List the potential costs of adding a third shift of workers. Then list the potential benefits. Write a summary of your analysis that provides a reasoned opinion you can provide to senior management.
10. Recall a moment in your life where you had to make a decision between several choices. What were the trade-offs and opportunity costs? What was your final decision?

College and Career Readiness

Communication Skills

Writing. Select three key terms from this chapter that you have not encountered before. Write a definition for each key term in your own words by drawing on your prior knowledge. *Prior knowledge* is experience and information you already possess about the term. Compare the definitions you wrote to those that appear in the glossary of this text.

Speaking. Developing effective communication skills requires individuals to be able to participate in and contribute to discussions. A *discussion* is a speaking situation in which two or more individuals share their ideas about a subject and talk about them with one another. Contribute thoughtful, relevant comments when participation is invited during class discussion. Ask questions if you need help determining or clarifying the meaning of the topics discussed during the lesson.

Listening. *Contextual clues* are hints that can help you define an unfamiliar word by considering the surrounding words or sentences. For example, consider how these sentences help explain the meaning of the word *clout*: "Celebrities often believe they have clout. Many think they have the power to get whatever they want." Using contextual clues can help you understand unfamiliar words you hear as well as read. When you hear an unfamiliar word during class, listen for contextual clues to help you understand its meaning.

Internet Research

Management Information System (MIS). Technology plays an important role in business planning. Businesses depend on a Management Information System (MIS) to store data and access information. Conduct a search on *Management Information System (MIS)*. Write a summary on what you learned about how technology influences business strategy.

Teamwork

As a requirement for a management position, knowledge of basic accounting terms is important. Working with your team, review the accounting terms in Figure 4-3. Identify terms that you think are missing and add them as you create a new chart. When you are finished, distribute the new illustration to the class and ask for their input.

College and Career Readiness

Portfolio Development

Hard-Copy Organization. As you collect materials for your portfolio, you will need an effective strategy to keep the items clean, safe, and organized for assembly at the appropriate time. Structure and organization are important when working on an ongoing project that includes multiple pieces. Photocopy each document that you want to include and file the original in a safe place for future reference. Never include an original document in a portfolio.

Plan to keep similar items together and label each category of items. For example, store documents that illustrate your writing skills together. Use notes clipped to the documents to identify each item and state why it is included in the portfolio. For example, a note might say, "Newsletter that illustrates desktop-publishing skills."

A large manila envelope works well to keep hard copies of documents, photos, awards, and other items safe. File folders and three-ring binders with divider tabs also work well.

1. Create a master spreadsheet to track each component that you add to your portfolio. Save the spreadsheet as MASTER_PORTFOLIO with your last name, for example, MASTER_PORTFOLIO_SMITH, or use a different naming convention that is suitable for your management system. Ask your instructor where you should save your file. It is recommended to use a flash drive as a backup, in addition to the school network, so that you have access to your information at all times.
2. Decide on a management system that works for you as you collect items. You may list each document alphabetically, by category, date, or other convention that helps you keep track of each document you are including. For each activity you complete, remember to update the spreadsheet.

EVENT PREP

CTSOs

Role-play and Interview. Some competitive events for Career and Technical Student Organizations (CTSOs) require that entrants complete a role-play or interview. Role-play is representing a situation by acting. An interview is a formal conversation during which one person asks questions and the other person answers them.

Those who participate will be provided information about a situation and given time to practice. A judge or panel of judges will review the presentations or conduct the interview.

To prepare for the role-play or interview event, complete the following activities.

1. Read the guidelines provided by your organization.
2. Visit the website of the organization and look for role-play or interview events from previous years. Many organizations post these events for students to use as practice for future competitions. Also, look for the evaluation criteria or rubric for the event. This will help you determine what the judge will be looking for in your presentation.
3. Practice in front of a mirror. Are you comfortable speaking without reading directly from your notes?
4. Ask a friend or an instructor to listen to your presentation or conduct an interview with you. Give special attention to how you present yourself, such as your posture. Concentrate on the tone of voice. Be pleasant and loud enough to hear, but do not shout. Make eye contact with the listener. Do not stare, but engage the person's attention.
5. After you have made your presentation, ask for constructive feedback.

UNIT 3 Organizing and Staffing

Chapters

Functions of Management Covered in This Unit

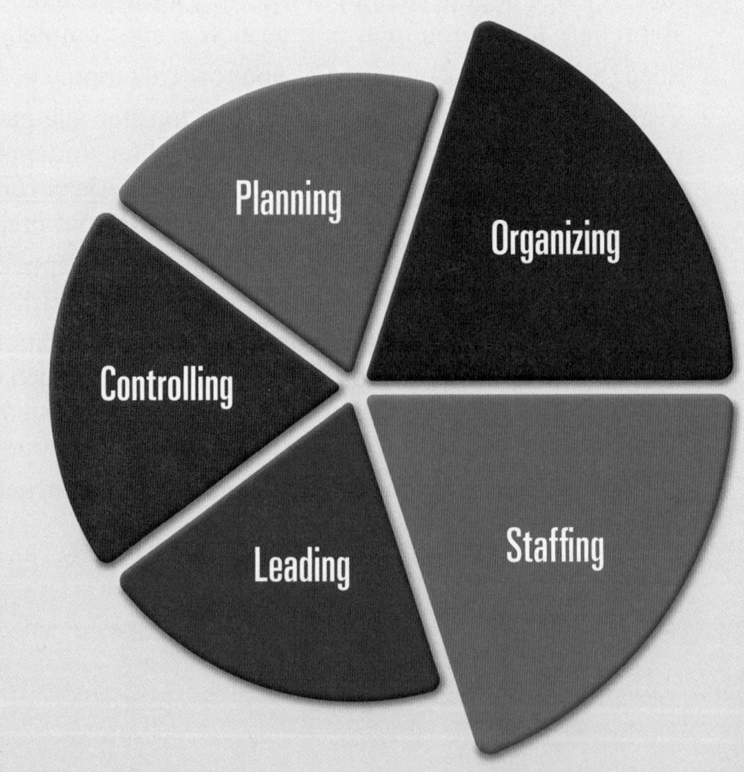

While studying, look for the activity icon for:

- Vocabulary terms with e-flash cards and matching activities

These activities can be accessed at www.g-wlearning.com/business/8417

Case Study

Delegation

pathdoc/Shutterstock.com

Mateo is a human resources manager for a sporting goods company. He has a great deal of success with the company and is respected by his direct reports. Mateo has also earned the trust of his fellow managers.

As part of the management team, Mateo participated in the writing of a five-year strategic plan for the company. In the plan, two tasks were identified that required immediate attention from HR. One of the tasks identified is the need to hire an employee to fill a vacant position in the accounting department. The other task is to update the company's employee benefits package to comply with new federal laws.

Mateo's schedule is busy and he realized he could not accomplish the assignments in a timely manner without assistance. His solution was to break the assignments into smaller, specific tasks that he could delegate to his staff.

He called on two of his most productive direct reports to meet with him. Mateo asked one employee to create the job description for the vacant position, post it to available jobsites, and screen applications for potential candidates. He asked another employee to compare the company's current benefits package to the new federal laws and summarize recommended changes needed to be in federal compliance.

Based on recommendations, Mateo conducted interviews to fill the open position. He also met with the company's senior managers to offer suggestions to update the benefits package for current employees based on his staff member's research. By working with others and delegating responsibilities, Mateo was able to accomplish multiple tasks in a short amount of time.

Critical Thinking

1. How does delegation relate to productivity?
2. At what point can delegation become micromanagement?

CHAPTER 5

Organizing

Sections

5.1 Importance of Organizing

5.2 Defining Corporate Culture

Reading Prep

Before reading this chapter, read the Essential Questions that appear in the section openers. Write a short paragraph in response to each question. Share your answers with a classmate. Discuss how each other's answers relate to the chapter topic.

Exploring Careers

Project Manager

Project managers are responsible for planning and executing a specific project. They have the responsibility of overseeing the development, creation, and fulfillment of an activity or project as assigned. One of the main goals of project managers is to organize and maintain a project's schedule and the tasks of team members. They also are responsible for reducing the risks of failure, maximizing benefits, and decreasing production costs.

Typical job titles for this position include *chief project manager*, *program manager*, and *project director*. Examples of tasks that project managers perform include:

- developing project plans;
- communicating project objectives clearly to the team;
- delegating tasks and assignments to the team;
- monitoring production and quality of project; and
- offering solutions to issues as they arise.

A project manager position requires a bachelor degree in management, business, or a related field. In addition, certification may be required for the position. The Project Management Institute and American Society for the Advancement of Project Management offer a variety of certifications for project managers. Project managers should have strong time-management, communication, and organizational skills.

wavebreakmedia/Shutterstock.com

Section 5.1

Importance of Organizing

What does an organizational structure look like for a typical business?

Learning Objectives

LO 5.1-1 Summarize the organizing function of management.
LO 5.1-2 Explain specialization.
LO 5.1-3 Identify types of departmentalization.
LO 5.1-4 Discuss chain of command.
LO 5.1-5 Define *span of control.*

Key Terms

organizational structure	departmentalization	teamwork
organization chart	chain of command	span of control
organizational design	unity of command	
specialization	project manager	

LO 5.1-1 Organizing Function

During the planning process, management creates tactical plans that define how an organization uses its resources to accomplish specific goals related to strategic plans. The tactical plan outlines precise details on how to accomplish goals, how work is accomplished, who will do it, and which organizational resources are used. This requires a number of well-trained employees on every level.

Organizing is the function of management that follows the planning process. It is the coordination of activities and resources needed to accomplish a plan. Organizing includes assigning tasks to members of a team and granting authority to employees to make decisions. When executed well, the benefits of the organizing function include:

- identifying where power exists in the organization;
- establishing who has authority and responsibility;
- creating structure; and
- clarifying job tasks for each employee.

Organizing creates the structure and ways of working together to help managers and employees achieve the organizational strategies. Through organizing, planning turns into reality.

Organizational Structure

Every business has an organizational structure. **Organizational structure** identifies the hierarchy of employees and determines their roles, authority, and communication flow within an organization. Structure helps identify responsibility and determines who should carry out a job. It also defines who has the authority to make decisions and how jobs are completed.

An **organization chart** is a diagram that shows the structure of an organization. The chart identifies departments, shows how tasks are identified, and indicates levels of authority. An example of an organization chart is illustrated in Figure 5-1.

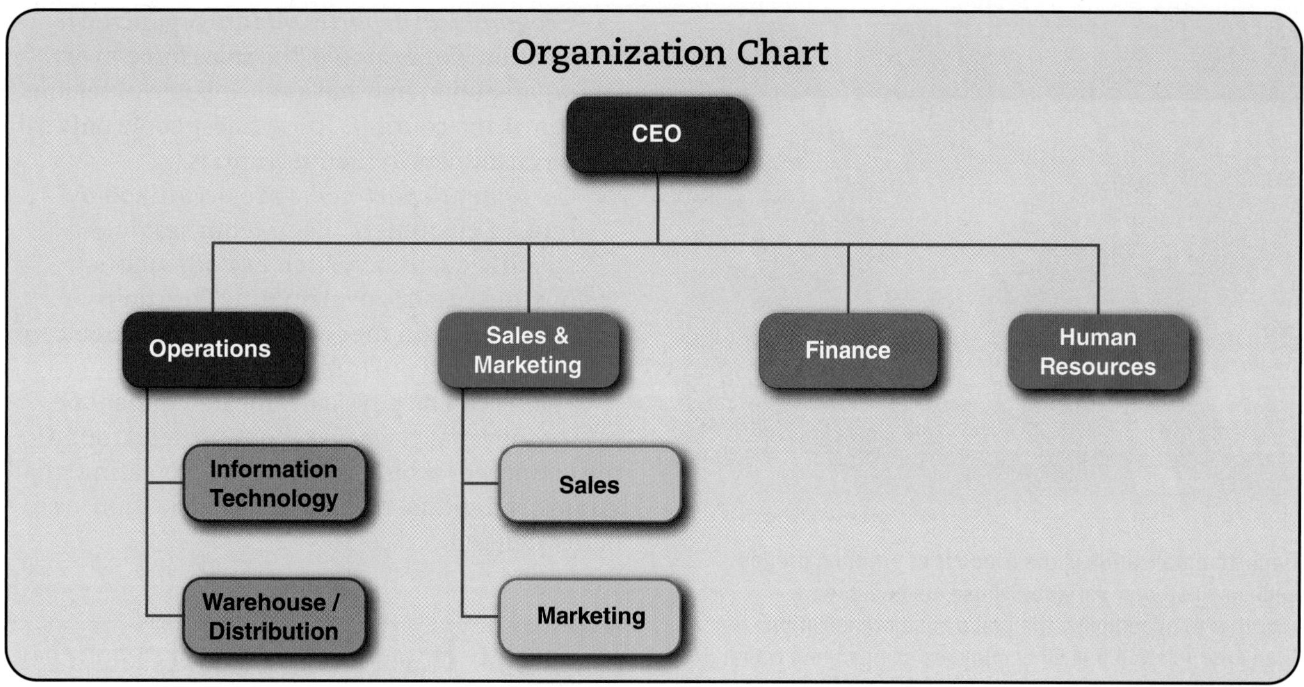

Goodheart-Willcox Publisher

Figure 5-1 An organization chart is a diagram that shows the structure of an organization.

Organizational Design

Organizational design identifies the hierarchy of employees within the business. Creating a structure for an organization includes identifying:

- specialization;
- departmentalization;
- chain of command; and
- span of control.

Organizational design is the process of making decisions about how goals are accomplished in an efficient manner.

LO 5.1-2 Specialization

Management must analyze the needs of the business and identify the types of jobs that will help the organization meet its goals. Management starts the process by defining the good or service offered and identifying the tasks needed to create the product. For example, Great Clips provides haircutting services that requires specific jobs, such as stylists. In addition, marketers, buyers, and accountants are needed. Each job is analyzed to determine the knowledge, skills, and abilities necessary to successfully perform functions of the job.

Most businesses require that employees are specialists at specific tasks. **Specialization** is a focus on the production of specific products so that a greater degree of efficiency is gained. Specialization enables workers to become efficient in their roles. *Division of labor* is the specialization of individuals who perform specific tasks. Employees who perform repetitive tasks generally become faster and more accurate because of the repetition. This, in turn, leads to increased productivity and profits for a company.

A typical organization may require specialists, such as accountants, marketing managers, customer service representatives, and salespeople. If a business manufactures goods, manufacturing and production specialists are needed. The types of specialization vary for each type of business.

wavebreakmedia/Shutterstock.com

Departmentalization is the process of creating groups, such as customer service, whose members work together to accomplish the goals of an organization. **If an organization has 50 employees as one team rather than multiple teams, how do you think the efficiency of the company would rate?**

LO 5.1-3 Departmentalization

After jobs are identified in an organization, management typically creates small groups of employees. This concept is known as departmentalization. **Departmentalization** is the process of creating groups whose members work together to accomplish the goals of an organization. There are various methods, or types, of departmentalization. Companies can organize departments by function, product, geography, or customer.

- *Functional departments* are comprised of employees with common job tasks. For example, a marketing department would include marketing managers, communication coordinators, and advertising directors. Functional teams are common in large organizations.
- *Product departments* include all functional areas required to create a good or service. They are sometimes referred to as product teams. Product departments typically operate as a *small business unit (SBU)* within the organization. Each team handles its own production, marketing, and finance. It makes its own decisions, has functional employees who are dedicated, and operates as its own independent business.
- *Geographical departments* are organized by location. For example, the sales force in an organization may have salespeople in regions across the country. Those salespeople only call on customers in their territories.
- *Customer departments* are organized by type of customers. Each team services a specific customer, such as consumers, businesses, or government. This helps a team focus on meeting the specific needs of each type of customer.

Teams can be physically located under one roof or they may have members located around the country or around the world. By creating small groups, individual roles in the organization are better defined.

LO 5.1-4 Chain of Command

There must be clear understanding of who is leading the team, roles of team members, and how decisions are made. The **chain of command** is the authority structure in a company from the highest to the lowest levels. It is also known as the *line of authority*. Chain of command helps clarify employee power as well as protocol for flow of information. It also defines *direct reports*, who are the employees who report to a manager.

Unity of command states that each employee reports to one manager. That manager reports to the next level of management and so on up the chain of command. Unity of command establishes clear lines of authority for an employee when receiving instructions on how to perform a task. The employee knows exactly from whom to take direction.

The division of authority within a company can vary depending on the type of business, size of the company, or wishes of owners or senior management. The authority within an organization can be centralized or decentralized.

In a *centralized organization*, all authority within a business rests with senior management. Decisions are made at the top and pushed down to each level of the organization. Advantages of this type of organization include a clear chain of command, focused company vision, and quick implementation of decisions. Potential disadvantages include a sense of dictatorial form of leadership and less employee creativity.

You Do the Math

Probabilistic Reasoning: Probability

Probability is the likelihood of an event occurring. In general, probability is stated as the number of ways an event can happen over the total number of outcomes. Flipping a coin, for example, can result in either heads or tails. The probability of the result being heads is one in two, or 1/2. There is only one side of the coin with heads, and there are two total possible outcomes. Probability can be expressed as a percentage. In the case of a flipped coin: $1/2 = 0.5 \times 100 = 50$ percent chance of heads being the result.

Solve the following problems.

1. An office supply vendor offers a discount to its regular customers. The discount may be 2 percent, 4 percent, 6 percent, or 25 percent. The discount is randomly selected by a computer. What is the probability that a customer will receive a 25 percent discount?
2. Of the 100 employees hired in a new factory, 20 of them need specialized training to run the factory equipment. What is the probability percentage the next employee hired will not need specialized training?
3. The manager of a vacation resort surveyed 100 resort guests to find out which resort feature was most liked. The manager found that of the resort's water park, spa, golf course, and restaurant, 42 preferred the water park to any other feature. What is the probability the next guest will prefer any other feature at the resort?

In a *decentralized organization,* authority is given to each manager of a department. An advantage of decentralized organization is middle and supervisory managers are granted decision-making power. A manager can make a decision without getting approval from senior management. This power facilitates a manager's ability to keep business moving with little to no delays. Granting power to middle and supervisory management enables senior managers to focus on overall company strategies. A potential disadvantage of this type of organization is that due to the delegation of power, senior management might feel a loss of control of the organization.

Organizational structures are based on company size, type of product, and other similar factors. Common types of organizational structures are line, line-and-staff, matrix, and team.

Line Structure

In a *line structure,* authority flows from top to bottom from manager to employee as shown in Figure 5-2. In this example, each person reports directly to the vice president (VP) of marketing who makes all final marketing decisions. A line structure is common in functional departments.

An advantage of line structure is a manager has control and can make decisions for the team. This creates efficiencies as well as places responsibility on a manager to meet company goals. However, it can be a disadvantage as a department's independence tends to minimize communication between other teams.

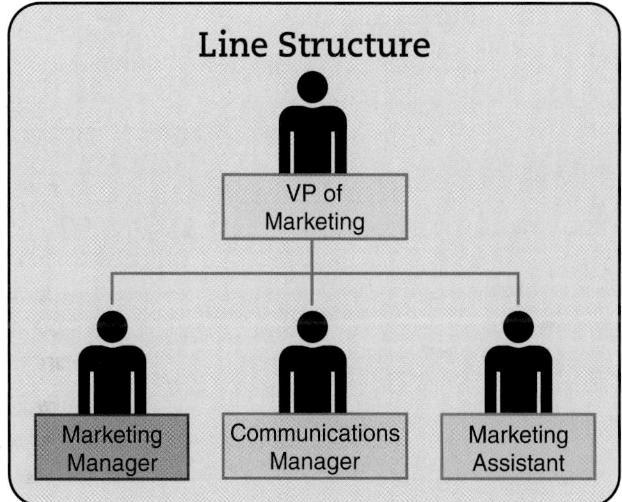

Goodheart-Willcox Publisher

Figure 5-2 Authority flows from the top to the bottom in a line structure.

The lack of communication can create isolation for departments in an organization.

Line-and-Staff Structure

Some large organizations have a *line-and-staff structure*, as shown in Figure 5-3. This structure includes *line managers* who have authority over those they supervise and *staff positions* that provide expertise and advise the line manager when needed. For example, when a manager needs expertise, such as accounting advice, the company accountant lends a hand. *Staff authority* is to advise only, not direct.

An advantage of this structure is a line manager can obtain expert advice when needed. Having experts on staff in an organization creates consistency and eliminates the need to hire outside consultants. However, it can create a disadvantage when a line manager and staff position have conflicting opinions on decision-making outcomes.

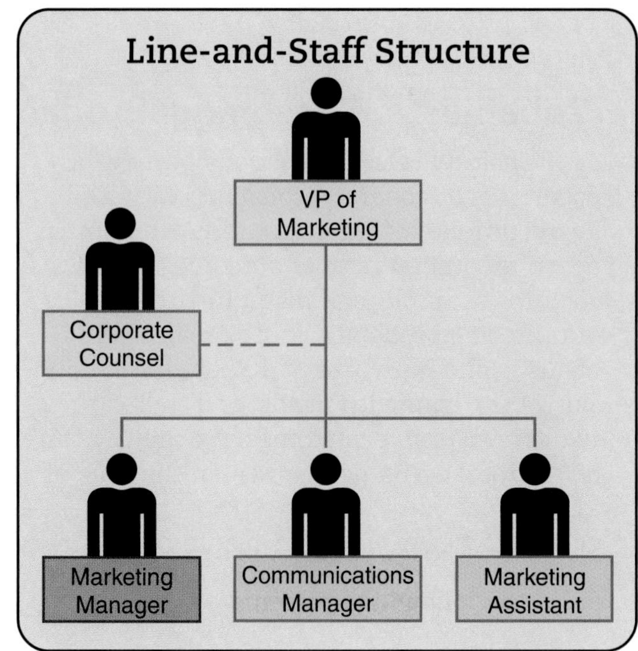

Goodheart-Willcox Publisher

Figure 5-3 A line-and-staff structure is an extension of the line-structure model.

Matrix Structure

In a *matrix structure*, employees from different functional groups come together to complete a project with a defined start and end date. Employees report to a manager of the functional team and a manager of the temporary team. Figure 5-4 shows a matrix structure.

An individual in charge of a temporary team is a project manager. A **project manager** is a person assigned to develop and execute a *project plan*. A project plan includes development, creation, and fulfillment of a specific good or service and

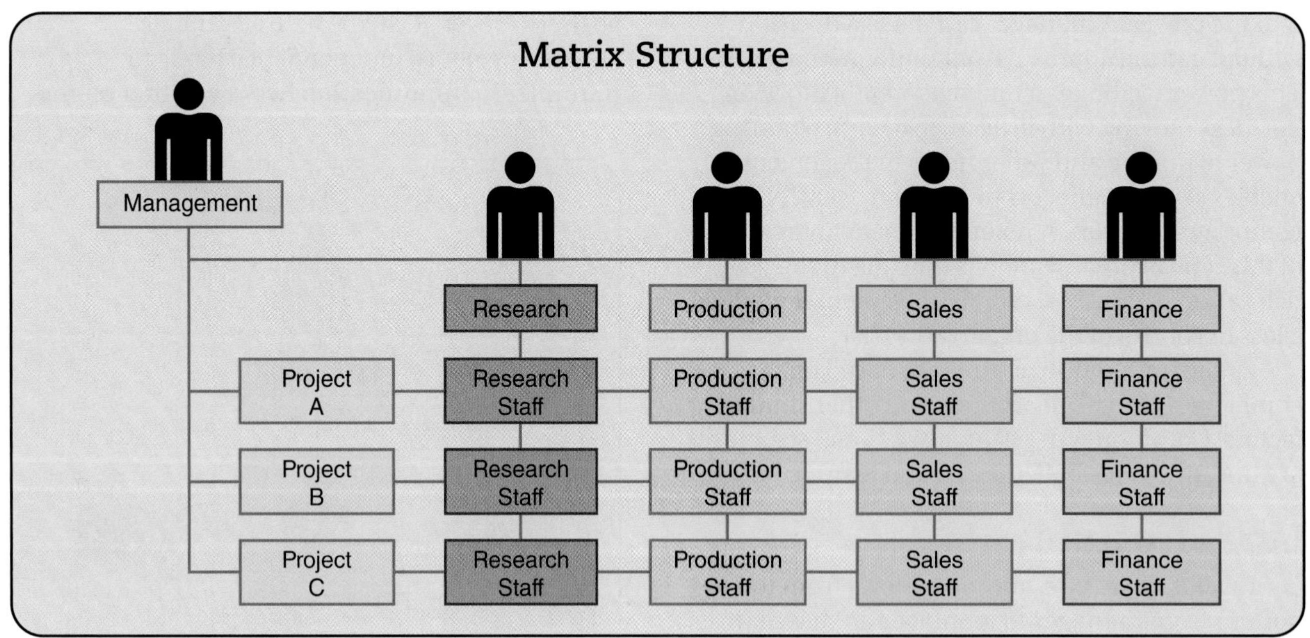

Goodheart-Willcox Publisher

Figure 5-4 A matrix structure is one in which employees from different functional groups are brought together to complete a project that has a defined start and end date.

identifies resources needed, such as people and other organizational resources. When a project is complete, the team disbands.

Project management is the action of overseeing activities to make sure they happen on schedule, on budget, and according to specifications. It follows a process similar to the one shown in Figure 5-5. *Project-management tools,* such as Gantt charts and Microsoft Projects, help keep a project on task.

An advantage of a matrix structure is large projects are completed quickly and efficiently by employees who are most suited for a specific project. The team then reverts to its original structure when the project is complete. A disadvantage is an employee reports to his or her manager in addition to reporting to a project manager, which can create conflict.

Team Structure

A *team structure* is one in which two or more people come together to achieve a common goal. Each team member shares accountability for reaching the overarching goals of the group. **Teamwork** is the cooperative efforts by individual members to achieve a goal. Members of a team share responsibilities, collaborate when making decisions, and take pride in their actions.

A team has a leader to whom each member reports. In this structure, the leader takes on more of a facilitator role than that of a traditional supervisor. Teams have the ability to make their own decisions rather than waiting on approval from senior management, which reduces some of the hierarchy that is present in other structures.

LO 5.1-5 Span of Control

Span of control is the number of employees who report to a manager. It is also called *span of management*. The number of employees who report to a manager is based on factors such as the size of the organization, number of employees, and mission of the company.

baranq/Shutterstock.com

A narrow span of control exists when a manager has only a few employees that he or she directs. **What is your opinion of a narrow span of control for managers in an organization?**

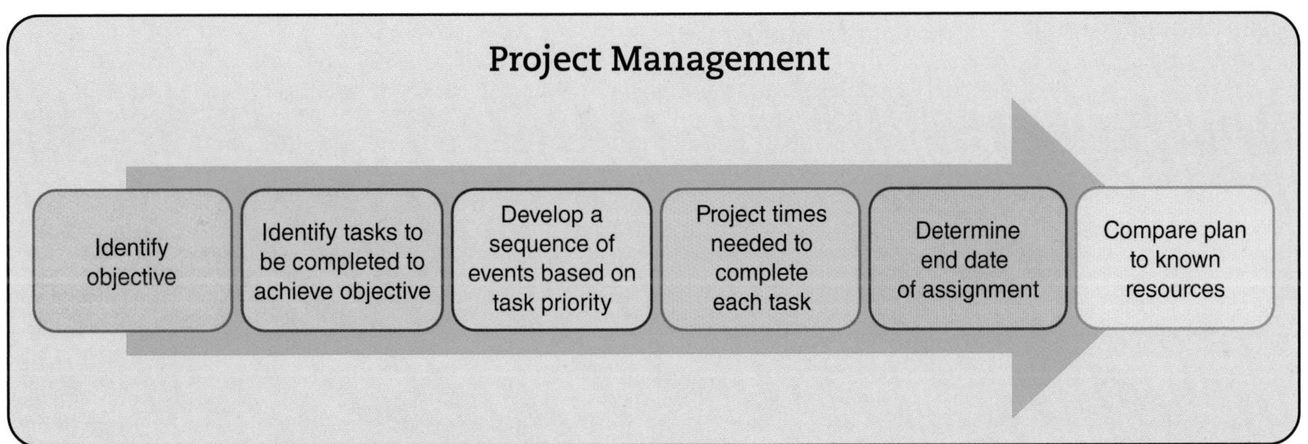

Goodheart-Willcox Publisher

Figure 5-5 Project management is the action of overseeing activities to make sure they happen on schedule, on budget, and according to specifications outlined.

If a person has too many reports, employees may not receive the direction they need.

A *narrow span of control* exists when a manager has only a few employees that he or she directs. For many organizations, four to six direct reports is an optimal number. This enables a manager to interact more frequently with employees. This is especially effective for supervisory management that requires directing employees who perform day-to-day operations.

A *wide span of control* exists when a manager directs many employees. This tends to work better for senior and middle levels of management. These levels have supervisory managers reporting to them who do not typically need day-to-day supervision, but rather regular check-ins and strategic interactions.

Section 5.1 Review

Check Your Understanding

1. Cite benefits of the organizing function of management.
2. How does specialization lead to increased productivity and profits for a company?
3. There are four types of organizational structure: line, line-and-staff, matrix, and team. Explain each type.
4. Define a *staff authority*.
5. Explain the difference between a narrow span of control and a wide span of control.

Build Your Vocabulary

As you progress through this text, develop a personal glossary of key terms. This will help you build your vocabulary and prepare you for a career. Write a definition for each of the following terms and add them to your personal glossary.

organizational structure
organization chart
organizational design
specialization
departmentalization
chain of command
unity of command
project manager
teamwork
span of control

Section 5.2

Defining Corporate Culture

Why should management be in tune to the corporate culture of their organization?

Learning Objectives

LO 5.2-1 Discuss corporate culture in an organization.

LO 5.2-2 Summarize ways an organization can create an ethical culture.

LO 5.2-3 Summarize ways an organization can create a customer-focused culture.

Key Terms

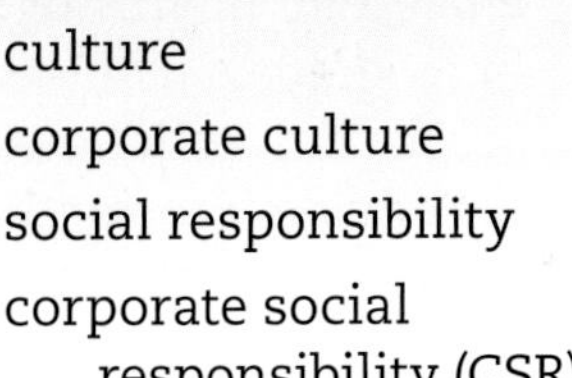

- culture
- corporate culture
- social responsibility
- corporate social responsibility (CSR)
- employee perception
- ethics
- integrity
- morals
- business ethics
- code of ethics
- conflict of interest
- proprietary information
- insider trading
- confidentiality
- stereotyping
- code of conduct
- customer service
- customer-focused mindset

LO 5.2-1 Corporate Culture

Culture is the shared beliefs, customs, practices, and social behavior of a particular group or nation. The term **corporate culture**, or *organizational culture*, describes how the owners and employees of a company think, feel, and act as a business. It is a set of shared values and practices held by the members of an organization.

Culture is reflected in how an organization operates and accomplishes its objectives. The culture of an organization is observed in some of these behaviors:

- how an organization conducts business;
- treatment of employees and customers;
- extent of employee freedom in decision-making and personal expression; and
- commitment of employees to the organization.

Human resources plays an important role in guiding management to create a healthy culture for an organization. Improving communication, engaging employees in their work, and expressing appreciation for performance are examples of actions that can be taken to nurture the culture of an organization.

Corporate Social Responsibility

Corporate culture includes social responsibility. **Social responsibility** is behaving with sensitivity to social, environmental, and economic issues.

Corporate social responsibility (CSR) includes all the actions taken by a business to promote social good. CSR is an *external strategy* used to enhance the brand of the organization, spread goodwill, and encourage customers to do business with them. Most customers prefer to do business with companies that demonstrate social responsibility. CSR is also an *internal strategy*. It provides employees with a sense of pride to work for a company that cares about others.

Employee Perception

Corporate culture influences employee perception. *Perception* is the way in which an individual interprets what he or she sees or hears and, as a result, forms an opinion or judgment. **Employee perception** is an employee's view of the organization and its impact on an individual. It can be about the culture or company leadership. It can also be about the respect an organization gives its employees.

The result of positive employee perception is greater employee engagement within the organization. An engaged employee is dedicated and enthusiastic about his or her job. Employees who perceive a quality workplace are more motivated and loyal to the success of fellow employees and the company as a whole. From an employee's perception, a simple "thank you" from management goes a long way.

There is a saying that goes, "perception is reality." If an employee perceives the culture to be negative, it becomes negative to that person. The result can be an unpleasant workplace when employees are unhappy.

wavebreakmedia/Shutterstock.com

Corporate social responsibility (CSR) includes all the actions taken by a business to promote social good, such as volunteering or donating to charity. **How does participating or not participating in CSR affect the reputation of an organization?**

Ethics

Insider Trading

Insider trading is using private company information to make stock trades for personal gain. Managers are often aware of information that will affect the price of the stock for the company for which they are employed. If the company has an event that will increase the price of stock, a person with insider information could buy it while the price is low and make a hefty profit. It is illegal to use this information as a basis for buying or selling company stock or to share it with others so they can make stock transactions. It is unethical and illegal to provide information to selected people who could make purchases resulting in profits that other investors cannot make.

LO 5.2-2 Creating an Ethical Culture

Managers are responsible for playing a role in creating the culture of an organization. A person in charge of a business, project, or team is expected to set an example and display ethical behavior. **Ethics** are rules of behavior based on a group's ideas about what is right and wrong. **Integrity** is the honesty of a person's actions. Those actions may be motivated by ethical, moral, or legal decisions. **Morals** are an individual's ideas of what is right and wrong. A person's morals guide his or her overall behavior and actions. Ethical actions result when a person, team, or organization applies ethical and moral behavior.

A business expects all employees to perform in an ethical manner. **Business ethics** are the rules for professional conduct and integrity in all areas of business. They are principles that help define appropriate behavior of management toward employees, stockholders, and the public. These principles help businesses, governments, and employees make decisions.

Employability Skills
Humility

Humility means being modest and not to think one is better than another person. A person who possesses humility does not judge other people as less important or competent. Possessing humility does not mean to be meek or have diminished self-esteem or self-image. Instead, it means treating people respectfully, being confident in one's abilities, and behaving as a professional. When soft skills are mastered, some aspects of humility naturally happen. For example, simply saying "thank you" to someone demonstrates humility.

Business ethics help guide managers and employees to make correct decisions for a company. Some ways an organization can create an ethical culture include establishing a code of ethics and a code of conduct.

Code of Ethics

Ethical workplace behavior is the actions of employees that impact the effectiveness of daily business of an organization. Most businesses adopt clear, written guidelines for the ethical behavior expected from their employees in the workplace. A **code of ethics** is a document that dictates how business is conducted within the organization. It is sometimes called a *statement of ethics*. Its goal is to establish a value system for the organization that enables employees to make sound ethical decisions. Ethical business practice includes the following examples.

- **Avoiding a conflict of interest.** A **conflict of interest** exists when an employee has competing interests or loyalties. Conflicts of interest can take many forms and be harmful to a business. Some are illegal; others are legal, yet still unethical.
- **Respecting proprietary information.** **Proprietary information** is information a company wishes to keep private. Also known as *trade secrets*, it can include many things, such as product formulas, customer lists, or manufacturing processes.
- **Avoiding insider trading.** **Insider trading** is when an employee uses private company information to purchase company stock or other securities for personal gain. Using company information that is not available to the public for personal gain is both unethical and illegal.
- **Honoring confidentiality.** In business, **confidentiality** means that specific information about a company or its employees is not shared except with those who have clearance to receive it. A *confidentiality agreement* typically states the employee will not share any company information with those outside the company. Confidentiality agreements can also prevent former employees from working for a competitor for a specified length of time.

Ethical behavior includes treating all people fairly and respecting diversity. *Diversity* means having representatives from different backgrounds, cultures, or demographics in a group. It includes age, race, nationality, gender, mental ability, physical ability, and other qualities that make an individual unique. **Stereotyping** is a belief or generalization about a group of people with a given set of characteristics. Ethical people refrain from stereotyping others.

Code of Conduct

Businesses typically have a code of conduct. A **code of conduct** is a document that identifies the manner in which employees should behave while at work or when representing the company. It outlines expectations of employee behavior when representing the company outside the workplace. Specific policies may include behavior such as "to avoid the appearance of conflicting interests, employees are not allowed to accept gifts from vendors."

Tom Wang/Shutterstock.com

A code of conduct outlines expectations of employee behavior when representing the company outside the workplace, such as not accepting gifts from vendors. **Why would an organization object to an employee accepting gifts from outside customers or suppliers?**

Companies may define specific issues as inappropriate or unethical. Ethical issues result when a person or organization is confronted with a situation in which decisions that involve applying integrity and moral behavior must be made. When making decisions that represent an organization, the following questions can be used to analyze if the action is ethical.

- Is the action legal?
- Will the privacy and confidentiality of the company be protected?
- Who is affected by these actions?
- Is the information presented factual and honest?

LO 5.2-3 Creating a Customer-Focused Culture

Successful organizations focus on their customers. Without customers, there would be no business. *External customers* are the people and businesses to whom the organization provides goods and services. *Internal customers* are the coworkers within the business with whom each employee works and collaborates. In a customer-focused culture, all customers are respected.

Customer-focused organizations train all employees to provide customer service. **Customer service** is the way in which a business provides services before, during, and after a sale. The phrase "going above and beyond" is often used to refer to exceptional customer service. A **customer-focused mindset** is the attitude that customer satisfaction always comes first.

Listening to customers, hearing their concerns, and meeting their needs are necessary for a company to exist and be profitable. Learning how to resolve complaints from external customers can help ensure that product is sold and customers return for future transactions. Understanding and collaborating with internal customers helps a business create products that meet customer needs and generates profits for the business. Both types of customers are necessary for a successful business.

Dmytro Zinkevych/Shutterstock.com

Successful organizations focus on their customers. Without customers, there would be no business. **What is the value of a customer-focused culture?**

Section 5.2 Review

Check Your Understanding

1. Provide an example of an action that can be taken to improve the culture of an organization.
2. How does an organization benefit from positive employee perception?
3. What is the goal of a code of ethics?
4. Summarize how to make ethical decisions.
5. Why is it necessary for a business to focus on both internal and external customers?

Build Your Vocabulary

As you progress through this text, develop a personal glossary of key terms. This will help you build your vocabulary and prepare you for a career. Write a definition for each of the following terms and add them to your personal glossary.

- culture
- corporate culture
- social responsibility
- corporate social responsibility (CSR)
- employee perception
- ethics
- integrity
- morals
- business ethics
- code of ethics
- conflict of interest
- proprietary information
- insider trading
- confidentiality
- stereotyping
- code of conduct
- customer service
- customer-focused mindset

Chapter 5 Review and Assessment

Chapter Summary

Section 5.1 Importance of Organizing

LO 5.1-1 **Summarize the organizing function of management.**
The organizing function follows the planning process. It is the coordination of activities and resources needed to accomplish a plan. Organizing creates the structure and ways of working together to help managers and employees achieve the organizational strategies.

LO 5.1-2 **Explain specialization.**
Specialization is a focus on the production of specific products so that a greater degree of efficiency can be gained. It enables workers to become more efficient and more accurate in their roles. This, in turn, leads to increased productivity and profits for a company.

LO 5.1-3 **Identify types of departmentalization.**
Types of departmentalization include organizing departments by function, product, geography, or customer.

LO 5.1-4 **Discuss chain of command.**
The chain of command is the authority structure in a company from the highest to the lowest levels. It helps clarify employee power as well as protocol for flow of information. Chain of command also defines direct reports, who are the employees who report to a manager.

LO 5.1-5 **Define *span of control.***
Span of control is the number of employees who report to a manager. A company can have a narrow span of control or wide span of control.

Section 5.2 Defining Corporate Culture

LO 5.2-1 **Discuss corporate culture in an organization.**
Corporate culture describes how the owners and employees of a company think, feel, and act as a business. It is a set of shared values and practices held by the members of an organization. Corporate culture includes social responsibility and influences employee perception.

LO 5.2-2 **Summarize ways an organization can create an ethical culture.**
A business expects all employees to perform in an ethical manner. An organization can create an ethical culture by establishing a code of ethics and a code of conduct. A code of ethics is a document that dictates how business is conducted within the organization. A code of conduct is a document that identifies the manner in which employees should behave while at work or when representing the company.

LO 5.2-3 **Summarize ways an organization can create a customer-focused culture.**
Customer-focused organizations listen to customers, hear their concerns, and meet their needs. Additional methods for creating a customer-focused culture include learning how to resolve complaints from external customers and understanding and collaborating with internal customers.

Review Your Knowledge

1. Summarize the organizing function of management.
2. Explain specialization.
3. Describe four types of departmentalization.
4. Discuss chain of command.
5. Explain the advantages and disadvantages of centralized and decentralized organizations.
6. Briefly explain span of control.
7. Discuss corporate culture in an organization.
8. Explain the concept of employee perception.
9. How can an organization create an ethical culture?
10. Summarize ways an organization can create a customer-focused culture.

Apply Your Knowledge

1. Write a paragraph to explain your interpretation of the following statement: Through organizing, planning turns into reality.
2. Specialization enables workers to become efficient in their roles. In what ways do you consider yourself a specialist? How might this specialization transfer to a future career?
3. Work groups are typically organized by function, product, geography, or customer. Create a chart with four columns. Label the columns *Functional*, *Product*, *Geographical*, and *Customer*. In each column, list potential advantages of organizing employees into each type of department.
4. Create a Venn diagram to compare and contrast centralized and decentralized organizations. Label one circle *Centralized* and the other circle *Decentralized*. List qualities unique to either type of organization in the appropriate circle. Then, list qualities that both types of organization share in the space where the circles overlap.
5. Span of control is the number of employees who report to a manager. There is no "magic number" of how many people report to a manager. What factors do you think would influence the appropriate number of direct reports for a manager?
6. Corporate culture describes how the owners and employees of a company think, feel, and act as a business. School culture describes how the students, instructors, and administrators think, feel, and act as a group. In your own words, write several paragraphs to describe your school's culture as you define it.
7. Employee perception is an employee's view of the organization and its impact on an individual. Student perception is a student's view of an educational institution and its impact on the individual. Write a few paragraphs to describe your perception of your school and how it influences your learning as a student.
8. The goal of a code of ethics is to establish a value system for the organization that enables sound ethical decisions to be made by employees. Choose a group with which you are familiar, such as your class, family, or sports team. Write a brief code of ethics that could be used by that group to guide decision-making.

9. How do you think "going above and beyond" for customers contributes to the success of an organization?
10. Internal customers are the coworkers with whom each employee works and collaborates. Why should a business be concerned with internal customers as well as external customers?

Communication Skills

Reading. *Print awareness* is the understanding that printed text is organized in a methodical way. For example, texts written in English contain individual letters that make up words, which are separated by spaces. Words are read from left to right and top to bottom. Print awareness helps readers understand that text can be broken up by images, page breaks, or other divisions. These breaks may or may not indicate a break in thought. Review the pages of this chapter. How does your understanding of print awareness help you read and understand the text?

Writing. *Rhetoric* is the study of writing or speaking as a way of communicating information or persuading someone. When you *persuade*, you convince a person to take a proposed course of action. There will be many instances when you will be required to write paragraphs to persuade a reader. Write a script you could use as the basis for a conversation with a classmate about whether a clean learning environment is important. Use your best persuasive techniques to argue for or against the value of a clean school. Use solid reasoning that will influence your classmate's understanding of the topic.

Speaking. What role do you think ethics and integrity have in decision-making? Think of a time when your ideals and principles helped you make a decision involving ethics. Do you think you made the correct decision? What was the impact of your decision? Deliver an informal speech to your class to narrate the situation that led to the decision. Describe your thoughts and opinions. Explain how ethics and integrity influenced your decision.

Internet Research

Project Management. Identify a school project or task you have that has a specific due date. Using the Internet, read about *project management* then how to write a *project plan*. Using the information you find, write a project plan for the task. Start by identifying resources needed to complete the project. Next, conduct a search for *project management tools*. Based on your research, select a tool to track your progress. Explain how you will use the tool to keep your project on task.

Ethical Workplace Behavior. Business ethics are rules for professional conduct and integrity in all areas of business. They help guide both managers and employees to make correct decisions for a company. Search for *ethical workplace behavior*. Explain in your own words what it means to behave ethically in the workplace.

Contemporary Ethics Cases. Research a contemporary case of a business dealing with a violation of ethics. Begin by searching for *business ethics violation* plus the current year, or a similar phrase. Summarize the situation and explain why it is an issue of ethics and explain what you think is the best solution.

Teamwork

Working with your team, create a chart to use as a visual aid to explain the advantages and disadvantages of types of organizational structures. Create a four-column chart and label each of the columns *Line*, *Line-and-Staff*, *Matrix*, and *Team*. List the advantages and disadvantages of each organizational structure in the appropriate column. Then, use this chart as a visual aid to explain each type of organizational structure to the class.

College and Career Readiness

Portfolio Development

Electronic Organization. Before you begin collecting items for an electronic portfolio, you will need to decide how you are going to present the final product. There are many creative ways to present an electronic portfolio. One option is to create an electronic presentation with slides for each item. Another option is to place the files on a CD. Websites also work well for presenting an electronic portfolio. The method you choose should allow the viewer to navigate and find items easily. For example, you could create an electronic presentation with slides for each section. The slides could have links to documents, videos, graphics, or sound files. Alternatively, you could use a CD or a flash drive to present the material.

Websites are another option for presenting an electronic portfolio. You could create a personal website to host the files and have a main page with links to various sections. Each section page could have links to pages with your documents, videos, graphics, or sound files. Be sure you read and understand the user agreement for any site on which you place your materials.

1. If you have not already done so, create a master spreadsheet to track each component that you add to your portfolio. Save the spreadsheet as MASTER_PORTFOLIO with your last name, for example MASTER_PORTFOLIO_SMITH, or use a different naming convention that is suitable for your management system. Ask your instructor where you should save your file. It is recommended to use a flash drive as a backup, in addition to the school network, so that you have access to your information at all times.
2. Decide on a management system that works for you as you collect digital files. You may list each document alphabetically, by category, date, or other convention that helps you keep track of each document you are including. For each activity you complete, remember to update the spreadsheet.
3. Begin collecting hard-copy files you will need to scan into the computer. As you scan each file, place in the appropriate folder or subfolder established in a previous portfolio activity. Remember, you can always add additional folders or subfolders as needed. When finished, update your spreadsheet.

EVENT PREP

CTSOs

Teamwork. Some competitive events for CTSOs have a teamwork component. When competing in a team event, it is important for the team to prepare to operate as a cohesive unit. Effective team members are individuals who contribute ideas and personal effort.

To prepare for teamwork activities, complete the following activities.

1. Review the rules to confirm if questions will be asked or if the team will need to defend a case or situation.
2. Practice performing as a team by completing the team activities at the end of each chapter in this text. This will help members learn how to interact with each other and participate effectively.
3. Locate a rubric or scoring sheet for the event on the website of your organization to see how the team will be judged.
4. Confirm whether visual aids may be used in the presentation and the amount of setup time permitted.
5. Make notes on index cards about important points to remember. Team members should exchange note cards so each person evaluates the other team members' notes. Use these notes to study. You may also be able to use these notes during the event.
6. Assign each team member a role for the presentation. Practice performing as a team. Each team member should introduce himself or herself, review the case, make suggestions for the case, and conclude with a summary.
7. Ask your instructor to play the role of a competition judge as your team reviews the case. After the presentation is complete, ask for feedback from your instructor. You may also consider having a student audience to listen and give feedback.

CHAPTER 6

Staffing

Sections

Reading Prep

Before reading this chapter, review the Learning Objectives for each section. Based on this information, write down two or three items you think are important to note while you are reading. How can this help you prepare to understand the content?

Exploring Careers

Human Resources Manager

Human resources managers are responsible for recruiting and hiring new employees as well as overseeing employee evaluations and the general management of personnel. They also analyze and modify compensation packages and organizational policies to follow legal requirements and compete with other companies in the marketplace. Human resources managers serve as the link between management and employees by handling questions, creating and distributing employment offers, and resolving work-related problems.

Typical job titles for this position include *employee relations manager* and *human resources director*. Examples of tasks that human resources managers perform include:

- overseeing the recruiting and hiring of new employees;
- handling the development of compensation and benefits offers for employees;
- ensuring employee safety and welfare;
- suggesting changes to organizational policies; and
- handling employee grievances or issues.

This position requires a bachelor degree and prior work experience. A master degree or professional certification in human resources can also be beneficial. Human resources managers spend time working with employees, as well as other managers, so they must have strong communication, listening, and relationship-building skills. As the position entails exposure to employee personal and sensitive information, confidentiality skills are required.

kurhan/Shutterstock.com

Section 6.1 Human Resources

When you hear the term *human resources*, what comes to mind?

Learning Objectives

LO 6.1-1 Summarize the staffing function of management.
LO 6.1-2 Define *human resources planning.*
LO 6.1-3 Explain the recruitment process used by human resources.
LO 6.1-4 Discuss training and development of employees.
LO 6.1-5 Discuss diversity in the workplace.

Key Terms

- human resources management (HRM)
- human resources (HR) department
- human resources planning
- talent management
- succession planning
- job analysis
- recruiting
- selection process
- employment verification
- background check
- compensation
- negotiate
- orientation
- onboarding
- job shadowing
- professional development
- personal development
- human capital
- inclusion

LO 6.1-1 Staffing Function

Organizational resources are all the resources available for an organization to perform its business processes. They include capital resources, raw materials, human resources, monetary resources, and information technology. Of all these resources, the human resource is the most important. *Human resources* are the employees who work for an organization. Employees are also referred to as *talent* in an organization.

Human resources management (HRM) is all the activities that lead to attracting, recruiting, hiring, training, evaluating, and compensating employees. This is the staffing function of management. The *staffing function* includes recruiting, hiring, training, evaluating, and compensating employees. One of the critical goals of HRM is identifying talent needed in an organization. After talent is identified, it is the responsibility of HRM to secure and retain that talent. This process includes multiple steps as shown in Figure 6-1.

The **human resources (HR) department** is the division that oversees the human resources within an organization. HR is responsible for hiring and supporting employees of an organization. However, it has evolved from a traditional department within an organization that handles the hiring and firing of employees to one that plays a strategic role in the organization.

Human Resources Management (HRM)

- Planning
- Completing job analysis and job description
- Recruiting and hiring new employees
- Overseeing employee compensation
- Conducting performance evaluation
- Maintaining employee relations
- Terminating, or firing, employees if needed

Goodheart-Willcox Publisher

Figure 6-1 Human resources management (HRM) is all the activities that lead to attracting, recruiting, hiring, training, evaluating, and compensating employees.

It is the role of HR to create an environment that is safe for all employees, as well as establish a place where people want to work. HR is also the place where employees should feel comfortable when help or counseling is needed.

LO 6.1-2 Human Resources Planning

Human resources planning is the process of creating a strategy to meet the employment needs of an organization. It begins with a review of the strategic plan created in the planning function. Management reviews the forecasted goods and services that will be produced and the revenue that will be generated. Using this information can help determine how many employees are needed to produce and sell the products.

Human resources planning starts with evaluating current employees and their skills. It includes reviewing potential internal promotions, potential terminations, resignations, retirements, and new or vacant positions that need staffing. The process is complicated and can be time consuming. Human resources planning uses the following criteria.

- **Current human resources supply.** The organization evaluates how many current employees it has, the qualifications of each employee, and the jobs those people are filling.
- **Future demand for employees.** After reviewing the current talent of an organization, a forecast of how many employees are needed in the future, and the job expectations of each position are created.
- **Demand forecast.** The number of current employees is compared with the demand for future employees.

Talent management is the anticipation of employees needed in an organization and planning required to meet those needs. Human resource managers seek to acquire talent for sufficient staffing to meet company goals. They also seek to retain those currently employed by the company. The planning process for acquiring and retaining talent is critical for organizations that desire to develop a culture of successful results.

Monkey Business Images/Shutterstock.com

Human resources planning is the process of creating a strategy to meet the employment needs of an organization. **Explain the importance of an organization creating a strategy to meet the employment needs for its company.**

Succession planning is a continuous process of identifying and developing new employees to replace employees in leadership positions who leave. By designing a succession plan, HR works to keep the organization functioning at its highest capacity.

Each position that is critical to an organizational structure is identified with a plan to ensure a key position is never without a qualified person. As part of the plan, some organizations bring in talent from another company, even a competing company. Other companies strive to promote from within, which creates motivation and loyalty of existing employees.

Job Analysis

Once the organization determines the need for new employees, a job analysis is completed. A **job analysis** is a process that identifies the job requirements for a position, employee qualifications needed, and metrics used to evaluate performance. The job analysis aligns with the planning process and type of positions to be filled.

For example, a job analysis for a sales representative begins by defining the specific skills needed for the job. In addition, the minimum personal qualifications and education necessary must be determined. Metrics are then determined on how the job performance will be evaluated, such as setting dollar or unit sales goals that a person in that position must meet.

Job Description

With the information from the job analysis, HR can develop a job description. A *job description* defines a position and expectations of a person hired to perform the job. Job descriptions are generally very detailed in terms of what a company requires from an employee. Most job descriptions list necessary skills and education required for the position. In addition, core responsibilities and day-to-day activities in which the employee will be involved are described. With a job description, HR will know which skills and qualifications to seek in a potential employee.

LO 6.1-3 Recruitment

A major responsibility of HR is recruiting and hiring employees. **Recruiting** is the process of finding people who are qualified for a position. It is a part of the staffing function in which the organization aims to hire the best talent available. It is well known that an organization is only as good as the people who work for it.

Recruiting is about finding the right person for the right position. Attracting prospective employees for a company is of great importance. Doing so can lead to their hiring, training, and evaluating, as well as providing their compensation and benefits. Organizations spend a great deal of time, resources, and money in hiring employees. Recruiting involves:

- advertising available positions;
- selecting and screening applicants;
- conducting interviews;
- verifying applicants' information and conducting background checks; and
- extending offers and negotiating compensation.

Advertising

Once a job description is created, it is posted for potential candidates to view. Job postings can be advertised on employment websites, social media, and company websites. Depending on the position, job-search websites can be a good source of potential candidates. *Job-search websites* are websites job seekers can use to find open positions. Companies can use these sites to recruit candidates for positions. CareerBuilder and Indeed are examples of job-search websites. Additional examples of places to advertise job postings are shown in Figure 6-2.

Candidates who respond to job postings are generally required to complete a job application. A *job application* is an employment form that requests contact information, education, degrees, certifications, relevant skills, and work experience. Even though much of this information may be included on a candidate's résumé, many organizations require an application to place on file.

Selecting

Selection is the next step in the recruiting process. The **selection process** is the act of reviewing job applications and résumés and choosing candidates for potential interviews. As part of this process, HR reviews job applications and selects applicants who appear to have the required qualifications based on the job description.

Interviewing

After selecting candidates, the top candidates are invited to participate in the interview process. An *interview* is an employer's opportunity to review a candidate's résumé and ask questions to see if he or she is qualified for the position. The first interview is the *screening interview*. A screening interview is usually conducted by HR to confirm a candidate's qualifications for a position. If an applicant meets the expectations for the position, he or she will likely be invited for a second interview.

Job Postings
• Career and college placement offices
• Organization websites
• Employment agencies
• Job fairs
• Online employment sites
• Social media

Goodheart-Willcox Publisher

Figure 6-2 There are numerous locations for HR to post available job positions.

Sergey Nivens/Shutterstock.com

A major responsibility of HR is recruiting and hiring employees. **How do you think recruiting and hiring employees relates to organizational success?**

The hiring manager typically conducts the second interview. The interview is an in-depth examination of a candidate's qualifications and how well he or she fits the position. Other managers, staff, or team members may participate in the process as well.

Testing may be a part of the interviewing process. It is generally conducted after deciding that a candidate meets the expectations of the position. For example, if specific skills are required, a skills test will be administered to see if he or she can perform the tasks needed for the job.

Employment Verification

After the top applicants are interviewed, management makes its selection of the final candidates. The next step in the process is employment verification. **Employment verification** is a process through which the information provided on an applicant's résumé is verified that previous employment information is correct. Former employers typically verify only the dates of employment, position title, and other objective data of employees who are no longer at the company. Professional references are also checked at this time. These people can provide greater insight about the applicant.

In addition, HR might conduct a background check before offering a position to a candidate. A **background check** is an evaluation of personal data that is publicly available. This can involve looking at governmental records, the applicant's social media pages, and other sources. An employer must ask for written permission from the applicant before obtaining a background check. It is the applicant's choice to either accept or deny the background check. While an applicant is not legally obligated to give permission, a business can deny him or her a job based on unknown or unverified information.

Some job positions, such as a finance job, may require an applicant to share his or her credit history. To request credit histories, an organization must show a viable business need to access this information. Similar to a background check, an employer is legally required to obtain an applicant's written permission before conducting a credit check.

Before making an offer, the organization might require that the candidate undergo screenings that test for drugs and alcohol. Laws related to these screenings vary by state. Screenings are commonly performed at a sterile, off-site location, such as a lab, and can be in the form of a blood, urine, or saliva test. A failed drug or alcohol test can result in a candidate being eliminated for consideration for a position.

Negotiating an Offer

If a candidate passes the interviews and verifications, a job offer is made. HR may make the job offer to the selected applicant by phone, letter, e-mail, or in person.

An offer for a job includes discussion of compensation. **Compensation** is payment to an employee for work performed including wages or salaries, incentives, and benefits. HR is responsible for making sure the compensation offered by a business is in line with its competition and industry standards.

For a candidate, an important part of a job offer is negotiating the compensation package. To **negotiate** is to have a formal discussion between two or more people in an attempt to reach an agreement. Negotiation involves working through the terms of the offer, such as work location, start date, and job expectations.

You Do the Math

Statistical Reasoning: Mean, Median, and Mode

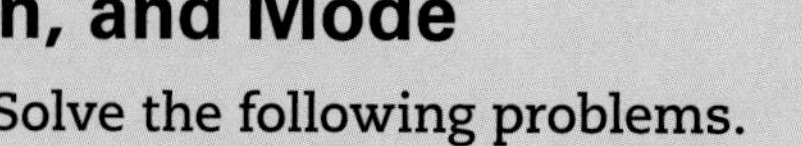

There are three measures of the center of a data set. A *data set* is a group of numbers that are related to a particular topic. The *mean* is the average of all values in the data set. Mean is calculated by adding all values and dividing the sum by the total number of values. The *median* is the middle number in a data set. To find the median, the numbers are listed in numerical order. The *mode* is the value that occurs most frequently in the data set.

Solve the following problems.

1. A recent survey of gasoline prices for a region reported these prices per gallon: $3.49, $3.67, $3.52, $3.58, and $2.56. What is the mean price per gallon?
2. What is the median of the prices listed in the previous question?
3. An online electronics retailer sold merchandise at the following prices during one hour: $99, $105, $75, $116, $99, $105, $105, and $116. What is the mode price?
4. What is the mean of the prices listed in the previous question?

It is up to the candidate to accept or decline the offer. Once the offer is accepted, HR usually notifies the other candidates the position has been filled. There is no law that requires HR to contact other candidates, but it is a professional gesture.

LO 6.1-4 Training and Development

After an employee is hired, training is provided to prepare the new hire for the job. HR is responsible for employee training and development. It starts with new employee orientation and onboarding.

Orientation

Organizations provide an orientation for new employees on their first day. **Orientation** is the welcoming of a new person to a company. It is a one-time event that provides an overview of the organization and its operations. New employees learn about the company's philosophy, mission statement, policies, and goals. Information is provided about employee benefits, such as health insurance, retirement plan, and vacation time.

Onboarding

Onboarding is the system or process of integrating a new employee into the organization. HR is in charge of the onboarding process and coordinates the equipment, training, and other important tools needed for the new employee.

Onboarding includes introducing the new employee to coworkers and managers and providing specific information regarding the role and its responsibilities, who to go to with questions, and other details relating to the company and position. It is an ongoing process to help the new employee become comfortable and acclimate to the organization and his or her day-to-day responsibilities.

Training

After an employee is hired, training to prepare the new employee for the job must be provided. *Job-specific training* focuses on achieving quality results, developing problem-solving processes, and learning how to work in a team environment. Job-specific training usually combines group learning in a classroom setting and hands-on training. *Hands-on training* often includes job shadowing. **Job shadowing** is observing a certain type of work by accompanying an experienced worker as he or she performs the assigned job.

The new employee works side-by-side with an experienced employee to learn the specific tasks of the job. HR may also offer cross-training. *Cross-training* is providing training in different tasks or skills than those usually needed so the employee can perform another job if the need arises.

Professional development is an important part of the training services provided by HR. **Professional development** is education for people who have already completed their formal schooling and training to gain new skills and knowledge needed for growth and career development. Some examples of professional development opportunities include:

- seminars on public speaking;
- conferences about new industry practices; and
- presentations on sexual harassment in the workplace.

Personal development is education that provides opportunities for an individual to develop talents and skills to become more confident and self-aware. Examples of personal development opportunities include:

- making improvements to time-management skills;
- improving *emotional intelligence (EI)*, which is the ability to understand personal emotions and the emotions of others; and
- enhancing listening skills.

Training can be offered to an employee by allowing him or her to attend a local conference or take a class at a university or training facility. HR may bring a trainer into the organization and offer sessions on site. Virtual classes may be another option for employee education. Generally, when these opportunities are offered, HR covers the tuition for the class.

Employers who support further training of employees can reap benefits for the organization. Providing educational opportunities for employees:

- reduces turnover because employees can advance themselves and their careers;
- reduces cost as employers can invest in employees and train for new positions, eliminating recruitment cost and training of new workers;
- increases operational effectiveness when employees learn and apply new skills; and
- keeps a business competitive.

Monkey Business Images/Shutterstock.com

Job shadowing is observing a certain type of work by accompanying an experienced worker as he or she performs the assigned job. **Why is job shadowing a good way to train new employees?**

Spending time and money on education is considered an investment in human capital. **Human capital** is the knowledge and skills that contribute to an individual's ability to produce economic benefit. Making an investment in education and training usually results in better and higher paying jobs than those who do not make the investment. When employers assist their employees in furthering education, it becomes a winning situation for both parties.

LO 6.1-5 Diversity

One responsibility of HR is to strive for a diverse workforce. *Diversity* means having representatives from different backgrounds, cultures, or demographics come together in a group. Diversity includes age, race, nationality, gender, mental ability, physical ability, and other qualities that make an individual unique.

Workplace diversity is achieved by employing people without regard to gender, age, ethnicity, or racial background. However, diversity for diversity's sake can hurt a business. Individuals should be hired based on their qualifications for the job.

A diverse workforce has many advantages. Diversity can help organizations be more creative, be receptive to customer needs, and find new and efficient ways of completing tasks. Diverse employees can help a company create goods or services that may be new in the marketplace. New ways of thinking and looking at business are some benefits of hiring people with varied backgrounds and experiences. Diversity also increases the pool of potential qualified candidates, which can result in a more-effective workforce.

Diversity, however, does not come without its challenges. Special training may be required for employees to learn how to communicate in a diverse workplace. Employees may have to adjust their way of thinking and daily habits to work with a diverse population.

In order to understand and embrace diversity, culture must be understood. *Culture* is the shared beliefs, customs, practices, and social behavior of a particular group or nation. Culture influences how people respond to the communication and behavior of individuals and organizations. It affects how people think, work, and interact with others.

HR must be aware of actions and behaviors that can negatively impact a diverse workplace. Examples include stereotyping and biases. A *stereotype* is a belief or generalization about a group of people with a given set of characteristics. Diversity benefits a business only when the unique qualities of its employees are recognized and put to their best uses. A *bias* is the strong preference or opinion of a person on a particular topic or issue, whether work related or not. HR plays a role in discouraging biases so they do not destabilize the organization or affect it in a negative way.

Inclusion is the practice of recognizing, accepting, valuing, and respecting diversity. It is the act of involving all people's work or social circles in responsibilities, functions, or activities. Inclusion means accepting diverse people who are different in gender, race, mental or physical ability, age, or other qualities that make an individual unique.

Monkey Business Images/Shutterstock.com

Workplace diversity can help organizations be more creative, be receptive to customer needs, and find new and efficient ways of completing tasks. **Why do you think diversity is valuable in the workplace?**

Section 6.1 Review

Check Your Understanding

1. What are examples of responsibilities of a human resources (HR) department?
2. Summarize tasks involved in recruiting employees.
3. Briefly explain the selection process for recruiting new employees.
4. What does *professional development* mean in the context of current employees of an organization?
5. Provide examples of benefits that come from having a diverse workforce.

Build Your Vocabulary

As you progress through this text, develop a personal glossary of key terms. This will help you build your vocabulary and prepare you for a career. Write a definition for each of the following terms and add them to your personal glossary.

human resources management (HRM)
human resources (HR) department
human resources planning
talent management
succession planning
job analysis
recruiting
selection process
employment verification
background check
compensation
negotiate
orientation
onboarding
job shadowing
professional development
personal development
human capital
inclusion

Section 6.2 Retaining Employees

Why should an organization focus on offering competitive compensation packages?

Learning Objectives

LO 6.2-1 Discuss compensation as provided to employees by an organization.

LO 6.2-2 Identify ways an organization can offer a work-life balance for employees.

Key Terms

wage	piecework	family leave
salary	benefit	flextime
incentive	work-life balance	job sharing
bonus	personal leave	telecommuting
commission		

LO 6.2-1 Compensation

An organization spends time and money developing employees to be positive contributors to the company. In order to retain the best and brightest people, employee compensation is of great importance. *Compensation* is payment to an employee for work performed including wages or salaries, incentives, and benefits. It can also include ongoing training opportunities for employees.

Wages or Salaries

A **wage** is payment for work and usually calculated on an hourly, daily, or weekly basis. Wages are paid on a schedule, such as every week or every two weeks. For example, an hourly wage is a fixed amount paid for each hour worked. An employee who is paid $12 an hour and works 40 hours during a week will earn $480 a week (40 hours × $12) before taxes.

Competitive wages are wages that are at least equal to those paid by similar businesses in an area. They are also called *market* or *industry wages*. For example, if most manufacturing businesses in an area pay associates $10 per hour, a manufacturing business needs to pay close to that amount to attract and keep employees.

A **salary** is a fixed payment for work and expressed as an annual figure. It is paid in periodic equal payments. The payment period is usually weekly, biweekly (every other week), semimonthly (twice a month), or monthly. The annual salary amount is divided by the number of pay periods in the year. For example, a project manager who earns $72,000 a year may be paid once per month. The manager's monthly salary, before taxes, would be $6,000 a month ($72,000 ÷ 12).

Incentives

An **incentive** is a type of compensation based on performance. Also known as *pay for performance*, it is usually based on the company's or employee's performance.

A **bonus** is money added to an employee's base wage or salary. Its purpose is to encourage and reward outstanding achievement. A bonus amount can be based on a worker's accomplishments, length of time with the company, or the organization's profits.

A **commission** is income paid as a percentage of sales made by a salesperson. This is another example of pay for performance. Some employees work on a commission-only basis. For these individuals, their sole wage or salary is dependent on the commission they earn for the work they perform. Others receive a combination of base pay plus commission. These employees receive some type of base wage or salary and are able to add commission to it based on their efforts.

Another form of incentive pay is the piecework system. **Piecework** is a wage based on a rate per unit of work completed. In the piecework system, an employee receives a specific dollar amount for each unit of work finished. For example, garment workers may be paid by the number of garments completed. Piecework systems are common in the manufacturing and agriculture industries.

Benefits

An employee **benefit** is a form of noncash compensation received in addition to a wage or salary. Many employees view benefits to be as important as actual pay. Benefits provided by employers may include:

- medical and dental insurance, including eye care;
- retirement plan;
- sick leave;
- vacation time; and
- a profit-sharing program.

Benefits are another way for a business to compete in the labor market, in addition to compensation of wage or salary. By offering competitive benefits, a business can attract qualified candidates and increase employee job satisfaction.

Employability Skills
Emotional Control

Emotional control is the process of directing one's feelings and reactions toward a desirable result that is socially acceptable. The lack of emotional control in a workplace situation can cost an individual his or her job. Learning how to manage emotions helps a person think logically and act appropriately.

baranq/Shutterstock.com

An employee benefit, such as vacation time, is a form of noncash compensation received in addition to a wage or salary. **What type of noncash compensation do you think is important to employees?**

Ongoing Training

New employees receive training when they begin their jobs with the company. However, experienced employees often need training as well. Organizations understand they must continuously update their operations, which requires new knowledge or skills. Many businesses will provide ongoing training to improve professional or personal development. This training may involve learning:

- how to use new computer hardware, software, and phone system;
- new or updated operating procedures; and
- best practices within the industry.

LO 6.2-2 Work-Life Balance

Many organizations recognize that employees have responsibilities and obligations outside of work. To create a positive organizational culture, employees may be offered various ways to balance job responsibilities with family and life responsibilities. A **work-life balance** is the amount of time an individual spends working compared to the amount of time spent in a personal life.

Some of the ways an organization may offer a work-life balance include personal leave, family leave, flextime, job sharing, and telecommuting.

- **Personal leave** is a few days each year employees can use for personal reasons. In most organizations, personal time can be taken an hour at a time or days at a time.
- **Family leave** is time off work for certain life events. These may include the birth or adoption of a child, caring for a sick family member, and other family-related emergencies.
- **Flextime** is a policy allowing employees to adjust work schedules to match personal schedules better. For example, it is more practical for some employees to begin work early in the morning and leave early in the afternoon.
- **Job sharing** is an arrangement in which two part-time employees handle the responsibilities of a single full-time position. Together, their hours and duties are equal to one full-time employee.
- **Telecommuting** is an arrangement in which employees work away from the business site. Most telecommuters work from home and use the Internet and telephone to communicate with managers, coworkers, and customers.

Section 6.2 Review

Check Your Understanding

1. What are competitive wages?
2. What is another term for incentives?
3. List examples of benefits provided by employers.
4. Why do organizations provide ongoing training?
5. State examples of how an organization can offer a work-life balance to employees.

Build Your Vocabulary

As you progress through this text, develop a personal glossary of key terms. This will help you build your vocabulary and prepare you for a career. Write a definition for each of the following terms and add them to your personal glossary.

wage	piecework	flextime
salary	benefit	job sharing
incentive	work-life balance	telecommuting
bonus	personal leave	
commission	family leave	

Section 6.3 Employee Performance

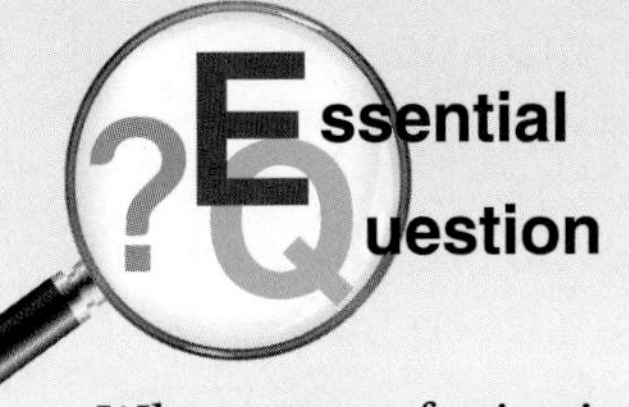

What types of criteria do you think employers use when they evaluate employees?

Learning Objectives

LO 6.3-1 Summarize performance management.
LO 6.3-2 Explain employee turnover.
LO 6.3-3 Discuss termination of employees.

Key Terms 

performance management
performance evaluation
turnover
turnover rate
exit interview
attrition
termination
downsizing

LO 6.3-1 Performance Management

Performance management is the manner in which a human resources department can measure the effectiveness of each employee. Employees are evaluated on their performances based on a set of metrics. *Metrics* are standards that outline what is expected for each position. Metrics are also called *key performance indicators (KPI)*. A manager uses these standards to evaluate how well the employee performed.

A **performance evaluation** is a formal assessment of an employee's job performance and progress made toward achieving set goals. It is also known as an *appraisal*. Performance evaluations are used to assess how well employees are performing their jobs. Typically, a performance evaluation form is used that includes the metrics for the position, as shown in Figure 6-3. The manager rates the employee for his or her performance on each standard.

Most organizations conduct employee performance evaluations on an annual basis. Pay raises, bonuses, and promotions are often based on performance evaluations. HR is responsible for developing an evaluation system that is reliable and fair.

RedSky Travel Employee Performance Evaluation			
Employee Information			
Name:			
Job Title:			
Review Period:			
Ratings			
	1 Poor	2 Acceptable	3 Excellent
Job Skills:			
Attendance:			
Initiative:			
Communication:			
Dependability:			
	Composite Score:		
Comments:			
Verification of Review			
Employee Signature			
Manager Signature			

Goodheart-Willcox Publisher

Figure 6-3 A performance evaluation is a formal assessment of an employee's job performance and progress made toward achieving set goals.

The employee's immediate supervisor usually conducts the performance evaluation. The supervisor discusses the results of the evaluation with the employee. During this time, the supervisor discusses what the employee is doing well and provides feedback to improve performance and professional development. A copy of the evaluation is forwarded to HR and placed in the employee's permanent personnel file.

Employees who perform their jobs well, are reliable, and are loyal to the company are generally in line to be promoted. A *job promotion* is an advancement by an employee within a company to a position of greater responsibility. A promotion also typically leads to increased pay and a higher status within the company.

The possibility of a promotion helps motivate employees to do their best work. Promotions also allow employees to apply their skills and talent and take ownership in the business. HR generally communicates to an employee the expectations of what it will take to be eligible for a promotion within the company.

LO 6.3-2 Employee Turnover

Turnover is when an employee leaves the organization because he or she chooses to do so or is terminated by the employer. The **turnover rate** is the percentage of employees leaving a company within a certain period of time, typically a year. Turnover is important for HR to control because there are major costs to the company in the hiring, training, and development of a new employee. Some studies show that each time a salaried employee leaves an organization, it costs the company six to nine months of the employee's salary in recruitment costs to refill the vacant position.

Constant turnover means ongoing costs that decrease a company's profits. Examples of ways to control turnover include:

- hire the right people for the right job;
- create compensation packages that are in line with the competition;
- recognize employee performance;
- provide job and professional support for employees;
- allow flexible schedules or meet the needs of the employees within reason; and
- communicate often with employees to uncover any conflicts that HR may be able to resolve.

Ethics

Nepotism

Nepotism is the practice of hiring individuals who have a familial relationship even when they do not have the qualifications for a position. Hiring family members is not unethical. However, favoring family members who are not qualified for a position is unacceptable.

Another way to help manage future turnover is to conduct exit interviews with employees who leave. **Exit interviews** are formal interviews with departing employees during which they are asked to provide information about their reasons for leaving and their experience with the organization. These interviews help HR become aware of any workplace conditions or situations that are detrimental to working in the organization.

Attrition is a reduction in staff as a result of employees retiring or resigning from an organization without plans to backfill those positions. One way HR actively forecasts employee supply is assessing those employees who potentially could retire. Retirement is a normal occurrence in all organizations and can sometimes be planned for as it generally depends on the ages of employees. In addition, many organizations estimate a percentage of employees who could potentially resign. These numbers are based on past records of the company.

Attrition is voluntary, but turnover can be voluntary or involuntary. Managing turnover and attrition is important for a company to stay competitive and achieve results needed to fulfill its mission.

LO 6.3-3 Termination of Employees

If an employee's performance does not meet expectations or the employee violates company policy, it may be necessary to terminate that person. **Termination** is the process of ending the relationship between an employer and an employee. Termination is often called *dismissal* or *firing* if it is the result of employee nonperformance.

It can be considered a *layoff* if the organization eliminates employees due to business reasons that do not include employee performance.

Termination is made with "cause," meaning the employee violated a policy or was involved in conduct that opposed company culture. For example, an employee falsifying data records can be cause for dismissal. It is the responsibility of HR to document all instances of unacceptable actions and place documentation of issues in the employee's file.

In some states, termination is made "without cause." This is called *employment at will.* Employment at will means an employer can terminate an employee at any time for any reason, except an illegal one, or for no reason, without incurring legal liability. Likewise, an employee is free to leave a job at any time for any or no reason with no adverse legal consequences. In this case, the employer has no obligation to provide a reason for the termination.

Downsizing is a general reduction in the number of employees within an organization. It is a result of an organization's decision, not a lack of employee performance.

The decision to downsize can be the result of new technology that requires fewer employees to create a product. However, downsizing usually occurs in economic conditions that require an organization to decrease spending. For example, in 2018, Tesla Inc. laid off about 4,000 employees and restructured the company. Tesla downsized to remove duplicate roles and selected positions no longer needed.

A positive result of downsizing is fewer employees and a smaller payroll. Payroll is one of the largest costs for a company. A negative result of downsizing is the resulting decreased morale and motivation of those who remain employed. Downsizing creates uncertainty and makes employees wonder if they are next to be dismissed. In addition, downsizing can affect the reputation of a company. Companies must carefully evaluate the effects of downsizing on operations and production, as well as on business finances, before taking this approach.

Section 6.3 Review

Check Your Understanding

1. What are metrics?
2. Why is it important for HR to control turnover?
3. What are some ways an organization can control turnover?
4. What is the meaning of *employment at will?*
5. State examples of reasons an organization would downsize.

Build Your Vocabulary

As you progress through this text, develop a personal glossary of key terms. This will help you build your vocabulary and prepare you for a career. Write a definition for each of the following terms and add them to your personal glossary.

performance management
performance evaluation
turnover
turnover rate
exit interview
attrition
termination
downsizing

Chapter 6 Review and Assessment

Chapter Summary

Section 6.1 Human Resources

LO 6.1-1 **Summarize the staffing function of management.**
Human resources management (HRM) is all the activities that lead to attracting, recruiting, hiring, training, evaluating, and compensating employees. This is the staffing function of management. The staffing function includes recruiting, hiring, training, evaluating, and compensating employees.

LO 6.1-2 **Define *human resources planning.***
Human resources planning is the process of creating a strategy to meet the employment needs of an organization. It starts with evaluating current employees and their skills. It includes reviewing potential internal promotions, potential terminations, resignations, retirements, and new or vacant positions that need staffing.

LO 6.1-3 **Explain the recruitment process used by human resources.**
Recruiting is the process of finding people who are qualified for a position. It involves advertising available positions, selecting and screening applicants, conducting interviews, verifying applicant's information and conducting background checks, and extending offers and negotiating compensation.

LO 6.1-4 **Discuss training and development of employees.**
HR is responsible for employee training and development. It starts with new employee orientation and onboarding. Then, the employee goes through job-specific training, which is a combination of group learning in a classroom setting and hands-on training.

LO 6.1-5 **Discuss diversity in the workplace.**
Diversity means having representatives from different backgrounds, cultures, or demographics come together in a group. Workplace diversity is achieved by employing people without regard to gender, age, ethnicity, or racial background. It has many advantages, such as helping organizations be more creative, be receptive to customer needs, and find new and efficient ways of completing tasks. In addition, inclusion is an important part of achieving a diverse workforce.

Section 6.2 Retaining Employees

LO 6.2-1 **Discuss compensation as provided to employees by an organization.**
In order to retain the best and brightest people, employee compensation is of great importance. Compensation is payment to an employee for work performed including wages or salaries, incentives, benefits, and ongoing training opportunities.

LO 6.2-2 **Identify ways an organization can offer a work-life balance for employees.**
Some of the ways an organization may offer a work-life balance include personal leave, family leave, flextime, job sharing, and telecommuting.

Section 6.3 Employee Performance

LO 6.3-1 **Summarize performance management.**
Performance management is the manner in which a human resources department can measure the effectiveness of each employee. Employees are evaluated on their performance based on a set of metrics. To evaluate employees, a performance

evaluation form is used to assess how well employees are performing their jobs. HR is responsible for developing an evaluation system that is reliable and fair.

LO 6.3-2 **Explain employee turnover.**
Turnover is when an employee leaves the organization because he or she chooses to do so or is terminated by the employer. Turnover is important for HR to control, as there are major costs to the company in the hiring, training, and development of a new employee.

LO 6.3-3 **Discuss termination of employees.**
Termination is the process of ending the relationship between an employer and an employee. It can be made with cause or without cause. It can also occur when the organization downsizes, or general reduction, number of employees due to business reasons that do not include employee performance.

Review Your Knowledge

1. Summarize the staffing function of management.
2. Discuss human resources planning.
3. Explain recruitment processes used by human resources.
4. Discuss training and development of employees.
5. Summarize diversity in the workplace.
6. Explain forms of compensation provided to employees by an organization.
7. Identify and explain ways an organization can offer a work-life balance for employees.
8. Summarize performance management.
9. Explain employee turnover.
10. Discuss termination of employees.

Apply Your Knowledge

1. Explain whether you agree with the following statement: Human resources are the most important organizational resources an organization utilizes.
2. A job analysis is a process that identifies the job requirements for a position, employee qualifications needed, and metrics used to evaluate performance. Assess your role as a student in your classroom. Perform a job analysis for the job of "student" and write a job description for the position.
3. Organizations spend a great deal of time and money in hiring employees. Explain how time and money spent by an organization to recruit and hire employees can be viewed as an investment in the future of the organization.
4. Recruiting involves seeking candidates who possess the necessary skills to perform a job. Discuss why it is the responsibility of management to ensure employees are properly trained for their jobs. Include your thoughts on why skilled employees, whether they are new or existing, may require additional training after being hired.
5. Diversity means having representatives from different backgrounds, cultures, or demographics in a group. Using your own words, explain the advantages of having a diverse workforce.
6. Part of the staffing function is to ensure the compensation package offered by an employer is in line with those of its competitors and with industry standards. Explain the role business competition plays when making decisions about employee compensation.

7. Some ways an organization may offer a work-life balance include personal leave, family leave, flextime, job sharing, and telecommuting. Which of these do you think is the most attractive to today's employees? Explain your selection.
8. A performance evaluation, or appraisal, assesses an employee's job performance and progress made toward achieving set goals. Why is it necessary for management to appraise the performance of employees?
9. There are major costs to the company in the hiring, training, and development of a new employee. Rationalize the costs a business must incur to respond to employee turnover.
10. It may be necessary to terminate employees whose performance does not meet expectations. Why is it the responsibility of a manager to assess whether an employee should be terminated?

College and Career Readiness

Communication Skills

Listening. *Active listening* is fully participating as you process what a person says. Listen actively to a classmate as he or she is talking with you and focus on what the person is saying. Provide feedback by asking for more explanation about anything you do not understand.

Reading. *Scanning* is done when you know the information you need is in a document, you just have to find it. Scan this chapter for information on employee compensation. Did scanning work for you? How long did it take you to find the information?

Writing. When taking notes, it is common to write down only key information, rather than every word. Select several pages of notes you have taken during class. Rewrite your notes as complete sentences and paragraphs. Use *transition words* to make smooth connections as your writing moves from one idea to the next.

Internet Research

SHRM. The Society for Human Resource Management (SHRM) is an organization that provides support, networking, and information for HR managers. Using the Internet, conduct a search for *SHRM.* Summarize examples of services offered to members. Why would it be important for HR managers to belong to SHRM?

Recruitment and Diversity. Recruitment and diversity are two topics that are frequently in the news. Using the Internet, perform a search on *case study on recruitment* and *case study on workplace diversity.* Identify a recent case for each and summarize the event. Summarize what you learned.

Downsizing. Downsizing can occur when an organization needs to reduce its expenses. Use the Internet to search for *examples of downsizing.* Select a news article about a company that has downsized recently. Write the name of the company, the reasons for downsizing, and related data, such as the percentage of employees released.

Teamwork

Performance evaluations are used to assess how well employees perform on the job. Working with your team, create a performance evaluation form for a student's overall class performance. Using Figure 6-3 as an example, include metrics, such as attendance or participation, and a ranking scale to create an evaluation form.

Portfolio Development

Checklist. Once you have established a method of collecting and organizing your documents, you will need to ensure nothing is left out or forgotten. Remember, a portfolio is a living document—one that is often customized for each job or academic program to which you apply. Unfortunately, this makes it easy to misplace, lose, or forget relevant information. It is helpful to use the master list of documents you created in a previous portfolio activity to serve as a checklist of components to be included in your portfolio. The checklist can also be used to record ideas for additional documents and other items that you may choose to include. It should *not* be included in your final portfolio, however.

Your checklist will likely need to be updated for each school or employer who will see your portfolio. Modifying your master list to appeal to each instance will result in greater chances of success. For example, if you were applying to a visual arts program at a university specializing in art, you would likely not present the same portfolio as if you were applying for a part-time job creating graphics for a marketing company.

As you move copies of documents from their original location to your customized portfolio, check the document off your list. This will help you make sure all relevant items are included.

1. Ask your instructor for a checklist. If one is not provided, use the Internet and research Student Portfolio checklists. Find an example that works for your purpose.
2. Print the master list of documents you created in a previous portfolio activity and compare that to the checklist you obtained in step 1. Make any necessary adjustments.
3. Using the master list, sample checklist, and any pertinent notes you made while comparing the two, create a checklist to serve as a road map for your portfolio.

CTSOs

Extemporaneous Speaking. Extemporaneous speaking is an event that demonstrates the ability to speak effectively on a topic with little preparation. This event allows you to display your communication skills, specifically your ability to organize and deliver an oral presentation.

At the competition, several topics will be presented from which to choose. Time limits will be in place for creating the speech and for delivering it. The evaluation will be based on your content, organization, coherence, and structure of the speech. In addition, verbal and nonverbal skills, as well as the tone and projection of voice, will be evaluated.

To prepare for an extemporaneous speaking event, complete the following activities.

1. Ask your instructor for several practice topics so you can practice making speeches.
2. After you have a practice topic, jot down the ideas and points to cover. An important part of making this type of presentation is that you will have only a few minutes to prepare. Being able to organize your main ideas quickly will enable you to focus on what you will actually say in the presentation.
3. Practice the presentation. You should introduce yourself, review the topic you will be presenting, defend the topic, and conclude with a summary.
4. Ask your instructor to play the role of competition judge as you give the presentation. Afterward, ask for feedback from your instructor. You may also consider having a student audience listen and give feedback.
5. For the event, bring paper and pencils to record notes. Supplies may or may not be provided.

CHAPTER 7

Managing Employees

Sections

7.1 Relationship Management

7.2 Employment Laws

Reading Prep

Before reading this chapter, review the key terms. They are listed at the beginning of each section and highlighted within the body of the chapter. As you read, determine the meaning of each key term.

Exploring Careers

Training and Development Manager

Training and development managers oversee the planning, direction, and coordination of training and development of an organization's employees. They select and assemble course content and materials for training programs. They also arrange on-the-job training for new employees and create courses to develop the skills of current employees. Sometimes, training and development managers will create courses to train management, who then train their direct reports.

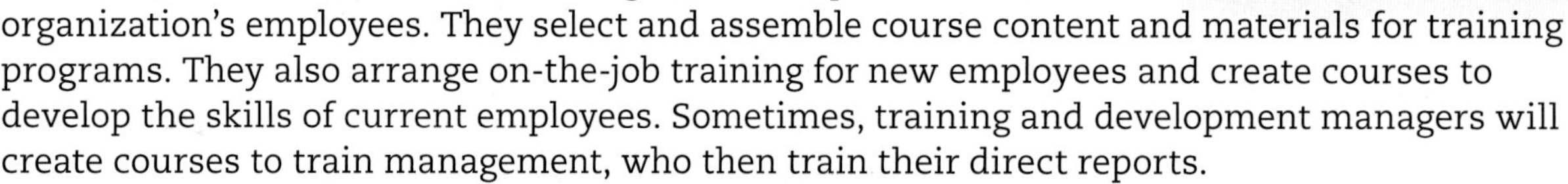

Typical job titles for this position include *education director* and *education development manager.* Examples of tasks that training and development managers perform include:

- assessing the needs of employees for training;
- creating and managing training budgets;
- developing training courses that make the best use of available resources; and
- evaluating the effectiveness of the training programs.

Training and development manager positions require a bachelor degree in human resources, education, business administration, or a related field. Some organizations prefer a master degree with a concentration on training and development, business management, or professional development. Prior work experience as training and development specialists or another human resources field may be required. Since training and development managers create instructional programs and often coach other employees, planning, organization, and communication skills are essential for this position.

Rawpixel.com/Shutterstock.com

Section 7.1 Relationship Management

What do you think it means for HR to manage employee relations in an organization?

Learning Objectives

LO 7.1-1 Explain relationship management.
LO 7.1-2 Identify characteristics of an adaptive organization.
LO 7.1-3 Discuss organizational change.
LO 7.1-4 Summarize managing change in an organization.
LO 7.1-5 Define *grievances*.

Key Terms 

employee relations
relationship management
workplace rules
employee handbook
workplace bullying
adaptive organization
organizational change
change management
communication plan
grievance

LO 7.1-1 Relationship Management

Employee relations is the organization's efforts to manage communication and cooperation between employees. Employee relations include relationships between managers and their employees, managers with other managers, or two employees. **Relationship management** is the processes that HR facilitates to ensure that employee relationships in an organization are productive and meet company goals. Relationship management is broad and requires HR to actively evaluate and anticipate the needs of employees.

A component of relationship management is workplace rules. Without rules, it would be difficult for employees to coexist in the work environment.

Workplace Rules

Workplace rules are established guidelines for behavior in the workplace. Rules are necessary for an organization to comply with federal, state, and local laws. Employers are required to have certain work rules in place that provide protection for employees. These rules establish guidelines on safety, time and attendance, and workplace interactions. In addition, work rules establish guidelines for appropriate behavior, which are guided by the culture of the organization.

Organizations usually communicate workplace rules in an employee handbook. An **employee handbook** translates the policies of the business into day-to-day information that the employees need to know. It is important to communicate policies and standards in writing. This eliminates any confusion or misunderstanding about appropriate conduct. Orientation for employees includes introduction to the employee handbook and the code of conduct. Generally, employees are required to sign a statement saying they have read the policies and understand the expectations of behavior.

To discourage undesirable behavior in the workplace, most businesses provide a set of employee guidelines with clear definitions of right and wrong actions. A *code of conduct* is a document that identifies the manner in which employees should behave while at work or when representing the company. This may be a separate document or a part of the employee handbook.

For example, Toyota's code of conduct explains the necessary attitude of employees to put the company's Guiding Five Main Principles of Toyota into practice. In addition, it also explains the social responsibilities and other key points for employees to follow.

The following list is examples of actions not acceptable in the workplace and could warrant immediate termination of employment. These may be in a code of conduct.

- Purposeful falsification or causing the falsification of any time, attendance, personnel, business, financial, or other records of the company.
- Disorderly conduct during work time or on company property, including fighting, threatening, yelling at, or otherwise abusing or harassing a coworker by word, act, or serious horseplay involving or having the potential for personal injury.
- Possession of weapons on company property, during company events, or while conducting company business.

Workplace bullying is a serious example of conduct that is unacceptable in the workplace. **Workplace bullying** is intentional or repeated mistreatment, verbal abuse, threatening, or any action that prevents a person from doing his or her job without fear. Such behavior can escalate to a point that endangers the well-being of an individual and instills fear of bodily harm. Avoiding workplace bullying may be a part of a code of conduct.

lightwavemedia/Shutterstock.com

Workplace bullying is a serious example of conduct that is unacceptable in the workplace. **What rules are in place at your school that address bullying?**

Employability Skills
Resilience

Resilience is a person's ability to cope with and recover from change or adversity. Resilient people are able to handle challenges aptly in one aspect of their lives while not letting it affect other aspects. They can bounce back even when they feel as if they have been knocked down.

Workplace Rule Violations

Ignorance of workplace rules is not an excuse for violating those rules. Each employee is responsible to read the company handbook and ask questions if a workplace rule is not clear.

Common workplace violations include excessive absenteeism, tardiness, productivity deficiencies, and negative workplace behavior.

Minor violations, such as cell phone usage during work hours, are typically handled by a supervisor. Serious violations, such as workplace bullying or employee theft, are addressed by HR. The consequences can be a reprimand or termination of employment.

Organizations often deploy a three-step process when issuing disciplinary action. Those steps may include the following.

1. A *verbal warning* is a discussion between the supervisor or HR and the employee outlining the need to change.
2. A *written warning* is a more formal disciplinary action that is in written form and signed by the manager or HR.
3. The *final written warning* is a written document addressed to an employee before termination.

Training of supervisors and managers on when and how to discipline employees is crucial for organizations. HR helps train managers on how to enforce workplace rules consistently throughout the organization.

LO 7.1-2 Adaptive Organization

The way in which business is conducted in the 21st century changes almost daily. The workplace is evolving with college graduates entering the workforce, rapidly changing technology, and social media becoming a source of news. We no longer live in a society of nine-to-five workers.

Organizations that do not adjust to the changing environment will more than likely be unsuccessful or simply fail. Successful businesses anticipate changes in the environment that influence the direction of the company. These events can be positive or negative, but the outcome is that adjustments are required. Management teams must be proactive and ready to adapt and move forward with the company goals.

An **adaptive organization** is an organization that has the ability to adjust to events in the internal and external environment that affect operation of a business. The goal of an adaptive organization is to create an environment that makes proper use of the capabilities of all employees and an operation that can be sustained and remain competitive far into the future.

Adaptive organizations are proactive and generally share similar attributes. Examples of those attributes are:

- open-minded leadership;
- managers who are eager to collaborate with peers, employees, and supervisors;
- management that is willing to try new ideas; and
- willingness to keep lines of communication open.

These organizations recognize when changes will or need to happen. They prepare for the transition by making it possible for individual employees and the organization as a whole to adjust to the changes.

fizkes/Shutterstock.com

An adaptive organization is an organization that has the ability to adjust to events in the internal and external environment that affect operation of a business. **What are some examples of events that could affect an organization?**

LO 7.1-3 Organizational Change

Change is constant in the workplace. Sometimes change happens quickly with little time for management to prepare employees for sudden events. For example, the CEO of the organization may suddenly be terminated with no warning. Such a sudden announcement can result in worker fear and unrest.

There are other times when change is planned and can be controlled. For example, a business announces to the employees that they are selling the company. The employees understand the plan and that there will be changes. The transition process usually takes time and management can lead employees through adjustments.

Life-changing events in a company are called organizational changes. **Organizational change** is any modification to the structure of an organization, its people, or technology.

Organizational Structure

Organizational structure identifies the hierarchy of employees and determines their roles, authority, and communication flow within an organization. There are times when an organization must change its structure to be competitive. A volatile economy, new competitors, and countless other events happen that require a company to change its structure to maintain or improve profit levels.

An outcome of change can be that employees are assigned different tasks or to different work teams. Some employees resist change and like their current routines and the people with whom they have direct work relations.

It is the responsibility of HR to help employees understand how such changes will benefit the business and how each individual can play a positive role in making the adjustments.

People

There are situations where good people are in the wrong positions. It is important that organizations have the right people in the right jobs. There are situations in which an employee is assigned to a job that is not a good fit for his or her talents. This can be corrected by reassigning the employee to a position in the organization in which opportunities for success may be greater. Change that affects people can also mean promotions for some or termination for others. An organization is only as strong as its human resource talent.

Technology

Technology changes every day. Changes in technology may include new software programs or updates to the Management Information System (MIS). By keeping technology current, businesses can increase productivity, improve communication, and broaden customer outreach. An organization will probably not survive if it does not keep up with evolving technology.

LO 7.1-4 Change Management

Change management is applying processes and techniques to help employees adjust to organizational changes. It is a systematic approach and application of knowledge, tools, and resources to deal with change and resistance to change. HR manages the process by helping individual employees and the organization transition from the current state to the desired state. To facilitate the process, the following steps can ensure a smooth transition in an organization.

- Planning and identifying what needs to change and when it will happen.
- Facilitating communication from management to employees on a timely basis.
- Helping employees understand the need for the change.
- Improving employee skills through proper training and development.
- Supporting employees through the change process.

Monkey Business Images/Shutterstock.com

Change management is applying processes and techniques to help employees adjust to organizational changes. **How can managers help employees adjust to changes in their organization?**

The *change process* involves defining and adopting new corporate strategies, structures, procedures, and technologies. Effective change management involves changes to workplace culture and the *people side* of an organization. The primary goal of change management is to implement new processes, products, and business strategies successfully while minimizing negative outcomes within the organization. A goal should be *innovative*, which means to use new methods. Communication is an important component of the change process that requires priority in the process. Educating employees about what will happen, why, and when can make transitions go more smoothly.

Having a communication plan in place can guide managers on appropriate protocol for communication and help facilitate change. A **communication plan** is a road map that includes objectives and goals that clearly outline the way in which communication takes place. Communication plans are discussed in Chapter 9.

LO 7.1-5 Grievances

A **grievance** is a written claim by an employee stating that he or she was adversely affected by the application of a written company policy. Sometimes grievances are genuine inequities in the workplace, such as company violation of safe working conditions. They can also be the result of organizational change.

Other times, a grievance can be the result of perceived inequities. *Perceived* means interpreted and not necessarily true. An example might be an unhappy employee overlooked for a promotion when he or she thought a promotion was deserved.

A *grievance procedure* is the formal process of communication designed to resolve grievances as soon as possible. HR facilitates the grievance procedure with managers, supervisors, and representatives of the organization.

All grievances, real and perceived, should be brought to HR by management to be reviewed and resolved. If a grievance is filed, it should be addressed quickly according to the procedure established by HR, similar to the steps outlined in Figure 7-1.

Grievances should be addressed and resolved promptly. Failing to address a grievance properly can lead to broken trust between the employer and employee or potential lawsuits.

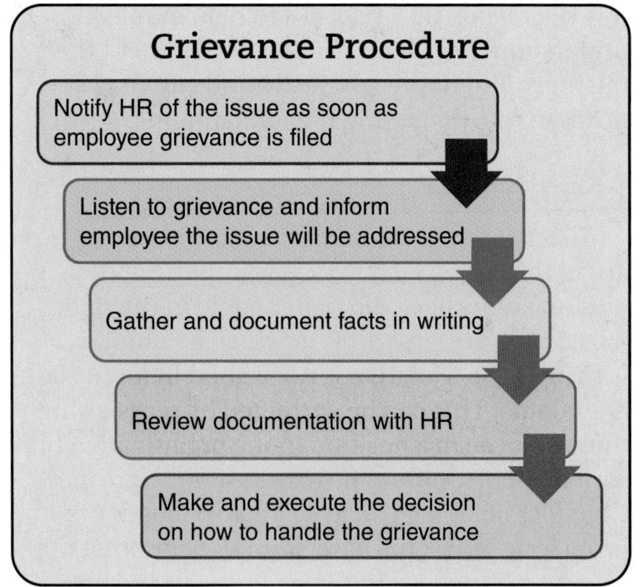

Figure 7-1 A grievance procedure is the formal process of communication designed to resolve grievances as soon as possible.

Section 7.1 Review

Check Your Understanding

1. Why do organizations often create an employee handbook for communicating rules?
2. Cite a three-step process deployed by an organization when issuing disciplinary action.
3. List examples of attributes of adaptive organizations.
4. What are three common types of organizational change?
5. Define a *grievance procedure.*

Build Your Vocabulary

As you progress through this text, develop a personal glossary of key terms. This will help you build your vocabulary and prepare you for a career. Write a definition for each of the following terms and add them to your personal glossary.

employee relations	employee handbook	change management
relationship management	workplace bullying	communication plan
workplace rules	adaptive organization	grievance
	organizational change	

Section 7.2 Employment Laws

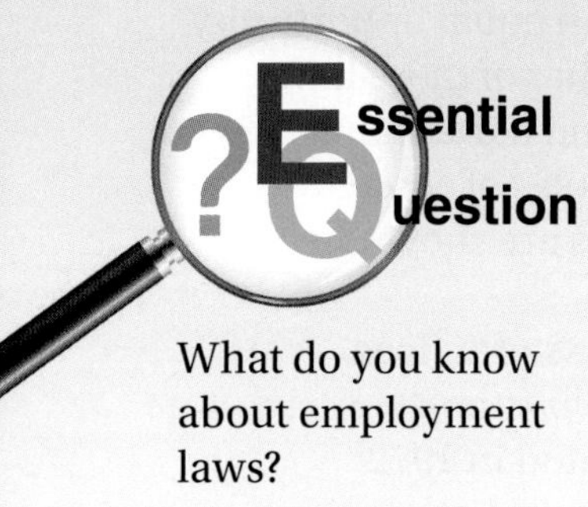

What do you know about employment laws?

Learning Objectives

LO 7.2-1 Explain labor relations and compensation and benefits laws.

LO 7.2-2 Discuss equal employment opportunity laws.

LO 7.2-3 Identify examples of employee health and safety regulations in the workplace.

LO 7.2-4 Summarize stress management.

Key Terms

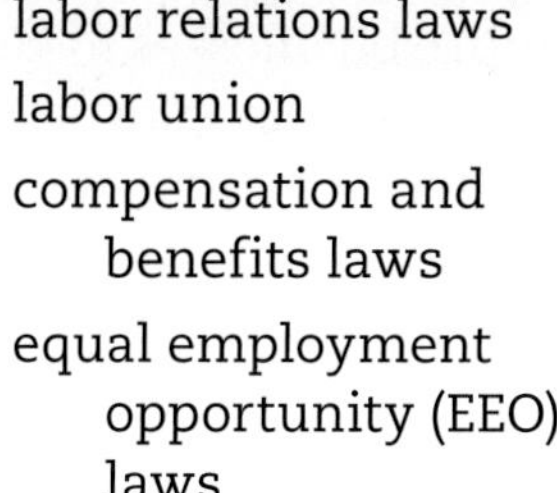

- labor relations laws
- labor union
- compensation and benefits laws
- equal employment opportunity (EEO) laws
- discrimination
- adverse impact
- harassment
- sexual harassment
- health and safety laws
- ergonomics
- stress
- stress management
- stress-management skills

LO 7.2-1 Labor Relations and Compensation

Businesses are required to protect and treat employees fairly. It is necessary for HR to stay up-to-date with labor acts and regulations. Employment laws change often and may vary from state to state. HR is often responsible for training managers to ensure they understand and follow the various regulations.

Government agencies may impose fines and penalties on a business for noncompliance of employment laws. In extreme cases of noncompliance, employees may file lawsuits or the government may shut down a business. Two examples of laws with which a business must be in compliance are labor relations laws and compensation and benefits laws.

Labor Relations Laws

Labor relations laws are laws that give employees the right to organize and collectively bargain for rights. These laws regulate the relationships between employees and their employers.

The *National Labor Relations Act (NLRA)* is an important labor law that gives employees the right to organize into a labor union. A **labor union**, also called *organized labor*, is a group of workers united as a single body to protect and advance the rights and interests of its members. In many industries, workers are part of a union that negotiates the terms of employment with employers. This is called *collective bargaining*. Representatives of the employees meet with an employer to discuss various topics, such as wages, hours of work, working conditions, and other business practices, that affect a group of workers.

Ethics

Misconduct

Misconduct is intentionally behaving in a way that puts an employer at risk. This type of unethical behavior can take many forms, such as racial discrimination, sexual harassment, and ignoring safety protocols. Misconduct is unethical and, depending on the specific action, may expose the business to legal consequences.

Compensation and Benefits Laws

Compensation and benefits laws cover fair wages and benefits for all employees. These laws address topics including work hours and overtime pay, child labor laws, leave time, and employee retirement income. Figure 7-2 explains examples of compensation laws that businesses must follow.

LO 7.2-2 Equal Employment Opportunity Laws

Equal employment opportunity (EEO) laws ensure that all workers have an equal opportunity for employment. A large number of these laws help reduce discrimination and harassment in the workplace. Some examples of equal employment opportunity laws are shown in Figure 7-3.

To regulate unfair business practices, the *US Equal Employment Opportunity Commission (EEOC)* was created in 1972 to enforce antidiscrimination and other employment-related laws. EEOC regulations also require businesses to keep records on personnel, payroll, and employee evaluation to ensure fair practices are applied.

Workplace Discrimination

Many US laws describe the proper treatment expected for employees in the workplace.

Compensation and Benefits Laws

Law	Year	Description
Social Security Act	1935	This act established programs to provide Federal benefits for people who are retired, unemployed, or disabled, as well as for children and families of those who receive aid.
Fair Labor Standards Act (FLSA)	1938	FLSA established the 40-hour workweek with overtime pay beyond that for hourly employees; established the minimum hourly wage; and set the employment rules for anyone under 16 years old.
Employee Retirement Income Security Act (ERISA)	1974	ERISA protects benefits of employees whose employers have created a retirement plan. It applies to most retirement plans established by private-sector employers.
Family and Medical Leave Act (FMLA)	1993	FMLA ensures eligible employees are able to take up to 12 weeks of unpaid, job-protected leave for SPECIFIED family and medical reasons.
Health Insurance Portability and Accountability Act (HIPPA)	1996	HIPPA ensures employees guarantee access to insurance coverage even if they have preexisting health conditions.

Goodheart-Willcox Publisher

Figure 7-2 Compensation and benefits laws cover fair wages and benefits for all employees.

Equal Employment Opportunity Laws		
Law	**Year**	**Description**
Equal Pay Act	1963	Employers cannot pay different wages to men and women if they perform equal work in the same workplace.
Title VII of the Civil Rights Act (Title 7)	1964	Employers cannot discriminate based on the race, color, religion, national origin, or gender of an individual.
Age Discrimination in Employment Act (ADEA)	1967	ADEA protects individuals who are 40 years of age or older from employment discrimination based on age.
Section 501 of the Rehabilitation Act	1973	The federal government cannot discriminate against a qualified employment candidate with a disability.
Pregnancy Discrimination Act	1978	This act is an addition to Title VII that makes it illegal to discriminate against a woman because of pregnancy, childbirth, or a medical condition related to pregnancy or childbirth.
Title I of the Americans with Disabilities Act (ADA)	1990	ADA prevents employers from discriminating against a qualified person with a disability in both the private sector and in governmental departments. Employers must make reasonable accommodations for known physical or mental limitations of an otherwise qualified individual.
Genetic Information Nondiscrimination Act of 2008 (GINA)	2008	GINA prevents employers from discriminating against employees or applicants because of genetic information, such as information about any disease, disorder, or condition of an individual's family members.

Goodheart-Willcox Publisher

Figure 7-3 The Equal Employment Opportunity Commission (EEOC) enforces antidiscrimination and other employment-related laws.

Discrimination occurs when an individual is treated unfairly because of his or her race, gender, religion, national origin, disability, or age. Examples of discrimination in the workplace include:

- excluding certain groups of people from employment;
- asking a woman during a job interview if she plans to have children;
- paying different wages to equally qualified employees in the same position;
- denying the use of company facilities to certain employees; and
- unfairly evaluating certain employees for promotions.

Affirmative action policies are those in which an organization actively engages in efforts to improve opportunities for historically excluded groups in American society. These programs seek to increase employment opportunities for women and minorities.

Most organizations respect comparable worth. *Comparable worth* is the idea that one group of individuals, such as women, should receive pay equal to men if they possess similar levels of education and perform the same work.

Adverse impact refers to employment decisions, practices, or policies that appear neutral but have a discriminatory effect on a protected group. Adverse impact can occur even if the employer had no intent to discriminate. For example, during the hiring process, a company is not permitted to test the reading ability of a protected group while not testing a nonprotected group. HR and managers must monitor and remove such practices even if the meaning is unintended. If not addressed properly, a company can face lawsuits based on adverse impact.

You Do the Math

Functions: Discrete and Continuous Functions

A function involves relating an input to an output. Each value in a *discrete function* is one of a specified set, usually a whole number. For example, the number of children in a family must be a whole number, so the function for how many children are in a family is a discrete function. The values in a *continuous function* do not have to be one of a specific set; they can include fractions, decimals, or irrational values. For example, the average age of students in a class does not need to be a whole number, so the function for average age is a continuous function.

Solve the following problems.

1. The sales tax in a particular town. Is this a discrete or continuous function?
2. The amount a vendor charges for delivery. Is this a discrete or continuous function?
3. The average age of a business's accounting staff. Is this a discrete or continuous function?
4. The speed at which a delivery truck travels. Is this a discrete or continuous function?

Harassment

Harassment can create an unhealthy work environment. **Harassment** is uninvited conduct toward a person based on his or her race, color, religion, sex, national origin, age, or disability. According to the Sexual Assault Prevention and Awareness Center, **sexual harassment** is defined as "unwelcome sexual advances, requests for sexual favors, and other verbal or physical conduct of a sexual nature when the conduct is made as a term or condition of an individual's employment, education, living environment, or participation in a University community." According to the EEOC, harassment becomes unlawful when:

- enduring offensive conduct becomes a condition of employment; *or*
- conduct creates a work environment that a reasonable person would consider intimidating, hostile, or abusive.

Examples of offensive conduct include inappropriate jokes, name-calling, physical assaults, threats, intimidation, and insults. Offensive conduct also includes displaying offensive gestures, pictures, or objects.

A person can be an indirect target, as well as direct target, of harassment. For example, a coworker who overhears a person telling an inappropriate joke in the workplace is a victim of harassment.

Harassment is unacceptable in the workplace. It is necessary that HR have policies in place to deter, as well as punish, behavior that negatively affects employees.

LO 7.2-3 Employee Health and Safety

Health and safety laws are laws that establish regulations to eliminate illness and injury in the workplace. Established by the US Department of Labor in 1970, the *Occupational Safety and Health Association (OSHA)* sets and enforces workplace safety standards. OSHA performs inspections to ensure workplaces are safe and healthy for employees, handles safety complaints, and investigates workplace accidents. It also provides and encourages training, outreach, education, and assistance to businesses.

Employers must maintain a safe and healthy work environment for their employees in accordance with OSHA standards. Workplace safety standards include practices such as safety precautions, protective equipment, and confined spaces for dangerous production tasks. Health regulations include protecting employees from chemicals, toxins, and allergens that could be dangerous to health. Regulations may also require medical attendants to be on-site in the event of accidents. The number and type of regulations for both safety and health standards vary depending on the industry. However, all businesses must provide work areas that are free from danger.

Accidents

Falls are the most common workplace accident in an office setting. Preventing workplace falls is relatively simple. Some ways to decrease falling accidents include the following actions.

- Close drawers completely.
- Do not stand on a chair or box to reach.
- Secure cords, rugs, and mats.
- Obey safety signs.

Lifting hazards are a source of potential injury from improperly lifting or carrying items. Most back injuries are caused by improper lifting. To avoid injuries from lifting, employees should be instructed to do the following.

- Make several small trips with items rather than one trip with a heavy load.
- Use dollies or handcarts whenever possible.
- Lift heavy items with the legs, not with the back.
- Do not carry an item that blocks vision.
- Obey safety signs.
- Request assistance from someone else whenever possible to avoid lifting heavy items alone.

Material-storage hazards are sources of potential injury that come from the improper storage of files, books, office equipment, or other items. A cluttered workplace is an unsafe workplace. Material stacked too high can fall on employees. Paper and files that are stored on the floor or in a hallway are a fire risk. Both employers and employees can prevent material-storage injuries. Some ways to avoid these hazards include the following.

- Do not stack boxes or papers on top of tall cabinets.
- Store heavier objects on lower shelves.
- Keep aisles and hallways clear.
- Obey safety signs.

Emergency Procedures

Emergency procedures are a series of actions taken to minimize risks during an emergency. Employees must be trained to react and take appropriate actions in a workplace emergency.

The first line of defense in all emergencies is for employees to stay calm and follow the emergency procedures. The seriousness of the emergency should first be evaluated to determine the type of action required. Employees and visitors in a place of employment should be aware of exits and how to evacuate the premises, if necessary. If there is a medical emergency, employees should understand the procedures for giving assistance and calling for help.

jaboo2foto/Shutterstock.com

Employers must maintain a safe and healthy work environment for their employees in accordance with OSHA standards. **In what ways do health and safety laws protect both employees and the business?**

Employees should be trained and prepared for common emergency situations, including:

- fires;
- natural disasters, such as a tornado, earthquake, or hurricane;
- medical emergencies, such as heart attack, stroke, fainting, burns, and cuts; and
- bomb threats and active shooters.

Ergonomics

Ergonomics is a science concerned with designing and arranging things people use so that they can interact efficiently and safely. In the workplace, this can include designing workstations to fit the unique needs of workers and the equipment they use. Applying ergonomic principles results in a comfortable, efficient, and safe working environment.

Ergonomics can improve the workspaces of employees who spend long periods of time working at computer stations. There are many types of ergonomic accessories that may improve the comfort of reading on a screen. These include wrist rests, specially designed chairs, and back supports. In addition, Figure 7-4 identifies actions that can be taken for comfort while working at computer stations and help prevent injury or strain to the worker's body.

LO 7.2-4 Stress Management

Organizational change is stressful for management and their direct reports. As part of change-management techniques, HR may offer help with stress management for its employees.

Stress is the body's reaction to increased demands or dangerous situations. It can manifest itself in many ways, including nervousness, anger, feeling overwhelmed, frequent headaches, upset stomach, or even high blood pressure.

Stress management is a variety of strategies used to cope with stress and limit its effects. A certain amount of stress can be positive in the workplace. Some people are driven to perform when pressured to meet a deadline. Others react to the release of adrenaline that stress triggers, which speeds up the heart and increases metabolism for endurance. The goal is to identify the good stress as well as the negative stress. When stress becomes negative, employees may need help.

Stress-management skills are the skills that enable an individual to identify and control stress. Figure 7-5 identifies some common techniques HR might offer employees for managing stress.

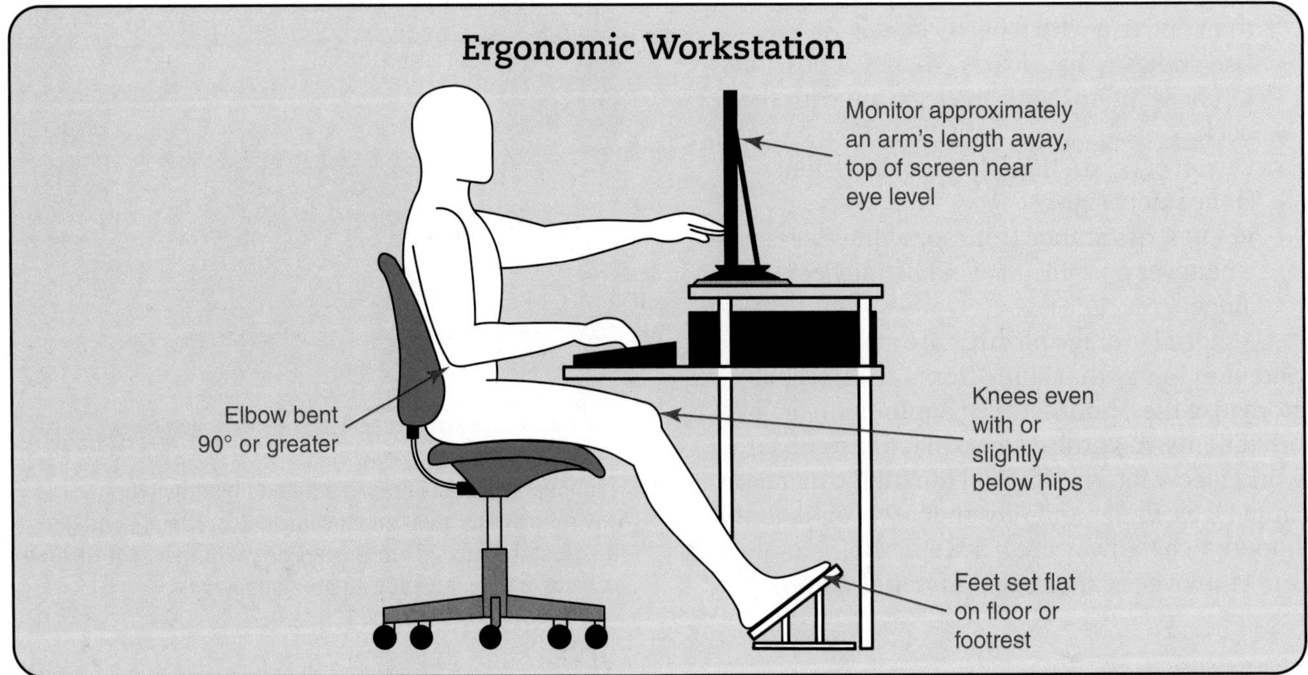

Goodheart-Willcox Publisher

Figure 7-4 Ergonomics can improve the workspaces of employees who spend long periods of time working at computer stations.

Stress-Management Strategies	
Identify stress triggers	• Identify where you were when you started feeling stressed. • Recall the activity in which you were engaged. • Remember if there was a particular situation or conversation involved. • Recognize if other people were around that may have contributed to your stress.
Attend to physical needs	• Get an adequate amount of sleep. • Eat regular and healthy meals. • Avoid foods providing a quick jolt of energy, such as sugar and caffeine. • Schedule regular exercise.
Be proactive, not reactive	• Focus on the positive. • Deal with the challenge rather than worry. • Set realistic goals. • Schedule tasks and commitments for the day. • Find balance in your personal, school, and work lives.

Goodheart-Willcox Publisher

Figure 7-5 Stress management skills are the skills that enable an individual to identify and control stress.

Section 7.2 Review

Check Your Understanding

1. What right does the National Labor Relations Act (NLRA) give employees?
2. Define *collective bargaining*.
3. What is the Equal Employment Opportunity Commission (EEOC)?
4. State examples of discrimination in the workplace.
5. Briefly explain the role of the Occupational Safety and Health Organization (OSHA).

Build Your Vocabulary

As you progress through this text, develop a personal glossary of key terms. This will help you build your vocabulary and prepare you for a career. Write a definition for each of the following terms and add them to your personal glossary.

- labor relations laws
- labor union
- compensation and benefits laws
- equal employment opportunity (EEO) laws
- discrimination
- adverse impact
- harassment
- sexual harassment
- health and safety laws
- ergonomics
- stress
- stress management
- stress-management skills

Chapter 7 Review and Assessment

Chapter Summary

Section 7.1 Relationship Management

LO 7.1-1 Explain relationship management.
Relationship management is the processes that HR facilitates to ensure that employee relationships in an organization are productive and meet company goals. It is broad and requires HR to actively evaluate and anticipate the needs of employees. One component of relationship management is workplace rules.

LO 7.1-2 Identify characteristics of an adaptive organization.
Adaptive organizations are proactive and generally share similar attributes. Examples of common attributes are open-minded leadership; managers who are eager to collaborate with peers, employees, and supervisors; management that is willing to try new ideas; and willingness to keep lines of communication open.

LO 7.1-3 Discuss organizational change.
Change is constant in the workplace. Sometimes change happens quickly with little time for management to prepare employees. Other times, change is planned and can be controlled. Life-changing events in a company are usually known as organizational changes, which are any modification to the structure of an organization, its people, or technology.

LO 7.1-4 Summarize managing change in an organization.
Change management is applying processes and techniques to help employees adjust to organizational changes. A goal is to be *innovative*. It is a systematic approach and application of knowledge, tools, and resources to deal with change and resistance to change. The change process involves defining and adopting new corporate strategies, structures, procedures, and technologies. Effective change management involves changes to workplace culture and the people side of an organization.

LO 7.1-5 Define *grievances*.
A grievance is a written claim by an employee stating that he or she was adversely affected by the application of a written company policy. A grievance can be genuine or perceived inequities.

Section 7.2 Employment Laws

LO 7.2-1 Explain labor relations and compensation and benefits laws.
Labor relations laws are laws that give employees the right to organize and collectively bargain for rights. These laws regulate the relationships between employees and their employers. Compensation and benefits laws cover fair wages and benefits for all employees. These laws address topics including work hours and overtime pay, child labor laws, leave time, and employee retirement income.

LO 7.2-2 Discuss equal employment opportunity laws.
Equal employment opportunity (EEO) laws ensure that all workers have an equal opportunity for employment. A large number of these laws reduce discrimination and harassment in the workplace.

LO 7.2-3 **Identify examples of employee health and safety regulations in the workplace.**
Employers must maintain a safe and healthy work environment for their employees in accordance with OSHA standards. Common types of health and safety regulations include reducing accidents caused by workplace falls, lifting hazards, or material-storage hazards; establishing emergency procedures; and creating an ergonomic workspace for employees.

LO 7.2-4 **Summarize stress management.**
Stress management is a variety of strategies used to cope with stress and limit its effects. The goal is to identify the good stress as well as the negative stress.

Review Your Knowledge

1. Explain relationship management.
2. Define an adaptive organization and its characteristics.
3. Discuss the need for organizational change.
4. Explain change management and the need for innovative strategies.
5. Summarize grievances in the workplace.
6. Explain labor relations and compensation laws.
7. Discuss equal employment opportunity laws.
8. Identify examples of employee health and safety regulations in the workplace.
9. Explain common emergency procedures.
10. Summarize stress management.

Apply Your Knowledge

1. Workplace rules establish guidelines for behavior in the workplace. Your school has rules that are guidelines for behavior while in school. Review the behavior policies established by your school. Write any additional rules you would include.
2. Organizations often deploy a process when issuing disciplinary action. The example given in this chapter includes a verbal warning, written warning, and final written warning. How does your school address students who behave in a way that requires disciplinary action?
3. Adaptive organizations generally share similar attributes including having open-minded leadership; managers who are eager to collaborate with peers, employees, and supervisors; management that is willing to try new ideas; and willingness to keep lines of communication open. Write a paragraph describing why you think or do not think that your school is considered an adaptive organization.
4. “There are situations where good people are in the wrong positions.” What do you think this statement means?
5. There are times when grievances voiced by an employee are genuine inequities in the workplace. Other times, a grievance can be the result of perceived inequities. What factors should be considered when determining if an inequity voiced by an employee is real or perceived?

6. A labor union is a group of workers united as a single body to protect and advance the rights and interests of its members. Identify a labor union with which you are familiar. Summarize what you know about the union and its members.
7. There are laws in place that prevent workplace discrimination and harassment. However, there are still cases of workplace discrimination and harassment reported by the news media. Write several paragraphs about examples of discrimination in the workplace that you have heard recently. What were they and why do you think these situations still exist?
8. It is the responsibility of an employer to provide a work environment that is safe and healthy for its employees. However, employees are responsible for following workplace rules. Explain how workplace rule violations by employees can affect the health and safety of the work environment and those with whom they work.
9. Ask your instructor for a copy of emergency procedures for your school. Evaluate the thoroughness of the policies. What would you suggest to improve the emergency procedures for your school?
10. Stress-management strategies are used to cope with stress and limit its effects. What do you do to manage stress in your own life? How can you carry your stress-management skills forward in your life to utilize them in your future career?

College and Career Readiness

Communication Skills

Speaking. *Impromptu speaking* is talking without advance notice to plan what to say. Turn to the person next to you and explain what you did over the weekend. Clarify anything the other person finds confusing or does not understand. Were you able to hold an impromptu conversation on this topic?

Listening. Active listening requires you to *show* you are listening. To do this, face the speaker and pay attention. Engage in eye contact but avoid staring, which can be intimidating and distracting. Nod when you understand a point. Practice showing you are listening by asking a friend or classmate about a familiar topic, such as his or her favorite movies. Identify important details of what he or she is saying.

Reading. *Reading for detail* involves reading all words and phrases, considering their meanings, and determining how they combine with other elements to convey ideas. Using this approach, read the first section in this chapter. Think through the way the author uses the words in each paragraph. After you have finished, decide if you have obtained a grasp of the content by reading for detail.

Internet Research

Adaptive Organization. An adaptive organization is an organization that has the ability to adjust to events in the internal and external environment that affect operation of a business. Search the Internet for *adaptive organizational design*. Based on the information you learned, write your suggestions on how to design an adaptive organization.

Federal Labor Legislation. Many laws protect the rights of employees in the workplace. Select one of the labor laws covered in this chapter, such as the *Fair Labor Standards Act* or the *Equal Pay Act*. Research the history of this law and describe how this piece of labor legislation affects the workplace.

Sexual Harassment. Sexual harassment is never acceptable in any situation. Search for *how to identify sexual harassment in the workplace*. List ways to identify this unacceptable behavior in the workplace. Summarize your research in a paragraph or two.

Teamwork

Workplace bullying is a serious example of conduct that is unacceptable in the workplace or at school. Together with your team, create a poster that promotes positive student behavior in your school.

Portfolio Development

References. A *reference* is a person who can comment on the qualifications, work ethic, personal qualities, and work-related aspects of another person's character. It is a person who knows your skills, talents, or personal traits and is willing to recommend you for a job, community service position, or perhaps entrance into a college program.

References can include your instructors, a manager at your part-time job, or counselors who know about your skills and interests. Someone you know from your personal life, such as a youth-group leader, can also be listed. However, you should *not* list relatives.

Always assume the interviewer will follow-up with your references. This means you should be selective when choosing them. Consider which references can best recommend you for the position for which you are applying. As a courtesy, always get permission from the person before using his or her name. Serving as a reference for someone is a responsibility that a person may not want. Getting permission to use someone as your reference verifies their willingness not only to be listed in your portfolio, but to recommend you for the position as well.

1. Ask several people who know you well if they are willing to serve as a reference for you. Using word-processing software, create a document that includes the names and contact information for those individuals. Each entry should include complete contact information for the person. Use the heading "Personal References" and your name. This page should follow your résumé when you are organizing your portfolio for presentation. Save this file as PERSONAL_REFERENCES with your last name, for example PERSONAL_REFERENCES_SMITH, or use a different naming convention that is suitable for the management system you implemented in Lesson 1. Back up the file on your flash drive.
2. Record the creation of your Personal References document on your master portfolio spreadsheet. In addition, record each person you contacted for a reference.

CTSOs

Ethics. Many competitive CTSO events include an ethics event or include an ethics component as a part of another event. Ethics is a set of rules that define what is wrong and right. Business ethics is a set of rules that help define appropriate behavior in a business environment.

The ethics component of an event may be part of an objective test. However, ethics may also be a part of the competition in which teams participate to defend a given position on an ethical dilemma or topic.

To prepare for an ethics event, complete the following activities.

1. Read the guidelines provided by your organization.
2. Make notes on index cards about important points to remember. Use these notes to study.
3. To get an overview of various ethical situations that individuals encounter, read each of the Ethics features that appear throughout this text.
4. Ask someone to practice role-playing with you by asking questions or taking the other side of an argument.
5. Use the Internet to find more information about ethical issues. Find and review ethics cases that involve business situations.

UNIT 4 | # Leading

Chapters

Functions of Management Covered in This Unit

While studying, look for the activity icon for:

- Vocabulary terms with e-flash cards and matching activities

These activities can be accessed at www.g-wlearning.com/business/8417

Case Study

Leadership

mimagephotography/Shutterstock.com

Sheila, an experienced manager, accepted a supervisory management position at an insurance company in a neighboring town. As a supervisory manager, she would be responsible for overseeing the daily activities of one of the claims units.

On her first day on the job, she was surprised to discover most of her direct reports were men. Concerned about how they would view reporting to a woman, Sheila decided to use an autocratic style of leadership. Through this style of leadership, Sheila maintained all of the power within her team. She was confident that if she showed them she was in charge, they would have no choice but to listen to her. She took total control of the group, maintained a firm grasp over the decisions and actions of the team, and avoided input from her employees.

At the end of her 90-day probation period, she met with her supervisor for her evaluation. She was surprised to learn her employees were complaining about her style of leadership. Sheila explained to her supervisor that she assumed the employees would be unwilling to listen to her or value her input. However, the result of her choice in leadership style was she alienated her staff. She told her supervisor she would make changes to her leadership style by allowing her employees to have more decision-making power and value their input.

Leadership style is the way in which a person leads a team, provides direction, motivates others, and plans actions. Experience helps managers learn by trial and error to develop the best approach that works for them, their team, and the organization as a whole.

Critical Thinking

1. How can employee feedback benefit a manager?
2. What could Sheila have done differently in her leadership style?

CHAPTER 8

Leading

Sections

Reading Prep

Prior knowledge is experience and information a person already possesses. It helps you to make sense of new information quickly. Before reading, look at the chapter title. What do you think you will be learning? How does this chapter relate to information you already know?

Exploring Careers

Management Analyst

Management analysts work to improve an organization's efficiency. They often evaluate an organization to help design or redesign systems and procedures, streamline workflow, and prepare operation manuals for management. Management analysts interview employees and managers to determine work functions and methods, equipment, and personnel needed to optimize productivity. They analyze collected data to develop new systems or procedures, which are documented and presented to senior management for implementation.

Typical job titles for this position include *administrative analyst* and *management consultant*. Examples of tasks that management analysts perform include:

- conducting on-site observations and interviewing managers and employees;
- analyzing financial data and other company reports;
- developing and recommending solutions to improve a company's system, procedures, or other organizational changes; and
- following up with managers to ensure changes are working.

Management analyst positions require a bachelor degree and prior work experience. Some organizations prefer a master degree in business administration as well as a Certified Management Consultant (CMC) designation. Management analysts must have good analytical, interpersonal, problem-solving, and communication skills.

OPOLJA/Shutterstock.com

Section 8.1 Importance of Leading

What do you think makes an effective leader?

Learning Objectives

LO 8.1-1 Summarize the leading function of management.
LO 8.1-2 Discuss leaders and power.
LO 8.1-3 Discuss leaders and empowering employees.
LO 8.1-4 Summarize leaders and motivating others.
LO 8.1-5 Explain leaders and creating effective teams.

Key Terms

trait
directing
empowerment
accountability
motivation
intrinsic motivation
extrinsic motivation
hierarchy of needs
collaboration skills
parliamentary procedure

LO 8.1-1 Leading Function

The *leading function* of management is the process of influencing others to work toward the attainment of common goals. Leaders set examples for behavior, work with others, and share ideas. They help with everyday tasks and develop solutions for challenges that arise in an organization.

Successful leaders possess a variety of effective traits. A **trait** is a characteristic that a person portrays. Organizations count on their managers to display leadership traits, such as honesty, loyalty, and decisiveness. Examples of traits of effective leaders are listed in Figure 8-1.

An organization cannot operate successfully without one or more individuals who lead and direct activities to drive business success.

Traits of Effective Leaders	
• Accountable	• Intuitive
• Collaborative	• Persistent
• Confident	• Self-assured
• Energetic	• Strategic
• Ethical	• Visionary

Goodheart-Willcox Publisher

Figure 8-1 A trait is a characteristic that a person portrays.

Without leadership, employees would work each day with no clear goal or direction.

Organizations strive to hire people for management positions who can manage *and* lead. A manager is a person hired for an officially defined position. A manager typically has employees, called *direct reports*, who report to him or her. It is this person's responsibility to carry out the job description and formally work on behalf of the organization. A manager, by definition, focuses on tasks. However, an effective manager knows how to manage tasks *and* lead and direct people.

Leaders direct the employees of an organization to meet its goals through the accomplishment of tasks. **Directing** is the process of influencing employees by supervising and overseeing them as they perform their job duties, providing motivation for them to be successful, and encouraging open communication.

LO 8.1-2 Leaders Earn Power

Leaders influence the people with whom they come in contact, such as their direct reports, peers, superiors, and even customers. *Influence* means to have power to cause an effect or outcome indirectly. Managers, by title, have a certain degree of power.

Power, in this situation, means they can influence what people think and how they behave when they interact with them. Managers must have power to make decisions and make things happen in an organization.

Types of Power

In 1959, social psychologists John French and Bertram Raven identified five sources of management power. These sources are legitimate, expert, referent, reward, and coercive power.

- *Legitimate power* comes by default because of the title or position the person holds in the organization. For example, the president of an organization has power because the president is in charge and is at the top of the organization. However, when the person loses the title, he or she also typically loses the power.
- *Expert power* is earned by developing expertise in a specific area. Managers who are experts in their areas generally receive respect when directing others because they genuinely have expertise in their areas.
- *Referent power* is power a person earns because others want to identify with that person. Managers who are popular sometimes create an image, similar to a celebrity, with which others want to be associated. If that desire to be connected to a specific manager disappears, so will that manager's power.
- *Reward power* comes to managers when they control the rewards others receive. Examples are benefits, new projects or training opportunities, better roles, and monetary benefits to influence people. When used ethically, it can be a positive way to encourage employees and help them develop their talents and skills.
- *Coercive power* involves the use of threats to make people do what one desires. It is considered an unwise use of power. Managers who coerce others may find themselves in illegal or unethical situations.

An effective manager learns how to use power appropriately and realizes that power gained can also be lost.

Wise Use of Power

A perceptive person will probably use different types of power at various times and learn to apply each type ethically and fairly. Management power, when used wisely, can help an organization accomplish great things for the business and for employees. Positive use of power enables a manager to:

- delegate tasks to others;
- contribute to business profit;
- make decisions when needed; and
- hire and terminate employees.

Abuse of power creates a negative environment for a business. Managers who use their power to intimidate employees or coworkers for any reason can be considered bullies.

You Do the Math

Problem Solving and Reasoning: Solution Accuracy

A manager may be tasked with checking the work of others for accuracy and effectiveness. For example, a business calculates the fuel economy of its delivery truck to be 19 miles per gallon. However, the amount of fuel used on a 20-mile delivery run is four gallons. This means either the calculation is incorrect or the reported usage is incorrect.

Solve the following problems.

1. A business sells 390 units of product for an average of $27.99 each. It reports the gross sales are $10,915. Determine if the reported sales figure is correct.
2. An employee drives a delivery vehicle 298 miles in eight hours. He uses 12 gallons of gasoline. He states his car gets 30 miles per gallon. Determine if the employee is correct.
3. A business spent a total of $43.87 on office supplies in one month and has decided to wait one month to pay the charge. The credit account accrues 2 percent interest per month on outstanding balances. The business estimates the finance charge will be $1.00. Determine if the finance charge is correct.

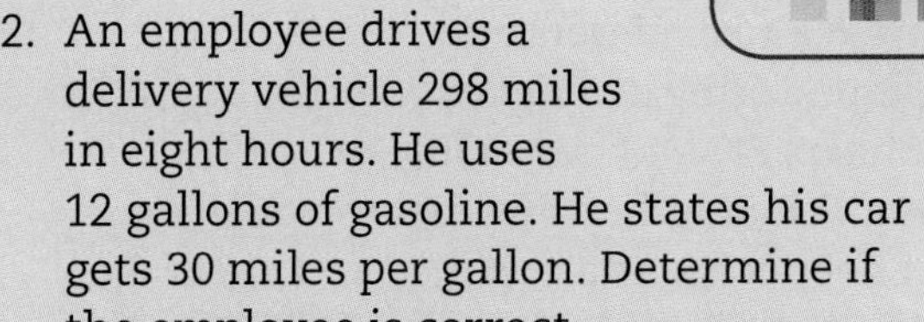

Ethics

Power

Managers hold power because they make decisions and direct the work of others. They are leaders who are trusted to use their power in an ethical manner to represent the company positively. When a manager uses power over other employees for negative reasons, such as for intimidation or personal gain, it is *abuse of power.* Abuse of power is unethical and can quickly become a situation of workplace bullying.

Workplace bullying is intentional or repeated mistreatment, verbal abuse, threatening, or any action that prevents a person from doing his or her job without fear. Those who use power for personal gain, to humiliate others, to cheat the business, or for other negative results will eventually be dismissed from their position.

LO 8.1-3 Leaders Empower Employees

Effective leaders empower employees. Today's leaders realize that empowering employees can be an effective method to make things happen. **Empowerment** is a management practice of giving decision-making authority to employees. However, empowerment is not given to just any employee. It is given only to ones who are qualified and experienced.

Empowering an employee encourages personal pride and ownership in work accomplished. When an employee realizes his or her decisions are valued and affect the success of an organization, that employee learns responsibility.

Empowering employees also helps prepare future leaders and management candidates. Training and promoting from within a company saves recruitment cost for an organization. It also contributes to a positive corporate culture.

Through employee empowerment, a manager can spend more time managing. Trusting a direct report to make more decisions frees a manager to focus on high-level issues. The result is higher productivity of the employee and manager. Empowering employees, however, does not release a manager from responsibility or accountability. **Accountability** is accepting responsibility for one's actions. Managers are ultimately responsible for the actions of employees and the success of their teams.

LO 8.1-4 Leaders Motivate Others

Leaders motivate others. **Motivation** is the force that inspires employees to want to perform their best and achieve results. It is a goal-oriented characteristic that helps a person accomplish his or her objectives. Motivation pushes an individual to work hard at achieving goals. Motivated employees are typically more productive and engaged in what they are doing.

Intrinsic and Extrinsic Motivation

There are two types of motivation: intrinsic and extrinsic. **Intrinsic motivation** is engaging in an activity that is personally rewarding. For instance, most people experience personal satisfaction from performing well on a task or doing the right thing. Praise from a peer or superior is not necessary. Motivation and satisfaction are internal and come from positive performance.

Black Salmon/Shutterstock.com

Extrinsic motivation is engaging in an activity in which an individual receives a reward from someone else. **Why do you think extrinsic motivation is an effective way to reward an employee?**

Extrinsic motivation is engaging in activity in which an individual receives a reward from someone else. Some individuals are motivated when they know they will receive something tangible for their performance. Examples of extrinsic rewards are a bonus, certificate of achievement, or promotion.

Theories of Motivation

There are multiple theories that attempt to establish how and why people are motivated. Understanding how a person becomes motivated is essential for a manager to get the best performance from that person. Three theories of motivation include Maslow's Hierarchy of Needs, Herzberg's Two-Factor Theory, and expectancy theory.

Maslow's Hierarchy of Needs

In the 1950s, psychologist Abraham Maslow developed a theory known as *Maslow's Hierarchy of Needs*. Maslow's theory states that unsatisfied needs motivate people to act. However, not all needs are equal, thus establishing a hierarchy of needs. A **hierarchy of needs** is an order in which certain needs are satisfied before others. Maslow observed that people tend to fulfill physical needs before needs that are less critical to survival are met. After physical needs, the needs for security, love and acceptance, esteem, and self-actualization are fulfilled in that order, as illustrated in Figure 8-2.

Herzberg's Two-Factor Theory

Psychologist Frederick Herzberg proposed a two-factor theory of motivation, also known as the *motivator-hygiene theory*. According to Herzberg, two factors have an effect on employee motivation and satisfaction.

- *Motivator factors* are the factors that lead to job satisfaction. Examples include recognition, opportunities for growth and achievement, and enjoyment of the job.
- *Hygiene factors*, or *dissatisfiers*, are those factors that lead to job dissatisfaction if they are *not* present and obvious. Examples include fair pay, good working conditions, and fringe benefits.

Expectancy Theory

Developed by Victor H. Vroom, the expectancy theory is one of the most widely accepted explanations of motivation.

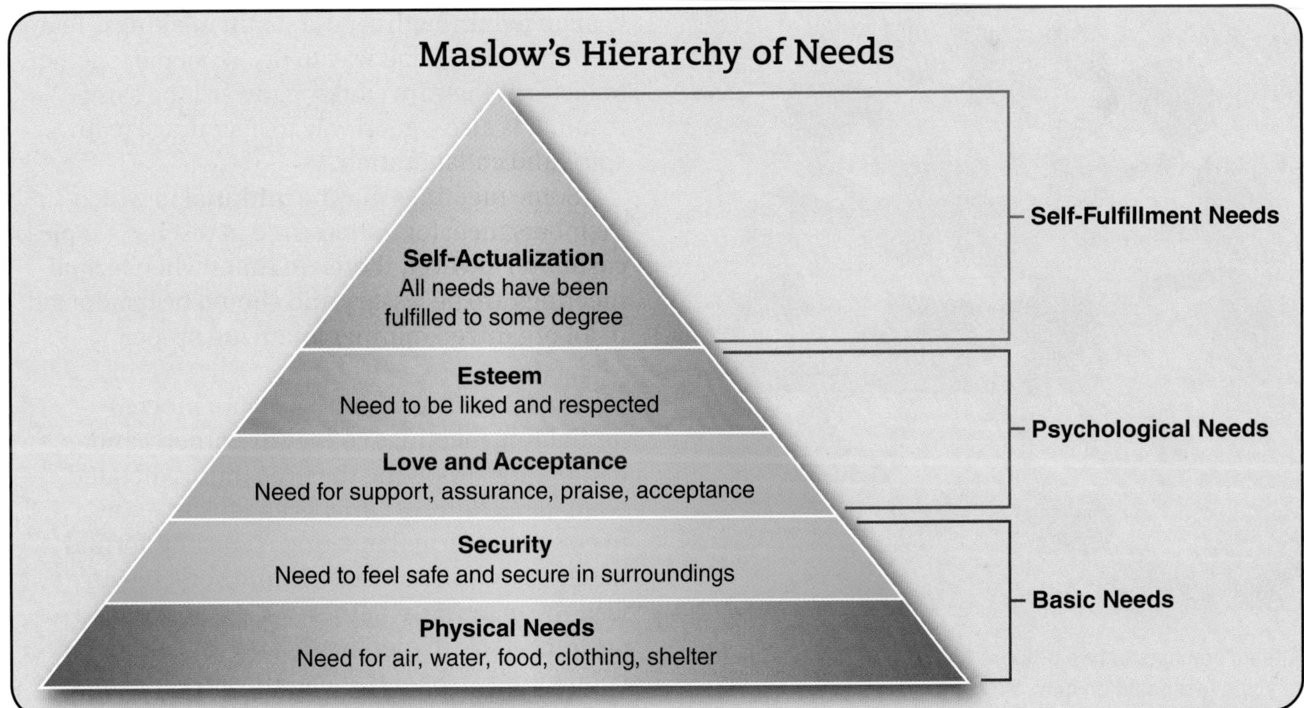

Goodheart-Willcox Publisher

Figure 8-2 Abraham Maslow believed physical needs must be met before other needs are met.

The expectancy theory says that an employee will be motivated to exert a high level of effort when he or she believes that:

- effort leads to a good performance appraisal;
- positive appraisal leads to organizational rewards; and
- organizational rewards lead to satisfaction of personal goals.

The key to the expectancy theory is the understanding of an individual's goals and the relationships between effort and performance, rewards and individual goal satisfaction, and performance connections to a reward. When an employee has a high level of expectancy and the reward is attractive, motivation is usually high.

LO 8.1-5 Leaders Create Effective Teams

Managers are typically responsible for a team of people. A *team* consists of two or more people working together to achieve a common goal. An effective leader creates effective teams by inspiring its members to work collaboratively to achieve common goals.

Rawpixel.com/Shutterstock.com

A team consists of two or more people working together to achieve a common goal. **Why are teams needed in the workplace?**

The terms *team*, *department*, and *group* are used interchangeably. Small businesses may only have one or two teams. Larger organizations may have multiple teams. Teams can be physically located under one roof or they may have members located around the country or the world. By creating teams, individual roles in the organization can be better defined.

Managers are the conduit between senior management and the team. Senior management determines the company's goals and objectives, which middle and supervisory managers then convey to their teams. In addition, managers share team successes, needs, and progress with senior management.

Teamwork is the cooperative efforts by individual team members to achieve a goal. Effective team members are individuals who contribute ideas and personal effort. They are team players and work well with others both on the team and outside of the team. Individuals who are positive contributors demonstrate leadership qualities even when they are not in leadership roles. They also possess collaboration skills. **Collaboration skills** are the skills that enable individuals to work with others to achieve a common goal. This can include sharing ideas and compromising for the greater good of the team.

Goals, objectives, and other information are exchanged through regular team meetings. Team meetings are a good way to bring people together to feel as if they are working toward the same result. It is also a good way to encourage team spirit and collaboration.

Some meetings may be informal in which members meet for a short time to discuss a topic casually. However, there are times when formal meetings are necessary and should be conducted in an organized manner following proper etiquette.

Parliamentary procedure is a process for holding meetings so they are orderly and democratic. Applying the procedures dictated by *Robert's Rules of Order* is an effective way to conduct a formal meeting. Typically, formal meetings require an agenda and someone to lead the meeting, whether it is a manager or a designated team member. Other guidelines for conducting an effective meeting are shown in Figure 8-3.

Guidelines for Effective Meetings		
Before the Meeting	**During the Meeting**	**After the Meeting**
• Identify meeting purpose • Select participants • Reserve room and time • Send meeting invitation • Prepare agenda • Send agenda to all participants	• Adhere to parliamentary procedure • Follow the agenda • Lead conversation • Respect others' time • End meeting on time	• Review notes • Send meeting notes to participants • Schedule follow-up meetings if all topics were not covered

Goodheart-Willcox Publisher

Figure 8-3 Applying the procedures dictated by *Robert's Rules of Order* is an effective way to conduct a formal meeting.

Sometimes, team meetings may include a virtual component for members not at the same location. These types of meetings are called *remote meetings*. The same rules of conducting a meeting should be followed when remote attendees are invited.

When the meeting begins, the leader should request permission from the participants to put them on speaker. Next, the leader should acknowledge those calling or logging in and make introductions. If appropriate, individuals can introduce themselves if there are not too many people in attendance for personal responses.

For those who are attending remotely, it is *polite* to put the phone or microphone on mute until ready to contribute to the conversations. It is *impolite* to be multitasking when a meeting is in progress rather than paying attention to what is transpiring in the conversations.

Section 8.1 Review

Check Your Understanding

1. Compare a manager to a leader.
2. Explain management power.
3. Cite examples of sources of management power.
4. State three theories of motivation.
5. Summarize the concepts of a team and teamwork.

Build Your Vocabulary

As you progress through this text, develop a personal glossary of key terms. This will help you build your vocabulary and prepare you for a career. Write a definition for each of the following terms and add them to your personal glossary.

trait	motivation	collaboration skills
directing	intrinsic motivation	parliamentary procedure
empowerment	extrinsic motivation	
accountability	hierarchy of needs	

Section 8.2 Leadership

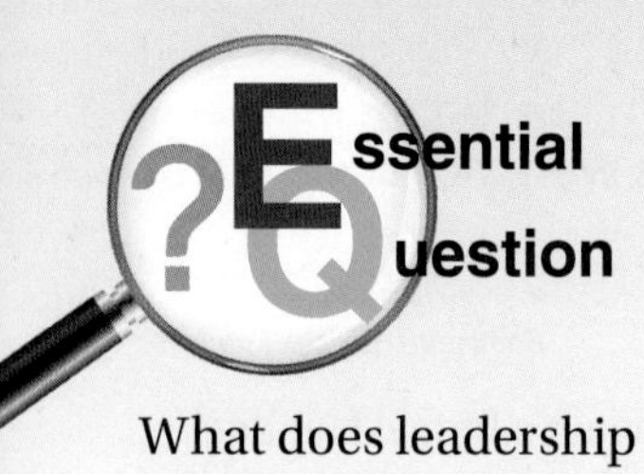

What does leadership style mean to you?

Learning Objectives

LO 8.2-1 Define different types of leadership styles.
LO 8.2-2 Cite examples of management styles.
LO 8.2-3 Identify types of difficult people encountered in the workplace.
LO 8.2-4 Discuss conflict resolution.

Key Terms

leadership	conflict-resolution skills	negotiation
conflict	emotional control	mediation
conflict resolution		ultimatum

LO 8.2-1 Leadership Style

Leadership is the ability to influence others to reach a goal. *Leadership style* is the way in which a person leads a team, provides direction, motivates others, and plans actions. Leadership style can be influenced by the personalities of the people with whom a manager works.

Experienced managers may learn by trial and error while developing the best approaches that work for them. Each individual has an opinion of how best to manage employees. Three common leadership styles are democratic, autocratic, and laissez-faire, as shown in Figure 8-4.

Democratic Style

Democratic leadership style is one in which the leader shares decision-making with the group. Democratic leaders encourage other team members to participate in the leadership process. This style is appropriate when employees are committed to their work, actively seek out more responsibilities, and are well-trained workers. However, it can become ineffective when too many team members want to be a part of decision-making and time becomes an issue when gaining a consensus.

Autocratic Style

The *autocratic* leadership style describes a leader who maintains all power within a team. Through this style, employees look to the manager to handle problems that arise. It works best in situations when control is necessary, such as emergencies or working with temporary employees.

Leadership Styles

Democratic Leadership
- Invites participation from team
- Open and collegial
- Shares decision-making with team members

Autocratic Leadership
- Handles problems that arise
- Keeps close control over members of the team
- Maintains power within the group

Laissez-faire Leadership
- Adapts a hands-off approach
- Makes decisions only if requested by the team
- Provides little or no direction

Goodheart-Willcox Publisher

Figure 8-4 Leadership style is the way in which a person leads a team, provides direction, motivates others, and plans actions.

Banana Oil/Shutterstock.com

Management style describes how a manager leads his or her team. **How do you think a leader evolves into his or her management style?**

It is also effective in groups where individual members lack leadership. However, it can be ineffective when it creates a situation in which the leader behaves as a dictator.

Laissez-faire Style

Laissez-faire leadership style is a hands-off approach to leadership. This style leaves the decision-making to the group to decide and manage. When members are highly skilled, motivated, and able to make decisions, this style works well. It is ineffective when no team member wants to make a decision or assume accountability for actions taken.

LO 8.2-2 Management Style

Closely associated with leadership style is *management style*, which describes how a manager leads his or her team. Managers have distinct views of their employees and the amount of supervision they need. Examples of management styles include close management, limited management, and flexible management.

- **Close management.** The manager believes employees will not perform unless watched over. They believe that employees will not work without someone telling them what to do.
- **Limited management.** The manager believes employees will perform their job and do not need close supervision. It is trusted that employees will work together when needed or ask for help.
- **Flexible management.** The manager adjusts his or her personal approach to employees depending on the situation. An employee who needs close supervision is managed differently than those who do not need supervision.

LO 8.2-3 Difficult People

As a member of the workforce, each worker meets many different types of people and personalities. To have an effective organization that meets its goals, employees must learn to work together as a cohesive unit. Managers are, in part, responsible for setting a tone and creating an environment where people perform their job tasks in a professional manner.

Most organizations have employees with whom others find it difficult to work. A *difficult person* is a person who resists cooperation and forces his or her opinions on others. A *difficult employee* is a person who does not behave in a professional manner in the workplace. Difficult people are hard to please, unkind, or argumentative. They may criticize everything and everybody. They may think they are never wrong or always need to have the last word on every issue. Difficult people can be annoying or, more seriously, can undermine another person's career.

Managing difficult employees can be a challenge and requires professionalism in all situations. A manager should try to stay focused on the issue and keep emotions out of the conversation. Sometimes it may be appropriate to ignore a difficult employee. However, difficult people who threaten the success of a business or someone's personal well-being should be addressed. Examples of types of difficult people in the workplace include complainers, angry employees, and bullies.

Complainers

The complainer never likes what is happening, whether it is as important as what the team is doing or something as simple as the temperature in the room. Complainers blame others when something goes wrong or they are unable to get the job finished or perform as required. These people are obnoxious and hard to please. This can be a challenging situation for a manager to handle. A private discussion with a complainer may help eliminate the circumstances that caused the issue. In other situations, it may be a personality issue that needs control in the workplace.

Angry Employees

Angry employees may display temper outbursts when things go off course, use profanity in conversations with others, or generally show aggressive behavior. This type of negative behavior in the workplace must be addressed so it does not escalate. A manager of an angry employee must learn the importance of remaining calm when an outburst happens. The manager should approach the employee stating the issue calmly and avoid using personal comments. If a solution cannot be found, help should be sought from the human resources department.

Bullies

One extreme type of difficult person is a bully. A bully is someone who is repeatedly unkind and cruel to another person whom the bully perceives as weak. The act of being a bully is called *bullying.* A bully may steal ideas, publicly criticize or humiliate others, or use abusive language. He or she may sabotage somebody's work to make the targeted person look bad. A bully may harass or even threaten someone with violence, both of which are illegal. If bullying happens to a team member, the manager should assist the person. The manager should document the time and place of each bullying incident, and describe the behavior. Witness names should be included in the documentation. If the bullying behavior does not stop, help should be sought from the human resources department.

baranq/Shutterstock.com

A difficult employee is a person who does not behave in a professional manner in the workplace. **What do you think motivates a person to be difficult when working with others?**

Employability Skills

Leadership

Leadership is the ability to influence others to reach a goal. It is a soft skill that reflects professionalism. Certain traits, such as honesty, competence, self-confidence, communication skills, problem-solving skills, and dependability, are examples of leadership characteristics. Setting goals, following through on tasks, and being forward-thinking are also important leadership abilities. *Leaders* are those who guide others to a goal.

LO 8.2-4 Conflict Resolution

When people work together, there is likely to be some conflict. A **conflict** is a strong disagreement between two or more people or a difference that prevents agreement. It is more than just a problem that needs solving or a minor incident that needs attention. Conflicts can happen between employees or between a manager and an employee.

Conflict that is ignored or not resolved can result in a person losing self-respect, being dismissed from a job, or exhibiting violent behavior. When conflict happens in the workplace, it is generally the responsibility of a manager to either facilitate a resolution or request assistance from human resources.

Conflict resolution is the process of recognizing and resolving disputes. **Conflict-resolution skills** are the skills required to resolve a situation that could lead to hostile behavior, such as shouting or fighting. Following a conflict-resolution model, as shown in Figure 8-5, can help managers guide individuals to work toward a resolution when disagreements arise.

Conflict resolution requires that each party involved exhibits emotional control. **Emotional control** means each person directs his or her feelings and reactions toward a desirable result that is socially acceptable. Emotional control is required to keep communication lines open. Listening to one another without interruption is important to resolve conflict.

Speaking clearly and in a calm manner can also help keep communication lines open. When a conflict cannot be resolved, a manager might need to go to the human resources manager for assistance.

Formal methods of conflict resolution, such as negotiation, may be required in extenuating circumstances. **Negotiation** occurs when individuals involved in a conflict come together to discuss a compromise. Negotiation requires that each party is willing to reach a compromise by giving something up and meeting the other party in the middle. During extreme conflicts when neither party is willing to compromise or a decision cannot be reached, mediation may be needed. **Mediation** is the inclusion of a neutral person, called a *mediator*, to help the conflicting parties resolve their dispute and reach an agreement.

Ultimatums are generally not a good solution when negotiating. An **ultimatum** is a final proposal or statement of conditions. Some situations require the negotiator risk all and give an ultimatum, but only if he or she is willing to lose. The result can be rejection and loss of an opportunity.

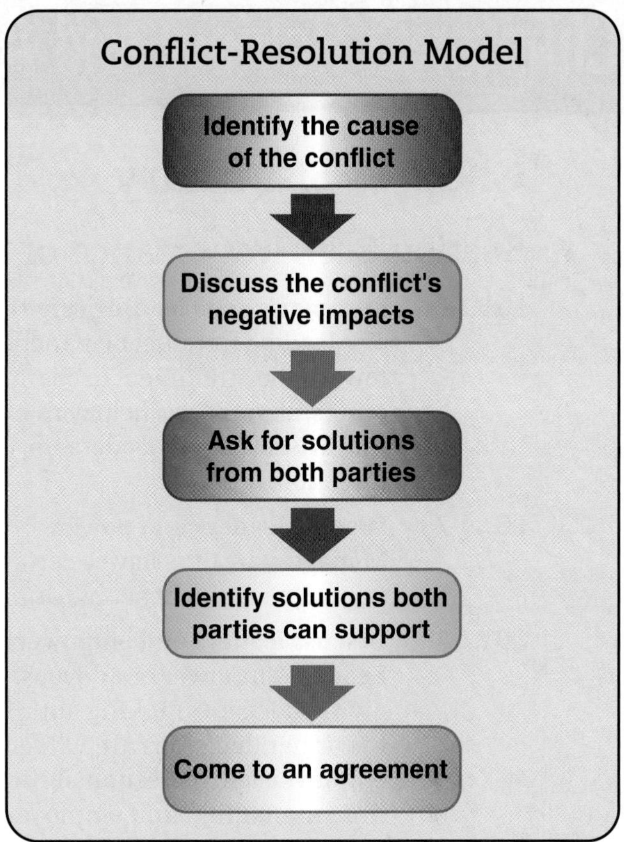

Goodheart-Willcox Publisher

Figure 8-5 A conflict-resolution model can help a team resolve issues efficiently.

Section 8.2 Review

Check Your Understanding

1. Define *leadership style.*
2. Identify three distinct management styles.
3. State examples of types of difficult people in the workplace.
4. Why is emotional control required in conflict resolution?
5. Why is giving an ultimatum generally not a good negotiation strategy?

Build Your Vocabulary

As you progress through this text, develop a personal glossary of key terms. This will help you build your vocabulary and prepare you for a career. Write a definition for each of the following terms and add them to your personal glossary.

leadership	conflict-resolution skills	negotiation
conflict	emotional control	mediation
conflict resolution		ultimatum

Chapter 8 Review and Assessment

Chapter Summary

Section 8.1 Importance of Leading

LO 8.1-1 **Summarize the leading function of management.**
The leading function of management is the process of influencing others to work toward the attainment of common goals. Leaders set examples for behavior, work with others, share ideas, help with everyday tasks, and develop solutions for challenges that arise. Without leadership, employees would work each day without a clear goal or direction.

LO 8.1-2 **Discuss leaders and power.**
Managers, by title, have a certain degree of power. Power, in this situation, means they can influence what people think and how they behave when they interact with them.

LO 8.1-3 **Discuss leaders and empowering employees.**
Leaders empower employees. Empowerment is a management practice of giving decision-making authority to employees. When an employee realizes his or her decisions are valued and affect the success of an organization, that employee learns responsibility. Empowerment allows managers to spend more time managing, and employees are prepared for becoming future leaders and management candidates.

LO 8.1-4 **Summarize leaders and motivating others.**
Leaders motivate others. Motivation is the force that inspires employees to want to perform their best and achieve results. It pushes an individual to work hard at achieving goals. Motivated employees are typically more productive and engaged in what they are doing. Two types of motivation are intrinsic motivation and extrinsic motivation.

LO 8.1-5 **Explain leaders and creating effective teams.**
A team consists of two or more people working together to achieve a common goal. An effective leader creates effective teams by inspiring its members to work collaboratively to achieve common goals.

Section 8.2 Leadership

LO 8.2-1 **Define different types of leadership styles.**
Different types of leadership styles are democratic, autocratic, and laissez-faire. Democratic leadership style is one in which the leader shares decision-making with the group. The autocratic leadership style describes a leader who maintains all power within a team. Laissez-faire leadership style is a hands-off approach. This style leaves the decision-making to the group to decide and manage.

LO 8.2-2 **Cite examples of management styles.**
Examples of management styles include close management, limited management, and flexible management.

LO 8.2-3 **Identify types of difficult people encountered in the workplace.**
Examples of types of difficult people in the workplace include complainers, angry employees, and bullies.

LO 8.2-4 Discuss conflict resolution.
Conflict resolution is the process of recognizing and resolving disputes. Following a conflict-resolution model can help managers guide individuals to work toward a resolution when disagreements arise. Conflict resolution also requires that each party involved exhibits emotional control. Formal methods, such as negotiation, may be required in extenuating circumstances.

Review Your Knowledge

1. Summarize the leading function of management.
2. Discuss leaders and power.
3. Explain leaders and empowering employees.
4. Summarize leaders and motivating others.
5. Explain the following theories of motivation: Maslow's Hierarchy of Needs, Herzberg's Two-Factor Theory, and expectancy theory.
6. Explain leaders and creating effective teams.
7. Define different types of leadership styles and when each is appropriate to use.
8. Explain three types of management styles.
9. Briefly explain types of difficult people encountered in the workplace.
10. Discuss conflict resolution.

Apply Your Knowledge

1. Identify someone you know who is in a leadership position. Discuss how this person uses his or her power wisely or unwisely. Cite examples of each type of behavior.
2. Empowerment is a management practice of giving decision-making authority to another person. Describe a time when a teacher, club sponsor, or another person empowered you to make decisions. How did that empowerment make you feel?
3. Managers sometimes use reward techniques to encourage employee performance. List potential employee rewards that could be used for motivation, such as promotions, empowerment, and monetary incentives. Describe each example and explain why you think it would work as a motivational technique.
4. Managers work closely with his or her direct reports. Sometimes a manager and employee become personal friends. What is your opinion about personal relationships between managers and employees and its impact on the workplace?
5. Teamwork is the cooperative efforts by individual team members to achieve a goal. Recall a time that you were on a team that did not successfully reach its goal. What prevented your team from reaching the goal? What do you think you and your team members could have done differently?
6. Leadership is the process of influencing others to work toward the attainment of common goals. On a scale of 1 to 10, with 10 being highest, rate your ability to lead others effectively. Provide examples that support your position.
7. Imagine you are a manager and have multiple direct reports. Which of the three motivation theories discussed in this chapter would you use to base your leadership and management style? Why do you think this model is the most useful in leadership?

8. Imagine you are president of your student organization that has 50 members. Which leadership style (democratic, autocratic, or laissez-faire) do you think would be most effective for you to use and why?
9. A difficult employee is a person who does not behave in a professional manner in the workplace. Write a paragraph to narrate how you would handle a difficult person if you were in a management role.
10. Identify a conflict that you had recently. Make a list of actions that you could have followed to find a solution based on the conflict-resolution model in Figure 8-5.

College and Career Readiness

Communication Skills

Writing. A *concept map* is a type of graphic organizer used to show how facts, concepts, and ideas fit together. Listen carefully to your instructor as a lesson is presented. Note each main point by drawing a large circle on paper and writing the main point inside. Write supporting details around the circle and draw connecting lines to it.

Listening. Listening with purpose will help you focus on important information that a speaker is conveying. Rather than speak during class, listen to the conversations around you. Make notes on which students contribute to discussions and the important points they make. What did you learn about your classmates by listening?

Speaking. Most people in the United States act as responsible and contributing citizens. How can a person demonstrate social and ethical responsibility in times when disaster relief is needed in the community? Participate in a group discussion about how citizens can go beyond the minimum expectations of helping others in the community.

Internet Research

Leadership Traits. Conduct an Internet search for *leadership traits.* What leadership traits do you think are required for success in a management role? Summarize your findings and explain your thoughts on what traits are necessary for a leader to be effective.

Famous Leaders. Who do you think of when you hear the word "leader"? Brainstorm a short list of famous people whom you consider leaders. Your list might include people like the president, a favorite athlete, or another famous person. Select one person to research from your list. Use Internet resources to find information about this person. Write a bulleted list of information about this person that illustrates how he or she is a leader.

Teamwork

Working as a team, participate in a discussion to distinguish the difference between extrinsic and intrinsic rewards. Why are these rewards important? Arrive at a consensus of the two extrinsic and intrinsic rewards that your team agrees would motivate an employee to perform. Why did your teammates pick these particular rewards?

Portfolio Development

Recommendations. After you have created a list of references, you will need to obtain letters of recommendation. A *letter of recommendation* is a letter in which your qualities and abilities to perform in a specific capacity are assessed by a person you know well. It highlights your achievements in your academic or professional career. The letter is usually written by an instructor, supervisor, or someone else who is familiar with your qualifications for a given job or application. The purpose of the letter is to advocate for you as a candidate.

A letter of recommendation will probably be written by a person who also agrees to serve as a reference for you. However, it is not required that your letters of recommendation come from your references. For example, if you are applying for enrollment into an academic program, you may choose to use your managers or former employers as references but elect to have a teacher write a letter of recommendation. This allows people from both your professional and academic careers to vouch for your abilities. Two or three letters of recommendation are sufficient.

1. Contact several people from your references and ask if they are willing to write a letter of recommendation for you. For those contacts who agree to write letters, suggest to them a date by which you would like to receive it. Writing the letter can, and should, take some time, so plan in advance. When organizing your portfolio, it is suggested that these letters follow your personal references document.

EVENT PREP

CTSOs

Parliamentary Procedure. *Parliamentary procedure* is a process for holding meetings so they are orderly and democratic. In this event, the participants must demonstrate understanding of these procedures, such as *Robert's Rules of Order.* Applying the procedures dictated by *Robert's Rules of Order* is an effective way to conduct a formal meeting.

This is often a team event in which the group demonstrates how to conduct an effective meeting. In addition, an objective test may be administered to each person on the team that will be evaluated and included in the overall team score.

To prepare for the parliamentary procedure competition, complete the following activities.

1. Read the guidelines provided by your organization.
2. Study parliamentary procedure principles by reviewing *Robert's Rules of Order.*
3. Practice proper procedures for conducting a meeting. Assign each team member a role for the presentation.
4. Visit the website of the organization and look for the evaluation criteria or rubric for the event. This will help you determine what the judges will be looking for in your presentation.

CHAPTER 9

Managing Communication

Sections

9.1 Communication Basics

9.2 Organizational Communication

Reading Prep

Before reading this chapter, review its opening pages and read the section titles. By previewing these, you can be prepared for the topics that will be presented. What do the titles reveal about what you will be learning?

Exploring Careers

Cybersecurity Manager

Cybersecurity managers are responsible for understanding an organization network system's vulnerabilities and creating security measures to protect it. They familiarize themselves with tactics used by cybercriminals so they can better avoid hacks, fix problems, and improve security. Cybersecurity managers are responsible for maintaining data integrity and ensuring information systems are not breached by hackers or infected with malware. They plan and implement security measures and establish network system policies of the organization.

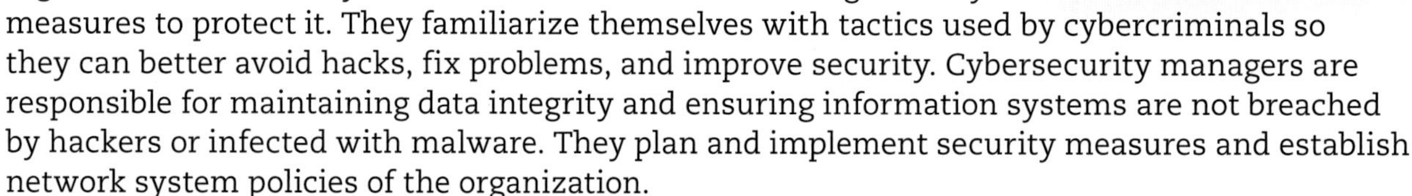

Typical job titles for this position include *IT security manager*, *information systems security manager*, and *information security manager*. Examples of tasks cybersecurity managers perform include:

- establishing network security policies and procedures;
- monitoring systems for security gaps and designing effective solutions;
- conducting risk assessments on networks;
- training employees on cybersecurity awareness, protocols, and procedures; and
- assessing, testing, and selecting new products and technologies that comply with security requirements.

Cybersecurity manager positions require a bachelor degree in information technology, computer science, engineering, or a related field as well as prior work experience. Some organizations may require a master degree. Cybersecurity managers must have excellent written and oral communication, critical-thinking, problem-solving, leadership, and organizational skills.

sakkmesterke/Shutterstock.com

Section 9.1 Communication Basics

How does the workplace environment affect the way in which communication is conducted in an organization?

Learning Objectives

LO 9.1-1 Discuss communication.

LO 9.1-2 Summarize the communication process.

LO 9.1-3 Identify types of communication.

LO 9.1-4 Define barriers to effective communication.

Key Terms 

communication skills
etiquette
intrapersonal communication
interpersonal communication
small-group communication
communication process
encoding
transmission
channel
decoding
feedback
Standard English
language
oral language
nonverbal communication
noise
barrier

LO 9.1-1 Communication

Communication is the sending and receiving of messages that convey information, ideas, feelings, and beliefs. **Communication skills** are skills that affect a person's ability to understand others, establish positive relationships, and perform in most situations. Being able to communicate skillfully, therefore, is essential to a successful career.

Purpose of Communication

All communication has a purpose. When people communicate, there is a specific reason for doing so. It is important for those who operate a business or manage a team to be able to communicate clearly so the purpose of a message is understood by those who are receiving it. Generally, communication informs, persuades, instructs, makes a request, or responds to a request from others.

- **Inform.** A message that informs provides information or education.
- **Persuade.** A message that persuades attempts to change the behavior of the receiver.
- **Instruct.** A message that instructs others attempts to provide direction or guidance.
- **Make a request.** A message that makes a request asks a question or for an action to occur.
- **Respond to a request.** Alternatively to making a request, there will be times an individual must respond to a request that has been made of him or her.

A person who does not have a good grasp of the purpose for communicating is likely to relay a confused and ineffective message. Clarifying ideas that are to be communicated helps focus the purpose of the message. It also guides how communication will take place.

Proper etiquette should be used for all communication. **Etiquette** is the art of using good manners in any situation. In addition, it is every employee's responsibility to maintain ethical behavior in all company communication.

LStockStudio/Shutterstock.com

Small-group communication occurs with 3 to 20 people who come together to share ideas and solve problems. **What value do you think the formation of small groups provides in a workplace?**

Forms of Communication

Communication can vary quite a bit from day to day. Sometimes a manager will talk with a single person. Other times a manager will participate in group conversations, like those that take place in a meeting with direct reports. These are all different examples of forms of communication. Forms of communication include intrapersonal, interpersonal, and small-group communication.

- **Intrapersonal communication** is the conversation a person has with himself or herself. Sometimes known as *self-talk*, this is how most individuals sort through the information they want to convey.
- **Interpersonal communication** occurs between two people. This form of communication allows individuals to participate in effective and meaningful one-on-one conversations.
- **Small-group communication** occurs with 3 to 20 people. It is communication that takes place when individuals come together to work with others to share ideas and solve problems.

LO 9.1-2 Communication Process

The **communication process** is a series of actions on the part of the sender and receiver of a message and path the message follows. The six elements of the process are the sender, message, channel, receiver, translation, and feedback, as shown in Figure 9-1.

Sender

The person who has a message to communicate is the *sender*. The sender initiates the communication process after deciding there is a need to relay information to the receiver. Before sending the message, the sender uses self-talk to plan what he or she wishes to convey. After the information is sorted in the sender's mind, it is assembled into the form of a message.

Message

The sender decides which format the message will take. The form might be written words, spoken words, pictures, or other visuals, such as a YouTube video. **Encoding** is the process of turning the idea for a message into symbols that can be communicated. Most people convert their messages into a language of written or spoken words or symbols the receiver can understand. In order for a message to be understood, both the sender and receiver must be able to interpret the words or symbols.

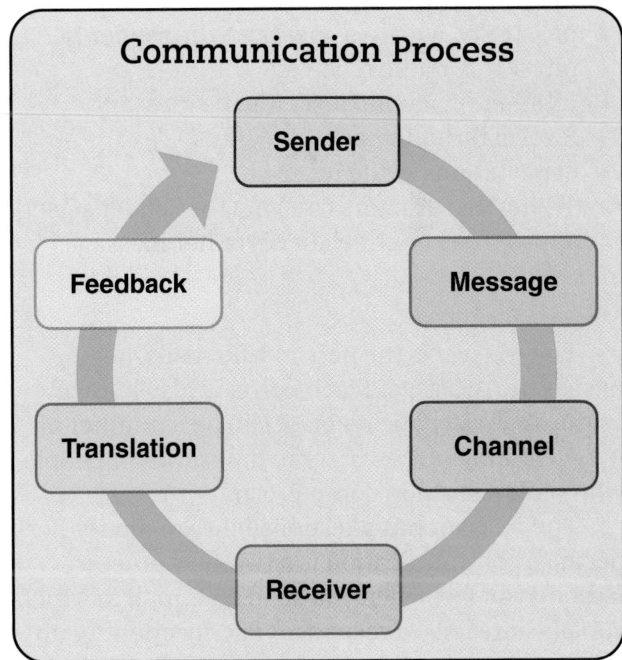

Goodheart-Willcox Publisher

Figure 9-1 The communication process is a series of actions on the part of the sender and receiver of a message and path the message follows.

Employability Skills
Etiquette

Etiquette is the art of using good manners and polite behavior in any situation. *Professional etiquette* is applying the rules of good manners in the workplace and in other work-related situations.

Channel

Once the message is encoded, it can be sent. The act of sending a message is called **transmission**. The **channel** is how the message is transmitted, such as face-to-face conversation, telephone, or any other vehicle that is appropriate for the situation. The sender determines the channel through which to send the message. Factors that influence how to transmit a message include:

- need for security or confidentiality;
- importance of having a record of the information;
- need for the receiver to have the information immediately;
- proximity, which is how close the sender is physically to the receiver;
- number of people receiving the message;
- level of formality necessary; and
- expectations of the receiver.

Analyzing these factors can help the sender select the appropriate channel for his or her message.

Receiver

The *receiver* is the person who reads, hears, or sees the message. The receiver is also known as the *audience*. The receiver can be a number of people, from one coworker to thousands of people who see a television commercial.

The receiver has a responsibility to the sender because communication is a two-way process. How do you feel when you send an e-mail to which you never receive a response? Paying attention to the sender is a matter of courtesy and necessity and is essential to the communication process.

Translation

Once the receiver receives the message, it is decoded. **Decoding** is the translation of a message into terms the receiver can understand. Decoding occurs in the receiver's mind. It is usually seen as the process of understanding a message. The message is not considered to be received if the receiver does not understand what has been read or heard.

Feedback

Feedback is the receiver's response to the sender and concludes the communication process. Providing feedback to a sender is a crucial step in the process. This tells the sender if the receiver understood the message as it was intended. If the sender does not receive feedback to be sure the message was understood, the communication process has failed.

LO 9.1-3 Types of Communication

The channel of communication is the manner in which a message is transmitted. In order to convey information, a type of communication is chosen, which includes written, visual, verbal, and nonverbal communication.

Written Communication

Managing a team or business requires a substantial amount of written contact with internal and external individuals. *Written communication* is recording words through writing to communicate.

Dean Drobot/Shutterstock.com

Body language is nonverbal communication through facial expressions, gestures, body movements, and posture. **What kinds of messages can nonverbal communication send to a listener?**

Because of its importance to the reputation and success of an organization, business writing requires the use of Standard English. **Standard English** refers to English language usage that follows accepted rules for spelling, grammar, and punctuation. Words are the tools of all written communication. How well these tools are used affects the success of the message.

Business writing may require the use of jargon in order to communicate effectively with an audience. *Jargon* is language specific to a line of work or area of expertise. Some industries have specific words and phrases familiar to their customers. For example, stockbrokers talk about bull and bear markets. Therefore, these would be appropriate words to use in a message being conveyed to professionals in the investment field.

Visual Communication

Visual communication is using visual aids or graphics to communicate an idea or concept. Visuals add clarity, understanding, and interest to attract and maintain the attention of the audience. Visual communication can be an important component of a business message. Examples of this are a report that includes charts and a business plan that has financial statements.

Verbal Communication

Verbal communication is the use of words and sound to convey a message. It is also known as *oral communication*. People use verbal communication to express themselves, along with nonverbal communication, when a message is transmitted to others. It is used in conversations, presentations, interviews, small group discussions, and meetings.

Verbal communication is based on language. **Language** is a system of symbols, signs, and gestures as a means of communication and the rules of using them. **Oral language** is a system in which words are spoken to express ideas or emotions. Oral language typically reflects an individual's tone and style.

This type of communication involves a variety of situations, such as conversations about work tasks, asking and answering questions, giving information, and participating in meetings. *Verbal skills* enable a person to communicate effectively using spoken words. They are also known as *speaking skills*.

An effective manager has command of verbal communication and is aware that if a voice is too loud or too soft, listeners will be distracted from the content of the message. A variety of techniques can be used to increase the effectiveness of interpersonal communication. *Modulation* is the act of changing the emphasis of words by raising and lowering the voice. *Pitch* describes the highness or lowness of a sound. Emphasis is made by raising or lowering the pitch of the voice. *Intonation* is the rise and fall in the pitch of the voice. Another effective technique is simply to pause so the word or phrase following the pause receives extra emphasis.

Nonverbal Communication

Nonverbal communication is the actions or behaviors, as opposed to words, that send messages. *Nonverbal skills* enable a person to communicate effectively using body language, eye contact, touch, personal space, behavior, and attitude, as shown in Figure 9-2. Nonverbal skills can be used to send messages with or without verbal communication.

Nonverbal Communication	
Type	**Definition**
Body language	Facial expressions, gestures, body movements, and posture
Eye contact	Two people look directly into each other's eyes while engaged in conversation
Touch	Physical contact, such as a handshake
Personal space	Physical space between two individuals
Behavior	Gestures, such as waving, pointing, or a shoulder shrug
Attitude	Body movements that reflect a person's mood, such as trembling, stepping closer to another person, and posture

Goodheart-Willcox Publisher

Figure 9-2 Nonverbal communication is the actions or behaviors, as opposed to words, that send messages.

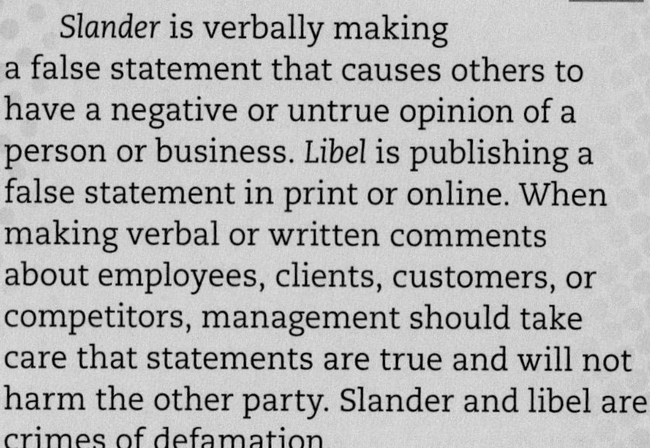

Ethics

Slander and Libel

Slander is verbally making a false statement that causes others to have a negative or untrue opinion of a person or business. *Libel* is publishing a false statement in print or online. When making verbal or written comments about employees, clients, customers, or competitors, management should take care that statements are true and will not harm the other party. Slander and libel are crimes of defamation.

A manager must be aware of what his or her nonverbal communications are telling receivers. If the message is positive, but the tone or mannerisms are negative, the entire message can be lost.

LO 9.1-4 Barriers to Effective Communication

Communication does not always go smoothly. **Noise** is anything that interferes with clear, effective communication. It does not prevent the communication, but interrupts it. Noise can be physical, such as a loud radio playing in the same room. Another example of noise is a person who suffers from hearing loss and struggles to hear a message. It can also be psychological, such as the receiver having other things on his or her mind.

In addition to noise, there are barriers to communication. A **barrier** is anything that prevents clear, effective communication. The difference between a *barrier* and *noise* is that a barrier prevents communication while noise interferes with the communication process. An example of a barrier is attitude when an individual refuses to listen to another person. Barriers can be destructive to the communication process.

Internal and External Barriers

Barriers can be internal or external. *Internal barriers* are distractions that occur within an individual, such as fatigue, hunger, or wandering thoughts. *External barriers* are distractions that occur in the surrounding environment. Examples of external barriers can include looking out the window or hearing another conversation. Be aware of the types of barriers that can occur.

Sending Barriers

A *sending barrier* can occur when the sender says or does something that causes the receiver to stop listening. This can happen when the receiver simply does not understand what the sender is saying. The words used may not be clear to the receiver. Such misunderstandings cause problems ranging from minor events to serious, costly errors.

Sending barriers for written and visual communication may include:

- using poor grammar or spelling;
- assuming too much or too little about what the receiver already knows; and
- using inappropriate language.

Tyler Olson/Shutterstock.com

While hearing is a physical ability, listening is a conscious action. **Why is it important to listen instead of simply hearing a message?**

For written documents, the rules of writing, grammar, and document formatting should be followed. A well-written and properly formatted document will send a positive message.

Face-to-face verbal and nonverbal communication barriers include:

- distracting mannerisms;
- facial expressions that conflict with the words being said;
- inappropriate dress or demeanor;
- sarcastic or angry tone of voice; and
- speaking too softly or too loudly.

In these situations, a sender's written or verbal message may be lost or undermined by competing nonverbal messages.

Receiving Barriers

A *receiving barrier* can occur when the receiver says or does something that causes a sender's message not to be received. These barriers can be just as harmful to the communication process as sending barriers. The receiver has a responsibility to give attention and respect to the sender.

Most receiving barriers can be overcome by paying attention and listening. While *hearing* is a physical ability, *listening* is a conscious action. Although senders are responsible for sending clear messages, listeners should be ready to recognize unclear messages. A listener who is willing to accept responsibility for getting clarification will be a more effective communicator.

Section 9.1 Review

Check Your Understanding

1. Identify purposes of communication.
2. What are the six elements of the communication process?
3. List four types of communication.
4. Explain the difference between internal and external barriers.
5. Cite examples of face-to-face verbal and nonverbal communication barriers.

Build Your Vocabulary

As you progress though this text, develop a personal glossary of key terms. This will help you build your vocabulary and prepare you for a career. Write a definition for each of the following terms and add them to your personal glossary.

communication skills
etiquette
intrapersonal communication
interpersonal communication
small-group communication
communication process
encoding
transmission
channel
decoding
feedback
Standard English
language
oral language
nonverbal communication
noise
barrier

Section 9.2 Organizational Communication

Why is communication management important for a person who manages direct reports?

Learning Objectives

LO 9.2-1 Discuss communication management.

LO 9.2-2 Explain a communication plan.

LO 9.2-3 Summarize communication competence.

LO 9.2-4 Identify effective ways to communicate in a diverse workplace.

Key Terms 

- communication management
- protocol
- formal communication
- peer
- informal communication
- communication competence
- listening
- critical thinking
- cultural sensitivity
- intercultural communication
- English as a second language (ESL)

LO 9.2-1 Communication Management

Communication management is the planning and execution of communication from an organization to its external and internal customers. *External customers* are individuals or other organizations with whom business is conducted. *Internal customers* are the employees of the company.

Successful employees understand the corporate culture of the business and acceptable way to communicate. Culture typically drives ethical communication within an organization. Communicating ethically involves telling the truth. Truthfulness creates trust, and trust is necessary for healthy, professional relationships.

Ethics are rules of behavior based on a group's ideas about what is right and wrong. *Morals* are an individual's ideas of what is right and wrong. Ethics help people determine the most appropriate behavior for situations in their personal and professional lives.

Ethical behavior refers to actions that adhere to a person's ethical standards. *Ethical communication* is applying ethics to messages to make sure all communication is honest in every way. Ethical communicators are accountable for their words and actions. They follow through on commitments and take responsibility when they default.

Formal Communication

Corporate culture influences the manner in which owners, management, and employees of a company interact with each other and conduct business based on its protocol. **Protocol** is a set of customs that define how certain levels of employees interact with each other. The way people talk to each other, their style of communication, and frequency of communication is usually the result of the corporate culture.

Communication within an organization is sometimes formal. **Formal communication** is the sharing of information that conforms to specific protocol. Formal communication usually happens according to levels within an organization. It flows in three directions, as illustrated in Figure 9-3.

- *Upward communication* is the flow of information from lower levels of an organization to people in higher levels.
- *Lateral communication* is communication that takes place between peers. A **peer** is a person of equal standing or work position.
- *Downward communication* is the flow of information from higher levels of an organization to people in lower levels.

It is necessary for employees to understand the flow of communication before initiating contact with management. For example, it may not be appropriate for a supervisory manager to bypass the vice president about an issue and go straight to the CEO.

Informal Communication

Communication within an organization can also be informal. **Informal communication** is the casual sharing of information without customs or rules of etiquette involved. Reporting hierarchy is not important in informal communication. People from various levels, divisions, and positions interact with each other in a casual way. Informal communication could be text messages, telephone calls, or just talking in the hallway. Informal communication is necessary to build teamwork and cooperation within an organization.

However, getting information from the "grapevine" should be avoided. The *grapevine* refers to unofficial circulation of information. It may or may not be a dependable source of facts. It is also known as gossiping and can cost a person his or her job if unethical information is passed on to others.

LO 9.2-2 Communication Plan

Managers play a role in creating the way in which information is shared with others. A *communication plan* is a road map that includes objectives and goals that clearly outline the way in which communication takes place.

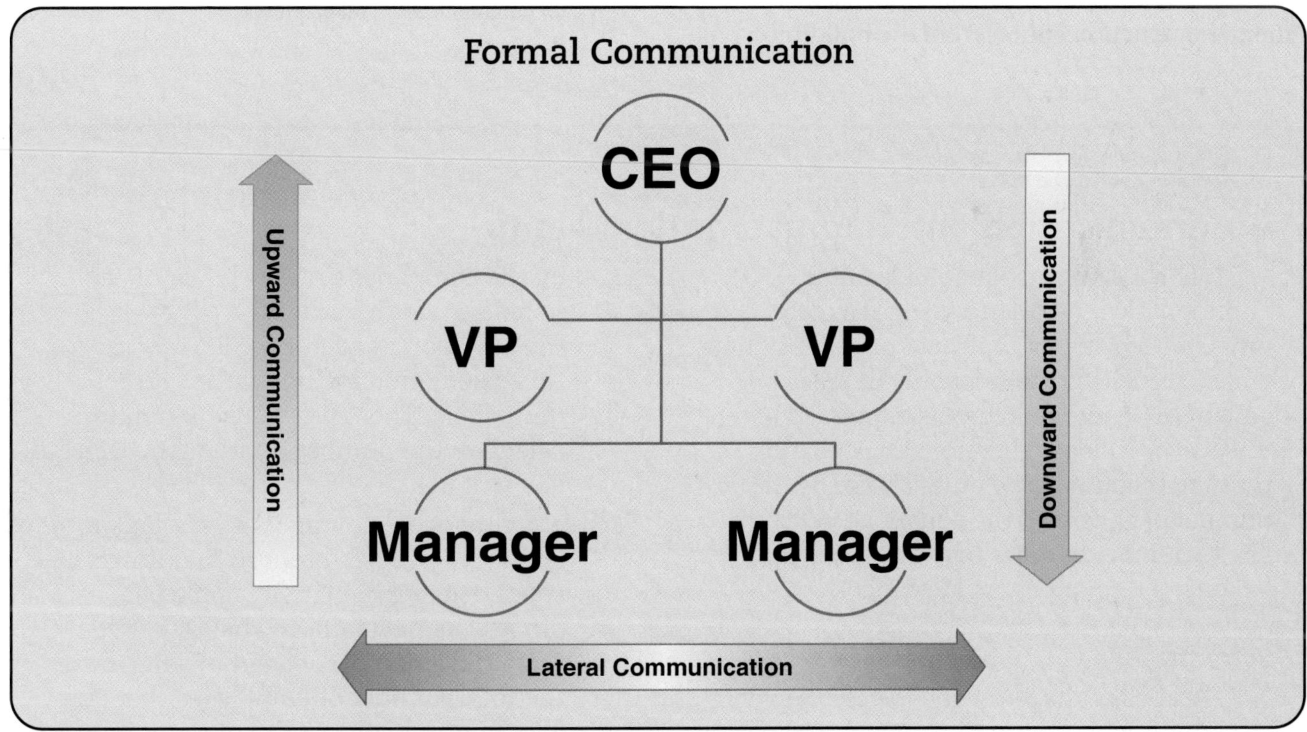

Goodheart-Willcox Publisher

Figure 9-3 Formal communication is the sharing of information that conforms to specific protocol.

It is a way of anticipating and providing specific information stakeholders of an organization need and when they should receive it. *Stakeholders* are people who have interest in the company, such as employees, vendors, and stockholders. Without a plan, clear information may not reach the people who need to hear a message.

An effective communication plan answers the questions of who, what, why, when, and how. Figure 9-4 highlights the process of creating a communication plan.

- Who is the audience who needs the information?
- What is the information that will be shared?
- Why must information be shared?
- When must information be transmitted to the audience?
- How will you decide which communication channel to use?

For internal communications, a communication plan identifies how information about organizational changes, policies, or company goals is shared with employees. It also identifies the channel in which the message should be sent, such as a company-wide e-mail or departmental team meetings. An example of an internal communication plan is one that is focused on emergency exit procedures from the building.

Communication Plan

Ask who, what, why, when, and how:

- Who? Identify the audience who requires the information
- What? Decide the information that needs to be shared
- Why? Ask why the information must be shared
- When? Identify when the message will be sent
- How? Select which communication channel will be used to deliver the information

Create and deliver the information in a message:

- Plan for obstacles, emergencies, or any other barriers that may interfere with the delivery of the information
- Create an action plan
- Decide how the effectiveness of the plan will be evaluated and adjust as needed

Goodheart-Willcox Publisher

Figure 9-4 A communication plan is a road map that includes objectives and goals that clearly outline the way in which communication takes place.

You Do the Math

Communication and Representation: Units

When solving an equation, careful attention must be paid to using the correct units in each step of the equation. For example, when calculating fuel economy in miles per gallon (MPG), the final unit is expressed as miles over gallons. Therefore, the equation must be the number of miles *divided* by the number of gallons. If the equation is expressed as the number of miles *times* the number of gallons, the solution would be incorrect.

Solve the following problems.

1. A sales manager needs to calculate the number of sales dollars generated per salesperson. State the equation needed for this calculation including the correct unit labels.
2. A company ships products that weigh 1.3 pounds each. Each shipping box used by the company is rated to hold 65 pounds. State the equation needed for this calculation including the correct unit labels. Then, use the equation to calculate the number of products each box will hold.

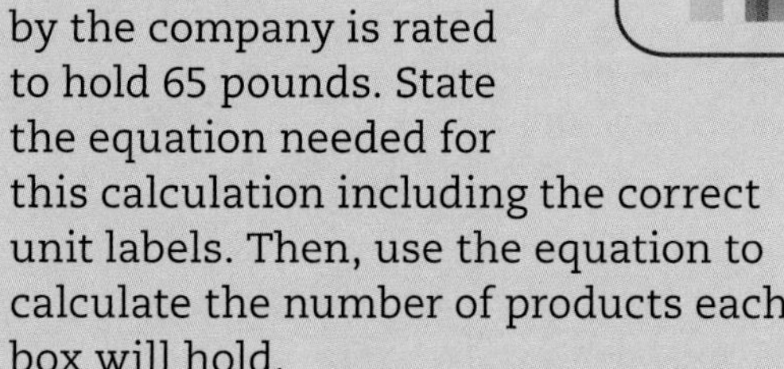

3. A company is moving its operations into a new building. In order to maximize space, there will be two people per office. The new building has 37 offices. State the equation needed to determine the total number of employees that can be accommodated in the new building, including the correct unit labels. Then, use the equation to calculate the number of employees.
4. What is the final unit for this equation: 12.8 feet × 3.6 feet ÷ 7.6 seconds?

The plan may consist of an e-mail to employees, posters displayed within the facility, and other tools to convey the importance of evacuation should an emergency arise.

For external communications, a communication plan identifies how information is provided to the public, the appropriate channels that should be used, and who has authority to make the communication. Many employees have regular communication with customers and other business contacts. However, public relations directors are often employed to share company information to the public.

Most external communication typically takes place in letters, e-mails, presentations, or other messages that are planned and put into words. Written documents are generally used when it is necessary to record and document information for future reference.

LO 9.2-3 Communication Competence

Communication competence is an individual's ability to understand basic principles of communication and apply them when interacting with others. It is a skill that enables a person to communicate well with others and build successful relationships on social and professional levels. People who possess communication competence understand the value of effective communication. Behaviors that contribute to communication competence are mindfulness, listening, emotional control, critical thinking, and cultural sensitivity.

Mindfulness

When someone is *mindful,* the person is aware of his or her action and understands how communication transpires with others. It is the act of a person paying attention to what he or she says and anticipating another person's potential reaction to his or her behavior. Mindful people think before they act and show respect to others.

Listening

Hearing is the physical process of sound waves reaching a person's ears, which sends signals to his or her brain. **Listening** is an intellectual process that combines hearing with evaluating. Just because a person hears another person speak does not mean that person is listening to what is said. When you *listen,* you make an effort to process what you *hear.*

Listening skills are some of the most important skills a person will develop in his or her personal and professional life. Listening to others when they speak is a demonstration of etiquette. Competent communicators are open to ideas of others and listen without interrupting.

Emotional Control

Emotional control is directing one's feelings and reactions toward a desirable result that is socially acceptable. Learning how to manage emotions helps a person think logically and act appropriately. It also helps keep communication lines open.

Critical Thinking

Critical thinking is the ability to analyze and interpret a situation and make reasonable judgments and decisions. When a person applies critical-thinking skills, emotions are eliminated and an open-minded frame of mind is applied.

Cultural Sensitivity

Cultural sensitivity is acting with respect and awareness toward cultures different from one's own. Failure to be sensitive to the cultures of others can lead to miscommunication, errors, missed opportunities, hurt feelings, and lost business.

Atstock Productions/Shutterstock.com

Communication competence is an individual's ability to understand basic principles of communication and apply them when interacting with others. **Why is communication competence an important skill to develop?**

LO 9.2-4 Communicating in a Diverse Workplace

Intercultural communication is the process of sending and receiving messages between people of various cultures. It is important to understand the culture of the person with whom you are communicating. Not understanding another person's culture may result in the misinterpretation of verbal and nonverbal communication.

For example, in the United States a topic is "tabled" if it is put off for another time. In contrast, the same phrase in Great Britain means to "bring it to the table" for discussion.

Additionally, the concept of time can be interpreted differently in some cultures. The workday may not be the 8-hour workday common in the United States.

Working with diverse people requires that individuals learn how to communicate clearly and concisely. This sometimes means taking extra time and patience to establish and maintain working relationships. It can also mean taking time to study another person's culture or language so that a spirit of understanding is developed. Diversity should never be a communication barrier or create situations of stereotyping. It is necessary to show respect and learn how to listen, speak, write, and communicate clearly with others in the workplace.

Listen Carefully

Listening is one of the most important skills a manager will use. When listening to diverse individuals, extra attention should be given. English may not be a person's first language. **English as a second language (ESL)** is the field of education concerned with teaching English to those whose native language is not English. Imagine yourself in another country trying to speak a foreign language. It could be frustrating trying to express a thought or idea if you are not fluent in the language. Show the same courtesy to others that you would want to be shown if you were in a similar situation.

val lawless/Shutterstock.com

Professional communication requires individuals to speak clearly and use simple language to avoid misunderstandings. **What does professional communication mean to you?**

Just as when listening to a friend or family member, basic courtesies should be applied when listening to coworkers.

- Do not interrupt.
- Ask for clarification for any point that is not understood.
- Watch for nonverbal cues.
- Concentrate on what he or she is saying.
- Provide appropriate feedback.

Listening is an important skill necessary for all situations.

Speak Clearly

Professional communication requires individuals to speak clearly. Simple language and short sentences can help avoid misunderstandings. Speak slowly and enunciate words. *Enunciation* is the practice of pronouncing words clearly.

Avoid humor and be aware of topics that are not appropriate in the workplace. Do not use technical terms, words, or expressions that someone from another country would not understand. Slang words and jargon are examples of words to avoid. Alternatively, do not speak in a condescending tone.

Be polite and use common courtesies. If the person does not seem to understand what was said, try to rephrase. Remember that talking loudly will not necessarily make the person understand what you are saying.

Write Clearly

If the situation requires written communication, apply the same rules as when speaking. Use short sentences, be brief, and avoid words that may be misunderstood. Confirm the appropriate method of written communication, such as a letter or an e-mail. The rules of good grammar and writing should be applied.

Be Aware of Body Language

Being aware of body language can help eliminate communication barriers. People from all cultures have specific meanings for nonverbal behavior. Often, two cultures do not always give the same meaning to an action. For example, direct eye contact is not acceptable in some cultures while it is favorable in others. Different cultures have varying standards of how much personal space should be given other people. Shaking hands may be inappropriate when meeting someone from one culture, while it is common in others. Whenever possible, conduct research to understand what body language cues are expected by coworkers from another culture. Social etiquette in one culture can be very different from what you are used to. Try to understand these differences before communication begins.

Section 9.2 Review

Check Your Understanding

1. Identify three directions in which formal communication flows.
2. Why should getting information from the grapevine be avoided?
3. What is a communication plan?
4. List examples of behaviors that contribute to communication competence.
5. What are basic courtesies that should be applied when listening to coworkers?

Build Your Vocabulary

As you progress through this text, develop a personal glossary of key terms. This will help you build your vocabulary and prepare you for a career. Write a definition for each of the following terms and add them to your personal glossary.

communication management
protocol
formal communication
peer
informal communication
communication competence
listening
critical thinking
cultural sensitivity
intercultural communication
English as a second language (ESL)

Chapter 9 Review and Assessment

Chapter Summary

Section 9.1 Communication Basics

LO 9.1-1 **Discuss communication.**
Communication is the sending and receiving of messages that convey information, ideas, feelings, and beliefs. Communication skills are skills that affect a person's ability to understand others, establish positive relationships, and perform in most situations. Being able to communicate skillfully is essential to a successful career.

LO 9.1-2 **Summarize the communication process.**
The communication process is a series of actions on the part of the sender and receiver of a message and path the message follows. The six elements of the process are the sender, message, channel, receiver, translation, and feedback.

LO 9.1-3 **Identify types of communication.**
Types of communication include written, visual, verbal, and nonverbal communication.

LO 9.1-4 **Define barriers to effective communication.**
A barrier is anything that prevents clear, effective communication. Internal barriers are distractions that occur within an individual, such as fatigue, hunger, or wandering thoughts. External barriers are distractions that occur in the surrounding environment. A sending barrier can occur when the sender says or does something that causes the receiver to stop listening. A receiving barrier can occur when the receiver says or does something that causes a sender's message not to be received.

Section 9.2 Organizational Communication

LO 9.2-1 **Discuss communication management.**
Communication management is the planning and execution of communication from an organization to its external and/or internal customers. Successful employees understand the corporate culture of the business and the acceptable way to communicate. Corporate culture influences the manner in which owners, management, and employees of a company interact with each other and conduct business based on its protocol.

LO 9.2-2 **Explain a communication plan.**
A communication plan is a road map that includes objectives and goals that clearly outline the way in which communication takes place. It is a way of anticipating and providing specific information stakeholders of an organization need and when they should receive it. An effective communication plan should answer the questions of who, what, why, when, and how.

LO 9.2-3 **Summarize communication competence.**
Communication competence is an individual's ability to understand basic principles of communication and apply them when interacting with others. It enables a person to communicate well with others and build successful relationships on social and professional levels. Behaviors that contribute to communication competence are mindfulness, listening, emotional control, critical thinking, and cultural sensitivity.

LO 9.2-4 Identify effective ways to communicate in a diverse workplace.
Working with diverse people requires that individuals learn how to communicate clearly and concisely. This sometimes means taking extra time and patience to establish and maintain working relationships. It can also mean taking time to study another person's culture or language so that a spirit of understanding is developed. It is necessary to show respect and learn how to listen, speak, write, and communicate clearly with others in the workplace.

Review Your Knowledge

1. Discuss communication, its purpose, and forms it takes.
2. Analyze the communication process.
3. Cite factors that influence how a message is transmitted.
4. Identify and explain types of communication.
5. Discuss barriers to effective communication.
6. Discuss communication management.
7. Compare and contrast formal and informal communication.
8. Explain a communication plan.
9. Summarize communication competence.
10. Identify effective ways to communicate in a diverse workplace.

Apply Your Knowledge

1. Being able to communicate skillfully is essential to a successful career. Why do you think it is essential for a manager to be able to communicate skillfully?
2. Describe your effectiveness as an interpersonal communicator. Why do you think you excel or need improvement in this form of communication?
3. The communication process is vital to our personal and professional lives. Using a graphic organizer, create a visual of the communication process. Analyze the process as you perceive it.
4. Describe a time when you either observed or created a communication barrier. What could have been done differently in the situation to avoid the barrier?
5. Ethical communication is important to a business. State an example of a communication from a business that advertises on TV that you would consider to be ethical or unethical. Write a paragraph that defends your position.
6. A communication plan is important in an organization. Discuss the components of an effective communication plan for a company.
7. Organizational culture typically drives the way communication takes place within an organization. How does the organizational culture of your school or classroom affect the communication that takes place within it?
8. Communication competence is an individual's ability to understand basic principles of communication and apply them when interacting with others. Evaluate your communication competence. How can you improve?

9. Emotional control is directing one's feelings and reactions toward a desirable result that is socially acceptable. Why is it important for an individual to have emotional control when communicating?
10. Words and phrases can mean different things in different cultures. What common words and phrases do you use that might mean something different in another culture? How can you avoid using certain words and phrases that may cause confusion in another culture?

Communication Skills

Reading. *Decoding* is applying knowledge of the relationships between letters and sounds, including letter patterns, to pronounce written words correctly. This is achieved by recognizing individual letters and combinations of letters and matching them to their respective sounds. When you *sound out* a word, you are decoding it. Look at the list of key terms and select one that is unfamiliar to you. Look at the letters that create the word and think about the sounds each one makes. Decode the term by sounding it out.

Listening. A *barrier* is anything preventing clear, effective communication. *Internal barriers* are distractions that occur within an individual, such as fatigue, hunger, or wandering thoughts. During class, attempt to recognize any internal barriers to listening. How can you fight internal barriers?

Writing. To become career ready, it is necessary to utilize critical-thinking skills in order to solve problems. Identify an example of a problem you needed to solve that was important to your success at work or school. Explain how you applied critical-thinking skills to arrive at a solution.

Internet Research

Communication Plan. A communication plan is a tool that helps an organization facilitate messaging to its employees and customers. Search the Internet for *how to create a communication plan*. After you have completed your research, create a list of steps that an organization might use if completing a new plan.

English as a Second Language (ESL). Being able to communicate skillfully is essential for a successful career as a manager. In the workplace, there are many people who have English as their second language. Research *English as a second language (ESL)* and ways to have a conversation with someone whose first language is not English. Based on your research, summarize how communication barriers can be avoided.

Teamwork

Communication plans can be used by any group or organization that needs to send information to external or internal customers. Working with a partner, create a communication plan that your principal could use when it becomes necessary to cancel school due to inclement weather. Begin the process by writing down who will send the message and how it should be sent, such as an e-mail, text, or prerecorded phone call. Include how a school determines when to cancel school and when the message should be sent. Then, write the plan as it would appear for students and their families.

Portfolio Development

Testimonials. A *testimonial* is a formal statement from a teacher, customer, or other professional that certifies a person's qualifications or character. A testimonial focuses on a specific action a person executed that was exceptional in nature. The person writing the testimonial may not know you personally, but is validating the work or service you provided.

For example, if you work part-time at a computer store and help a customer set up a computer, the customer may be very happy with your work and may contact your supervisor through an e-mail with a testimonial that conveys his or her appreciation. If your employer forwards any positive written customer comments about you, save these for inclusion in your portfolio.

You may also have testimonials from instructors who made complimentary remarks on a paper you wrote or a project in which you participated. A former employer may have sent you an e-mail with congratulations on a personal accomplishment of yours. These are all testimonials that validate your abilities.

Newspaper articles that summarize a contribution, service, or personal accomplishment are also testimonials of your character, skills, and talents. Include newspaper articles in which you are the subject.

You can also include employer evaluations in your portfolio. Evaluations serve as a snapshot of your performance as an employee. They reflect your work habits, strengths, and contributions to an employer. If you decide to include an evaluation, be selective in the one you choose.

1. Sort through testimonials you have collected. Include assignments that have an instructor's written comments about your work. Print any e-mails from community members or other professionals who complimented your actions on something you did for that person. Attach notes to each document to identify (1) what it is and (2) why it is included in the portfolio. For example, a note on a research paper you wrote might say, "Research paper, Professor Dansby commenting on my writing skills." Be sure to update your master portfolio spreadsheet as you add testimonials to your portfolio.
2. If you have any evaluations from supervisors of any jobs you may have, review and decide if these would be appropriate to include.

CTSOs

Communication Skills. Competitive events may also judge the participants' communication skills. Presenters must be able to exchange information with the judges in a clear, concise manner. The evaluation will include all aspects of effective writing, speaking, and listening skills.

To prepare for the communication portion of an event, complete the following activities.

1. Visit the website of the organization and look for specific communication skills that will be judged as a part of a competitive event.
2. Spend time reviewing the essential principles of business communication, such as grammar, spelling, proofreading, capitalization, and punctuation.
3. If you are making a written presentation, ask an instructor to evaluate your writing. Review and apply the feedback so your writing sample appears professional and correct.
4. If you are making an oral presentation, ask an instructor to review and listen for errors in grammar or sentence structure. After you have received comments, adjust and make the presentation several times until you are comfortable with your presentation.
5. Review the Communication Skills activities that appear at the end of each chapter of this text as a way to practice your reading, writing, listening, and speaking skills.
6. To practice listening skills, ask your instructor to give you a set of directions. Then, without assistance, repeat those directions to your instructor. Did you listen closely enough to be able to do what was instructed?

CHAPTER 10

Soft Skills for Management

Sections

10.1 Human Relations

10.2 Self-Management Skills

Reading Prep

Before reading this chapter, preview the headings. Make a list of questions you have about the topics mentioned or the terms used in them. Search for answers to your questions as you read the chapter.

Exploring Careers

Business Management & Administration

Sales Manager

Sales managers hire, train, and direct salespeople to achieve a company's sales goals. They establish sales territories and quotas for sales representatives, monitor sales potential and inventory requirements, and analyze sales statistics. In addition, they develop training programs for the salespeople to help them become more familiar with the products. In larger organizations, sales managers often report directly to company executives.

Typical job titles for this position include *director of sales, sales supervisor*, and *sales executive.* Examples of tasks sales managers perform include:

- monitoring customer preferences to help focus the efforts of sales representatives;
- preparing sales budgets;
- completing performance evaluations of sales representatives; and
- resolving customer complaints.

Sales manager jobs typically require a bachelor degree, as well as considerable experience or on-the-job training. They must be able to manage and motivate employees effectively to maximize individual potentials. They should understand the principles, techniques, and methods of selling and marketing. Sales managers should have extensive familiarity with a company's products and the competition products in the marketplace. Communication, critical-thinking, and problem-solving skills are also essential for this position.

lightwavemedia/Shutterstock.com

Section 10.1 Human Relations

What soft skills do you think are important for a manager to possess?

Learning Objectives

LO 10.1-1 Cite examples of soft skills important for professionals.

LO 10.1-2 Differentiate between passive listening and active listening.

Key Terms

professionalism
attitude
resilience
confidence
passive listening
active listening
empathy

LO 10.1-1 Soft Skills

Management is a challenging job. A major responsibility of this position is to ensure that work is accomplished efficiently and effectively so the business is profitable. A manager's job includes interacting with employees, vendors, customers, and other stakeholders of the organization to meet goals. To accomplish this job effectively, soft skills are required.

Soft skills are skills used to help an individual find a job, perform in the workplace, and gain success in a job or career. They are also known as *interpersonal skills, human relations skills*, and *employability skills*. These skills enable a person to interact with others in a positive manner.

Like all other employees, managers must conduct themselves with professionalism in the workplace. **Professionalism** is the act of exhibiting appropriate character, judgment, and behavior by a person trained to perform a job. It is an acquired soft skill of knowing how to interact with others in a manner that is conducive for everyone to be successful in their responsibilities. Professionals have the skills and abilities to perform specific job tasks and work well with others. The following attributes are exhibited by professionals.

- Professionals show *initiative* and make the first step to take charge. When they see a task that needs attention or a decision to be made, they are comfortable making the first move to find a solution.
- Professionals are *responsible*, which means they are accountable for their actions, accepting when they have made good decisions or bad decisions.
- Professionals are *confident* in their abilities to lead and motivate others.
- Professionals *dress* in a manner appropriate for the job and workplace. Self-representation is the behavior in which a person reflects his or her personal image. It includes good grooming and hygiene.

In all situations, professionals apply soft skills. Examples of soft skills important for professionals to exhibit include a positive attitude, confidence, and professional etiquette.

Positive Attitude

Professionals exhibit a positive attitude in their job performance and workplace interactions. **Attitude** is how personal thoughts or feelings affect a person's outward behavior. It is a combination of how you feel, what you think, and what you do. Attitude is how an individual sees himself or herself, as well as how he or she perceives others. An individual with a *positive attitude* is optimistic and looks at the upside of a situation rather than the downside.

Attitude influences the way a manager performs in a job situation. Positive people are enthusiastic and show interest in their jobs and the activities in which they participate. They are eager to learn new tasks and make an effort to have productive relationships with those around them.

Monkey Business Images/Shutterstock.com

Professionalism is the act of exhibiting appropriate character, judgment, and behavior by a person trained to perform a job. **How does a person develop professionalism?**

People who have positive attitudes are generally more resilient. **Resilience** is a person's ability to cope with and recover from change or adversity. Managers face many challenges in the workplace. Having resilience helps them aptly handle challenges in one aspect of their lives while not letting it affect other aspects. They can bounce back even when they feel as though they have been knocked down.

Confidence

An important element to the professional image of a manager is confidence. **Confidence** is being certain and secure about one's own abilities and judgment. Effective managers have confidence and know what they are good at doing and how to best use their abilities to achieve goals of the organization. Successful managers are confident, humble, and take charge of situations. An important role of a leader is to be in control and responsible for business activities.

Professional Etiquette

Managers are expected to have good manners in their dealings with customers as well as those who work in the organization. *Etiquette* is the art of using good manners in any situation. *Professional etiquette* is using good manners in a professional or business setting. It means to be courteous as well as acting and speaking appropriately in all situations. Examples of professional etiquette expected from managers are shown in Figure 10-1.

Part of etiquette also involves having proper telephone etiquette. *Telephone etiquette* is using good manners when speaking on the telephone. It involves being courteous to the person on the other end of the phone. Volume and tone of voice are also important when participating in a phone call for business. Additional telephone etiquette techniques include the following.

- A caller should smile when on the phone to make his or her voice sound more pleasant.
- A ringing phone should be answered on the first or second ring.
- The person answering the call should identify himself or herself immediately after picking up the phone.
- A caller should not be placed on speakerphone unless it is a conference call with multiple participants. If speakerphone is necessary, permission should be requested from the person.
- Callers should not be placed on hold unless necessary. If the situation requires that a call be placed on hold, an explanation should be given and assurance that the wait will be brief.
- If leaving a voice mail, speak clearly and slowly. A person should state his or her name, job title, phone number, and a brief message.
- If a call is missed, return it promptly within 24 hours. Failing to return a call implies the caller is not important.

Professional Etiquette

- Show kindness and courtesy to each person with whom you come in contact
- Compliment those around you when they contribute in a positive manner
- Arrive on time to every meeting and appointment
- Address each person to whom you speak by his or her name
- Turn off your digital devices when in a meeting or conversation
- Shake hands when meeting someone for the first time
- Show you are listening when engaged in a conversation

Goodheart-Willcox Publisher

Figure 10-1 Professional etiquette is using good manners in a professional or business setting.

LO 10.1-2 Listening

Listening is an intellectual process that combines hearing with evaluating. It is a critical soft skill for managers. A person who is listening makes an effort to pay attention and process what is heard. There are two types of listening: passive listening and active listening.

Passive listening is casually listening to someone talk and is appropriate when interaction is not required with the person speaking. For example, a person in an audience listening to a speaker probably will not converse with that person during the presentation. The audience simply listens rather than having an interactive conversation with the speaker. Passive listeners *hear* rather than *listen* to a speaker.

Active listening is fully processing what a person says and interacting with the person who is speaking.

DGLimages/Shutterstock.com

Empathy is having the ability to share someone else's emotions and showing understanding of how the other person is feeling. **How can empathy play a role in developing relationships with people in the workplace?**

You Do the Math

Connections: Percentages

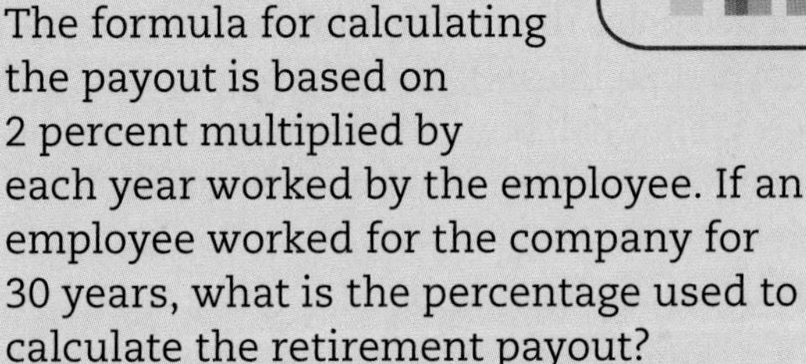

Many calculations related to employee salary, retirement planning, and taxes involve percentages. A percentage is a part of 100 and is the same as a fraction or decimal. For example, 15 percent is the same as 15 ÷ 100, which is 0.15. To calculate the percentage of a number, change the percentage to a decimal and multiply by the number. For example:

15 percent of 200 = $15 \div 100 \times 200$

or

$0.15 \times 200 = 30$

Solve the following problems.

1. The HR director for a company is calculating the profit-sharing payout for an employee who is retiring. The formula for calculating the payout is based on 2 percent multiplied by each year worked by the employee. If an employee worked for the company for 30 years, what is the percentage used to calculate the retirement payout?
2. Social Security tax is a standard withholding from employee paychecks. An assistant manager earns $650 per week before withholdings. Social Security tax rate is 6.2 percent. How much will be withheld from the assistant manager's paycheck for Social Security?
3. A supervisor worked in the same position for three years earning a salary of $29,500. The supervisor was promoted to manager and was given an 11 percent raise. What is the new salary?

Active listening is used to obtain information, respond to requests, receive instructions, and evaluate what another person is saying.

For example, when a manager is speaking to an employee, interaction will take place. Each person will talk and contribute to the conversation. Actively listening to a direct report can make the difference between successful and unsuccessful performance at work. Actively listening to a supervisor can affect future job promotions. Following specific listening techniques, as outlined in Figure 10-2, can lead to productive interactions.

An important component of listening is to demonstrate empathy. **Empathy** is having the ability to share someone else's emotions and showing understanding of how the other person is feeling. This often results in better relationships including those with friends, family, and coworkers.

Active Listening

- Face the person who is talking and give your full attention
- Let the person finish speaking before you contribute to the conversation
- Engage in eye contact to signal you are listening
- Avoid staring, which can be intimidating and distracting
- Lean toward the person who is talking to indicate you are paying attention
- Be appropriately responsive
- Nod your head when you understand a point

Goodheart-Willcox Publisher

Figure 10-2 Active listening is fully processing what a person says and interacting with the person who is speaking.

Section 10.1 Review

Check Your Understanding

1. List examples of attributes exhibited by professionals.
2. Why is having resilience helpful for a manager?
3. How can managers exhibit confidence?
4. What is professional etiquette?
5. What is the result of having empathy?

Build Your Vocabulary

As you progress through the text, develop a personal glossary of key terms. This will help you build your vocabulary and prepare you for a career. Write a definition for each of the following terms and add them to your personal glossary.

professionalism	confidence	active listening
attitude	passive listening	empathy
resilience		

Section 10.2 Self-Management Skills

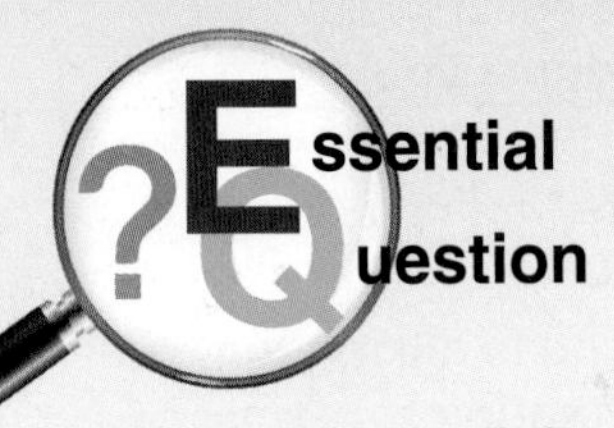

How would you define *self-management skills*?

Learning Objectives

LO 10.2-1 List examples of time-management practices.

LO 10.2-2 Explain the proper way to make introductions in professional settings.

LO 10.2-3 Discuss professional success.

Key Terms

time management
introduction
office politics

LO 10.2-1 Time Management

Time management is the practice of organizing time and work assignments to increase personal efficiency. It is a *self-management skill* which is a skill that enables an individual to control and make the best of his or her time and abilities. Time-management skills help managers work efficiently, meet deadlines, and keep appointments. Without time-management skills, it would be nearly impossible for a manager to accomplish what is necessary to keep a team or company operating efficiently. Time-management practices include setting goals, prioritizing, using a calendar or day-planner, and creating to-do lists.

Set Goals

Setting goals helps facilitate time management. A *goal* is something to be achieved in a specified timeframe. *Goal setting* is the process of deciding what needs to be achieved and defining the time period in which to achieve it.

Goals can be set for a short term or long term. A *short-term goal* is one to be achieved in less than one year. A *long-term goal* is one that will take a longer amount of time to achieve, usually more than one year. Well-defined goals follow the SMART goal model as described in Chapter 3.

Prioritize

To *prioritize* tasks means to determine the order of importance in which tasks are to be completed. Tasks are prioritized by deciding which ones should be completed before others. For example, you *have* to attend a department meeting. You *do not have* to check personal social media sites while you are at work. Therefore, checking social media should not be on your list of tasks for the day.

Use a Calendar

All appointments and meetings should be recorded on a calendar, preferably in the calendar that is part of an e-mail program. Personal vacations or appointments should also be noted on the same calendar. Entering all commitments on one calendar helps avoid missed meetings and scheduling conflicts.

Create a To-Do List

Creating a list of tasks to do each day is one simple way to manage time and an easy way to track tasks. As each task is finished, a line should be drawn through it. Any listings that are not deleted should be forwarded to the next day.

Stuart Jenner/Shutterstock.com

As a professional, a manager should initiate introductions when an unfamiliar person is encountered. **Why is it the responsibility of a manager to initiate introductions with new people who enter a meeting or a room in which business is being conducted?**

LO 10.2-2 Introductions

Successful managers are confident and take charge of situations. An important role of a manager is to be in control and responsible for business activities. When a situation calls for colleagues to gather, managers make introductions and put others at ease.

An **introduction** is making a person known to someone else by sharing the person's name and other relevant information. It may be necessary for a manager to introduce direct reports, coworkers, other managers, employees, or customers to each other. A proper introduction can create a positive first impression, and a negative impression can be created if protocol is not followed. When making professional introductions, the situation might be informal, but the language should always be formal and appropriate for the workplace.

Introducing Yourself

As a professional, a manager should initiate introductions when an unfamiliar person is encountered. When making a personal introduction, proper etiquette is to tell the person your full name and your role in the company. For example, a person might introduce herself by saying, "Hello, my name is Annabella Mellory, a manager for XYZ Company."

If a person is in rank above you, use professional protocol. Using a title like "Mr." or "Ms." or "Mrs." may be appropriate. When the other party gives his or her name, repeat the person's name as you greet him or her. For example, saying, "It is great to meet you, Mr. Gardner" is a polite way to respond when being introduced to someone in a professional situation. Saying a person's name after an introduction will help you remember it. Remembering a person's name is important to career success.

Always stand when introducing yourself or introducing others. Professionals extend their hand when meeting a person for the first time, as well as when greeting people they already know. In the United States, handshakes are customary when greeting both men and women. A customary handshake is performed by two people extending their right hands and grasping the other person's hand firmly. Applying the right amount of pressure is important. A handshake that is too strong makes a person seem overbearing and rude, while a handshake that is too weak makes a person seem timid or submissive.

Ethics

Time Theft

Employees of a company are paid for the use of their time. They are expected to arrive on time and ready to work. It is equally important to arrive on time to meetings. A well-known saying is, "If you're early, you're on time. If you are on time, you are late. If you are late, it is unacceptable." Arriving late and leaving early without permission is time theft. *Time theft* occurs when an employee uses paid work time for unapproved personal reasons.

Employability Skills

Self-Management Skills

Self-management skills are skills that enable an individual to control and make the best use of his or her time and abilities. They are important because they facilitate productivity, help ensure employee success, and provide assurance for an employer that the employee will help the business meet its goals. An individual has complete control over the development and use of self-management skills. Some important self-management skills are emotional control, problem solving, time management, and goal setting.

When you approach someone you may have met before but do not know well, introduce yourself again. This saves embarrassment for all parties if names are forgotten. Doing so puts everyone at ease and shows you are a professional.

Introducing Others

When introducing two people to each other, clearly state each person's full name. Professional protocol is to introduce the lower-ranking person to the higher-ranking person. For example, if introducing a new intern to an executive, a manager would say: "Marcus, this is Ms. Sophia Royer, vice president. Sophia, this is Marcus Zamora. Marcus is working as our social media intern this summer."

In addition, providing more information about a person can help the two people easily make conversation. For example, an individual might say: "Olivia Price, I would like to introduce to you Joshua Morgan. Joshua is a set designer for a local theater. He has a great idea about how we can improve our displays."

Introducing Speakers

On occasion, managers will be responsible for making formal introductions for speakers at events. If you are introducing another person as a speaker, request information about the person in advance. Use the information to develop your introduction. Select information from the speaker's notes that will complement the person's presentation. Write the points you wish to express on an index card so you do not forget to include them. Be specific in what you convey to the audience. For example, you might say what city the person is from or where he or she went to college.

Conversely, you could be the speaker and required to make your own introduction. If you are introducing yourself, give a brief background of who you are and why you are making a presentation. Keep it short, but interesting. This time should not be used as a bragging session.

LO 10.2-3 Professional Success

Professional success means different things to different people. A personal sense of accomplishment and satisfaction gained from working in a chosen profession is a sign of success for many people. Others seek professional advancement as an indicator of success. Advancement can be measured by a promotion, new job title, or other forms of recognition that help an individual attain a desired career status. Each individual has his or her own measure of job success.

To attain advancement, it is important to exhibit confidence in personal performance and the ability to interact in the workplace. It also requires taking control of your career and learning how to manage up and appropriately deal with office politics within the organization.

Manage Up

"Manage up" is a common term in the workplace. *Managing up* is the efforts of an employee to establish a working relationship with a supervisor so his or her professional needs are met as well as the employee's own needs. It is the act of demonstrating professional behavior and working toward the goals of a supervisor and the company.

To manage up is to show basic respect toward your supervisor. It is the act of maintaining a good attitude, volunteering your services when needed, and learning how to make a supervisor look good. Successful employees determine what the manager wants and how to show support. This includes being proactive in situations that demand attention. Knowing how to help a manager can make an employee an asset to the team and to the company. It can also position an individual for promotions when they arise.

WAYHOME studio/Shutterstock.com

Some people seek professional advancement, such as a promotion, as an indicator of success. **In addition to promotions, what are some other indicators of professional success?**

Some people confuse "managing up" with "playing up." *Playing up* is going through the motions of building a relationship with a supervisor and displaying professional behavior, but the motivation behind the actions is not genuine. Someone who plays up to a superior is only looking to gain influence and does not have the best interests of the company in mind. This is often demonstrated through flattery, insincere praise, and eager attentiveness toward a supervisor. Playing up is often called *brown-nosing.*

Office Politics

Office politics are inevitable in most organizations. **Office politics** are the behaviors that individuals practice to gain advantages over others in the workplace. It is a struggle for power. Engaging in office politics is considered inappropriate at best and is often unethical. Some individuals believe the more they know about company business, the more power they will have. Others want to secure a friendship with upper managers or with those who can help them climb the ladder for promotions. Gossipers may say unkind things about coworkers to try to make them look worse. Some workers withhold information from a coworker to maintain an advantage over him or her. Many times office politics result in a coworker being the target of someone's negative behavior. Unfortunately, while an employee can avoid participating in office politics, he or she cannot prevent others from engaging in them.

Section 10.2 Review

Check Your Understanding

1. How are time-management skills helpful for managers?
2. What does it mean to prioritize tasks?
3. Why is it helpful to introduce yourself again to someone you have met?
4. State the protocol if you are introducing yourself as a speaker.
5. What does managing up mean?

Build Your Vocabulary

As you progress through this text, develop a personal glossary of key terms. This will help you build your vocabulary and prepare you for a career. Write a definition for each of the following terms and add them to your personal glossary.

time management introduction office politics

Chapter 10 Review and Assessment

Chapter Summary

Section 10.1 Human Relations

LO 10.1-1 Cite examples of soft skills important for professionals.
Examples of soft skills important for professionals to exhibit include a positive attitude, confidence, and professional etiquette.

LO 10.1-2 Differentiate between passive listening and active listening.
Passive listening is casually listening to someone talk and is appropriate when interaction is not required with the person speaking. Active listening is fully processing what a person says and interacting with the person who is speaking. It is used to obtain information, respond to requests, receive instructions, and evaluate what another person is saying.

Section 10.2 Self-Management Skills

LO 10.2-1 List examples of time-management practices.
Time-management practices include setting goals, prioritizing, using a calendar, and creating to-do lists.

LO 10.2-2 Explain the proper way to make introductions in professional settings.
If you are introducing yourself, tell a person your full name and role in the company. Always stand and extend your hand when introducing oneself. If introducing other people, say each person's full name and information to help the two people make conversation. If introducing a speaker, information about the person should be requested in advance to develop the introduction.

LO 10.2-3 Discuss professional success.
Professional success means different things to different people. A personal sense of accomplishment and satisfaction gained from working in a chosen profession or professional advancement are signs of success. To attain advancement, it is important to exhibit confidence in personal performance and the ability to interact in the workplace. It also requires taking control of your career and learning how to manage up and appropriately deal with office politics within the organization.

Review Your Knowledge

1. Define *soft skills* and provide examples of soft skills important for professionals to exhibit.
2. Why do managers need soft skills?
3. Why is it important for a manager to have a positive attitude?
4. Provide examples of ways proper telephone etiquette can be applied when using the phone in the workplace.
5. Differentiate between passive listening and active listening.
6. List and explain examples of time-management practices.
7. Discuss how to properly introduce yourself.
8. How would someone introduce two people to each other?
9. State the protocol for introducing a speaker.
10. Summarize professional success.

Apply Your Knowledge

1. Create a list of soft skills you possess. Rate each one on its strength. What can you do to improve these skills?
2. Describe a person who you think models professionalism. What traits does this person have that influenced your opinion?
3. Recall a situation in which you observed a person in a management or other leadership position exhibit unprofessional behavior. Identify what this person did and the effect the behavior had on the situation.
4. Describe your personal level of self-confidence. Reflect on a situation or event during which confidence played a role in your behavior or decision-making.
5. A person who is actively listening makes an effort to pay attention and process what is heard. How would your friends and family describe your ability to listen?
6. Summarize the methods you use for time management. Explain why these methods work for you. If you think your time management could be improved, create a strategy for doing so.
7. You have been given the opportunity to speak at a school assembly on the importance of soft skills for students. You are required to make your own introduction. Write a paragraph you could use as an introduction for yourself.
8. Professional success means different things to different people. Write several paragraphs to explain your interpretation of professional success.
9. Summarize the difference between *managing up* and *playing up* in your own words.
10. Office politics are often the result of a struggle for power in an organization. Explain how you think office politics would influence your skills as a manager.

Communication Skills

Listening. Your purpose for listening will change depending on the situation. You will become a better listener if you know your purpose for listening and change your behavior accordingly. What was your purpose for listening to your instructor lecture to the class today?

Speaking. An *introduction* is making a person known to someone else by sharing the person's name and other relevant information. Create a script you might use to introduce yourself to another classmate whom you do not know well. What information will you tell this person about yourself? Then, use the script to introduce yourself to a classmate.

Writing. *Tone* is the way a writer expresses an attitude toward a topic in his or her writing. Just as you can tell a person's tone of voice when you listen, you can often tell a writer's tone when reading his or her writing. The tone might be happy, solemn, or humorous. Write several paragraphs that describe your usual tone when completing a typical writing assignment that you submit to your instructor for a grade.

Internet Research

Soft Skills. Soft skills are necessary for success at all levels of a company, especially for managers. Conduct a search for *soft skills for the workplace.* Which soft skills do you think you possess? Which ones are you lacking?

Empathy versus Sympathy. There is a fine line between empathy and sympathy. Conduct an online search for *empathy versus sympathy.* Based on your research, recall a past conversation that you had with someone. Did you display empathy or sympathy while listening? Explain.

Teamwork

Telephone etiquette is using good manners when speaking on the telephone. The voice mail greeting on your phone should reflect a polite message. There is always the chance that a potential employer or other important call could arrive on your personal phone. An inappropriate voice mail message could cost you a career opportunity. Working with a partner, write a script you could use to create a voice mail message on your phone. Practice by reading the script aloud. Then, record the message for your voice mail greeting. How would you rate your use of good manners?

Portfolio Development

Schoolwork. Academic samples are important to include in a portfolio in order to show your accomplishments in school. Include items related to your schoolwork that support your portfolio objective and the job or program for which you are presenting your portfolio. These items might be report cards, completed assignments, list of classes, or honor roll reports. Diplomas should also be included.

This is a particularly important part of a portfolio, especially for those interested in visual mediums of work, such as graphic design or sculpting. Samples of work completed for school are just as valuable as samples of work done for payment. For example, if a school assignment required you to design a menu for a fake restaurant, including the assignment shows your ability to design both visual and textual media. Even if your interest is not in visual art or something similar, showing your ability to create good work in that area demonstrates a variety of skills and well-roundedness.

1. Create a Microsoft Word document that lists notable classes you have taken and activities you have completed. Use the heading "Schoolwork" on the document along with your name.
2. Scan hard-copy documents related to your schoolwork, such as report cards, to serve as samples. Place each document in an appropriate folder.
3. Place the hard-copy documents in the container for future reference.
4. Update your spreadsheet.

CTSOs

Public Speaking. Public speaking is delivering a prepared speech to a large group or audience. This event enables participants to demonstrate communication skills of speaking, organizing, and making an oral presentation.

The topic for this event will typically be posted on the website of the CTSO. You will be given time to research, prepare, and practice before going to the competition. Review the specific guidelines and rules for this event for direction as to topics and props that are permitted for the presentation.

To prepare for a public speaking event, complete the following activities.

1. Read the guidelines provided by your organization. Review the topics from which you may choose to make a speech.
2. Locate a rubric or scoring sheet for the event on the website of your organization.
3. Confirm if visual aids may be used in the presentation and the amount of setup time permitted.
4. Review the rules to confirm if questions will be asked or if you will need to defend a case or situation.
5. Make notes on index cards about important points to remember. Use these notes to study. Verify whether you will be able to use these notes during the event.
6. Practice the presentation. You should introduce yourself, review the topic that you are presenting, defend the topic, and conclude with a summary.
7. After the presentation is complete, ask for feedback from your instructor. You may consider also having a student audience listen and give feedback.

UNIT 5 Controlling

Chapters

11 Controlling

12 Operations Management

Functions of Management Covered in This Unit

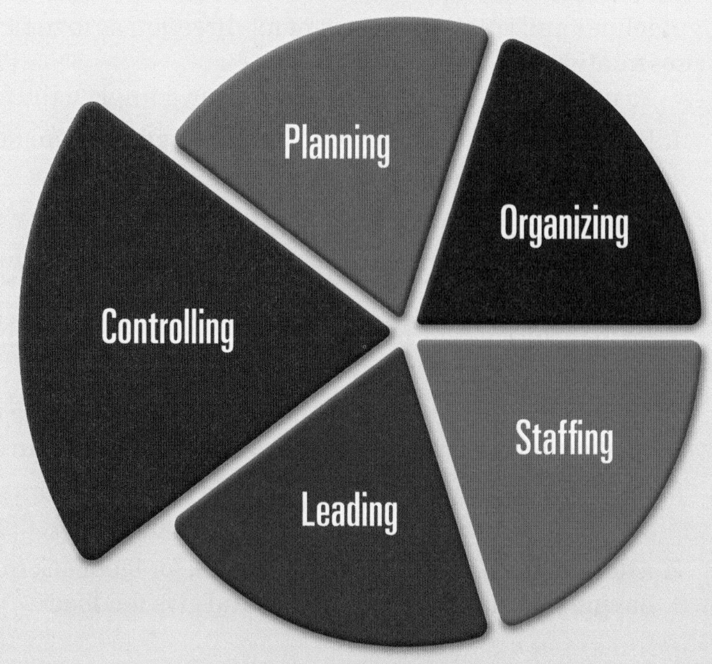

While studying, look for the activity icon for:

- Vocabulary terms with e-flash cards and matching activities

These activities can be accessed at www.g-wlearning.com/business/8417

Case Study

Responsibility

mavo/Shutterstock.com

Kai is an assembly line leader at a manufacturing company. He has been in his position for three years and is a valuable member of the management team.

When Kai arrived at work one morning, he noticed a box of nails had tipped over on the supply shelf and spilled, creating piles of loose nails all along the belts of the assembly line. When his employees arrived to begin work, he had them investigate their respective work areas to ensure there were no additional conditions that could cause a work stoppage or worker injury.

Production stopped for nearly three hours in the morning. However, the employees were able to begin production after completing the additional checks. By the afternoon, the assembly line was running at full speed.

When Kai reported that production stopped for a few hours, his supervisor called for an explanation. Kai explained there was a safety issue and the well-being of the employees took precedence. He was uneasy putting his crew on an assembly line that could pose potential hazards, and expressed his desire to maintain a safe and productive line. The supervisor, while not happy about the production delay, understood Kai's concern for safety and commended him for making a difficult management decision.

Responsibility is an important soft skill for leadership. Managers are responsible for controlling the environment in which their employees work. It includes being responsible for employees as well as the physical workspace. By applying a problem-solving process, appropriate decisions can be reached that are effective for both the workers and the organization as a whole.

Critical Thinking

1. How did Kai control the working environment of his crew?
2. What could have been the result of not stopping the production line?

CHAPTER 11

Controlling

Sections

11.1 Importance of Controlling

11.2 Organizational Control

Reading Prep

To *skim* is to glance through material quickly to get an overview. It is also called *prereading*. Before reading this chapter, skim the material by reading the first sentence of each paragraph. Use this information to create an outline for the chapter before you read it.

Exploring Careers

Financial Manager

Financial managers are responsible for directing and coordinating the monetary activities for a business. Their primary task is to oversee the financial health of the organization. They analyze and prepare information related to finances to assist the management team to make sound decisions. In addition, they investigate ways to improve profitability and research business opportunities, such as mergers or acquisitions.

Typical job titles for this position include *financial center manager* and *finance officer*. Examples of tasks financial managers perform include:

- ensuring compliance with laws and procedures;
- approving an organization's expenditures;
- evaluating financial data to create budgets;
- providing assistance to customers or vendors when financial discrepancies appear; and
- preparing operational and financial risk reports.

Financial manager positions require a bachelor degree in economics, finance, accounting, or a related field. Some organizations may require a master degree in finance, accounting, economics, or business administration. In addition, certifications or licenses can be beneficial. Extensive mathematical and accounting skills are essential for this position. Financial managers must have excellent listening, critical-thinking, and communication skills, as well as an understanding of customer service.

Pressmaster/Shutterstock.com

Section 11.1 Importance of Controlling

Why is controlling necessary for an organization?

Learning Objectives

LO 11.1-1 Summarize the controlling function of management.
LO 11.1-2 Identify examples of standards set in the controlling function.
LO 11.1-3 Discuss measuring performance against standards.
LO 11.1-4 Identify actions taken by management when performance standards are not met.

Key Terms

standard
time standard
quantity standard
cost standard
quality
quality standard
variance

LO 11.1-1 Controlling Function

An effective organization is largely the result of good management. A business reaches its goals, in part, because a strong management team executes the functions of management. It is necessary that *planning*, *organizing*, *staffing*, and *leading* responsibilities are the focus of every manager in an organization.

The final function of management is *controlling*, which is the continuous process of comparing actual outcomes with planned outcomes and taking corrective action when goals are not met. Controlling attempts to keep an organization on track by providing the means to monitor the performance of individuals, divisions, departments, and the organization as a whole.

Even though controlling is the last function of management, it is closely related to the first function of management, which is planning. *Planning* determines the goals of an organization and maps out the strategies and tactics necessary to achieve those goals. *Controlling* helps evaluate the effectiveness of the planning process.

An ongoing controlling process provides the information needed for effective decision-making. Benefits of controlling include the following.

- Plans created in the planning process can be measured for their effectiveness and success against the standards created in the controlling process.
- Departments and units in an organization work together better because they each follow the same direction as designated by the planning process.
- Departments and units in an organization are more efficient because standards are in place that everyone follows.
- The outputs of each department or unit are evaluated equally on performance standards set by the controlling process.
- Controls provide the basis on which decisions can be made.

An important component of control is that management focuses on critical items that influence the overall efficiency and success of the organization. Controls should be implemented that assist and encourage employees to accomplish their jobs rather than slow down their performances.

Some organizations "get in the weeds" and attempt to control unimportant details that cause poor morale and lack of success. It is the responsibility of management to focus on standards that utilize monetary and human resources in the best-possible manner for the company.

Controlling helps an organization manage productivity. By creating standards, measuring performance, and taking corrective actions, a business can monitor and manage its productivity. When a business loses track of how much it is producing, it cannot project accurate sales potential or growth opportunities. The result could be loss of profits or even the failure of the company. By keeping track of productivity levels and tracking plans for improvement, a company can manage growth and profits.

As with other processes, controlling has multiple steps, as shown in Figure 11-1. The three basic steps of the *control process* are:

- set standards;
- measure performance; and
- take action to correct inadequacies.

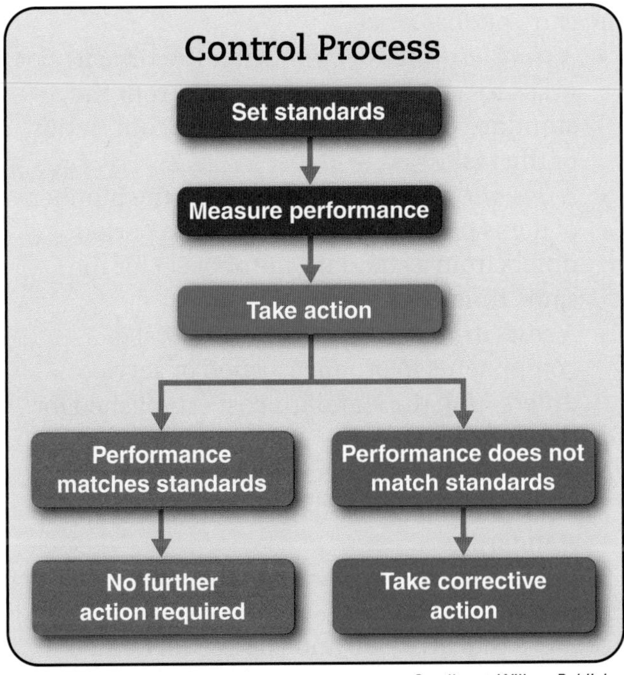

Figure 11-1 The control process has three basic steps.

LO 11.1-2 Set Standards

The first step of the controlling process is to set standards. A **standard** is an established measure against which performance can be compared. Standards are also called *controls*. They establish operational guidelines for a business to follow to help it meet the quality measures for the goods and services it produces. In addition, standards help monitor costs, improve efficiencies in production, and comply with federal and state requirements.

Standards can be *internal*, which are ones an organization writes for its specific business. Each company determines which standards are necessary to accomplish its goals efficiently. An example of an internal standard is a requirement that each employee wear a name badge and uniform vest. This is a standard that many retail businesses, such as Walmart, set to ensure the appearance of employees is appropriate and results in positive customer interactions.

Standards can also be *external*, such as laws and regulations mandated by federal, state, and local laws. An example of an external standard is that all businesses must follow Equal Employment Opportunity Commission (EEOC) regulations. EEOC regulations require that employers keep all personnel or employment records for one year. This is a standard imposed on all businesses.

For many businesses, industry standards dictate processes and procedures. Examples of these standards include food purity in the food-processing industry and automobile safety in the automotive industry.

The standards a business develops to control operations depend on the size of the business and the nature of its operations. The major types of standards are time, quantity, cost, and quality.

Time Standard

A **time standard** is an estimated or predetermined amount of time necessary to complete a single task or activity. It is often said that "time is money." The more time it takes to complete a task or activity, the greater its cost. The result can be a decrease in company profit. By developing and following realistic time standards, a business can reduce costs and thereby increase profit.

For example, in a manufacturing business, standards are set to project how many minutes it *should* take to produce one part of a unit. If the standard is 10 minutes per part and employees take 9 minutes per part, the standard is exceeded.

Quantity Standard

A standard somewhat related to a time standard is a quantity standard. A **quantity standard** is an estimated or predetermined quantity of work to be completed in a specified amount of time. *Quantity* refers to a number or amount of an item.

For example, a car manufacturer sets a standard to project how many units are produced in an hour. If the quantity standard is to produce 350 car doors in one eight-hour shift and a factory produces that number, the quantity standard is met.

Cost Standard

A **cost standard** is an estimated or predetermined cost to produce a good or deliver a service. Each good or service consists of multiple parts that have individual associated costs.

For example, a shipping service packs boxes to ship for its customers. The price for the service is based on the cost of the box, filler, and tape for the box. The standard cost of components for one box is $2.25. If the actual cost of components for a box exceeds $2.25, the standard is exceeded. The business must increase its selling price to customers to cover the additional costs or suffer a reduction in profit.

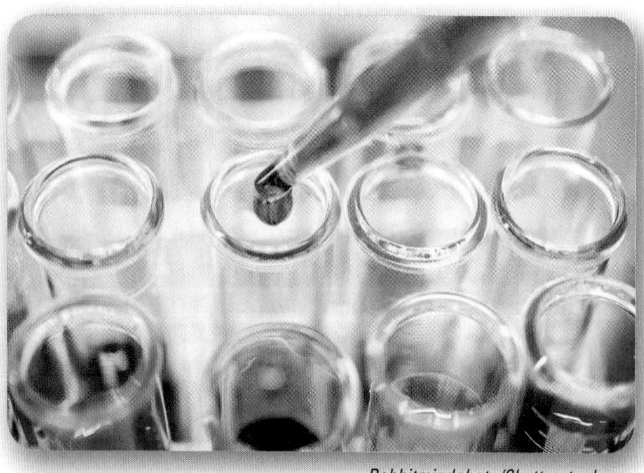

Rabbitmindphoto/Shutterstock.com

Standards establish operational guidelines for a business to follow to help it meet the quality measures for the goods and services it produces. **What standards do you use to measure your performance in school or at work?**

Quality Standards

Quality is an indicator of a product's excellence. A **quality standard** is an established level of acceptability for the production of goods and services. Some businesses define quality as a minimal amount of flaws. Other businesses define quality as perfect, or having no flaws. Each type of business sets standards based on what its customers will accept.

For example, management sets a standard that says the quality of items produced should meet 100 percent accuracy. If employees achieve 90 percent accuracy on production, the quality standard is not met.

LO 11.1-3 Measure Performance

After standards are set, the next step in the control process is to measure actual performance against the standards. Generally, not all established standards are met 100 percent of the time. A **variance** is the difference between the standard and the actual performance. Variances of time, quantity, cost, and quality are used to measure performance.

- A *time variance* occurs when the time it takes to complete a task differs from the standard amount of time set for completion of the task.
- A *quantity variance* occurs when the number of items produced or sold during a period differs from a standard number set for the same time.
- A *cost variance* occurs when the cost of components to produce a good or service differs from the standard cost established for that product.
- A *quality variance* occurs when the quality of the items produced deviates from the standards set.

Businesses study both favorable and unfavorable variances. *Favorable variances* are those that are good and contribute to the profitability of a business. The favorable variances are evaluated to determine which factors or conditions led to the positive outcome. Factors that lead to a favorable outcome can become "best practices" in an effort to continue reaching those results.

Unfavorable variances are those that are detrimental to profits and operating efficiency of a business. The unfavorable variances are evaluated to determine why a standard was not met and which factors or conditions led to the negative outcome. The information is used to determine adjustments needed in the future to meet the standard.

Variances are important because they can influence profits. For example, if an employee is evaluated on the number of units produced and he or she fails to reach the set standard, production decreases. The result is fewer products to sell, which means revenue decreases. Alternatively, if the employee exceeds the standard and produces more units, revenue can increase.

Various techniques are used to measure actual performance against standards to determine variances. Two widely used techniques to measure performance include observations and reports.

Employability Skills
Protocol

Protocol is a set of customs or rules of etiquette that explains proper conduct or procedures in formal situations. *Business protocol* refers to the customs and etiquette rules found in the professional world. It requires employees to show respect and courtesy when interacting with coworkers, customers, clients, or other business contacts. As a new employee, it can be challenging to learn business protocol on the job. Many aspects of business protocol are not in written format and, therefore, must be learned from experience.

Observations

Observations are a way to make first-hand evaluations and produce immediate information. Observation involves watching individuals interact with their surroundings or other people. For example, if employee-performance standards are used, a manager can observe how well an employee performs assigned tasks. If the employee is doing well, the manager can confirm the performance. If the employee is not meeting the standard, corrections can be made. The outcome of the observation is part of a performance evaluation.

PKpix/Shutterstock.com

A time standard is an estimated or predetermined amount of time necessary to complete a single task or activity. **What is the value of an organization establishing time standards?**

Even though observation is a good way to measure some standards, it is a time-consuming activity. In addition, observation results can be influenced by personal biases of those who conduct the observations.

Reports

Reports are another good tool that can be used to measure actual performance against standards. A budget is an example of a report created in the planning function that reflects anticipated revenue and how it is allocated in the operation of the business. By comparing the planned budget to actual results, management can make judgments on performance based on data and determine variances. In addition, other reports generated by the organization, such as graphs and statistics, are valuable when evaluating standards against performance.

LO 11.1-4 Take Action

The final step in the control process is to take action. If management determines the actual performance does not meet standards, corrective action is necessary. One way in which corrective action is taken is to revise the standard. Another option for corrective action is to adjust performance.

Revise the Standard

Corrective action often starts with an examination of the standard to evaluate if the standard is realistic. Perhaps the standard was set too low or too high. If a standard is *routinely met* at a high percentage, perhaps the standard is set too low. If a standard is *rarely met*, the standard may be set at an unrealistically high level.

Alternatively, extenuating circumstances can prevent the organization from meeting a standard. For example, a business established a standard for each member of its sales force to sell 1,000 units each month. Three salespeople did not meet this standard because the product was out of stock. Because there were no products to sell, the salespeople could not perform their jobs. Therefore, this was not an issue of employee performance, rather an out-of-stock situation.

The question must be asked why there was no stock. The variance could be the result of a factory production standard that was set too low and not enough units produced to sell. Alternatively, a variance could be the result of an uncontrollable external issue that resulted in components not arriving for assembly. No matter the cause, there was a shortage of stock that prevented sales from being made. In this situation, the standard for units sold should be adjusted and decreased. In addition, the standard for quantity of units produced should be adjusted and increased.

Adjust Performance

If a standard is reasonable, fair, and achievable, the corrective action is to adjust the performance of an employee, department, or a business as a whole so a standard can be met. Managers can evaluate the situation by analyzing work procedures that influence performance. Perhaps employees need better technology or equipment to perform their jobs. There may be some employees who need additional training. Other employees may simply not be qualified and need to be removed from their positions.

Conducting evaluations to adjust performance can be challenging. It often involves bringing in an outside expert to review current operating procedures and make recommendations for improvement.

Section 11.1 Review

Check Your Understanding

1. Briefly explain how the controlling function relates to the planning function.
2. List three basic steps of the control process.
3. What are internal and external standards?
4. State the difference between favorable variances and unfavorable variances.
5. What are two ways management can take corrective action if it determines actual performance does not meet standards?

Build Your Vocabulary

As you progress through this text, develop a personal glossary of key terms. This will help you build your vocabulary and prepare you for a career. Write a definition for each of the following terms and add them to your personal glossary.

standard	cost standard	quality standard
time standard	quality	variance
quantity standard		

Section 11.2 Organizational Control

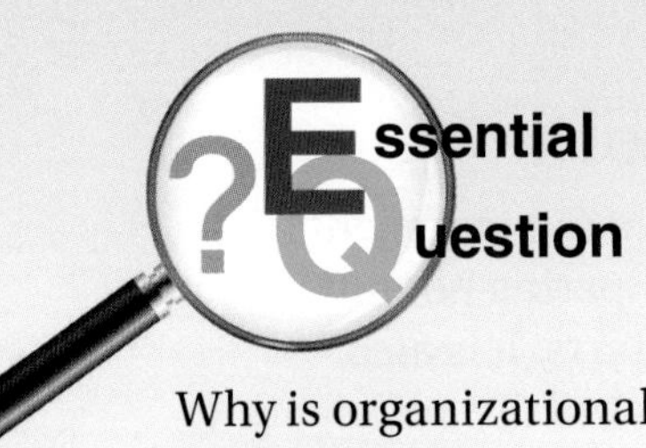

Why is organizational performance a responsibility of managers?

Learning Objectives

LO 11.2-1 Discuss organizational performance.
LO 11.2-2 Define types of organizational controls.
LO 11.2-3 Identify examples of financial controls used to measure financial performance.
LO 11.2-4 Summarize information technology control.

Key Terms

feedforward control
concurrent control
cyberloafing
feedback control
financial control
financial statement analysis
ratio
ratio analysis
financial ratio
current ratio
debt ratio
net profit ratio
operating ratio
data security
cyberattack
cybersecurity

LO 11.2-1 Organizational Performance

In Chapter 1, the term *management* was introduced as the process of controlling and making decisions about an organization, as well as overseeing others to make sure activities are performed efficiently and effectively. Through *planning, organizing, staffing, leading,* and now *controlling,* managers can evaluate if the work completed has been efficient and effective for the organization. The function of controlling asks the question, "Has the organization performed?"

Organizational performance is the result of all the activities that transpire in a business to reach a desired outcome. Performance measures are used to review how well an organization performed and achieved its desired outcome. Measures include efficiency, effectiveness, and productivity.

- **Efficiency.** Efficiency means to use resources to get a job done with minimal waste of time and effort. Has the organization used its resources to get a job done with minimal waste of time and effort?
- **Effectiveness.** Effectiveness means the intended goals or objectives were achieved or targeted challenges solved. Has the intended goal or purpose been accomplished?
- **Productivity.** Productivity is a measure of output accomplished by an employee in a specific timeframe. Is the output by employees in a specific period adequate to meet the goal?

All managers are responsible for the performance of the organization. Organizational performance standards are used to measure how efficient, effective, and productive an organization has been for a specific period of time. The control process helps identify behaviors that resulted in positive performance and the ones that were not effective.

Internal controls help an organization measure its effectiveness. There are five components of internal control typically used by management. These components are described as follows.

- **Control the environment:** ensure that all employees have workplace ethics, are committed to the organization, and policies are followed
- **Be prepared for risk:** perform risk assessment on all levels and prepare for changes that are necessary to minimize risks, which is the possibility of suffering loss or harm

wavebreakmedia/Shutterstock.com

Organizational performance measures are used to review how well an organization performed and achieved its desired outcome. **Why are standards necessary to measure performance?**

- **Control activities of the business:** institute data security, accounting systems, policies, and procedures to ensure the organization operates properly
- **Be communicative with the employees:** share information, have open communication policies, and respect all workers
- **Set monitoring standards:** conduct ongoing controls to monitor the organization and the productivity of employees

Implementing internal controls helps to ensure the organization will perform as desired.

LO 11.2-2 Organizational Controls

Even though control is the last of the functions of management, managers control performance every day in one form or another. They can set controls *before* an activity starts, *during* the performance of the activity, or *after* the activity is completed. Examples of organizational controls are feedforward control, concurrent control, and feedback control, as illustrated in Figure 11-2.

Feedforward Control

A **feedforward control** is a management technique that involves anticipating potential problems before an activity starts. It is also referred to as *preventative control.* By anticipating problems before an activity begins, management is in a better position to prevent a problem or deal with it more effectively should it occur.

For example, a checklist of parts can be reviewed before a job begins. If parts are missing, they can be requested before the job starts. This is a preventative measure to keep production from stopping once it has begun.

Concurrent Control

A **concurrent control** is a management technique that focuses on identifying and correcting problems that may occur while an activity is in progress. Concurrent controls are *steering controls.* The objective of concurrent controls is to identify problems as they develop and take immediate corrective action to prevent interruptions in work.

An example of concurrent control is *managing by walking around (MBWA).* A manager who walks around can sometimes identify problems by observing how work is accomplished. If equipment is observed as not working properly, repairs can be made. When an employee is observed as not performing tasks as assigned, a manager can talk to the employee and attempt to correct the employee's behavior.

Organizational Controls

Feedforward Control	Concurrent Control	Feedback Control
Anticipates problems *before* they happen	Controls problems *as* they happen	Corrects problems *after* they happen

Goodheart-Willcox Publisher

Figure 11-2 Managers can set controls *before* an activity starts, *during* the performance of the activity, or *after* the activity is completed.

However, for employees who are cyberloafing, identifying an activity while it is in progress can be difficult. **Cyberloafing** occurs when an employee uses the Internet at work for personal use instead of performing required work tasks. A manager observing an employee working at a computer can be deceiving. An employee can pretend to be working when in fact, he or she may be surfing the Internet.

It is estimated that cyberloafing costs US companies upward to $90 billion a year in lost employee productivity. Some companies have responded by tracking employee time on the Internet and the sites they visit. Many organizations have strict policies, and cyberloafing can be grounds for dismissal.

Feedback Control

Feedback control is a management technique in which control happens *after* the activity is completed. It is also called *post-action control.* If actual results are less than planned, managers can use feedback to adjust the work process to increase productivity or improve the quality of a product.

For example, an employee was tasked with applying postage to letters that were being sent to customers. When the letters were returned by the post office as undeliverable, it was discovered that the employee used the incorrect amount of postage. The manager gave the employee feedback on how to fix the error and not make it again.

Feedback control is the most popular type of control. However, since it is applied after the completion of a task or activity, it is the least-desirable type of control when damage or mistakes actually occur.

Pressmaster/Shutterstock.com

Feedback control is a management technique in which control happens *after* the activity is completed. **What is the importance of feedback control for a business?**

Ethics

Fraud

Managers who are responsible for approving checks for suppliers and vendors may have access to company checking accounts. Greed can sometimes influence an individual to write a personal check to a family member to cash for individual use. Known as *check forgery*, this is an example of a fraudulent act that is unethical and illegal. *Management fraud* is a wrongful act by a manager with the intent of financial or personal gain.

LO 11.2-3 Financial Controls

Financial controls are the policies and procedures used by an organization to manage its finances. They play an important role in ensuring the accuracy of information, eliminating fraud, and protecting the organization's resources. Financial controls hold managers accountable for their individual departments and the overall financial success of a business.

Organizations use key data extracted from financial statements to evaluate performance. **Financial statement analysis** is the process of reviewing information provided in financial statements to analyze the performance of the business. Accountants in the organization prepare financial statements and extract information in formats that managers can review and use to make conclusions and recommendations. Two examples of information used to evaluate performance are financial ratios and budget analysis.

Financial Ratios

A **ratio** is a comparison of one figure to another. **Ratio analysis** is the process of using ratios to compare the relationship between financial statement items. Businesses use various ratios for planning and decision-making.

Financial ratios evaluate the overall financial condition of the business by showing the relationships between selected figures on financial statements. By analyzing financial ratios, specific areas can be identified in which the business is strong and where improvements are needed.

Financial ratios provide a benchmark of company performance compared to earlier years of the business. Ratios are also a good way to show comparisons with competitors in the same industry. Examples include current ratio, debt ratio, and profitability ratios.

Current Ratio

A **current ratio** shows the relationship of current assets to current liabilities. A *current asset* is any asset that will be collected, sold, or used up in the next 12 months. Equipment is not a current asset because it typically has a life longer than one year. A *current liability* is any debt due in the next 12 months. A long-term notes payable is not a current liability because it is usually paid over several years. This information comes from the balance sheet, shown in Figure 11-3. A current ratio shows the degree to which a company can pay its current liabilities. The formula for finding a current ratio follows.

current assets ÷ current liabilities = current ratio
$58,000 ÷ $24,000 = 2.42:1

A current ratio of 2.42 is commonly expressed at 2.42:1, which is read as *2.42 to 1*. This means the business has $2.42 in current assets for each $1.00 in current liabilities.

A current ratio of 2:1 or higher is considered good. However, the business should compare this ratio with those of other similar businesses in the same industry to see if it meets industry norms. Knowing this information can help determine if the business is doing well or needs improvement.

Debt Ratio

A **debt ratio** shows the percentage of dollars owed compared to assets owned. This information comes from the balance sheet, shown in Figure 11-3. The formula for finding a debt ratio follows.

total liabilities ÷ total assets = debt ratio
$42,000 ÷ $73,000 = .58:1

This ratio shows that for every dollar of assets, the business owes creditors 58 cents. The business can compare this ratio with industry guidelines to see if the ratio is healthy.

A high debt ratio means a company is carrying a lot of debt compared to its assets. This may make getting additional credit more difficult or more expensive. A low debt ratio means a company is not carrying a lot of debt compared to its assets. Companies with low debt ratios have lower financial risks.

Countryside Corporate **Balance Sheet** **December 31, 20--**		
ASSETS		
Cash	$36,000	
Accounts Receivable	22,000	
Equipment	15,000	
Total Assets		$73,000
LIABILITIES		
Accounts Payable	$24,000	
Notes Payable	18,000	
Total Liabilities		$42,000
OWNERS' EQUITY		
Capital		31,000
Total Liabilities and Owner's Equity		$73,000

Goodheart-Willcox Publisher

Figure 11-3 A balance sheet reports the assets, liabilities, and owner's equity of a business.

Profitability Ratios

Profitability ratios are an important indicator of progress. The higher the profitability ratio, the more sales dollars end up as profit. Profitability differs widely from industry to industry but for most, it is between 4 and 5 percent.

If management thinks their profitability is too low, they look for ways to improve it. Possible ways include expanding the product line, cutting unnecessary expenses, and increasing overall sales.

Profit margin ratios include the net profit ratio and the operating ratio. This information comes from the income statement, shown in Figure 11-4.

Net Profit Ratio. A **net profit ratio** illustrates profit generated per dollar of sales. The formula for finding a net profit ratio follows.

net income ÷ sales = net profit ratio
$35,000 ÷ $68,000 = .51:1

This ratio shows that for every dollar of sales, the business is producing 51 cents in profit. This ratio of 51 cents is above average.

Operating Ratio. Comparing expenses to sales is another important ratio. An **operating ratio** shows the relationship of expenses to sales.

expenses ÷ sales = operating ratio
$33,000 ÷ $68,000 = .49:1

This ratio shows that for every dollar of sales, 49 cents goes toward expenses.

Budget Analysis

Another type of financial control used by organizations is budget analysis. A *budget* is a financial plan that reflects anticipated revenues and how it will be allocated in the operation of the business. A budget is often used during planning as a way to allocate resources. It is a forecast that enables management to meet objectives, plan for growth, and use in the control function for evaluation purposes. A budget provides measurable data to compare to the actual company financial statements at the end of the period. This enables managers to evaluate performance and how well they managed finances.

Countryside Corporate
Income Statement
For Year End December 31, 20--

Revenue		
Sales		$68,000
Operating Expenses		
Advertising Expense	$ 5,000	
Rent Expense	20,000	
Insurance Expense	6,000	
Supplies Expense	200	
Utilities Expense	1,800	
Total Expenses		33,000
Net Income		$35,000

Goodheart-Willcox Publisher

Figure 11-4 An income statement reports the revenue and expenses of a business for a specific period of time and shows a net income or net loss.

You Do the Math

Numeric Reasoning: Multiplication

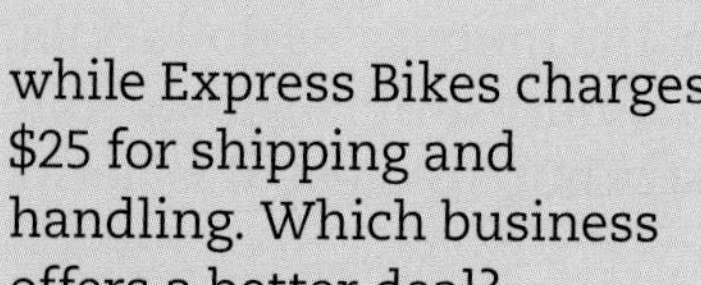

In multiplication, the number that is going to be multiplied by another number is called the *multiplicand*. The number by which the multiplicand is multiplied is called the *multiplier*. To multiply whole numbers and decimals, place the numbers, called *factors*, in pairs in a vertical list.

Solve the following problems.

1. The marketing manager of a bicycle manufacturer, Sunbeam Cycles, is creating a competitive analysis. The manager is comparing Sunbeam's prices to an online competitor, Express Bikes. Sunbeam Cycles has a popular model available for $265. A similar model is on sale at Express Bikes for 15 percent less. The sales tax rate for both is 6 percent. Sunbeam Cycles ships its products free, while Express Bikes charges $25 for shipping and handling. Which business offers a better deal?
2. An electronics retailer is evaluating its competition and has recorded the following information. Store A has 36" televisions on sale at two for $550. Store B has them on sale for 25 percent off their normal price of $350 each. Store C is running a promotion in which one free television is given for each television purchased at the regular price of $500.
   A. How much does one television cost at each store?
   B. Which store has the lowest price for one television?
   C. Which store charges the highest price for one television?

For example, a *budgeted income statement* is compared to the *actual income statement* at the end of the period. Managers can compare their forecasts to the actual results. It is especially important to forecast revenue and expenses in an accurate manner as they directly influence profit for the business.

LO 11.2-4 Information Technology Control

Chapter 4 introduced the importance of information housed in the management information systems of a business. *Information technology (IT) control* is the procedures an organization follows to ensure information technology is used as intended, data is accurate, and information is in legal compliance.

Most organizations use a Management Information System that facilitates these procedures. A *Management Information System (MIS)* is an integrated system of computer hardware and software that gathers information and presents it for use in the decision-making process. In order to have an effective MIS, organizations must address many security issues. Two particular areas of importance are data security and cybersecurity.

ra2studio/Shutterstock.com

Cybersecurity is protecting an information system against unintended or malicious changes or use. **What are examples of damages a company can incur as a result of a cyberattack?**

Data Security

Entering information accurately and securely is of crucial importance to an organization. **Data security** is the measures used to protect the privacy and prevent unauthorized access to the computers, databases, and websites of a business. Doing so protects data from being corrupted or stolen. Data security also protects a business from being a victim of a cyberattack. A **cyberattack** is an attempt to steal, damage, or destroy data or a computer system.

Data-security measures ensure the data used by a company is of acceptable quality and available only to those who need it. There are multiple practices for assuring data security in an organization. An important security practice is backing up information. Some organizations store information on a server at the business locations with a back-up server off-site. The cloud is a common choice for a secure off-site method for storing information.

Another data-security practice is restricting employee access to information systems. Only designated employees should have permission to input information. Information entered by those without permission can corrupt or crash the system.

In addition, the output of data must be protected. Only employees who have clearance should be able to extract company information. Reports accessed by those who do not have clearance can create a risky situation. Sensitive information in the hands of the wrong people could jeopardize a business.

Cybersecurity

Information systems must be protected from outside threats. **Cybersecurity** is protecting an information system against unintended or malicious changes or use. Cybersecurity issues include attacks on phone systems, computer viruses, data theft, malware, and computer hacks.

Corporations are at high risk for cybersecurity attacks. Many organizations send their management teams for training so they can be proactive in protecting company data.

Section 11.2 Review

Check Your Understanding

1. What do managers evaluate through the control process?
2. List three organizational controls used by managers.
3. Briefly explain financial statement analysis and its use by managers.
4. List examples of financial ratios used to review the overall financial condition of a business.
5. What can happen if people without clearance access information crucial to an organization?

Build Your Vocabulary

As you progress through this text, develop a personal glossary of key terms. This will help you build your vocabulary and prepare you for a career. Write a definition for each of the following terms and add them to your personal glossary.

feedforward control
concurrent control
cyberloafing
feedback control
financial control
financial statement analysis
ratio
ratio analysis
financial ratio
current ratio
debt ratio
net profit ratio
operating ratio
data security
cyberattack
cybersecurity

Chapter 11 Review and Assessment

Chapter Summary

Section 11.1 Importance of Control

LO 11.1-1 **Summarize the controlling function of management.**
The controlling function is the continuous process of comparing actual outcomes with planned outcomes and taking corrective actions when goals are not met. Controlling attempts to keep an organization on track by providing the means to monitor the performance of individuals, divisions, departments, and the organization as a whole.

LO 11.1-2 **Identify examples of standards set in the controlling function.**
Examples of standards set in the controlling process are time, quantity, cost, and quality standards.

LO 11.1-3 **Discuss measuring performance against standards.**
A variance is the difference between the standard and the actual performance. Variances of time, quantity, cost, and quality are used to measure performance. In addition, using observations and reports can help a business measure its performance and compare outcomes to the standards set.

LO 11.1-4 **Identify actions taken by management when performance standards are not met.**
Actions taken by management when performance standards are not met include revising the standards and adjusting performance.

Section 11.2 Organizational Control

LO 11.2-1 **Discuss organizational performance.**
Organizational performance is the result of all the activities that transpire in a business to reach a desired outcome. Organizational performance standards are used to measure how efficient, effective, and productive an organization has been for the period. The control process helps identify behaviors that resulted in positive performance and the ones that were not effective.

LO 11.2-2 **Define types of organizational controls.**
Types of organizational controls include feedforward control, concurrent control, and feedback control. Feedforward control involves anticipating potential problems before an activity starts. Concurrent control focuses on identifying and correcting problems that may occur while an activity is in progress. Feedback control is a management technique in which control happens after the activity is completed.

LO 11.2-3 **Identify examples of financial controls used to measure financial performance.**
One example of a financial control includes financial ratios, which includes current ratio, debt ratio, and profitability ratio. Another example is a budget analysis.

LO 11.2-4 **Summarize information technology control.**
Information technology (IT) control is the procedures an organization follows to ensure information technology is used as intended, data is accurate, and information is in legal compliance. Most organizations use a Management Information System (MIS) that facilitates these procedures. Two particular areas of importance in IT control are data security and cybersecurity.

Review Your Knowledge

1. Summarize the controlling function of management.
2. Explain the importance of managing for productivity and growth.
3. Identify and explain examples of standards used in the controlling process.
4. Discuss measuring performance against standards.
5. Identify actions taken by management when performance standards are not met.
6. Discuss organizational performance.
7. Define three types of organizational control.
8. How is information on financial statements used and interpreted for managerial decision-making?
9. Identify and explain examples of financial controls used to measure financial performance.
10. Summarize information technology control.

Apply Your Knowledge

1. The functions of management are planning, organizing, staffing, leading, and controlling. Explain how you think controlling relates to each of the other functions of management.
2. Controls can assist employees and encourage them to accomplish their jobs. However, some controls can reduce employee performance. Create a two-column chart. In column one, list actions a manager could take to encourage employees. In column two, list actions a manager could take that might discourage employees.
3. Identify a time when you set an action or task that you wanted to accomplish. It can be preparing for a final exam or getting a part-time job. Using the steps of the control process, examine how you set standards, measured your performance, and what actions you took to adjust any inadequacies.
4. Internal standards are ones the company has written for its specific business. Consider a business with which you are familiar, such as a grocery store or gas station. Write several standards you think a similar business would set for itself.
5. A time standard is an estimated or predetermined amount of time it should take to complete a single task or activity. List several industries that you think use time standards. Create an example of a possible time standard that might be set for use in that industry.
6. A quantity standard is a predetermined or estimated quantity of work to be completed in a specified time. How do you think quantity standards can help a business stay profitable?
7. A cost standard is an estimated or predetermined cost to produce a good, create a service, or perform an activity. What are some possible consequences of a business routinely breaking cost standards?
8. A quality standard is an established level of acceptability for the production of goods and services. What kind of quality standards do you think a company such as Apple has set for itself?
9. Some organizations store data at off-site locations, such as an off-site server or a cloud server. Why would an organization want to use off-site storage for its data?
10. Cyberattacks are reported each day in the news, and the damage that organizations face can be damaging to business. Summarize what you know about cybersecurity based on what you have heard from others and in the news.

Communication Skills

College and Career Readiness

Speaking. Select three of your classmates to join a formal discussion panel. Assign each person a specific role, such as leader, timekeeper, or recorder. Hold a panel discussion on the pros and cons of teens being allowed to drive at age 16. The leader should keep the panel on task and encourage fair discussion. The recorder should make notes of the information discussed. Afterward, hold an informal discussion to decide the most important information to include in the notes. Create a final document of the discussion notes to distribute to the class.

Writing. *Figurative language* is a word or phrase used in a way that is different from its normal or literal meaning. Figurative language makes the idea more interesting to the reader. An example is to say snow is a "clean, white blanket." The literal translation would be, "snow is on the ground." Select a section of this chapter and rewrite selected paragraphs in your own words. Highlight the sentences in which you used figurative language.

Reading. A *prefix* is added to the beginning of a word to create a new meaning. A *suffix* is added to the end of an existing word to create a new meaning. *Affix* means to add a prefix or suffix to a root word. Locate three words in this chapter that have a prefix or suffix. Determine the meaning of the prefix and suffix, and then the meaning of the whole word. Look for clues in the surrounding text to help you understand what the word means.

Internet Research

Analyzing Data. Using the Internet, search for financial statements for a business, such as Target or JC Penney. Analyze and interpret the data that appears in the financial statements that could be used for managerial decision-making. Calculate information such as ratios and breakeven analysis. What did you learn from this exercise?

Data Security. Data security measures protect an organization's data from being corrupted or stolen. There are multiple practices for assuring data security in an organization. Use the Internet to conduct a search for *data security practices*. List specific measures or practices a business can adopt to help keep its data secure.

Cybersecurity. Cyber threats are a major security concern for businesses both in the United States and around the world. Search for *cybersecurity threats*. Review the web pages that appear in your search results. Summarize your findings.

Teamwork

There are five components of internal control that are used by management. They are control the environment, be prepared for risk, control activities of the business, be communicative with the employees, and set monitoring standards. Together with your team, create a poster or another type of visual display that illustrates these five primary controls.

Portfolio Development

Writing Samples. As you collect academic samples to include in your portfolio, you may want to emphasize samples of your best writing. Writing skills are necessary for success in every part of life including academics and career. Regardless of occupation, industry, or position, at some point, every job will require written communication. Even jobs that are not done on a computer require writing skills. For example, an automotive mechanic or welder will undoubtedly have to write or summarize the scope of work for a given job. It is important to demonstrate your ability to communicate ideas and information through the written word.

As you review documents, collect those that highlight your writing skills. Select items you have written, such as essays, stories, or poems. Each person is different in terms of writing styles. Some can be as unique as a fingerprint. Focus on selecting items that not only positively demonstrate your writing abilities but also provide a glimpse of your signature writing style.

1. Select writing examples that demonstrate your writing style. Be critical and choose your best creative writing sample, an article you have written for the school newspaper, or other documents of which you are proud.
2. For each document, attach a note that (1) describes what the sample is and (2) states why it is included in your portfolio. For example, a note on an article you wrote for the school newspaper might say, "Example of journalistic and investigative reporting skills."
3. Update your master portfolio spreadsheet to include your academic work samples.

CTSOs

Written Events. Many competitive events for CTSOs require students to write a paper and submit it either before the competition or after the student has arrived at the event. Written events can be lengthy and take a lot of time to prepare, so it is important to start early.

To prepare for a written event, complete the following activities.

1. Visit the website of your organization and select a written event in which you might be interested. The research topic will be specified in detail.
2. Read the guidelines provided by the organization. All final-format guidelines, including how to organize and submit the paper, will be provided. Make certain you ask questions about any points you do not understand. Create a checklist of guidelines that you must follow for this event.
3. Research the topic and then complete an outline. Conduct your research early. Research may take days or weeks, and you do not want to rush the process. If you are still interested, move forward and start the writing process.
4. Set a deadline for yourself that allows you to write at a comfortable pace.
5. After you write the first draft, ask an instructor to review it and provide feedback for revision. Repeat this step as necessary until you have a final version of your paper.
6. Once you have the final version, review the checklist for the event to make sure you have covered all of the details. Your score will be penalized if you do not follow instructions.

CHAPTER 12

Operations Management

Sections

12.1 Role of Operations

12.2 Quality

Reading Prep

Special features focus on topics of interest related to the material presented in the content. Before reading this chapter, preview the special features so you can relate the information to the main text as you read.

Exploring Careers

Operations Manager

Operations managers are responsible for planning, directing, and coordinating the operations that convert resources into finished products. They oversee production, monitor and analyze an organization's current production system, and check the system's efficiency. Part of the job responsibilities include managing the supply chain and resources to maximize efficiency and minimize cost. While performing their duties, operations managers must also ensure that all operations comply with safety and environmental regulations.

Typical job titles for this position include *facility manager*, *operations supervisor*, and *operations director*. Examples of tasks that operations managers perform include:

- formulating policies;
- managing daily operations and quality assurance of products;
- planning the use of materials and human resources; and
- monitoring and managing operation costs by reviewing financial statements or other performance data.

Operations managers typically require a bachelor degree in operations or a field related to business administration, management, accounting as well as prior work experience. Some companies may require a master degree. Operations managers must have managerial, interpersonal, monitoring, and leadership skills as well as a focus on quality.

NicoElNino/Shutterstock.com

Section 12.1 Role of Operations

Why is operations management important for all businesses?

Learning Objectives

LO 12.1-1 Summarize operations management.
LO 12.1-2 Discuss job responsibilities of an operations manager.
LO 12.1-3 Explain inventory management.
LO 12.1-4 Recognize benefits of effective operations management.

Key Terms

- operations management
- production process
- manufacturing operations
- supply chain
- service operations
- operations manager
- sourcing
- quality characteristic
- quality control
- inventory
- inventory management
- raw materials inventory
- work in process inventory
- finished goods inventory
- perpetual inventory system
- just-in-time (JIT) inventory-control system
- distribution

LO 12.1-1 Operations Management

Operations are the activities of an organization that transforms resources into goods and services with a focus on quality. Goods are tangible items, and services are tasks or activities provided for a fee. Collectively, goods and services are called *products.*

Operations management is an area of management that focuses on the production of goods and services. *Production* is activity related to creating a product. The **production process** is all the activities required to create a product.

A major component of production involves a transformation process. The *transformation process* takes inputs and transforms them into outputs, as illustrated in Figure 12-1. *Inputs* are resources of labor, equipment, technology, materials, and information. *Outputs* are the finished goods and services produced. The transformation process is applied by both manufacturing and service businesses.

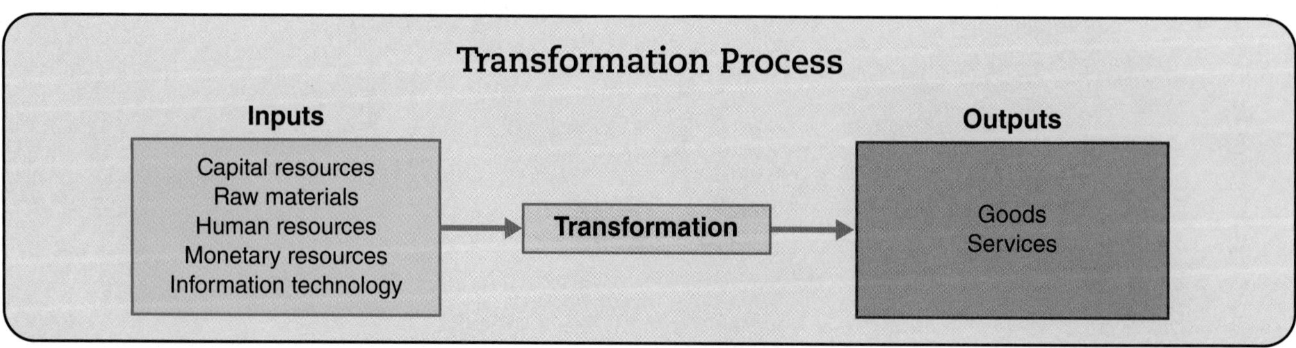

Goodheart-Willcox Publisher

Figure 12-1 The transformation process takes inputs and transforms them into outputs.

Kodda/Shutterstock.com

Service operations are all the activities involved in delivering a service to a customer, such as transportation. **What activities do you think make up service operations for a company, such as a taxi business?**

Manufacturing Businesses

A *manufacturer* is a producer that uses raw materials from other producers to convert into finished products. An example of a manufacturing business is an automobile producer, such as General Motors or Ford.

Critical to manufacturing are resources of raw materials, labor, and overhead costs of the production process. With the use of resources, manufacturers transform materials into finished goods, such as cell phones and clothing.

Manufacturing operations are all the activities involved in operating a manufacturing facility, often a factory. Examples include receiving raw materials into stock and using machinery to produce goods. These activities make it possible for the transformation process to happen.

Manufacturing is important because it creates form utility. *Utility* is the characteristics of a product that satisfy a want or need. *Form utility* is the value, or usefulness, of a finished product. It is the difference between the inputs and outputs of the transformation process.

Manufacturers are a part of the supply chain. The **supply chain** is the businesses, people, and activities involved in turning raw materials into products and delivering them to end users. A manufacturer is at the beginning of that chain as the producer of products. Manufacturers typically do not sell directly to the end user, but instead sell to wholesalers. A *wholesaler* is a business that purchases large amounts of goods directly from manufacturers and sells to retailers.

Service Businesses

Output is not always as clear for service businesses as it is for manufacturing businesses. Manufacturing businesses produce goods that are tangible, which means goods exist physically and can be touched. A service business provides services. A service is intangible, meaning it is not physical, and cannot be touched.

A *service business* earns profits by providing consumers with services that meet their needs and wants. **Service operations** are all the activities involved in delivering a service to a customer. Its output is the action or task offered for sale. Service businesses are also a part of the supply chain. However, they generally sell directly to the end user. An example of a service business is Uber that offers transportation to its customers.

LO 12.1-2 Operations Manager

An **operations manager** is the person who is responsible for overseeing the production of goods and services for an organization. This person's primary role is to guide decision-making for all aspects of operations as well as plan and control the processes. The tasks performed are extensive and include planning, identifying resources, scheduling, and overseeing quality control.

Ethics

Sourcing Operations

Ethical managers purchase raw materials or goods from reputable suppliers whose products are created sustainably and in safe conditions. Factories in which products are created should be clean and safe for all employees. Manufacturers in other countries may have different work-safety standards than those established in the United States. It is unethical to purchase products that are made cheaply at the expense of someone's health or well-being.

Planning

Similar to other managers in an organization, operations managers perform the functions of management, which are planning, organizing, staffing, leading, and controlling. Planning is an important management function that is necessary to determine resources needed for production. It requires determining how the short-term and long-term goals stated in the business plan will be met.

Resources

The planning process helps identify resources required for production. Examples of resources include labor, physical location, equipment, and raw materials. *Business purchasing* is the activity of acquiring materials, supplies, or services necessary to create a product.

Sourcing is finding suppliers of materials needed for production. A *supplier*, or *vendor*, is a business that sells materials, supplies, or services to an organization that creates products. For example, items such as cardboard boxes are needed for packing goods. Vendors must be sourced from which to buy those supplies.

Scheduling

Scheduling personnel, shipments, and many other items are key to business operation. For example, manufacturing businesses must have enough raw materials on hand to meet production requirements. A shortage of raw materials will slow down the production process. An excessive amount of raw materials could potentially go to waste and have a harmful impact on profits. In addition, an adequate number of employees must be hired and scheduled to work. Too few employees will result in a shortage in production. Too many employees will cause an unnecessary increase in the cost of labor.

Different types of scheduling techniques are used to monitor processes. One example is a Gantt chart. A *Gantt chart* is a type of bar chart used to show when a task should be completed and compares it to the actual completion of the task. Using this tool helps a manager evaluate if a job is on schedule or behind schedule. An example of a Gantt chart is shown in Figure 12-2.

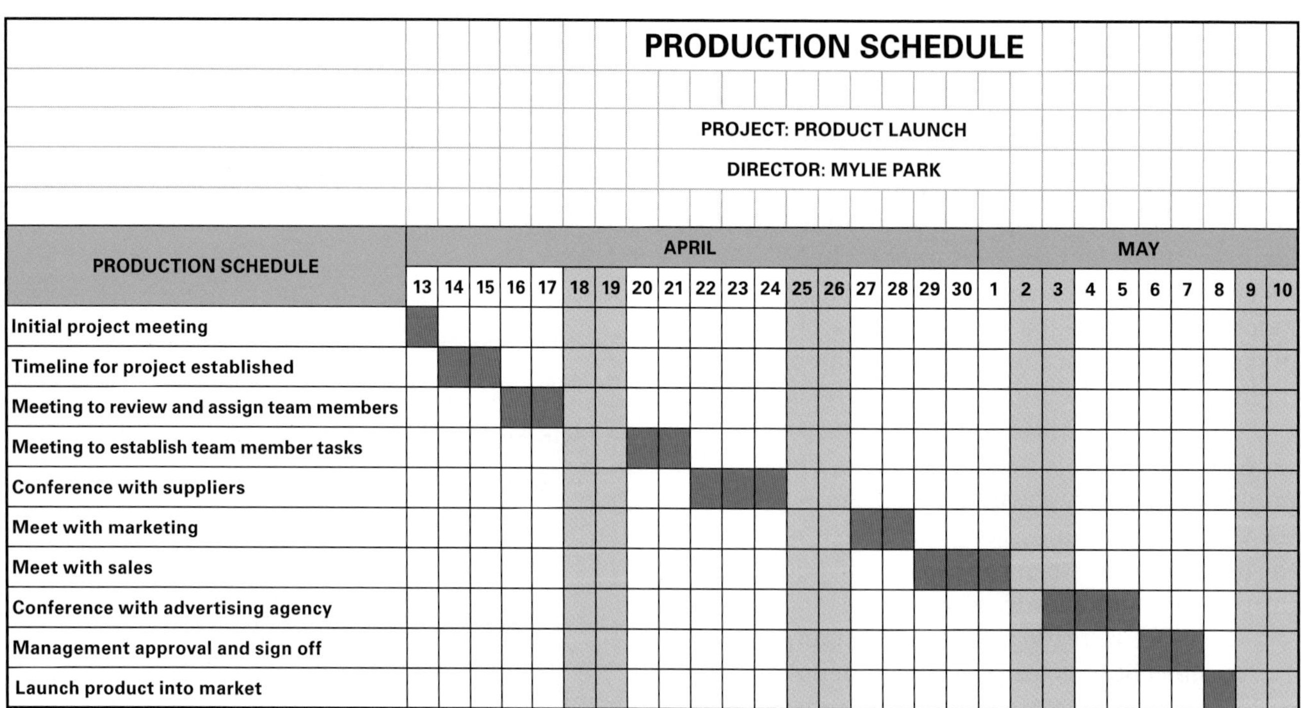

Goodheart-Willcox Publisher

Figure 12-2 A Gantt chart is an example of a scheduling technique used to monitor processes.

You Do the Math

Statistical Reasoning: Qualitative and Quantitative Data

Qualitative data includes items that can be observed, but not measured. Smell, taste, color, appearance, and texture are examples of qualitative data. On the other hand, *quantitative* data includes items that can be measured. Distance, weight, cost, speed, and temperature are examples of quantitative data.

Solve the following problems.

1. The catalog description of a product is as follows: attractive, blue model has a smooth finish, is 5 inches wide, and weighs 14 ounces. List the qualitative data and quantitative data in this description.
2. A business describes its customer-service team as follows: a staff of 17 well-trained and helpful representatives, which includes five certified technicians and two master technicians. List the qualitative data and quantitative data in this description.

Quality Control

Quality is an indicator of a product's excellence. A **quality characteristic** is something that makes an item distinctive. Examples of quality characteristics are shown in Figure 12-3. For example, a quality characteristic of a glass bottle is that it is scratch resistant.

A quality characteristic is an item on a checklist used when performing quality control. **Quality control** is the activity of checking raw materials received or products produced to ensure the quality meets expectations. Checking products for damages, shortages, and overages is an important part of the production process for which a manager is responsible.

Quality control may involve visual inspection or physical testing. It takes place from the time raw materials are received to when the finished goods are completed. Quality control is important for building a strong business that can deliver products that meet or exceed end-user expectations. In addition, it ensures products are sold at the most reasonable prices.

Quality Characteristics	
• Performance	• Durability
• Features	• Serviceability
• Reliability	• Aesthetics
• Conformance	• Perception

Goodheart-Willcox Publisher

Figure 12-3 A quality characteristic is something that makes an item distinctive.

A business that sells a poorly manufactured good or delivered service risks reducing the value of its brand. A *brand* is the name, term, or design that sets a business or product apart from the competition. A brand includes unique design, customer service, product reliability, and customer satisfaction. It creates an *image*, which is the idea that people have of a business. The image of a business can be positive if it has strong and reliable products. It can also be negative from poorly designed products.

LO 12.1-3 Inventory Management

In addition to planning, identifying resources, scheduling, and overseeing quality control, an operations manager is responsible for overseeing inventory. **Inventory** is the assortment or selection of items a business has on hand at a particular point in time. **Inventory management** is the area of management involved in ordering items, receiving them on arrival, and paying vendors. It also includes managing the costs of shipping, storage, and other activities to keep inventory-related costs low.

mavo/Shutterstock.com

Inventory is the assortment or selection of items a business has on hand at a particular point in time. **Why do you think it is necessary to have a specific person in charge of monitoring inventory?**

Types of Inventory

As shown in Figure 12-4, manufacturers have three types of manufacturing inventory: raw materials, work in process, and finished goods.

- **Raw materials inventory** is the selection of raw materials needed to produce a finished product. This inventory is the materials that are part of the production process but have not yet been put in use.
- **Work in process inventory** consists of products that are partially completed. This is the inventory moving through the production process and in various stages of completion.
- **Finished goods inventory** is the assortment or selection of finished products for sale that a business has in stock. These items move through the supply chain. The manufacturer sells to wholesalers, who sell to retailers, who sell to the end user.

Inventory Control

Maintaining accurate amounts of raw materials inventory is important to keep production on schedule. Without raw materials, the transformation process cannot happen. A **perpetual inventory system** is a method of tracking inventory that shows the quantity on hand at all times. This system tracks each item when it is received, placed in inventory, and removed from inventory. An operations manager can check inventory levels at any time for an accurate count of items available.

Production managers have a fiscal responsibility for managing and controlling inventory. *Fiscal* means related to generating revenue. Running short of raw materials inventory holds up production. This could have a direct impact on profits if a finished good is not delivered for sale. Finished goods are the source of revenue for a manufacturing business. Without finished goods to sell, there are no profits.

Too much inventory can be detrimental to profits. If products cannot be sold, they could ruin, become out of date, or not sell for other reasons. This decreases revenue for a business.

Controls must be in place to make sure inventories are at appropriate levels. In addition, levels of finished goods inventory are monitored for accuracy.

Raw Materials Strategy

The **just-in-time (JIT) inventory-control system** is a strategy of managing inventory that keeps a minimal amount of raw materials on hand to meet production needs. In a JIT system, raw materials are received *just in time* for the production needs of the day. Manufacturing companies that use JIT systems aim to operate with a minimum amount of raw materials in storage. The goal is to receive raw materials right before they are needed in the production process.

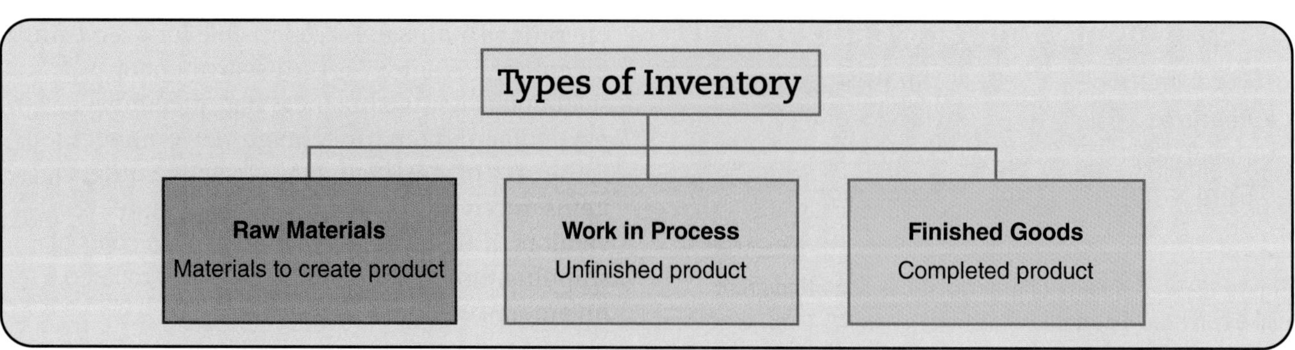

Goodheart-Willcox Publisher

Figure 12-4 Manufacturers have three types of manufacturing inventory.

Advantages of using a JIT system include increased efficiency, reduced waste and storage space, and increased cash available for other purposes. A disadvantage of using a JIT system occurs when production or delivery is timed incorrectly. If raw materials are late in arriving, a manufacturing production line may be forced to shut down until materials arrive. JIT systems can be difficult to implement because many suppliers cannot meet demands for frequent deliveries.

Employability Skills

Positive Attitude

Professionals exhibit a positive attitude in their job performance and workplace interactions. *Attitude* is how personal thoughts or feelings affect a person's outward behavior. It is a combination of how you feel, what you think, and what you do. Attitude is how an individual sees himself or herself as well as how he or she perceives others.

LO 12.1-4 Benefits of Effective Operations Management

The major goal of operations management is to assure the production of goods and services meet quality standards, produced at the lowest possible cost, and stay on schedule. Benefits of effective operations management include:

- increased employee productivity;
- finished goods;
- improved quality;
- accurate distribution;
- increased flexibility to meet customer needs; and
- increased profitability.

Increased Employee Productivity

Effective management results in productivity. *Productivity* is the amount of output employees produce in a specified period of time. The fewer inputs it takes to produce a good or service, the greater the productivity. Increased productivity results in lower costs and increased profits. Productivity also plays a major role in the ability of a business to stay competitive in an expanding global economy. Operations managers study goals and develop the most efficient ways to achieve them. They also monitor production processes to minimize waste, eliminate production errors, and re-work costs.

Finished Goods

Efficient operations management results in a more-accurate inventory of finished goods. When a manager successfully plans for production and monitors the outcome, a more-accurate level of finished goods are available for sale.

Travel mania/Shutterstock.com

Distribution involves determining when, where, and how products progress through the supply chain. **What importance does the supply chain play in distribution?**

Improved Quality

Effective operations managers add value to a business's goods and services by focusing on quality control and improvement at every phase of production. The efficient production of quality goods and services without wasting the business's resources results in competitively priced outputs.

Accurate Distribution

Distribution refers to the activities involved in getting a good or service to the end user. It is also known as *place*. Distribution involves determining when, where, and how products progress through the supply chain. A benefit of effective operations management in manufacturing is the reliable delivery of goods and services to the wholesaler or end user.

Increased Flexibility

Increased flexibility to meet customer needs is a benefit of operations management. Customer needs and wants are constantly changing. Businesses must be flexible and ready to adapt to evolving operating environments and changing market conditions. Effective operations managers stay current on the latest:

- production techniques;
- software applications;
- laws and pending legislation;
- market conditions; and
- customer preferences.

Companies that are not able to determine market trends and quickly adapt to changing conditions often fall behind competitors, and many do not survive.

Increased Profitability

One of the main objectives of operations management is to reduce costs while maintaining or improving product quality. For each dollar decrease in costs, profits rise by the same amount. Through cost monitoring and increased productivity, production managers are able to reduce costs, and thereby increase profit.

Section 12.1 Review

Check Your Understanding

1. What is the transformation process?
2. Explain service operations.
3. Explain the importance of quality control.
4. Discuss just-in-time (JIT) inventory-control system.
5. List examples of benefits gained from effective operations management.

Build Your Vocabulary

As you progress through this text, develop a personal glossary of key terms. This will help you build your vocabulary and prepare you for a career. Write a definition for each of the following terms and add them to your personal glossary.

operations management
production process
manufacturing operations
supply chain
service operations
operations manager
sourcing
quality characteristic
quality control
inventory
inventory management
raw materials inventory
work in process inventory
finished goods inventory
perpetual inventory system
just-in-time (JIT) inventory-control system
distribution

Section 12.2 Quality

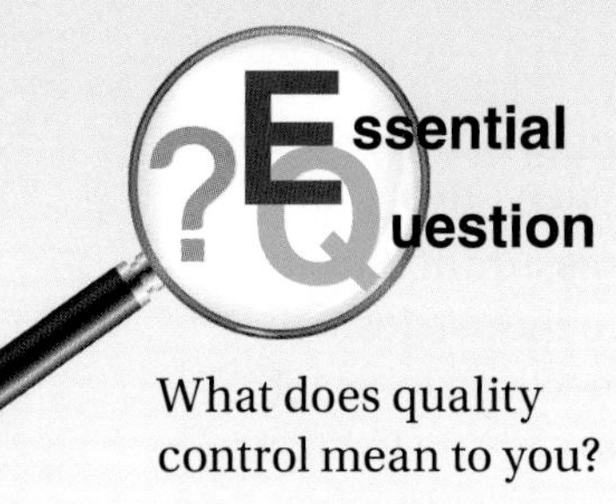

What does quality control mean to you?

Learning Objectives

LO 12.2-1 Explain quality management.
LO 12.2-2 Discuss ISO Quality Management standards.
LO 12.2-3 Summarize quality improvement.
LO 12.2-4 Recognize two major awards for quality.

Key Terms 

quality management
continuous improvement plan
International Organization for Standardization (ISO)
ISO 9000
ISO 14000
Six Sigma
lean manufacturing
Malcolm Baldrige National Quality Award (MBNQA)
Deming Prize

LO 12.2-1 Quality Management

Quality management is a formal system that documents each step of processes and procedures to achieve company goals and standards. Quality-management systems help an organization be efficient, lower costs, encourage employee engagement, and operate in a strategic manner.

Total quality management (TQM) is a management philosophy in which the success of an organization is directly related to customer satisfaction. The goal of TQM is to have all members of an organization committed to improving processes, improving quality of products, and reducing waste. TQM integrates customer satisfaction into every part of business operations through customer focus, continuous improvement, and teamwork.

Customer Focus

Organizations have two classifications of customers. External customers are organizations or individuals with whom business is conducted. Internal customers are the employees of the company. *Customer focus* means that the entire business, at all levels, is directed to meet the needs of all customers.

Continuous Improvement

Continuous improvement is an ongoing effort to increase the quality of goods and services by constantly reviewing and updating the production process. A **continuous improvement plan** is a set of activities designed to enhance the production process through constant review and product testing. Common aspects of a continuous improvement plan include:

- making quality decisions based on measurements, not personal judgments;
- monitoring activities related to the manufacturing processes for continuous improvements;
- creating a culture of cooperation among employees who aim to improve quality; and
- increasing employee involvement in identifying quality-related issues.

Through continuous improvement, companies are able to find effective and efficient ways to improve products to meet customer needs.

Teamwork

A *team* consists of two or more people working together to achieve a common goal. Teamwork is an essential part of TQM because the business as a whole produces goods or services.

Nestor Rizhniak/Shutterstock.com

Continuous improvement is an ongoing effort to increase the quality of goods and services by constantly reviewing and updating the production process. **Why is it important for a business to continuously improve the goods or services it offers?**

Teamwork means that every employee, department, and division of the company must work together to improve product quality and customer satisfaction.

LO 12.2-2 ISO Quality Management Standards

Quality management requires that processes and standards be created so results can be measured. Through the implementation of standards, an organization can ensure customer needs are met as well as the organization's requirements for profits and growth.

The **International Organization for Standardization (ISO)** is a worldwide network composed of members from 162 countries that develops and publishes international standards. The ISO Quality Management standards are some of the most recognized standards in the world. These standards provide guidelines to ensure goods and services meet the purposes for which they are produced.

To date, ISO has published in excess of 22,000 International Standards that cover almost every industry. This includes technology, food safety, health care, and many others. ISO Standards ensure goods and services are safe, reliable, and of good quality.

ISO certification is voluntary. However, many countries and companies now require ISO certification before they will conduct business with an organization. Well-known ISO Standards include ISO 9000 and ISO 14000.

ISO 9000

ISO 9000 is a series, or group, of international quality standards that define, establish, and maintain an effective quality assurance system for manufacturing and service industries. The standards provide guidance and tools for companies and organizations wishing to ensure their products and services consistently meet quality standards and customer expectations.

ISO 14000

ISO 14000 is a series of international standards designed to promote effective environmental management systems in organizations, regardless of size or industry. The ISO 14000 standards address environmental aspects of quality management in both the public-sector and private-sector organizations. The standards provide planning tools that help organizations make use of best-practices methods for environmental management.

LO 12.2-3 Quality Improvement

Organizations must provide value and quality in their goods and services in order to be attractive to customers. *Value* is the relative worth of something. *Quality* is an indicator of a product's excellence. If a good or service does not provide value and quality to customers, they will not buy it. Businesses must constantly work to improve the value and quality of their products to stay in business.

Quality improvement is the goal of most organizations. The resources coming into the manufacturing process, such as raw materials, must be controlled. In addition, internal resources, such as employees, must be controlled. To achieve this result, various techniques can be used. Two well-known quality-improvement techniques are Six Sigma and lean manufacturing.

Six Sigma

Six Sigma is a trademarked quality-improvement program that uses a set of tools designed to improve business processes by finding and eliminating errors that lead to defects in a product. To reduce errors, Six Sigma uses statistical analysis, rather than trial and error, in the production and delivery of a good or service. Reductions in errors mean less re-work and a reduction in costs. This, in turn, leads to a more efficient and profitable operation.

Six Sigma is based on a five-step approach to problem solving called DMAIC, which stands for:

- **define** the problem and the project goals;
- **measure** precisely the various aspects of the current process;
- **analyze** data to find defects in the process;
- **improve** the process; and
- **control** the process.

Six Sigma was first introduced in 1986 by engineer Bill Smith while he was working at Motorola. In 1995, business executive and chemical engineer Jack Welch made Six Sigma a primary business strategy at General Electric.

A formal certification program is offered for Six Sigma. There are various levels of Six Sigma certification, as shown in Figure 12-5.

Petr Vaclavek/Shutterstock.com

Six Sigma is a trademarked quality-improvement program that uses a set of tools designed to improve business processes by finding and eliminating errors that lead to defects in a product. **Why would a person in business work to earn Six Sigma certification?**

Six Sigma Certification	
Certification Name (Highest to Lowest)	**Certification Definition**
Master Black Belt	• Develops key project metrics and strategies • Acts as Six Sigma consultant • Trains and coaches black belts and green belts
Six Sigma Black Belt	• Leads projects • Coaches and supervises project members • Understands DMAIC problem solving model • Demonstrates leadership for DMAIC model
Six Sigma Green Belt	• Helps with statistical analysis • Leads projects when needed • Supports project improvements
Six Sigma Yellow Belt	• Possess foundational knowledge of Six Sigma • Participates as a project team member • Supports project improvements

Goodheart-Willcox Publisher

Figure 12-5 There are various levels of Six Sigma certification.

Lean Manufacturing

Lean manufacturing is a business practice that involves a continuous effort to reduce waste or any activity or practice that uses resources that do not add to the overall value of goods or services produced. It is also known as *lean production*. While Six Sigma focuses on *streamlining* and *improving processes* to reduce defects and waste, lean manufacturing focuses on *waste reduction*.

The practice of lean manufacturing involves analyzing tasks and processes and removing steps that do not add value to the goods or services produced. Examples include decreasing machine set-up times between processes, monitoring the amount of materials needed to reduce storage costs from excessive purchases, and matching qualified employees to tasks based on skill levels. Lean manufacturing involves manufacturing the appropriate amount of goods needed to meet customer demand. If too much is produced, inventory levels back up, storage costs rise, money is tied up, and the possibility of goods not being sold increases. If too little is produced, sales could be lost and customers could seek other sources of supply.

The lean manufacturing process involves three main steps:

- identifying waste and inefficient practices;
- analyzing the waste and inefficient practices to find the cause; and
- taking steps to eliminate the cause of identified waste and inefficient practices.

These steps are repeated during the design, production, and delivery of goods or services. Lean manufacturing increases revenue by producing a better-quality good or service more quickly and with fewer errors. In the final analysis, lean manufacturing does more with less.

LO 12.2-4 Quality Awards

Various governments grant annual quality awards to companies that have achieved high levels of TQM. The awards are part of a larger effort to make a country's businesses more competitive in international markets. Two major awards are the Malcolm Baldrige National Quality Award and the Deming Prize.

Malcolm Baldrige National Quality Award

The **Malcolm Baldrige National Quality Award (MBNQA)** is an award that raises awareness of quality management and recognizes US organizations that have implemented successful quality-management systems. It was established by the United States Congress in 1987. The award was named after Secretary of Commerce Malcolm Baldrige, who was an advocate of quality management.

The MBNQA is presented annually by the President of the United States to organizations that demonstrate quality and performance excellence.

Baldrige Criteria for Performance Excellence	
Leadership	How management leads an organization.
Strategy	How an organization creates and implements strategic plans.
Customers	How an organization establishes and maintains relationships with customers.
Measurement, Analysis, and Knowledge Management	How an organization uses its data to support processes and manage company performance.
Workforce	How an organization motivates its workforce.
Operations	How an organization designs and improves key operational processes.
Results	How an organization performs overall in the following areas: customer satisfaction, human resources, partner performance, finances, operations, governmental and social responsibility, and rank among competitors.

Goodheart-Willcox Publisher

Figure 12-6 Recipients of the Malcolm Baldrige National Quality Award (MBNQA) are judged on their achievement and improvement in seven areas known as the Baldrige Criteria for Performance Excellence.

Recipients of the award are judged on their achievement and improvement in seven areas known as the Baldrige Criteria for Performance Excellence, as shown in Figure 12-6. Awards are given in each of the following six categories:

- manufacturing;
- service company;
- small business;
- education;
- health care; and
- nonprofit.

Deming Prize

The **Deming Prize** is a Japanese award given to organizations that make the greatest strides in TQM. Established in 1951, the prize is named after Dr. W. Edwards Deming, who brought statistical quality-control methods to Japan after World War II. Awards are moderated by the Union of Japanese Scientists and Engineers (JUSE). The organization named the award after Deming to commemorate the relationship between them and as thanks for donating the royalties for his TQM lectures to the JUSE. Two categories of awards are made annually.

- The *Deming Prize for Individuals* is awarded to individuals who have made outstanding contributions to the study of TQM.
- The *Deming Prize* is awarded to public-sector and private-sector organizations that have implemented TQM systems suitable to their management philosophy and operation. Florida Power and Light and GC America are examples of American companies that have won the award.

Section 12.2 Review

Check Your Understanding

1. How does total quality management (TQM) integrate customer satisfaction into every part of business operations?
2. What do the ISO standards provide?
3. Describe the problem-solving approach on which Six Sigma is based.
4. State three main steps involved in the lean manufacturing process.
5. Name two major awards given for quality management.

Build Your Vocabulary

As you progress through this text, develop a personal glossary of key terms. This will help you build your vocabulary and prepare you for a career. Write a definition for each of the following terms and add them to your personal glossary.

quality management
continuous improvement plan
International Organization for Standardization (ISO)
ISO 9000
ISO 14000
Six Sigma
lean manufacturing
Malcolm Baldrige National Quality Award (MBNQA)
Deming Prize

Chapter 12 Review and Assessment

Chapter Summary

Section 12.1 Role of Operations

LO 12.1-1 **Summarize operations management.**
Operations management is an area of management that focuses on the production of goods and services. Production is activity related to creating a product. The production process is all the activities required to create a good or service. A major component of production involves a transformation process, which takes inputs and transforms them into outputs. It is applied by both manufacturing and service businesses.

LO 12.1-2 **Discuss job responsibilities of an operations manager.**
An operations manager's primary role is to guide decision-making for all aspects of operations as well as plan and control the processes. The tasks performed include planning, identifying resources, scheduling, and overseeing quality control.

LO 12.1-3 **Explain inventory management.**
Inventory management is the area of management involved in ordering items, receiving them on arrival, and paying vendors. It also includes managing the costs of shipping, storage, and other activities to keep inventory-related costs low.

LO 12.1-4 **Recognize benefits of effective operations management.**
Benefits of effective operations management include increased employee productivity, finished goods, improved quality, accurate distribution, increased flexibility to meet customer needs, and increased profitability.

Section 12.2 Quality

LO 12.2-1 **Explain quality management**
Quality management is a formal system that documents each step of processes and procedures to achieve company goals and standards. Quality-management systems help an organization be efficient, lower costs, encourage employee engagement, and operate in a strategic manner.

LO 12.2-2 **Discuss ISO Quality Management standards.**
The International Organization for Standardization (ISO) is a worldwide network composed of members from 162 countries that develops and publishes international standards. These standards provide guidelines to ensure goods and services meet the purposes for which they are produced, are safe, reliable, and of good quality. Well-known ISO Standards include ISO 9000 and ISO 14000.

LO 12.2-3 **Summarize quality improvement.**
Quality improvement is the goal of most organizations. The resources coming into the manufacturing process and internal resources must be controlled. Two well-known quality-improvement techniques are Six Sigma and lean manufacturing.

LO 12.2-4 **Recognize two major awards for quality.**
Two major awards given for quality management are the Malcolm Baldrige National Quality Award (MBNQA) and the Deming Prize.

Review Your Knowledge

1. Summarize operations management.
2. Explain the role that manufacturers play in the supply chain.
3. Discuss examples of job responsibilities an operation manager performs.
4. Explain inventory management.
5. Describe examples of benefits an organization can gain from effective operations management.
6. Explain quality management.
7. Define two ISO Quality Management standards.
8. Summarize quality improvement.
9. Briefly explain the Malcolm Baldrige National Quality Award (MBNQA).
10. What is the Deming Prize?

Apply Your Knowledge

1. The transformation process, when applied to manufacturing, takes raw materials and other inputs and turns them into outputs in the form of usable goods. Create a flowchart that illustrates how you think a simple finished good, such as a chair, undergoes the transformation process.
2. Critical to manufacturing operations are resources of raw materials, labor, and overhead cost of the production process. Create a flowchart and analyze each component of manufacturing operations.
3. A service business provides an action or task that satisfies the needs or wants of its customers. Name a service business that you or your family uses and describe the services it provides.
4. Discuss quality-related characteristics as you define it. Identify a product that you use frequently. Using the characteristics in Figure 12-3, define the quality-related characteristics as reflected in the product you chose.
5. Production managers are responsible for controlling the inventory of raw materials as well as the fiscal implications of too much or too little inventory. Fiscal means related to generating revenue. Use your own words to define inventory control in the context of management and fiscal responsibility.
6. Create a Gantt chart for a term paper or other extended assignment that you must complete. Assume the assignment must be completed in a four-week timeframe. Break down the steps needed to complete your assignment on a day-by-day or week-by-week basis.
7. *Continuous improvement* is an ongoing effort to increase the quality of goods and services by constantly reviewing and updating the production process. What techniques do you think an organization could apply to ensure that the company is always aiming for continuous improvement in its operations?
8. Why do you think many countries and companies require ISO certification of the other organizations with which they do business?
9. Six Sigma and lean manufacturing are techniques that can be implemented for quality improvement. Assume you are a manager of a manufacturing business. Explain which you would prefer to implement and why.
10. How do you think the governments that issue awards for manufacturing quality, such as the MBNQA and Deming Prize, benefit from issuing these awards?

Communication Skills

Writing. *Writing style* is the way in which a writer uses language to convey an idea. Select a page or pages of notes you have taken during a class. Evaluate your writing style and the relevance, quality, and depth of the information. What did you do well? What do you need to improve?

Speaking. Being able to *retell* or *summarize* what you read can help you confirm your understanding of the material and demonstrate that you comprehend the subject. Select a visual from this chapter such as a table, photo, or other illustration. Explain to the class what the visual means and how it relates to the chapter topic.

Reading. Reading word by word is slow, and it lessens both concentration and the ability to connect concepts to form meaning. Active readers read groups of words, or *phrases*, rather than individual words. Practice reading this chapter phrase by phrase, rather than word by word. How does this affect your understanding of the chapter?

Internet Research

Deming's 14 Points. Dr. William Edwards Deming developed 14 points for managers to view their roles in an organization in a new way. Research *Deming's 14 points*. Read the 14 points and summarize how they relate to total quality management (TQM).

Quality Awards. Using the Internet, research the *recent winner of the Malcolm Baldrige National Quality Award*. Then, research the *recent winner of the Deming Prize*. For each award, select an organization and critique how they represent the values of the award.

Teamwork

There are major factors considered in operations management, such as total quality management (TQM), lean manufacturing, and just-in-time inventory. Working with a team member, compare and contrast these three options. Record the information in either a chart, Venn diagram, or another form of visual display.

Portfolio Development

Transcripts. A *transcript* is an official academic record of the courses a student has completed, the school where the courses were taken, grades received, dates the courses were taken, and a cumulative grade point average (GPA). Including a transcript as part of your portfolio provides evidence of your scholastic achievements. Transcripts reflect academic successes and confirm the candidate's statements that courses of study have been completed as indicated on a résumé.

It is a given that universities will want to see your transcripts, but employers may also ask for a transcript at some point in the interviewing process. By including a copy in your portfolio, it shows organization and anticipation on the part of the candidate, which are signs of leadership.

When you contact your school for a copy of your transcript, you will likely be asked if you want an unofficial or official copy. An unofficial copy can generally be received by a student at no cost. For an official transcript, there may be a small fee requested. However, some schools may not release official transcripts to students. Each school has different guidelines regarding transcripts, so check with your advisor regarding transcript policies.

1. Determine if you should request an unofficial or official transcript.
2. Contact and obtain transcripts from your school. This may require a wait time, so plan accordingly.
3. Add dates for when you requested and received your transcript to your master portfolio spreadsheet.

CTSOs

Case Study. A case study is an analysis of a person, group, or specific situation that is reviewed in order to learn information. Case study events are an opportunity to demonstrate strategic analysis and decision-making skills. The activity may be a decision-making scenario for which your team will provide a solution. The presentation will be interactive with the judges.

To prepare for a case study event, complete the following activities.

1. Conduct an online search for *case studies.* Your team should select a case that seems appropriate to use as a practice activity. Look for a case that is no more than a page long. Read the case and discuss it with your team members. What are the important points of the case?
2. Make notes on index cards about important points to remember. Team members should exchange note cards so each person evaluates the other team members' notes. Use these notes to study. You may also be able to use these notes during the event.
3. Assign each team member a role for the presentation. Ask your instructor to play the role of competition judge as your team reviews the case.
4. Each team member should introduce himself or herself, review the case, make suggestions for the case, and conclude with a summary.
5. After the presentation is complete, ask for feedback from your instructor. You may also consider having a student audience to listen and give feedback.

UNIT 6 Environment of Management

Chapters

Functions of Management Covered in This Unit

While studying, look for the activity icon for:

- Vocabulary terms with e-flash cards and matching activities

These activities can be accessed at www.g-wlearning.com/business/8417

Case Study

Social Responsibility

AshTproductions/Shutterstock.com

Maria is a public relations manager at a nonprofit organization. She is a good fit for the job as it was always her goal to work for a company that supported the public good.

Her organization focuses on diminishing starvation in the United States. One of her tasks is to find ways to generate money to support the cause. Having minored in fashion design in college, Maria had an idea to create reusable tote bags to sell to the public. Her plan involved the organization selling the tote bags on its website and donating the proceeds to worthy charities or other like-minded organizations. The executives of the organization, while impressed with her initiative, decided that donating the proceeds would look like they were playing favorites to specific charities. Unfortunately, her proposal was rejected.

Undeterred, Maria decided to continue with her plan as a project on her own time. Her goal was to start her own nonprofit to donate the proceeds from her product. She contacted a tailor and graphic designer to create a prototype bag. The final design included a strong message, as well as print statistics, about world hunger. She showed the prototype to a distributor, explaining her goal to donate the proceeds to multiple nonprofits. The distributor was interested in her idea and the business began.

Within several years, Maria raised thousands of dollars. Her employer was impressed with her determination and success. They reconsidered the idea and offered to merge her organization with theirs and put her in charge of the project's operations.

Social responsibility is behaving with sensitivity to social, environmental, and economic issues. Businesses that demonstrate social responsibility have the benefits of creating a positive work environment, increasing customer engagement, and creating goodwill.

Critical Thinking

1. Working for a nonprofit was an advantage for Maria when pitching her idea. Assume she was employed by a for-profit business. How do you think she could have pitched this idea to a for-profit business?
2. Maria could have become discouraged when her idea was rejected. How do you think persistence and dedication kept her focused and determined to be successful?

CHAPTER 13

Managing in a Business Environment

Sections

13.1 Environment of Business

13.2 Legal Aspects of Business

13.3 Responsible Business Practices

Reading Prep

Review questions serve as a self-assessment tool that can help you evaluate your comprehension of the material you have read. As you read this chapter, stop at the Check Your Understanding questions. Try to think of potential answers to these questions without referring to the chapter content.

Exploring Careers

Compliance Manager

Business Management & Administration

Compliance managers are responsible for planning and coordinating activities to ensure an organization is compliant with legal regulations and standards. They evaluate data and maintain documentation that confirms the organization meets standards. Compliance managers conduct audits and enforce regulations in all levels of the business. Their goal is to ensure that the business is ethical and lawful in their operations.

Typical job titles for this position include *compliance officer* and *director of compliance*. Examples of tasks compliance managers perform include:

- maintaining documentation of compliance-related information;
- filing reports with governmental or regulatory agencies;
- conducting internal investigations or audits;
- identifying problems that require further investigation or follow-up; and
- reporting any noted violations to authorized enforcement agencies as appropriate or required.

Most compliance manager positions require a degree in law, finance, or related field. Some organizations may also prefer a master degree. Certifications are not required for this occupation, but compliant certification is usually desirable. Compliance managers must have excellent critical-thinking, problem-solving, communication, and active listening skills. In addition, the position requires in-depth knowledge of industry standards and legal regulations.

Monkey Business Images/Shutterstock.com

Section 13.1 Environment of Business

What comes to mind when you hear the phrase *business environment*?

Learning Objectives

LO 13.1-1 Summarize the business environment.

LO 13.1-2 Identify the functions of business.

LO 13.1-3 Discuss business types.

LO 13.1-4 List forms of business organization.

Key Terms 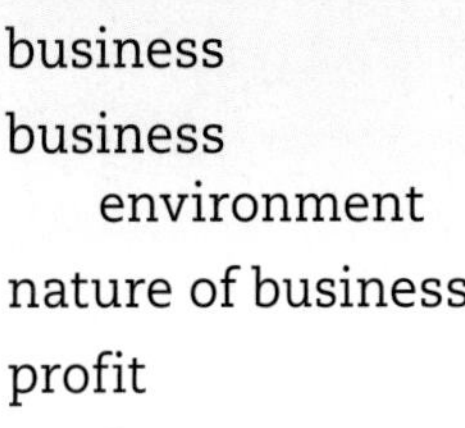

- business
- business environment
- nature of business
- profit
- producer
- extractor
- manufacturer
- intermediary
- wholesaler
- retailer
- sole proprietorship
- partnership
- corporation
- S corporation
- limited liability company (LLC)
- franchise

LO 13.1-1 Business Environment

Successful managers realize the importance of studying and understanding the business environment. Without knowledge of how business works in an economy, success will not be achieved. **Business** is the term for all activities involved in developing and exchanging goods and services.

The **business environment** is the internal and external factors that affect an organization. The *internal business environment* is composed of factors the organization has some control over, such as employees or management. The *external business environment* includes factors an organization cannot control, such as the economy and the competition.

A *business* is an organization of one or more people that works toward developing goods and services that are sold to customers. It sells goods or services, manages people, makes financial decisions, and decides what and how much to produce.

Business can be conducted domestically or globally. A *domestic business* is one that only sells products in the country in which it is located. A *global business* is one that sells its products to other countries as well as the country in which it is located.

In the United States, businesses are generally categorized as for-profit or not-for-profit. A *for-profit business* is an organization that generates revenue. One of its sole purposes is to be productive and generate profit for its owners. A *not-for-profit organization* is an organization that exists to serve some public purpose. The money it raises supports a cause rather than makes money for its owners. To be successful, both types of businesses need competent managers.

LO 13.1-2 Functions of Business

All businesses perform specific functions in their operations. A *function* is a general term for a category of activities. The *functions of business* are management, production, marketing, and finance, as illustrated in Figure 13-1. Each of these functions must be coordinated and work together to meet the goals established for operation.

Management

Without the *management function*, it would be difficult for an organization to survive. A manager is needed to provide guidance and direction to reach the goals a business sets for itself. *Management* is the process of controlling and making decisions about an organization as well as overseeing others to ensure activities are performed efficiently and effectively. It includes all the activities required to plan, coordinate, and monitor a business, as well as hiring and training employees. Managers are the individuals who guide a business to success.

American Red Cross
Together, we can save a life

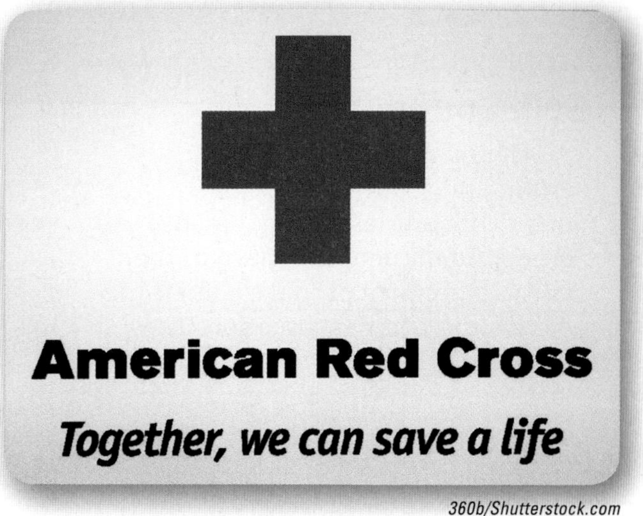

360b/Shutterstock.com

A not-for-profit organization is an organization that exists to serve some public purpose, such as the American Red Cross. **What do you think would be the impact on society if nonprofit organizations did not exist?**

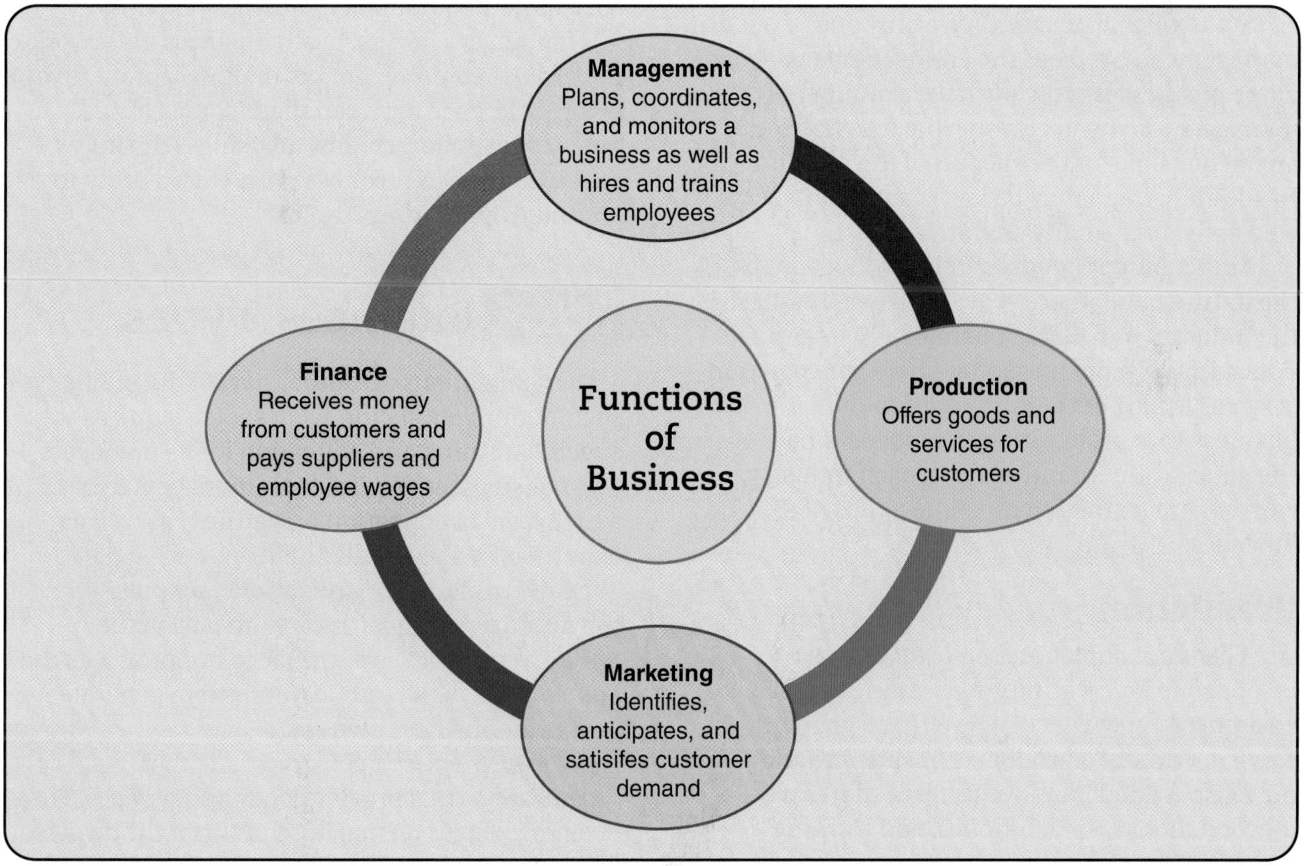
Management
Plans, coordinates, and monitors a business as well as hires and trains employees
Functions of Business
Finance
Receives money from customers and pays suppliers and employee wages
Production
Offers goods and services for customers
Marketing
Identifies, anticipates, and satisifes customer demand

Goodheart-Willcox Publisher

Figure 13-1 The four functions of business must be coordinated and work together to meet the goals established for operation.

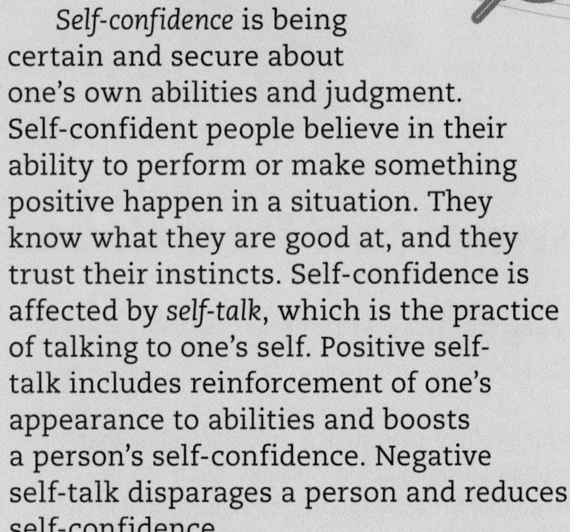

Employability Skills

Self-Confidence

Self-confidence is being certain and secure about one's own abilities and judgment. Self-confident people believe in their ability to perform or make something positive happen in a situation. They know what they are good at, and they trust their instincts. Self-confidence is affected by *self-talk*, which is the practice of talking to one's self. Positive self-talk includes reinforcement of one's appearance to abilities and boosts a person's self-confidence. Negative self-talk disparages a person and reduces self-confidence.

Small businesses may have only one manager who oversees the entire company. Large businesses typically have a number of managers who oversee a specific function and are responsible for the success of the division. In addition, there may be lower-level managers who assist in the daily operations.

Management needs are also influenced by the nature of business. The **nature of business** is the industry in which a business is categorized. For example, a business that offers construction services is part of the construction industry. A business that produces music videos is part of the entertainment industry. In each industry, workers are trained to meet the needs of a business.

Production

The *production function* of business is responsible for creating goods and services for customers. A *product* can be either a good or service. Without a product, a business would not exist. A good is a physical item that can be touched. Books, smartphones, and clothing are examples of goods. A service is an action performed, usually for a fee. For example, a hair stylist provides a service of cutting hair.

Marketing

The *marketing function* connects a business with its customers. *Marketing* consists of all activities that identify, anticipate, and satisfy customer demand while making a profit. It includes learning about customers, developing products, and pricing them for sale. Marketing is the function that promotes and sells products and follows up with customers to determine their degree of satisfaction. It ensures that the product is in the right place, at the right time, and being sold for the right price.

Finance

In order to remain profitable and in operation, the finances of a business must be managed. *Finance* includes all business activities that involve money. The *finance function* includes receiving money from customers, paying money to suppliers, and paying wages to employees. It also includes raising money from investors and lenders for items such as new equipment or business expansion.

Employees in a for-profit business must work toward the common goal of making a profit. **Profit** is the difference between the income earned and expenses incurred by a business during a specified time. A business must earn a profit to continue operations.

LO 13.1-3 Business Types

Organizations are either part of the public sector or private sector. Each sector requires specific training and education for its managers. Most businesses require their managers to have a high level of education or training, as well as expertise, in a particular field.

Governmental organizations, schools, the military, and health care are part of the *public sector*. They are similar to nonprofits as the goal is to serve the public rather than generate profits for business owners.

The *private sector* consists of all other organizations that provide goods and services. These businesses focus on making a profit for the owners. Businesses in the private sector are classified by *type* or *category*. Types of businesses include producers, intermediaries, and service businesses.

Producers

Producers are businesses that create goods and services used by individuals, other businesses, and the government. Producers include farmers, extractors, and manufacturers.

- *Farmers* raise crops and livestock to sell to either end users or other producers.
- **Extractors** are businesses or people that take natural resources, or *raw materials*, from the land. They then sell the natural resources to manufacturers.
- **Manufacturers** are businesses that use raw materials from other producers to convert them into finished products that can be sold to customers. With assembly lines, they are able to mass-produce goods for consumers.

Intermediaries

Intermediaries are businesses that purchase goods from producers and resell them to individuals or businesses. The most common types of intermediaries are wholesalers, retailers, and agents.

- A **wholesaler** is a business that purchases large quantities of products directly from producers and sells the products in smaller quantities to retailers. They are often called *distributors*.
- **Retailers** are businesses that buy products from wholesalers or directly from producers and sell them to consumers, or end users, to make a profit.
- An *agent*, also known as a *broker*, brings buyers and sellers together. They buy and sell goods for a commission, never take direct ownership of the products, and can work for either the buyer or seller. Their overall goal is to create a favorable exchange for both parties.

Service Businesses

A *service business* earns profits by providing consumers with services that meet their needs and wants. This type of business does not typically sell a physical product, but instead performs a task or service for its customers. Examples of service businesses include accounting, landscaping, and transportation businesses.

Nejron Photo/Shutterstock.com

Farmers are a type of producer that raises crops and livestock to sell to either end users or other producers. **What role do farmers play in our economy?**

Another example of a service business is the trade industry. The trade industry provides labor based on specialized knowledge and skills. Trade laborers include carpenters, electricians, mechanics, and plumbers. They provide services for many different businesses.

LO 13.1-4 Business Organization

Business organization, also referred to as *structure*, is the way in which an organization is legally organized. Three major forms of business structures are sole proprietorship, partnership, and corporation.

Sole Proprietorship

A **sole proprietorship** is a business owned by one person. The owner, or *sole proprietor*, has total responsibility for the business and receives all the profit. This structure is advantageous for a person who wants to own and manage a business with total control. However, a disadvantage is the owner is personally liable for all debts incurred by the business. This is referred to as *unlimited liability*.

Ken Wolter/Shutterstock.com

A franchise is a license to sell a company's goods or services within a certain territory or location. A UPS store is an example of a franchise. **Why do you think buying a franchise could be a good way to start a business?**

Partnership

A **partnership** is an association of two or more people who own a business with the objective of earning a profit. In a partnership, there must be at least two parties who own the business. However, there is no limit to the number of partners who can be a part of the organization.

An advantage of a partnership is the organization benefits from the contributions of its member's skills, talents, and financial resources. A disadvantage of this organization is that each partner is personally liable for all debts of the partnership and responsible for decisions made by the other partners. In addition, if a partner leaves the business, the partnership ends. A new partnership must be formed in order for the business to continue.

Corporation

A corporation is a more complex business structure than a sole proprietorship or partnership. Corporations are often referred to as *C corporations*. A **corporation** is defined by the US Supreme Court as "an artificial being, invisible, intangible, and existing only in contemplation of the law." It is a business legally separate from its owners. It is also known as an "artificial person" because it has most of the legal rights of an actual person. A corporation is owned by shareholders, also known as stockholders, who purchase shares of stock in the business.

An advantage of this type of structure is that a stockholder is not personally responsible for the debts incurred by the entity. Another advantage is a corporation has unlimited life. This means that if a shareholder is no longer part of the company, the business continues.

A disadvantage is the corporation itself pays a corporate income tax on profits. If part of the company's profit is paid as a dividend to stockholders, the stockholders must report the dividend on their personal tax returns, which results in double taxation. A *dividend* is a portion of the corporation's earnings distributed to stockholders. Another disadvantage is the formation of a corporation is typically more time-consuming and costly than other structures.

Alternative Forms of Ownership

There are business ownership structures that combine elements of sole proprietorships, partnerships, and corporations. They include S corporations, limited liability companies (LLCs), and franchises.

S Corporation

An **S corporation** is a form of business ownership that is organized as a corporation but is taxed as a partnership. An important advantage of this structure is the limited liability an S corporation provides to shareholders. Another advantage is since each owner's share of the profit is reported as income on his or her personal tax returns, the S corporation does not pay corporate income taxes. This eliminates the double taxation feature of C corporations.

A disadvantage of this structure is that S corporations are restricted to no more than 100 shareholders, all of whom must be US citizens or residents. In addition, most fringe benefits provided by the S corporation are taxable as income to shareholders who own more than two percent of the shares.

Limited Liability Company

A **limited liability company (LLC)** is a form of business ownership that combines features of a corporation with those of a sole proprietorship and partnership. An advantage of the LLC structure is, like corporations, it provides limited liability to its owners, who are called *members*. Also like a corporation, an LLC has unlimited life. This means if a member leaves the business, the LLC is not dissolved and does not have to be reformed in order for business activity to continue.

A disadvantage of the LLC structure is some states restrict the types of professions that can operate as an LLC. Another disadvantage is, like partnerships and sole proprietorships, members of an LLC must pay self-employment taxes on their share of business profit. The self-employment tax consists of the same Social Security and Medicare taxes paid by wage earners, but at double the rates.

Franchise

A **franchise** is a license to sell a company's goods or services within a certain territory or location. Buying a franchise gives a person the right to sell an established product or service. A *franchisee* is a person or company that buys a franchise. A franchisee pays for the use of a logo, name, and products. A *franchisor* is the person or company that grants a franchise.

An advantage of owning a franchise is that marketing direction, training, and other services are provided by the franchisor. However, owning a franchise means the owner must abide by the rules of the franchise. In addition, he or she will have less say on operation of the business.

Section 13.1 Review

Check Your Understanding

1. Explain the difference between internal and external environmental factors that influence the business environment.
2. List the functions of business.
3. How are businesses in the private sector classified?
4. What is business organization?
5. List examples of alternative forms of business ownership.

Build Your Vocabulary

As you progress through this text, develop a personal glossary of key terms. This will help you build your vocabulary and prepare you for a career. Write a definition for each of the following terms and add them to your personal glossary.

business
business environment
nature of business
profit
producer
extractor
manufacturer
intermediary
wholesaler
retailer
sole proprietorship
partnership
corporation
S corporation
limited liability company (LLC)
franchise

Section 13.2 Legal Aspects of Business

Why is a contract needed when entering into business transactions?

Learning Objectives

LO 13.2-1 Define *contract.*

LO 13.2-2 Discuss US laws.

LO 13.2-3 Explain legal procedure.

Key Terms 

contract	contract law	lease
offer	breach of contract	employment contract
acceptance	sales and service contracts	employer identification number (EIN)
consideration		
capacity		

LO 13.2-1 Contracts

A **contract** is a legally binding agreement between two or more people or businesses. Each person who participates in a contract agreement is called a *party.* The purpose of a contract is to formalize an agreement between the parties involved. Business contracts protect the interests of the organization and help to ensure all parties perform as expected. Contracts ensure that:

- customers understand their role and rights in a sales transaction;
- businesses have the materials and resources needed to operate; and
- all parties understand the terms of the agreement and consequences for not performing.

A contract may be a written document or a verbal agreement. Whether written or verbal, all parties involved in a contract are expected to perform according to the contract agreement. Legal experts recommend that all contracts be in writing because written contracts are easier to enforce and can avoid misinterpretations. Electronic contracts are as legal and enforceable as contracts printed on paper.

Elements of a Contract

Certain elements must be included in a contract for it to be enforceable. The following are some of the required elements of a legal contract.

- **Offer.** An **offer** is a proposal to provide a good or service.
- **Acceptance. Acceptance** means that all parties involved must agree to the terms of the contract.
- **Consideration. Consideration** means that something of value is promised in return for something of value received.
- **Intention of legal consequences.** The parties entering into the contract must understand that it can be enforced by law.

Additionally, the goods, services, and actions involved in a contract must be legal.

In order for a contract to be legally binding, all parties involved must enter the contract voluntarily and be competent. **Capacity** means that a person is legally able to enter into a binding agreement. Persons must be of legal age and of sound mind to understand their actions.

The US legal system provides a framework for creating and enforcing legal contracts.

Shawn Hempel/Shutterstock.com

A lease is a contract to rent an item or property. **Why is it wise to have a written contract rather than a verbal contract?**

Contract law regulates how contracts are written, executed, and enforced. A **breach of contract** is when one or more parties do not follow the agreed terms of a contract without having a legitimate reason. Breach is basically a broken promise. A breach-of-contract lawsuit is a civil action, and damages are usually settled in the form of money.

Business Contracts

Contracts are used in many areas of business and professional activities, such as with product vendors, business partners, property-leasing companies, and landscape contractors. Some contracts commonly used for business include:

- sales and service contracts;
- property or equipment leases;
- partnership agreements; and
- employment contracts.

Sales and Service Contracts

Sales and service contracts list the goods or services provided by a business and the price the customer pays in exchange. This type of contract can be a receipt that is printed for, or e-mailed to, the customer after a retail purchase. Other types of sales and service contracts can include more detail, such as a list of all materials and labor provided to a business. They can also include a timeframe for delivery, payment terms, and a product guarantee.

Leases

A **lease** is a contract to rent an item or property. This type of contract typically applies to real estate and vehicles used by a business. For example, if a business needs to rent office space, a property lease is issued. A property lease includes the type of activities that will take place in the space. It also includes the length of time the space will be provided and how much will be paid in rent to use the space.

A *software license* is a type of lease because the software publisher keeps ownership of the software. The software can only be used as described in the software license. The user agrees to this contract when the software is installed.

Partnership Agreements

A *partnership agreement* is a contract used when two or more individuals create a business. The agreement states how much each partner will invest in the business, each partner's responsibilities, and how profits and losses are distributed.

Employment Contracts

An **employment contract** describes the terms of employment between a business and an employee. The contract describes how long employment will last, how much the employee will be paid, and the benefits provided by the business. An employment contract can also include information related to trade secrets and termination of employment.

LO 13.2-2 US Laws

All businesses are subject to various laws and regulations set by local, state, and national governments. Some examples of laws include fair competition, e-commerce, business finance, environmental protection, and zoning and building codes.

Fair Competition

The Federal Trade Commission Act of 1914 created the *Federal Trade Commission (FTC)* to enforce US antitrust laws. *Antitrust laws* are laws that promote fair trade and competition among businesses. Antitrust laws, such as the Sherman Act and Clayton Act, regulate against unfair business practices that prevent competition in the marketplace. *Unfair business practices* include forming monopolies and exclusive distribution agreements. Enforcement of these laws enable consumers to choose goods and services that range in quality and price in an open and fair marketplace.

The Wheeler-Lea Act of 1938 prohibits unfair competition in order to protect businesses and consumers. It is also known as the advertising act as it restricts businesses from using false advertising to sell products.

Fair pricing plays a role in fair competition. The Sherman Act of 1890 imposed regulations on price fixing and predatory pricing in place. *Price fixing* occurs when two or more businesses in an industry agree to sell the same good or service at a set price, which eliminates price competition. *Predatory pricing* is setting very low prices to remove competition. It is illegal for businesses to intentionally price products to mislead customers or to force a competitor out of business.

The Robinson-Patman Act of 1936 prevents price discrimination among distributors and sellers. *Price discrimination* occurs when a company sells the same product to different customers at different prices without justifiable cause. By law, businesses must sell their products at the same price to all buyers, regardless of who the buyers are.

Ethics

Embezzlement

Managers often have access to financial records and transactions that occur in an organization. Because of that access, it might be tempting to take money from business accounts for personal use thinking no one will notice. *Embezzlement* is theft or misappropriation of funds from one's employer. Falsifying expense accounts or using a company credit card for personal purchases are examples of embezzlement. Embezzlement is not only unethical, it is a form of fraud.

E-Commerce

Businesses that operate online have additional e-commerce guidelines and laws that they must follow. Examples of e-commerce laws are listed in Figure 13-2. Typically, these laws regulate how online business is conducted including the use of customer information, data security, and online advertising.

E-Commerce Laws

Law	Year	Description
Electronic Fund Transfer Act	1978	Protects consumers who use electronic fund transfer (EFT) services including ATMs, point-of-sale terminals, automated bill-payment arrangements, and remote banking programs
Children's Online Privacy Protection Act (COPPA)	1998	Protects the personal information of children under 13 years old who are using online services or websites
Electronic Signatures in Global and National Commerce Act (ESIGN)	2000	Allows electronic signatures to be used for interstate and international commerce transactions that require written signatures
CAN-SPAM Act	2003	Sets rules for commercial e-mail messages and gives recipients the right to stop receiving unwanted e-mails
US Safe Web Act	2006	Increases the scope of cooperation to enforce regulations related to spam, spyware, false advertising, breaches in security, and consumer privacy

Goodheart-Willcox Publisher

Figure 13-2 E-commerce laws regulate how online business is conducted including the use of customer information, data security, and online advertising.

Mark Van Scyoc/Shutterstock.com

The Federal Trade Commission Act of 1914 created the Federal Trade Commission (FTC) to enforce US antitrust laws. **Why do you think it is important to have laws that promote fair trade and competition?**

Finance

There are many US laws that regulate the financial activities of businesses. Examples of finance laws are listed in Figure 13-3. Two governmental agencies that regulate financial activities are the Internal Revenue Service (IRS) and US Securities and Exchange Commission (SEC).

Internal Revenue Service (IRS)

The *Internal Revenue Service (IRS)* is a bureau of the US Department of Treasury. It is responsible for enforcing US tax laws. Businesses are required to pay taxes on their profits and file federal and state tax documents on a regular basis. In addition, businesses are responsible for collecting employment taxes from employee paychecks and sales taxes from customers.

Most businesses are required to have an employer identification number (EIN). An **employer identification number (EIN)** is a number assigned by the IRS for businesses to use when preparing federal tax returns and forms. Partnerships and corporations must have an EIN. Sole proprietorships with at least one employee must also have an EIN. The Internal Revenue Service and the Department of Revenue in each state provides information and resources to help businesses understand their legal tax obligations.

US Securities and Exchange Commission (SEC)

Securities laws regulate businesses that have publicly traded stocks and bonds. Securities include stocks and other financial investments. These regulations are enforced by the *US Securities and Exchange Commission (SEC)* and cover areas such as financial reports, issuance of securities, and use of information by company insiders.

Finance Laws

Law	Year	Description
Truth in Lending Act	1968	Requires the disclosure of terms and costs on all consumer credit agreements and in advertisements for credit plans
Fair Credit Reporting Act	1970	Regulates the collection of credit information and who can access consumer credit reports
Sarbanes-Oxley Act	2002	Prevents companies from fraudulent accounting practices that would mislead investors as to the strength of a company

Goodheart-Willcox Publisher

Figure 13-3 There are many US laws that regulate the financial activities of businesses.

Environmental Protection

Environmental control is protection of the environment through policies and laws concerning the control of the environment. Environmental law is the body of US laws, regulations, and international treaties that address the impact of human activity on the environment. These apply to every type of business in every industry. Some issues environmental laws address include:

- handling and removing of asbestos;
- importing and exporting materials that pose a risk to the environment;
- toxic chemicals released by industrial businesses;
- vehicle emissions;
- use of pesticides; and
- quality of drinking water.

All businesses must make responsible decisions about their actions that relate to the environment. The *Environmental Protection Agency (EPA)* is a governmental agency that enforces federal laws concerning the environment and human health. The EPA offers information and resources for communities, businesses, and individuals about environmental protection. Examples of environmental laws are listed in Figure 13-4.

Zoning and Building Codes

Local governments create zoning laws and regulations that define how property can be used in specific geographic zones. Zoning seeks to protect public health, safety, and welfare. Common property zones are residential, commercial, industrial, agricultural, and recreational. For example, residential zoning prohibits high-traffic activities in residential neighborhoods. In some cases, different types of business may have different zoning restrictions within residential areas. This may include the nature of the business, number of employees, hours of operation, and noise and delivery issues. Commercial and industrial zones are usually limited to those forms of business.

Local government may also control the physical structure of a business through building codes. They are in place to protect the health, safety, and welfare of the building's occupants. Building codes mainly specify the maximum height, minimum and maximum square footage

Environmental Laws		
Law	**Year**	**Description**
Clean Air Act	1970	Establishes the allowable air-pollutant levels emitted by US businesses
Clean Water Act	1972	Establishes the allowable water-pollutant levels emitted by US businesses
Noise Control Act	1972	Protects the public from excessive noise created by business operations
Pollution Prevention Act	1990	Forces the government, businesses, and public attention on reducing the amount of pollution through cost-effective changes in raw material use, production, and operation
Energy Policy Act	2005	Provides tax incentives for companies that use energy-efficient methods in the operation of their businesses

Goodheart-Willcox Publisher

Figure 13-4 Environmental law is the body of US laws, regulations, and international treaties that address the impact of human activity on the environment.

of space, and types of building materials used in a structure. Both zoning and building codes vary with local governments. However, most regulations and codes are the same across a city, township, or county.

LO 13.2-3 Legal Procedure

The US legal system interprets and enforces laws and regulations, including those that apply to businesses. The role of the legal process is to resolve disputes between people, businesses, and even those that involve agencies of the government. *Legal procedures* are the steps and methods involved in the legal process. This includes:

- informing parties of legal action;
- holding hearings;
- conducting trials;
- presenting evidence;
- making motions; and
- determining facts.

A standard legal procedure ensures the fair handling of every legal action. This applies to both civil and criminal proceedings.

Section 13.2 Review

Check Your Understanding

1. What do contracts ensure?
2. List examples of elements required in a legal contract.
3. What act created the FTC? What was the purpose for its creation?
4. Which government agency is responsible for enforcing US tax laws?
5. Cite examples of issues addressed by environmental laws.

Build Your Vocabulary

As you progress through this text, develop a personal glossary of key terms. This will help you build your vocabulary and prepare you for a career. Write a definition for each of the following terms and add them to your personal glossary.

contract
offer
acceptance
consideration
capacity
contract law
breach of contract
sales and service contract
lease
employment contract
employer identification number (EIN)

Section 13.3

Responsible Business Practices

What role does business have in society?

Learning Objectives

LO 13.3-1 Explain the role of business in society.
LO 13.3-2 Discuss social responsibility of businesses.

Key Terms

market	philanthropy	carbon footprint
standard of living	social audit	sustainability

LO 13.3-1 Role of Business in Society

In addition to making a profit for the owners, business plays a role in society. It provides products, creates markets, and generates economic benefits.

Provides Product

Businesses provide goods and services for its customers. Without a product, a business would not exist. A major task of business is to provide utility to products. *Utility* describes the characteristics of a product that satisfy a want or need. It means *usefulness*. If a product is not in the correct form, in the right place, at the right time, the end user will not be able to purchase it and take possession.

Creates Markets

Businesses create markets so consumers can decide which products they want to buy. A **market** is anywhere buyers and sellers meet to buy and sell goods and services. It can be a brick-and-mortar business like a Vans shoe store in a mall. It can also be an online market such as Amazon.com or eBay.

In the marketplace, businesses compete with each other to offer products and prices that appeal to customers. Competition provides choices and varieties of products and prices from which a customer can select.

Generates Economic Benefits

Economic benefits are gains measured in terms of money. One economic benefit of business is that it provides employment and rewards workers with wages. *Wages* are money earned in exchange for work. Workers use their wages to buy goods and services to satisfy their needs and wants. This, in turn, supports other businesses.

Businesses create products that enable consumers to determine their standard of living. **Standard of living** is a level of material comfort measured by the goods, services, and luxuries available. By earning a wage and having money to spend, consumers can decide the standard of living they can afford.

A profitable business pays taxes to the federal, state, and local governments. These taxes help fund services that benefit the community. A business also pays real-estate taxes if it owns the property on which the business operates. In addition, workers pay payroll taxes, which also help fund governmental activities.

Franck Boston/Shutterstock.com

Standard of living is a level of material comfort measured by the goods, services, and luxuries available. **How would you describe your current standard of living? What would you like your future standard of living to be?**

LO 13.3-2 Social Responsibility of Business

Social responsibility is behaving with sensitivity to social, environmental, and economic issues. Socially responsible businesses are civic-minded and work with the community in multiple ways. *Corporate social responsibility (CSR)* includes all the actions taken by a business to promote social good. These actions go beyond the profit interests and legal requirements of a business. A business may work to address social, economic, and environmental issues as a component of their social responsibilities.

Socially responsible management policies are not always initiated just by management alone. An employee in an organization can also make recommendations. These initiatives can be simple, such as placing recycling bins around the building. Other times they may be complicated and require more development, such as a company-wide volunteer project of building homes for the homeless. Most organizations make social responsibility a part of their corporate cultures. They encourage employees to create task forces to identify projects they can undertake in an organization and make a difference in the community. In addition, socially responsible policies boost employee engagement, improve an organization's reputation in a community, and promote philanthropy.

Philanthropy is promoting the welfare of others. Protecting natural resources or donating money or products are examples of ways businesses give back to society. Many organizations encourage employees to volunteer their time for charitable organizations. Giving back to the community creates goodwill for a business. Goodwill is the advantage a business has due to its positive reputation.

Businesses that support the economy also support themselves. Hiring employees from the community or using local vendors are both good business practices. Providing jobs for local people helps keep the community employment rate stable and strengthens the local economy. Hiring local vendors also contributes to the employment of a community. Both actions generate money from taxes that goes back to the local economy.

A **social audit** is a review of a company's involvement in socially responsible activities. It is an optional review managers can conduct to measure the social responsibility level of a business. Social audits evaluate an organization's record of charitable giving, volunteer activities, work environment, worker pay and benefits, and energy use. Additionally, an organization can determine if it wishes to release the social audit publicly or use it internally.

Human Rights

Businesses have a social responsibility to prevent human rights violations in their supply chains. A *supply chain* is the businesses, people, and activities involved in turning raw materials into products and delivering them to end users. *Human rights* are rights inherent to everyone, such as freedom from slavery, of expression, and to an education, regardless of nationality, race, or gender.

You Do the Math

Geometric Reasoning: Volume

Three-dimensional figures have length, width, and height. In other words, they have volume. Volume is an important measurement for shipping boxes, bottles, containers, and many other items. The volume of a rectangular figure is calculated by multiplying its length, height, and width. The volume of a cylinder is calculated by multiplying the area of its base by its height.

Solve the following problems.

1. The inside of a shipping container is 6 feet by 18 feet by 8 feet. If a single box is 1 foot by 2 feet by 6 inches, how many boxes can fit inside the shipping container?
2. If a rectangular box has a volume of 161.28 cubic inches and its base measures 3.5 inches by 7.2 inches, what is the height of the box?
3. If a cylindrical fuel tank is 4.25 feet tall and holds 122.6 cubic feet of fuel, what is the area of the base of the cylinder?

A *human rights violation* occurs if a person, business, state, or country acts to deprive someone of his or her human rights. According to the United Nations Guiding Principles on Business and Human Rights, businesses should not infringe on the rights of anyone involved in the production, sale, or consumption of their product. If they do, they must work to fix the issue and help anyone who may have been hurt by their actions.

One of the most prominent abuses of human rights is child labor. *Child labor* is defined as any work that prevents a child from having a normal childhood, abuses his or her dignity, or hurts his or her physical or mental development. This includes work that prevents children from attending school or exposes them to hazardous conditions.

Environment

Social responsibility includes concern for the environment. Air, water, noise, and land pollution are examples of environmental issues with which socially responsible businesses should be concerned. A **carbon footprint** is a measurement of how much the everyday behaviors of an individual, company, or community impact the environment. This includes the amount of carbon dioxide put into the air from the consumption of energy and fuel used in homes, for travel, and for business operations.

Online carbon footprint calculators are used to determine areas and practices that need to change. Companies can reduce their carbon footprints by recycling, reducing waste, and using responsible energy options. For example, video communication can be used to hold meetings among departments in locations across the country. This reduces the fossil fuel emissions for travel by automobile, train, or airplane.

Electronic waste includes computers, cell phones, and batteries of all kinds. All electronic waste can and should be recycled. Batteries in electronic devices contain hazardous chemicals that will harm the environment if discarded in a landfill. Many electronics retailers, such as Best Buy, and community groups provide electronics recycling services.

Sustainability

Environmental resources are limited, and corporate responsibility requires that businesses respect the environment. Many socially responsible businesses work to increase sustainability. **Sustainability** is creating and maintaining conditions under which humans and nature can coexist both now and in the future. It defines the use of resources that meet current needs without using up a resource or reducing the ability to meet future needs.

Goodmorning3am/Shutterstock.com

Using solar energy and wind energy are examples of sustainable business practices. **What sustainable practices does your school or work apply?**

Sustainable business practices include:

- energy conservation by using solar energy instead of natural gas;
- fossil fuel conservation by opting for hybrid vehicles for company use; and
- paper conservation by using digital communication rather than printing documents.

Businesses that provide packing for products can opt for sustainable packaging. The definition of *sustainable packaging* is broad, but includes these criteria:

- designed to reduce the amount of material used;
- uses recycled or recyclable materials;
- uses biodegradable and compostable materials; and
- material used remains safe and healthy for people and the environment throughout its life cycle.

Recycling is the reprocessing of resources so they can be used again. Many items used in daily business operations can be recycled, such as paper, printer cartridges, and plastic. Businesses can make small changes in their daily operations that will make an impact in sustainability efforts. Environmentally friendly products or components are both used in business operations and for product packaging. Businesses can offer customers reusable shopping bags, reuse cardboard boxes when shipping products, and use environmentally safe cleaning products in the maintenance of their facilities.

Section 13.3 Review

Check Your Understanding

1. What role does business play in society?
2. What are economic benefits?
3. What do social audits evaluate?
4. Define *human rights*.
5. List examples of sustainable business practices.

Build Your Vocabulary 

As you progress through this text, develop a personal glossary of key terms. This will help you build your vocabulary and prepare you for a career. Write a definition for each of the following terms and add them to your personal glossary.

market	philanthropy	carbon footprint
standard of living	social audit	sustainability

Chapter 13 Review and Assessment

Chapter Summary

Section 13.1 Environment of Business

LO 13.1-1 **Summarize the business environment.**
The business environment is the internal and external factors that affect an organization. The internal business environment includes factors that the organization has some control over. The external business environment includes factors an organization cannot control.

LO 13.1-2 **Identify the functions of business.**
The functions of business are management, production, marketing, and finance.

LO 13.1-3 **Discuss business types.**
Organizations are either part of the public sector or private sector. Governmental organizations, schools, the military, and health care are part of the public sector. The private sector consists of all other organizations that provide goods and services and are classified as producers, intermediaries, and service businesses.

LO 13.1-4 **List forms of business organization.**
Three major forms of business structures are sole proprietorship, partnership, and corporation. Alternative forms of ownership include S corporations, limited liability companies (LLCs), and franchises.

Section 13.2 Legal Aspects of Business

LO 13.2-1 **Define *contract*.**
A contract is a legally binding agreement between two or more people or businesses. The purpose of a contract is to formalize an agreement between the parties, or people, involved.

LO 13.2-2 **Discuss US laws.**
All businesses are subject to various laws and regulations set by local, state, and national governments. Some examples of laws include fair competition, e-commerce, business finance, environmental protection, and zoning and building codes.

LO 13.2-3 **Explain legal procedure.**
Legal procedures are the steps and methods involved in the legal process. This includes informing parties of legal action, holding hearings, conducting trials, presenting evidence, making motions, and determining facts.

Section 13.3 Responsible Business Practices

LO 13.3-1 **Explain the role of business in society.**
Business plays a role in society by providing products, creating markets, and generating economic benefits.

LO 13.3-2 **Discuss social responsibility of businesses.**
Social responsibility is behaving with sensitivity to social, environmental, and economic issues. Socially responsible businesses are civic-minded and work with the community in multiple ways. Businesses have a social responsibility to address issues related to human rights, the environment, and sustainability.

Review Your Knowledge

1. Summarize the business environment.
2. Identify and explain each of the four functions of business.
3. Discuss business types.
4. Identify an advantage and disadvantage for a business being organized as a sole proprietorship, partnership, and corporation.
5. Define contract and provide examples of contracts commonly used for business.
6. Explain types of laws that businesses must follow.
7. Summarize a legal procedure.
8. Explain the role of business in society.
9. How are socially responsible management policies initiated and implemented?
10. Summarize the role of businesses in protecting human rights.

Apply Your Knowledge

1. Would you rather work for a for-profit business or not-for-profit organization? Explain your reasoning.
2. The functions of business are management, production, marketing, and finance. Explain how the duties of a manager relate to each function of business.
3. Create a list of businesses or organizations with which you are familiar in the public sector. Next, repeat the process for businesses or organizations operating in the private sector. Summarize identifying features of each organization that confirms whether it is public or private.
4. Create a Venn diagram with three circles. Label each of the circles with three types of business ownership: sole proprietorship, partnership, and corporation. Using the diagram, record what the forms of ownership have in common and what makes each one unique.
5. A contract is a legally binding agreement between two or more people or businesses. The receipt that you received from your last purchase is a type of contract. Explain how the receipt from your last purchase is considered a contract.
6. Businesses create markets so consumers can decide which products they want to buy. It also creates competition for consumers to have a variety of choices and prices to select. As a consumer, explain why it is important to you to have a variety of choices when buying products.
7. A social audit is a review of a company's involvement in socially responsible activities. An organization can decide to release the social audit publicly or use it internally. Write an explanation of why you think executive management might choose either option.
8. Socially responsible businesses are civic-minded and work with their communities in many different ways. Identify a business in your community that actively engages in social responsibility. Describe the activities of this business that positively impact social-responsibility issues.
9. Discuss your opinion of the overall nature of social responsibility as it relates to issues of human rights.
10. Describe an idea for a social-responsibility initiative that could benefit a club or organization to which you belong. Explain how you would initiate the idea with your sponsor, and assuming the idea was approved, how you would implement it.

Communication Skills

Reading. *Visual support* is used to communicate an idea using images or objects. It can be used instead of words or in addition to them. Illustrations that accompany written text are visual supports that help you understand the content. Select an illustration from this chapter that serves as a visual support. Analyze and evaluate if the information is easy to understand. How does it relate to the written text?

Writing. Everyone has a stake in protecting the environment. Taking steps as an individual to become more environmentally conscious is a behavior of responsible citizens. From a business standpoint, it may also help a company be more profitable. Write a list of actions a business can take to minimize risk to the environment.

Speaking. Self-confidence is being certain and secure about one's own abilities and judgment. Practice your speaking skills and self-confidence by volunteering to read a special feature in this chapter aloud to your classmates. Stand in the front of the room, control your voice, and read loudly and clearly. How would you rate your speaking skills?

Internet Research

Elements of a Contract. A partnership agreement is a contract used when two or more individuals create a business. Conduct a search for a *partnership agreement sample.* Review the contract and note its elements. Summarize what you learned.

Contemporary Social Responsibility Cases. Research a contemporary case about business and social responsibility. Begin by searching for *social responsibility* plus the current year, or a similar phrase. Summarize the situation and explain why it is an example of social responsibility.

Teamwork

Working with your team, list three current legal issues related to businesses that have been in the news recently. Indicate if the legal issues involve the owner, employees, or other individuals. Discuss the business laws that may have been violated in each of the three situations.

Portfolio Development

Social Responsibility. *Social responsibility* is a cause that many businesses support and encourage from their employees. Workplace studies show that socially responsible employees are, by nature, productive, generally ethical, and loyal.

Social responsibility can be demonstrated in many ways, and you can start with activities at your current job or school. For example, you organized a green team at your school to initiate a recycling program, or you participated in a campaign to "turn off the lights" and conserve energy at home or school. Documentation of these activities reflects social responsibility.

Participating in community service is an example of social responsibility. This can sometimes be a criteria that employers or universities use when screening potential candidates. Serving the community shows a candidate is well-rounded, socially aware, and capable of teamwork. For some individuals, volunteer work could substitute for actual paid employment. In some situations, showing that you spent regular hours supporting a social cause is as valuable as paid work experience. By including evidence of these kinds of activities, a candidate can attract the attention of a person reviewing job applicants and climb the list of interviewees.

For a digital portfolio, consider creating a video that informs viewers about it. Suppose you volunteer with a group that helps repair homes for elderly homeowners. The video could show scenes from the worksites and comments from the residents. Be sure you have permission to include other people in your video before doing so.

1. Using word-processing software, create a document that lists socially responsible projects in which you have taken part at school, work, or in your community. Use the heading "Service Projects," or something similar, along with your name. List the name of the programs, date(s) of service, and activities that you performed. If you received an award related to this service, mention it here.
2. Update your master portfolio spreadsheet to include your service projects. Back up your files on your f lashdrive.

EVENT PREP

CTSOs

Business Law. Business law is a competitive event you might enter with your Career and Technical Student Organization (CTSO). It is an individual event in which participants take an objective test that covers multiple legal topics. Participants are usually allowed one hour to complete the event.

To prepare for a business law event, complete the following activities.

1. Visit the website of the organization well in advance of the date of the event.
2. Download any posted practice tests.
3. Conduct research on the Internet regarding the legal topics that will be covered on the test. Print out the information you find to use as study material.
4. Visit the website of the organization often to make sure information regarding the event has not changed.

CHAPTER 14

Managing in the Economic Environment

Sections

14.1 Basics of Economics

14.2 Our Economy

Reading Prep

The Chapter Summary, located at the end of the chapter, highlights the most important concepts of the content. Before reading, review the Chapter Summary. Based on this information, write down two or three items you think are important to note while you are reading.

Exploring Careers

Supply Chain Manager

Business Management & Administration

Supply chain managers are responsible to oversee and manage the supply chain, logistics, and inventory operations of an organization. They coordinate the activities of the production, purchasing, warehousing, distribution, and logistics teams to ensure that products flow from production through distribution. They manage supplier relationships as well as negotiate prices. It is their responsibility to maximize efficiency and cost of the organization's supply chain.

Typical job titles for this position include *forecasting manager, logistics manager*, and *purchasing manager*. Examples of tasks supply chain managers perform include:

- determining equipment and staffing needed to load, unload, move, or store materials;
- analyzing inventories to determine how quickly products are turned over;
- creating supply and demand plans to ensure timely availability of materials or products; and
- monitoring industry forecasts to identify trends that could affect the supply chain.

Most supply chain manager positions require a bachelor or master degree in business management or a related field, as well as prior experience. Certification as a Certified Purchasing Manager or production and inventory is desirable. Supply chain managers must have sound knowledge of production processes, understand the flow of distribution, and be able to maximize efficient manufacturing of products.

Harry Painter/Shutterstock.com

Section 14.1 Basics of Economics

How does the economic environment affect business operation?

Learning Objectives

LO 14.1-1 Define *economic environment*.

LO 14.1-2 Recognize the factors of production.

LO 14.1-3 Identify types of economic systems.

LO 14.1-4 Explain the forces of supply and demand.

LO 14.1-5 Discuss economic competition.

Key Terms

economic environment	economic system	communism
economics	capitalism	socialism
factors of production	market economy	law of supply and demand
scarcity	mixed economy	market structure
economic problem	command economy	

LO 14.1-1 Economic Environment

A primary goal of private businesses is to generate revenue by producing goods and services that meet the needs and wants of consumers. Effective managers realize the economy has a direct impact on what a business produces and the profits generated from the sale of those products. In general, if the economy is strong, consumers have money to buy goods and services and businesses do well. If the economy is weak, consumers may save their money and buy fewer products. Businesses consider economic conditions when planning what will be produced and the prices that will be demanded. These plans are revisited often and adjustments made accordingly.

Businesses operate in an economic environment. The **economic environment** consists of external factors outside the organization that directly influences its success. This environment is comprised of macroeconomic and microeconomic components.

- The *macroeconomic environment* consists of external factors a business cannot control and affect a nation as a whole. Inflation, taxes, unemployment rates, and interest rates are macroeconomic factors that directly affect the success of a business.
- The *microeconomic environment* consists of external factors that determine decisions made by a business. They typically do not affect the nation as a whole but affect specific businesses. Competition, demographics, and size of the market are microeconomic factors about which management must make decisions before creating products.

Light And Dark Studio/Shutterstock.com

The macroeconomic environment consists of external factors a business cannot control and affect a nation as a whole, such as interest rates. **What external factors do you believe are currently affecting the nation as a whole?**

Organizations are reliant on the knowledge and direction provided by the management team. Management must understand the economic environment to help make decisions that will provide a positive influence to drive profit.

LO 14.1-2 Factors of Production

By studying economics, a manager can make better decisions that can have a positive impact on business. **Economics** is a science that examines how goods and services are produced, sold, and used. The study can begin with the factors of production.

Factors of production are the economic resources used to make goods and services for a population. Each of these resources is limited. The factors of production include the following.

- *Land* is all the natural resources found in nature, such as soil, water, minerals, plants, and animals. Every good produced uses some form of natural resources.
- *Labor* is work performed by people. It is also called *human resources*. This includes workers producing goods, human resources managers hiring and training new employees, senior managers creating goals for a company, and all other business activities performed by people.
- *Capital* is all the tools, equipment, and machinery used to produce goods or provide services. *Capital goods* are the products businesses use to produce other goods. The production of capital goods is *capital formation*.
- *Entrepreneurship* is the willingness and ability to start a new business. *Entrepreneurs* are people who start a new business or purchase an existing business.

Businesses create products using the factors of production to meet the unlimited needs and wants of customers. However, unlimited needs and wants create a challenge for businesses as economic resources required to create products are limited. Decisions must be made on how best to use economic resources that are available.

Scarcity is a situation that develops when there are not enough resources to meet needs and wants which, in turn, creates an economic problem, as illustrated in Figure 14-1.

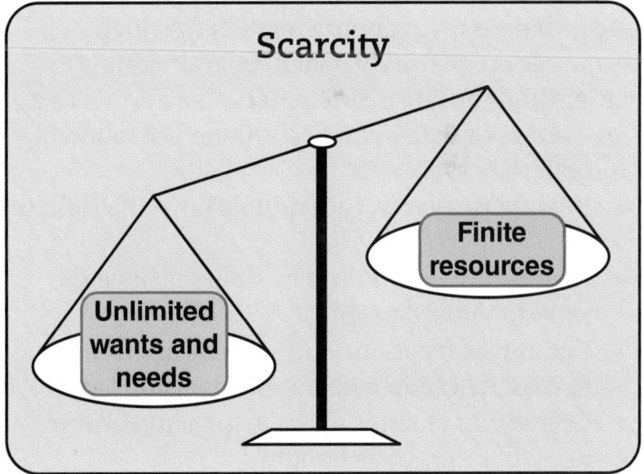

Goodheart-Willcox Publisher

Figure 14-1 Scarcity is a situation that develops when there are not enough resources to meet needs.

The **economic problem** is the concept that resources are limited and needs and wants are unlimited. As a result of scarcity, businesses are forced to answer three economic questions.

- What should we produce?
- How should we produce it?
- For whom should we produce it?

Without asking and answering these questions, a business could potentially develop products for which adequate resources are not available. In addition, they may develop a product for the wrong customer, resulting in poor performance of the company.

kikovic/Shutterstock.com

A market economy is an economic system in which individuals and businesses are free to make their own economic decisions. **Explain what market economy means to you.**

LO 14.1-3 Economic Systems

The United States, like other nations in the world, is a part of an economic system. An **economic system** is the structure in which resources are used to create goods and services. Economic systems differ, in part, based on who owns the factors of production. Does the government own the resources or do the people? Economic systems can be defined as capitalist or command economies.

Capitalism

The United States is part of a capitalist society. **Capitalism** is an economic system in which resources are privately owned by individuals rather than the government. It is also known as a *free-enterprise system* and is built on the following characteristics.

- **Private property.** Individuals have the right to own property.
- **Profit.** Individuals and businesses have the right to make a profit.
- **Economic freedom.** Individuals are free to make their own economic decisions and decide what to buy, when to buy, and how to use what they have bought.
- **Voluntary exchange.** Individuals and businesses have the right to buy and sell in a marketplace where prices are freely set by supply and demand.
- **Competition.** Businesses can compete to sell goods and services and decide what to produce, how to produce, and for whom to produce.

Capitalism is based on the market economy concept. A **market economy** is an economic system in which individuals and businesses are free to make their own economic decisions. People and businesses decide what and how much to produce. They also choose what to buy based on how much money they have. The government does not set prices; instead, consumers in the marketplace determine prices by how much they are willing to pay for items.

The United States is also considered a mixed economy. In a **mixed economy**, both the government and individuals make decisions about economic resources. In most countries, for example, public roads are built and maintained by the government. The government also handles law enforcement and national defense. However, private businesses operate with little governmental involvement and citizens are free to make their own economic decisions. The degree of government involvement in mixed economies can vary from one economy to another.

Command Economy

A **command economy** is an economic system in which the government makes all economic decisions for its citizens and answers the three economic questions. This economy is also called a *centrally planned economy* because a central government makes all the plans and decisions. Command economies are in communist and socialist countries.

Employability Skills
Self-Esteem

Self-esteem is how an individual feels about his or her value as a person. It is your sense of self-worth and how you see yourself when you look in the mirror. The more comfortable you are with yourself as a person, the more self-confidence you will exhibit.

Communism

Communism is a system in which the government's goal is to distribute the country's wealth among all its citizens equally or according to need. The government tries to achieve this objective by taking control of all the economic resources and redistributing them among the people. Citizens have few individual freedoms. The government owns all the property, decides what to produce, where people will work, and what jobs they will do. It also sets prices for goods and services.

Socialism

Socialism is a system in which the government owns and controls most of the factors of production but allows more ownership of personal property. Even though it is a type of command economy, it is less extreme than communism. Socialist governments do not control where people can work or what they do. Wealth is distributed based more on an individual's contribution to society.

LO 14.1-4 Supply and Demand

In a market economy, supply and demand is an important concept critical to business because it determines the price of goods and services. Consumers in the marketplace determine prices by how much they are willing to pay for items.

Supply is the quantity of goods and services available for purchase at a specific time and specific price. If the supply is low, the price will usually be high. If the supply is high, the price will be low.

Demand is the quantity of goods and services that consumers want to purchase. As the price increases, demand usually falls. As the price decreases, demand will rise.

The **law of supply and demand** states the price of a product is determined by the relationship of the supply of a product and the demand for a product. When supply and demand are relatively equal, the market is in *equilibrium*. The equilibrium determines the market price. The law of supply and demand is illustrated by a supply and demand curve, as shown in Figure 14-2. The *supply curve* shows that producers are willing to supply a greater quality of goods at higher prices. The *demand curve* shows consumers are willing to buy fewer goods at higher prices. The point at which the supply and demand are equal is the market price. The equilibrium is where the supply curve and demand curve intersect.

Generally, higher demand results in higher prices, and lower demand results in lower prices. Greater supply often lowers prices, while lower supply results in higher prices. Businesses often operate in a market in which the forces of supply and demand cause frequent price changes.

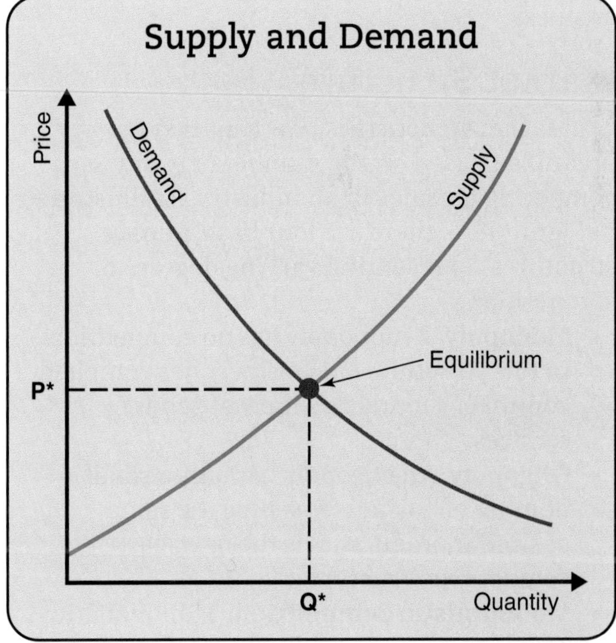

Goodheart-Willcox Publisher

Figure 14-2 The law of supply and demand states that the price of a product is determined by the relationship of the supply of a product and the demand for a product.

Supply and demand help businesses set prices for goods and services so a profit can be made. *Profit* is the difference between income earned and expenses incurred by a business during a specified time. The ability to earn a profit is one of the driving forces that influence producers to create goods and services to sell to consumers.

In a capitalistic system, individuals and businesses are rewarded for producing and selling goods, which is known as the profit motive. *Profit motive* is the desire to earn and maximize profit.

LO 14.1-5 Economic Competition

In a market economy, individuals and businesses have a right to offer competing goods and services for sale. *Economic competition* is the action taken by two or more businesses attempting to attract the same customers. It occurs when two or more sellers offer similar goods and services for sale in the marketplace. Since consumers have the freedom to choose which goods and services they buy, businesses work to win each consumer's business.

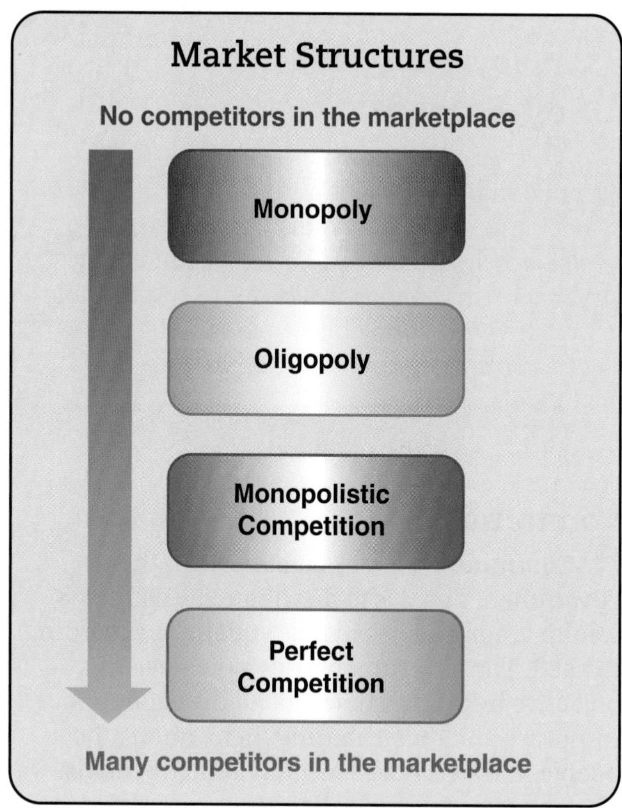

Goodheart-Willcox Publisher

Figure 14-3 There are four basic market structures representing varying degrees of competition.

Market Structure

Market structure is how a market is organized based on the number of businesses competing for sales in an industry. As illustrated in Figure 14-3, there are four basic market structures representing varying degrees of competition.

- **Monopoly.** A monopoly has no competition. In this structure, one business has complete control of a market's supply of goods or services.
- **Oligopoly.** An oligopoly has only a small number of businesses selling the same or similar products. It is the next least-competitive structure.
- **Monopolistic competition.** Monopolistic competition is more competitive with a larger number of businesses selling similar, but not the same, products and at different prices. This is also known as *imperfect competition*.
- **Perfect competition.** Perfect competition is the most-competitive market structure. It is characterized by a large number of businesses selling the same products at the same prices.

Most industries in the United States operate in a market structure of monopolistic competition.

Price and Nonprice Competition

In a free-enterprise system, sellers work to take away business from their competitors. Competition encourages producers to offer more products, wider selections, and prices that are appealing to customers.

Price competition is a situation that occurs when a lower price is the main reason for customers to buy from one business over another. It is also known as *pure competition*. For example, a computer store may lower prices to attract more customers. The store may sell more units than a competitor, but because they lowered prices, profits can suffer. Lowering prices may attract more customers, but it can have a negative effect on overall business profits.

Nonprice competition is a strategy to gain a competitive advantage through factors other than price. This might include better service, improved product assortment or quality, or more customer convenience. For example, an automobile dealer may not lower prices but instead, offer free oil changes and other services to attract customers. People buy from them not based on price but on service.

Section 14.1 Review

Check Your Understanding

1. What is the difference between the macroeconomic environment and the microeconomic environment?
2. Name the factors of production.
3. List characteristics on which a capitalist, or free-enterprise system, is built.
4. Define *supply* and *demand*.
5. Cite four basic market structures that represent varying degrees of competition.

Build Your Vocabulary

As you progress through this text, develop a personal glossary of key terms. This will help you build your vocabulary and prepare you for a career. Write a definition for each of the following terms and add them to your personal glossary.

economic environment
economics
factors of production
scarcity
economic problem
economic system
capitalism
market economy
mixed economy
command economy
communism
socialism
law of supply and demand
market structure

Section 14.2

Our Economy

Why is having a strong economy good for citizens of the country?

Learning Objectives

LO 14.2-1 Cite examples of economic indicators used to measure economic activity.

LO 14.2-2 Summarize the business cycle.

LO 14.2-3 Explain how the government can correct economic problems.

Key Terms

economic indicator
gross domestic product (GDP)
inflation
inflation rate
deflation
interest
interest rate
labor force
unemployment rate
business cycle
expansion
peak
recession
trough
fiscal policy
monetary policy

LO 14.2-1 Economic Indicators

Before business decisions can be made, the macroeconomic environment must be considered. As stated earlier, the macroeconomic environment consists of external factors that a business cannot control and affects a nation as a whole. Inflation, taxes, unemployment rates, and interest rates are situations that directly affect the success of a business.

The strength of the economy can be evaluated using economic indicators. An **economic indicator** is a statistic used to measure certain types of economic activities. Some of the most widely followed indicators of the economy are gross domestic product (GDP), inflation, interest rates, and the unemployment rate.

Gross Domestic Product

Gross domestic product (GDP) is a measure of the value of all goods and services produced by a nation during a specific timeframe, usually one year. GDP includes:

- consumer spending;
- gross private domestic investment, which is money invested by businesses;
- net exports of goods and services, which is exports minus imports; and
- government spending.

The economic growth rate shows the amount and direction of the change in GDP over a specific timeframe, such as a quarter or year. GDP is closely followed because it gives a picture of the overall performance of the economy.

- When GDP is rising, the economy is growing.
- When GDP growth is above average, it indicates a strong economy.
- When the rate of GDP growth is below average, it is a sign that the economy is weakening.
- When economic growth turns negative and GDP falls, it indicates a recession.

In the United States, economic growth has averaged about three percent a year since the late 1920s, excluding inflation. This is the typical range growth for many industrialized countries. Many fast growing countries, however, have growth rates that are higher than the average three percent a year.

Inflation

Inflation is the general rise in prices throughout an economy. It reduces the value of the dollar, which means a dollar buys fewer products. Inflation negatively affects people because they have less purchasing power. The result is decreased consumer spending, which, in turn, has a direct impact on revenue for businesses.

The **inflation rate** is the rate of change in prices calculated on a monthly or yearly basis. It is expressed as a percent. When the inflation rate is between zero to three percent, prices are stable. This is known as *price stability*, which is when prices or products in the marketplace are changing very slowly or not at all.

When the inflation rate increases to four percent or higher, it signals that there are economic problems. Higher inflation leads to higher interest rates, which makes borrowing money more expensive. In general, high inflation adds uncertainty to an economy and makes financial planning difficult.

Two indices used to measure inflation are Consumer Price Index (CPI) and Producer Price Index (PPI).

- *Consumer Price Index (CPI)* measures the average change in prices over time of goods and services purchased by households. It is also known as the cost of living index.
- *Producer Price Index (PPI)* measures the average change in selling prices over time of goods and services produced.

Inflation can be divided into four levels: low, moderate, severe, and hyperinflation. Each level is based on an inflation rate and is used to measure the strength of an economy. Figure 14-4 identifies each level and what it indicates about an economy's strength.

- During low-level inflation, the economy and prices are stable.
- Moderate-level inflation shows the economy starting to see problems and prices of products begin to rise.
- During a severe level of inflation, problems in the economy increase and purchasing power rapidly decreases.
- Although it occurs rarely, hyperinflation destroys an economy and the value of money.

Level of Inflation	
Level	**Effect**
Low	Economy remains stable
Moderate	Prices rise faster than wages
Severe	Purchasing power decreases
Hyperinflation	Economy and the value of money is destroyed

Goodheart-Willcox Publisher

Figure 14-4 Inflation can be divided into four levels: low, moderate, severe, and hyperinflation.

Stockr/Shutterstock.com

Gross domestic product (GDP) includes government spending, such as spending on road construction. **How does government spending contribute to the overall economy?**

Deflation is a general decline in prices throughout an economy. This is the opposite of inflation. Deflation usually occurs when the economy is very weak. The Great Depression in the 1930s was the last time the United States saw a significant deflation in the economy.

Interest

Interest is the amount a borrower pays to a lender for a loan. An **interest rate** is the cost of a loan. It is expressed as a percent of the amount borrowed. There are many different interest rates in an economy because there are many different borrowers, lenders, and types of loans.

- Borrowers include individuals, businesses, and the government.
- Lenders include banks, financial companies, and investors.
- Loans typically appear in the form of auto loans, school loans, home mortgages, and business loans.

The forces of supply and demand determine the interest rate on a loan. Interest rates tend to rise when there is an increase in demand to borrow money. When the demand to borrow money falls, interest rates tend to decline. As a result, interest rates typically rise during a strong economy when there is greater demand to borrow money to make purchases. Interest rates typically fall when the economy is weak and there is less demand to borrow money.

Rawpixel.com/Shutterstock.com

All people in a nation who are capable of working, and want to work, are called the labor force. **How would you define the statement "capable of working"?**

Labor

All people in a nation who are capable of working and want to work are called the **labor force**. It does not include children, individuals who are retired, or people who choose not to work. The total labor force includes civilian workers as well as those in the military.

The civilian labor force is segmented as those who are employed and those who are unemployed. *Employed* includes everyone who is working. *Unemployed* includes those who do not have a job but are actively looking for one. The **unemployment rate** is the percentage of the civilian labor force that is unemployed.

An unemployment rate between 4 and 5 percent indicates a healthy economy. A rising unemployment rate indicates a weakening economy because it means businesses are not hiring or are eliminating part of their labor force. Higher levels of unemployment cause consumer spending to weaken, which reduces the rate of economic growth.

LO 14.2-2 Business Cycle

The economy in the United States, like all other nations, does not grow at the same rate each year. In many years, it grows faster than the average. In other years, it grows slower than average or may even decline. The **business cycle** is the alternating periods of economic expansion and contraction. The business cycle of a country has a direct impact on decisions an organization makes for its operation.

The four stages in the business cycle are expansion, peak, recession, and trough. Each one can vary in length. Understanding these stages can help managers make better economic decisions for the business. The graph in Figure 14-5 illustrates the cyclical movement in our economy.

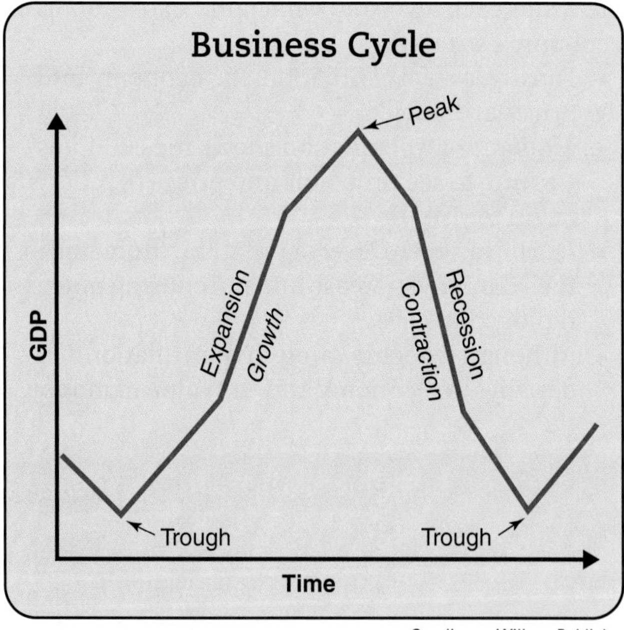

Goodheart-Willcox Publisher

Figure 14-5 Expansion, peak, recession, and trough are the four stages of the business cycle.

You Do the Math

Probabilistic Reasoning: Fundamental Counting Principle

The *fundamental counting principle* is a way to calculate the sample space for multiple independent events. The *sample space* is the set of all possible outcomes when determining probability. To use the fundamental counting principle, multiply the total possible outcomes of all events to find the sample space. For example, a printing company offers five types of printed banner material in one of seven sizes and four choices of fonts.

$5 \times 7 \times 4 = 140$ possible combinations

Solve the following problems.

1. The manager of a construction company must choose the model and features of a new truck to be used by employees. The dealership offers 3 choices for engine size, 14 choices for paint color, 2 choices for drive train, 5 choices for wheels and tires, and 3 choices for seat configuration. How many total combinations are possible for the truck?
2. A printing company offers a package in which a company's logo is printed as stickers in one of three sizes, magnets in one of five shapes, key chains in one of two styles, and water bottles in one of four styles. How many different packages are available?
3. A manager must price the printing of the annual report. The printer selected offers four choices of page size, three choices for binding, and nine choices for paper. How many total combinations are possible?

Expansion

Economic **expansion** is a period of growth when GDP is rising. Consumer confidence in the economy creates a sense of prosperity. It usually begins with an increase in consumer demand for goods and services. Businesses react to the rising demand by increasing production and hiring more workers. In addition, wages also begin to increase during an expansion. More workers and higher wages produce more demand for goods and services, which fuels more growth and continuous expansion.

Peak

The **peak** is the highest point in the business cycle and occurs at the end of an economic expansion. At this point in the business cycle, consumer demand for goods and services starts to slow. Businesses react cautiously and start cutting unnecessary expenditures. Wage growth tends to slow or stop. During the peak phase, overall economic growth slows.

Recession

Following the peak is a recession. A **recession** is a period of slow or no economic growth. It is marked by a contraction, or decline, across the economy. During this stage, inflation rates decline. Consumer demand decreases and causes businesses to drop their prices. Businesses must cut back on hiring and wages fall. On average, a recession can last anywhere from 12 to 18 months, but it may be less. When there is a severe economic contraction that lasts for a long period of time, it is called a *depression*.

Trough

The **trough** is the lowest stage of a business cycle and occurs at the end of a recession. A trough marks a period of renewed expansion called an *economic recovery*. The reason a recession ends is not always clear. However, through the increase of consumer demands for goods and services, the economy begins to grow again. Businesses often plan to increase production during a recovery and the cycle begins again.

LO 14.2-3 Correcting Economic Problems

The government takes an active role in trying to manage and stabilize the economy to reduce the length and effects of recessions in the business cycle. This happens through both fiscal and monetary policies.

Fiscal Policy

Fiscal policy is the taxation and spending decisions made by the president and Congress. Often, the government uses fiscal policy to smooth business cycles and lessen the impacts of recessions. Taxation and spending decisions are made to boost the GDP and reverse an economic contraction.

The economic theory is that when taxes are low, consumers and businesses have more money to spend. However, there is no guarantee that lowering taxes will increase consumer or business spending. They might choose to save the extra money or pay off debt instead.

Governmental spending of tax revenues creates demands for goods and services. For example, the government pays for highways with tax dollars. Private contractors build the highways with materials produced by private companies.

Ethics

Collusion

It is unethical and illegal for management to participate in acts of collusion. *Collusion* is an agreement between individuals or organizations to act illegally to deceive or cheat others. An example of collusion is two businesses working together to set prices so they can dominate the marketplace. Collusion is not only unethical, it is a form of fraud.

Ben Jeayes/Shutterstock.com

Monetary policy is the actions taken by a central bank, which is the Federal Reserve Bank, to regulate the money supply and interest rates. **Why is monetary policy important to the economy?**

The spending generates money that is put into the economy and helps create jobs and demand for goods and services.

Monetary Policy

Monetary policy is the actions taken by a central bank to regulate the money supply and interest rates. In the United States, the Federal Reserve is the central bank. The *US Federal Reserve System*, also called the *Fed*, was created in 1913. It is composed of 12 regional Federal Reserve Banks located in major cities throughout the country. The Federal Reserve System carries out the nation's monetary policy "to promote effectively the goals of maximum employment, stable prices, and moderate long-term interest rates."

When the economy is slowing, the Fed can use different tools to increase the growth of the money supply and help lower interest rates. The economic theory is that lowing interest rates makes borrowing easier. Lower interest rates can increase business investment and consumer spending. Likewise, the Fed can use tools to slow the growth of the money supply. It can increase interest rates to slow the economy and, hopefully, prevent inflation.

Section 14.2 Review

Check Your Understanding

1. Name two indices used to measure inflation.
2. When do interest rates rise, and when do they decline?
3. Why does a rising unemployment rate indicate a weakening economy?
4. List four stages of the business cycle.
5. How does the government use fiscal policy to help the economy?

Build Your Vocabulary

As you progress through this text, develop a personal glossary of key terms. This will help you build your vocabulary and prepare you for a career. Write a definition for each of the following terms and add them to your personal glossary.

economic indicator
gross domestic product (GDP)
inflation
inflation rate
deflation
interest
interest rate
labor force
unemployment rate
business cycle
expansion
peak
recession
trough
fiscal policy
monetary policy

Chapter 14 Review and Assessment

Chapter Summary

Section 14.1 Basics of Economics

LO 14.1-1 **Define *economic environment*.**
The economic environment consists of external factors outside the organization that directly influence its success. It is comprised of macroeconomic and microeconomic components.

LO 14.1-2 **Recognize the factors of production.**
Factors of production are the economic resources used to make goods and services for a population. They include land, labor, capital, and entrepreneurship.

LO 14.1-3 **Identify types of economic systems.**
An economic system is the structure in which resources are used to create goods and services. Economic systems can be defined as capitalist or command economies.

LO 14.1-4 **Explain the forces of supply and demand.**
Supply and demand determine the price of goods and services for a business. The law of supply and demand states the price of a product is determined by the relationship of the supply of a product and the demand for a product. Generally, higher demand results in higher prices, and lower demand results in lower prices. Greater supply often lowers prices, while lower supply results in higher prices.

LO 14.1-5 **Discuss economic competition.**
Economic competition is the action taken by two or more businesses attempting to attract the same customers. It occurs when two or more sellers offer similar goods and services for sale in the marketplace. Four basic market structures representing varying degrees of competition include monopoly, oligopoly, monopolistic competition, and perfect competition. Two forms of competition include price and nonprice competition.

Section 14.2 Our Economy

LO 14.2-1 **Cite examples of economic indicators used to measure economic activity.**
Examples of some of the most widely followed indicators used to measure economic activity are gross domestic product (GDP), inflation, interest rates, and the unemployment rate.

LO 14.2-2 **Summarize the business cycle.**
The business cycle is the alternating periods of economic expansion and contraction. It has a direct impact on the decisions an organization makes for its operation. The four stages of the cycle are expansion, peak, recession, and trough.

LO 14.2-3 **Explain how the government can correct economic problems.**
The government takes an active role to correct economic problems through both fiscal policies and monetary policies. Fiscal policy is the taxation and spending decisions made by the president and Congress. Often, the government uses fiscal policy to smooth business cycles and lessen the impacts of recessions. Monetary policy is the actions taken by a central bank to regulate the money supply and interest rates.

Review Your Knowledge

1. Summarize the economic environment.
2. Identify and define each factor of production.
3. Summarize types of economic systems.
4. Explain the forces of supply and demand.
5. Discuss economic competition.
6. What is the difference between price competition and nonprice competition?
7. Briefly explain economic indicators used to measure economic activity.
8. What does gross domestic product (GDP) indicate about the economy?
9. Summarize the business cycle.
10. Explain how the government can correct economic problems.

Apply Your Knowledge

1. Explain, in your own words, why it is important for a manager to understand the economic environment in which an organization operates.
2. Take a look at the current economy in which we live. Identify a resource that is scarce, such as gasoline or labor. Write a paragraph that explains how this scarcity personally affects you.
3. An economic system is the structure in which resources are used to create goods and services. Compare and contrast the following economic systems: capitalism, communism, socialism, and mixed economy. Create a graphic organizer to visually display the information.
4. How has supply and demand affected purchases that you have made over the last few months?
5. Market structure is how a market is organized based on the number of businesses competing for sales in an industry. Compare and contrast the market structures of monopoly, oligopoly, monopolistic competition, and perfect competition.
6. Perfect competition is characterized by a large number of businesses selling the same products, at the same prices. Identify a product sold by multiple stores at a similar price. Why do you think the selling price is similar for all the businesses?
7. Price competition is a situation that occurs when a lower price is the main reason for customers to buy from one business over another. Identify a time when you made a purchase based on price. How did price competition influence your purchasing decision?
8. Nonprice competition is a strategy to gain a competitive advantage through factors other than price. It may include better service, improved product assortment, or customer convenience. Select a store you shop at often. Identify examples of nonprice factors that can influence your purchasing decisions.
9. Some of the most widely followed indicators of the economy are gross domestic product (GDP), inflation, interest rates, and the unemployment rate. Select one of the indicators and summarize its influence on the current economy.
10. Is the current economy experiencing inflation, deflation, or neither? Explain your answer.

Communication Skills

College and Career Readiness

Listening. Begin a conversation with a classmate you do not already know very well. Ask the person about the clubs, sports teams, or other groups to which he or she belongs. Actively listen to what this person says. Build on his or her ideas by sharing your own thoughts. Next, summarize and retell what the person said in the conversation. Did you really hear what was being said? How is having a conversation with someone with whom you do not normally speak different from having a conversation with a friend or family member?

Reading. After you read this chapter, analyze how the author unfolds a series of ideas. Study the order in which the points are made, as well as how they are introduced and developed. How are the individual ideas related or connected? Draw a conclusion about the author's purpose for writing this material.

Writing. Being able to *retell* or *summarize* what you read can help you confirm your understanding of the material and demonstrate that you comprehend the subject. Summarizing is a technique that entails writing about the main points that you read. Summarizing involves identifying the most important ideas in the material and retelling them in your own words. Reread the first section in this chapter. Summarize the information in several paragraphs.

Internet Research

Economic Indicators. Search the Internet for current information on GDP, inflation rate, interest rates, and unemployment rate. What do these figures indicate about the overall economic health of the United States? At what stage of the business cycle would you say the economy is currently? Explain your reasoning.

Economic Recession and Depression. Search the Internet for *Great Recession of 2008* and read about this economic event. Then, search for *Great Depression of the 1930s* and read about this economic event. What economic conditions led to each event? How did the US work to grow its economy again after each one? Then, compare and contrast these economic events.

Teamwork

Working with a team, create a poster to explain the business cycle. Include a graphic illustration of the business cycle that identifies each stage. Use the material in this chapter as a basis for your information. Describe the condition of the economy during each stage of the business cycle.

Portfolio Development

College and Career Readiness

Skills and Talents. Candidates are reviewed based on their qualifications, including their skills and talents. Communication and interpersonal skills are often qualities that interviewers seek in applicants. These types of qualities are called soft skills. *Soft skills*, also called *employability skills* or *foundational skills*, are applicable skills used to help an individual find a job, perform in the workplace, and gain success in any job or career.

Acceptance committees also look for candidates who have the necessary skills to be successful in a position, such as the ability to use software programs or machinery. These abilities are called hard skills. *Hard skills*, or *job-specific skills*, are measurable, observable, and critical skills necessary to perform required, work-related tasks.

Additionally, you should showcase your *technical skills*. Examples of technical skills include working with computers and creating videos. Technical skills are very important for succeeding in school or at work.

Talents give insight into who an applicant is. In addition, some talents rely on different methods of processing information. For example, playing a musical instrument requires a different way of thinking than rebuilding an engine. Depending on the purpose of the interview, your talents may be criteria used to evaluate your qualifications.

Include samples of your skills or talents in your portfolio. Talents may be challenging to prove. One way to document your talents is to create a video. For example, if you are a musician, create a video with segments from your performances. Obtain permission to include other people in your video before doing so.

1. Conduct research about soft skills and their value in helping people succeed.
2. Create a Microsoft Word document and list the soft skills you currently possess that are important for a job or career. Use the heading "Skills" and your name. For each skill, write a paragraph that describes your abilities. Include soft skills, hard skills, and technical skills. Give examples to illustrate your skills. Save the document.
3. Create a Microsoft Word document that lists your talents. Use the heading "Talents" along with your name. Next to each talent listed, write a description of an assignment and explain how your talent was involved in completing it.
4. Scan hard-copy documents related to your talents to serve as samples. Save the documents in an appropriate folder.
5. Place the hard copies in the container for future reference.
6. Update your master spreadsheet.

CTSOs

Community Service Project. Many competitive events for CTSOs include a community service project. This project is usually created and executed by the entire CTSO chapter. In addition, it will take several months to complete. This project will probably span the school year. There will be two parts of the event, written and oral. The chapter will designate several members to represent the team at the competitive event.

To prepare for a community service project, complete the following activities.

1. Read the guidelines provided by your organization.
2. Contact the association immediately at the end of the state conference to prepare for next year's event.
3. As a team, select a theme for your chapter's community service project. Verify whether the chapter needs to gain approval on the project before moving forward. Depending on the organization, the CTSO may establish the theme for the project at the national level.
4. Decide which roles are needed for the team. There may be one person who is the captain, one person who is the secretary, and any other roles that will be necessary to create the plan. Ask your instructor for guidance in assigning roles to team members.
5. Identify your target audience, which may include business, school, and community groups.
6. Brainstorm with members of your chapter. List the benefits and opportunities of supporting a community service project.

CHAPTER 15

Managing in a Global Environment

Sections

College and Career Readiness

Reading Prep

Before reading this chapter, read the Apply Your Knowledge questions located in the Review and Assessment section. Use these questions to help you focus on the most important concepts as you read the content.

Exploring Careers

Global Manager

Global managers advance a company's efficiency and competitiveness on a global scale. They manage complex activities that occur when business is conducted across multiple time zones and diverse cultures. Global managers strategize, build assets and resources, and coordinate transactions across the world. They have general knowledge of all the organization's functions, even though they may specialize in one specific area.

Typical job titles for this position include *global project manager, international manager*, and *global accounts manager*. Examples of tasks global managers perform include:

- ensuring employee and business practices follow country, regional, and international regulations;
- verifying compliance in trade, imports and exports, and customs laws;
- reviewing reports, analyzing markets, and determining a course of action; and
- negotiating contracts.

Global manager positions require a bachelor degree, but many organizations may require a master degree and prior experience. Global managers need to understand industry operations and global business customer behavior. They must display cultural competency and the willingness to travel, since they often operate in foreign cultures. Communication, negotiation, diversity, diplomacy, and multitasking skills are essential for this career.

Syda Productions/Shutterstock.com

Section 15.1

Understanding the Global Environment

What does globalization mean to you?

Learning Objectives

LO 15.1-1 Explain the concept of globalization.

LO 15.1-2 List ways a business can enter into international trade.

LO 15.1-3 Summarize examples of regulations that govern international trade.

Key Terms 

globalization
international trade
absolute advantage
comparative advantage
licensing
joint venture
multinational corporation
contract manufacturing
trade policy
protectionism
trade barrier
embargo
trade sanction
tariff
quota
trade agreement
trading bloc

LO 15.1-1 Globalization

Globalization is the connection made among nations worldwide when economies freely move goods, labor, and money across borders. Modern technology enables countries to trade and conduct business beyond their borders. Globalization creates opportunities to open new markets, create new job positions, and recruit talent from other countries.

Absolute and Comparative Advantage

International trade is the buying and selling of goods and services between two or more countries. A primary reason why countries and businesses depend on international trade is that most do not have enough factors of production to produce all the goods and services needed by their population. Land, labor, capital, and entrepreneurship resources vary by country. Technology and modern transportation make it possible for businesses to trade goods and services easily with other countries so that needs and wants of its citizens are met.

An **absolute advantage** exists when a country or business can produce goods more efficiently, using the same amount of resources, and at a lower cost than the other country or business. For example, kiwifruit grows well in New Zealand. The kiwi market is an economically profitable export for them.

A **comparative advantage** exists when a country or business specializes in products that it can produce efficiently. These are goods and services that have the lowest opportunity cost but may not be produced at the highest volume. For example, the US has an advantage over other countries in the production of jet engines. While the volume of production may be relatively low, manufacturers can effectively produce enough engines for use in the US and for export to other countries.

Exporting and Importing

The *global economy* is the economic activity that transpires between countries. It has created opportunities for businesses to expand market potential, to create and sell products, and increase profitability.

An important reason why countries participate in international trade is to generate profits. An *export* is a product produced within a country's borders and sold in another country. By selling products outside the home country, a business can increase its sales and profitability. If sales increase, production increases, and new employees are needed. Employees earn wages,

Benny Marty/Shutterstock.com

The US has comparative advantage in the production of helicopters. **Why do you think the US has an advantage over other countries for this product?**

owners generate profits, and all pay taxes that benefit the community. People have money to spend, which benefits the community. The ripple effect of international trade affects all.

Importing is another way a company can increase potential profits. An *import* is a product brought into a country from outside its borders. It is sometimes less expensive for a manufacturer to import parts and assemble a product than to produce all the parts themselves. By importing less expensive parts, the profit level of the finished product can grow.

Alternatively, a business can import a finished product for a lesser price and sell it for a greater profit than if the business manufactures it. This saves time and overhead expenses rather than creating a product from the ground up. In addition, importing unique products can increase the appeal of a product line that a business might not normally have.

Importing, however, can be perceived as a negative for the citizens of a home country. Imported items brought into a home country generally mean those items are no longer manufactured in that country. People become unemployed and cannot contribute to the economy.

LO 15.1-2 Entering International Trade

In addition to exporting and importing, a company may decide to enter international trade through licensing, a franchise, a joint venture, a multinational corporation, or contract manufacturing as illustrated in Figure 15-1.

Licensing

Licensing occurs when a business sells the right to manufacture its products or use its trademark. Licensing involves selling the rights in exchange for a fee, also known as a royalty. A *royalty* is an amount of money paid to the original creator of an item. The company that sells the license is the *licensor*. The buyer of the license is the *licensee*. Licensing can benefit both parties because the licensor earns revenue, often for little to no extra work, and the licensee gets product into the market quickly.

Global Business				
Licensing	**Franchise**	**Joint Venture**	**Multinational Corporation**	**Contract Manufacturer**
• Disney • Ford Motor Company • Mattel • The Sharper Image • Warner Brothers	• Ace Hardware Corp. • Hilton Hotel and Resorts • Kumon Math & Reading Centers • RE/MAX LLC • The UPS Store	• BMW and Daimler • Dow Chemical and Corning Glass • Exxon Mobil and Royal Dutch Shell • Nissan and Renault • Toshiba Corporation and Hitachi Limited	• Amazon • Chevron Corporation • Hyundai Motor Company • Sony • United Airlines	• Celestica • Flextronics • Hon Hai Precision Industry (Foxconn) • Jabil Circuit • Sanmina - SCI

Goodheart-Willcox Publisher

Figure 15-1 There are numerous types of businesses involved in international trade.

FotograFFF/Shutterstock.com

Multinational corporations, such as IKEA, often have their corporate headquarters in one country and divisions of the business in another country. **What are some advantages a multinational corporation might realize?**

An example of a licensing agreement is Walt Disney entering into the Japanese market as the licensor of Tokyo Disneyland. The park was built and operated by Oriental Land Company, but the amusement park carries the Disney name.

Franchise

A *franchise* is the right to sell a company's goods or services in a specific area in return for royalty fees. The *franchisor* is the parent company that owns the chain and the brand. The *franchisee* is the company that buys the rights to use the brand. A franchisee pays an initial fee to the franchisor in addition to royalties based on the dollar volume of sales. Franchising enables the franchisee to enter a market where the good or service is already known. The franchisor provides standards and procedures to the franchisee to help get the company organized and in operation.

Joint Venture

A **joint venture** is a partnership of two or more companies that work together for a specific business purpose. Each company remains independent, but they share the profits or losses. It allows a company in one country to enter a foreign market without assuming all the risks. Joint ventures can be formed between two domestic businesses or between a domestic and foreign company. Some countries do not allow a foreign business to enter unless it has a joint venture with a domestic company.

An example of a joint venture is Campbell Soup Company entering into a joint venture with local companies in Japan and Malaysia. This allows Campbell to expand their markets into other countries without assuming all risks.

Multinational Corporation

A **multinational corporation** is a business that operates in more than one country. Multinational corporations often have their corporate headquarters in one country and divisions of the business in another country, or located offshore. *Offshoring* is the practice of basing selected company processes or services in other countries to enable them to take advantage of lower costs. Examples of multinational corporations are General Motors and Toshiba.

Contract Manufacturer

Contract manufacturing is transferring production work to another company. This is also known as *outsourcing*. Companies outsource production to avoid capital expenditures, reduce costs, or improve product quality. Many companies outsource work to foreign companies because the operating costs in other countries are lower. This can include the manufacture or assembly of final products or parts. Unfortunately, foreign outsourcing results in the loss of domestic jobs.

LO 15.1-3 Regulations

Governments regulate many aspects of international trade for various reasons, mostly to protect domestic companies from foreign competitors. There may also be political issues with foreign countries that influence how trade is conducted. Trade policies, trade regulations, trade agreements, and trade blocs are ways in which governments play a role in international trade.

Trade Policy

Trade policy is the body of laws related to the exchange of goods and services for international trade. Governments are constantly negotiating trade terms with one another. Most governments believe that fair and open trade among nations benefits everyone.

Trade Regulations

The nature of trade regulations is to promote fair competition and honest business practices in the global marketplace. Trade regulations can be used to prevent hazardous products from entering a country. They are also used to put political pressure on foreign governments and protect domestic businesses from foreign competitors.

Protectionism is a policy of protecting a country's domestic industries by enforcing trade regulations on foreign competitors. Protectionist policies can work against the goal of free trade.

Governmental policies that regulate trade can restrict or discourage import activity through trade barriers. A **trade barrier** is any governmental action taken to control or limit the amount of imports. There are several types of trade barriers including embargos, tariffs, and quotas.

- An **embargo** is a governmental order that prohibits trade with a foreign country. A *total embargo* is the most severe trade restriction. A **trade sanction** is an embargo that affects only certain goods. For example, trade sanctions can prohibit the import of a specific product for public health reasons.
- A **tariff** is a governmental tax on imported goods. A tariff is also known as a *duty, customs duty*, or *import duty*. One of the main reasons governments impose tariffs is for a source of revenue. Tariffs generate revenue for the government because the tax is paid on each related product. Imposing tariffs also protects domestic businesses. The additional tax makes imported products more expensive for consumers than competing products available from domestic businesses.
- A **quota** is a limit on the amount of a product imported into a country during a specific timeframe. For example, the United States has quotas on sugar, some textiles, tuna, beef, certain dairy products, and peanuts. Import quotas are meant to protect domestic producers by limiting foreign competition.

Kei Shooting/Shutterstock.com

Governments use import regulations to protect the health and safety of citizens from dangerous imported products. **Why do you think laws are needed to control imports into a country?**

Ethics

Confidentiality

Managers lead an organization. By default, they possess privileged, confidential information about a business and its employees. *Confidential* means that information is private and only shared with people who have clearance to receive it. Confidential business information should not be shared with anyone outside the management team. Doing so could harm the success of the business or its employees.

Governments use import regulations to protect the health and safety of citizens from dangerous imported products. For example, the United States has laws controlling firearms, drugs, and hazardous materials coming into the country. Additionally, there are laws regulating plants, animals, and food that may bring pests or diseases into the country. Endangered plant and animal species and products made from them are banned under the US Endangered Species Act.

Trade Agreements

The United States has trade agreements and partnerships with many individual nations and regions across the globe. A **trade agreement** is a document listing the conditions and terms for importing and exporting products between countries. The goal of trade agreements is to create economic benefits and opportunities for all participating nations by allowing free trade and investing across their borders.

The *World Trade Organization (WTO)* is a global organization that negotiates trade agreements and enforces a system of trade rules for its member countries. It is composed of over 160 nations around the world that have signed the WTO's international commerce agreements. These agreements outline the rights and responsibilities of member nations that engage in international trade with each other. In addition, the WTO handles trade-related disputes that arise between members. Most countries that engage in international trade belong to the WTO.

Established in 1994, the *North American Free Trade Agreement (NAFTA)* is a trade agreement between the United States, Canada, and Mexico. The agreement lowered trade barriers and opened markets among the three countries. Since NAFTA went into effect, trade has increased dramatically among the three nations. The ultimate goal of NAFTA was to reduce costs of trading and make North America more competitive in the global economic marketplace.

In 2018, President Trump renegotiated NAFTA with Canada and Mexico, establishing a new agreement. In accordance with the Office of the United States Trade Representative, "the *United States-Mexico-Canada Agreement (USMCA)* is a mutually beneficial win for North American workers, farmers, ranchers, and businesses. When finalized and implemented, the agreement will create more balanced, reciprocal trade that supports high-paying jobs for Americans and grows the North American economy." The USMCA has a 16-year expiration date and requires a review of the agreement every six years. Major points of the agreement are listed in Figure 15-2.

United States-Mexico-Canada Agreement (USMCA)

- New automobile rules by which the US, Canada, and Mexico must complete 75 percent of a car's production for it to pass through the countries duty-free
- Commitments to not engage in currency manipulation
- Modernizing and strengthening food and agricultural trade in North America
- Easing of rules regarding US exports of foods and dairy
- Support of a 21st century economy through new protections for US intellectual property

Goodheart-Willcox Publisher

Figure 15-2 The new United States-Mexico-Canada Agreement (USMCA) is a mutually beneficial win for North American workers, farmers, ranchers, and businesses.

Trading Blocs

A **trading bloc** is a group of countries joined together to trade as if they were a single country. A trading bloc is usually a free-trade zone as well. A *free-trade zone* is a group of countries that have reduced or eliminated trade barriers among themselves.

The *European Union (EU)* is a major trading bloc and free-trade zone in the modern global economy. It is the largest trade sector in the world. The EU has one of the largest gross domestic products (GDPs) and is the largest importer and exporter of goods and services. Many of the EU countries share the euro as the common currency.

Section 15.1 Review

Check Your Understanding

1. What is a primary reason why countries and businesses depend on international trade?
2. State the difference between exports and imports.
3. Why do companies outsource production?
4. What is the purpose of trade regulations?
5. What is the goal of trade agreements?

Build Your Vocabulary

As you progress through this text, develop a personal glossary of key terms. This will help you build your vocabulary and prepare you for a career. Write a definition for each of the following terms and add them to your personal glossary.

globalization	multinational corporation	embargo
international trade	contract manufacturing	trade sanction
absolute advantage	trade policy	tariff
comparative advantage	protectionism	quota
licensing	trade barrier	trade agreement
joint venture		trading bloc

Section 15.2

Operating in a Global Environment

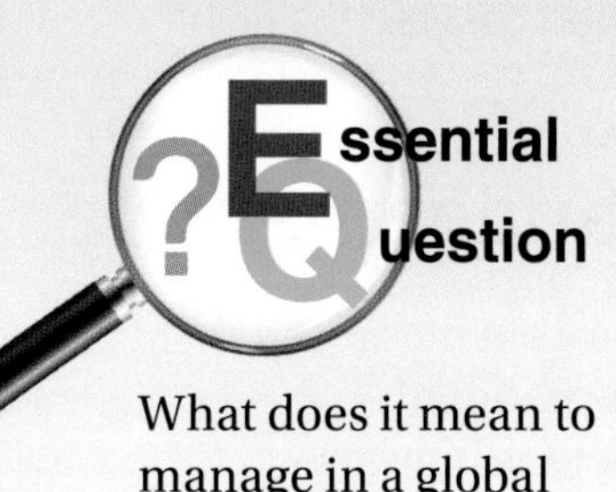

What does it mean to manage in a global environment?

Learning Objectives

LO 15.2-1 Discuss the global environment.

LO 15.2-2 Summarize global management.

LO 15.2-3 Identify examples of challenges when operating in a global environment.

Key Terms 

political environment
legal environment
sociocultural environment
culture
technological environment
global management
global manager
cultural competency
foreign exchange rate
letters of credit
logistics

LO 15.2-1 Global Environment

The *global environment* is made up of factors that influence a business when conducting international business. Organizations that opt to participate in international business must be aware of the global environment. What might be a good situation today for conducting global business can become a negative situation overnight.

There are multiple factors that comprise the global environment. Examples of those factors include the political, legal, sociocultural, and technological environments.

Political Environment

The **political environment** refers to the economic and governmental actions that affect the operations of business. Capitalist and command economies each function differently. The type of economic system in which a country operates may require changes to the way in which an organization conducts business.

Political structure is an important factor for conducting global business. The level of stability in a country's government affects the success of businesses that operate within it. Stability also affects the willingness and ability of consumers to purchase products.

Political instability usually occurs because country elections are not fair to its citizens. When the politics of a country fluctuates dramatically, it can result in military conflicts, changes in political leadership, and poor economic conditions. Conducting business with a politically unstable country can be difficult, as well as dangerous.

Legal Environment

The **legal environment** is the laws and regulations of a country that can affect business operations. The legal environment, such as laws relating to trade, has a significant impact on businesses. Trade regulations determine the extent to which a company can engage in business within certain markets. A country's tax policy affects the potential success of a business expanding overseas. Some countries have tax policies created to attract foreign businesses, while the tax laws of other countries make it more difficult for a business to be successful.

Sociocultural Environment

The **sociocultural environment** refers to the external environment that focuses on the society and culture of a country. **Culture** is the shared beliefs, customs, practices, and social behavior of a particular group or nation. It affects how people think, work, interact, and communicate with others.

Mike Flippo/Shutterstock.com

Culture is the shared beliefs, customs, practices, and social behavior of a particular group or nation. **How can culture influence the success or failure of an organization?**

The cultural beliefs and values of potential customers in a market affect how they make economic decisions and set economic goals. Attitudes toward spending, saving, and borrowing money can vary drastically. In addition, topics such as health, environmental issues, and leisure time can have a significant impact on whether a business is successful.

Social factors include the customs and expected behaviors related to carrying out business activities, such as meetings, financial transactions, developing business relationships, and other business functions. Social and business etiquette may differ in foreign countries. For example, in some countries it is customary to bring a gift to the host of a business meeting. In others, this would be an awkward and uncomfortable gesture.

Technological Environment

The **technological environment** is the external factors in technology that affect the way business is conducted. It includes equipment, software, and storage devices required to operate a business. Organizations must adapt their processes and embrace the technological environment to stay competitive and profitable.

Technology has provided means for the transaction of business around the clock and around the world. Companies have instant access to employees, customers, and suppliers regardless of their locations. Translation software has improved communication when conducting business with those who speak another language. In addition, working in the cloud enables teams around the world to work in real time.

With the increasing importance of the technological environment, security becomes an ongoing concern. Cybersecurity requires an investment of money, people, and time. Organizations can be at risk without the investment in protection of their assets.

LO 15.2-2 Global Management

Organizations that conduct business globally typically employ international managers. **Global management** is how an organization manages and directs its businesses internationally. This includes managing the sales, marketing, hiring, and financial practices of businesses in other countries outside of the one of domain. Global management is also known as *international management*. A **global manager** is a person who manages a business across country borders. He or she is a leader who is aware of the economic, cultural, and legal aspects of the country in which a business operates.

Global management is approached from different angles depending on the organization. Some businesses prefer to send their own management team to other countries to manage the operations. These organizations typically send managers to a training program to prepare them for the culture of the new country to which they are going. A typical six-week course prepares them for the culture, food, transportation, and other challenges they will encounter.

Pressmaster/Shutterstock.com

Global management is how an organization manages and directs its businesses internationally. **What factors do you think an organization must consider when planning global management strategies?**

Other organizations prefer to hire local talent in the country of business. These managers typically attend a training program at the home office to learn how business is conducted. These managers learn the culture of the United States, operations of the company, and other training required to manage the business.

LO 15.2-3 Challenges in a Global Environment

To be successful in a global market, there is much information that a manager needs to understand, depending on the level of involvement in international business. For example, a manager for a manufacturing business that imports parts may require an understanding of currency and the metric system. For a manager of a business that exports finished product, mastery of a foreign language and country culture may be required to transact business. Common challenges that management must address when conducting global business are culture, currency, labor laws, legal documents, logistics, and time zones.

Culture

As companies continue to expand globally, it is important to understand the culture that workers may face. *Culture* is the shared beliefs, customs, practices, and social behavior of a particular group or nation. As workers interact with other companies on a global scale, awareness of these cultures is necessary as business communication takes place. Shaking hands, exchanging business cards, and dining together are examples of important communication that can have a positive or negative impact on an international business meeting. Knowing what is acceptable to a coworker from another culture will help facilitate positive interaction.

Cultural competency is the acknowledgment of cultural differences and the ability to adapt one's communication style to successfully send and receive messages despite those differences. For example, corporations operating on a global scale often hold meetings with representatives from different countries. If a language barrier does exist, the culturally competent action is to have an *interpreter* present to avoid any miscommunication.

You Do the Math

Measurement Reasoning: Currency Conversion

It may be necessary to convert amounts of money from one currency to another when conducting business internationally. Exchange rate quotes are expressed as one country's currency in relation to the other currency. A unit of the *base currency* is valued at one. The equivalent amount is called the *counter currency* or *quote*. For example, the exchange rate of US dollars to European euros (EUR or €) is as follows.

$1.00 = €0.85

The exchange rate of European euros to US dollars is as follows.

€1.00 = $1.17

Currency exchange rates change every day, and can be found online.

The exchange rates needed to complete the following calculations are provided.

Solve the following problems.

1. An operations manager is purchasing raw materials from a supplier in Sweden. The price of the raw materials is in euros. The cost of the materials is €1,798.00. The current exchange rate is $1.00 = €0.85. What is the cost of the raw materials in US dollars? (Round to the nearest cent.)
2. A manufacturer of small appliances needs to purchase $3,500 worth of circuit boards from a supplier in India. The supplier's prices are listed in Indian rupees (INR or ₹). The current exchange rate is $1.00 = ₹66.00. What is the cost of the circuit boards in rupees?

Employability Skills

Cultural Competency

Cultural competency is the acknowledgment of cultural differences and the ability to adapt one's communication style to successfully send and receive messages despite those differences. The first step in becoming culturally competent involves recognizing cultural barriers. Being aware of potential disruptions is the best way to prevent or avoid them. The second step of cultural competency involves the willingness to adapt to those barriers.

Achieving cultural competence may not always be an easy task. In general, treating people with respect and patience and using best practices in the workplace will ultimately help in attaining cultural competence.

Currency

When negotiating business prices, currency must be considered. *Currency* is money. Most countries have their own currencies, which is typically required for business exchanges. For example, a US business that buys from the United Kingdom needs to exchange US dollars for British pounds to complete a financial transaction.

The **foreign exchange rate** is the cost to convert one currency into another. Exchange rates are needed because currencies have different values. For example, the value of one US dollar (USD) is not equal to one European euro (EUR). The exchange rate helps determine how much in European euros is needed to equal one US dollar. Figure 15-3 shows examples of five foreign currency exchange rates over time.

Labor Laws

If hiring labor in another country, there are many issues related to a country's labor force that can impact the success of conducting business abroad. Each country has unique labor laws that determine who can work, number of days and hours of work, and minimum rates of pay. The standard of acceptable working conditions also varies from country to country. Businesses must comply with the labor laws in each country in which they operate as well as US labor laws that apply to doing business in foreign countries. The US Bureau of International Labor Affairs (ILAB) and the Office of International Relations (OIR) offer organizations assistance with labor laws in other countries.

Legal Documents

Sales transactions require documents to accompany the goods or services sold globally. Many businesses and governmental agencies require special documentation to trade and transport products. These organizations include foreign customs offices, airports, harbors, and law enforcement and security agencies. Some of the documents required include air waybills, certificates of origin, dock receipts, ocean bills of lading, proof of insurance, and special packing lists. **Letters of credit** are documents used to guarantee payment in other countries. In a letter of credit, a bank guarantees the funds are paid as expected.

Currency Exchange Rates (Value per USD)			
Currency	**June 1, 2016**	**June 1, 2017**	**June 1, 2018**
British Pound (GBP)	£1.44	£1.29	£1.34
Canadian Dollar (CAD)	$1.31	$1.35	$1.29
European Union Euro (EUR)	€1.12	€1.12	€1.17
Japanese Yen (JPY)	¥109.55	¥111.24	¥109.49
Mexican Peso (MXN)	$18.55	$18.58	$19.86

Source: Board of Governors of the Federal Reserve System; Goodheart-Willcox Publisher

Figure 15-3 Foreign exchange rate is the cost to convert one currency into another.

Logistics

Logistics is planning and managing the flow of goods, services, and people to a destination. When a business sells products overseas, products must be moved over at least one country's border by air, rail, water, or truck. This is much more complex than transporting products domestically and may require the services of external professionals as well as longer shipping times and greater expenses.

Avigator Fortuner 887/Shutterstock.com

Logistics is planning and managing the flow of goods, services, and people to a destination. **Why is logistics an important consideration for global businesses?**

Time Zones

Not all countries are in the same time zone. Countries may be one hour to several hours apart. Conducting business with countries in other time zones presents challenges. Some of these challenges include scheduling meetings, traveling to conduct business, or simply mailing an item and determining when it will reach its destination.

Technology offers a wealth of options for conducting operations across time zones. It is a strong tool for managers to use to engage in business in different time zones. E-mails, video conferences, and other forms of telecommunication can keep people on different time zones connected and current.

Section 15.2 Review

Check Your Understanding

1. List examples of factors that comprise the global environment.
2. Briefly explain political instability.
3. What are examples of challenges that must be addressed when working in a global environment?
4. Why is it important to know and understand cultural differences in a business setting?
5. Cite examples of legal documents required for international business.

Build Your Vocabulary

As you progress through this text, develop a personal glossary of key terms. This will help you build your vocabulary and prepare you for a career. Write a definition for each of the following terms and add them to your personal glossary.

- political environment
- legal environment
- sociocultural environment
- culture
- technological environment
- global management
- global manager
- cultural competency
- foreign exchange rate
- letters of credit
- logistics

Chapter 15 Review and Assessment

Chapter Summary

Section 15.1 Understanding the Global Environment

LO 15.1-1 Explain the concept of globalization.
Globalization is the connection made among nations worldwide when economies freely move goods, labor, and money across borders. The global environment in which businesses operate has created opportunities to expand and increase profits by opening new markets for products, creating jobs for employees in the home country, and recruiting talent from other countries around the world.

LO 15.1-2 List ways a business can enter into international trade.
A company may decide to enter international trade through licensing, a franchise, a joint venture, a multinational corporation, or contract manufacturing.

LO 15.1-3 Summarize examples of regulations that govern international trade.
Governments regulate many aspects of international trade for various reasons, mostly to protect domestic companies from foreign competitors. Trade policies, trade regulations, trade agreements, and trade blocs are ways in which governments play a role in international trade.

Section 15.2 Operating in a Global Environment

LO 15.2-1 Discuss the global environment.
The global environment is made up of factors that influence a business when conducting international trade. Organizations that opt to participate in international business must be aware of the global environment. There are multiple factors that comprise the global environment including the political, legal, sociocultural, and technological environments.

LO 15.2-2 Summarize global management.
Global management is how an organization manages and directs its businesses internationally. This includes managing the sales, marketing, the hiring process, and financial practices of businesses in other countries outside of the one of domain.

LO 15.2-3 Identify examples of challenges when operating in a global environment.
Common examples of challenges that management must address when conducting global business are culture, currency, labor laws, legal documents, logistics, and time zones.

Review Your Knowledge

1. Briefly explain the concept of globalization.
2. How do businesses benefit from exporting and importing goods?
3. Identify ways a business can enter into international trade.
4. Summarize examples of regulations that govern international trade.
5. What is the World Trade Organization (WTO)?
6. Explain the global environment.
7. What are examples of cultural beliefs that can affect the success of an international business?
8. Summarize global management.
9. Briefly explain examples of challenges faced by management when operating in a global environment.
10. State an example of cultural competency in a business environment.

Apply Your Knowledge

1. Create a list of absolute advantages for the US. Next to each, explain why you think an advantage exists.
2. Create a list of five examples of comparative advantages for the US. Next to each, explain why you think an advantage exists.
3. The global economy is the economic activity that transpires between countries. Analyze the impact of the global economy on business profitability.
4. Offshoring is the practice of basing selected company processes or services in other countries to enable them to take advantage of lower costs. Discuss your opinion of offshoring. How does it help or hurt the US economy?
5. In your own words, explain what this statement means. "Governments regulate many aspects of international trade for various reasons, mostly to protect domestic companies from foreign competitors." Why would companies need protection?
6. What is the current political environment of the US? How do you think this affects businesses that export products to other countries?
7. Technology has obviously had a positive impact on global business. It has provided the means for business transactions to occur around the clock and around the world. What technology do you think will play an important role in the future of the global environment?
8. In your own words, write several paragraphs describing why you would or would not want to have a position as a global manager for an organization.
9. Describe business culture in the United States. Include any important information an employee from another country would need to understand to be successful.
10. Using a scale of 1–10 with 10 being highest, describe your level of cultural competency.

Communication Skills

College and Career Readiness

Speaking. An effective strategy for committing information to memory is to recite the information you want to remember. After reading this chapter, choose important information to commit to memory. This may be definitions or information you anticipate to be included on a test. Then, recite the information aloud until you have committed it to memory.

Listening. *Implicit* means hinted at without being expressed. When information is implicit, there may be hints or related ideas, but it is not said directly. For example, suppose you ask your instructor what will be on an exam. Your instructor responds that he or she cannot tell you what will be on the test but suggests studying specific topics. The implicit idea is the list of suggested topics will be on the test. Have a conversation with a classmate about tonight's homework. Identify any implicit information from him or her. How were you able to understand the implicit messages?

Reading. Being able to respond to questions about what you read demonstrates that you comprehend the information. After reading each section of the chapter, stop to answer the Check Your Understanding questions and complete the Build Your Vocabulary activity without looking back at the information covered in the chapter. Then, look back at the information to check your work.

Internet Research

Global Environment. There are many challenges that a business encounters when doing business internationally. Perform an Internet search for *business in a global environment.* Summarize some of the challenges to consider when conducting business in another country.

Trade Agreements. Established in 1994, the North American Free Trade Agreement (NAFTA) is a trade agreement between the United States, Canada, and Mexico. In 2018, NAFTA made headlines when the agreement was renegotiated to the new United States-Mexico-Canada Agreement (USMCA). Conduct an online search for *NAFTA*. Summarize the information that you found.

Teamwork

Working with your team, discuss the impact of imports and exports on the United States. Identify ways you and your team believe imports and exports help the United States. In addition, include any negative effects of the United States participating in import and export activities. Create a chart with pros on the left side and cons on the right side. Record the team's responses on the chart.

Portfolio Development

Diversity Skills. As part of an interview with a school or business, you may be asked about your travels or experiences with people from other cultures. Many different organizations serve people from a variety of geographic locations and cultures. Some have offices or facilities in more than one region or country. Representatives of these organizations may travel to facilities in different countries. You may need to interact with people from diverse cultures.

When applying for both work and school, the interviewer will want to know that you have the ability to work or get along with any person you may encounter. Therefore, having traveled, studied, or worked in other countries can be valuable assets. It is in the school's or company's best interest to have culturally competent representatives. In an academic setting, you could work as an English as a second language (ESL) instructor. In a professional setting, you may be able to understand the needs and wants of diverse people. You may also be better able to communicate and get along with others.

1. Identify travel or other educational experiences that helped you learn about another culture, such as foreign languages studied or trips taken.
2. Create a Microsoft Word document that describes the experience. Use the heading "Diversity Experience" and your name. Explain how the information you learned might help you better understand classmates, customers, or coworkers from this culture. Save the document in an appropriate folder.
3. Place a printed copy in the container for future reference.
4. Update your checklist to reflect the file format and location of the document.

CTSOs

Business Calculations. The business calculations event is an objective test that covers multiple problems related to various business applications. Participants are usually allowed one hour to complete the event.

To prepare for a business calculations test, complete the following activities.

1. Visit the website of the organization well in advance of the date of the event.
2. Download any posted practice tests.
3. Time yourself taking the tests with the aid of a calculator. Check the answers and correct any mistakes you may have made.
4. Review the Math Skills Handbook in this text.
5. Visit the website of the organization often to make sure information regarding the event has not changed.

UNIT 7

Small Business Management

Chapters

Functions of Management Covered in This Unit

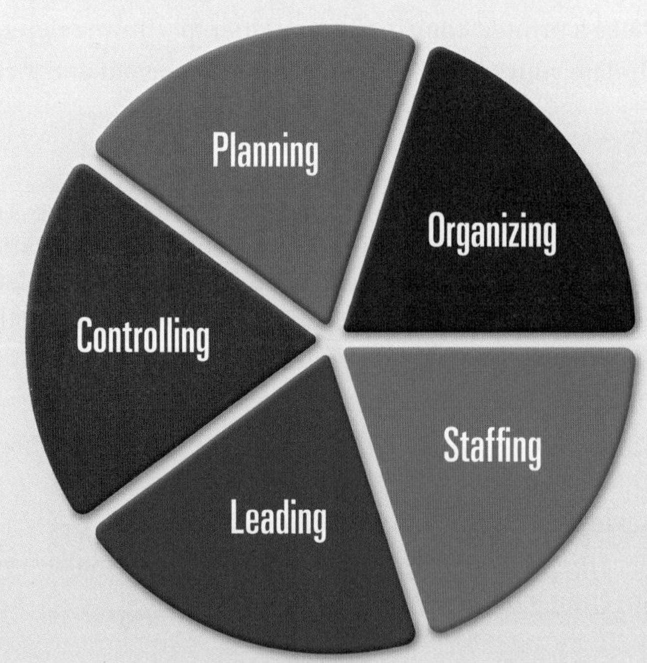

While studying, look for the activity icon for:

- Vocabulary terms with e-flash cards and matching activities

These activities can be accessed at www.g-wlearning.com/business/8417

Case Study

Professionalism

Minerva Studio/Shutterstock.com

Jason is a talented cybersecurity specialist who works for a securities firm. He has worked there for ten years and enjoys his job but is looking for a new career opportunity. Even though Jason is happy with his career choice, he looks toward the future and dreams of having his own cybersecurity business. He is well known in the cybersecurity profession, and his reputation has spread in the corporate workspace. He is confident that he could be successful on his own.

Jason made an appointment to speak with his employer about resigning from his position and to share plans to start his own business. It was time for him to leave and go on his own. He thanked his manager for the opportunity to work for her and expressed his appreciation for the career growth provided to him by the company. He wanted to be honest rather than resign without a conversation and walk out.

His manager was impressed with his honesty and consideration to share the news. She expressed her appreciation and offered support for him to create a new business. Because she respected his integrity and his talent, she urged him to register as an independent contractor for her company.

Professionalism is the act of exhibiting appropriate character, judgment, and behavior by a person trained to perform a job. It means conducting oneself in a manner that exhibits responsibility, integrity, and excellence. By demonstrating professionalism, Jason took the initial step to signing his first client for his new business.

Critical Thinking

1. Why is it important for individuals, whether an employee or a manager, to demonstrate professionalism?
2. Jason was honest with his employer about why he was resigning. Discuss the importance of honesty for career success.

CHAPTER 16

Managing a Startup

Sections

Reading Prep

Before reading this chapter, review the Learning Objectives for each section as well as the major headings. Compare the objectives to the headings. What did you discover?

Exploring Careers

Entrepreneur

Entrepreneurs are those who start new businesses or purchase existing businesses. Most entrepreneurs have started out working for someone else before going out on their own. They can open a business by creating a new business, buying an existing business, or buying a franchise. In any case, they are most often the responsible parties for drafting a business plan and securing business funding.

Typical job titles for this position include *principal*, *owner*, and *proprietor*. Examples of tasks entrepreneurs perform include:

- conducting research into the desired marketplace;
- applying for a business loan;
- performing necessary business-related tasks; and
- hiring employees to assist with operations.

Anyone can become an entrepreneur, and there is no required diploma or certification needed for this career. However, having a background or degree in business helps exponentially. Entrepreneurs must have the essential hard skills needed for the business they desire to open. For example, a person starting a computer repair business must have computer repair skills. Additionally, entrepreneurs must have exceptional soft skills, including communication skills, empathy, perseverance, and a sense of independence and accountability.

Dragon Images/Shutterstock.com

Section 16.1 Entrepreneurship

Why would a person want to start a business instead of working for an established organization?

Learning Objectives

LO 16.1-1 Define what it means to be an entrepreneur.

LO 16.1-2 Summarize a startup.

LO 16.1-3 Discuss startup strategies.

Key Terms

entrepreneur

entrepreneurship

startup

LO 16.1-1 Entrepreneurs

Many large businesses start as a small business owned by one person. As a small business becomes successful, there is potential that it can grow, hire employees, and even potentially incorporate and evolve into a large business. For example, at age 16, Michael Kittredge began hand-making candles for presents in his family's kitchen. He eventually opened his own small retail store with the help of friends and family. Over time, the small business expanded into the Yankee Candle Company with over 575 retail stores.

In the United States, any individual who is creative, willing to take a chance, and has a good idea can be an entrepreneur. An **entrepreneur** is a person who risks his or her own resources to start and operate a business. Creating a business takes time, and it does not happen overnight. Many entrepreneurs begin their careers by working for an existing company to gain experience before going out on their own. Working for another person or organization is a great way to learn the fundamentals of managing a company.

Entrepreneurship is the capacity to take the risks and responsibilities of starting a new business. It refers to the personal qualities that help an individual create, operate, and assume the risk of a new business.

A person starting a business must have the hard skills required for the profession. *Hard skills* are the critical skills necessary to perform the tasks of the position. For example, an entrepreneur starting a company that completes income tax returns needs to understand accounting and tax laws. During the early days of a startup, the owner will probably perform most of the job tasks. More than likely, there will not be funds to hire an employee to perform services. The owner must be able to perform every duty that is required to operate the business.

An entrepreneur must also possess good soft skills. *Soft skills* are the skills used to communicate and work with others. It includes understanding how to communicate and act in professional situations. These are the skills that enable a person to interact with others in a positive manner.

Ethics

Favoritism

Favoritism is the act of showing preferential treatment to one person or group over another. Managers who show favoritism with employees create a negative work environment. All employees should be treated fairly and equally. In addition, if the act of favoritism violates company policies, such as giving one employee an extra vacation day, the act could be considered illegal.

jejim/Shutterstock.com

As a small business becomes successful, there is potential that it can grow, hire employees, and even potentially incorporate and evolve into a large business, such as the Yankee Candle Company. **Discuss the advantages and disadvantages of growing a small business into a large business.**

LO 16.1-2 Startup

A **startup** is an entrepreneurial venture of creating a new business. It begins with the discovery process of identifying a need to be met in the marketplace. Not every idea can evolve into a business. Whether an idea is for a new good, service, or an improvement of an existing product, it must stand out from the competition.

There must be a ready market, or a current demand, for a new good or service. It takes much market research to recognize an opportunity that can be successful enough to generate a profit. Understanding the market enables an entrepreneur to focus on the most effective way to develop, advertise, and deliver a product. When an idea is confirmed as profitable, and an entrepreneur is ready to start a business, a decision will be made as to the type of business that will be created. Types of businesses for consideration include producers, intermediaries, and service businesses, as shown in Figure 16-1.

- **Producer.** A producer creates goods and services. This includes manufacturers who take materials and turn them into a product. It also includes farmers who raise crops or livestock.
- **Intermediary.** An intermediary takes goods and services from producers to the end user. Two common intermediaries are a wholesaler and retailer. A *wholesaler* is an intermediary that takes products from the producer to the retailer. A *retailer* is the business that buys product from the wholesaler and sells them to consumers to make a profit.
- **Service business.** A service business provides services to its customers. Hairdressers, electricians, and computer programmers are examples of service providers.

LO 16.1-3 Startup Strategies

After deciding the good or service a business will provide, an entrepreneur must decide the best way of starting the business. Will it be starting a business from the ground up? Perhaps there is a similar business for sale that can be purchased. Buying a franchise is another way to start a new business.

Start a New Business

When most people think of a new business, they usually think of starting from the ground up. Entrepreneurs who choose this option have the unique opportunity to build a reputation and establish a customer base on their own terms.

Types of Businesses		
Producers	**Intermediaries**	**Service Businesses**
• Automobile manufacturer • Iron ore extractor • Logging company • Organic farmer	• Apparel outlet • Electric supplies wholesaler • Grocery store • PC parts distributor	• Currency exchange • Event planning service • Lawn care company • Tax accounting firm

Goodheart-Willcox Publisher

Figure 16-1 Types of businesses include producers, intermediaries, and service businesses.

Starting from nothing puts the owner in complete charge of all aspects of the startup, such as finding a location, setting operating policies, purchasing needed assets, negotiating a lease, and hiring employees.

Buy an Existing Business

For a person looking to start a business, one option for ownership is to look for a business that is for sale. Buying an existing business can accelerate the start-up time. Taking over an operation that has an established customer base, location, and employees can help an entrepreneur get started quickly.

Buy a Franchise

Some entrepreneurs choose to buy a franchise. A *franchise* is a license to sell a company's goods or services within a certain territory or location. Buying a franchise gives a person the right to sell an established good or service. A *franchisee* is a person or company that buys a franchise. A *franchisor* is a person or company that grants a franchise. Examples of franchises include H&R Block and Ace Hardware.

A franchisee pays for the use of a logo, name, and products. In return, the franchisor provides marketing services, training, and perhaps assistance with funding. According to the Small Business Administration (SBA), a franchise gives the entrepreneur guidance but less control. Owning a franchise means that the owner must abide by the rules of the franchise and have less input on business operation.

Mark Van Scyoc/Shutterstock.com

The Small Business Administration (SBA) is a valuable resource for entrepreneurs. **Why do you think a person starting a business would need help from a resource, such as the SBA?**

Section 16.1 Review

Check Your Understanding

1. Who can be an entrepreneur?
2. How do many entrepreneurs begin their careers?
3. What types of businesses can an entrepreneur consider creating?
4. Name three startup strategies.
5. Define *franchise*, *franchisee*, and *franchisor*.

Build Your Vocabulary

As you progress through this text, develop a personal glossary of key terms. This will help you build your vocabulary and prepare you for a career. Write a definition for each of the following terms and add them to your personal glossary.

entrepreneur　　entrepreneurship　　startup

Section 16.2 Planning

If an entrepreneur does not have enough personal funds for a new business, what options for funding would a person have?

Learning Objectives

LO 16.2-1 Discuss the planning function as it applies to an entrepreneur.
LO 16.2-2 Summarize funding a new business.
LO 16.2-3 Identify examples of legal considerations when starting a new business.

Key Terms 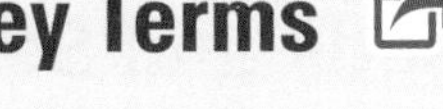

pro forma statement
self-funding
equity financing
venture capital
angel investor
debt financing
peer-to-peer lending

LO 16.2-1 Planning Function

All successful businesses start with a plan. *Planning* is the process of setting goals and objectives and deciding how to accomplish them. A *plan* is an outline of the actions needed to accomplish a goal. Without planning, a new business would likely not be successful. The planning process begins by writing a business plan.

A *business plan* is a written document that describes a business, how it operates, and how it makes a profit. A business plan defines the organization and serves as a blueprint for operation. It helps an entrepreneur decide how to start and operate his or her business successfully. In addition, a business plan is used when applying for financing with banks and other financial institutions. A typical business plan outline is shown in Figure 16-2.

The *Small Business Administration (SBA)* is a good source of information for new business owners. The SBA offers entrepreneurs templates and information for writing a business plan. The SBA recommends that a business plan include an executive summary, company description, market analysis, organization and management documentation, list of goods and services offered, marketing and sales information, and a financial plan.

Business Plan

Title Page
I. Table of Contents
II. Executive Summary
III. Company Description
IV. Market Analysis
V. Organization and Management
VI. Goods and Services Offered
VII. Marketing and Sales
VIII. Financial Plan
VIX. Bibliography
X. Appendices

Goodheart-Willcox Publisher

Figure 16-2 A business plan is a written document that describes a business, how it operates, and how it makes a profit serving as a blueprint for operation of the business.

Executive Summary

The executive summary is a description of the business and summary as to why it will be successful. The executive summary includes a *mission statement,* which is a sentence describing the purpose of the business. The mission statement is the organization's message to customers about why the business exists. It describes the business, identifies the potential customers, and shows how the business adds value.

A *vision statement* is what the business aspires to accomplish. The vision statement is like looking into a crystal ball and seeing the future of the company.

Company Description

A company description identifies problems the business will solve, target customers, and the competitive advantages the business provides. It also describes the business as a physical location, online store, or a combination. The company description also highlights the advantages a business has over its competitors.

Market Analysis

The market analysis provides an overview of the industry and market the business will serve. It presents the current and projected size of the entire market and identifies competitors. It also includes an estimate of how much of the market the entrepreneur plans to capture. The market analysis section also provides an indication of growth potential within the industry.

Organization and Management

The organization and management section details how the company is organized and operated. Is it a new business, purchase of an existing business, or a franchise? Is the business a sole proprietorship, a partnership, a corporation, or an alternative form of ownership? If there are employees, the organization chart is included.

Iakov Filimonov/Shutterstock.com

The goods and services portion of the business plan provides an in-depth description of what the business will sell. **Why would a bank or other funding source be interested in reading the entrepreneur's thorough description of product in a business plan?**

Employability Skills

Self-Awareness

Self-awareness is a sense of being aware of one's feelings, behaviors, needs, and other elements that make up the whole person. In order to promote yourself to others, you have to be aware of who you are and what your ultimate goal may be in the organization.

Goods and Services Offered

The goods and services portion of the business plan provides an in-depth description of what the business will sell. This section also includes each product's life cycle and a plan for pricing. In addition, an explanation is included that explains the competition and how it will be overcome.

Marketing and Sales

The marketing and sales strategy section describes how the business will reach its customers. The plan for promoting and selling products, average sale per customer needed to make a profit, and strategy for business growth is included.

Financial Plan

If asking for funding, this section explains how much cash is needed, how it will be used, and if debt or equity funding is being requested. The financial plan also defines when the loan must be repaid.

Funding requests should include pro forma statements. A **pro forma statement** is a financial statement based on estimates of future business performance, sales, and expenses. It should cover a cost estimate of one year, as well as a summary of start-up costs. *Start-up costs* are the initial expenses necessary to open a business. These can include costs of purchasing equipment or paying rent for the location of the business. Projections for a startup generally forecast the first year of business. Commonly prepared pro forma statements include the following.

- A *pro forma balance sheet* projects the future amount of assets, liabilities, and net worth for the business.
- A *pro forma income statement* projects future revenues and expenses for the business.
- A *pro forma cash flow statement* is the estimated amount of cash that will flow in and out of the business.

LO 16.2-2 Funding

Projecting start-up expenses is an important task when creating a business plan. Calculating expenses enables an owner to estimate profits, obtain funding, and prepare for tax filings. A first step in determining start-up costs is to decide if the business will be brick-and-mortar, online, or both. For example, a brick-and-mortar business requires floor space, equipment, utilities, and inventory. An online business may have similar requirements for business operations, but it will also need money invested in technology. Understanding the expenses to be covered is a necessary step to obtain the proper funding for a business.

An entrepreneur needs money to start, operate, and grow a business. Some entrepreneurs self-fund their business. **Self-funding**, also known as *bootstrapping*, means the owner uses his or her own money to start a business. Examples could be personal savings, investments, retirement funds, or other personal resources. With self-funding, the owner has full ownership interest in the business.

Some entrepreneurs finance their business. *Financing*, also known as *funding*, is necessary to obtain enough cash to start the business. Two common ways of funding are equity financing and debt financing, as shown in Figure 16-3.

Equity Financing

Equity financing is capital brought into the business in exchange for a percentage of ownership in the business. When equity financing is used, the person investing funds into the business gains a percentage of ownership. The business owner does not repay the investor. Examples of equity financing include partners, venture capital, and angel investors.

- **Partners.** To help with funding a business, an entrepreneur can take on partners. Partners offer additional funding and share responsibilities and operations of a business. In exchange, they are granted some ownership stake in the business.
- **Venture capital. Venture capital** is investment from others who are willing to help fund a business in exchange for an ownership share and an active role in the company. Venture capital usually comes from individual investors, investment banks, and other financial institutions.
- **Angel investor.** An **angel investor** is a private investor who provides funding for a new business in exchange for an ownership interest.

Funding Options			
Type of Funding	**Repay**	**No Repay**	**Gains Part of Ownership**
Partner		X	Yes
Venture capital		X	Yes
Angel investor		X	Yes
Small business loan	X		No
Peer-to-peer lending	X		No

Goodheart-Willcox Publisher

Figure 16-3 Two common ways of funding are equity financing and debt financing.

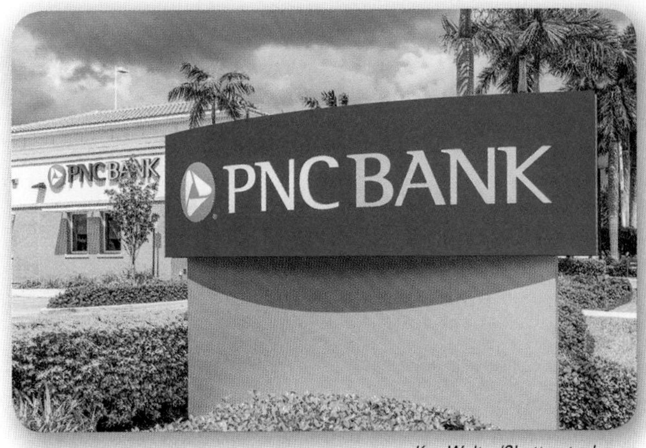

Ken Wolter/Shutterstock.com

An entrepreneur can apply for debt financing in the form of a small business loan from a bank. **Summarize the pros and cons of getting a loan from a bank rather than a loan from a friend or family.**

Debt Financing

Another way to fund a business is through debt financing. **Debt financing** is borrowing money that is repaid in the future. Otherwise known as a *loan*, debt financers do not own shares of the business. The entrepreneur retains full ownership of his or her business.

Loans can be obtained from friends, family, or financial institutions. Examples of debt financing include small business loans and peer-to-peer lending.

- **Small business loan.** A small business loan can be obtained from a bank, credit union, or with the help of the SBA.
- **Peer-to-peer lending.** Also known as *social lending*, **peer-to-peer lending** is borrowing money from investors via a website. These loans typically offer lower interest rates and shorter repayment timeframes than bank loans.

LO 16.2-3 Legal Considerations

There are a number of legal considerations when starting a small business. A good rule of thumb is to meet with an attorney for advice to avoid any legal issues. Some of these legal issues include:

- obtaining a business license;
- establishing the business structure;
- selecting a business name;
- obtaining a Federal Employer Identification Number (EIN);
- opening a business bank account;
- researching employment laws; and
- filing for trademark protection.

Business License

Business licenses or permits are likely required in the locality where the business operates. One example of a business license is a doing business as (DBA) license. A *doing business as (DBA) license* may be required if using a business name other than the owner's name. The DBA license, also known as *fictitious name registration*, allows the owner to register the business with a name different from his or her own.

Some types of business activities may require certain licenses or permits from the local or state government. For example, hairstylists are typically required to have a state-issued cosmetology license to provide their services to customers. In addition, most companies need an operating license from the city or county in which the business is located.

Business Structure

Most small business startups are structured as sole proprietorships. A business can also be a partnership if two or more people share ownership. Other business structures include registering as a small business corporation or a limited liability company (LLC). These structures can protect personal assets from business-related liabilities.

Business Name

Choosing an original business name is important because it could attract customers. Additionally, a well-named business is easy to remember. Because of federal trademark law, however, you should choose a business name that is not the same, or similar, to another registered business name. To verify the availability of a business name, search the prospective name at the US Patent and Trademark Office and perform a comprehensive search in local and state governmental business databases.

Federal Employer Identification Number (EIN)

A *Federal Employer Identification Number (EIN)* is a nine-digit unique identification number issued by the Internal Revenue Service (IRS). It identifies the business for taxation purposes and must be included on all tax returns and reports filed with the IRS. However, sole proprietors without employees are *not* required to obtain an EIN. In most states, a state employer identification number is also needed.

It is recommended that a proprietor does not use his or her personal Social Security number when conducting banking and other business transactions. Business transactions should be kept separate from personal activities.

Milosz Maslanka/Shutterstock.com

Choosing an original business name is important because it could attract customers. **There is an old saying, "What's in a name?" What does this potentially mean to an entrepreneur when naming a business?**

Vytautas Kielaitis/Shutterstock.com

Registering a trademark with the US Patent and Trademark Office (USPTO) is recommended to protect an asset. **Do you believe a business should register for a trademark? Why or why not?**

Banking

After an EIN is obtained, a proprietor can open a business bank account. This separates the business funds from the owner's personal funds. A business bank account can make it easier for the business to obtain lines of credit. In addition, a business bank account enables the business to accept customer credit cards, which can increase sales.

Employment Laws

Employers have certain legal obligations to their employees. Familiarity with federal and state laws regarding payroll, compensation and benefits, equal employment opportunities, safety, and other employment-related issues is essential. The IRS and many state governments offer free seminars regarding legal and other issues related to starting and operating a small business.

Trademark Protection

A *trademark* protects taglines, names, graphics, symbols, or any unique method used to identify a product or company. Filing for trademark protection is not required for new businesses. However, registering a trademark with the *US Patent and Trademark Office (USPTO)* is recommended to protect an asset. An *asset* is property or items of value a business owns.

Once a trademark or service mark has been registered, the symbol ® can be used with the mark. This symbol notifies the public that the creator claims exclusive rights to the brand and its use. It also makes it easy to prove infringement, which is use of protected material without permission, and discourages others from using the mark.

Section 16.2 Review

Check Your Understanding

1. State examples of items that should be included in a business plan.
2. Identify names of common pro forma statements.
3. What is equity financing?
4. List and discuss some examples of debt financing.
5. Briefly explain a DBA license.

Build Your Vocabulary

As you progress through this text, develop a personal glossary of key terms. This will help you build your vocabulary and prepare you for a career. Write a definition for each of the following terms and add them to your personal glossary.

pro forma statement	venture capital	debt financing
self-funding	angel investor	peer-to-peer lending
equity financing		

Section 16.3

Organizing, Leading, and Controlling

Essential Question

In what ways do the functions of management apply to an entrepreneur when creating a startup?

Learning Objectives

LO 16.3-1 Discuss the organizing function of management as it applies to an entrepreneur.

LO 16.3-2 Explain the leading function of management as it applies to an entrepreneur.

LO 16.3-3 Summarize the controlling function of management as it applies to an entrepreneur.

LO 16.3-4 List common types of exit strategies.

Key Terms

organic growth	diversification	merger
market penetration	succession plan	acquisition
market development	harvest strategy	liquidation
inorganic growth		

LO 16.3-1 Organizing Function

Organizing is the coordination of activities and resources needed to accomplish a plan. Basically, the organizing function asks the question, "What will be done, who will do it, and when?"

An entrepreneur will encounter various business organization issues. One issue is choosing the legal form of organization for the business. A common legal form of business for a small owner is a sole proprietorship. A *sole proprietorship* is a business owned and operated by one individual, known as the *proprietor*. Proprietorships are the simplest and most common form of business structure. Advantages of a proprietorship include the following.

- All profits belong to the owner.
- The owner has complete control of the business.
- It is the easiest form of business to start compared to a partnership or a corporation.

However, being a sole proprietor of a business is not always easy. It also has some disadvantages.

- The owner is personally responsible for any expenses and debts the business incurs.
- Complete control is great to have, but self-management skills are required. An owner will probably work long hours, make all the decisions, and take responsibility for everything that happens in the business. Liability comes with ownership.
- A proprietor is personally responsible for funding the business, whether it is from personal funds or borrowed money from a bank or individuals. Funding may be a challenge.

LO 16.3-2 Leading Function

Leading is the process of influencing others to work toward the attainment of common goals. To accomplish goals, entrepreneurs need to do more than just plan, organize, staff, and control. They must also lead the venture.

An entrepreneur is a leader, but a leader is not automatically an entrepreneur. There is one specific characteristic that distinguishes a leader from an entrepreneur. An entrepreneur is a risk-taker willing to *personally invest* in a business. If the business fails, the owner is responsible

Diego Cervo/Shutterstock.com

An entrepreneur is a risk-taker willing to personally invest in a business. **Briefly explain if you would or would not describe yourself as a risk-taker.**

and takes the loss. Managers may take risks with money belonging to a business, but it is not their money at stake. Generally, they are not personally responsible for financial losses of a company.

Leadership includes optimism. Entrepreneurs are generally optimistic and see the glass as "half full." Leadership also includes vision. Entrepreneurs are visionaries who understand that the success of the business is on them. They are creative and make things happen. Entrepreneurs must be able to think through situations and visualize a desired outcome. They must also be able to project into the future and work with others to lead their efforts to achieve the desired goals.

A business rarely becomes a success solely because of the efforts of the owner. In most cases, an entrepreneur leads a team of capable and dedicated employees who are willing to follow. Most successful businesses need a team of suppliers, lenders, and others who are willing to trust the leadership of the owner.

LO 16.3-3 Controlling Function

The controlling function is necessary in all businesses. *Controlling* is the continuous process of comparing actual outcomes with planned outcomes and taking corrective action when goals are not met. Controlling attempts to keep a business on track by providing the means to monitor the performance of the organization as a whole. By creating standards, measuring performance, and taking corrective actions, a business owner can monitor and manage productivity. By keeping track of productivity levels and tracking plans for improvement, a company can manage growth and profits.

The objective of business is to grow and prosper. However, controlling growth is a challenge faced by entrepreneurs. The way in which an owner controls business growth often determines if it survives. Two strategies for managing growth are organic growth and inorganic growth.

Organic Growth

Many businesses begin expanding through organic growth. **Organic growth** occurs by expanding the current business. Organic growth involves increasing number of customers, number of locations, or other growth that comes from the current business. Strategies include market penetration, market development, and product development.

Market Penetration

Market penetration involves increasing sales in the existing target market. Instead of acquiring new customers, an organization focuses on current customers. It is a relatively low-risk growth strategy and includes:

- convincing customers to buy more product per purchase and make purchases more often;
- working to take away business from competitors;
- increasing marketing activities; and
- continuing to develop relationships with existing customers.

Market Development

Market development is expanding existing products to new physical locations or target markets. This strategy focuses on finding new customers. If successful, a business can add to their customer base by appealing to nonbuying consumers already within a target market. Strategies include the following:

- adding another location;
- promoting different product benefits;
- adding new customer channels;
- franchising the business; and
- creating a public corporation.

You Do the Math

Communication and Representation: Circle Graph

A *circle graph* is a type of graph that looks like a divided circle and shows how a whole object is cut into parts. Circle graphs are also called *pie charts* and are often used to illustrate percentages.

Solve the following problems using the circle graph.

1. What is the largest percentage of market share?
2. What is the smallest percentage of market?
3. How many companies make up the bottom 50% of this market?
4. How many companies make up the top 50% of this market?

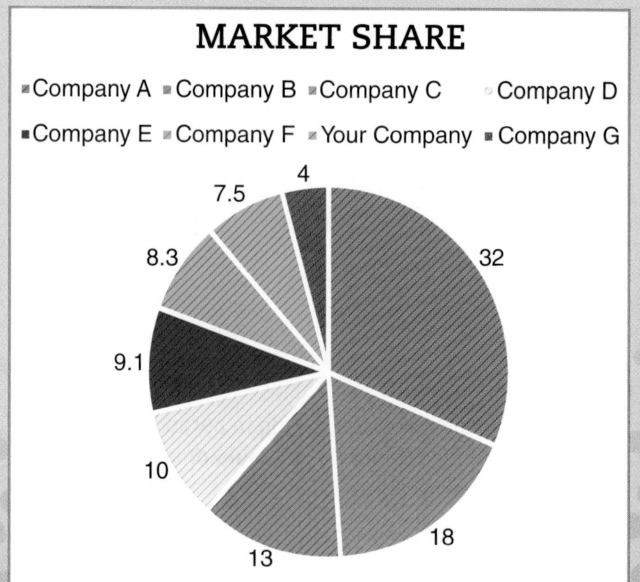

Product Development

Another organic growth strategy is to engage in product development. This may mean creating new products to sell to the current market. It may also mean replacing older products with updated ones. Updating a product may simply mean improving a current product to make it more appealing. It could also mean redesigning the product to meet a change in the market.

Inorganic Growth

Inorganic growth occurs when a company buys a new product line, buys another business, or merges with another company. This can be a good option if an entrepreneur is interested in expanding the types of offerings. For example, if a store sells computers and wants to expand into the office furniture business, it might be easier to buy an established office furniture company than start one from scratch.

When a company has reached its limit on current product sales, it may choose to diversify. **Diversification** is a way to reduce risk that involves adding different goods, services, locations, or markets. Diversification can help reduce the risk to a company. If one product line experiences slow sales, the other product lines may still be selling steadily. Sales may even continue to increase. This can help balance the ups and downs of sales cycles.

LO 16.3-4 Exit Strategy

Many entrepreneurs start businesses with the goal of building the business and someday selling it for a large profit. Other entrepreneurs may decide at a certain point that they would like to sell and move on to a new venture. Still other business owners reach the point where they wish to sell the business and retire.

It is important for an entrepreneur to know when to leave the business. All business owners should have an exit strategy. Ending a business can be emotionally and financially painful, and having a plan in place can make transition easier. Common types of exit strategies include succession plans, harvest strategies, merger or acquisition, and liquidation of a business.

Succession

A **succession plan** details who will operate the company in the event the owner leaves the company, retires, or passes away. It helps ensure that the owner's company will continue. A succession plan describes how ownership will be transferred when the owner exits the business. The transfer could be to family, employees of the business, or investors.

Harvest

A **harvest strategy** is a plan for extracting the cash from a business, brand, or product line. This can be a way to repay investors as well as provide an exit for the owner. A harvest strategy might include selling the company to an outside party or allowing employees to buy the company.

Merger or Acquisition

A **merger** is combining two companies into one new company. For example, Company X merges with Company Y to form a new company, Company Z. Both companies dissolve and a new one is created.

An **acquisition** is the outright purchase of one business by another business. For example, an owner sells a business to another company. The original owner can potentially stay with the business or exit, but the ownership changes to a new organization.

Carolyn Franks/Shutterstock.com

Liquidation refers to the sale of all assets of a business, including inventory, equipment, and buildings. **Why would an entrepreneur liquidate a business?**

Liquidate the Business

For some business owners, transferring ownership or selling the business are not options. For these owners, the plan is to close the business. **Liquidation** refers to the sale of all assets of a business, including inventory, equipment, and buildings. When this occurs, the business ceases to exist.

Section 16.3 Review

Check Your Understanding

1. What one characteristic distinguishes a leader from an entrepreneur?
2. Name two strategies for managing growth.
3. List examples of market penetration strategies.
4. State examples of market development strategies.
5. Why would an entrepreneur decide to exit a business?

Build Your Vocabulary

As you progress through this text, develop a personal glossary of key terms. This will help you build your vocabulary and prepare you for a career. Write a definition for each of the following terms and add them to your personal glossary.

organic growth	diversification	merger
market penetration	succession plan	acquisition
market development	harvest strategy	liquidation
inorganic growth		

Chapter 16 Review and Assessment

Chapter Summary

Section 16.1 Entrepreneurship

LO 16.1-1 **Define what it means to be an entrepreneur.**
Any individual who is creative, willing to take a chance, and has a good idea can be an entrepreneur. An entrepreneur is a person who risks his or her own resources to start and operate a business.

LO 16.1-2 **Summarize a startup.**
A startup is an entrepreneurial venture of creating a new business. It begins with the discovery process of identifying a need to be met in the marketplace and conducting market research. When an idea is confirmed as profitable and an entrepreneur is ready to start a business, a decision will be made as to the type of business that will be created, such as producers, intermediaries, and service businesses.

LO 16.1-3 **Discuss startup strategies.**
Options for startup strategies include starting a new business, buying an existing business, or buying a franchise.

Section 16.2 Planning

LO 16.2-1 **Discuss the planning function as it applies to an entrepreneur.**
Planning function of management, as it applies to an entrepreneur, is the process of setting goals and objectives and deciding how to accomplish them. Without planning, a new business would likely not be successful. The planning process begins by writing a business plan, which describes a business, how it operates, and how it makes a profit.

LO 16.2-2 **Summarize funding a new business.**
An entrepreneur needs money to start, operate, and grow a business. Some entrepreneurs self-fund their business. Others finance their business. Financing, also known as funding, is necessary to obtain enough cash to start the business. Two common ways of funding are equity financing and debt financing.

LO 16.2-3 **Identify examples of legal considerations when starting a new business.**
Examples of legal considerations an entrepreneur should consider when starting a new business include obtaining a business license, establishing the business structure, selecting a business name, obtaining a Federal Employer Identification Number (EIN), opening a business bank account, researching employment laws, and filing for trademark protection.

Section 16.3 Organizing, Leading, and Controlling

LO 16.3-1 **Discuss the organizing function of management as it applies to an entrepreneur.**
Organizing function of management, as it applies to an entrepreneur, is the coordination of activities and resources needed to accomplish a plan. It asks the question, "What will be done, who will do it, and when?" An entrepreneur will encounter various business organization issues, such as choosing the legal form of organization for the business.

LO 16.3-2 **Explain the leading function of management as it applies to an entrepreneur.**
Leading function of management, as it applies to an entrepreneur, is the process of influencing others to work toward the attainment of common goals. Entrepreneurs must lead the venture. Leadership includes optimism. Entrepreneurs are generally optimistic and see the glass as "half full." Leadership also includes vision. Entrepreneurs are visionaries who understand that the success of the business is on them.

LO 16.3-3 Summarize the controlling function of management as it applies to an entrepreneur.
Controlling function of management, as it applies to an entrepreneur, is the continuous process of comparing actual outcomes with planned outcomes and taking corrective action when goals are not met. Controlling attempts to keep a business on track by providing the means to monitor the performance of the organization as a whole. Through controlling, a business owner can monitor and manage productivity and track plans for improvement to achieve growth and increase profits.

LO 16.3-4 List common types of exit strategies.
Common types of exit strategies include a succession plan, harvest strategy, merger, acquisition, and liquidation.

Review Your Knowledge

1. What does it mean to be an entrepreneur?
2. Summarize a startup.
3. Discuss examples of startup strategies.
4. Discuss the planning function as it applies to an entrepreneur.
5. Explain funding a new business.
6. Identify examples of legal considerations when starting a new business.
7. Discuss the organizing function of management as it applies to an entrepreneur.
8. Explain the leading function as it applies to an entrepreneur.
9. Summarize the controlling function as it applies to an entrepreneur.
10. Identify and explain examples of exit strategies.

Apply Your Knowledge

1. Make a list of both hard skills and soft skills you possess that would make you a good entrepreneur.
2. An entrepreneur can start a new business from the ground up, buy an existing business, or buy a franchise. Create a chart for each type of startup and summarize the advantages and disadvantages you would share with a person contemplating a startup.
3. Many new businesses fail due to incomplete or incorrect research. What types of research sources would you recommend an entrepreneur use when planning a business?
4. Identify examples of costs that you think an entrepreneur would encounter when starting a new business.
5. There are multiple sources for securing financing to start and operate a business. What types of funding would you recommend for a startup and why?
6. Identify important legal considerations that should be researched when starting a new business. What would be the consequences if these issues were not addressed before starting a business?
7. In your own words, explain the value of a trademark for a business owner. What could happen if a business name or product does not obtain a trademark?
8. To what extent do you agree or disagree with the following statement: An entrepreneur is a leader, but a leader is not automatically an entrepreneur.
9. At some point in the life of a business, the owner may decide to exit. Discuss why an owner would want to withdraw from a personal business. What options would this person have when exiting and the issues that may be a part of that decision?
10. Take a look around your community. What resources are available to help entrepreneurs?

Communication Skills

Writing. Critical thinking is necessary for success as a student and in your future career. Learning how to apply critical-thinking skills now will help you develop the ability to use them to handle challenges throughout your life. Recall a problem you needed to solve that was important to your success at school or work. Write several paragraphs to describe the problem and explain how you applied critical-thinking skills to arrive at a solution. Summarize the pros and cons of your choice.

Speaking. A *presentation* is usually a speech given to a group of people. This chapter discussed different ways to start a business. Plan and deliver a speech about an idea you have to start a business. Be clear in your perspective for the idea and demonstrate solid reasoning.

Listening. A *barrier* is anything preventing clear, effective communication. *External barriers* are those that exist outside of a person, such as hearing other noises in the room or being distracted by looking out the window at something that is occurring outside. During class, attempt to recognize any external barriers to listening. How can you avoid external barriers?

Internet Research

Business Plan. Using the Internet, visit the *Small Business Administration (SBA)* website. Research information on the site that describes how to start your own business. Design, write, modify, and evaluate a business plan that includes a detailed description of products and/or services offered, risk analysis, short- and long-term profits, and marketing plan. In addition, identify investment needed to start and maintain the business, plans to obtain working capital, legal licenses, and vendor contracts. Include a company organization chart, job description and skills needed of main employees, physical equipment and facilities required, and any future expansion plans.

Bankruptcy. Over the course of the last decade, multiple well-known businesses were forced to file for bankruptcy protection. Examples include RadioShack, Borders, and Toys"R"Us. Conduct online research into a company that recently filed for bankruptcy protection and summarize why the company was unable to continue doing business. Write several paragraphs describing whether you think this business could have been a good candidate for an entrepreneur to purchase and revive.

Teamwork

Working with a partner, create a five-column chart. Label each column one of the functions of management: planning, organizing, staffing, leading, and controlling. Under each heading, explain in your own words how entrepreneurship relates to each function of management.

Portfolio Development

Foreign-Language Skills. In some situations, individuals who are fluent in a foreign language may have an advantage over other candidates in an application process or other competitive situations. As part of an interview with an organization, you may be asked about your ability to speak multiple languages or experience with people who speak a language other than your own. Many organizations are interested in this information because they often serve people from a variety of geographic locations, cultures, and languages.

People who speak more than one language or have traveled, studied, or worked in other countries can be valuable assets to an organization. For example, an employer may or may not have offices or factories in more than one region or country. A candidate who notes multilingual skills can be considered to have a competitive edge over other candidates with similar experience.

It is important to be specific and accurate when you list the language skills you possess. By being proactive and noting any experiences you have in working with people in other cultures, you may catch the eye of the interviewer even before the interviewing process begins.

1. If you are fluent in another language, create a document that describes the language in which you are proficient, where you received your training, and your level of fluency. Use the heading "Languages Spoken" and your name.
2. If you have limited language proficiency, create a document that says "Limited Language Proficiency" and list each language and your ability to communicate using it. For example, you may have only a limited proficiency in German that could be helpful in a business situation.
3. Update your master portfolio spreadsheet to include your foreign-language skills documentation.

EVENT PREP

CTSOs

Business Financial Plan. Creating a business financial plan is a competitive startup (entrepreneurship) event that may be offered by your Career and Technical Student Organization (CTSO). This may be an individual or team event. There may be two parts to this event: the written plan and the oral presentation of the plan.

The event calls for the development of a written business plan that will likely be judged prior to the competition. Written events can be lengthy and take a lot of time to prepare. Therefore, it is important to start early.

The rules for this event are similar to other business plan presentations. However, writing this plan requires research on the means of financing a business and the institutions and individuals that provide such financing.

To prepare for writing a financial plan, complete the following activities.

1. Visit the website of your CTSO and read the guidelines provided by your organization. There will be specific directions given as to the parts of the business plan and how each should be presented. Ask yourself: Does this event interest me? Can I do what is necessary to be successful at the event? If you answered "yes," move forward with the process.
2. Create a checklist of the guidelines you must follow. All final-format guidelines will also be given, including how to organize and submit the business plan. Be sure to ask any questions about points you do not understand.
3. Conduct research into business funding early. Research may take days or weeks, and you do not want to rush the process. Study this chapter to learn about financial plans.
4. Set a deadline for yourself so you write at a comfortable pace.
5. After you write your first draft, ask a teacher to review it and give you feedback. Repeat this step as needed until you have a final version of the plan.
6. Once you have the final version of your finance plan, review the checklist you prepared. Make sure you have addressed all the requirements. Your score will be penalized if a direction is not followed exactly.
7. Practice presenting the presentation.

CHAPTER 17

Risk Management

Sections

Reading Prep

To *read for detail* is to read all words and phrases, consider their meanings, and determine how they combine with other elements to convey ideas. Other elements might include sentences, headings, or graphics. Read this chapter for detail to learn the concepts being taught.

Exploring Careers

Risk Manager

Risk managers are responsible for analyzing, controlling, and managing business risk. They identify and measure operational risk for a company and make decisions regarding the best way to lessen the business's loss or exposure. Additionally, they develop and implement plans, policies, and strategies to minimize loss and avoid future risk.

Typical job titles for this position include *risk-management director* and *risk-management specialist*. Examples of tasks risk managers perform include:

- developing contingency plans;
- assessing the organization for potential areas of risk;
- compiling and analyzing data to support findings of potential risks;
- documenting and presenting risk assessments to leadership groups; and
- maintaining risk-management systems.

Most risk manager positions require a bachelor degree in business administration, risk management, or a related field. Some organizations may desire additional degrees or certifications. Risk managers must be familiar with various types of software used to analyze and mitigate risk as well as excellent problem-solving and analytical skills. They also need to be able to communicate their findings and plans effectively, so interpersonal and communication skills are necessary.

Tashatuvango/Shutterstock.com

Section 17.1 Insurance Basics

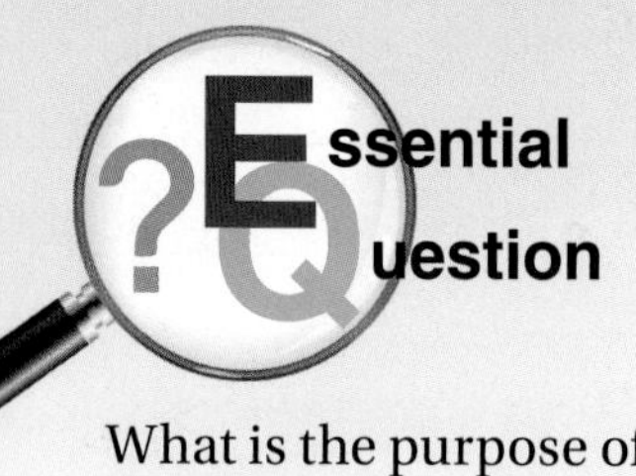

What is the purpose of insurance?

Learning Objectives

LO 17.1-1 Discuss insurance.

LO 17.1-2 List common types of insurance coverage available for purchase by a business.

LO 17.1-3 Identify types of insurance for employees a business might purchase.

Key Terms

risk
business risk
insurance
insurance policy
premium
claim
deductible

LO 17.1-1 Insurance

A business faces risk every day, even on days when it is closed. A **risk** is the possibility of suffering loss or harm. Some risk can be major and endanger the future operation of a business. Some risk has lesser consequences and may cause a short period of discomfort for the business rather than financial loss.

A **business risk** is the possibility of loss or injury that might occur in an organization. For example, an employee could be injured on the job, a natural disaster could damage or destroy business property, or a business could be sued because of an alleged product defect. For these and other reasons, a business must have adequate insurance to protect itself.

Insurance is a financial service used to protect against loss. When a business purchases insurance, they transfer risk to the insurance company. Without adequate insurance, an otherwise profitable business could be forced into bankruptcy because of a single disaster or lawsuit. Even an unsuccessful lawsuit against a business can do substantial harm because of costs associated with going to court.

An **insurance policy** is a contract that defines the types of losses covered, amount of coverage in dollars, and other conditions to which the parties agree. The insurance company, the *insurer*, provides protection against economic loss to the policyholder, the *insured*.

A **premium** is the amount the insured pays for insurance coverage. Money collected from premiums is invested by the insurance company, and the earnings are used to pay claims of insured individuals or businesses. A **claim** is a formal request to an insurance company for compensation related to a covered loss or event. When an insured suffers a loss, a claim is made to the insurance company.

Most policies carry a deductible. A **deductible** is the amount the insured is responsible for paying before the insurance pays a claim. In general, the higher the amount of the deductible, the lower the premium.

LO 17.1-2 Business Insurance

Insurance policies are available to cover most types of risk that a business may encounter. The amount of insurance coverage needed for a business depends on the size, location, type of operations, and probable risks of the business. The goal is to buy the correct amount of insurance at a reasonable rate that will cover the insurable risks of the business.

Common business insurance includes general liability insurance, product liability insurance, professional liability insurance, property insurance, commercial vehicle insurance, and umbrella policies, as shown in Figure 17-1.

General Liability Insurance

General liability insurance protects a business against financial losses that arise from legal issues. This includes lawsuits for accidents and injuries that occur on business premises, medical costs of injured parties, and attorney costs related to defending lawsuits. This type of insurance can protect the owner and the business. It also provides coverage in the event of copyright infringement or damage to the professional reputation of an individual or a company.

Product Liability Insurance

A business is liable for the safety of all products it makes, sells, or distributes. *Product liability insurance* protects against financial losses due to a product defect that may cause injury or harm to the user of the product. The amount of coverage needed varies with the type of product involved. For example, products produced by a pharmaceutical company carry higher risks than those of a clothing manufacturer. As a result, the pharmaceutical company should carry a larger amount of product liability insurance.

T-I/Shutterstock.com

Property insurance covers losses and damage to the assets of a business caused by a variety of events, such as floods. **What type of potential events could affect businesses in your community?**

Professional Liability Insurance

Professional liability insurance protects service-based businesses from financial losses caused by errors or negligence in the services provided to customers. It is also known as *errors and omissions (E & O) insurance.* Many states require certain professions, such as healthcare professionals and lawyers, to carry professional liability insurance.

Business Insurance	
Insurance	**Protection**
General Liability	Protects against financial losses arising from legal issues
Product Liability	Protects against financial losses due to a product defect that causes injury or harm to customers
Professional Liability	Protects service-based businesses from financial losses from errors or negligence in the services provided
Property	Covers losses or damages to business assets caused by a variety of events, such as natural disasters and vandalism
Commercial Vehicle	Protects business-owned vehicles from theft, injuries or damage caused by vehicles, certain weather events, and vandalism
Umbrella Policy	Covers the loss of amounts that are higher than those covered by the primary insurance policy

Goodheart-Willcox Publisher

Figure 17-1 Common business insurance is available to cover most types of risk that a business may encounter.

Ethics

Snooping

Managers are often in positions to have access to confidential company and employee information. Obtaining confidential information can bring a sense of power and inspire a person to become greedy and snoop for data. *Snooping* is trying to gain unauthorized access to a company's data or a person's private information. Snooping is not only unethical, but it can pose a security threat to an organization if a person gains sensitive company information and uses it for personal gain.

Property Insurance

Property insurance covers losses and damage to the assets of a business caused by a variety of events, such as floods, wind, hail, fire, smoke, theft, and vandalism. The definition of property is broad. It usually includes physical assets, such as buildings, equipment, documents, and money. In addition to covering physical assets, property insurance also typically covers income lost from lack of sales due to property losses. For example, a flood causes a company to close for several months while repairs were made. Property insurance may cover the income lost by the company during the time it was closed.

Commercial Vehicle Insurance

All vehicles used in the operation of a business should be insured. *Commercial vehicle insurance* covers trucks, cars, trailers, and other forms of vehicles used in a business. The coverage includes theft of vehicles; medical bills for drivers and passengers injured while using vehicles; and damage to vehicles caused by factors, such as collisions, certain weather events, and vandalism. It also includes property damage and bodily injuries of others caused by accidents involving the vehicles.

Umbrella Policies

Many insurance policies have a maximum limit, or ceiling, that is paid for claims during the term of a policy. In such situations, an umbrella policy can help protect the business. An *umbrella policy* covers the loss of amounts that are higher than those covered by the primary policy. These policies are relatively inexpensive but often require business owners to purchase the maximum limits on all other policies in effect.

LO 17.1-3 Employee Insurance Coverage

Businesses can offer their employees various types of insurance as part of employment benefits. These can include health insurance, dental insurance, and life insurance. However, there are certain types of insurance coverage that businesses with employees are required by law to carry. This usually includes workers' compensation insurance and unemployment insurance.

Gino Santa Maria/Shutterstock.com

Workers' compensation insurance covers medical expenses and lost wages for employees injured on the job or suffering from work-related illnesses. **What types of legal situations could an organization encounter if workers comp is not provided for employees?**

Employability Skills
Polite Language

When speaking to others at work, use respectful and polite language at all times. Use polite phrases such as "please," "thank you," and "you are welcome" whenever possible. Choose words that show respect to others. Never use profane words or phrases. To do so is inappropriate and unacceptable workplace behavior.

Workers' compensation insurance covers medical expenses and lost wages for employees injured on the job or suffering from work-related illnesses. Depending on the state, insurance can be purchased by an employer from an approved private insurance company, a state fund, or both. Each state has a workers' compensation commission or board that regulates and enforces these laws.

Unemployment insurance provides certain benefits to workers who have lost their jobs through no fault of their own. Employers pay for this insurance through a payroll tax based on employee earnings. A small percentage of the tax is paid to the federal government with a larger percentage paid to the state in which the business is located. Each state administers a separate unemployment insurance program within guidelines established by federal law.

Some states require employers to provide disability insurance for their employees. *Disability insurance* is an earnings continuation policy for employees who become sick or injured due to a non-work related event or condition. In most cases, disability insurance is purchased from an insurance company approved by the state. Some states also have a state insurance fund from which employers can purchase disability insurance for their employees. Depending on the state, premiums for the insurance can be paid solely by the employer, solely by employees, or employer and employees share the cost.

Section 17.1 Review

Check Your Understanding

1. When a business purchases insurance, to whom is the risk transferred?
2. How does a business decide the amount of insurance coverage needed?
3. What is another name for professional liability insurance?
4. List specific vehicles covered by a commercial vehicle insurance policy.
5. Which types of employee insurance are businesses required by law to carry?

Build Your Vocabulary

As you progress through this text, develop a personal glossary of key terms. This will help you build your vocabulary and prepare you for a career. Write a definition for each of the following terms and add them to your personal glossary.

risk	insurance policy	claim
business risk	premium	deductible
insurance		

Section 17.2 Risk

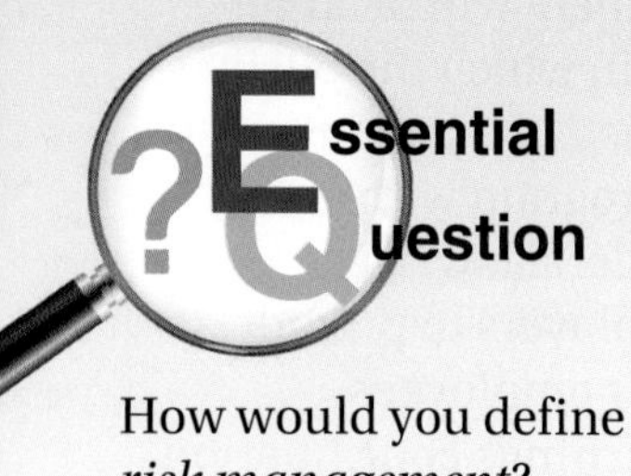

How would you define *risk management*?

Learning Objectives

LO 17.2-1 Explain risk management.

LO 17.2-2 Identify methods used to classify risk.

LO 17.2-3 Discuss cybersecurity risk management.

LO 17.2-4 Cite ways a company can manage customer credit risk.

Key Terms

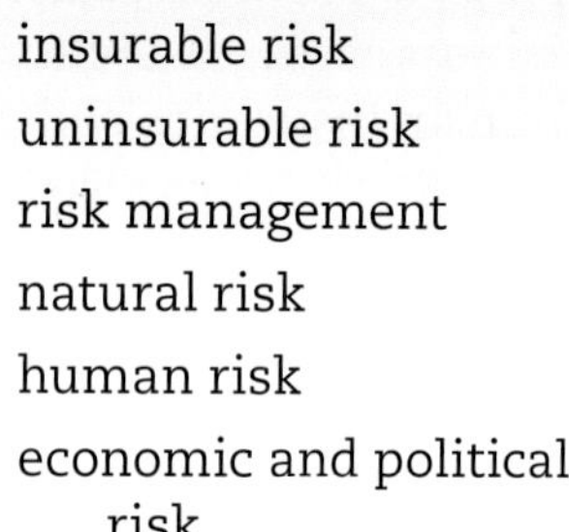

- insurable risk
- uninsurable risk
- risk management
- natural risk
- human risk
- economic and political risk
- market risk
- pure risk
- speculative risk
- controllable risk
- uncontrollable risk
- cybersecurity risk management
- credit
- credit risk
- collection agency
- trade credit
- credit report
- credit bureau

LO 17.2-1 Risk Management

A *risk* is the possibility of suffering loss or harm. A *business risk* is the possibility of loss or injury that might occur in a business. Some risks are insurable, such as flood insurance, whereas other risks are not insurable, such as an economic recession. An **insurable risk** is one that insurance will cover in the event of loss. An **uninsurable risk** is a loss that insurance will not cover.

Risk management is the process of evaluating risks and taking steps to avoid or minimize loss should it occur. The first step in risk management is to identify the risks a business is likely to encounter. Once risk is identified, plans can be made to avoid, reduce, transfer or assume the risk, as shown in Figure 17-2.

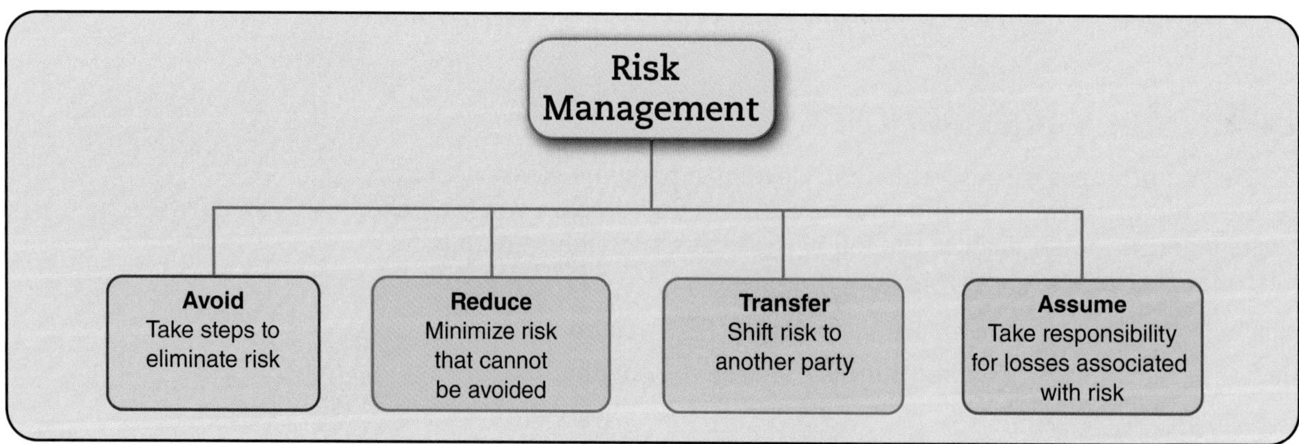

Figure 17-2 Risk management is the process of evaluating risks and taking steps to avoid or minimize loss should they occur.

pixinoo/Shutterstock.com

To reduce risk is a strategy of minimizing risks that cannot be avoided, such as installing security cameras. **How can security equipment reduce risk for a business?**

Avoid Risk

To avoid risk is to take steps to eliminate it. For example, market research shows that selling snowboards in Florida is a business that will fail. Risk management would recommend avoiding the risk and not selling snowboards in Florida. A better choice might be to sell them in locations with snow like Colorado or Utah.

Reduce Risk

To reduce risk is a strategy for minimizing risks that cannot be avoided. For example, a retail store runs a risk of shoplifting from people who walk into the store. Risk management would recommend reducing the risk by installing security cameras and hiring plain-clothed security officers. These precautions could reduce some of the loss potential caused by shoplifters.

Transfer Risk

To transfer risk is a strategy that involves shifting risk to another party. Insurance is the most common way of transferring risk. Businesses that purchase insurance become members of a large group of businesses that transfer risk to an insurance company.

Assume Risk

To assume risk is to take responsibility for all losses associated with risk that cannot be avoided, reduced, or transferred. Economic and market risks are examples of risks that are considered uninsurable.

In order to assume risk, a business must have sufficient financial resources to cover losses should the risk materialize. An example would be to have a separate bank account set up with emergency funds.

You Do the Math

Numeric Reasoning: Rounding

When a number is rounded, some of the digits are changed, removed, or changed to zero so the number is easier to work with. Rounding is often used when precise calculations or measurements are not needed. To round a number, identify the place to which you are rounding, such as tens or hundreds. If the digit to the *right* of this place is 5 or greater, add 1 to the digit in the identified place. If the digit to the right is less than 5, do not change the digit in the identified place. Then, change all the digits to the right of the identified place to zero.

Solve the following problems.

1. A company's utilities expenses were $16,285.22 last year. The finance manager of the company is preparing a budget for next year and wants to round this amount to the nearest 1,000. What number should be included in the budget?
2. The same company's marketing expenses were $27,620.25. The finance manager wants to round this amount to the nearest 10,000 for next year's budget. What number should be included in the budget?

LO 17.2-2 Classifying Risk

Before a risk can be managed, it must first be classified. There are many ways that the classification can be made. An organization is responsible to select the method that works for its specific industry and needs. Some methods used to classify risks are based on the:

- source of the risk;
- result of the risk; or
- controllability of the risk.

Source of Risk

One basic starting point is to consider the source of the risk. Is it a natural, human, economic and political, or market risk? In addition, is the risk insurable or uninsurable? Figure 17-3 illustrates four common sources of risk.

Natural Risk

Natural risk is a situation caused by acts of nature. Extreme weather conditions like floods, tornadoes, hurricanes, and earthquakes may damage or demolish a business. Natural risk is insurable.

Human Risk

Human risk is a situation caused by human actions. Employees and customers pose potential risks of embezzlement, theft, fraud, or accidental injury. Human risk can be predicted, and some human risk is insurable.

Economic and Political Risk

Economic and political risk is a situation that occurs when the economy suffers due to negative business conditions in the United States or the world. Political conditions in the United States or other countries may create risk for global businesses. This may negatively affect the ability of US businesses to sell products. Some examples of political risk are new import or export laws, tariffs, and taxes. Economic and political risk is difficult to forecast and is uninsurable.

Market Risk

Market risk is the potential that the target market for new goods or services is much less than originally thought. Market risk is difficult to predict and is uninsurable.

Result of Risk

Another way to classify a risk is to consider the result of a situation. A **pure risk** is a risk with a possibility of loss but no possibility of gain. The only two possible outcomes of pure risk are something bad can happen or nothing will happen. If someone steals from the business or a natural disaster happens, for example, there is no possibility of gain from these events. Some pure-risk events can also be a *liability risk*, which results from possibility of losing money, property, or other assets because of legal proceedings. Pure risk is insurable.

A **speculative risk** is a risk that can result in financial gain, financial loss, or nothing.

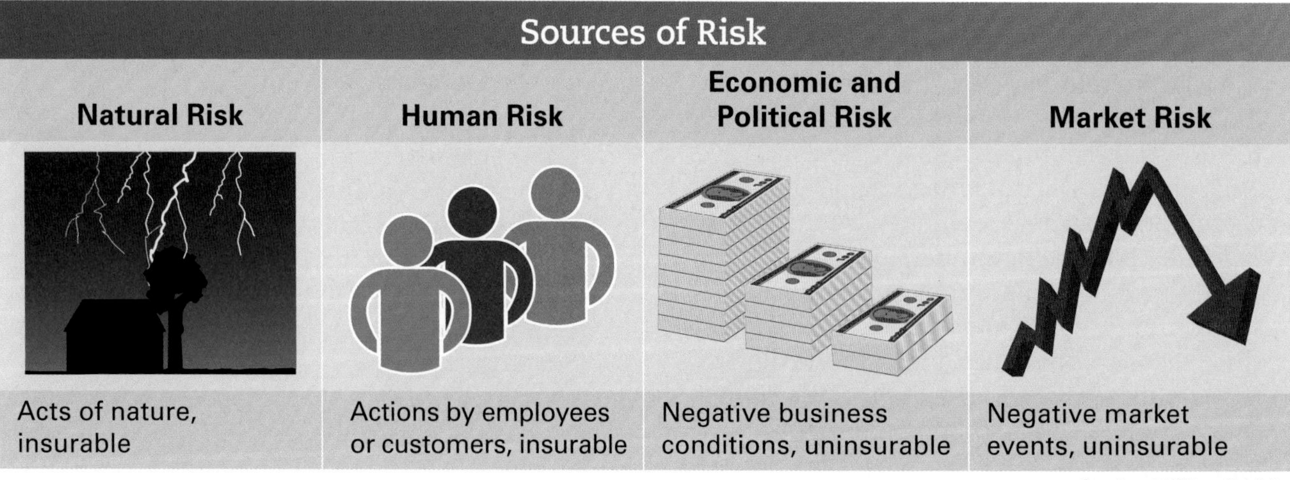

Figure 17-3 Sources of risk include natural, human, economic and political, and market risks.

For example, becoming an entrepreneur and opening a business is a speculative risk because the business may be successful or unsuccessful. Investing in the stock market is another example of speculative risk. An owner can earn money, lose money, or break even. Most speculative risks are not insurable because they are taken willingly in hopes of making a gain.

Controllability of Risk

Some businesses classify risk based on if it can be controlled or not controlled. A **controllable risk** is a situation that can be minimized by actions or avoidance. *Avoidance* is taking steps to eliminate risk. For example, data security risk can be minimized by installing firewalls and virus protection software on a network. For other risk, such as risk of a fire, insurance can be purchased.

An **uncontrollable risk** is a situation that cannot be predicted or covered by purchasing insurance. This type of risk cannot be minimized by taking action. For example, if the economy declines and customer purchasing decreases, there is no action to take to prevent this risk. Insurance cannot be purchased to protect the business from this event.

LO 17.2-3 Cybersecurity Risk Management

There are many types of risk that an organization encounters. All risks are important, and many can have a devastating effect on a business if not addressed and resolved. One significant risk a business encounters is the potential that the organization's information technology system could be jeopardized.

Information technology (IT) plays a critical role in the operation of businesses. Therefore, it must be protected. Failure or breach of an IT system can cause serious problems including identify theft, loss of customer data, delayed payrolls, legal liability, and other negative consequences.

Cybersecurity is protecting an information system against unintended or malicious changes or use. It is the set of measures used to protect an organization's networks, programs, and data from attack, misuse, damage, or unauthorized access. **Cybersecurity risk management** is the process of evaluating risk and taking steps to avoid or minimize loss to the information technology system of an organization. Examples of IT risks include the following.

- *Hackers* are people who illegally break into computer systems.
- *Malware* is malicious software designed to disrupt computer operation and damage, destroy, or steal data. An example of malware is ransomware, which is a type of malicious software designed to block access to a computer system until a sum of money is paid.
- *Computer viruses* are codes that can copy themselves and spread from one computer to another with the intent of causing harm.
- *Phishing* is the use of fraudulent e-mails and copies of valid websites to trick people into providing private and confidential data. It also includes scamming people into buying fraudulent goods.
- *Human error* is the result of factors such as entering incorrect information into the system, negligent disposal of important data, and opening infected e-mail attachments.
- *Hardware failure* occurs when a computer or any of its components fails to operate efficiently.
- *Software failure* occurs when programs fail to work as intended.

one photo/Shutterstock.com

Computer viruses are codes that can copy themselves and spread from one computer to another with the intent of causing harm. **What are examples of consequences of a computer virus that attacks the IT system of an organization?**

Once a business has identified the IT risks it is likely to encounter, strategies can be developed to deal with them should they materialize. Some risks, such as hardware and software failures, can be reduced by regular maintenance and testing of new hardware and software programs before they are put into application. Businesses should also prioritize security updates and set up firewalls against viruses as well as alerting employees about scams and risks and educating them on how to identify potential risks.

LO 17.2-4 Managing Customer Credit Risk

Extending credit to customers creates another type of business risk, especially for small organizations. **Credit** is an agreement or contract to receive goods or services before actually paying for them. The *debtor*, or borrower, is the individual or business who owes money for goods or services received. The *creditor*, or lender, is the individual or business to whom money is owed for goods or services provided.

Credit risk is the potential of credit to the business not being repaid. Customers who fail to pay bills on time may cause a cash-flow problem for the business. For those customers who do not eventually pay their debts, it may be necessary for the creditor to hire a collection agency.

Dan Kosmayer/Shutterstock.com

Customers should complete a credit application that provides credit history, work history, and other information necessary to qualify for credit. **What do you believe are the benefits and risks of extending credit to customers?**

A **collection agency** is a company that collects past-due bills for a fee or a percentage of the amount collected. Businesses may also attempt to collect payments in small claims court, which is a special court where debts under a certain amount can be collected quickly and inexpensively. Each state sets a dollar limit for debts that can be brought to a small claims court.

Each business must weigh the benefits of extending credit against the risks and decide if extending credit to customers is a wise business decision. Some businesses choose only to accept cash or checks and avoid offering credit to customers. When granting credit to customers, it is important to establish a credit process that reduces risk.

Customer guidelines that include specific terms of repayment, interest rates, late fees, penalties, and actions for nonpayment should be set. Guidelines should include a policy of salespeople checking customer identification before accepting credit cards. This can help avoid credit card fraud.

Trade credit is credit offered by a business to its customers that enables customers to buy now and pay later. Credit limits and guidelines are typically set based on how much credit the business can afford to extend. Most importantly, when extending credit, the cash flow of the business should be monitored. Most credit customers pay on time. However, some pay late and some fail to pay altogether. Both late payments and uncollected amounts hurt cash flow.

Create a Credit Policy

Before extending credit, a business should write clear directions and explanations for the staff regarding policies for extending credit to customers. Dollar figures for credit limits should be established based on how much credit a business can afford to extend.

Customers approved for credit should receive a copy of the credit policies for a business. This is necessary so the customer knows his or her responsibilities in repaying the credit. Included may be a payment schedule, interest rate, and late payment penalties. The *Truth in Lending Act* requires that businesses convey all information on the credit terms and costs to customers before the first transaction. If the customer is *not* approved for credit, businesses must convey that message as well.

Require a Credit Application

It is important to check the financial backgrounds of all customers who apply for credit. Customers should complete a credit application that provides credit history, work history, and other information necessary to qualify for credit. Depending on the loan amount or trade credit extended, the business may also request personal financial statements that show net worth and financial status. Bank statements are also commonly requested as part of the application process.

Obtain a Credit Report

Before a business extends credit, the credit history of an applicant should be checked. A credit history may provide information about his or her likelihood of repaying the credit. A **credit report** is a record of a business or person's credit history and financial behavior.

Credit reports are issued by credit bureaus. A **credit bureau** is a private firm that maintains consumer-credit data and provides credit information to businesses for a fee. There are three national credit-reporting agencies: Equifax, Experian, and TransUnion LLC.

Evaluate the Information

Once information is obtained about the customer, the credit worthiness of the applicant is evaluated based on the *three Cs of credit*. The three Cs of credit are as follows.

- **Character.** The individual or business has a good record of paying bills and repaying debt on time.
- **Capacity.** The individual has a stable employment history or the business has consistent earnings that would allow the individual or business to repay a loan.
- **Capital.** The individual or business has a positive net worth in the form of assets that can be used to repay the loan in case of default.

Section 17.2 Review

Check Your Understanding

1. How can risk be managed?
2. Which sources of risk are insurable?
3. Define a *liability risk*.
4. What is the difference between a debtor and a creditor?
5. What are the three Cs of credit?

Build Your Vocabulary

As you progress through this text, develop a personal glossary of key terms. This will help you build your vocabulary and prepare you for a career. Write a definition for each of the following terms and add them to your personal glossary.

insurable risk	market risk	credit
uninsurable risk	pure risk	credit risk
risk management	speculative risk	collection agency
natural risk	controllable risk	trade credit
human risk	uncontrollable risk	credit report
economic and political risk	cybersecurity risk management	credit bureau

Chapter 17 Review and Assessment

Chapter Summary

Section 17.1 Insurance Basics

LO 17.1-1 **Discuss insurance.**
Insurance is a financial service used to protect against loss. When a business purchases insurance, they transfer risk to the insurance company. Without adequate insurance, an otherwise profitable business could be forced into bankruptcy because of a single disaster or lawsuit.

LO 17.1-2 **List common types of insurance coverage available for purchase by a business.**
Common business insurance available for purchase includes general liability insurance, product liability insurance, professional liability insurance, property insurance, commercial vehicle insurance, and umbrella policies.

LO 17.1-3 **Identify types of insurance for employees a business might purchase.**
There are certain types of insurance coverage that businesses with employees are required by law to carry. These include workers' compensation insurance and unemployment insurance. Some states require businesses to provide disability insurance as well for employees.

Section 17.2 Risk

LO 17.2-1 **Explain risk management.**
Risk management is the process of evaluating risks and taking steps to avoid or minimize loss should it occur. The first step is to identify the risks a business is likely to encounter. Once risk is identified, plans can be made to avoid, reduce, transfer, or assume the risk.

LO 17.2-2 **Identify methods used to classify risk.**
Some methods used to classify risks include source of the risk, result of the risk, and the controllability of the risk.

LO 17.2-3 **Discuss cybersecurity risk management.**
Cybersecurity risk management is the process of evaluating risks and taking steps to avoid or minimize loss to the information technology system of an organization. Once a business has identified the IT risks it is likely to encounter, strategies can be developed to deal with them should they materialize.

LO 17.2-4 **Cite ways a company can manage customer credit risk.**
To manage customer credit risk, businesses can create a credit policy, require a credit application, obtain a credit report, and evaluate the information to review the credit worthiness of the applicant.

Review Your Knowledge

1. Summarize insurance.
2. Identify and explain common types of insurance coverage available for purchase by a business.
3. State examples of items protected under general liability insurance.
4. What items does property insurance cover?
5. Briefly explain types of employee insurance coverage a business might purchase.
6. Summarize risk management.
7. Identify methods used to classify risk.
8. Explain cybersecurity risk management.
9. Briefly explain ways a business can manage customer credit risk.
10. What is the Truth in Lending Act?

Apply Your Knowledge

1. Write two to three paragraphs in your own words explaining what risk means to you.
2. Write two to three paragraphs in your own words explaining why you think insurance is important for individuals as well as for businesses.
3. Imagine going to a grand opening at a local electronics store. As you are entering the store, you see someone slip and fall on ice on the sidewalk in front of the store. To what extent do you think the store's general liability insurance is responsible for any injury sustained in this fall?
4. When a consumer buys an appliance or digital device, the salesperson usually offers an insurance policy that can be purchased for that item. Why is this a good idea or bad idea to purchase an insurance policy on appliances or digital devices?
5. Visualize a large employer in your area. List examples of potential work-related injuries or illnesses that could be sustained from working conditions or the environment from working there.
6. Risk management includes avoiding risks. What are some ways you can avoid risk in your life?
7. Human risks is a negative situation caused by people. What kinds of human risks do you think a business must be prepared to handle?
8. Cybersecurity is protecting an information system against unintended or malicious changes or use. How do you protect your electronic devices, such as your tablet or smartphone, from unwanted cyberattacks?
9. Imagine a scenario in which a business approves a person with limited income for a line of credit beyond his or her means of income. To what extent should the business be held accountable if this person fails to pay his or her debt?
10. The three Cs of credit are used by businesses to evaluate a person's ability to repay credit. List each of the Cs and rate yourself. Explain why you deserve credit if applying for it to make a major purchase.

Communication Skills

Reading. Good readers are able to reflect on their own reading abilities and make changes to improve them. They often monitor their comprehension, adjust their speed to match the difficulty of the text, and self-evaluate any comprehension problems they encounter. Students who are able to self-evaluate their reading skills ultimately comprehend more in all areas of communication. Review your own reading habits to identify where you can improve. This can include timing yourself as you silently read this chapter, paying attention to how often you interrupt yourself, or staying on topic when your thoughts begin to wander. What did your self-assessment reveal about your reading skills?

Writing. Writing is an academic skill applied each day in both personal and professional lives. Using standard English, write a paragraph about why writing is considered an academic skill. How do you think writing skills will help you in your professional career?

Listening. *Reflective listening* occurs when the listener shows an understanding of what was said. Engage in a conversation with a classmate about how this person spends free time. After the conversation, restate what your classmate said. How much did you remember?

Internet Research

Cybersecurity Risk Management. Cybersecurity risks can vary from hardware and software failures to human errors. Using the Internet, research *cybersecurity risk management*. Summarize your findings on how a business can reduce cybersecurity risks.

Teamwork

Working with a team, select one local business in your area. Identify any natural, human, economic, and market risks that could affect the business. Use a graphic organizer to present the information. Then, explain how the business could manage each type of risk.

Portfolio Development

Certificates. A *certificate* is a document that serves as evidence of completion of an activity, training, or other accomplishment. For example, a certificate might show that you passed an examination testing your knowledge of cybersecurity. Another one might show that you can key data at a certain speed.

Certificates are sometimes awarded to an individual as proof of receipt of scholarships, grants, or other recognition. For example, those who participated in competitive events for a Career and Technical Student Organization (CTSO) will probably have certificates that reflect leadership positions, awards, or other honors that were earned.

Some certificates provide evidence of specialized training without a degree being granted. These programs are designed for individuals who are not seeking a degree, but are looking to update their current skills or taking courses specifically for employment.

Certification is a professional status earned by an individual after passing an exam focused on a specific body of knowledge. Some jobs *require* certification. For example, a position as an information technology specialist may require industry specific hardware or software certifications. Already having and displaying a certification makes it more likely you will be seriously considered for the position.

1. Collect certificates of accomplishment that you have earned that are not associated with a degree or certification. You can arrange them in order of importance or dates earned.
2. Collect diplomas, proof of certification, and other examples that relate to educational accomplishments. This could mean making photocopies or digital scans of the original documents. If scanning, be sure to follow the naming conventions you established for your digital portfolio. These documents should be arranged in a logical order.
3. Update your master portfolio spreadsheet.

CTSOs

Proper Attire. Some Career and Technical Student Organization (CTSOs) require appropriate business attire from all entrants and those attending the competition. This requirement is in keeping with the mission of CTSOs: to prepare students for professional careers.

To be sure the attire you have chosen to wear at the competition is in accordance with event requirements, complete the following activities.

1. Visit the website of the organization and look for the most current dress code.
2. The dress code requirements are very detailed and gender specific. Some CTSOs may require a chapter blazer be worn during the competition.
3. Conduct a dress rehearsal when practicing for your event. Are you comfortable in the clothes you have chosen? Do you present a professional appearance?
4. In addition to selecting the appropriate style of clothing, be sure the clothes are clean and pressed. You do not want to undermine your appearance or event performance with wrinkled clothes that may distract judges.
5. Make sure your hair is neat and styled conservatively. If you are a male, you should be clean-shaven. Again, you do not want anything about your appearance detracting from your performance.
6. As far in advance of the event as is possible, share your clothing choice with your organization's advisor to ensure you are dressed appropriately.

CHAPTER 18

Marketing

Sections

Reading Prep

Read the chapter title and tell a classmate what you have experienced or already know about the topic. Then, write a paragraph describing what you would like to learn about the topic. After reading the chapter, share two things you learned with the classmate.

Exploring Careers

Marketing Manager

Business Management & Administration

Marketing managers identify potential customers and develop strategies to market the company's products effectively to these customers. Additionally, marketing managers help keep the company on track by monitoring customer wants and needs and suggesting new goods or services to satisfy those needs.

Typical job titles for this position include *marketing director*, *brand manager*, and *market development manager*. Examples of tasks marketing managers perform include:

- coordinating marketing activities and policies to promote the company's goods or services;
- developing marketing and pricing strategies;
- conducting market research and analysis; and
- coordinating or participating in promotional activities and trade shows to showcase the company's products.

A bachelor degree in marketing, advertising, communications, or a related field is required. Some organizations also require one to five years of work experience. Marketing managers need a strong background in sales and marketing strategy, as well as in principles of customer service and employee management. They need a solid knowledge of the English language, business and management principles, and media production and communication. Marketing managers must also be able to think creatively and use critical-thinking skills to solve problems.

Debby Wong/Shutterstock.com

Section 18.1 Introduction to Marketing

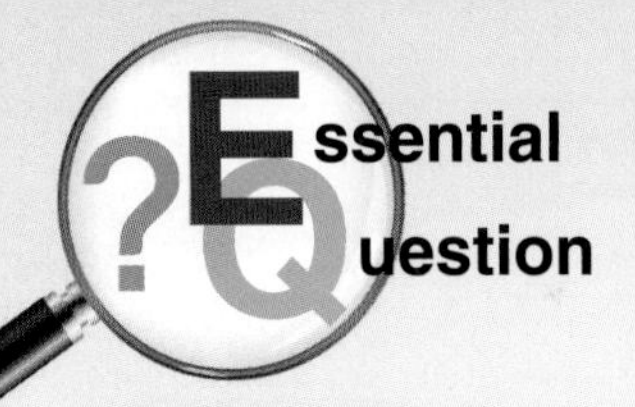

Why is marketing important for business success?

Learning Objectives

LO 18.1-1 Discuss marketing.

LO 18.1-2 List and define the four Ps of marketing.

Key Terms

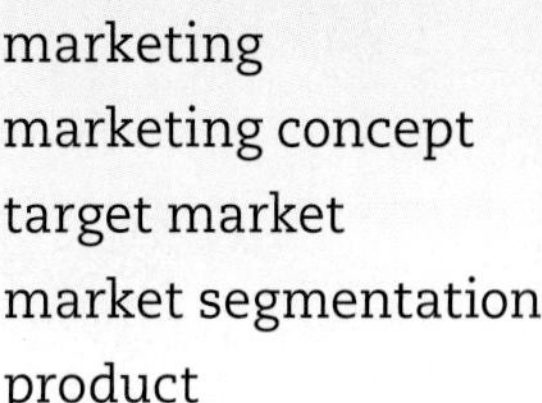

marketing	price	break-even point
marketing concept	place	markup
target market	promotion	channel of distribution
market segmentation	marketing mix	promotional mix
product	value proposition	

LO 18.1-1 Marketing

Marketing plays a major role in the success of a business. Because of its importance, organizations typically hire a manager to direct the activities of marketing. However, the owner of a startup may not be able to afford the costs of hiring a marketing manager. In this situation, the business owner may need to take on the responsibility of marketing tasks.

Marketing consists of dynamic activities that identify, anticipate, and satisfy customer demand while making a profit. It consists of hundreds of activities and can be organized in many different ways. Marketing activities can be categorized into seven functions of marketing. The functions of marketing are:

- channel management;
- marketing-information management (MIM);
- market planning;
- pricing;
- product/service management;
- promotion; and
- selling.

An organization, large or small, startup or established, must have a plan to inform customers of their products. If customers are unaware of the goods and services a business offers, they will not be able to buy them. Marketing activities focus on the customer. The goal of marketing is to meet customer needs and wants with products they can and will buy.

The **marketing concept** is an approach to business that focuses on satisfying customers as the means of achieving profit goals for the company. *Customer satisfaction* is the degree to which customers are pleased with a company's goods or services. Customer satisfaction results in increased profit for a business.

Target Market

Before a business can decide how best to satisfy its customers, it must first identify the customer. There are three basic types of customers:

- consumers, also known as the *business-to-consumer (B2C) market*;
- other businesses, also known as the *business-to-business (B2B) market*; and
- governments and institutions.

A business can sell to one or more of these customers. *Market identification* is the process of identifying customers as consumer, business, or governmental.

A *market* is the group of people who might buy a product. A **target market** is the specific group of customers whose needs and wants a company will focus on satisfying. These are the individuals most likely to buy goods or services a business produces. For example, a business that manufactures running shoes targets its marketing efforts on people who are athletic. Marketing to consumers who are not interested in the sport of running would not be a good use of time or money. A target market has four characteristics.

- Customers have clearly defined wants and needs.
- Customers have enough money to buy the product.
- Customers are willing and have the ability to buy the product.
- There are enough customers in the market for the product to be profitable.

Daniel M Ernst/Shutterstock.com

A target market is the specific group of customers whose needs a company will focus on satisfying, such as high school students. **Identify and describe factors that make up the target market to which you typically belong.**

Market Segmentation

After a target market is identified, the market is segmented. **Market segmentation** is the process of dividing a large market into smaller groups. A market can be segmented by lifestyle factors, locations, demographics, or another set of factors unique to the business as shown in Figure 18-1.

By breaking the market into smaller segments, marketing messages can focus on specific customers who are most likely to buy the product. In addition, a message can be customized to address multiple segments. For example, the business that sells running shoes might further segment the customer as men, women, and teens. There may be three different messages, each addressing an individual segment.

LO 18.1-2 Four Ps of Marketing

Most people think of marketing as advertising, but advertising is just one aspect of the role marketing plays in an organization. Marketing includes deciding what to produce, how to price goods and services, how to get products to the end user, and how to promote goods and services.

Market Segmentation			
Geographic Segmentation	**Demographic Segmentation**	**Psychographic Segmentation**	**Behavioral Segmentation**
• Region • Climate • Population density	• Age • Gender • Income • Ethnicity • Education level • Occupation • Marital status • Family size	• Values • Activities • Interests • Personality • Beliefs	• Benefits sought • Usage rate • Buying status • Brand loyalty • Occasion • Attitude

Goodheart-Willcox Publisher

Figure 18-1 Market segmentation is the process of dividing a large market into smaller groups.

The answers to these questions are called the *four Ps of marketing*, which are product, price, place, and promotion.

- **Product** is a good or service that can be bought or sold.
- **Price** is an amount of money requested or exchanged for a good or service.
- **Place** includes the activities involved in getting products to end users.
- **Promotion** is the process of communicating with potential customers in an effort to influence their buying behavior.

The **marketing mix** is the strategy for using the elements of product, price, place, and promotion, as shown in Figure 18-2. These elements are used individually, or in a combination, to create marketing strategies. The marketing mix can be developed for a single product, a group of products, or an entire company.

Nemanja Zotovic/Shutterstock.com

The promotional mix is a combination of the elements used in a promotional campaign to market products. **Identify a business, such as Samsung, and describe some of the elements of the promotional mix they might use to sell the Galaxy phone.**

Product

A product is a good or service that can be bought or sold. Collectively, goods and services are *products*. Goods are tangible, which means they physically exist and can be touched, such as shoes, laptops, and furniture. A service is intangible, meaning it is not physical and cannot be touched, such as a concert, accounting service, and medical care.

Businesses sell products to satisfy customer needs. Product is the primary *P* of the marketing mix because it is the first element to be decided. Other marketing mix decisions about price, place, and promotion are based on the product decision. If a business does not have a product to sell, other elements of the marketing mix are not needed.

Price

Price is the amount of money requested or exchanged for a product. One goal of marketing is to set competitive prices that will help the company increase its sales and profits. Every business faces the challenge of correctly setting the prices of goods and services.

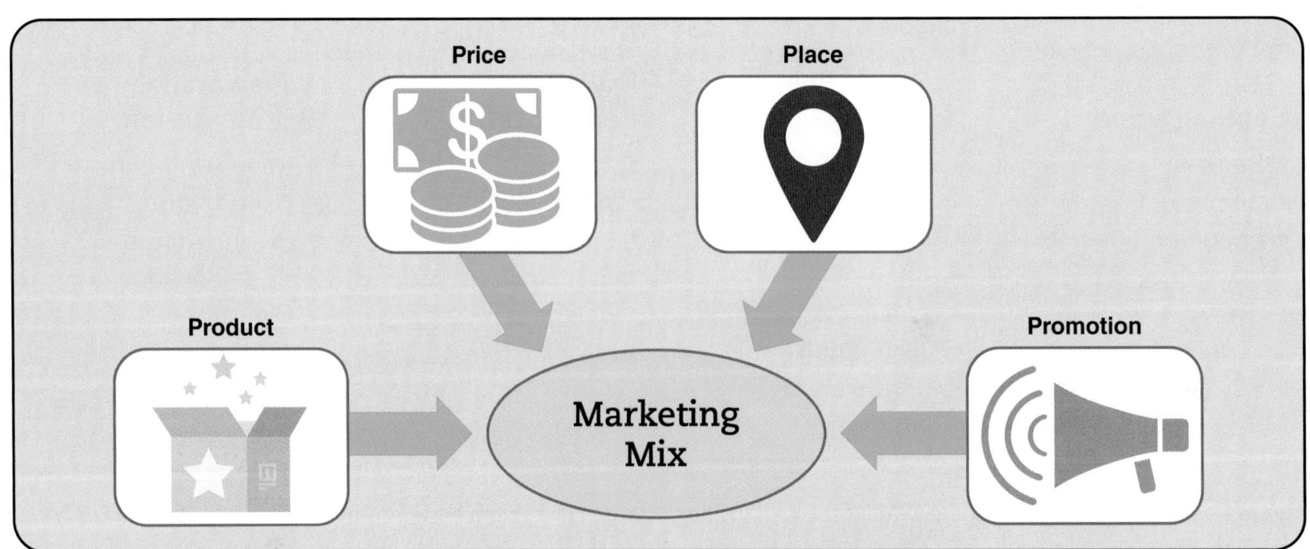

[Credits for Shutterstock images from left to right] howcolour/Shutterstock.com; Aha-Soft/Shutterstock.com; Maksym Drozd/Shutterstock.com; Blan-k/Shutterstock.com; Goodheart-Willcox Publisher

Figure 18-2 The marketing mix is the strategy for using the elements of product, price, place, and promotion.

Pricing strategies are business decisions about how prices are set to be competitive while making a profit. The price of a product should:

- cover costs of producing and selling the product;
- generate desired level of profit for the business; and
- match what customers are willing to pay for the product.

Price is usually associated with value. *Value* is the relative worth of something. A **value proposition** is an explanation of the value of a certain product over others that are similar. Each customer has a personal opinion of the value he or she thinks a product possesses.

Business must set the selling price of an item at a point at which the business generates profits. The *selling price* is the amount a customer pays for an item. The selling price of products is needed to determine the break-even point. The **break-even point** is the point at which revenue from sales is equal to the cost of manufacturing, transporting, and selling products. At the break-even point, costs are recovered. A company does not make or lose money at this point. Sales revenue beyond the break-even point results in profit.

To determine the selling price for an item, a business begins with cost and adds a markup. **Markup** is the amount added to the cost to determine the selling price. The markup can be a dollar amount or percentage. To calculate selling price using a dollar amount, the formula is as follows.

cost +markup dollars = selling price
$80 + $55 = $135

Businesses may decide to use a percentage of profit rather than a dollar amount. Using a *percentage markup method* is a common technique to determine markup. To calculate selling price using a percentage, the formula is as follows.

(cost × percentage of markup) + cost = selling price
($40 × .65) + $40 = $66

Place

Place refers to the activities involved in getting a good or service to the end user. Place is also known as *distribution*. Determining when, where, and how products get to customers is part of place decisions.

You Do the Math

Problem Solving and Reasoning: Adequate Information

When solving word problems, the elements of the math problem must be identified. An important key to solving word problems is to determine whether the information available is sufficient to solve the stated problem. If some information is not provided, the problem cannot be solved.

Solve the following problems.

1. A business sells smartphones in packaging that measures 6 inches by 4 inches by 1 inch. The products are shipped to resellers in cartons that measure 18 inches by 12 inches by 12 inches. The cartons can hold a maximum of 15 pounds. The company wants to know how much each full carton weighs. Is there enough information to solve this problem? If not, what information is missing?
2. An office manager orders supplies every Monday. This week he must order 23 reams of paper, 2000 envelopes, and 12 boxes of tape. He wants to know how much this will cost. Is there enough information to solve this problem? If not, what information is missing?
3. A sales manager travels for work. On Monday, she drove 48 miles. On Tuesday, she drove 37 miles. On Thursday, she drove 76 miles. She is reimbursed for gasoline at a rate of $0.53 per mile. She wants to determine how many miles per gallon she averaged while traveling. Is there enough information to solve this problem? If not, what information is missing?

Distribution is part of the supply chain process. A *supply chain* is the businesses, people, and activities involved in turning raw materials into products and delivering them to end users. The path goods take through the supply chain is the **channel of distribution**. Many different organizations help move products through the channel of distribution to the end users. The channel of distribution may be short or long, as illustrated in Figure 18-3.

An important decision of distribution is selecting the appropriate mode of transportation to ensure a product travels through the supply chain. *Transportation* is the physical movement of products through the channel of distribution.

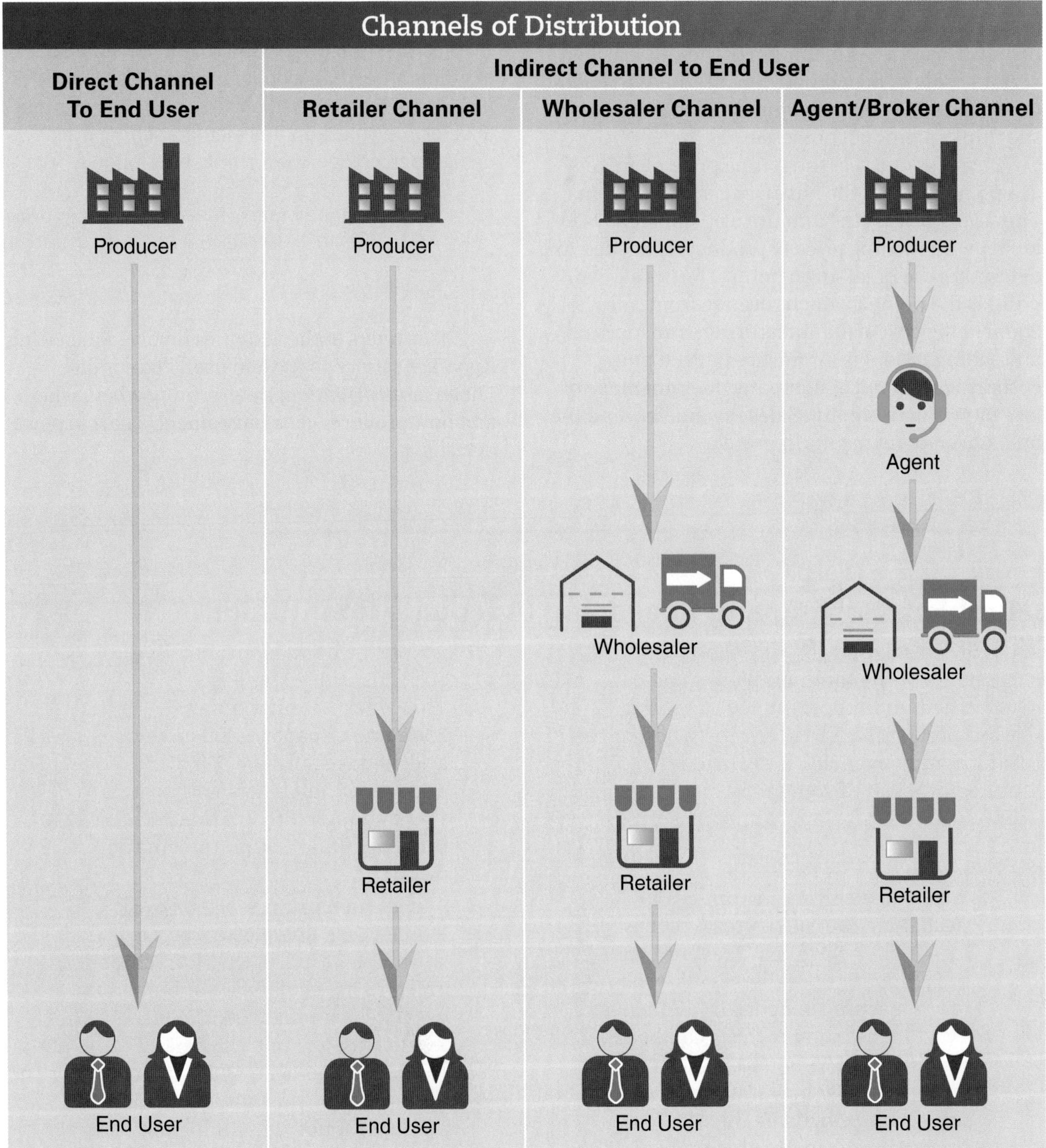

Figure 18-3 The channel of distribution is the path goods take through the supply chain.

It can include road, rail, air, water, digital, or pipeline. Transportation is expensive and has a direct impact on the final price the customer pays for a product.

Promotion

Promotion is the process of communicating with potential customers with the goal of influencing their buying behaviors. Businesses aim to do this by promoting a product's price, its features and benefits, and the place where it is offered. If customers do not know that a product exists or where to find a product, they cannot buy it.

Promotion is the most visible of the four Ps of marketing. The **promotional mix** is a combination of the elements used in a promotional campaign to market products. These elements include advertising, direct marketing, sales promotion, public relations, and personal selling.

- *Advertising* is any nonpersonal communication paid for by an identified sponsor. It provides information about the features and benefits of a product, including prices and descriptions. Examples of advertising are newspaper ads, television or radio commercials, billboards, and Internet advertisements.
- *Direct marketing* is a type of advertising sent directly to individual customers without the use of a third party. Examples include brochures, coupons, flyers, e-mails, and postcards.
- *Sales promotion* is the efforts used to encourage customers to buy a product within a specific timeframe, usually as soon as possible. A sales promotion can include coupons, rebates, promotional items, samples, loyalty programs, contests and sweepstakes, trade shows, and displays.
- *Public relations (PR)* consists of the marketing activities promoting goodwill between a company and the public. Unlike advertising, public relations is unpaid media coverage.
- *Personal selling* is any direct contact between a salesperson and a customer with the objective of making a sale. By meeting customer needs with a product, a company can grow its sales.

The promotional mix is determined based on the goals, budget, target market, and marketing mix for the product. Decisions are made as to which elements will be used to reach the customer in the target market. This means that advertising, direct marketing, sales promotion, public relations, and personal selling must all work together.

Section 18.1 Review

Check Your Understanding

1. List seven functions of marketing.
2. Define *customer satisfaction.*
3. Identify the four Ps of marketing.
4. The price of a product should accomplish what three objectives?
5. Name elements of the promotional mix.

Build Your Vocabulary

As you progress through this text, develop a personal glossary of key terms. This will help you build your vocabulary and prepare you for a career. Write a definition for each of the following terms and add them to your personal glossary.

marketing	price	break-even point
marketing concept	place	markup
target market	promotion	channel of distribution
market segmentation	marketing mix	promotional mix
product	value proposition	

Section 18.2 Marketing Plan

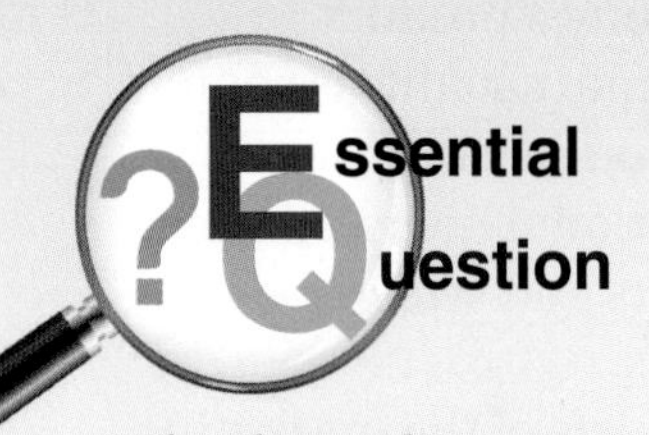

Why does a business need a marketing plan?

Learning Objectives

LO 18.2-1 Explain the concept of a marketing plan.

LO 18.2-2 Name sections of a marketing plan.

Key Terms

marketing plan
marketing strategy
action plan
marketing tactic
metrics

LO 18.2-1 Marketing Plan

A **marketing plan** is a document that describes business and marketing objectives and the strategies and tactics used to achieve them. All organizations create marketing plans. A typical marketing plan outline is shown in Figure 18-4.

For established organizations, a marketing plan is written as a part of the strategic planning process. It is written each year and updated throughout the year as needed. For a startup, a marketing plan is written as a required part of the business plan. It is reviewed by potential investors to show evidence of plans to generate sales.

Research is required to write a marketing plan and includes the creation of a situation analysis. As you recall, a *situation analysis* is a review of the internal and external factors that affect a business. It is completed by conducting SWOT and PEST analyses.

- A *SWOT analysis* is the identification of an organization's strengths, weaknesses, opportunities, and threats. It helps identify both internal and external factors that can affect the success of a business.
- A *PEST analysis* is an evaluation of the political, economic, social, and technological factors in a certain market or geographic region that may affect the success of a business. It is an example of an environmental analysis, also called *environmental scan,* which examines external factors that are beyond the control of a business.

Marketing Plan

Title Page
Table of Contents

- I. Executive Summary
- II. Business Description
  - A. Overview
  - B. Vision Statement
  - C. Mission Statement
  - D. Company Goals
- III. Market Analysis
  - A. SWOT Analysis
  - B. Environmental Scan (PEST Analysis)
  - C. Competitive Analysis
- IV. Sales Analysis
  - A. Sales History and Projection
  - B. Best Opportunities
  - C. Sales Goals
- V. Marketing Strategies
  - A. Marketing Goals
  - B. Target Market
  - C. Marketing Mix
    1. Product Strategies
    2. Price Strategies
    3. Place Strategies
    4. Promotion Strategies
  - D. Product Positioning
- VI. Action Plan
  - A. Timeline
  - B. Budget
  - C. Metrics
- VII. Bibliography
- VIII. Appendices

Goodheart-Willcox Publisher

Figure 18-4 A marketing plan is a document that describes business and marketing objectives and the strategies and tactics used to achieve them.

Peshkova/Shutterstock.com

Research is required to write a marketing plan and includes the creation of a situational analysis. **How does research contribute to success of a marketing plan?**

In addition, a competitive analysis is completed. A *competitive analysis* is a tool used to compare the strengths and weaknesses of a business with those of competing businesses. In the analysis, competitors are evaluated on factors, such as physical locations, product lines, pricing, and market share. Using this information, an organization can determine how it will compete with others to gain its share of sales in the market.

Learning about the competition includes estimating the portion of the market that each competitor holds.

- *Market size* is the total sales per year for a specific product held by all the competing businesses.
- *Market share* is the percentage of total sales in a market held by one business.
- *Market potential* is the maximum number of customers and amount of sales that can be generated from a specific segment in a defined timeframe.

LO 18.2-2 Creating a Marketing Plan

Creating a marketing plan takes time and research. Some of the information from the plan can be found in the existing business plan. Other sections of the marketing plan require information to be gathered and analyzed.

In an established organization, the marketing team typically writes the marketing plan. In the case of a startup, the writing and development of the marketing plan is the responsibility of the business owner. A marketing plan typically contains these sections: opening, analysis, marketing strategies, and action plan.

Opening

The opening section of a marketing plan summarizes information from the business plan. This section reiterates the vision statement, mission statement, and goals of the organization. The purpose of summarizing this information is to create a foundation on which the marketing plan is based.

Analysis

The analysis section details information from market and sales analyses obtained during research for the strategic plan. This section includes the SWOT, PEST, and competitive analyses. It also summarizes the findings of each. The analysis section helps an organization define both the environment in which the business is operating and the business goals to be met.

Marketing Strategies

A **marketing strategy** is a decision made about how to execute the marketing plan and meet the goals of the business. Marketing strategies outline who, what, where, when, and how of the marketing process. Strategies include establishing marketing goals, identifying the target market, and defining components of the marketing mix.

Action Plan

The **action plan** is a list of the marketing tactics with details about how to execute each tactic. A **marketing tactic** is a specific activity implemented to carry out a marketing strategy. An example of a marketing tactic is to air a television commercial for three weeks to promote a sale.

Employability Skills
Telephone Etiquette

Telephone etiquette is using good manners when speaking on the telephone. Always be courteous to the person on the other end of the call. Be aware of the volume and tone of your voice. Smile when you are talking on the phone; it will make your voice sound more pleasant.

Sidewalk Fashion Company Action Plan						
Promotional Item	**In Creative**	**Finished Date**	**Mail or Launch Date**	**Lead Person**	**Budget**	**Metrics**
Social media page	1-Apr	1-May	3-May	Jordan	$2,000	5,000 followers
Brochure	1-May	1-Jun	3-Jun	Susan	$5,000	1,000 customer responses
E-mail campaign	1-Jul	5-Jul	7-Jul	Jim	$1,000	2,500 website hits
Pamphlets	1-Aug	1-Sep	4-Sep	Kiara	$4,000	1,000 customer responses
Coupons	1-Oct	4-Oct	6-Oct	Alonso	$3,500	1,500 purchases made with coupon
Mobile site	1-Oct	30-Nov	1-Dec	Ashleigh	$3,000	3,000 website hits

Goodheart-Willcox Publisher

Figure 18-5 An action plan is a list of the marketing tactics with details about how to execute each tactic.

An action plan can take many forms depending on the organization's needs. A spreadsheet, similar to the one in Figure 18-5, is a convenient format. Important components include a timeline, marketing budget, and metrics.

- A *timeline* lists when each activity starts, where it happens, its end date, and the person responsible. This helps keep a marketing team on track and moves the plan forward.
- A *marketing budget* shows the costs to implement the planned marketing tactics and promotional activities. Most organizations base the budget on a percentage of sales generated for the company or other factors related to sales.
- **Metrics** are standards of measurement. They are used to determine the success rate of each marketing activity.

The action plan is a detailed section of the marketing plan. Having an action plan helps ensure marketing efforts are carried out in the way it was planned and that money spent on marketing is used wisely.

Section 18.2 Review

Check Your Understanding

1. What is a situation analysis?
2. What is a competitive analysis?
3. Explain market size, market share, and market potential.
4. What information appears in the opening section of a marketing plan?
5. Name three components of an action plan.

Build Your Vocabulary

As you progress through this text, develop a personal glossary of key terms. This will help you build your vocabulary and prepare you for a career. Write a definition for each of the following terms and add them to your personal glossary.

marketing plan
marketing strategy
action plan
marketing tactic
metrics

Section 18.3

Product Development

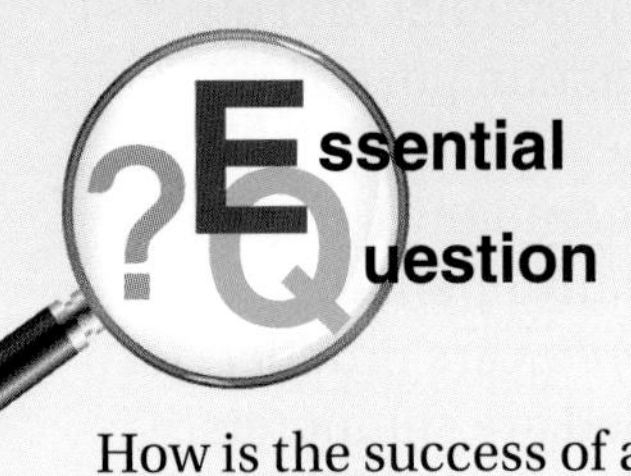

How is the success of a business impacted by its products?

Learning Objectives

LO 18.3-1 Discuss products.
LO 18.3-2 Differentiate between consumer and business products.
LO 18.3-3 Summarize new-product development.
LO 18.3-4 List stages in the product life cycle.

Key Terms 

product mix	product manager	maturity stage
new product	introduction stage	saturated market
product life cycle	growth stage	decline stage

LO 18.3-1 Product

Businesses sell tangible goods or intangible services to generate revenue and satisfy customer needs. Products are distinguished by their features, usage, and protection.

- A *feature* is a fact about a product. For example, a feature of a pair of boots is they are made of leather. An optional feature, or *option*, is a feature added to a product by customer request. An example of an optional feature is adding an electronic navigation system to a new car. The *quality* of a product is an indicator of its excellence. A product's level of quality can be considered a feature. Price and quality are often directly related. Generally, the higher the quality, the higher the price.
- *Usage* is the way a product is used. The usage of a product can distinguish it from similar products offered by other companies. Businesses help their customers use a product correctly by providing instructions, installation, and technical support.
- *Protection* refers to measures that protect the product, the user, or both. It includes safety inspections, packaging, warranties, and product maintenance and repair services.

Product planning is the process of deciding which products will appeal to the target market. It is deciding the features and benefits that will help a product be successful. It also involves monitoring a product through its life cycle.

Product planning includes decisions about the product mix. A **product mix** is all the goods and services a business sells. Typically, the product mix consists of goods and services that relate to one another in some way. For example, the product mix for Famous Footwear offers athletic shoes, dress shoes, and casual shoes for men and women.

LO 18.3-2 Consumer and Business Products

Products are necessary for a business to generate revenue. Some products are intended for consumers, whereas other products are created for business use.

Consumer Products

Consumer products are those sold to individuals for their personal use, which makes the consumers the end users. These types of products include the following.

- *Convenience goods* are typically for immediate use. These goods are often bought with little effort. Examples of convenience goods include most grocery items and gasoline.

antoniodiaz/Shutterstock.com

Consumer products are those sold to individuals for their personal use, which makes the consumers the end users. **When did you or your family last purchase consumer products? How did you or your family decide what products to purchase?**

- *Shopping goods* are goods usually purchased after making the effort to compare price, quality, and style in more than one store. These goods are purchased less often than convenience goods. Examples of shopping goods include home appliances and electronics.
- *Specialty goods* are unique items that consumers are willing to spend considerable time, effort, and money to buy. Examples of specialty goods include luxury vehicles and antiques.

Consumers have a wide variety of needs and wants. A business must have the right goods and services to meet these needs and wants, or customers will choose to shop elsewhere.

Business Products

Business products are items sold to businesses, government agencies, and other organizations for use in their operations. These products include the following.

- *Raw materials* are natural or man-made materials that become part of a manufactured product. Raw materials include wood, plastic pellets, metal, and other substances. These are sold to manufacturers for various uses.
- *Process materials* are used in product manufacturing but are not readily identifiable in the finished product. Examples of process materials include food preservatives and industrial glue.
- *Component parts* are already assembled and become a part of a finished product. These parts are typically sold to companies that produce final products. Examples include computer chips and tires.
- *Major equipment* is large machines and other equipment used for production purposes. Equipment includes cranes, furnaces, and conveyers. Manufacture companies require different equipment for daily operation.
- *Office equipment and supplies* are products for basic office needs. Included are computers, pens, paper, and other office items. All businesses, big or small, need these products.
- *Business services* are the tasks necessary to keep a business operating. Examples include building maintenance, equipment repair, and accounting services.

LO 18.3-3 New-Product Development

A **new product** is a product that is different in some way from existing products. A new product may replace a product that is no longer salable. Alternatively, it can be a brand new product that does not currently exist.

A startup may research a competitive product, decide how it can be improved, and introduce a new product to the marketplace. An established business may research a current product it sells, determine how to improve it, and relaunch it to the marketplace.

Sheila Fitzgerald/Shutterstock.com

Changing something as basic as packaging can be considered as *added value*, such as single serve packaging for oatmeal containers. **Why would consumers buy a product, such as oatmeal, that was repackaged for added value? What is the value and what is it worth in terms of price?**

Even a small change to an existing product can add value and transform it into a new product. Changing something as basic as packaging can be considered as *added value*. The difference between new and existing products can be small or significant. There are six categories of new products, as shown in Figure 18-6.

Developing new products does not happen overnight. The new-product development process generally follows seven steps, as shown in Figure 18-7.

1. **Idea generation.** A new product idea is often a result of research, observation, customer feedback, or brainstorming. *Brainstorming* is a creative process that focuses on new product ideas.
2. **Idea screening.** Once an idea is generated, it must be reviewed to determine if it is feasible. During this step, new product ideas are reviewed from a customer's viewpoint.
3. **Business analysis.** A business analysis is completed that includes projected costs and forecasts of product sales. Also included is how the new product aligns with the image and goals of a company.
4. **Product design.** After the business analysis is complete, the product is designed. The product idea becomes a reality and the name, image, logo, slogan, and packaging of the product are created.

New Product	
Category	**Description**
New to the world	New product or invention with never-before-seen technology
Minor variation	Improvement or revision of existing product
New line	New product line to enter an existing market
Addition to existing line	New product added to existing product lines
Reposition	Existing product marketed in a new way
Less-expensive version	Product created with less-expensive material or methods to reduce cost and lower prices

Goodheart-Willcox Publisher

Figure 18-6 There are six categories of new products.

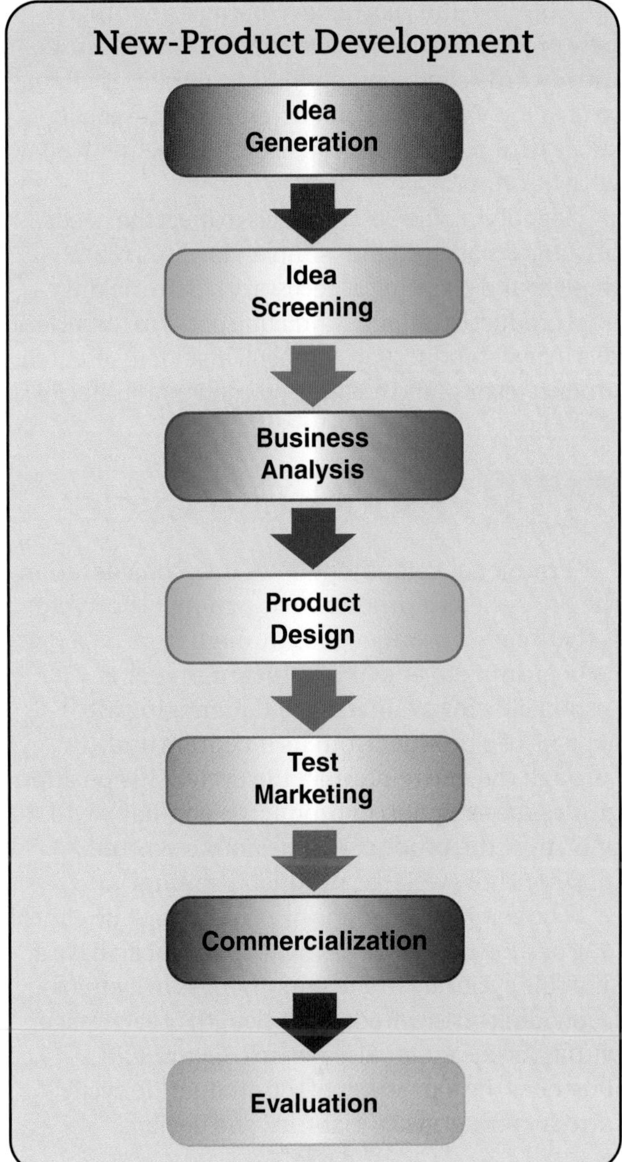

Goodheart-Willcox Publisher

Figure 18-7 A new-product development process generally follows seven steps.

5. **Test marketing.** During test marketing, a new product is introduced to a portion of the target market to learn how it will sell. Test marketing can test the entire marketing mix for the product.
6. **Commercialization.** Commercialization brings attention to the product and creates demand. This is also the introduction stage of the product life cycle.
7. **Evaluation.** After a product is in the market, its success is evaluated. Success can be based on how well it met the sales and other goals established for the product during the business analysis.

The cost and risk of developing a genuinely new product is high. However, if it is successful, the rewards can be great. Many companies choose to develop variations on currently or previously successful products because of the risk involved with developing new ideas.

Identifying the best products to meet the needs of a target market sounds simple. However, much thought and planning is necessary before making final product decisions. Marketing plays an important role in new-product development, including research, product testing, and creating promotional strategies.

LO 18.3-4 Product Life Cycle

Product development takes into consideration the life cycle of a product. The **product life cycle** is the stages a product goes through from its beginning to end. A **product manager** is responsible for evaluating and managing all aspects of a product from its inception and through the entire product life cycle. This position guides the selection of products a company will offer, how the product will be marketed, and monitors how well the product is selling.

The complete life cycle of a product can be either long or short. For example, smartphones can have a short life cycle due to constant changes in technology. Depending on the product, the length of each stage within the life cycle varies as well. Figure 18-8 illustrates the four stages of the product life cycle: introduction, growth, maturity, and decline.

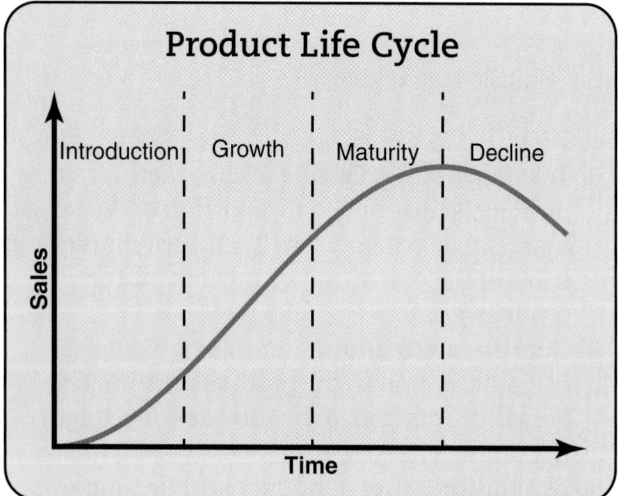

Goodheart-Willcox Publisher

Figure 18-8 The product life cycle is the stages a product goes through from its beginning to end.

Ethics

Bribery

Bribery is giving or receiving an item of value in order to influence someone when engaging in a business transaction. An example of a bribe is offering money to a person to post a negative online review about a competitor. Another example is accepting money in return for hiring a friend as an employee. Participating in an act of bribery for personal or business reasons while representing an organization is unethical and potentially illegal.

Introduction Stage

The **introduction stage** is the time when a new product is first brought to market. Usually, very few people know about the product. At this stage in the life cycle, marketing focuses heavily on promotions explaining the new product and its benefits. Sales tend to be low until more people learn about why they should buy the product. Profits are also lower in the introduction stage due to low sales and high costs.

Production costs for a new product tend to be high because fewer units are produced until demand increases. In addition, the company has already invested a large amount of money on market research, product development, production, and promotion. It is expected that the investment will be recovered as the product begins to sell. Profits tend to rise later in the product life cycle due to increased sales and decreased production costs.

Growth Stage

The **growth stage** is the period in which product sales increase rapidly. To keep product sales high, a new model of the product may be introduced. Modifications may also be made to the product to keep customers interested or meet new needs or wants. During the growth stage, marketers focus on promotions distinguishing their brands from the competition. They also use strategies to build *brand loyalty,* which is customer dedication to a certain brand or product.

Maturity Stage

The **maturity stage** occurs when product sales are stable. During this stage, competition for customers is intense. Sales are no longer increasing quickly, nor are they decreasing. Maturity can happen when the market becomes saturated with a product or when a newer, better product is introduced to fill the consumer's needs. A **saturated market** is one in which most of the potential customers who need, want, and can afford a product have bought it. At this stage, businesses look for new ways a product could be used or try to identify new markets for the product to avoid losing revenue.

BrAt82/Shutterstock.com

Mature products eventually enter the decline stage in which product sales begin to decrease and become obsolete, such as the typewriter. **Identify a product that has become obsolete in your lifetime and explain why you think it is now obsolete.**

Decline Stage

Mature products eventually enter the **decline stage** in which product sales begin to decrease. If sales decline rapidly, the company may stop making or selling the product. Decline often occurs when a new technology is growing rapidly, so the older products become obsolete quickly.

Deciding whether a product is truly at the end of its life cycle can be tricky. A decline in sales does not always mean the product is in the decline stage. For example, in an economic recession, sales for expensive products like video game systems may decline quickly because consumers need to save money. However, that does not mean that video game systems are at the end of the product life cycle.

Section 18.3 Review

Check Your Understanding

1. How are products distinguished?
2. What is product planning?
3. List examples of consumer products.
4. List the steps of the new-product development process.
5. Define *brainstorming.*

Build Your Vocabulary

As you progress through this text, develop a personal glossary of key terms. This will help you build your vocabulary and prepare you for a career. Write a definition for each of the following terms and add them to your personal glossary.

product mix	product manager	maturity stage
new product	introduction stage	saturated market
product life cycle	growth stage	decline stage

Chapter 18 Review and Assessment

Chapter Summary

Section 18.1 Introduction to Marketing

LO 18.1-1 **Discuss marketing.**
Marketing plays a major role in the success of a business. It consists of dynamic activities that identify, anticipate, and satisfy customer demand while making a profit. Marketing activities focus on the customer. The marketing concept is an approach to business that focuses on satisfying customers as the means of achieving profit goals for the company.

LO 18.1-2 **List and define the four Ps of marketing.**
The four Ps of marketing are product, price, place, and promotion. Product is any good or service that can be bought or sold. Price is an amount of money requested or exchanged for a good or service. Place includes the activities involved in getting products to end users. Promotion is the process of communicating with potential customers in an effort to influence their buying behaviors.

Section 18.2 Marketing Plan

LO 18.2-1 **Explain the concept of a marketing plan.**
A marketing plan is a document that describes the business and marketing objectives and the strategies and tactics that will be used to achieve them. For established organizations, the marketing plan is written as a part of the strategic planning process. For a startup, marketing plans are written as a required part of the business plan. A marketing plan is reviewed by potential investors to show evidence of plans to generate sales.

LO 18.2-2 **Name sections of a marketing plan.**
A marketing plan typically contains these sections: opening, analysis, marketing strategies, and action plan.

Section 18.3 Product Development

LO 18.3-1 **Discuss products.**
Businesses sell products, whether tangible goods or intangible services, to generate revenue. Products are distinguished by their features, usage, and protection. Making decisions about which products will appeal to the target market is known as product planning.

LO 18.3-2 **Differentiate between consumer and business products.**
Consumer products are products sold to individuals for their personal use. Business products are items sold to businesses for use in their operations.

LO 18.3-3 **Summarize new-product development.**
The new-product development process generally follows seven steps: idea generation, idea screening, business analysis, product design, test marketing, commercialization, and evaluation. The cost and risk of developing a genuinely new product is high. However, if it is successful, the rewards can be great.

LO 18.3-4 **List stages in the product life cycle.**
The four stages of the product life cycle are introduction, growth, maturity, and decline.

Review Your Knowledge

1. Discuss marketing.
2. Name three basic types of customers.
3. List and explain the four Ps of marketing.
4. Discuss a marketing plan.
5. Explain each section of a marketing plan.
6. Discuss products.
7. Explain the difference between consumer products and business products.
8. Summarize new-product development.
9. What is the role of a product manager?
10. Explain each stage in the product life cycle.

Apply Your Knowledge

1. Marketing is an important function of every business. Explain why you would or would not want the responsibility of being a marketing manager for a business.
2. The marketing concept is an approach to business that focuses on satisfying customers as the means of achieving profit goals for the company. Assume you are the owner of a startup. How would you make customers the focus of your business activities?
3. Select a product that interests you. The product you choose can be a good or a service. Create a poster that describes the company and the product. On the poster, describe each of the four Ps of marketing as they might be applied in the marketing mix for the product.
4. Product is the most important of the four Ps of marketing. Assume you are in charge of product development for a company. What product would you choose to sell and why?
5. The channel of distribution is the path goods take through the supply chain. Choose a good that you have purchased recently. Using Figure 18-3 as a reference, create a flowchart of the distribution channel the good followed from production to your purchase.
6. The promotional mix is a combination of the elements used to market products. These elements include advertising, direct marketing, sales promotion, public relations, and personal selling. Select a product that you see promoted on television, radio, or other media. Create a chart and identify examples of each component of the promotional mix that is used to promote the product.
7. Explain how writing a marketing plan relates to the planning function of management.
8. If you are selling a good, there are three product elements on which you will focus: features, usage, and protection. Create a chart for your smartphone and define each product element as it pertains to the phone.
9. Name a product with which you are familiar that you think could be repositioned by making some small changes, such as packaging. Define what the change is and why you think it would be a good strategy.
10. Summarize the challenges you think a business might face as its products go through the different phases of the product life cycle.

College and Career Readiness

Communication Skills

Reading. *Environmental print* refers to the words you come across in your daily life, such as signage, logos, and advertisements. Locate an example of environmental print in your classroom or school and read the words. What is the purpose or meaning of the environmental print?

Writing. *Compare* means to look at two things to find what is the same between them. *Contrast* means to look at two things in order to find what is different between them. Write one paragraph comparing working part-time while in school to not working while in school. Write another paragraph contrasting these scenarios. Develop and strengthen your ideas as needed by revising and editing your writing.

Speaking. What do you think the saying, "necessity is the mother of invention" means? Provide an example of how the need for a product sparked its creation. Identify an example of the need for a new product, and invent one to meet the need. Present your invention to your class. Make use of a poster, visual display, or demonstration to improve the presentation.

Internet Research

Pricing Strategy. Pricing strategies are business decisions about how competitive prices are set while making a profit. Using the Internet, research *pricing strategies.* Based upon your findings, summarize examples of pricing strategies that can be used for pricing products.

Marketing Plans. Numerous marketing plan templates are found on the Internet. Conduct an Internet search of *marketing plan templates.* Compare the templates you find and examine each. Select the one that you prefer for use in the teamwork activity that follows.

Product Life Cycle. Fashion, entertainment, and technology trends change regularly. Choose a product that was once popular but has fallen out of demand, such as CD players or Tickle Me Elmo™ dolls. After you select the product, research its life cycle. Document your findings.

Teamwork

Writing a marketing plan is an important task that every business must undertake. Working with your team, select a business and write a marketing plan. Use the outline in Figure 18-4 as you identify information that needs to be included. Each team member should assume responsibility for one section of the plan. Then, each part should be combined into one succinct marketing plan.

Portfolio Development

Clubs and Organizations. Participation in an organization, academic club, or sport demonstrates that you have the skill set to work with others and be a team player. Many soft skills, such as appreciation for diversity, leadership, and social responsibility, are learned from participating in a club or group. Documenting that you have been a member of an organization shows an employer that you are responsible, a hard worker, and a team player.

Networking skills can also be learned from interacting with club members and its leadership. *Networking* means talking with people and developing relationships that can lead to potential career opportunities. This is an important skill that will help you in both your academic and professional careers.

Showing evidence that you have participated in competitive events, such as those organized by CTSOs, is a valuable addition to a portfolio. These competitions support lifelong learning and the application of the skills learned in real-world situations. Participation in competitive events encourages leadership, teamwork, and career development. If you have participated in an event for a club or sports team, write a summary of your role and what you learned from the experience.

1. Identify organizations, academic clubs, or sports teams to which you belong. Create a document that lists each membership using word-processing software. Include the name of each organization, its contact information, and the dates that you were active. Use the heading "Clubs and Organizations," or another appropriate title, and your name. Save the document, and update your master portfolio spreadsheet. Remember to back up each document on your flash drive.

EVENT PREP

CTSOs

Careers. Many competitive events for CTSO competitions offer events that include various careers. This competitive event may include an objective test that covers multiple topics. Participants are usually allowed one hour to complete the event.

To prepare for the careers component of an event, complete the following activities.

1. Read the careers features in each chapter of the text. As you read about each career, note an important fact or two that you would like to remember.
2. Conduct an online search for *careers*. Review careers that may be a choice for the event. Make notes on important facts about each.

UNIT 8 Managing Your Career

Chapters

Functions of Management Covered in This Unit

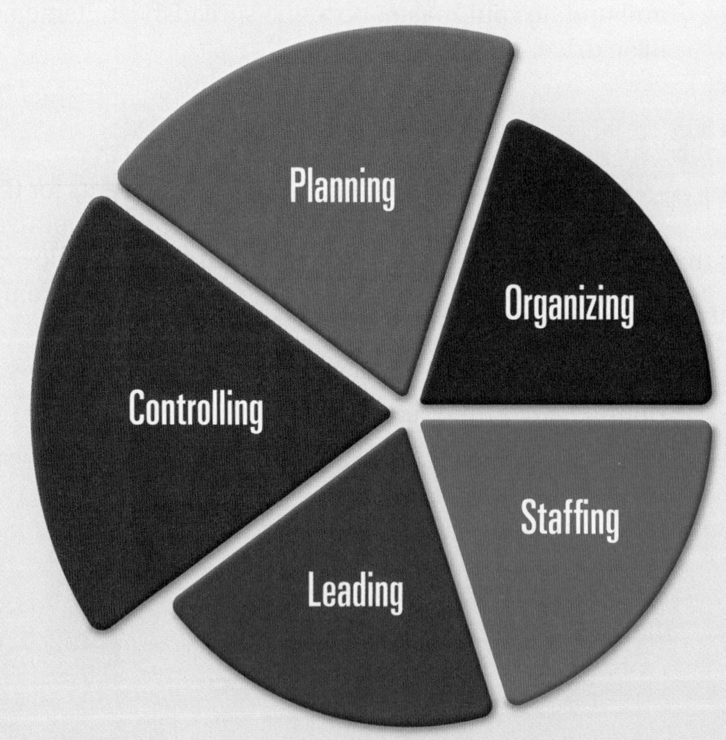

While studying, look for the activity icon for:

- Vocabulary terms with e-flash cards and matching activities

These activities can be accessed at www.g-wlearning.com/business/8417

Case Study

Truthfulness

El Nariz/Shutterstock.com

June was recently hired as a team leader at a prestigious software development firm. She was selected based on experience listed in her résumé. Her work experience listed extensive time spent working for competing organizations, and her education boasted both undergraduate and graduate degrees from well-known and respected universities.

As June began her role, her actions did not demonstrate the competencies she proclaimed to possess. Her direct reports immediately questioned her experience and noticed obvious discrepancies in her work. They found themselves having to correct multiple coding errors and fix inconsistencies. In addition, she seemed unaware of the production processes for software, which should have been second nature for her.

Her direct reports went to HR with their concerns. After listening to their feedback, the HR director made follow-up phone calls to previous employers. It was discovered that June embellished the facts on her résumé. While she did work at competing organizations, she was not in a management position. Furthermore, the university from which she claimed to have a graduate degree confirmed that she enrolled in classes but never graduated. When presented with the discrepancies, June explained that she was confident she could do the job even though she had not previously held a management position. Because of her dishonesty, and lack of solid experience and required education, June's employment was immediately terminated.

Telling untruths to gain employment is unethical. If hired for a position for which qualifications were falsified, it can be grounds for dismissal. Lying on a résumé is a risk that could cost a person future career opportunities. It is better to be honest and focus on actual skills and talents rather than embellish those that do not exist.

Critical Thinking

1. What impact can résumé fraud have on a person's employment opportunities?
2. What suggestions would you offer a job candidate about how to focus on strengths and not embellish talents or skills that the person does not possess?

CHAPTER 19

Career Planning

Sections

Reading Prep

Before reading this chapter, preview the illustrations. Translate the information in the illustrations into words. In what ways do you think the illustrations support the content?

Exploring Careers

Product Manager

Business Management & Administration

Product managers are responsible for the strategy of a product through its life cycle. They provide guidance to keep the product profitable or remove it from a company's product offerings. In addition, product managers direct new product development from concept to delivery. They work with developers to create prototypes, forecast costs, and project future sales. Product managers are also responsible for conducting research, which includes investigating new products and analyzing buying trends.

Typical job titles for this position include *merchandise manager*, *purchasing manager*, and *procurement specialist*. Examples of tasks product managers perform include:

- using spreadsheet software to organize and analyze sales figures on product lines;
- meeting with sales employees to get information about customer wants and needs;
- analyzing sales records and trends to determine future demand; and
- setting markups and selling prices for the products.

Product manager positions require a bachelor degree in business or related fields. Product managers must be able to use financial information to analyze product performance. They need to possess good communication, negotiation, and research skills as well as be able to work under pressure, meet deadlines, and demonstrate good judgment.

Syda Productions/Shutterstock.com

Section 19.1 Choosing a Career

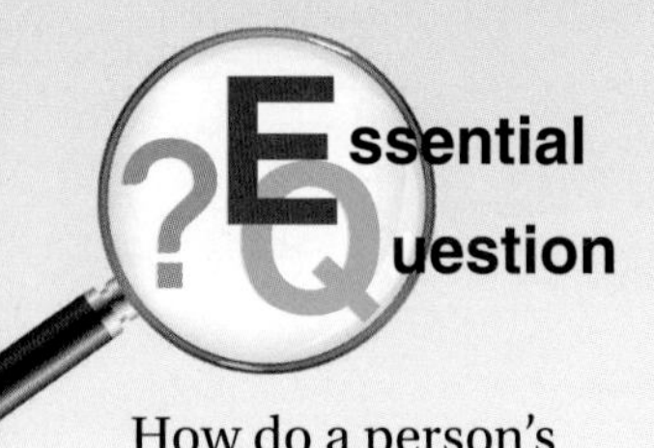

How do a person's skills contribute to career success?

Learning Objectives

LO 19.1-1 Determine skills needed for the workplace.

LO 19.1-2 Discuss career planning.

LO 19.1-3 Explore sources of career information.

LO 19.1-4 Summarize how CTSOs can prepare a student for a career.

Key Terms 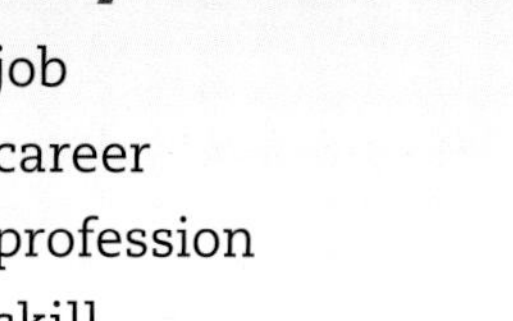

job	career pathway	interest
career	career ladder	networking
profession	career plan	informational interviewing
skill	aptitude	career and technical student organization (CTSO)
employability skills	ability	
career cluster	values	

LO 19.1-1 Skills for the Workplace

A **job** is the work a person does regularly in order to earn money. A job may be a part-time position you go to after school. A **career** is a series of related jobs in the same profession. **Profession** is a job that requires special training or skills and usually a high level of education. A career is a position for which you prepare by attending school or completing specialized training. Over time, a job can turn into a career.

All employment opportunities require skills. A **skill** is something an individual does well. Skills are the foundational elements of all career fields. *Job-specific skills* are critical skills necessary to perform the required work-related tasks of a position. These are also known as hard skills. Job-specific skills are acquired through work experience and education or training. Without them, an individual will be unlikely to perform the job successfully.

Employability skills are applicable skills used to help an individual find a job, perform in the workplace, and gain success in a job or career. Employability skills are known as *foundational, transferable,* or *soft skills.* You have already acquired many of these skills. However, some of them are acquired through life experiences. Others come from working at a job or partaking in social situations. These skills are not specific to one career, but are transferable to many different jobs and professional positions. Examples of employability skills are shown in Figure 19-1.

Employability Skills			
Basic Skills	**Thinking Skills**	**People Skills**	**Personal Qualities**
• Reading • Writing • Speaking • Listening • Technology • Mathematics	• Decision-making • Creative thinking • Problem solving • Visualization • Reasoning	• Social perceptiveness • Leadership • Teamwork • Cultural competence	• Self-management • Integrity • Honesty • Social responsibility

Goodheart-Willcox Publisher

Figure 19-1 Employability skills are applicable skills used to help an individual find a job, perform in the workplace, and gain success in a job or career.

Career Clusters

Studying the career clusters is a good way to begin analyzing the principles of career fields. The **career clusters**, shown in Figure 19-2, are 16 groups of occupational and career specialties that share common knowledge and skills. Career clusters are centered on related career fields.

Within each of the 16 career clusters are multiple career pathways. A **career pathway** is a subgroup within a career cluster that reflects occupations requiring similar knowledge and skills.

The 16 Career Clusters	
Careers involving the production, processing, marketing, distribution, financing, and development of agricultural commodities and resources. Agriculture, Food & Natural Resources	Careers involving management, marketing, and operations of foodservice, lodging, and recreational businesses. Hospitality & Tourism
Careers involving the design, planning, managing, building, and maintaining of buildings and structures. Architecture & Construction	Careers involving family and human needs. Human Services
Careers involving the design, production, exhibition, performance, writing, and publishing of visual and performing arts. Arts, A/V Technology & Communications	Careers involving the design, development, support, and management of software, hardware, and other technology-related materials. Information Technology
Careers involving the planning, organizing, directing, and evaluation of functions essential to business operations. Business Management & Administration	Careers involving the planning, management, and providing of legal services, public safety, protective services, and homeland security. Law, Public Safety, Corrections & Security
Careers involving the planning, management, and providing of training services. Education & Training	Careers involving the planning, management, and processing of materials to create completed products. Manufacturing
Careers involving the planning and providing of banking, insurance, and other financial-business services. Finance	Careers involving the planning, management, and performance of marketing and sales activities. Marketing
Careers involving governance, national security, foreign service, revenue and taxation, regulation, and management and administration. Government & Public Administration	Careers involving the planning, management, and providing of scientific research and technical services. Science, Technology, Engineering & Mathematics
Careers involving planning, managing, and providing health services, health information, and research and development. Health Science	Careers involving the planning, management, and movement of people, materials, and goods. Transportation, Distribution & Logistics

Source: States' Career Clusters Initiative 2008; Goodheart-Willcox Publisher

Figure 19-2 Each of the 16 career clusters contains multiple career pathways.

These pathways, or *career areas*, include careers ranging from entry-level to those requiring advanced college degrees and years of experience. All of the careers within the pathways share a common foundation of knowledge and skills.

Levels of Careers

In each career area, positions are generally grouped by skill level or education. A **career ladder** is a series of jobs organized in order of education and experience requirements. Often each job in an individual's career path requires more education and experience than the previous one. The steps on the career ladder are called *career levels*. There are five levels of careers that make up a career ladder, as illustrated in Figure 19-3.

- An *entry-level* position is usually a person's first or beginning job. These positions require the least amount of education and experience.
- A *career-level* position requires an employee to have the skills and knowledge for continued employment and advancement in the field.
- A *specialist-level* position requires specialized knowledge and skills in a specific field of study. However, someone in this position does not supervise other employees.
- A *supervisory-level* position requires specialized knowledge and skills and has management responsibility over other employees. An example of this level is a supervisory management position.
- An *executive-level* position is the highest level. This position is responsible for the planning, organization, and management of a company. An example of this level is a senior management position.

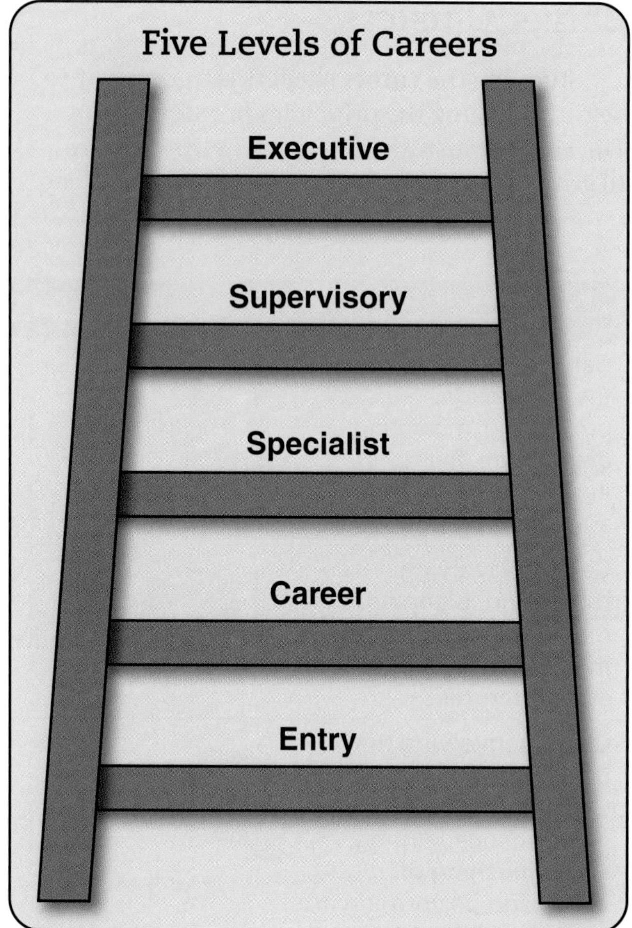

Goodheart-Willcox Publisher

Figure 19-3 Most careers have different levels of positions based on education, years of experience, and technical skills.

Employability Skills
Networking

Networking means talking with people you know and developing new relationships that can lead to potential career or job opportunities. A *professional network* is a group of professionals you know and who know you. These people are supportive in your career endeavors and may or may not be social friends.

LO 19.1-2 Career Planning

Planning for your career can be exciting. Your career choice will direct many other decisions in your life. It will affect decisions about your education and even where you will live. To determine the careers that will be enjoyable for you, you must first learn about yourself.

A **career plan** is a list of steps on a timeline to reach each of your career goals. It is also known as a *postsecondary plan*. A career plan should take into account the options for continuing your education. Education options include four-year colleges, two-year colleges, or technical schools. It should also address current job opportunities in your career of interest.

A career plan is similar to a map used to guide an individual to a career goal. There is no set format for writing a career plan. Many free career-plan templates are found on the Internet. Figure 19-4 shows action items for a career plan for a person who wants to become a sales manager. To create a plan, you should first conduct a self-assessment and then set career SMART goals. You will continue revising the career plan as you achieve your goals and set new ones.

Conducting a Self-Assessment

A *self-assessment* is the first step in evaluating your aptitudes, abilities, values, and interests. By conducting a self-assessment, you can focus your energy on what is necessary for you to become successful in a career. Some self-assessment techniques are thinking or writing exercises. Others are in the form of tests, such as a personality test. Your career counselor can help you conduct a self-assessment.

Consider what you like to do and what you do well. This can provide you with clues to aid in your self-assessment. If you always do well in math class, you may find success in a career that requires you to work with numbers. On the other hand, if you do not do well in English class, a career that requires writing may not be your best match. Identifying a career in which you will excel and find enjoyment in begins with identifying what you like to do.

What is your *work style*? Some individuals prefer to work independently. Others need constant direction to accomplish a task. Mornings are more productive for some workers, whereas others perform better in the afternoons. Casual dress influences some people to perform well. Business dress makes others more effective on the job.

When taking a self-assessment, strive to identify your aptitudes, abilities, values, and interests. Learning this information can reveal careers for which you are well suited.

Aptitudes

An **aptitude** is a characteristic that an individual has developed naturally. Aptitudes are also called *talents*. When a person naturally excels at a task without practicing or studying, he or she has an aptitude for it. For example, a person with an aptitude for music may be very good at accurately humming a tune or keeping a beat, even if he or she has never studied music. Aptitude tests can help you discover natural strengths and weaknesses.

Knowing your aptitudes can lead to job success and job satisfaction. Some examples of aptitudes are mathematics, drawing, writing, and sports.

Action Items for a Career Plan: Sales Manager

	Work Experience	Education and Training	Extracurricular and Volunteer Activities
During High School	• Seek a part-time position that allows application of business and communication skills	• Enroll in business classes in addition to required graduation courses • For optional or extra credit work, select topics and projects related to business management and writing	• Be a part of the logistics team for an organization • Volunteer with a local nonprofit group to help with fundraisers
During College	• Apply to work as an intern at a local business	• Follow the bachelor degree path for Business Management & Administration	• Assist an organization or nonprofit group with budgets to maximize their funds
After College	• Work as an entry-level employee in a sales department of a local business	• Take part in appropriate professional development opportunities • Consider obtaining a master degree in business	• Attend local business professionals and chamber of commerce events

Goodheart-Willcox Publisher

Figure 19-4 This table illustrates action items to use for a potential career plan in the Business Management & Administration career cluster.

Billion Photos/Shutterstock.com

A self-assessment can help an individual focus on what is necessary to become successful in a career field of his or her interest. **What is the value of a person being introspective when looking ahead to a future career?**

Abilities

An **ability** is the mastery of a skill or the capacity to do something. Having aptitudes and skills are supported or limited by a person's abilities. For instance, a student who has musical aptitude and skill might not have the ability to perform under pressure in musical concerts. Examples of abilities include teaching others, multitasking, logical thinking, and speaking multiple languages.

While an aptitude is something a person is born with, an ability can be acquired. Often, it is easier to develop abilities that match your natural aptitudes. For example, someone with an aptitude for acquiring languages may have the ability to speak French. A person without an aptitude for acquiring language can also learn to speak French, but it may be more difficult. Aptitudes and abilities do not always match. Someone with an aptitude for repairing machines may not enjoy doing this type of work and never develop the ability.

Values

The principles and beliefs that an individual considers important are **values**. They are beliefs about the things that matter most to an individual. Values are developed as people mature and learn. Your values will affect your life in many ways. They influence how you relate to other people and make decisions about your education and career.

Your work values can provide great insight into what kind of career will appeal to you. *Work values* are the aspects of work that are most important to a person. For some individuals, work values include job security. For others, the number of vacation days is important. Everyone has a set of work values that are taken into consideration when choosing a career path. For example, a person who values the environment may want to pursue a career in green energy or conservation. Examples of values are perfection, equality, harmony, and commitment.

Closely related to values are family responsibilities and personal priorities. These can have a direct impact on a career choice. For example, if you expect to have a large family, you may decide that time is a family responsibility. You may want to spend as much time as possible with your children as they grow. This may mean choosing a career that does not typically require travel or working long hours. On the other hand, it may be important to you to live in an expensive house and drive an expensive car. This personal priority will require a career with an income level that supports these choices.

Interests

An **interest** is a feeling of wanting to learn more about a topic or to be involved in an activity. Interests are things that capture your attention and you are willing to spend time doing. Your interests might include a subject, such as history. You may be interested in local politics or cars. Your interests can also include hobbies, such as biking or cooking. There is a good chance there is a career that would enable you to apply your creative talents or hobbies. Examples of interests include art, technology, sports, adventure, and collecting.

Your interests may change over time. You may find new hobbies or topics that interest you. Try to determine if there is a uniting theme to your interests. When considering your interests, look at the "big picture." For example, you may enjoy being on the cross-country team right now. In a few years, a career as an arborist might suit you because you enjoy physical activity and being outdoors.

Setting Career SMART Goals

Another step in the career-planning process is to set goals. A *goal* is something a person wants to achieve in a specified time period. Remember there are two types of goals: short term and long term. A *short-term goal* is one that can be achieved in less than one year, such as getting an after-school job for the fall semester.

A *long-term goal* is one that will take a longer period of time to achieve, usually more than one year. An example of a long-term goal is to attend college to earn a four-year degree.

Goal setting is the process of deciding what a person wants to achieve. Your goals should be based on what you want for your life. Well-defined career goals follow the SMART goal model. Recall that *SMART goals* are specific, measurable, attainable, realistic, and timely, as illustrated in Figure 19-5.

Specific

A career goal should be specifically defined and stated. For example, "I want to have a career" is not a specific goal. Instead, you might say, "I want to have a career as an accounting manager." When the goal is specific, it is easier to track progress.

Measurable

It is important to measure your progress so you know when you have reached your goal. For example, "I want to earn a bachelor degree in business management" is a measurable goal. When you earn the degree, you will know the goal was accomplished.

Attainable

Goals need to be attainable. For example, "I want to be a communications manager when I graduate from college." This is not reasonable for that point in a person's career. Gaining work experience is necessary before obtaining a management position.

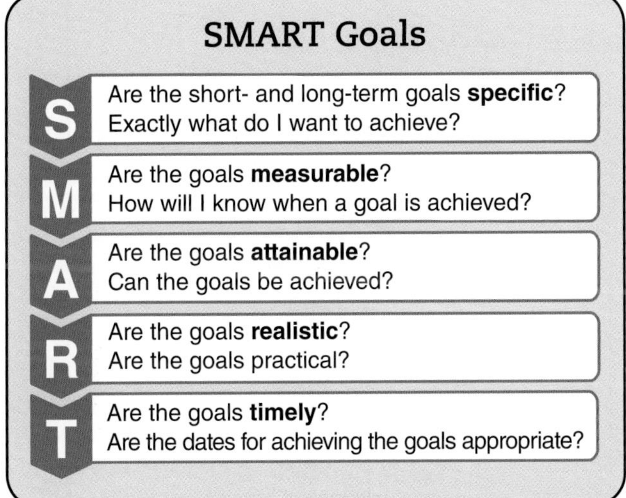

Goodheart-Willcox Publisher

Figure 19-5 The SMART goal model can help a person create well-defined career goals.

This goal becomes more attainable when coupled with a plan to gain the necessary aptitudes, skills, and experience required for a job position.

Realistic

Goals must be realistic. Obtaining a position as marketing communications manager may be practical with proper planning. It is not realistic for a new college graduate. Finding an entry-level position as an assistant and working your way up to a communications manager over a period of years makes this a realistic goal.

Timely

A goal should have a starting point and an ending point. Setting a timeframe to achieve a goal is the step most often overlooked. An end date can help you stay on track. For example, you may want to be an accounting manager by the time you are 35 years old. Aiming to get the experience and education to achieve this position by a specific age will help you remain motivated to reach the goal on time.

LO 19.1-3 Finding Career Information

There are many resources for career research. Resources will help you evaluate which careers make the best use of your talents, skills, and interests. They can also help you see what careers are available in a certain field as well as the education and experience requirements. Some examples of resources include the Internet, career handbooks, networking, and informational interviews.

Internet Research

The Internet is a good place to start when you begin finding information about your future career. Researching various professions, employment trends, industries, and prospective employers provides insight to careers that may interest you. Many postsecondary schools have websites that provide career information.

The Occupational Information Network (O*NET) is a valuable resource for career information. The most comprehensive database of occupational information, O*NET OnLine, was created by the US Department of Labor and is updated regularly. This website contains data on salaries, growth, openings, education requirements, skills and abilities, work tasks, and related occupations for more than 1,000 careers. The database can be searched by career cluster.

An additional online resource offered by the Department of Labor is CareerOneStop. This resource helps job seekers find jobs and employers find workers. The CareerOneStop Toolkit offers information for making smart career decisions, such as how to find schools, training, and scholarships.

The Internet is also a great tool to use when you begin applying for jobs. You can search for available jobs in almost any career field. Indeed and CareerBuilder are examples of job-search sites. When you find a job that interests you, you can submit a résumé, job application, and cover message via the Internet.

Career Handbooks

The US Bureau of Labor Statistics publishes the *Occupational Outlook Handbook* and the *Career Guide to Industries*. An *industry* is a group of businesses that produce the same type of goods or services. These handbooks describe the training and education needed for various jobs. They provide up-to-date information about careers, employment trends, working conditions, and even salary outlooks.

You Do the Math

Communication and Representation: Line Graph

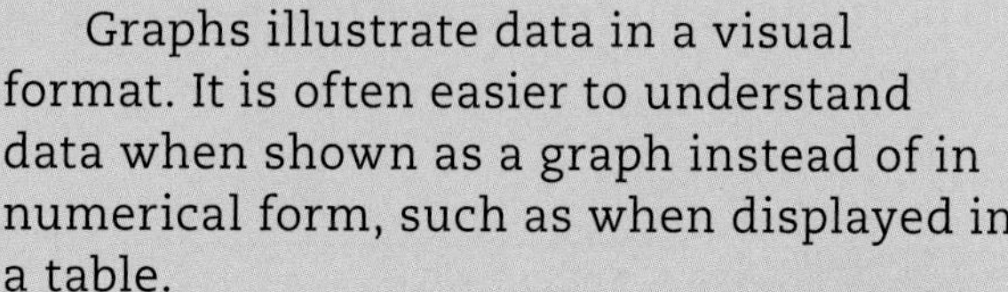

Graphs illustrate data in a visual format. It is often easier to understand data when shown as a graph instead of in numerical form, such as when displayed in a table.

A *line graph* organizes information on vertical and horizontal axes. The data are graphed as a continuous line. Line graphs are often used to show trends over a period of time.

Solve the following problems using the graph.

1. Which branch had the highest performance?
2. Which branch experienced the highest growth in foot traffic?
3. Which branch experienced a decline in foot traffic?
4. Which month had the highest average sales across all branches?

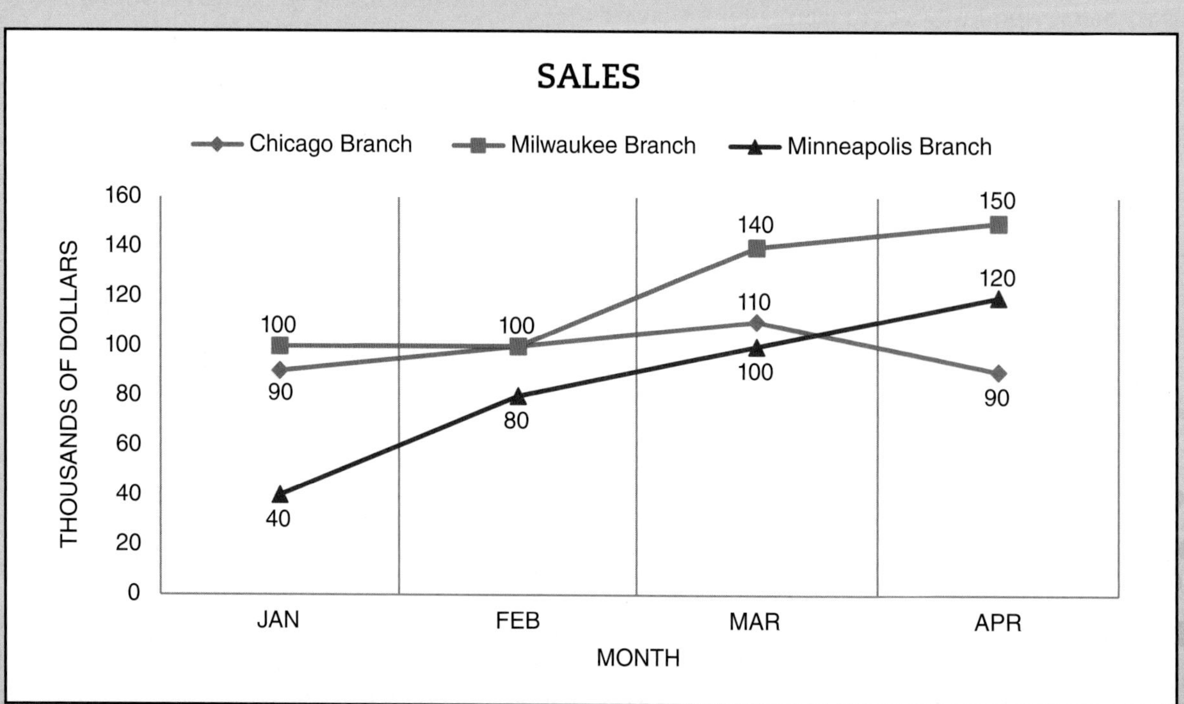

AshTproductions/Shutterstock.com

There are many resources for career research. **What value does researching multiple sources provide when researching a career?**

The average person spends 30 percent of his or her time working every day. Understanding the industry of a chosen career is an important step to take. Career handbooks offer a great place to begin researching specific careers, their industries, and the areas of the country or world in which these industries thrive.

Networking

Networking is talking with others and establishing relationships with people who can help you achieve career, educational, or personal goals. People in your network can be family members, friends, instructors, coworkers, and counselors who know about your skills and interests.

Networking can lead to job opportunities. The more contacts you make, the greater your opportunities for finding career ideas. Talking with people you know can help you evaluate career opportunities. It also may lead to potential jobs.

Informational Interviews

Informational interviews can give you unique insight into a career. **Informational interviewing** is a strategy used to interview a professional to ask for advice and direction rather than for a job opportunity. This type of interview will help you get a sense of what it is like to work in that profession.

It can also be a valuable networking opportunity. By talking with someone in the field, you can learn more about what is expected. You can also learn what types of jobs are available and other information about an industry.

Before an informational interview, prepare a list of questions. These questions should cover what you most want to know about the career. At the interview, be as professional and polite as you would in any other interview situation. Follow up with your contact after an interview. Send a thank-you message to show appreciation for his or her time.

LO 19.1-4 Career and Technical Student Organizations

Career and technical student organizations (CTSOs) are national student organizations, with local school chapters, that are related to career and technical education (CTE) courses. Internships and other cooperative work experiences may be a part of the CTSO experience. CTSOs can help prepare high school graduates for their next step, whether it is college, training, or a job.

CTSO Goals

The goal of CTSOs is to help students acquire knowledge and skills in different career and technical areas. They also help students develop leadership skills and gain work experience important for professional development. In addition, they guide students in identifying and developing effective interpersonal skills.

michaeljung/Shutterstock.com

Participating in CTSO programs can encourage a lifelong interest in community service. **Summarize the importance of being a contributing citizen and participating in community service.**

Interpersonal skills are the skills that enable a person to communicate and work effectively with coworkers, supervisors, and subordinates. These organizations guide student members to become competent, successful members of the workforce.

Support for local CTSO chapters is often coordinated through each state's education department. Local chapters elect officers and establish a program of work. The CTSO advisors help students run the organization and identify the best programs that meet the goals of the educational area.

CTSO Opportunities

Participating in a CTSO and its activities can promote a lifelong interest in community service and professional development. Student achievement is recognized in specific areas, such as leadership or patriotism, with certificates or award ceremonies. Other professional development opportunities may include:

- completing a school or community project related to the field of study;
- training in the field;
- supporting a local or national philanthropic organization;
- attending CTSO state meetings; and
- participating in leadership conferences.

These events measure the use of decision-making, problem-solving, and leadership skills. They also provide opportunities for team-building skills and collaboration skills. Possession of these skills lay the groundwork for future interactions in a career with coworkers, supervisors, and subordinates.

Competitive events sponsored by CTSOs recognize outstanding student performance. Competing in events enables students to show mastery of specific content. Students may receive recognition awards for participating in events. In some cases, scholarships are awarded at state and national competitions.

Your participation in a CTSO can help you learn more about a profession. These organizations provide students firsthand experience with the demands of a career.

Section 19.1 Review

Check Your Understanding

1. Explain the difference between a job and a career.
2. Name five levels of careers on the career ladder.
3. What qualities of an individual does a self-assessment identify?
4. List types of data that can be found on O*NET OnLine.
5. Cite examples of professional development opportunities available through CTSO programs.

Build Your Vocabulary

As you progress through this course, develop a personal glossary of key terms. This will help you build your vocabulary and prepare you for a career. Write a definition for each of the following terms and add it to your personal glossary.

job
career
profession
skill
employability skills
career cluster
career pathway
career ladder
career plan
aptitude
ability
values
interest
networking
informational interviewing
career and technical student organization (CTSO)

Section 19.2

Planning for Your Education

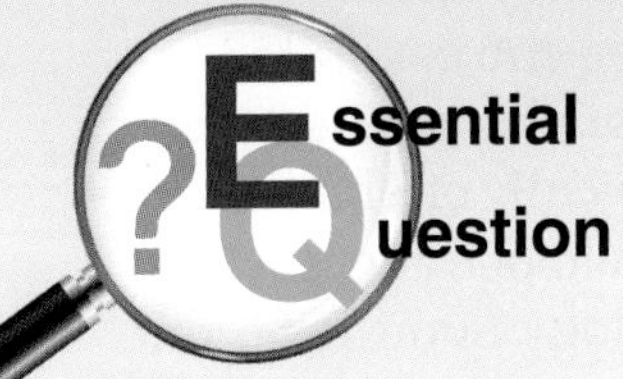

Why is planning for education, training, or certification a worthwhile investment of time?

Learning Objectives

LO 19.2-1 Discuss the role of education, training, and certification in career choices.

LO 19.2-2 Summarize college access.

LO 19.2-3 Identify sources of funding when pursuing an education.

Key Terms

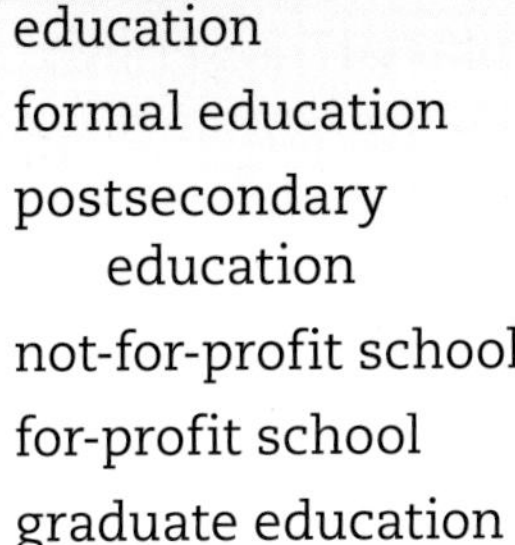

education	postgraduate education	college access
formal education	lifelong learning	529 plan
postsecondary education	occupational training	grant
not-for-profit school	internship	scholarship
for-profit school	apprenticeship	work-study program
graduate education	certification	need-based award

LO 19.2-1 Education, Training, and Certification

There are many steps to take as you plan your career. Your educational needs will depend on your career interests and goals. Some careers require a high school diploma followed by technical training or a bachelor degree. Others require a master degree as well. Still others require professional certification. Early career planning can help you make decisions about your education.

Education

Education is the general process of acquiring knowledge and skills. Education can occur anywhere and continues throughout your life. **Formal education** is the education received in a school, college, or university. Most careers require a college degree. However, for an entry-level position, a high school diploma may get you in the door. Jobs higher up on the career ladder often require additional formal education.

High School

The minimum educational requirement for most entry-level jobs is a high school diploma. During high school, a variety of subjects are taken. This gives students a well-rounded education to serve as a foundation for lifelong learning. English, mathematics, and science are some of the subjects all students study in high school. At the end of four years, students graduate and receive a high school diploma. To an employer, a diploma indicates that you have basic reading, writing, and math skills.

Postsecondary Education

Postsecondary education is any education achieved after high school. This includes all two- and four-year colleges and universities. Common postsecondary degrees are an associate degree and a bachelor degree. An associate degree is a two-year degree. A bachelor degree is a four-year degree.

Area of Study. Students in postsecondary schools choose an area of study that suits an interest or meets a career goal. This is referred to as a *major area of study* or a *major*.

For example, a student who wants to eventually become an operations manager may major in business administration, management, or accounting.

When considering a major, research the income potential of various related careers. Some careers start at a low salary and steadily increase over the course of the career. Other careers may start high and continue to increase. In addition to income potential, look into the number of jobs that are available in the area, both for new graduates and for those with experience.

In addition to major areas of study, postsecondary students are typically required to take a wide variety of classes in other subjects. These courses are referred to as *general education courses*. They cover many of the same subject areas as high school courses. The courses also cover subjects not often offered at the high-school level, such as political science and psychology.

Not-for-Profit and For-Profit Schools. A postsecondary school may be either a not-for-profit school or a for-profit school. A **not-for-profit school** is one that invests the money it earns back into the school. These schools receive funding from student tuition and fees, donations, and governmental programs. A not-for-profit school is what most people think of in terms of "college." It may be a public school, such as a state university. Others may be private, such as a private college or university. Not-for-profit schools tend to encourage academic exploration and personal growth beyond the specific requirements of a student's major.

AN NGUYEN/Shutterstock.com

Formal education is the education received in a school, college, or university. **Identify and discuss potential postsecondary options that could help you reach your career goals.**

A **for-profit school** is one that is set up to earn money for investors. It sells a product, which is education. In return for providing education, for-profit schools receive money from their customers, which are students. For-profit schools are also known as *proprietary schools*. They tend to focus on specific skills and do not require general education courses. A trade school is an example of a for-profit school. They typically offer a two-year degree specialized in a field of trade, such as automotive repair or cosmetology. Some for-profit schools offer graduate degree programs.

Requirements and Costs. When considering a college or university, be aware of what is needed to apply. Requirements may include:

- official transcripts;
- college entrance exam scores;
- essays; and
- interviews.

For all requirements, be sure to know the deadlines for completing and submitting the information. Missing a deadline can mean not being accepted to the school.

The costs of a postsecondary education must be considered. In addition to tuition, there are fees for many classes. Some majors include many laboratory classes. These classes can have more fees than other courses. Living expenses must also be considered as part of the cost of a postsecondary education.

Graduate and Postgraduate Education

Education received after an individual has earned a bachelor degree is **graduate education**. Master degrees are graduate degrees. Education beyond a master degree is **postgraduate education**. Doctoral degrees are postgraduate degrees.

Graduate study often builds on the same subject area or a closely related subject in which a bachelor degree was earned. For example, a student who earned a Bachelor of Arts in Business Administration may pursue a Master of Business Administration (MBA) degree.

Continuing Education

Learning does not stop when you have reached your educational goals. In order to advance in your career, you must continually improve your job skills. Some careers that have professional licenses require *continuing education classes*. Completing these classes earns the student *continuing education units (CEUs)*. These classes are necessary to maintain a license. For example, a school system may require that its teachers earn a specified number of CEUs every year.

Another form of continuing education is more commonly called *adult education* or *adult ed.* These classes are for people age 18 or older and traditionally focus on basic skills. Classes are offered on a wide variety of topics. They can range from learning computer skills to the English language.

Lifelong Learning

Lifelong learning is the voluntary attainment of knowledge throughout life. It typically refers to adults who are learning for the sake of learning in a variety of situations. Lifelong learning often relates to hobbies and interests, including art, cooking, foreign languages, outdoor recreation, and physical fitness.

There are numerous benefits to lifelong learning. The primary benefit is the knowledge gained, or learning for learning's sake. Learning more allows you to achieve goals you have established outside of your career or education and improve your self-esteem. Additional benefits include maintaining communication and social skills, expanding your interests, and mental acuity.

Training

A college degree is not necessary for all career paths. Before taking on the expense of college classes, decide if college is right for you and your career goals. There are many options for career training, including occupational training, internships, apprenticeships, and military service.

Occupational Training

Training for a specific career can be an option for many technical, trade, and technology fields. **Occupational training** is education that prepares an individual for a specific type of work. This type of training typically costs less than a traditional college education. It can also be completed in less time.

Internships

An **internship** is a short-term position with a sponsoring organization that provides an opportunity to gain on-the-job experience in a certain field of study or occupation. Internships can be paid or unpaid. High schools, colleges, and universities often offer school credit for completing internships. Internships are an opportunity for students to gain hands-on work experience while completing an education.

Pamela Au/Shutterstock.com

Some students choose to enter the armed forces through the Reserve Officers' Training Corps (ROTC) to receive skilled training. **Explain what type of training would be helpful for your career path.**

Apprenticeships

An **apprenticeship** is a combination of on-the-job training, work experience, and classroom instruction. Apprenticeships are typically available to those who want to learn a trade or a technical skill. The apprentice works on mastering the skills required to work in the trade or field under the supervision of a skilled tradesperson.

Military Service

Service in the military can provide opportunities to receive skilled training, often in highly specialized technical areas. In addition to receiving this training, often it can be transferred into college credit or professional credentials. After completing military service, there are many benefits available to veterans. For example, the *GI Bill* is a law that provides financial assistance for veterans pursuing education or training. Other forms of tuition assistance are also available.

Some students choose to enter the armed forces through the *Reserve Officers' Training Corps (ROTC)*. Each branch of the military has an ROTC program at selected colleges and universities. Some high schools have Junior ROTC (JROTC) programs that are elective courses. The purpose of the ROTC program is to train commissioned officers for the armed forces. It can provide tuition assistance in exchange for a commitment to military service. Students enrolled in this program take classes just like other college students. However, students also receive basic military and officer training.

Information is available on the Today's Military website sponsored by the US Department of Defense. In addition, opportunities in the armed forces are outlined in the *Occupational Outlook Handbook*.

Professional Certification

Some professional organizations offer certifications. **Certification** is a professional status earned by an individual after passing an exam focused on a specific body of knowledge. The individual usually prepares for the exam by taking classes and studying content that will be tested. Certification requirements should be considered when making a career plan.

Some jobs *require* a professional certification. There are many types of certifications in most industries and trades. Figure 19-6 shows examples of certifications in the business field. For example, an accounting agency might require an accountant be certified as a Certified Public Accountant (CPA) as a qualification for the job. Other employers may prefer, but not require, certification.

There are certifications that must be renewed on a regular basis. For example, many certifications sponsored by Microsoft are only valid for the specific version of software. When the next version is released, another exam must be taken to be certified for the update. Other certifications require regular continuing education classes to ensure individuals are current with up-to-date information in the profession.

Some certifications are not subject-specific. Instead, they verify that an individual has employability skills. These certifications confirm that the person possesses the skills to be a contributing employee. The focus of these certifications is on soft skills. Individuals who earn this type of certification have demonstrated they possess the qualities necessary to become effective employees.

Monkey Business Images/Shutterstock.com

The National Council Licensure Examination for Registered Nurses (NCLEX-RN) is an example of a professional certification required for registered nurses. **Why would some careers require certification, in addition to a degree, to work in a specific industry?**

Quality of Education

Colleges, universities, and training programs can vary significantly in the quality and type of education offered. There are many resources available that rank schools and provide other tools to help you evaluate an institution.

As you begin to make decisions about your education after high school, analyze the quality of the education that institutions offer.

Business Certifications	
Accounting	Certified Public Accountant (CPA) Certified Management Accountant (CMA)
Administrative	Certified Administrative Professional (CAP)
Business Analyst	Certified Business Analysis Professional (CBAP)
Human Resources	Professional in Human Resources (PHR) Senior Professional in Human Resources (SPHR)
Project Management	Project Management Professional (PMP) Certified Associate in Project Management (CAPM)
Supply Chain Management	Certified Supply Chain Professional (CSCP)

Goodheart-Willcox Publisher

Figure 19-6 Many certifications are available for a business career.

This can ensure that the education you receive will be well worth the investments of both time and money. Some of the criteria include:

- academic reputation;
- credentials of the faculty;
- graduation statistics;
- potential earning power of graduates; and
- student activities and opportunities on and around the campus.

LO 19.2-2 College Access

College access refers to building awareness about college opportunities, providing guidance regarding college admissions, and identifying ways to pay for college. College access includes access to many types of postsecondary institutions. This includes colleges, universities, and trade schools. Attending a postsecondary school to further your education can be a critical step in your career plan. However, preparing to go to college can present challenges to students and families, both academically and financially. The sooner you begin planning, the better. It is never too early.

Academic preparation includes taking the right classes and doing your best. If you have always been a good student, keep up the good work and habits. If you have not been performing to your potential, demonstrate your abilities and commitment by showing improvement. Along with strong academics, involvement in organizations at your high school or in your community will also provide greater access to college. Most schools are looking for well-rounded individuals. As you plan for your education, learn as much as possible about what it takes to be accepted to the college of your choice.

Many websites provide information to help you gain access to college. You can begin by searching the Internet for resources offered in your state. Search using the term *college access* plus the name of your state. If you have already been thinking about a specific school, check its official website to learn about admission requirements and to find out what financial help might be available to you. The US Department of Education, the College Board, and the National College Access Network have websites that include a wealth of information about college access. Topics include applying to college and paying for college. If you have not already done so, talk to your family, friends, and guidance counselor for information to begin planning for college.

Ethics

Cyberbullying

Cyberbullying is using technology to harass or threaten an individual. It includes sending hurtful words or pictures over social media, text, or e-mail to harass or scare a person. Even though a victim may not be harmed physically, cyberbullying is a form of harassment. *Harassment* is uninvited conduct toward a person based on a protected characteristic such as race, religion, nationality, age, gender, disability, genetic information, and citizenship, family, or veteran status.

LO 19.2-3 Funding Your Education

Whether you attend a trade school, community college, or university, someone has to pay the cost of the education. As you are making decisions about which type of education to pursue, you will need to create a financial plan for paying for it. An online college-cost calculator can help you estimate how much money you will need for educational expenses.

Funds to pay for education can come from a variety of sources. You will need to determine which sources are available to you and fit your needs. Each student's financial situation is different.

Some families can afford to pay for college with current income or savings. If your parents or other family members are able and willing to pay for a college education for you, take advantage of their generosity. Thank them by studying hard and earning your degree.

Saving money for a college education is an investment strategy for the future. Someone in your family may have established a 529 plan to fund your college education. A **529 plan** is a savings plan for education operated by a state or educational institution. These plans are tax-advantaged savings plans and encourage families to set aside educational funds for their children. Each state now has at least one 529 plan available. Plans vary from state to state because every state sets up its own plan. There are restrictions on how the money can be used, so make sure you understand how the plan works before spending the money. There are penalties if money invested in a 529 plan is used for a purpose other than educational expenses.

Even if your family has a 529 plan, the amount saved might not be enough to pay for all of your college expenses. Many families pay for college using a combination of savings, current income, and loans. Parents, other family members, and students often work together to cover the cost of college. You might contribute money you have saved, money you earn if you work while attending school, and money for loans you will have to repay. More than half of students attending college get some form of financial aid. Figure 19-7 shows potential sources of funding for your education.

Financial aid is available from the federal government, as well as from nonfederal agencies. Some states also offer college money to attend a state school if you have good grades in high school. There is more than $100 billion in grants, scholarships, work-study, need-based awards, and loans available each year.

Potential Sources of Funding a College Education

Source	Brief Description	Repayment
529 Plan	Tax-advantaged savings plan designed to encourage saving for future college costs. Plans are sponsored by states, state agencies, and educational institutions.	No repayment.
Grants	Money to pay for college provided by governmental agencies, corporations, states, and other organizations. Most grants are based on need and some have other requirements.	No repayment.
Scholarships	Money to pay for college based on specific qualifications including academics, sports, music, leadership, and service. Criteria for scholarships vary widely.	No repayment.
Work-study	Paid part-time jobs for students with financial need. Work-study programs are typically backed by governmental agencies.	No repayment.
Need-based awards	Aid for students who demonstrate financial need.	No repayment.
Governmental educational loans	Loans made to students to help pay for college. Interest rates are lower than bank loans.	Repayment is required. Repayment may be postponed until you begin your career.
Private educational loans	Loans made to students to help pay for college. Interest rates are higher than governmental loans for education.	Repayment is required.
Internships	Career-based work experience. Some internships are paid and some are not. In addition to experience, you will likely earn college credit.	No repayment.
Military benefits	The US military offers several ways to help pay for education. It provides education and training opportunities while serving and also provides access to funding for veterans. The US Reserve Officers' Training Corps (ROTC) programs and the military service academies are other options to consider.	No repayment; however, a service commitment is required.

Goodheart-Willcox Publisher

Figure 19-7 Funds to pay for education can come from a variety of sources.

A **grant** is a financial award that is not repaid and is typically provided by a nonprofit organization. Grants are generally need-based and usually tax exempt. A Federal Pell Grant is an example of a grant from the government.

A **scholarship** is financial aid that can be based on financial need or some type of merit or accomplishment. There are scholarships based on standardized test scores, grades, extracurricular activities, athletics, and music. There are also scholarships available for leadership, service, and other interests, abilities, and talents.

It is surprising how many scholarships and grants go unused because no one has applied for them. Do not fail to apply for help just because you do not want to write the essay or fill out the application. Talk to your school counselor to learn more about scholarship and grant opportunities. Be persistent if you think you might qualify for a scholarship.

Work-study programs are part-time jobs on a college campus and subsidized by the government. Wages earned at a work-study job go toward paying for tuition and other college expenses, such as dormitory expenses and purchasing textbooks.

Need-based awards are financial-aid awards available for students and families who meet certain economic requirements. Income and other demographics are used to determine if a student qualifies for this assistance.

The *Free Application for Federal Student Aid (FAFSA)* is the application form used to determine a student's eligibility for federal financial aid. Many institutions require the FAFSA form if you are applying for any type of financial aid. You can file your application online at the Federal Student Aid website, which is an office of the US Department of Education. The FAFSA website also has resources to help you plan for college.

Section 19.2 Review

Check Your Understanding

1. Compare and contrast a not-for-profit school and a for-profit school.
2. List the levels of education that are available after receiving a bachelor degree.
3. What does an individual earn after completing continuing education classes?
4. How is an internship different from an apprenticeship?
5. What is the Free Application for Federal Student Aid (FAFSA)?

Build Your Vocabulary

As you progress through this text, develop a personal glossary of key terms. This will help you build your vocabulary and prepare you for a career. Write a definition for each of the following terms and add them to your personal glossary.

education
formal education
postsecondary education
not-for-profit school
for-profit school
graduate education
postgraduate education
lifelong learning
occupational training
internship
apprenticeship
certification
college access
529 plan
grant
scholarship
work-study program
need-based award

Chapter 19 Review and Assessment

Chapter Summary

Section 19.1 Choosing a Career

LO 19.1-1 Determine skills needed for the workplace.
Skills for the workplace require both job-specific skills and employability skills. Job-specific skills are specific to the tasks related to a position. These are also known as hard skills. Employability skills are transferrable to any career. These skills help an individual find a job, perform in the workplace, and gain success in a job or career.

LO 19.1-2 Discuss career planning.
A career plan is a list of steps on a timeline to reach each of your career goals. A career plan should take into account the options for continuing your education as well as address current job opportunities in your career of interest. To create a plan, you should first conduct a self-assessment and then set personal SMART goals. Continue revising the career plan as you achieve goals and set new ones.

LO 19.1-3 Explore sources of career information.
There are many resources for career research to help evaluate which careers would make the most of your talents, skills, and interests. Internet resources, career handbooks, networking, and informational interviews are ways to gain insight into a career.

LO 19.1-4 Summarize how CTSOs can prepare a student for a career.
The goal of CTSOs is to help students acquire knowledge and skills in different career and technical areas. They also help students develop leadership skills and gain work experience important for professional development. In addition, they guide students in identifying and developing effective interpersonal skills.

Section 19.2 Planning for Your Education

LO 19.2-1 Discuss the role of education, training, and certification in career choices.
Your educational needs will depend on your career interests and goals. Most careers require a college education. However, there are many options for career training, including occupational training, internships, apprenticeships, and the military. Certification is a professional status earned by an individual after passing an exam focused on a specific body of knowledge. Some jobs require a professional certification.

LO 19.2-2 Summarize college access.
College access refers to building awareness about college opportunities, providing guidance regarding college admissions, and identifying ways to pay for college. It includes access to many types of postsecondary institutions, including colleges, universities, and trade schools.

LO 19.2-3 Identify sources of funding when pursuing an education.
Sources of funding for pursuing an education include a 529 plan, grants, scholarships, work-study programs, and need-based awards.

Review Your Knowledge

1. Discuss skills needed for the workplace.
2. Explain the relationship between career clusters and career pathways.
3. Identify and explain items that should be included in a career plan.
4. Describe examples of sources of career information.
5. Summarize how CTSOs can prepare a student for a career.
6. Individuals preparing for careers may seek formal education, training, and potential certification opportunities. Describe each option.
7. What are the benefits of lifelong learning?
8. How can military service provide career training?
9. Summarize college access.
10. Identify and explain sources of funding for an education.

Apply Your Knowledge

1. Two important types of skills that are foundational to your career are job-specific skills and employability skills. Create a chart with two columns. In column one, list the job-specific skills you currently possess. In column two, list the employability skills that you possess. Use this chart as a source of information when you create a career plan.
2. Refer to the Career Clusters in Figure 19-2. Review the Business Management and Administration, Marketing, and Finance clusters. How are different careers within the cluster related to one another?
3. People who start their careers in entry-level positions can work their way up to managerial roles. Describe your career plan for moving up to a managerial position.
4. Conduct an informal self-assessment by defining your work style, aptitudes, values, and interests. Next, evaluate your individual talents, abilities, and skills. This will help prepare you to write a career plan.
5. Analyze your interests to identify potential careers that you would like to pursue. Write three SMART goals based on these careers. Specify how each of these goals is specific, measurable, attainable, realistic, and timely.
6. Write a list of action items you might consider following for the next five years to pursue a career of your choice. State your career. Include your career objectives and the strategies you will use to accomplish your goals.
7. Describe the advantages and disadvantages of going from high school to each of the following: college, occupational training, internship, apprenticeship, and the military.
8. Explain whether you consider yourself to be a lifelong learner.

9. Preparing for college and career requires that an individual identify and practice interpersonal skills. Of special importance is learning team-building skills necessary for future situations that involve coworkers, supervisors, and subordinates. Reflect on interpersonal skills that you currently possess. How can you identify and practice skills necessary for the future as you prepare for a career?
10. Think about your future career plans, such as a career in business management. Consider how your personal priorities and family responsibilities would influence the type of career you would pursue. Make a list of the priorities and responsibilities that would have the most influence on a future career.

College and Career Readiness

Communication Skills

Writing. The way you communicate with others will have a lot to do with the success of the relationships you build. Write a couple of paragraphs that you could use when introducing yourself to a counselor at a local college. The counselor should be a person you have never met. Exchange your response with a classmate and read each other's information. How did the style, words, and phrases used influence the way the audience responded to your information?

Reading. When engaging in active reading, it is important to relate what you are reading to your *prior knowledge,* which is what you already know or have already experienced. This helps you understand and form judgments about what you are reading. Select one of the sections of this chapter to read again. Assess whether your prior knowledge helped you understand the content.

Speaking. Demonstrating leadership qualities is a way to make a helpful contribution to a team. Identify leadership characteristics you believe all team members should have. Create a graphic organizer to present your ideas visually. Develop a short presentation that focuses on the use of your leadership graphic to explain the topic. As you are presenting, adjust your presentation length to fit the attention of the audience.

Internet Research

Employment Opportunities. Using the Internet, explore a career that is of interest to you. Research the education, training, and certification requirements of the career. Next, compare this career with a career in the same career cluster. What opportunities are currently available for each career? Evaluate salaries, career paths, and demand for the careers.

Career Match. Self-assessment tools can help decide which career opportunities might be a good fit for you. Visit the O*NET Resource Center online and select the Advance Search option. Under the Browse by O*NET Data, research careers that fall under the abilities, knowledge, interests, or skills of your choice. Select a career that interests you. Record the skills you currently possess and the skills you will need to require for this position.

Career Plan. It is important that you take ownership of a career plan that matches your interests and skills. Using the Internet, research how to create a career plan. Select a template that meets your needs. Create a career plan that aligns a career pathway to your educational goals. Using your list of SMART goals, create a career plan for the next five years.

Teamwork

By joining a CTSO, you can participate in student leadership activities and learn how to prepare for school and career opportunities. Working with your team, make a list of the CTSOs that are available at your school. What leadership opportunities are provided for students in each organization? What professional development activities are available? How can your school CTSOs help you prepare for life after graduation?

College and Career Readiness

Portfolio Development

Portfolio Introduction. After you have collected materials for your portfolio, you are ready to start organizing the content inside the portfolio. The first document in your portfolio should be an *introduction* that gives an overall snapshot of who you are. This will set the tone for your presentation, so you want to make a good impression. Tell the reader who you are, your goals, and any relevant biographical information, such as schools attended, titles or certifications earned, or degrees completed. You may want to highlight information by referencing specific sections or page numbers of items in the portfolio.

This document should also include links regarding your online presence. If you are creating an electronic portfolio, create a home page to house the introduction. This should be the first page a visitor to your portfolio site will encounter. In addition to the introduction, provide live links to your pages. You should also link to any pages containing documents of importance.

1. Create a thorough, comprehensive document that introduces yourself, outlines your goals and qualifications, and entices the employer to continue reading your portfolio. Include the heading "Introduction" and your name.
2. Update your master portfolio spreadsheet.

CTSOs

Job Interview. Job interviewing is an event you might enter with your CTSO. By participating in the job interview event, you will be able to showcase your presentation skills, communication talents, and ability to listen actively to the questions asked by the interviewers. For this event, you will be expected to write a letter of application, create a résumé, and complete a job application. You will also be interviewed by an individual or panel.

To prepare for a job interview event, complete the following activities.

1. Use the Internet or textbooks to research the job-application process and interviewing techniques.
2. Write your letter of application and résumé, and complete the application form (if provided for this event). You may be required to submit this before the event or present the information at the event.
3. Make certain that each piece of communication is complete and free of errors.
4. Solicit feedback from your peers, instructor, and parents.

CHAPTER 20

Writing for Employment

Sections

20.1 Résumés, Cover Messages, and Applications

20.2 Job Interviews and the Employment Process

Reading Prep

Before reading, write the main heading for each section, leaving space under each. As you read the chapter, write three points you learned that relate to each heading.

Exploring Careers

Social Media Manager

Social media managers are responsible for monitoring, contributing to, filtering, maintaining, and guiding a company's social media presence. This includes the social media channels for the company as well as its products. They are responsible for ensuring the brand and online reputation of the business are upheld. Social media managers create and maintain web pages, as well monitor new goods, services, and news on social media sites. Additionally, they may work with the marketing managers to initiate web-based campaigns and report the results.

Typical job titles for this position include *social media editor* and *social media specialist*. Examples of tasks performed by social media managers include:

- uploading or posting videos and images to promote a company's products or brand;
- monitoring traffic on social media pages;
- responding to user comments;
- documenting which posts get the most attention; and
- performing analytics.

Social media manager positions require a bachelor degree in marketing, communication, public relations, or journalism. Employers may also seek candidates with experience in search-engine optimization (SEO) or trend research. Social media managers must possess technological literacy as well as excellent communication and graphic design skills.

stockfour/Shutterstock.com

Section 20.1

Résumés, Cover Messages, and Applications

What can a person's résumé reveal about his or her potential career success?

Learning Objectives

LO 20.1-1 Discuss writing a résumé.

LO 20.1-2 Explain submission of a résumé as part of the application process.

LO 20.1-3 Summarize how to write a persuasive cover message to accompany a résumé.

LO 20.1-4 Explain how to apply online and in person.

Key Terms

résumé
career objective
chronological résumé
job application
reference
keyword
cover message
portfolio

LO 20.1-1 Writing a Résumé

When looking for employment, you must sell your talents and skills to a potential employer. You must persuade the hiring manager that your skills and experience match the qualifications of the job you are seeking. A **résumé** is a document that profiles a person's career goals, education, and work history. Think of a résumé as a snapshot that shows who you are and why you would be an asset as an employee.

A résumé is the first impression that potential employers will have of you. It must be well-written and error-free. The *four Cs of communication* should be applied when writing for employment: clarity, conciseness, courtesy, and correctness. Take the time to proofread your documents and check each line for correct grammar, vocabulary, and punctuation. Communication that contains typographical errors or poor language usage reflects negatively on the applicant.

A general rule is a résumé should be one page. A simple format should be used with top and bottom margins approximately one inch. Side margins should also be one inch but can be adjusted as needed to fit the résumé on one page. Font selection should be conservative and professional, such as Calibri 11pt. or Times New Roman 12pt. Decorative fonts are distracting and should never be used on a résumé.

Résumés have standard parts that employers expect to see. A typical résumé is organized into the following sections:

- name and personal information;
- career objective;
- work experience or volunteer experience;
- education; and
- honors, awards, and publications.

An example of a résumé is shown in Figure 20-1. In this example, a student is applying for a job as an accountant's assistant.

Name and Personal Information

The top of the résumé page should present your name, address, telephone number, and e-mail address. Use an e-mail address that is your real name, or at least a portion of it. E-mails with nicknames or screen names do not make a professional impression. Before you begin applying for jobs through e-mail, set up an e-mail address that you will use only for professional communication.

Jake Barton
123 Eastwood Terrace
Saratoga Springs, NY 60123
518-555-9715
jbarton@e-mail.edu

CAREER OBJECTIVE
A mature and responsible high school senior seeks an entry-level job as an accountant's assistant.

WORK EXPERIENCE
Saratoga Springs City Online Newspaper, Saratoga Springs, NY
September 2020 to present
Accounting Intern

- Track subscriptions revenue for newspaper.
- Assist with the setup of billing processes.
- File invoices as needed.
- Prepare accounts receivable and payable schedules.

Hunter High School, Saratoga Springs, NY
September 2019 to September 2020
Student Office Volunteer

- Answered telephone calls.
- Sorted and filed vendor invoices as they were received.
- Updated spreadsheets to track student fees.
- Recorded fees for parking permits.

EDUCATION
Hunter High School, Saratoga Springs, NY
Expected graduation date: May 2021
Relevant coursework: Accounting I and II, Financial Math

HONORS

- Hunter High School Honor Roll, 8 quarters
- FBLA Most Valuable Student of the Year, 2018

ACTIVITIES

- Saratoga High School FBLA, two years

Goodheart-Willcox Publisher

Figure 20-1 A chronological résumé lists information in reverse chronological order, with the most recent information listed first.

Career Objective

A **career objective** is a summary of the type of job for which the applicant is looking. An example of an objective is, "To gain industry experience as a sales associate while earning my business degree." The career objective should match or be related to the position for which you are applying.

Work Experience

The work experience section of a résumé includes details about the jobs you have held in the past as well as your current job. The information in this section is typically the main focus of an employer's attention.

To compose this section, list your current or most recent employer first. This format is known as a chronological résumé. A **chronological résumé** lists information in reverse chronological order, with the most recent information listed first.

For each work experience entry, include the company name, your job title, and the duration of time you worked in that position. List the responsibilities and details about the position you held. Do not list the addresses or telephone numbers of previous employers. This contact information will be provided on a job application.

mangostock/Shutterstock.com

For each work experience entry on your résumé, include the company name, your job title, and the duration of time you worked in that position. **Why do you think potential employers are interested in your previous work experience?**

Ethics

Applications and Résumés

When applying for a job, to a college, or for a volunteer position, it is important to be truthful on applications and résumés. Fabricating experience or education is unethical and could cost an individual the opportunity to be a part of that organization. This means a person should always tell the truth about his or her skills, experience, and education. Do not embellish. He or she should play up his or her strengths without creating the illusion of being someone he or she is not. Information is presented in a positive light, but is also honest.

A **job application** is a form with spaces for contact information, education, and work experience.

Volunteer work may also be listed as work experience. Employers are especially interested in community-oriented applicants who do volunteer work. Be certain to list any volunteer activities and the length of time you have participated in the activities.

Education

The education section should list the name of your high school and where it is located. Indicate the year in which you will graduate. Briefly describe any courses you have taken that are relevant to the job for which you are applying. List any certifications you have earned, special courses or training programs completed, and any other educational achievements related to the job you are seeking. The education section is also a good place to list relevant skills, both hard and soft skills, which highlight your qualifications for the job.

Honors, Activities, and Publications

Employers look for well-rounded individuals. Include information on your résumé that shows your involvement in activities outside of work or school.

These can be separate sections, or they can be combined into one section. List applicable honors, activities, or publications with the corresponding year in which each occurred. If you have been a leader in an organization, note that experience. If you are a member of a career and technical student organization (CTSO), include the name of the organization and number of years you have been a member.

References

A **reference** is a person who can comment on the qualifications, work ethic, personal qualities, and work-related aspects of another person. References will most likely be someone from your professional network.

Atstock Productions/Shutterstock.com

A manager or a coworker is a good choice to ask to be a reference when applying for a position. **Identify three to four people that you would choose to be references. Explain why you selected each person.**

Your references should include individuals for whom you have worked or with whom you provided community service. However, you should not list relatives as references. Your list of references should present each person's name, title, and contact information. Request permission from the people you intend to use as references in addition to notifying them the companies and positions for which you are applying.

It is customary for references to be provided only when requested by the employer. For that reason, your list of references should be separate from your résumé. Create a separate document for your list of references.

To be prepared, bring copies of your list of references to the job interview. Employers who require references in advance usually indicate this in the job advertisement. Otherwise, you will be told during the interview process when references are needed.

LO 20.1-2 Submitting a Résumé

The traditional way to submit a résumé is by mail or in person. However, most people submit résumés online. To do this, you may need to send your résumé as an e-mail attachment or upload it to a website.

Employers may use a software program to screen the résumés submitted electronically. These programs look for keywords to screen applicants. A **keyword** is a word or term that specifically relates to the functions of the position for which the employer is hiring. These words are typically nouns rather than verbs. For example, for an accounting position you may include words such as *spreadsheet, financial statements,* and *net profit*.

Be sure to include keywords in your résumé to increase your chance of being invited to an interview. Start with the job description and underline the specific terms related to the position. If you have the relevant experience, use the same words to describe it in your résumé. Remember to be truthful.

LO 20.1-3 Writing Cover Messages

A **cover message** is a letter or e-mail sent with a résumé to introduce the applicant and summarize his or her reasons for applying for a job. It is also sometimes called a *cover letter* or a *letter of application*. A cover message is a sales message written to persuade the reader to grant an interview. It provides an opportunity to focus a potential employer's attention on your background, skills, and work experience that match the job you are seeking.

Writing a cover message is an important part of applying for a job. It sets the tone for the résumé that follows. A cover message should focus on your qualifications without being boastful. It should not repeat the details listed in the résumé. Rather, it should highlight your key qualifications that are specific to the job for which you are applying. The message also explains how you heard about the position.

A cover message must be completely error-free. Take the time to proofread your cover message before sending it to a potential employer. If you are submitting an application by mail, follow the guidelines for formatting a letter. If you are submitting it by e-mail, write a message that follows professional etiquette and attach the résumé. Figure 20-2 shows an example of a cover message sent by e-mail.

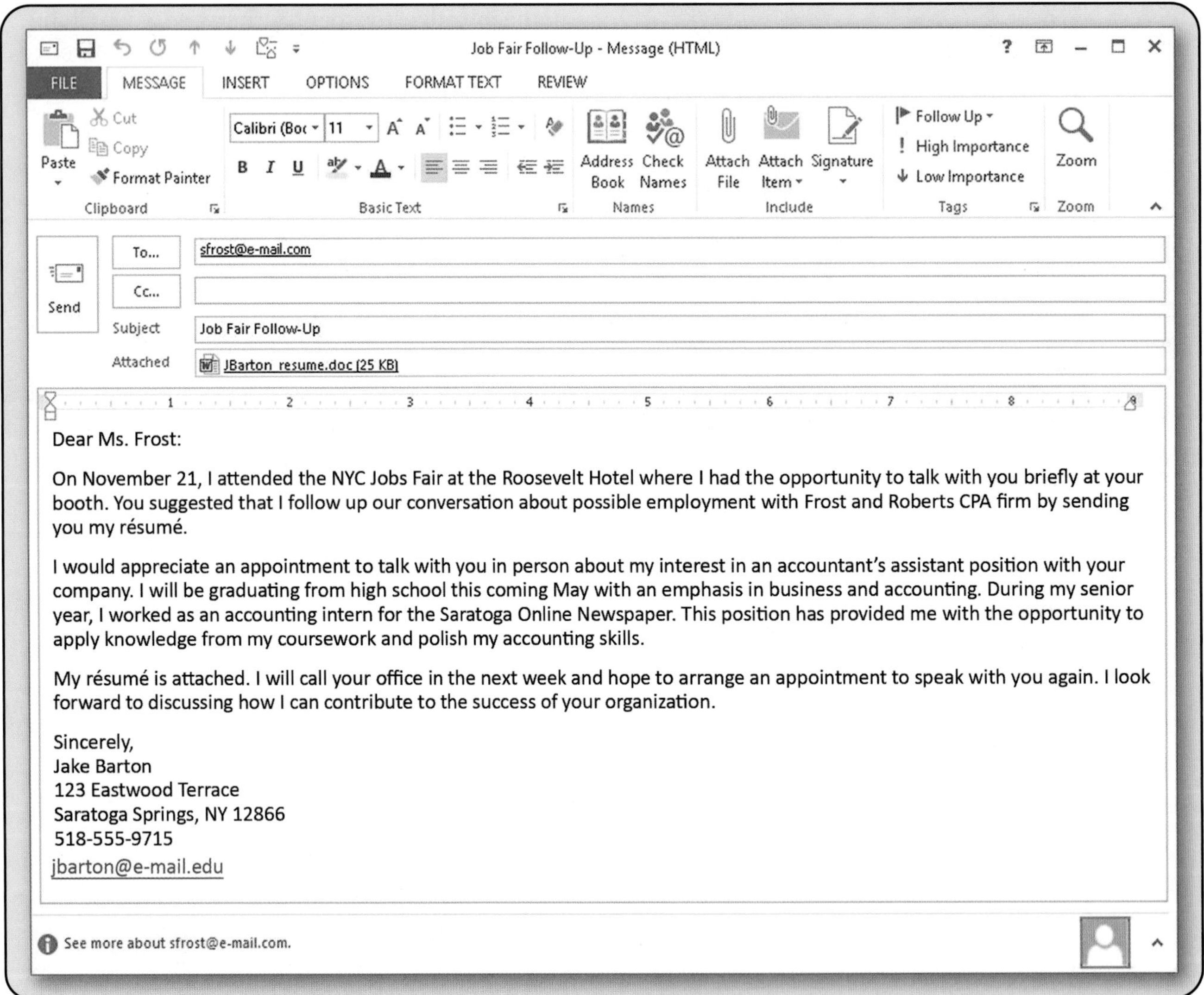

Job Fair Follow-Up - Message (HTML)

To... sfrost@e-mail.com

Cc...

Subject: Job Fair Follow-Up

Attached: JBarton_resume.doc (25 KB)

Dear Ms. Frost:

On November 21, I attended the NYC Jobs Fair at the Roosevelt Hotel where I had the opportunity to talk with you briefly at your booth. You suggested that I follow up our conversation about possible employment with Frost and Roberts CPA firm by sending you my résumé.

I would appreciate an appointment to talk with you in person about my interest in an accountant's assistant position with your company. I will be graduating from high school this coming May with an emphasis in business and accounting. During my senior year, I worked as an accounting intern for the Saratoga Online Newspaper. This position has provided me with the opportunity to apply knowledge from my coursework and polish my accounting skills.

My résumé is attached. I will call your office in the next week and hope to arrange an appointment to speak with you again. I look forward to discussing how I can contribute to the success of your organization.

Sincerely,
Jake Barton
123 Eastwood Terrace
Saratoga Springs, NY 12866
518-555-9715
jbarton@e-mail.edu

See more about sfrost@e-mail.com.

Goodheart-Willcox Publisher

Figure 20-2 A cover message sent in an e-mail should have the résumé included as an attachment.

You Do the Math

Connections: Break-Even Point

Making connections with math involves understanding the use of mathematics in a variety of careers and professions. A manager may need to use math skills to calculate the break-even point for his or her organization. A *break-even point* is the number of units a company must sell to cover its costs and expenses and earn a zero profit. Use the following formula to find a company's break-even point.

(costs × number of units) ÷ selling price = break-even point

Solve the following problems.

1. It costs $8.50 to manufacture one unit. A business produced 500 units. The product sells for $17.00 each. What is the break-even point for this product?
2. It costs $1.70 to produce a unit. A business produced 10,000 units. The product sells for $5.00 each. What is the break-even point for this product?
3. It costs $3.00 to produce one unit. A business produced 280 units. The product sells for $7.00 each. What is the break-even point for this product?

Introduction

A cover message should begin with an introduction. The introduction tells the employer who you are, the position for which you are applying, and why you are applying. If responding to a job advertisement, note where you found the ad. For example, you could be responding to an online job posting.

If sending a general letter of application, explain in specific terms how you identified the company and why you are interested in working there. If someone gave you the name of the employer to contact, mention the person and his or her connection to the company in your message.

Body

In the body of the cover message, demonstrate your positive work behaviors and qualities that make you employable. This may illustrate your ambition, determination, and abilities. Focus on the positive traits and skills the employer is seeking and included in the job description. Explain why you are qualified and how your skills and experience make you the best candidate for the job.

Do not expect the reader to infer why you are the right person to hire—point it out. Remember that your résumé accompanies the cover message, so it is not necessary to repeat the facts in it. Offer enough information to encourage the reader to read the résumé. Show genuine interest in the organization.

Conclusion

The cover message should end with a conclusion. The conclusion has two purposes: to request an interview and to make it easy for the reader to grant an interview. Leave no doubt in the reader's mind about your desire to be contacted for an interview. State how and when you can be reached for an interview. Supply the employer with the information necessary to arrange an interview. You may also state how and when you will follow up to schedule an interview.

LO 20.1-4 Applying for Employment

The process of applying for employment typically involves completing a job application along with submitting a résumé and cover message. Some job advertisements might request candidates to submit a portfolio as part of the application process. A **portfolio** is a selection of related materials that an individual collects and organizes to show his or her qualifications, skills, and talents that support an individual's career or personal goals.

Portfolios are used in many professions to demonstrate an applicant's credentials. Some common elements included in a portfolio are photocopies of certificates of accomplishment and diplomas. Samples of work, letters of recommendation, and any documents showing a talent or skill appropriate for the position should also be included. Examples of portfolio items are listed in Figure 20-3.

You have been creating a portfolio throughout this course. Each chapter in this text has a Portfolio Development activity as part of the end-of-chapter exercises. Your finished portfolio can be a part of the application materials you use to apply for a job.

Phovoir/Shutterstock.com

When applying in person, bring with you a copy of your résumé, cover message, and portfolio to hand deliver to a potential employer. **When applying in person, why is it important to hand deliver your résumé and other materials instead of e-mailing the items to human resources after completing a job application?**

Applying Online

In today's market, the job application process is typically completed online. Some employers require that a candidate complete a digital application and attach a résumé. Other employers require sending an e-mail application with a résumé attached.

Digital Application

Some companies have potential candidates complete a digital application. When completing a digital application, you can copy and paste the required information from your résumé, list of references, or additional materials. Be aware that copying and pasting text into a form usually strips out the formatting, such as bold type and tabs. You may need to adjust the layout of your résumé after pasting it into an online application form.

In addition to the application, you may be requested to submit a résumé, portfolio, or other information. Carefully review the documents before clicking the submit button. Applying online does not mean you can ignore proper spelling, grammar, and usage. Your application materials will be the employer's first impression of you. Submitting an application with misspellings or other errors may persuade an employer to eliminate you as a serious candidate. Once you hit the submit button, you cannot return to the application to make corrections.

Portfolio Elements

- Awards
- Copy of diploma, certificates, or degrees
- Final school transcripts
- Job evaluations
- Letter of introduction
- Letters or recommendation
- List of volunteer work or memberships to organizations
- Samples of original written, artistic, or photographic work
- SAT, ACT, or GRE scores

Goodheart-Willcox Publisher

Figure 20-3 A portfolio is a selection of related materials that an individual collects and organizes to show his or her qualifications, skills, and talents that support an individual's career or personal goals.

E-mail Application

Some organizations request job candidates to respond to a job posting by sending an e-mail cover message with a résumé in either a Word document or PDF format attached, as shown in Figure 20-2. A portfolio may also be included as an attachment to an e-mail. The e-mail can be sent to a specific person within the company or to a general human resources e-mail address.

Applying in Person

The traditional way to apply for employment is to visit the human resources office of a business to which you are applying. When you arrive, be prepared to complete a job application. Have your personal data, information about your citizenship status, and locations and names of past employers in hand. Use blue or black ink and your best printing. Carefully review the form before submitting it.

Bring with you a copy of your résumé, cover message, and portfolio to hand deliver to a potential employer. All documents should be on the same high-quality white or off-white paper using a laser printer. Do not fold or staple the documents. Instead, use a large envelope, file folder, or paper clip to keep the pages together. If using an envelope or folder, print your name on the outside and list the components included.

Section 20.1 Review

Check Your Understanding

1. List sections of a résumé.
2. Who should be included on your list of references?
3. Explain the purpose of a cover message.
4. What information is contained in the body of a cover message?
5. State examples of elements included in a portfolio.

Build Your Vocabulary

As you progress through this course, develop a personal glossary of key terms. This will help you build your vocabulary and prepare you for a career. Write a definition for each of the following terms and add it to your personal glossary.

résumé	job application	cover message
career objective	reference	portfolio
chronological résumé	keyword	

Section 20.2

Job Interviews and the Employment Process

What types of questions should you be most prepared to answer during a job interview?

Learning Objectives

LO 20.2-1 Explain how to prepare for a job interview.
LO 20.2-2 Discuss steps to take at the conclusion of an interview.
LO 20.2-3 Summarize the employment process.

Key Terms 

mock interview | hypothetical question | behavioral question

LO 20.2-1 Preparing for a Job Interview

A *job interview* is an employer's opportunity to review a candidate's résumé and ask questions to see if he or she is qualified for a position. Being invited to a company for an interview is an important accomplishment. It means that the employer is interested in your résumé or job application and wants to learn more about you. This is your opportunity to sell yourself in person and demonstrate professionalism. Your answers to interview questions are important in the employer's decision-making process.

Company Information

The first step in preparing for a job interview is to learn as much as you can about *not* only the position but the company as well. There are several ways to do this. If the company has a website, thoroughly study the site. Pay special attention to the *About Us* section for an overview of the company. This section of the website may include press releases, annual reports, and information on the company's goods or services.

While a company website can be a valuable source of information, do not limit your research to just the company site. Use your network of friends and relatives to find people who are familiar with the employer. Get as much information as you can from them.

You can also call the company's human resources department for additional information. The human resources department often has materials specifically developed for potential employees. When you call a company, use your best telephone etiquette while speaking with the person who answers the phone. Introduce yourself, state your purpose for calling, and be prepared with a list of questions to ask. Be polite and say "please" and "thank you" when speaking with each person so that you project a positive impression.

While preparing for an interview, it is helpful to be mentally prepared in the event that a performance test is required as part of the interviewing process. For example, a graphic artist may be asked to create a design using the software the company uses as a production tool. This will not only test the person's design abilities, but also his or her ability to use the design software. Be prepared to take a performance test, if requested.

Dress for the Interview

An interview is a meeting in which you and the employer discuss the job and your skills. Interviews are usually in person, but initial interviews are sometimes conducted by phone. A face-to-face interview is typically the first time you see a company representative. First impressions are important, so dress appropriately. You should be well-groomed and professionally dressed.

Your appearance communicates certain qualities about you to the interviewer. When dressing for an interview, consider what you wish to communicate about yourself.

The easiest rule to follow is to dress in a way that shows you understand the work environment and know the appropriate attire. It is better to dress more conservatively than to dress in trendy clothing. Employers understand that interviewees want to put their best foot forward. Dressing more conservatively than needed is not likely to be viewed as a disadvantage. However, dressing too casually, too trendy, or wearing inappropriate clothing is likely to cost you the job. Additionally, personal expressions such as visible tattoos or piercings may be seen as inappropriate for the workplace by the employer. Figure 20-4 provides general guidelines for dressing for an interview.

Interview Questions

Interview questions are intended to assess your skills and abilities and explore your personality. Your answers to interview questions help determine whether you will fit in with the company team and the manager's leadership style. Interviewers also want to assess your critical-thinking skills. They may ask you to cite specific examples of projects you have completed or problems you have solved.

Verbal communication is speaking words to communicate. It is also known as *oral communication*. In the course of a workday, most people spend at least some portion of time talking with coworkers, supervisors, managers, or customers. This communication involves a variety of situations, such as conversations about work tasks, asking and answering questions, making requests, giving information, and participating in meetings. Communicating effectively in an interview requires specific skills to be mastered.

Common Questions

Before the interview, try to anticipate questions the interviewer is likely to ask you. The following are some common interview questions.

- What are your strengths?
- What are your weaknesses?
- What about this position interests you?
- What do you plan to be doing five years from now?
- Why do you want to work for this organization?

Appropriate Attire for an Interview

Women

- Wear a suit or a dress of a conservative length
- Choose solid colors over prints
- Wear pumps with a moderate heel or flats
- Keep any jewelry small
- Have a well-groomed hairstyle
- Use little makeup
- Avoid perfume or apply it very lightly
- Nails should be manicured and of moderate length without decals
- Cover all tattoos

Men

- Wear a conservative suit of a solid color
- Wear a long-sleeved shirt, either white or a light color
- Choose a tie that is a solid color or conservative print
- Wear loafers or lace-up shoes with dark socks
- Avoid wearing jewelry
- Have a well-groomed hairstyle
- Avoid cologne
- Nails should be neatly trimmed
- Cover all tattoos

Viorel Sima/Shutterstock.com; YURALAITS ALBERT/Shutterstock.com; Goodheart-Willcox Publisher

Figure 20-4 When dressing for an interview, consider what you wish to communicate about yourself.

michaeljung/Shutterstock.com

A job interview is an employer's opportunity to review a candidate's résumé and ask questions to see if he or she is qualified for a position. **What steps would you take to prepare for a job interview?**

Write down your answers to these questions. Practice answering the questions while in front of a mirror. An important part of the communication process is nonverbal communication. Practicing in front of a mirror allows you to see your nonverbal communication.

Another way to prepare for an interview is to conduct a mock interview with a friend or an instructor. A **mock interview** is a practice interview conducted with another person. Practice until you can give your planned responses naturally and without reading them off the page. The more prepared you are, the more relaxed, organized, competent, and professional you will appear to the interviewer.

Hypothetical Questions

Interviewers may also ask hypothetical questions. **Hypothetical questions** are questions that require a candidate to imagine a situation and describe how he or she would act. Frequent topics of hypothetical questions relate to working with and getting along with coworkers. For example, "How would you handle a disagreement with a coworker?" You cannot prepare specific answers to these questions, so you need to rely on your ability to think on your feet.

When a hypothetical question is asked, the interviewer is aware that you are being put on the spot. In addition to what you say, he or she considers other aspects of your answer. Body language is first and foremost. *Body language* is nonverbal communication through facial expressions, gestures, and body movements. Avoid fidgeting and looking at the ceiling while thinking of your answer. Instead, look at the interviewer and calmly take a moment to compose your thoughts. Keep your answer brief. If your answer runs on too long, you risk losing your train of thought. Try to relate the question to something that is familiar to you and answer honestly.

Do not try to figure out what the interviewer wants you to say. Showing that you can remain poised and project confidence carries a lot of weight, even if your answer is not ideal. In many cases, the interviewer is not as interested in *what* your response is as much as *how* you responded. Was your answer quick and thoughtful? Did you ramble? Did you stare blankly at the interviewer before responding?

Behavioral Questions

Interviewers may ask behavioral questions. **Behavioral questions** are questions that draw on an individual's previous experiences and decisions. Your answers to these types of questions indicate past behavior, which may be used to predict future behavior and success in a position. The following are some examples of behavioral questions.

- Tell me about a time when you needed to assume a leadership position in a group. What were the challenges, and how did you help the group meet its goals?
- Describe a situation where you needed to be creative in order to help a client with a problem.
- Describe a situation when you made a mistake. How did you correct the mistake and what measures did you put in place to ensure it did not happen a second time?

Again, you cannot prepare specific answers to these questions. Remain poised, answer honestly, and keep your answers focused on the question. Making direct eye contact with the interviewer can project a positive impression.

Questions an Interviewer Should Not Ask

State and federal laws prohibit employers from asking questions on certain topics. It is important to know these topics so you can be prepared if such a question comes up during an interview.

It is illegal for employers to ask questions about a job candidate's religion, national origin, gender, or disability. Questions about age can only be asked if a minimum age is required by law for a job. The following are some examples of questions an employer is *not* permitted to ask a candidate.

- What is your religion?
- Are you married? If so, what is the name of your spouse?
- What is your nationality?
- Do you have any physical impairments?
- Do you have children?
- How much do you weigh?
- Have you ever filed a workers' compensation claim or been injured on the job?
- How many days where you absent from work last year due to an illness?

If you are presented with similar questions during the interview, remain professional. You are not obligated to provide an answer. You may choose to calmly respond by saying, "Please explain how that relates to the job." You could also completely avoid the question by saying, "I would rather not answer personal questions."

Questions to Ask the Interviewer

It is beneficial to prepare a list of questions to ask the interviewer. Write down any questions you have about the position, the job responsibilities, and company policies. Keep in mind that the questions you ask and how you ask them reveal details about your personality. Asking questions can make a positive impression. Good questions cover the duties and responsibilities of the position. Be aware of how you word questions.

Your questions should demonstrate that you would be a valuable employee and are interested in learning about the company. The following are some questions you may want to ask.

- What are the specific duties of this position?
- What is company policy or criteria for employee promotions?
- Do you have a policy for providing on-the-job training?
- When do you expect to make your hiring decision?
- What is the anticipated start date?

Some questions are not appropriate until after you have been offered the job. Usually, questions related to pay and benefits, such as health insurance or vacation time, should not be asked in the interview unless the employer brings them up. These can be asked after an offer of employment is made to you.

Monkey Business Images/Shutterstock.com

A good way to prepare for an interview is to conduct a mock interview with a friend or an instructor. **Discuss how role playing in a mock job interview situation can help prepare you for a real interview with an employer.**

Sometimes, however, an interviewer asks what salary you want or expect. It is also common for salary requirements to be requested in the job posting, in which case you would address this in your cover letter. Prepare for questions about salary by researching the industry. If you prefer to not answer at the time of the interview, you can simply tell the interviewer that the salary is negotiable.

LO 20.2-2 After an Interview

When the interview concludes, thank the interviewer for his or her time. Express your appreciation for the opportunity and your interest in the position. Inquire about next steps of the process and actions required from you when you leave. Shake the hand of each person in the room and then exit.

Evaluating the Interview

Evaluate your interview performance as soon as you can after it is completed. Every job interview is an opportunity to practice. If you discover that you are not interested in the job, do not feel as though your time was wasted.

Make a list of the things you feel you did right and things you would do differently next time. Asking yourself the following questions can help in evaluating your performance.

- Was I adequately prepared with knowledge about the company and the position?
- Did I remember to bring copies of my résumé, a list of references, my portfolio, and any other requested documents to the interview?
- Was I on time for the interview?
- Did I talk too much or too little?
- Did I honestly and completely answer the interviewer's questions?
- Did I dress appropriately?
- Did I display nervous behavior, such as fidgeting, or forgetting things I wanted to say?
- Did I come across as composed and confident?
- Which questions could I have handled better?

Monkey Business Images/Shutterstock.com

When a job interview concludes, shake the hand of each person in the room and then exit. **How does shaking hands with an interviewer demonstrate professionalism?**

Write a Follow-Up Message

After an interview, you should always write a *thank-you message* to each person who interviewed you. Thank the interviewer for taking the time to talk with you about the job and your career interests. Restate any important points that were made, and if you are still interested, reinforce your enthusiasm for the job. A thank-you may be in the form of a printed letter sent through the mail or an e-mail. Business thank-you letters should be keyed and formatted in business style. Keep the letter brief and to the point. Remind the interviewer of your name and reiterate your enthusiasm, but do not be pushy. An example of a thank-you message is shown in Figure 20-5.

Employment decisions can take a long time. Some companies notify all applicants when a decision is made, but some do not. If you have not heard anything after a week or two, it is appropriate to send a brief follow-up message. Be sure your tone is positive. Avoid sounding impatient or demanding. Simply restate your interest in the job and politely inquire whether a decision has been made.

Accepting a job is one of the most fulfilling messages you will ever write. Think of this as your first official act as a new employee. It remains important to present an image of intelligence, organization, courtesy, and cooperation.

Dear Ms. Frost:

Thank you for the opportunity to discuss the position of accountant assistant.

I am very excited about the possibility of working for Frost and Roberts CPA firm. The job is exactly the sort of challenging opportunity I had hoped to find. I believe my educational background and internship experience will enable me to make a contribution, while also learning and growing on the job.

Please contact me if you need any additional information. I look forward to hearing from you.

Sincerely,

Goodheart-Willcox Publisher

Figure 20-5 A thank-you message is an appropriate way to follow up the interview. Thank the interviewer for taking the time to meet with you, and restate your interest in the job.

In writing an acceptance message, let your natural enthusiasm show. Be positive and thank the person who has been the bearer of good news. Say that you look forward to the job.

LO 20.2-3 Employment Process

The employment process can take a substantial amount of time. There are tasks that the employer completes to make sure a candidate is a fit for the position. Most companies make a job offer based on employment verification, background checks, and credit checks. If the applicant passes the screenings, the job offer is generally made official. In addition, there are forms that the employee must complete before starting a position.

Employment Verification

The employer will complete an employment verification using the information on your job application or résumé. *Employment verification* is a process through which the information provided on an applicant's résumé is checked to verify that it is correct. A person's former employers typically verify only the dates of employment, position title, and other objective data. Most employers will not provide opinions about employees, such as whether or not he or she is considered a good worker. Reference checks are also made at this time.

Another important part of the employment process is a background check. A *background check* is an evaluation of personal data that is publicly available. It is an investigation into personal data about a job applicant. This information is available from governmental records and other sources, including public information on the Internet. The employer should inform you that a background check will be conducted. The company must ask for written permission before obtaining the background check report. Sometimes employers also run a check of your credit. You must give permission for them to conduct a credit check as well. A person is not legally obligated to give permission, but an employer can reject a candidate based on insufficient or unverified background information.

In addition to governmental sources, many employers use Internet search engines, such as Google, to search for your name. Employers may also check social networking websites, such as Facebook and Twitter. Be aware of this before posting any personal information or photos. These checks might work to your advantage or against you, depending on what the employer finds. It is up to you to ensure that the image you project on social media is not embarrassing or, worse, preventing you from achieving your career goals.

Employability Skills

Inside Voice

Be aware of the volume of your voice when speaking to a coworker or talking on the phone. Often, others are within earshot of your conversation. Talking in the hallways, outside an office, or in a cubicle can be disturbing to those around you. If a conversation requires more than a few words, move into a conference room or another space where a door can be closed.

Evaluating an Offer

If the employment verification and background checks are successful, the employer will typically make a job offer. An initial offer may be extended by mail, e-mail, or telephone. This is the time when salary, benefits, and other details are discussed between an employer and an applicant. Evaluate the offer in terms of your career goals and expectations. Consider the position and whether it is right for you. Compare the position and salary with others in the industry. Be sure to understand the demands that will be placed on you if you accept the position.

If both parties accept the terms of the offer, a formal job offer will be made as a written, legal document. Once you receive the document, you will be requested to sign, date, and return it in a timely manner. It is customary to include a letter of acceptance with the job offer document. If you decide to decline an offer, return the job offer document and include a letter of refusal stating you are declining the position. You do not have to go into detail explaining why you are declining the offer. However, your letter should express appreciation for the consideration, and provide a brief reason for declining.

Employment Forms

The first day on the job, you will spend a considerable amount of time in the human resources department completing necessary forms for your employment. Common employment forms include Form I-9, Form W-4, and benefit forms. Come prepared with the personal information required for a multitude of forms. You will need your Social Security number, contact information for emergencies, and other personal information.

Form I-9

A *Form I-9 Employment Eligibility Verification* is used to verify an employee's identity and that he or she is authorized to work in the United States. This form is from the US Citizen and Immigration Services, a government agency within the US Department of Homeland Security. Both citizens and noncitizens are required to complete this form. An example of a Form I-9 is shown in Figure 20-6.

The Form I-9 must be signed in the presence of an authorized representative of the human resources department. Documentation of identity must be presented at the time the form is signed. Acceptable documentation commonly used includes a valid driver's license, a state-issued photo ID, or a passport.

Form W-4

A *Form W-4 Employee's Withholding Allowance Certificate* is used by the employer for the information necessary to withhold the appropriate amount of taxes from an employee's paycheck.

Employment Eligibility Vertification

Department of Homeland Security
U.S. Citizenship and Immigration Services

USCIS
Form I-9
OMB No. 1615-0047
Expires 03/31/20XX

▶ START HERE. Read instructions carefully before completing this form. The instructions must be available during completion of this form.

ANTI-DISCRIMINATION NOTICE. It is illegal to discriminate against work-authorized individuals. Employers **CANNOT** specify which document(s) they will accept from an employee. The refusal to hire an individual because the documentation presented has a future expiration date may also constitute illegal discrimination.

Section 1. Employee Information and Attestation *(Employees must complete and sign Section 1 of Form I-9 no later than the* ***first day of employment****, but not before accepting a job offer)*

Last Name *(Family Name)*	First Name (Given Name)	Middle Initial	Other Names Used *(if any)*

Address *(Street Number and Name)*	Apt. Number	City or Town	State	Zip Code

Date of Birth *(mm/dd/yyyy)*	U.S. Social Security Number	E-mail Address	Telephone Number
	☐☐☐-☐☐-☐☐☐☐		

I am aware that federal law provides for imprisonment and/or fines for false statements or use of false documents in connection with the completion of this form.

I attest, under penalty of perjury, that I am (check one of the following):

☐ A citizen of the United States

☐ A noncitizen national of the United States *(See instructions)*

☐ A lawful permanent resident (Alien Registration Number/USCIS Number): ____________

☐ An alien authorized to work until (expiration date, if applicable, mm/dd/yy) ____________. Some aliens may write "NA" in this field. *(See instructions)*

For aliens authorized to work, provide your Alien Registration Number/USCIS Number ***OR*** *Form 1-94 Admission Number:*

Source: US Department of Homeland Security; Goodheart-Willcox Publisher

Figure 20-6 The Employment Eligibility Verification Form I-9 confirms an employee's identity. All new employees are required to complete this form.

Deductions are based on marital status and the number of dependents claimed, including the employee. The amounts withheld are forwarded to the appropriate government agency.

At the end of the year, the employer sends the employee a *Form W-2 Wage and Tax Statement* to use when filing income tax returns. This form summarizes all wages and deductions for the year for an individual employee.

Benefits Forms

The human resources department will provide a variety of forms that are specific to the compensation package offered by the employer. These forms may include health insurance, life insurance, corporate membership, or profit-sharing enrollment forms. If the position involves driving, you may need to fill out additional forms related to your driving record. Be prepared to complete multiple forms on your first day.

Section 20.2 Review

Check Your Understanding

1. Explain the purpose of a job interview for both the employer and the applicant.
2. What is the easiest rule to follow when dressing for an interview?
3. Cite examples of behavioral questions.
4. What should be included in a thank-you message after an interview?
5. List forms that must be completed by a newly hired employee.

Build Your Vocabulary

As you progress through this course, develop a personal glossary of key terms. This will help you build your vocabulary and prepare you for a career. Write a definition for each of the following terms and add it to your personal glossary.

mock interview   hypothetical question   behavioral question

Chapter 20 Review and Assessment

Chapter Summary

Section 20.1 Résumés, Cover Messages, and Applications

LO 20.1-1 **Discuss writing a résumé.**
A general rule is a résumé should be one page. Font selections should be conservative and professional. Typical sections to include on your résumé include name and personal information; career objective; work experience or volunteer experience; education; and honors, awards, and publications. In addition, a résumé should use correct grammar, vocabulary, and punctuation.

LO 20.1-2 **Explain submission of a résumé as part of the application process.**
The traditional way to submit a résumé is by mail or in person. However, most people submit résumés online by attaching it to an e-mail, uploading it to a website, or copy and pasting it to an online application form.

LO 20.1-3 **Summarize how to write a persuasive cover message to accompany a résumé.**
A cover message provides an introduction to who you are and why you are the right person for the position you are seeking. A cover message should focus on your qualifications without being boastful. It does not repeat the details listed in the résumé, but instead highlights your key qualifications that are specific to the job for which you are applying. The message also explains how you heard about the position.

LO 20.1-4 **Explain how to apply online and in person.**
Applying for a job can be completed online or in person. In today's market, the job application process is typically completed online. Some employers require that a candidate complete a digital application and attach a résumé, while other employers require sending an e-mail application with a résumé attached. The traditional way of applying in person requires the job candidate to visit the human resources department and fill out a job application. In addition, the applicant should bring a copy of his or her résumé, cover message, and portfolio to hand deliver to a potential employer.

Section 20.2 Job Interviews and the Employment Process

LO 20.2-1 **Explain how to prepare for a job interview.**
The first step in preparing for a job interview is to learn as much as you can about not only the position but the company as well. The *About Us* section on a company's website as well as the human resources department are valuable sources for information. You should prepare an outfit for the interview that shows you understand the work environment and know the appropriate attire. Additionally, practice answering potential interview question in addition to preparing questions to ask the interviewer.

LO 20.2-2 **Discuss steps to take at the conclusion of an interview.**
When the interview concludes, thank the interviewer for his or her time. An individual should express appreciation for the opportunity and interest in the position. He or she should shake the hand of each person in the room and then exit. After leaving, the job candidate evaluates the interview performance to prepare for future opportunities. Additionally, a job candidate should write a thank-you message to the interviewer to thank him or her again for the opportunity, restate any important points that were made, and reinforce enthusiasm for the job.

LO 20.2-3 **Summarize the employment process.**
The employment process can take a substantial amount of time. Employers must conduct employment verification and a background check to make sure the candidate is qualified for the position. After employment verification and background check are completed, an official job offer is extended for the candidate to accept or decline. In addition, employment forms must be completed by an employee when beginning a new job.

Review Your Knowledge

1. Summarize writing a résumé.
2. How is a résumé submitted as part of the application process?
3. Explain keywords and the role they play in writing a résumé.
4. Discuss how to write a persuasive cover message to accompany a résumé.
5. Explain how to apply online and in person.
6. Describe ways a person can prepare for a job interview.
7. If an employer asks an interviewee a question that is illegal, how should an interviewee handle the situation?
8. Why is it beneficial to ask questions during an interview?
9. Discuss steps to take at the conclusion of an interview.
10. Summarize the employment process.

Apply Your Knowledge

1. Create a draft of a résumé for a business position of your choice. List all your past work experiences. Refer to Figure 20-1 as an example. Write a brief description of your responsibilities at each job to demonstrate your positive work behaviors and qualities that make you employable. Use appropriate keywords. If you have any special licenses or certifications, note these also. List your educational background and any other information you think should be included.
2. After the draft of your résumé is complete, format the document. Using Figure 20-1 as an example, create your final résumé. Demonstrate use of appropriate content, concepts, and vocabulary. Check the final document for grammar.
3. A résumé may be required during the application process for college or a community service position. How would you modify your résumé for a college application? For a volunteer position?
4. Write a cover message that you would attach with your résumé if applying for a business position. Use the example as shown in Figure 20-2. Explain how your positive work behaviors and other qualities make you employable. Demonstrate use of appropriate content, concepts, and vocabulary. Check the final document for grammar and formatting.
5. Describe what you would wear to an interview and explain why the choice is appropriate.
6. Write an answer for each of the following potential interview questions.
   - What makes you a good employee?
   - What are your strengths?
   - What are your weaknesses?

7. Create a list of five questions you might ask during an interview. Be aware of how you word questions to make the best impression.
8. Ask a friend or an instructor to conduct a mock interview with you. Dress as you would for an actual job interview. Before the interview begins, give your résumé to the interviewer. As you answer questions for the interviewer, demonstrate your professionalism by applying appropriate verbal skills and conducting yourself in a manner that is acceptable in the workplace.
9. You have recently been interviewed for the position of assistant manager at a local business. Write a thank-you message to the interviewer.
10. You have been offered the position of assistant manager. Write an acceptance message to show your interest in receiving the position.

College and Career Readiness

Communication Skills

Writing. Many college applications require an essay as part of the application process. Write a 500-word essay explaining why a chosen career is the perfect one for you. Be mindful of Standard English grammar and spelling rules as you write.

Speaking. Beginning a career calls for an individual to be able to stay motivated during a job search. Prepare a one- to two-minute speech you might deliver to a friend who is becoming discouraged while searching for a job. Deliver the speech to a classmate, using note cards if necessary. Practice correct pronunciation and grammar.

Listening. When taking notes in class, discretion must be used to decide which keywords and main ideas are important so they can be recorded. It is not necessary to write down every word you hear. A first rule of note taking is to practice active listing. You must not only hear what is said, but comprehend the information. One way to determine importance is to listen to repetition by the instructor. If information is repeated, it must be important. Listen closely to the lectures by your instructor. What have you noticed that he or she consistently repeats?

Internet Research

Online Job Advertisement. Using the Internet, locate job advertisements for a company that is hiring for positions that interest you. Select one that would fit your criteria if you were to apply for it. Summarize how you found this particular job using the Internet, such as what search terms you used.

Lawful Interview Questions. Research the term *lawful interview questions*. Give examples of federal laws regarding employment interviews. Write several paragraphs explaining what you learned from this research.

Multiple Intelligence. Multiple intelligence research indicates that intelligence is not just I.Q. and that individuals exhibit how smart they are by exhibiting behaviors in various ways. Using the Internet, research the topic of multiple intelligence. Write several paragraphs about your findings, and evaluate the validity and reliability of sources.

Teamwork

Work in pairs or teams as assigned by your teacher to conduct mock interviews. Take turns acting as the interviewer and the interviewee. Refer to the typical interview questions given in this chapter, but come up with your own questions as well. When all interviews are completed, write a brief summary evaluating how you performed in the interview. Describe what you could do better in the future.

Portfolio Development

Presenting the Print Portfolio. Once you have collected items for your portfolio, it is time to organize the contents. Print the documents that you created as evidence of your abilities, such as your Skills and Talents document. Review and select the documents you want to include in your final portfolio.

After determining the appropriate order for documents, create divider pages for each section. This helps organize the material.

Prepare a title page, which should consist of the word *Portfolio* followed by the phrase *Prepared by* and your full name. Next, create a table of contents.

Conclude your portfolio with a résumé and generic cover letter. Insert your references and letters of recommendation after.

Decide what you want to use to house your portfolio. You will need multiples because you will often leave a copy with the interviewer. You should initially create two or three. Remember, a portfolio is a living document and will be updated regularly. As your education and career progress, there will be changes you want to make. If you created too many initial versions, you may find yourself discarding them.

1. Review the documents you have collected. Select the items you want to include in your portfolio. Make copies of certificates, diplomas, and other important documents. Keep the originals in a safe place.
2. Organize the documents in the order that you wish them to appear. The title page will appear first. Then, create a table of contents based on your selected order.
3. Place the items in a folder, binder, or other container.
4. Submit the portfolio to an instructor or other person who can give constructive feedback. Review the feedback you received. Make necessary adjustments and revisions.

CTSOs

Preparing for an Event. No matter what competitive events you will participate in for a CTSO, you will have to be well-organized and prepared. Of course, you will have studied the content exhaustively before the event, but you also have to prepare by making sure all the tools you need for the event have been secured and travel arrangements to the event have been made. Confirming details well in advance of an event will decrease stress and leave you free to concentrate on the event itself.

To prepare for a competition, complete the following activities.

1. Pack appropriate clothing, including comfortable shoes and professional attire.
2. Prepare all technological resources, including anything that you might need to prepare or complete. Double-check to make sure that any electronic presentation material is saved in a format that is compatible with the machines that will be available to you at the event. Consider also packing hard copies in the event your technology fails to function properly.
3. If the event calls for visuals, make sure you have them prepared in advance, packed, and ready to take with you.
4. Bring registration materials, including a valid form of identification.
5. Bring study materials, including flash cards and any other materials you have used to study for the event. If note cards are acceptable when making a presentation, make sure your notes are complete and easy to read. Have a backup set in case of an emergency.
6. At least two weeks before you go to the competition, create a checklist of what you need for the event. Include every detail down to a pencil or pen. Review this checklist before you go into the presentation so you do not forget anything.

CHAPTER 21
Digital Citizenship

Sections

Reading Prep

Rereading can clarify the content you have read and strengthen your understanding of it. Scan the content for passages that contain information that may raise questions or cause confusion. Reread these sections of this chapter.

Exploring Careers

Webmaster

Webmasters are responsible for creating and managing an organization's website. They are responsible for designing and maintaining a visually pleasing and easy-to-use website for internal and external customers. Webmasters oversee the building of the site as well as maintain the site after it becomes active. In addition, webmasters are responsible to ensure that the website stays safe and secure.

Typical job titles for this position include *website manager* and *corporate webmaster*. Examples of tasks webmasters perform include:

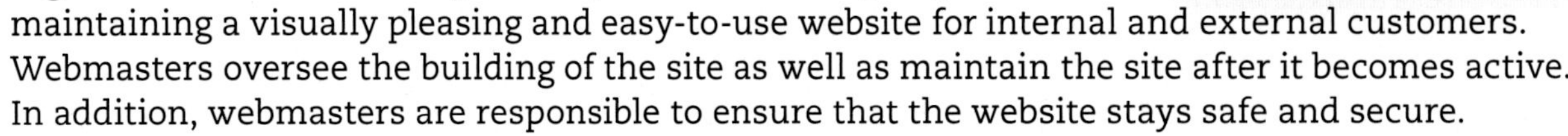

- working with web development teams to provide an easy-to-use interface and solve usability issues;
- installing updates and upgrades as needed;
- troubleshooting web page and server problems, keeping downtime to a minimum;
- implementing and monitoring firewalls and other security measures; and
- updating content and links as requested or needed by the company.

Most webmaster positions require a bachelor degree in web design or a related field. Exceptional skills with computers and computer programs are a must. Webmasters must be proficient in application-server software, graphics software, payment-processing software, and web page-creation software. They need a good understanding of graphic design, website design, and programming. They must also have good customer service, communication, problem-solving, and math skills.

wavebreakmedia/Shutterstock.com

Section 21.1

Communicating in a Digital Society

What implications does digital citizenship have for society as a whole?

Learning Objectives

LO 21.1-1 Identify elements of digital communication.

LO 21.1-2 Explain intellectual property and what it includes.

Key Terms 

digital communication	slander	piracy
digital literacy	libel	infringement
digital citizenship	digital footprint	public domain
cyberbullying	intellectual property	open source
netiquette	plagiarism	

LO 21.1-1 Digital Communication

Digital communication is the exchange of information through electronic means. Using technology to communicate in the workplace, as well as in one's personal life, requires users to be responsible. This involves the knowledge and skills to successfully navigate the Internet and interact with individuals and organizations. Digital communication requires digital literacy and digital citizenship.

Digital Literacy

Digital literacy is the ability to use technology to locate, evaluate, communicate, and create information. According to the federal government, digital literacy skills include:

- using a computer or mobile device, including the mouse, keyboard, icons, and folders;
- using software and applications to complete tasks, such as word processing and creating spreadsheets, tables, and databases;
- using the Internet to conduct searches, access e-mail, and register on a website;
- communicating online, including sharing photos and videos, using social media networks, and learning to be an informed digital citizen; and
- helping children learn to be responsible and make informed decisions online.

To learn more about digital literacy skills, visit the Digital Literacy website maintained by the United States government for information, resources, and tools.

Digital Citizenship

Digital citizenship is the standard of appropriate behavior when using technology to communicate. Good digital citizenship focuses on using technology in a positive manner rather than using it for negative or illegal purposes. People who participate in the digital society have a legal responsibility for their online actions, whether those actions are ethical or unethical. *Ethics* are the principles of what is right and wrong that help people make decisions. Ethical actions are those that apply ethics and moral behavior. Unethical actions are those that involve immoral behavior, crime, or theft. These actions can be punishable by law.

It is important to understand the difference between ethical and unethical digital activities. For example, it is sometimes difficult for someone to know where joking stops and bullying starts. **Cyberbullying** is using the Internet to harass or threaten an individual. It includes using social media, text messages, or e-mails to harass or scare a person with hurtful words or pictures. A target of cyberbullying cannot be physically seen or touched by the bully. However, this does not mean the person being targeted cannot be harmed by the bully's actions.

Monkey Business Images/Shutterstock.com

Digital literacy is the ability to use technology to locate, evaluate, communicate, and create information. **What do you consider the most important aspect of digital literacy skills?**

Cyberbullying is illegal in most states and can be prosecuted.

Other unacceptable online behaviors include spamming, flaming, and trolling.

- *Spamming* is sending unwanted mass e-mails or intentionally flooding an individual's social media site or e-mail inbox with unwanted messages.
- *Flaming* is purposefully insulting someone and inciting an argument on social media.
- *Trolling* is posting offensive, irrelevant, or provocative messages or comments with the goal of upsetting a person or group of people. It is less personal than flaming, which is usually a personal attack on one person.

Etiquette is the art of using good manners in any situation. **Netiquette** is etiquette used when communicating electronically. It is also known as *digital etiquette.* Netiquette includes accepted social and professional guidelines for Internet-based communication. These guidelines apply to e-mails, social networking, and other contact with customers and peers via the Internet. For example, using all capital letters in a message, which has the effect of yelling, is not acceptable. Always use correct capitalization, spelling, and grammar.

Having poor netiquette can also have legal ramifications. **Slander** is speaking a false statement about someone that causes others to have a bad opinion of him or her. **Libel** is publishing a false statement about someone that causes others to have a bad or untrue opinion of him or her. Slander and libel are crimes of defamation. It is important to choose words carefully when making comments about others, whether online or in person.

Content you post on the Internet never really goes away. A **digital footprint** is a data history of all an individual's online activities. Even if you delete something you have posted on the Internet, it still affects your digital footprint. Always think before posting to social media sites or sending an e-mail. Content you post online today could risk your future college and job opportunities.

LO 21.1-2 Intellectual Property

The Internet provides countless sources for obtaining text, images, video, audio, and software. Even though this material is easily obtainable, this does not mean it is available for you to use any way you choose. Laws exist to govern the use of media and creative works. The creators or owners of this material have certain legal rights. **Intellectual property** is something that comes from a person's mind, such as an idea, invention, or process. Intellectual property laws protect a person's or a company's inventions, artistic works, and other intellectual property.

Plagiarism is claiming another person's material as your own, which is both unethical and illegal. If you must refer to someone else's work, follow intellectual property laws to ethically acquire the information. This includes using standard methods of citing sources. Citation guidelines in *The Chicago Manual of Style* and the *MLA Style Manual and Guide to Scholarly Publishing* can be helpful to prevent plagiarism.

Piracy is the unethical and illegal copying or downloading of software, files, and other protected material. Examples of protected material include images, movies, and music. Piracy carries a heavy penalty, including fines and incarceration.

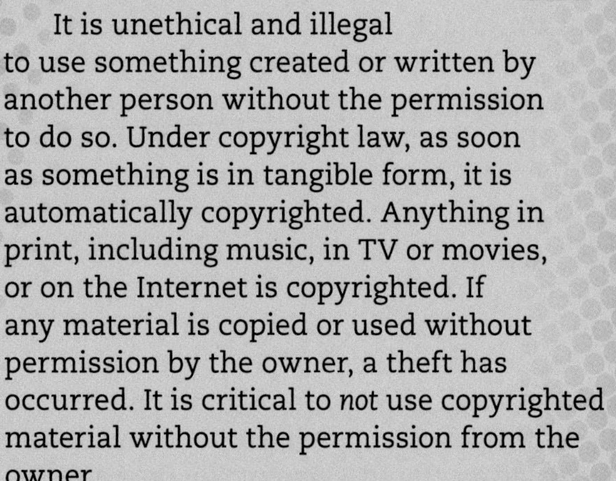

Ethics

Copyright

It is unethical and illegal to use something created or written by another person without the permission to do so. Under copyright law, as soon as something is in tangible form, it is automatically copyrighted. Anything in print, including music, in TV or movies, or on the Internet is copyrighted. If any material is copied or used without permission by the owner, a theft has occurred. It is critical to *not* use copyrighted material without the permission from the owner.

Copyright

A *copyright* acknowledges ownership of a work and specifies that only the owner has the right to sell the work, use it, or give permission for someone else to sell or use it. Any use of copyrighted material without permission is **infringement**. Copyright laws cover all original work, whether it is in print, on the Internet, or in any other form of media. Scanning a document does not make the content yours.

All original material is automatically copyrighted as soon as it is in a tangible form. This means that, for example, an essay is copyrighted as soon as it is written and saved or printed. Similarly, a photograph is copyrighted as soon as it is taken. An idea cannot be copyrighted.

When a copyright expires and is not renewed, the material enters the public domain. **Public domain** refers to material not owned by a specific person and can be used without permission. Much of the material created by federal, state, or local governments is in the public domain. This is because taxpayer money was used to create it. In addition, an owner of the material may choose to give up ownership and place the material in the public domain.

Copyrighted material that is published is often indicated by the © symbol or the statement "copyright by." Lack of the symbol or statement does not mean the material is not copyrighted. Original material is still legally protected whether or not the copyright is registered. A copyright can be registered with the US Copyright Office, which is part of the Library of Congress.

Fair Use

A *fair use doctrine* allows individuals to use copyrighted works without permission in limited situations under very strict guidelines. It allows material to be used for the purpose of describing or reviewing the work. A student writing about the material in an original report is an example of fair use. Another example is a product-review website providing editorial comments. Fair use doctrine does not change the copyright or ownership of the material used under the doctrine.

Creative Commons

In some cases, individuals or organizations may wish to allow others to use their intellectual property without needing permission. This type of use assignment is called *copyleft,* which is a play on the word *copyright.*

One popular method of allowing use of intellectual property is a Creative Commons license. A *Creative Commons (CC) license* is a specialized copyright license that allows free distribution of copyrighted work. Figure 21-1 shows the Creative Commons symbol that often appears on material bearing this license.

Creative Commons

Figure 21-1 The Creative Commons (CC) license allows free sharing of intellectual property.

If the creator of the work wants to give the public the ability to use, share, or advance his or her original work, a Creative Commons license provides that flexibility. The creator maintains the copyright and can specify how the copyrighted work is used. For example, one type of Creative Commons license prohibits original work from being used for commercial use.

Most information on the Internet is copyrighted, whether it is text, graphics, illustrations, or digital media. This means it cannot be used without obtaining permission from the owner. Sometimes, the owner places the material on the Internet to be used by others. However, if this is not explicitly stated, assume the material is copyrighted and cannot be freely used.

patat/Shutterstock.com

Patents protect an invention that is functional or mechanical, such as LEGO building blocks. **Why are patents important for a person or business to acquire?**

Patent

A *patent* gives a person or company the right to be the sole producer of a product for a defined period of time. Patents protect an invention that is functional or mechanical. The invention must be considered useful and inoffensive, and it must be operational. This means that an idea cannot be patented. However, a process can be patented under certain conditions. The process must be related to a particular machine or transform a substance or item into a different state or thing. In the United States, patents are granted by the *US Patent and Trademark Office (USPTO).*

lightpoet/Shutterstock.com

Reusing material without permission, such as photocopying pages out of a textbook, is unethical. **Summarize why reusing material without permission is unethical behavior.**

Trademark

A *trademark* protects taglines, slogans, names, symbols, and any unique method to identify a product or company. A *service mark* is similar to a trademark, but it identifies a service rather than a product. Trademarks and service marks do not protect a work or product. They only protect the way in which the product is described. The term "trademark" is often used to refer to both trademarks and service marks. Trademarks never expire. Just as with patents, trademarks and service marks are registered with the USPTO.

The symbols used to indicate a trademark or service mark are called *graphic marks*, as shown in Figure 21-2. Some graphic marks can be used without being formally registered.

Licensing Agreement

A *licensing agreement* is a contract that gives one party permission to market, produce, or use the product or service owned by another party.

Graphic Marks	
™	Trademark, not registered
SM	Service mark, not registered
®	Registered trademark

Goodheart-Willcox Publisher

Figure 21-2 Graphic marks are symbols that indicate legal protection of intellectual property.

Software Type			
Characteristics	**For-Purchase**	**Freeware**	**Shareware**
Cost	• Must be purchased to use • Demo may be available	• Never have to pay for it	• Free to try • Pay to upgrade to full functionality
Features	• Full functionality	• Full functionality	• Limited functionality without upgrade

Goodheart-Willcox Publisher

Figure 21-3 Each type of software has specific licensing permissions.

The agreement grants a license in return for a fee or royalty payment. For example, Disney may give a clothing manufacturer permission to print the image of Mickey Mouse on T-shirts.

When buying software, the purchaser agrees to follow the terms of a license. A *license* is the legal permission to use a software program. All software, and many websites, list rules called the *terms of use* or *terms of service* that explain how and when the software or downloaded files may be used. The terms of use agreement may come up automatically, for example, when downloading a file or software application. If, however, you are copying an image or a portion of text from a website, you will need to look for the terms of use information. Figure 21-3 explains the characteristics of various software licensing.

Alternative usage rights for software programs are typically covered by the *GNU General Public License (GNU GPL)*. The GNU GPL guarantees all users the freedom to use, study, share, and modify the software. The term **open source** applies to software that makes its source code available to the public at no charge. Open-source software can be downloaded and used for free and can be modified and distributed by anyone. However, part or all of the code of open-source software may be owned by an individual or organization.

Section 21.1 Review

Check Your Understanding

1. What two items does digital communication require?
2. What actions are considered cyberbullying?
3. Name two unethical uses of another person's intellectual property.
4. What is fair use doctrine?
5. Define a *licensing agreement*.

Build Your Vocabulary

As you progress through this text, develop a personal glossary of key terms. This will help you build your vocabulary and prepare you for a career. Write a definition for each of the following terms and add them to your personal glossary.

digital communication	slander	piracy
digital literacy	libel	infringement
digital citizenship	digital footprint	public domain
cyberbullying	intellectual property	open source
netiquette	plagiarism	

Section 21.2 Internet Use in the Workplace

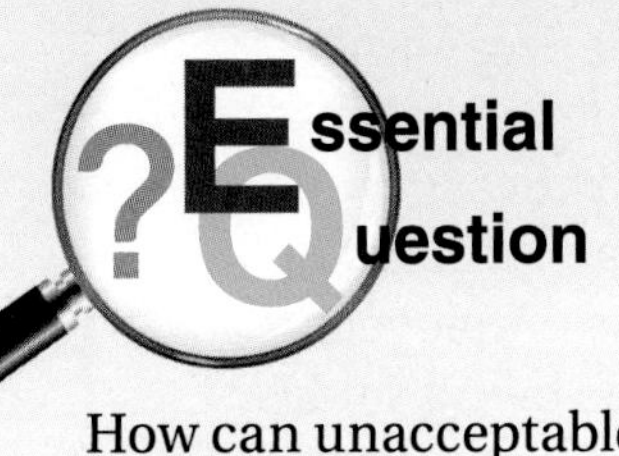

How can unacceptable Internet use by an employee affect a company as a whole?

Learning Objectives

LO 21.2-1 Discuss acceptable use of the Internet.

LO 21.2-2 List potential online security risks.

LO 21.2-3 Summarize digital security.

Key Terms

acceptable use policy	cookies	software virus
cloud computing	phishing	ransomware
Internet protocol address	malware	identity theft
hacking	spyware	firewall

LO 21.2-1 Acceptable Internet Use

An important aspect of digital citizenship is respecting your employer's electronic resources and time spent using them. Internet access provided by a company should be used only for business purposes. For example, checking personal e-mail or playing a game online is not acceptable. Most companies have an established acceptable use policy. An **acceptable use policy** is a set of rules that explains what is and is not acceptable use of company-owned and company-operated equipment and networks. Employees are typically made aware of acceptable use policies during training before they are allowed access to the company's computers and network.

Many organizations allow cloud computing to support collaboration and working remotely. **Cloud computing** is using Internet-based resources to store and access data rather than on a personal computer or local server. Cloud computing makes private digital information accessible from an Internet-enabled device. This allows users to access personal content, such as saved files, from any device that has an Internet connection.

Employers are legally allowed to censor information that employees read on the Internet accessed through company computers during work hours. *Censorship* is the practice of examining material, such as online content, and blocking or deleting anything considered inappropriate. It is common for companies and schools to use *filters* that prevent unauthorized Internet surfing or visiting selected websites during working hours, such as social media sites.

LO 21.2-2 Online Risks

When used correctly, the Internet can be a valuable tool for communication, research, and efficiency. However, it can also be an inherently dangerous place. As cyberattacks become more prevalent, it is increasingly important that people and businesses develop methods of online security.

One way to practice secure online activity is to use discretion. Whether at work or at home, each time you access a search engine or visit a web page, the computer's identity is revealed. The **Internet protocol address**, known as the *IP address*, is a unique number used to identify an electronic device connected to the Internet. While your personal information cannot be easily discovered, an IP address can reveal your approximate geographic location. All e-mails you send, comments you post, or photos you upload from a computer or mobile device have an IP address associated with them.

Another way to protect yourself online is to ensure that you are transmitting data over a secure connection. When transmitting private information to a website, check that the site is secure. A secure address begins with https. The s stands for secure. This is not 100 percent foolproof but generally is a sign of protection. If the connection is secure, the browser will also display an icon somewhere, usually in the address bar, to indicate that the communication is secure. Be wary of providing personal information to sites that are not secure. When possible, avoid public Wi-Fi hotspots. While convenient, these networks are generally not secure and put your devices at risk of inadvertently exposing data to others on the wireless network. Potential security risks of which you must be aware include hacking, cookies, phishing, and malware.

Hacking

One definition of **hacking** is illegally accessing or altering digital devices, software, or networks. Hackers can create illicit hotspots in locations where free or paid public Wi-Fi exists. Users might unknowingly connect to the incorrect network, which allows the hacker access to any data transmitted over that connection. The signal with the best strength may not always be a legitimate hotspot. An easy way to avoid illicit hotspots is to check with an employee of the business that provides the Wi-Fi access. Ask the employee for the name of the network and the access key. If a Wi-Fi authentication screen asks for credit card information, confirm that the Wi-Fi connection is legitimate before providing a credit card number.

Lighthunter/Shutterstock.com

Use caution and protect your privacy when using technology to communicate.

Employability Skills
Listening

Hearing is a physical process. *Listening* is an intellectual process that combines hearing with evaluating. When an employee listens, he or she makes an effort to process what was heard. Companies lose millions of dollars every year because employees are not listening to what is being said by customers, managers, or peers. Paying attention is important in the workplace. Not learning how to listen effectively can cost you your job.

Cookies

Cookies are bits of data stored on a computer that record information about the websites the user has visited. Cookies can also contain personal information you have entered on a website. For example, if you configure your e-mail account to remember or store your password, a cookie is created on your computer that stores the password. The next time you log into your e-mail, the website will find and read the cookie to retrieve your password so you do not have to enter it manually. Most cookies are from legitimate websites and will not harm your computer. Some advertisers place them onto your computer for research and selling purposes. However, if a hacker gains access to your cookies, you are at risk. The cookies can be used to steal information stored or saved from a website. Cookies also can be used to target you for a scam based on your Internet history.

As a precaution, there are ways to protect your computer from cookie theft. One way is to prevent cookies from being accepted by the browser. Most Internet browsers allow you to set a preference to never accept cookies. Check your browser for specific instructions. Another way to protect your computer is to delete cookies on a regular basis. Cookies can also be removed by running a disk cleanup utility.

Phishing

Phishing is the use of fraudulent e-mails and copies of valid websites to trick people into providing private and confidential data.

A common form of phishing is sending a fraudulent e-mail that appears to be from a legitimate source, such as a bank. The e-mail asks for certain information, such as a Social Security number or bank account number. Sometimes it provides a link to a web page. The linked web page looks real, but its sole purpose is to collect private information that will be used to commit fraud.

Most legitimate organizations do not use e-mail to request this type of information. Never provide confidential information in response to an unsolicited e-mail. Avoid clicking a link to a website in an e-mail. It is better to manually enter the website URL into a web browser.

Malware

Malware, short for *malicious software*, is a term given to software programs that are intended to damage, destroy, or steal data. Beware of an invitation to click on a website link for more information about an advertisement, as the link may trigger malware. One click can activate the malware, and your computer could be hacked or infected. Malware comes in many forms, including spyware, Trojan horses, software viruses, worms, and ransomware.

Spyware

Spyware is software that spies on a computer. Spyware can capture private information, such as e-mail messages, usernames, passwords, bank account information, and credit card information. Often, affected users are not aware that spyware is on their computer.

Trojan Horse

A *Trojan horse* is malware usually disguised to appear as a useful or common application in order to convince people to download and use the program. However, the Trojan horse performs malicious actions on the user's computer, such as destroying data or stealing information. Trojan horses do not self-replicate, nor do they infect other files, but they do provide a form of backdoor access to a person's computer.

Software Virus

A **software virus** is a computer program designed to negatively affect a computer system by infecting other files. A virus may destroy data on the computer, cause programs to malfunction, bring harm to a network, or steal information. Viruses are introduced to a computer in many ways, such as by downloading infected files from an e-mail or website. Never open an e-mail attachment that you are not expecting.

Worms

Worms are similar to software viruses, except they self-replicate. This allows them to infect other computers and devices without interaction from the user. For example, if a worm infects a computer, it can self-replicate and send itself to everyone listed in an e-mail address book.

You Do the Math

Numeric Reasoning: Reducing Fractions

Fractions are reduced to make them easier to work with. Reducing a fraction means writing it with smaller numbers or in *lowest terms*. Reducing a fraction does not change its value.

To find the lowest terms, determine the largest number that *evenly* divides both the numerator and denominator so there is no remainder. Then use this number to divide both the numerator and denominator.

Solve the following problems.

1. The manager of a service business asks ten customers if they were satisfied with the service they recently received. Eight customers said they were satisfied. What is the fraction of satisfied customers reduced to lowest terms?
2. The manager distributes an online survey to 560 customers via e-mail. The survey asked customers if they were "likely" or "unlikely" to patronize the business again. There were 35 survey responses of "unlikely." What is the fraction of customers who responded "unlikely" reduced to lowest terms? What is the fraction of customers who responded "likely" reduced to lowest terms?

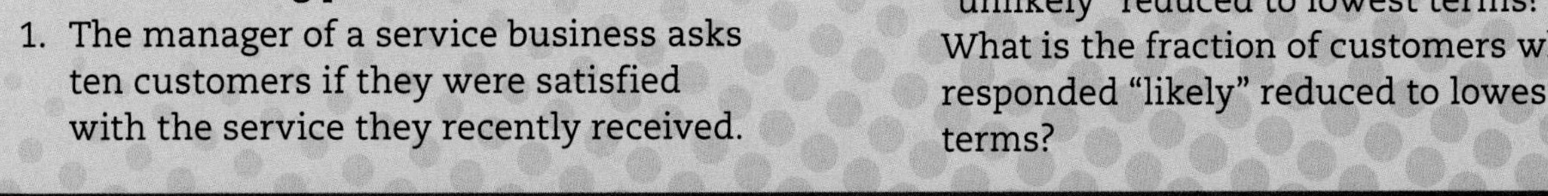

It could then repeat the process on each addressee's computer. Because of this, worms can spread quickly and easily across computers in a network and networks connected to the Internet. Unlike software viruses, however, worms do not infect other files.

Ransomware

Ransomware is a type of malware that seizes control of a computer and demands payment from the owner to unlock it. Often, payment must be made using *cryptocurrency*, which is digital currency that is difficult to trace. Ransomware encrypts all files on the computer, which makes them unusable. If the ransom is paid, the criminals will hopefully unlock the computer by decrypting the files. Always report a ransomware attack to law enforcement officials. Do not pay to unlock the computer without first consulting experts.

Kues/Shutterstock.com

A general security plan should be in place for your computer, databases you maintain, and mobile devices you have. **What consequences could you suffer if you do not have a security plan in place for your digital devices?**

LO 21.2-3 Digital Security

Do not be lulled into a false sense of security when communicating with others online. Be especially careful with those whom you do not personally know. Avoid opening e-mails that look suspicious. Use common sense when deciding what personal details you share, especially your address and Social Security number. Resist the urge to share too much information, which could be stolen.

If you have any suspicions about communicating with someone or giving your information via a website, do not proceed. Investigate the person or company with whom you are dealing. You may be able to avoid a scam.

Avoid Identity Theft

Identity theft is an illegal act that involves stealing someone's personal information and using it to commit theft or fraud. There are many ways that your personal information can be stolen without your knowledge. A lost credit card or driver's license can provide thieves with the information they need to steal a person's identity. Criminals also steal physical mail or garbage to commit identity theft. This method is often called *dumpster diving*. However, computer technology has made identity theft through digital means the most prevalent. Be wary of how much information you share on social networking websites, such as birthdates or locations, as it could potentially be used against you.

If you suspect your identity has been stolen, visit the identity theft website provided by the Federal Trade Commission (FTC) for resources and guidance. Timing is important, so if this unfortunate situation happens to you, act immediately.

Create a Security Plan

A general security plan should be in place for your computer, databases you maintain, and mobile devices you have. Your employer will assist in creating a plan for your workplace equipment.

Consider downloading and running antivirus software for your mobile device, especially if you rely on it to complete daily tasks. It is important to guard them against viruses that would disrupt a primary means of communication and expose personal data.

You must also plan to protect your mobile devices from theft. If you become careless and leave your smartphone or other device in an unexpected location, your identity can be stolen. You may also be stuck with a large telephone bill. If it is an employer-issued device, you may be responsible for replacing it using your personal funds. To protect your mobile device from use by a thief, create a password to lock it. Have the number of your mobile device in a safe place so that if the unexpected happens, you can contact your service provider. Always be cognizant of how much information you store on your mobile devices, as they are easily stolen.

Virus-protection software helps safeguard a computer against malware and should be used on any computer or electronic device that is connected to the Internet or any type of network. This software is also referred to as *antivirus* or *antimalware* software.

A firewall should also be used. A **firewall** is a program that monitors information coming into a computer. It helps ensure that only safe information gets through.

Secure Passwords

Unfortunately, many people have weak passwords for even their most important accounts, such as banking or credit card accounts. Your employer will have guidelines for creating passwords for work accounts. When creating new passwords, use the tips shown in Figure 21-4.

Security Settings

Become familiar with the security settings and features of your Internet browser. Change the browser settings to protect your computer and information. Enabling a *pop-up blocker* prevents the browser from allowing pop-up ads, which can contain malware.

Secure Passwords

- Do not be careless or in a hurry.
- Do not use passwords that contain easily guessed information.
- Do not use the same passwords for multiple accounts or profiles.
- Do change your passwords often.
- Do record your passwords on a dedicated and secure hard-copy document.

Goodheart-Willcox Publisher

Figure 21-4 Use these tips to create safe, secure passwords.

Back Up Your Computer

An important part of a security plan is backing up the data on your computer. If a virus invades your computer or the hard disk crashes, it may be too late to retrieve your files and computer programs.

Your employer will request regular backups of files on your work computer. For your personal computer, put a plan in place to perform regular backups. Decide on a storage device and method for backing up your files. Place the backup in a fireproof container and store it at a location other than your home, such as a safety deposit box at a bank.

Section 21.2 Review

Check Your Understanding

1. What is the purpose of an acceptable use policy in the workplace?
2. A secure address begins with https. What does the s stand for?
3. What is the difference between spyware and a software virus?
4. How can a mobile device be protected from theft?
5. Why should a computer be backed up on a regular basis?

Build Your Vocabulary

As you progress through this text, develop a personal glossary of key terms. This will help you build your vocabulary and prepare you for a career. Write a definition for each of the following terms and add them to your personal glossary.

acceptable use policy	cookies	software virus
cloud computing	phishing	ransomware
Internet protocol address	malware	identity theft
hacking	spyware	firewall

Chapter 21 Review and Assessment

Chapter Summary

Section 21.1 Communicating in a Digital Society

LO 21.1-1 **Identify elements of digital communication.**
Digital communication requires digital literacy and digital citizenship. Digital literacy is the ability to use technology to locate, evaluate, communicate, and create information. Digital citizenship is the standard of appropriate behavior when using technology to communicate.

LO 21.1-2 **Explain intellectual property and what it includes.**
Intellectual property is something that comes from a person's mind, such as an idea, invention, or process. Intellectual property laws protect a person's or a company's inventions, artistic works, and other intellectual property. Copyrights, patents, and trademarks can protect intellectual property.

Section 21.2 Internet Use in the Workplace

LO 21.2-1 **Discuss acceptable use of the Internet.**
Internet access provided by a company should be used only for business purposes. Most companies have an established acceptable use policy. An acceptable use policy is a set of rules that explains what is and is not acceptable use of company-owned and company-operated equipment and networks.

LO 21.2-2 **List potential online security risks.**
Potential online security risks include hacking, cookies, phishing, and malware.

LO 21.2-3 **Summarize digital security.**
Do not be lulled into a false sense of security when communicating with others online. Identity theft is an illegal act that involves stealing someone's personal information and using that information to commit theft or fraud. Be wary of how much information is shared on social networking websites, such as birthdates or locations. It is also important to protect equipment and data against theft by putting a security plan in place.

Review Your Knowledge

1. Identify and explain elements of digital communication.
2. State two examples of digital literacy skills.
3. Explain the importance of digital citizenship.
4. Explain what intellectual property is and what it includes.
5. What is open source and what does it allow?
6. Describe measures companies put in place to ensure their employees use the Internet appropriately while at work.

7. Briefly explain types of potential online security risks.
8. How can a digital citizen protect his or her computer from cookies?
9. What is a common form of phishing?
10. Summarize digital security methods.

Apply Your Knowledge

1. Prepare a presentation to illustrate your understanding of digital literacy and digital citizenship and its implications for individuals, society, and business. Explain to your audience how digital literacy and digital citizenship can be exhibited by an individual in any personal or professional situation.
2. Analyze the legal and ethical responsibilities for digital citizenship that you have as a student.
3. Create a list of acceptable behaviors that are considered to be good examples of netiquette. Next to each, explain why these behaviors are necessary in a digital society.
4. Your digital footprint is important to your personal life as well as your future professional career. List examples of activities that may have a negative impact on your life if you posted about them on a social media website. After putting these actions in writing, will you think more seriously about what you post? Explain your answer.
5. Photocopying copyrighted material is illegal and unethical. What is your opinion of a friend photocopying a textbook chapter instead of buying the textbook? Demonstrate your understanding of ethical and legal issues by writing a letter to your friend about whether the fair use doctrine would apply in this situation.
6. Review the citation guidelines in a style guide, such as *The Chicago Manual of Style* or the *MLA Handbook*. Use these guidelines to cite a book, newspaper article, or copy on a website. How is the citation unique for each type of source?
7. Locate your school or district's policy on acceptable Internet use. This is often located in the student handbook. What policies does your school have in place regarding appropriate Internet use? How are these policies enforced?
8. When shopping online, you may notice that with each new site you browse, you see advertisements for previous sites and products that you have searched. This is due to the presence of cookies on your computer. Marketers use this information for selling purposes. That is why you are likely to see those products appear repeatedly when shopping online. Is this an ethical practice? Why or why not?
9. Secure passwords are crucial to digital security. Describe your experiences creating passwords for various online accounts or electronic devices, such as an e-mail account, social media website, or cell phone. What were the requirements for these passwords? How do you keep track of them?
10. Create your own digital security plan. Make a list of the actions you will take to protect your online identity as well as your private information.

Communication Skills

Reading. Identify the main idea of this chapter as well as the key supporting details. Analyze the development of the main idea over the course of the chapter. How do details shape or refine the presentation of the main idea?

Writing. *Reasoning* is thinking about something in a logical or orderly way to form a conclusion about it. Using the information in this chapter, generate your own idea or opinion about what it means to be safe online. Write several paragraphs describing your thoughts with specificity and detail. Be sure to use reasoning as you form your conclusions.

Speaking. Most people in the United States act as responsible and contributing citizens. How can a person demonstrate social and ethical responsibility in a digital society? Can you think of ways that are not discussed in this chapter? Share your opinions with the class.

Internet Research

Copyright. Copyright laws protect intellectual property. Conduct an Internet search for *copyright law violation example*. Select an example and discuss the law and how it was violated. What copyright issues were at stake? Write your findings and cite your sources using *The Chicago Manual of Style* or your choice of style guide.

Password Strength. Use the Internet to locate a password strength meter. Test the passwords that you use for your online accounts. How strong are your passwords? What strategies can you apply to make your password stronger?

Teamwork

Working with your team, identify and analyze examples of ethical responsibilities that a professional person in business has to society. Make a list of applicable rules your team thinks are appropriate for professional conduct. How can a professional exhibit ethical conduct?

Portfolio Development

Presenting the Electronic Portfolio. After your print portfolio is assembled, decide how to present your electronic portfolio. Review the files you have collected, select the ones you want to include, and remove those you do not. Next, decide how you want to present the materials. You could create a slideshow and store it on a CD or flash drive, or you can create a portfolio website. The method in which you choose to present your electronic portfolio may dictate the file types you use.

Your electronic portfolio will contain documents you created digitally as well as scanned, hard-copy documents. Decide which file formats to use for both types of documents. Before you begin, consider the technology that you might use for creating and scanning documents. This may require access to desktop-publishing software, scanners, cameras, or other digital equipment or software.

For hard-copy files you are scanning, consider saving them in portable document format, or PDF. For documents you create, consider using the default format to save the files. For example, you could save letters and essays created in Microsoft Word in the default DOCX format. If your presentation will include graphics or video, verify the native file formats for each item.

Keep in mind that the person reviewing your electronic portfolio will need programs that open these formats to view your files. One option is to save *all* files as PDF files. Having all of the files in the same format can make viewing them easier for those who need to review your portfolio.

1. Create the slide presentation, website, or other vehicle for presenting your electronic portfolio.
2. View the completed electronic portfolio to check the appearance and functionality.
3. Write a short summary about the format of your electronic portfolio. Include brief instructions on how to navigate or view the portfolio.
4. Give the portfolio to an instructor, counselor, or other person who can give constructive feedback. Review the feedback you received. Make necessary adjustments and revisions.

CTSOs

Day of the Event. You have practiced all year for this CTSO competition, and now you are ready. Whether it is an objective test, written test, report, or presentation, you have done your homework and are ready to shine.

To prepare for the day of the event, complete the following activities.

1. Get plenty of sleep the night before the event so you are rested and ready to compete.
2. Use your event checklist before you go into the presentation so you do not forget any of your materials needed for the event.
3. Find the room where the competition will take place and arrive early. If you are late and the door is closed, you will be disqualified.
4. If you are making a presentation before a panel of judges, practice what you are going to say when you are called on to speak. State your name, your school, and any other information requested. Be confident, smile, and make eye contact with the judges.
5. When the event is finished, thank the judges for their time.

Writing a Management Report

Table of Contents

Reports

Reports are documents used to present information in a structured format to a specific audience for a defined purpose. In the workplace, they are often used to convey information used as the basis for making business decisions. Reports provide facts and information from which conclusions are drawn. They also discuss problems and recommend solutions.

Company reports usually have a deadline. If you are not given a deadline by a supervisor, establish one for yourself. Schedule enough time to finish the writing process. Use the calendar in your personal information management (PIM) system to schedule your report-writing tasks. A *personal information management (PIM)* is a system that individuals use to acquire, organize, maintain, retrieve, and use information. An example of a PIM system is Microsoft Outlook.

A *formal report* is a document that focuses on a broad main topic that is divided into subtopics for complete and clear coverage. These reports are often supported by formal research or gathering of information. They may require formal components, such as a table of contents and a bibliography. Formal reports are often created by a team. Individuals assume responsibility for designated sections and then work collaboratively to create the final document.

An *informal report* is a document that does not require formal research or documentation. Informal reports are typically short, no more than a few pages long. They are commonly a part of the regular work routine. Informal reports are typically written in the first person when the writer is reporting his or her own actions, ideas, or conclusions.

Prewriting

The first step in the writing process is prewriting. Prewriting is the planning stage of the writing process. It involves identifying:

- the purpose of the report;
- audience for the report;
- the message to be communicated; and
- research required.

Taking time to plan thoroughly will help make the writing process go smoothly. After you have completed the prewriting steps, you will be able to begin the research.

Purpose

Reports are written for a specific and defined purpose. There are three common purposes for writing a report.

- *Informational reports* contain facts, data, or other types of information. Informational reports do not attempt to analyze the data or persuade the reader.
- *Analytical reports* contain both information and analysis of the data. These reports often provide conclusions or recommendations drawn from the analysis.
- *Proposals* typically contain an idea and attempt to persuade the reader to take a certain course of action. Extensive research and analysis often go into a proposal.

Most reports state in the introduction why the report is being written. This helps the audience focus on why they are reading the report.

Audience

Analyzing the audience is an important step in the writing process. It will help you make decisions about the approach, style, tone, and level of formality of the report. It will also affect how the content is presented as well as how the report is published.

The first question to ask is will the audience be internal, external, or both? An *internal audience* is composed of employees in the organization. They are familiar with the business and can relate to the information conveyed. An *external audience* is composed of people outside the company, such as customers or vendors, and will probably need more background information about your topic.

The second question to ask is will there be a primary audience, secondary audience, or both? The *primary audience* is directly involved in the purpose of the communication. These people will act on the content of the message. After reading, the primary audience should feel like their points of view were considered and their concerns were addressed. The *secondary audience* is indirectly involved in the purpose of the communication and may or may not be interested in the details. They receive copies of the communication, read it, and generally do not respond.

Message

Determine the message you want the reader to take from the report. Knowing what ideas you want to communicate helps focus on the purpose of the message. What do you want the reader to do as a result of reading the information? Answering this question will help narrow down the subject area so that you can select the specific topic that will be covered.

Consider the proper scope of the content for the message. The *scope* of the report is the guideline of how much information will be included. Is it detailed or general? Which key points will be included? Scope defines the boundaries in which a report should be kept.

Research

Collecting data is an important step in preparing to write a report. *Data* are the pieces of information gathered through research. Information usually falls into one of two categories: qualitative or quantitative data.

- *Qualitative data* are the information that provides insight into how people think about a particular topic. An example of qualitative data is a customer's feelings after speaking with a customer service agent.
- *Quantitative data* are facts and figures from which conclusions can be drawn. An example of quantitative data is the number of customers who requested to speak with a customer service agent after using a certain product.

Research techniques include conducting surveys, focus groups, or interviews, and studying written information on the topic. Research might include collaboration with other departments, consulting outside experts, or convening a taskforce. The report dictates where you must look for source material.

Primary research is first-hand research conducted by the writer in preparation for writing a report. The most common methods of primary research for a business report are interviews, surveys, observations, and experiments.

Secondary research is data and information already assembled and recorded by someone else. This might include published materials or resources available to you in the organization. Primary research is conducted when secondary research is not productive.

Structure

As you prepare to write, select a structure that supports your material. The direct approach or indirect approach should be chosen in order to achieve the desired outcome. When using the *direct approach,* start with a general statement of purpose. Follow this with supporting details. The direct approach is desirable when the reader is expecting a straightforward message. When using the *indirect approach,* discuss supporting details upfront. This will prepare the reader for your general statement of purpose or conclusions.

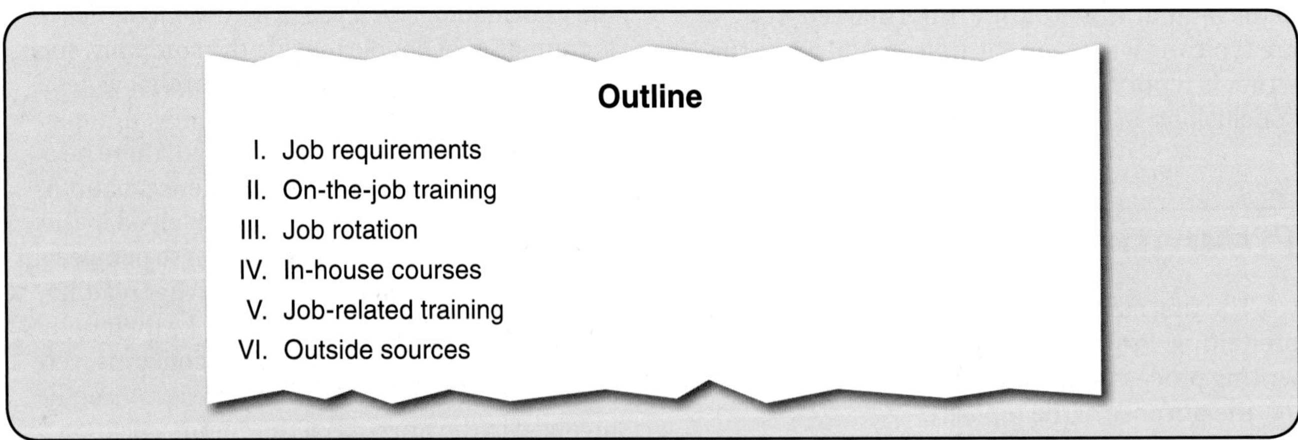
Outline

I. Job requirements
II. On-the-job training
III. Job rotation
IV. In-house courses
V. Job-related training
VI. Outside sources

Goodheart-Willcox Publisher

Figure 1 Outline

After the approach is decided, the next step is creating an outline. Figure 1 shows a basic outline for a short report. For a long report, the outline might consist of key points with details. Think ahead and plan the introduction and conclusions you want to make. Note the main points you want or need to be covered. Once you have all the information, arrange it in the order that will make the report effective.

There are several approaches to organization that can be applied to reports. You can choose to organize a report by chronological or sequential order, order of importance, cause and effect, or problem-solution. A combination of two or more organizational orders can be used to accomplish your goal.

- **Chronological or sequential order.** When you are reporting events or discussing a process, the chronological or sequential order is a good choice. *Chronological* means in order of time. *Sequential* means in order of sequence. In this order, start with the earliest events and proceed to the most recent. A variation is to use the reverse order, where the most recent events are presented first.
- **Order of importance.** When organizing by order of importance, present information from most to least important. Readers can easily follow this logic. In some cases, it is better to present information in the reverse order, from least to most important.
- **Cause-and-effect order.** The cause-and-effect organization is useful when your report reflects an investigation. This approach lists facts or ideas followed by conclusions. You should report your opinions only after careful research and fact-finding.
- **Problem-solution order.** This organization type works well when the report will describe a problem and offer a solution or multiple solutions. By presenting the problem, you communicate to the reader why an action is needed. You can then offer the reader options for solving the problem. This approach is very common in the professional world when writing a report to a superior.

Writing Formal Reports

Once your research is finished and your sources are organized, you are ready to continue the writing process and compose the report. The writing stage includes creating the first draft. You will complete the first draft and revise it as many times as necessary to create the final product. Once you have finished revising the report, it will be necessary to edit the document. Where revising focuses on constructing the content, editing is polishing the document until it is in finished form.

When you prepare a report, ask if there are guidelines that must be followed. Formal reports are written in the third person. They follow a structured format that adheres to standards used by most businesses. There may be templates you need to use to create a new report. A company template may include text fields or a letterhead, for example. If there are no guidelines to follow, you might use the templates provided in your word processing software. You can also look for examples online.

The parts of a formal report vary according to its purpose and topic. There are several common parts that appear in a formal report.

Title Page

All formal reports should have a title page designed for readability and visual appeal, as shown in Figure 2. The information that should be listed on the title page include the:

- report title;
- person or group for whom the report was written;
- author of the report; and
- date the report is distributed.

Sometimes other information, such as the location of the company, may also be needed on the title page.

Table of Contents

A table of contents is necessary so the reader knows what is included in the report. The *table of contents* lists the major sections and subsections within the report with page numbers, as shown in Figure 3. This page can be referred to as *table of contents* or *contents*.

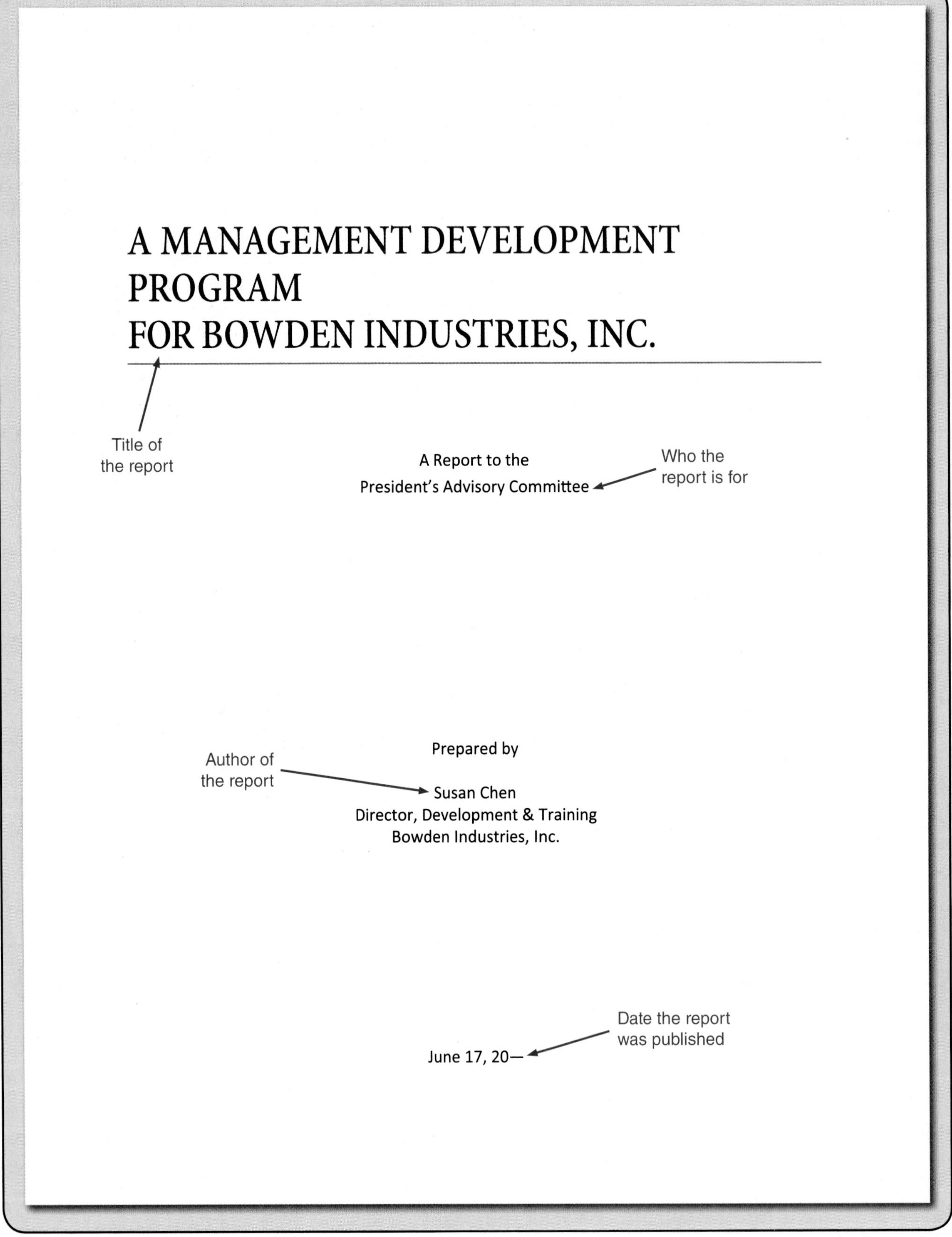
A MANAGEMENT DEVELOPMENT PROGRAM FOR BOWDEN INDUSTRIES, INC.

A Report to the
President's Advisory Committee

Prepared by

Susan Chen
Director, Development & Training
Bowden Industries, Inc.

June 17, 20—

Goodheart-Willcox Publisher

Figure 2 Title Page

Begin introduction on page 1 and use Roman numerals for preceding pages

CONTENTS

ii

Goodheart-Willcox Publisher

Figure 3 Table of Contents

Executive Summary

The *executive summary* summarizes the main points in the report, as shown in Figure 4. It is sometimes referred to as a *summary* or *abstract.* The summary should be an overview for some recipients who may not read the entire report. It appears at the beginning of the report, before the introduction.

Introduction

The reader's attention should be captured by giving an overview of the content of the report. An introduction usually discusses the purpose of the report and the benefits of the ideas or recommendations you are presenting. The introduction of the report often covers:

- a history or background of the situation that led to the preparation of the report;
- the purpose for which the report was written, including the need or justification for the report;
- the scope of the report, including what is covered and, if necessary, what is not covered;
- definitions of terms that may present problems for certain readers; and
- descriptions of methods used to gather information, facts, and figures for the report.

An example of an introduction is in Figure 5.

Body

The body of the report contains all the information, data, and statistics you assemble. Your outline will help you organize ideas and information in a logical manner. Providing supporting data from reliable sources will help the audience understand the content.

If the topic about which you are writing is very high level, a formal tone is more likely to achieve this goal. You want to convince the reader you have thoroughly studied the matter and that your information is highly trustworthy. If, on the other hand, you are writing a report about employee activities that boost morale and create a sense of team, a conversational tone would be appropriate. This friendlier tone will help set the stage for the theme of the report.

Your place in the organization will influence the tone of the content. A report addressed to the company president is likely to be formal in tone. If you have a friendly relationship with your supervisor, a report you write for her or him may be more conversational.

Bias

Sometimes bias on the part of the reader will influence your handling of the topic. A *bias* is a tendency to believe that some ideas or people are better than others. Consider biases the reader might bring to the subject matter, and develop content to address them. For example, your reader is known to be very timid about innovations. In this case, recommendations for new product designs should concentrate on facts rather than appealing to trends.

Knowledge

Assess the level of knowledge the audience will bring and if there is variation within the audience. The amount of background information and the need to define terms depends on your assessment of the audience's prior knowledge. A lesser degree of prior knowledge will require additional explanation on the part of the writer.

Readability

Another aspect of preparing the body of your report is readability. Readability is a measure of how easy it is for the audience to understand your writing and locate information within the report.

Conclusions and Recommendations

The conclusion of a report summarizes the key points. In some cases, you will want to close with conclusions and recommendations based on your study or analysis. *Conclusions* are the writer's summary of what the audience should take away from the report. *Recommendations* are actions the writer believes the reader should take. Both of these should follow logically from the information presented in the body, as shown in Figure 6. If you make a leap in logic, you risk losing credibility with the audience.

EXECUTIVE SUMMARY

The President's Advisory Committee of Bowden Industries, Inc., requested a study to determine the reasons the company has had difficulty filling management positions and to find solutions to the problem. If Bowden is to continue on a path to future expansion, a concerted effort must be made to hire and develop the necessary managerial expertise.

Research

A thorough examination of hiring, training and development, management, and promotion practices was conducted. The research looked at why vacancies occurred, how they were filled, and the success rate of these hirings. The data suggest that management positions at Bowden require a high level of training, experience, and education and that there is no established route to provide this combination of preparedness for those entering management.

Findings

Findings showed that the majority of openings had to be filled from the outside because current staff had not been prepared to accept the greater responsibilities of management. The studies also revealed that those hired from outside required extensive training once they came onboard. The lack of inside promotions had a negative impact on morale and the on-the-job adjustment period for employees recruited from outside was very expensive.

Recommendations

The attached report recommends that the company create a formal, well-rounded training program under the guidance of an appointed director and a Management Education Committee for the purpose of training candidates for managerial positions.

iii

Goodheart-Willcox Publisher

Figure 4 Executive Summary

INTRODUCTION

Bowden Industries, Inc., is often referred to as "a family that keeps outgrowing its home." This implies little planning, innovation, and management leadership in the company's twelve years of existence, which is simply not true. Product diversification, innovative marketing and manufacturing, and sound financial management all attest to the effective leadership with which the company has been blessed.

At the May 9 meeting of the President's Advisory Committee, the question was asked, "where will the managerial expertise needed for future growth and expansion come from?" The purpose of this report is to provide possible answers to that vital question.

History

In the past, Bowden has depended largely on universities and executive placement agencies for sources of managerial talent—and, of course, on its own promotion-from-within policy. By and large, these have been good sources of talent and, no doubt, will continue to be used. However, training and developing those new management hires has been through hit-or-miss, largely unstructured, on-the-job supervision. The results are mixed. Some people were well trained and quickly moved up when positions became available. Others languished and, seeing no opportunity for growth, left the company.

Scope

The term "management" in this report refers to all positions from first-line supervisors (classified as Levels 13 and 14 by the Human Resources Department) right on up to the top executive positions. No attention has been given to lower-level jobs in this report, although this is obviously a subject that deserves full exploration later.

Statement of Problem

During the past year, 44 vacancies occurred in management positions. Of that number, 22 were the result of retirement because of age or health, 13 resigned to accept positions in other companies, and the remaining nine were the result of newly created positions within the company.

It is interesting to find that 27 of the 44 openings had to be filled from the outside. In other words, only 17 employees were considered ready to accept the greater responsibilities of management. Actually, few of the people recruited from the outside were actually ready either (the unknown often looks better than the known); many required a long break-in period. Besides having a negative effect on employees who were denied promotion, outside recruiting and on-the-job adjustment are very expensive.

Goodheart-Willcox Publisher

Figure 5 Introduction

RECOMMENDATIONS

On the basis of this study, there would appear to be a definite need for a well-rounded education program at Bowden Industries, Inc. There are numerous possible methods of operating and conducting it. The following recommendations are offered.

1. Appoint a Director of Management Development, preferably a person with sound academic credentials (possibly a Ph.D.), teaching experience in management at the undergraduate and graduate levels, and broad business experience in supervision and management. The appointed person would report directly to the Executive Vice President or to the President.

2. Appoint a Management Education Committee, consisting of the top executive of each of the six divisions in the company and the Executive Vice President (ex officio). This committee would advise the Director of Management Development in planning and operating the program, using as many of the sources described in this report as feasible.

Goodheart-Willcox Publisher

Figure 6 Recommendations

Citations

If your report contains information from sources you have researched, these sources should be acknowledged. A *citation* is a reference to another person's work. It is acceptable to reference material from other sources provided proper credit is given. Citations summarize the work in your own words or by directly quoting part of it.

A citation includes the:

- author's name;
- publication title;
- name and location of the publisher;
- publication year; and
- website name, URL, and date of retrieval.

Citations are listed in footnotes on the page where the reference occurs or in a bibliography at the end of the report. Examples of citations are shown in Figure 7. It is necessary to provide citations for both print and electronic sources.

WORKS CITED

Arbor, Jonathan Cole, "Training that Works." *Train the Trainer (*March 20—) pp. 23–25.

Coletta, Nicole, *The Essentials of Performance Management*. New York: Future Publishing, 2010.

Newberg, Alexis, "Formal Training Programs at Bowden Industries," Report Submitted to the Executive Board, Bowden Training Department, 2009.

Goodheart-Willcox Publisher

Figure 7 Citations

Optional Elements

Complex reports may contain other elements that help the reader find information and understand the contents.

- **List of visuals.** A report can be greatly enhanced with the use of visuals, such as tables and figures. If visuals are used, include a list at the front of the report with page references. This will aid readers in quickly finding information.
- **Glossary.** If terminology used in the report may be unfamiliar to some readers, include a list at the end of the report to define important terms.
- **Appendices.** Information that users might want to refer to, but is not integral to the body, may be included at the back of the report in an appendix. For example, if your report includes survey results, you might provide the survey questionnaire in an appendix.

These optional elements are opportunities to include extra information that may not fit into the scope of the report body.

Feedback

The writing process also includes soliciting feedback. If there is someone available to read the report, have that person give it a final review. Ask for feedback and suggestions that will make the report more effective.

Finalizing Formal Reports

The final step in the writing process is preparing the report for distribution. Formatting and publishing a report are part of the final step in the writing process. It is important to format your report so it appears polished and professional. Publishing a report in the correct format ensures it will be read by its audience, either inside or outside the organization.

Formatting

The final appearance of a report is important. Some organizations have formatting guidelines for reports. Other organizations use templates provided in Microsoft Word or other word-processing software.

If the topic covers more than one key point or important issue, consider using headings as a design element. *Headings* are words and phrases that introduce sections of text. Headings are leveled to organize blocks of information in a document and serve as guideposts to alert the reader to what is coming. Most narrative text can be divided into main topics and subtopics with no more than three levels of headings. Figure 8 shows examples of how to display these levels using heading styles in Microsoft Word.

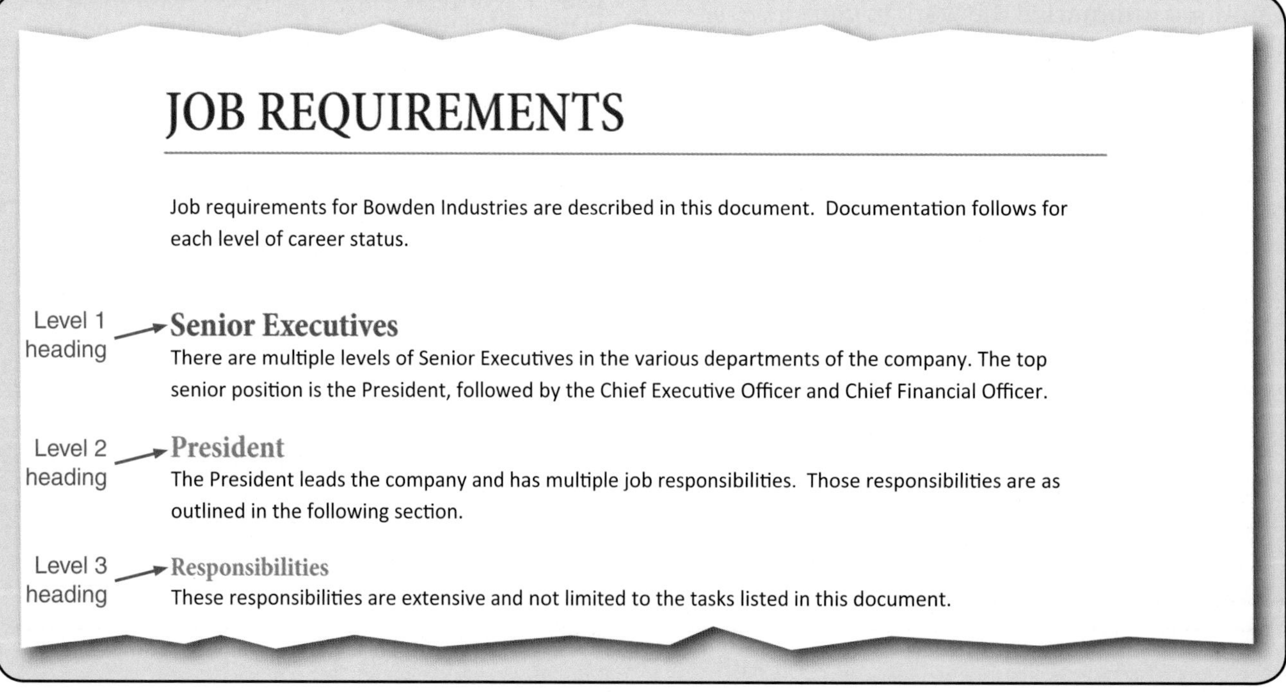

JOB REQUIREMENTS

Job requirements for Bowden Industries are described in this document. Documentation follows for each level of career status.

Level 1 heading → **Senior Executives**

There are multiple levels of Senior Executives in the various departments of the company. The top senior position is the President, followed by the Chief Executive Officer and Chief Financial Officer.

Level 2 heading → **President**

The President leads the company and has multiple job responsibilities. Those responsibilities are as outlined in the following section.

Level 3 heading → **Responsibilities**

These responsibilities are extensive and not limited to the tasks listed in this document.

Goodheart-Willcox Publisher

Figure 8 Headings

The use of white space is important for readability. This includes margins, space between paragraphs, and other blank space on the page. Style manuals, like *The Chicago Manual of Style* or the *MLA Handbook*, include formatting guidelines. You can also use the default spacing in Microsoft Word. The report should be formatted to the preferred style of an organization.

Publishing

Formal reports are often posted on the *intranet site* of an organization. This makes it convenient for those within the organization who need to read the report to have access at their convenience. Alternatively, reports intended for the public may be posted on the organization's *public* website. The electronic file of the report should be a PDF so unauthorized changes cannot be made. The audience can read the report online or print a copy.

If the report will be presented at a meeting, it may be bound to make the presentation polished and highly professional. Binding may be handled through a company's graphics department or an outside service.

Writing Informal Reports

An informal report does not require the research that a formal report requires. It is generally prepared for use inside the organization. These reports use a casual tone and personal pronouns. An informal report does not have a table of contents, appendices, or other components of a formal report. However, these reports have an introduction, body, and conclusion and are only a few pages long.

Introduction

The introduction states the purpose of the report. This is typically where the rest of the paper is briefly summarized. If the report is being written at the request of someone, you might mention that person in the introduction. For example: Following is a report on my visit to the new conference facility we are considering for next month's meeting on digital media and advertising.

Body

The body contains the information of the report. Decide if the content has subtopics that will help the reader scan and skim for information. For example, a short report on a site visit to view a facility might be divided into sections such as location, facility description, and cost. The body of the report should be of sufficient length to communicate the purpose of the document.

Conclusion

Reports should end with a brief summary of main points from the writer's point of view. If you use headings, this section, might be labeled *Conclusion*, *Recommendation*, or *Summary*. If your report does not have headings, the conclusion is the last paragraph. In the example stated in the Introduction section, the writer would likely conclude with a recommendation about whether or not to use the facility.

Types of Informal Reports

It is not possible to list the many types of informal reports used in the workplace. Some of the types of informal reports used in business are described as follows.

Periodic Reports

Periodic reports are written according to a specified schedule, such as daily, weekly, monthly, or quarterly. A periodic report generally provides the status of a project, reports data over a specified period, or summarizes an ongoing activity.

An example of a periodic report is a progress report. A *progress report* tracks the status of a project, is written in a specified format, and is periodically submitted to a manager. Progress reports are also known as *status reports*. These types of reports can be as simple as a monthly one-page update using a template. They can also be as complex as an annual report from a corporation written for its stockholders.

An informal report can be incorporated as part of an e-mail or as an e-mail attachment. In Figure 9, the report is incorporated in the body of an e-mail. While this format is not difficult to read, the layout makes it hard to make comparisons. Additionally, the report will need to be created from scratch each quarter. Another option is to send the report as an e-mail attachment. When attaching a report, use the report file name as the e-mail subject line. This helps the receiver manage his or her e-mail more efficiently.

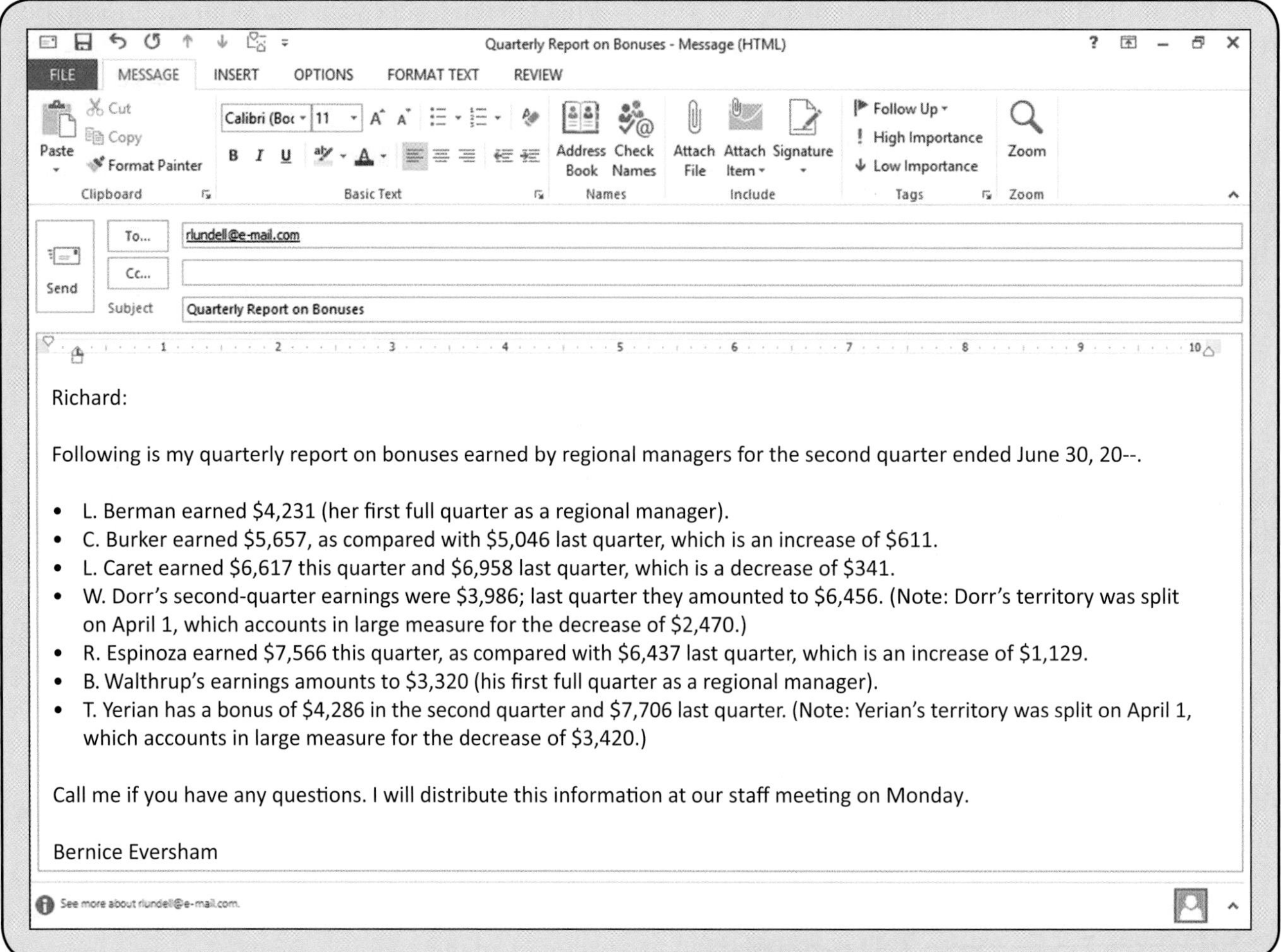

Quarterly Report on Bonuses - Message (HTML)

To... rlundell@e-mail.com

Cc...

Subject Quarterly Report on Bonuses

Richard:

Following is my quarterly report on bonuses earned by regional managers for the second quarter ended June 30, 20--.

- L. Berman earned $4,231 (her first full quarter as a regional manager).
- C. Burker earned $5,657, as compared with $5,046 last quarter, which is an increase of $611.
- L. Caret earned $6,617 this quarter and $6,958 last quarter, which is a decrease of $341.
- W. Dorr's second-quarter earnings were $3,986; last quarter they amounted to $6,456. (Note: Dorr's territory was split on April 1, which accounts in large measure for the decrease of $2,470.)
- R. Espinoza earned $7,566 this quarter, as compared with $6,437 last quarter, which is an increase of $1,129.
- B. Walthrup's earnings amounts to $3,320 (his first full quarter as a regional manager).
- T. Yerian has a bonus of $4,286 in the second quarter and $7,706 last quarter. (Note: Yerian's territory was split on April 1, which accounts in large measure for the decrease of $3,420.)

Call me if you have any questions. I will distribute this information at our staff meeting on Monday.

Bernice Eversham

Goodheart-Willcox Publisher

Figure 9 Report in E-mail

Informal Study Reports

An *informal study report* provides information gathered by the writer through methods other than formal research. These methods of research may include reading documents, conducting informal interviews, reviewing competitive products, or attending a meeting. Informal study reports may be initiated by the writer or prepared at the request of someone higher in the organization, such as a senior manager. Informal reports about activities are sometimes written in the first person to state your own actions, conclusions, and ideas.

Informal study reports can be incorporated into a memo or e-mail or created as a separate document. Figure 10 is an example of a report based on an informal study. Note that the report uses appropriate headings to guide the reader.

Idea and Suggestion Reports

Idea and suggestion reports are written when an employee is asked for ideas and suggestions for making improvements. Examples of areas where input is often requested include improving employee morale, saving time, and cutting costs. In responding to such requests, follow these guidelines.

- Be assertive in offering your opinion. You would not have received an invitation to contribute your ideas if your ideas were not considered valuable.
- Begin with positive remarks about the present situation and tactfully proceed with your suggestions for change.
- Be specific in your recommendations. The reader should not have to guess what you have in mind.
- When appropriate, group your ideas according to subject. Prominently display the subjects.

Review of Customer Correspondence

I have completed the review of customer correspondence you requested on December 16 for the period of November 1 through December 15, 20--. As you suggested, I read all outgoing letters and e-mails written by the six Customer Care Specialists. During this period, 64 pieces of communication (18 letters and 46 e-mails) were written and mailed to customers on issues not covered by our form letters.

Method

As I read each letter, I assigned a grade to it:

- A (excellent)
- B (good)
- C (passable)
- D (poor)

The elements considered in assigning these grades were: tone (friendliness), helpfulness, accuracy of information, organization, and correct mechanics (grammar, spelling and punctuation).

Findings and Conclusions

Number of Letters and E-mails	Grade Assigned
14	A
13	B
25	C
12	D

My evaluations were subjective; however, the distribution of grades I assigned supports the types of criticisms we have been hearing from the sales staff. As they mentioned to us at the last meeting, there are many examples of indifference, carelessness with facts, lack of clarity, and negativism. It seems apparent, based on the 64 pieces of correspondence that were examined, that the standard of customer correspondence is much lower than it should be.

Recommendations

Based on this informal study, I recommend we set up a written communications course for all Customer Care Specialists. I have contacted Dorothy Fairchild in Human Resources Training about setting up and teaching the course. Last year, she organized and taught a course for the Credit Department and, according to the credit manager, Clark Pinson, it was a great success. I will be happy to assist in setting up the course and will help the instructor in any way I can, if you think this is a feasible solution.

Goodheart-Willcox Publisher

Figure 10 Informal Study Report

APPENDIX B Math Skills Handbook

Table of Contents

Getting Started

Math skills are needed in everyday life. You will need to be able to estimate your purchases at a grocery store, calculate sales tax, or divide a recipe in half. This section is designed to help develop your math proficiency for better understanding of the concepts presented in the textbook. Using the information presented in the Math Skills Handbook will help you understand basic math concepts and their application to the real world.

Using a Calculator

There are many different types of calculators. Some are simple and only perform basic math operations. Become familiar with the keys and operating instructions of your calculator so calculations can be made quickly and correctly.

Shown below is a scientific calculator that comes standard with the Windows 10 operating system. To display this version, select the **Settings** pull-down menu and click **Scientific** in the menu.

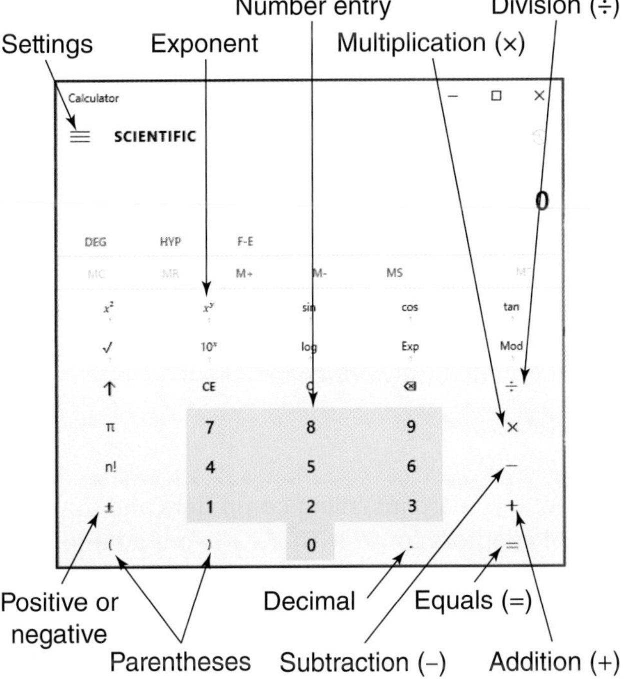

Solving Word Problems

Word problems are exercises in which the problem is set up in text, rather than presented in mathematical notation. Many word problems tell a story. You must identify the elements of the math problem and solve it.

Strategy	How to Apply
List or table	Identify information in the problem and organize it into a table to identify patterns.
Work backward	When an end result is provided, work backward from that to find the requested information.
Guess, check, revise	Start with a reasonable guess at the answer, check to see if it is correct, and revise the guess as needed until the solution is found.
Substitute simpler information	Use different numbers to simplify the problem and solve it, then solve the problem using the provided numbers.

There are many strategies for solving word problems. Some common strategies include making a list or table; working backward; guessing, checking, and revising; and substituting simpler numbers to solve the problem.

Number Sense

Number sense is an ability to use and understand numbers to make judgments and solve problems. Someone with good number sense also understands when his or her computations are reasonable in the context of a problem.

Example

Suppose you want to add three basketball scores: 35, 21, and 18.

- First, add 30 + 20 + 10 = 60.
- Then, add 5 + 1 + 8 = 14.
- Finally, combine these two sums to find the answer: 60 + 14 = 74.

Example

Suppose your brother is 72 inches tall and you want to convert this measurement from inches to feet. Suppose you use a calculator to divide 72 by 12 (number of inches in a foot) and the answer is displayed as 864. You recognize immediately that your brother cannot be 864 feet tall and realize you must have miscalculated. In this case, you incorrectly entered a multiplication operation instead of a division operation. The correct answer is 6.

Numbers and Quantity

Numbers are more than just items in a series. Each number has a distinct value relative to all other numbers. They are used to perform mathematical operations from the simplest addition to finding square roots. There are whole numbers, fractions, decimals, exponents, and square roots.

Whole Numbers

A whole number, or integer, is any positive number or zero that has no fractional part. It can be a single digit from 0 to 9, or may contain multiple digits, such as 38.

Place Value

A digit's position in a number determines its *place value.* The digit, or numeral, in the place farthest to the right before the decimal point is in the *ones position.* The next digit to the left is in the *tens position,* followed by the next digit in the *hundreds position.* As you continue to move left, the place values increase to thousands, ten thousands, and so forth.

Example

Suppose you win the lottery and receive a check for $23,152,679. Your total prize would be *twenty-three million, one hundred fifty-two thousand, six hundred seventy-nine dollars.*

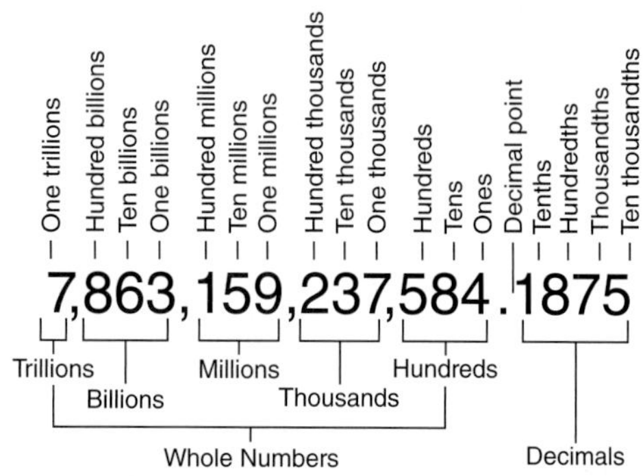

Addition

Addition is the process of combining two or more numbers. The result is called the *sum.*

Example

A plumber installs six faucets on his first job and three faucets on his second job. How many faucets does he install in total?

$$6 + 3 = 9$$

Subtraction

Subtraction is the process of finding the *difference* between two numbers.

Example

A plumber installs six faucets on her first job and three faucets on her second job. How many more faucets did she install on the first job than the second? Subtract 3 from 6 to find the answer.

$$6 - 3 = 3$$

Multiplication

Multiplication is a method of adding a number to itself a given number of times. The multiplied numbers are called *factors,* and the result is called the *product.*

Example

Suppose you are installing computers and need to purchase four adaptors. If the adaptors are $6 each, what is the total cost of the adaptors? The answer can be found by adding $6 four times:

$$\$6 + \$6 + \$6 + \$6 = \$24$$

However, the same answer is found more quickly by multiplying $6 times 4.

$$\$6 \times 4 = \$24$$

Division

Division is the process of determining how many times one number, called the *divisor,* goes into another number, called the *dividend.* The result is called the *quotient.*

Example

Suppose you are installing computers and buy a box of adaptors for $24. There are four adaptors in the box. What is the cost of each adaptor? The answer is found by dividing $24 by 4:

$$\$24 \div 4 = \$6$$

Decimals

A decimal is a kind of fraction with a denominator that is either ten, one hundred, one thousand, or some power of ten. Every decimal has three parts: a whole number (sometimes zero), followed by a decimal point, and one or more whole numbers.

Place Value

The numbers to the right of the decimal point indicate the amount of the fraction. The first place to the right of a decimal point is the tenths place. The second place to the right of the decimal point is the hundredths place. As you continue to the right, the place values move to the thousandths place, the ten thousandths place, and so on.

Example

A machinist is required to produce an airplane part to a very precise measurement of 36.876 inches. This measurement is *thirty-six and eight hundred seventy-six thousandths* inches.

36.876

Addition

To add decimals, place each number in a vertical list and align the decimal points. Then add the numbers in each column starting with the column on the right and working to the left. The decimal point in the answer drops down into the same location.

Example

A landscaper spreads 4.3 pounds of fertilizer in the front yard of a house and 1.2 pounds in the backyard. How many pounds of fertilizer did the landscaper spread in total?

$$\begin{array}{r} 4.3 \\ +\ 1.2 \\ \hline 5.5 \end{array}$$

Subtraction

To subtract decimals, place each number in a vertical list and align the decimal points. Then subtract the numbers in each column, starting with the column on the right and working to the left. The decimal point in the answer drops down into the same location.

Example

A landscaper spreads 4.3 pounds of fertilizer in the front yard of a house and 1.2 pounds in the backyard. How many more pounds were spread in the front yard than in the backyard?

$$\begin{array}{r} 4.3 \\ -\ 1.2 \\ \hline 3.1 \end{array}$$

Multiplication

To multiply decimals, place the numbers in a vertical list. Then multiply each digit of the top number by the right-hand bottom number. Multiply each digit of the top number by the bottom number in the tens position. Place the result on a second line and add a zero to the end of the number. Add the total number of decimal places in both numbers you are multiplying. This will be the number of decimal places in your answer.

Example

An artist orders 13 brushes priced at $3.20 each. What is the total cost of the order? The answer can be found by multiplying $3.20 by 13.

$$\begin{array}{r} \$3.20 \\ \times\quad 13 \\ \hline 960 \\ +\ \ 3200 \\ \hline \$41.60 \end{array}$$

Division

To divide decimals, the dividend is placed under the division symbol, the divisor is placed to the left of the division symbol, and the quotient is placed above the division symbol. Start from the *left* of the dividend and determine how many times the divisor goes into the first number. Continue this until the quotient is found. Add the dollar sign to the final answer.

$$\begin{array}{rl} 3.20 & \\ 3\overline{)9.60} & \\ 9\downarrow & \text{Product of } 3 \times 3 \\ \hline 06 & \text{Bring down the 6} \\ 6\downarrow & \text{Product of } 2 \times 3 \\ \hline 0 & \text{No remainder} \end{array}$$

Example

An artist buys a package of three brushes for $9.60. What is the cost of each brush? The quotient is found by dividing $9.60 by 3.

$$\begin{array}{r} 3.20 \\ 3\overline{)9.60} \\ -9\downarrow \\ \hline 06\downarrow \\ \hline 00 \end{array}$$

Rounding

When a number is rounded, some of the digits are changed, removed, or changed to zero so the number is easier to work with. Rounding is often used when precise calculations or measurements are not needed. For example, if you are calculating millions of dollars, it might not be important to know the amount down to the dollar or cent. Instead, you might *round* the amount to the nearest ten thousand or even hundred thousand dollars. Also, when working with decimals, the final answer might have several more decimal places than needed.

To round a number, follow these steps. First, underline the digit in the place to which you are rounding. Second, if the digit to the *right* of this place is 5 or greater, add 1 to the underlined digit. If the digit to the right is less than 5, do not change the underlined digit. Third, change all the digits to the right of the underlined digit to zero. In the case of decimals, the digits to the right of the underlined digit are removed.

Example

A company's utility expense last year was $32,678.53. The owner of the company is preparing a budget for next year and wants to round this amount to the nearest 1,000.

Step 1: Underline the digit in the 1,000 place.

$3<u>2</u>,678

Step 2: The digit to the right of 2 is greater than 5, so add 1.

2 + 1 = 3

Step 3: Change the digits to the right of the underlined digit to zero.

$33,000

Fractions

A fraction is a part of a whole. It is made up by a numerator that is divided by a denominator.

$$\frac{\text{numerator}}{\text{denominator}}$$

The *numerator* specifies the number of these equal parts that are in the fraction. The *denominator* shows how many equal parts make up the whole.

Proper

In a *proper fraction,* the numerator is less than the denominator.

Example

A lumberyard worker cuts a sheet of plywood into four equal pieces and sells three of them to a carpenter. The carpenter now has 3/4 of the original sheet. The lumberyard has 1/4 of the sheet remaining.

Improper

An *improper fraction* is a fraction where the numerator is equal to or greater than the denominator.

Example

A chef uses a chili recipe which calls for 1/2 cup of chili sauce. However, the chef makes an extra-large batch that will serve three times as many people and uses three of the 1/2 cup measures. The improper fraction in this example is 3/2 cups of chili sauce.

Mixed

A mixed number contains a whole number and a fraction. It is another way of writing an improper fraction.

Example

A chef uses a chili recipe that calls for 1/2 cup of chili sauce. However, the chef makes an extra-large batch that will serve three times as many people and uses three of the 1/2 cup measures. The improper fraction in this example is 3/2 cups of chili sauce. This can be converted to a mixed number by dividing the numerator by the denominator:

The remainder is 1, which is 1 over 2. So, the mixed number is 1 1/2 cups.

$$\begin{array}{r} 1 \\ 2\overline{)3} \\ \underline{-2} \\ 1 \end{array}$$

Reducing

Fractions are reduced to make them easier to work with. Reducing a fraction means writing it with smaller numbers, in *lowest terms.* Reducing a fraction does not change its value.

To find the lowest terms, determine the largest number that *evenly* divides both the numerator and denominator so there is no remainder. Then use this number to divide both the numerator and denominator.

Example

The owner of a hair salon asks ten customers if they were satisfied with the service they recently received. Eight customers said they were satisfied, so the fraction of satisfied customers is 8/10. The largest number that evenly divides both the numerator and denominator is 2. The fraction is reduced to its lowest terms as follows.

$$\frac{8}{10} = \frac{8 \div 2}{10 \div 2} = \frac{4}{5}$$

Addition

To add fractions, the numerators are combined and the denominator stays the same. However, fractions can only be added when they have a *common denominator.* The *least common denominator* is the smallest number to which each denominator can be converted.

Example

A snack food company makes a bag of trail mix by combining 3/8 pound of nuts with 1/8 pound of dried fruit. What is the total weight of each bag? The fractions have common denominators, so the total weight is determined by adding the fractions.

$$\frac{3}{8} + \frac{1}{8} = \frac{4}{8}$$

This answer can be reduced from 4/8 to 1/2.

Example

Suppose the company combines 1/4 pound of nuts with 1/8 cup of dried fruit. To add these fractions, the denominators must be made equal. In this case, the least common denominator is 8 because $4 \times 2 = 8$. Convert 1/4 to its equivalent of 2/8 by multiplying both numerator and denominator by 2. Then the fractions can be added as follows.

$$\frac{2}{8} + \frac{1}{8} = \frac{3}{8}$$

This answer cannot be reduced because 3 and 8 have no common factors.

Subtraction

To subtract fractions, the second numerator is subtracted from the first numerator. The denominators stay the same. However, fractions can only be subtracted when they have a *common denominator.*

Example

A snack food company makes a bag of trail mix by combining 3/8 pound of nuts with 1/8 pound of dried fruit. How much more do the nuts weigh than the dried fruit? The fractions have common denominators, so the difference can be determined by subtracting the fractions.

$$\frac{3}{8} - \frac{1}{8} = \frac{2}{8}$$

This answer can be reduced from 2/8 to 1/4.

Example

Suppose the company combines 1/4 pound of nuts with 1/8 cup of dried fruit. How much more do the nuts weigh than the dried fruit? To subtract these fractions, the denominators must be made equal. The least common denominator is 8, so convert 1/4 to its equivalent of 2/8. Then the fractions can be subtracted as follows.

$$\frac{2}{8} - \frac{1}{8} = \frac{1}{8}$$

This answer cannot be reduced.

Multiplication

Common denominators are not necessary to multiply fractions. Multiply all of the numerators and multiply all of the denominators. Reduce the resulting fraction as needed.

Example

A lab technician makes a saline solution by mixing 3/4 cup of salt with one gallon of water. How much salt should the technician mix if only 1/2 gallon of water is used? Multiply 3/4 by 1/2:

$$\frac{3}{4} \times \frac{1}{2} = \frac{3}{8}$$

Division

To divide one fraction by a second fraction, multiply the first fraction by the reciprocal of the second fraction. The *reciprocal* of a fraction is created by switching the numerator and denominator.

Example

A cabinet maker has 3/4 gallon of wood stain. Each cabinet requires 1/8 gallon of stain to finish. How many cabinets can be finished? To find the answer, divide 3/4 by 1/8, which means multiplying 3/4 by the reciprocal of 1/8.

$$\frac{3}{4} \div \frac{1}{8} = \frac{3}{4} \times \frac{8}{1} = \frac{24}{4} = 6$$

Negative Numbers

Negative numbers are those less than zero. They are written with a minus sign in front of the number.

Example

The number –34,687,295 is read as *negative thirty-four million, six hundred eighty-seven thousand, two hundred ninety-five.*

Addition

Adding a negative number is the same as subtracting a positive number.

Example

A football player gains nine yards on his first running play (+9) and loses four yards (–4) on his second play. The two plays combined result in a five yard gain.

$$9 + (-4) = 9 - 4 = 5$$

Suppose this player loses five yards on his first running play (–5) and loses four yards (–4) on his second play. The two plays combined result in a nine yard loss.

$$-5 + (-4) = -5 - 4 = -9$$

Subtraction

Subtracting a negative number is the same as adding a positive number.

Example

Suppose you receive a $100 traffic ticket. This will result in a –$100 change to your cash balance. However, you explain the circumstance to a traffic court judge, and she reduces the fine by $60. The effect is to subtract –$60 from –$100 change to your cash balance. The final result is a –$40 change.

$$-\$100 - (-\$60) = -\$100 + \$60 = -\$40$$

Multiplication

Multiplication of an odd number of negative numbers results in a *negative* product. Multiplication of an even number of negative numbers results in a *positive* product.

Example

If you lose two pounds per week, this will result in a –2 pound weekly change in your weight. After five weeks, there will be a –10 pound change to your weight.

$$5 \times (-2) = -10$$

Suppose you have been losing two pounds per week. Five weeks ago (–5) your weight was 10 pounds higher.

$$(-5) \times (-2) = 10$$

Division

Division of an odd number of negative numbers results in a *negative* quotient. Division of an even number of negative numbers results in a *positive* quotient.

Example

Suppose you lost 10 pounds, which is a –10 pound change in your weight. How many pounds on average did you lose each week if it took five weeks to lose the weight? Divide –10 by 5 to find the answer.

$$-10 \div 5 = -2$$

Suppose you lost 10 pounds. How many weeks did this take if you lost two pounds each week? Divide –10 by –2 to find the answer.

$$-10 \div -2 = 5$$

Percentages

A percentage (%) means a part of 100. It is the same as a fraction or decimal.

Representing Percentages as Decimals

To change a percentage to a decimal, move the decimal point two places to the left. For example, 1% is the same as 1/100 or 0.01; 10% is the same as 10/100 or 0.10; and 100% is the same as 100/100 or 1.0.

Example

A high school cafeteria estimates that 30% of the students prefer sesame seeds on hamburger buns. To convert this percentage to a decimal, move the decimal point two places to the left.

$$30\% = 0.30$$

Representing Fractions as Percentages

To change a fraction to a percentage, first convert the fraction to a decimal by dividing the numerator by the denominator. Then convert the decimal to a percentage by moving the decimal point two places to the right.

Example

A high school cafeteria conducts a survey and finds that three of every ten students prefer sesame seeds on hamburger buns. To change this fraction to a percentage, divide 3 by 10, and move the decimal two places to the right.

$$3 \div 10 = 0.30 = 30\%$$

Calculating a Percentage

To calculate the percentage of a number, change the percentage to a decimal and multiply by the number.

Example

A car dealer sold 10 cars last week, of which 70% were sold to women. How many cars did women buy? Change 70% to a decimal by dividing 70 by 100, which equals 0.70. Then multiply by the total number (10).

$$0.70 \times 10 = 7$$

To determine what percentage one number is of another, divide the first number by the second. Then convert the quotient into a percentage by moving the decimal point two places to the right.

Example

A car dealer sold 10 cars last week, of which seven were sold to women. What percentage of the cars were purchased by women? Divide 7 by 10 and then convert to a percentage.

$$7 \div 10 = 0.70$$

$$0.70 = 70\%$$

Ratio

A ratio compares two numbers through division. Ratios are often expressed as a fraction, but can also be written with a colon (:) or the word *to*.

Example

A drugstore's cost for a bottle of vitamins is $2.00, which it sells for $3.00. The ratio of the selling price to the cost can be expressed as follows.

$$\frac{\$3.00}{\$2.00} = \frac{3}{2}$$

$$\$3.00{:}\$2.00 = 3{:}2$$

$$\$3.00 \text{ to } \$2.00 = 3 \text{ to } 2$$

Measurement

The official system of measurement in the United States for length, volume, and weight is the US Customary system of measurement. The metric system of measurement is used by most other countries.

US Customary Measurement

The following are the most commonly used units of length in the US Customary system of measurement.

- 1 inch
- 1 foot = 12 inches
- 1 yard = 3 feet
- 1 mile = 5,280 feet

Example

An interior designer measures the length and width of a room when ordering new floor tiles. The length is measured at 12 feet 4 inches (12′ 4″). The width is measured at 8 feet 7 inches (8′ 7″).

Example

Taxi cab fares are usually determined by measuring distance in miles. A recent cab rate in Chicago was $3.25 for the first 1/9 mile or less, and $0.20 for each additional 1/9 mile.

Metric Conversion

The metric system of measurement is convenient to use because units can be converted by multiplying or dividing by multiples of 10. The following are the commonly used units of length in the metric system of measurement.

- 1 millimeter
- 1 centimeter = 10 millimeters
- 1 meter = 100 centimeters
- 1 kilometer = 1,000 meters

The following are conversions from the US Customary system to the metric system.

- 1 inch = 25.4 millimeters = 2.54 centimeters
- 1 foot = 30.48 centimeters = 0.3048 meters
- 1 yard = 0.9144 meters
- 1 mile = 1.6093 kilometers

Example

A salesperson from the United States is traveling abroad and needs to drive 100 kilometers to meet a customer. How many miles is this trip? Divide 100 kilometers by 1.6093 and round to the hundredth place.

```
                 62.138
1.6093.) 100.0000.000
          -96558
           34420
          -32186
            22340
           -16093
             62470
            -48279
             141910
            -128744
              13169
```

Estimating

Estimating is finding an *approximate* answer and often involves using rounded numbers. It is often quicker to add rounded numbers, for example, than it is to add the precise numbers.

Example

Estimate the total miles a delivery truck will travel along the following three segments of a route.

- Detroit to Chicago: 278 miles
- Chicago to St. Louis: 297 miles
- St. Louis to Wichita: 436 miles

The mileage can be estimated by rounding each segment to the nearest 100 miles.

- Detroit to Chicago: 300 miles
- Chicago to St. Louis: 300 miles
- St. Louis to Wichita: 400 miles

Add the rounded segments to estimate the total miles.

300 + 300 + 400 = 1,000 miles

Accuracy and Precision

Accuracy and precision mean slightly different things. *Accuracy* is the closeness of a measured value to its actual or true value. *Precision* is how close measured values are to each other.

Example

A machine is designed to fill jars with 16 ounces of peanut butter. The machine is considered accurate if the actual amount of peanut butter in a jar is within 0.05 ounces of the target, which is a range of 15.95 to 16.05 ounces. A machine operator tests a jar and measures the weight to be 16.01 ounces. The machine is accurate.

Suppose a machine operator tests 10 jars of peanut butter and finds the weight of each jar to be 15.4 ounces. The machine is considered precise because it fills every jar with exactly the same amount. However, it is not accurate because the amount differs too much from the target.

Algebra

An *equation* is a mathematical statement that has an equal sign (=). An *algebraic* equation is an equation that includes at least one variable. A *variable* is an unknown quantity.

Solving Equations with Variables

Solving an algebraic equation means finding the value of the variable that will make the equation a true statement. To solve a simple equation, perform inverse operations on both sides and isolate the variable.

Example

A computer consultant has sales of \$1,000. After deducting \$600 in expenses, her profit equals \$400. This is expressed with the following equation.

$$\text{sales} - \text{expenses} = \text{profit}$$
$$\$1{,}000 - \$600 = \$400$$

Example

A computer consultant has expenses of \$600 and \$400 in profit. What are her sales? An equation can be written in which sales are the unknown quantity, or variable.

$$\text{sales} - \text{expenses} = \text{profit}$$
$$\text{sales} - \$600 = \$400$$

Example

To find the value for sales, perform inverse operations on both sides and isolate the variable.

$$\begin{array}{lcccc} \text{sales} & - & \$600 & = & \$400 \\ & + & \$600 & + & \$600 \\ \hline \text{sales} & & & = & \$1{,}000 \end{array}$$

Order of Operations

The order of operations is a set of rules stating which operations in an equation are performed first. The order of operations is often stated using the acronym *PEMDAS.* PEMDAS stands for parentheses, exponents, multiplication and division, and addition and subtraction. This means anything inside parentheses is computed first. Exponents are computed next. Then, any multiplication and division operations are computed. Finally, any addition and subtraction operations are computed to find the final answer to the problem. The equation is solved from left to right by applying PEMDAS.

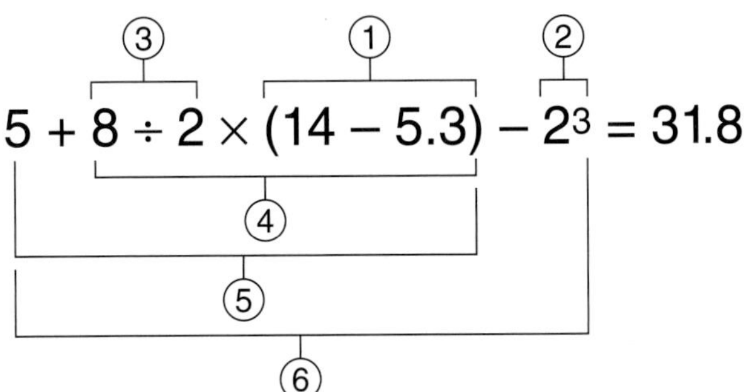

Recursive Formulas

A *recursive formula* is used to determine the next term of a sequence, using one or more of the preceding terms. The terms of a sequence are often expressed with a variable and subscript. For example, a sequence might be written as a_1, a_2, a_3, a_4, a_5, and so on. The subscript is essentially the place in line for each term. A recursive formula has two parts. The first is a starting point or seed value (a_1). The second is an equation for another number in the sequence (a_n). The second part of the formula is a function of the prior term (a_{n-1}).

Example

Suppose you buy a car for \$10,000. Assume the car declines in value 10% each year. In the second year, the car will be worth 90% of \$10,000, which is \$9,000. The following year it will be worth 90% of \$9,000, which is \$8,100. What will the car be worth in the fifth year? Use the following recursive equation to find the answer.

$$a_n = a_{n-1} \times 0.90$$
$$\text{where } a_1 = \$10{,}000$$
$$a_n = \text{value of car in the } n^{th} \text{ year}$$

Year	Value of Car
n = 1	$a_1 = \$10{,}000$
n = 2	$a_2 = a_{2-1} \times 0.90 = a_1 \times 0.90 = \$10{,}000 \times 0.90 = \$9{,}000$
n = 3	$a_3 = a_{3-1} \times 0.90 = a_2 \times 0.90 = \$9{,}000 \times 0.90 = \$8{,}100$
n = 4	$a_4 = a_{4-1} \times 0.90 = a_3 \times 0.90 = \$8{,}100 \times 0.90 = \$7{,}290$
n = 5	$a_5 = a_{5-1} \times 0.90 = a_4 \times 0.90 = \$7{,}290 \times 0.90 = \$6{,}561$

Geometry

Geometry is a field of mathematics that deals with shapes, such as circles and polygons. A *polygon* is any shape whose sides are straight. Every polygon has three or more sides.

Parallelograms

A *parallelogram* is a four-sided figure with two pairs of parallel sides. A *rectangle* is a type of parallelogram with four right angles. A *square* is a special type of parallelogram with four right angles (90 degrees) and four equal sides.

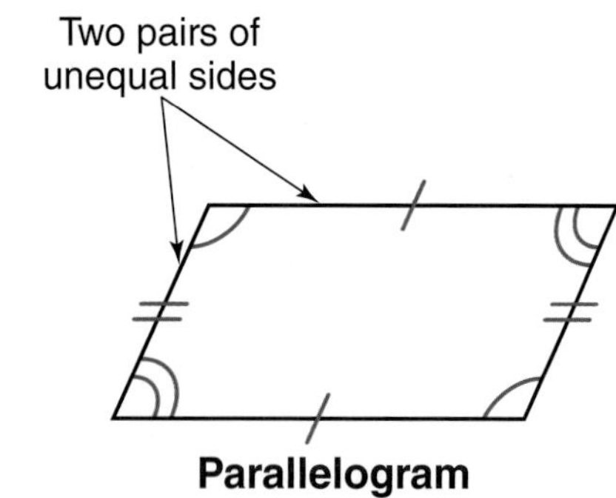

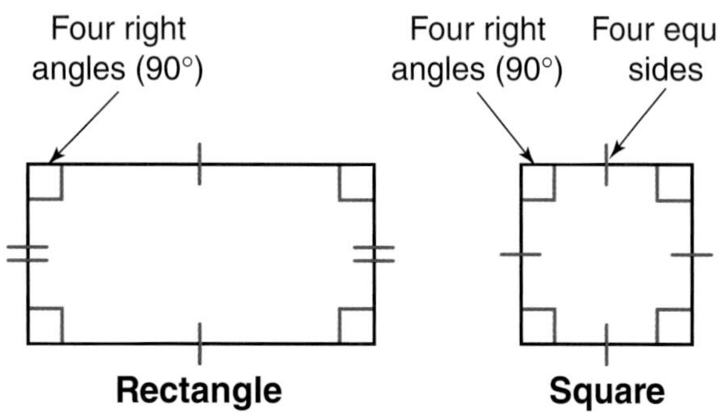

Example

Real-life examples of squares include ceramic floor and wall tiles, and each side of a die. Real-life examples of a rectangle include a football field, pool table, and most doors.

Circles and Half Circles

A *circle* is a figure in which every point is the same distance from the center. The distance from the center to a point on the circle is called the *radius.* The distance across the circle through the center is the *diameter.* A half circle is formed by dividing a whole circle along the diameter.

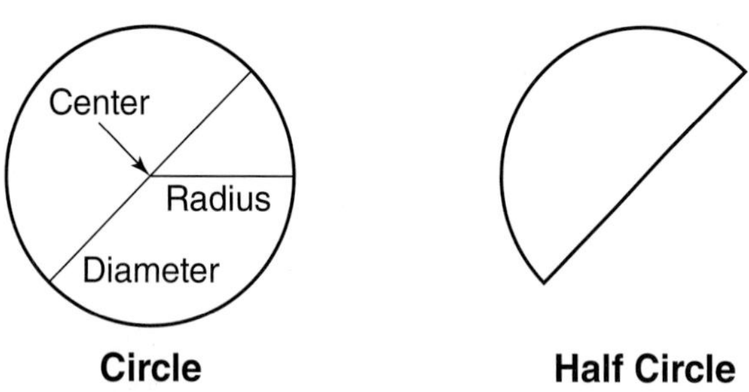

Example

Real-life examples of circles include wheels of all sizes.

Triangles

A three-sided polygon is called a *triangle.* The following are four types of triangles, which are classified according to their sides and angles.

- *Equilateral:* Three equal sides and three equal angles.
- *Isosceles:* Two equal sides and two equal angles.
- *Scalene:* Three unequal sides and three unequal angles.
- *Right:* One right angle; may be isosceles or scalene.

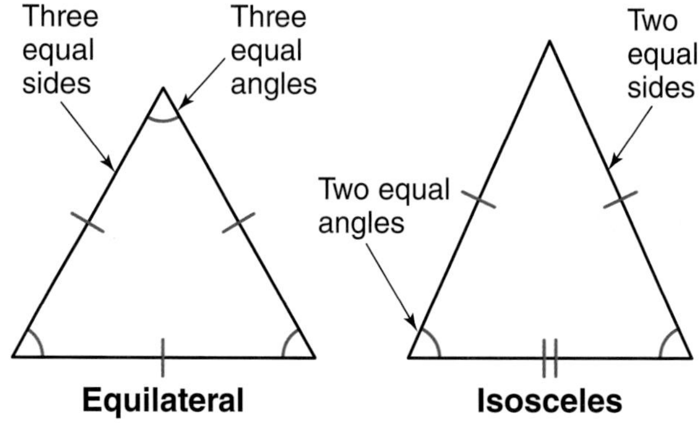

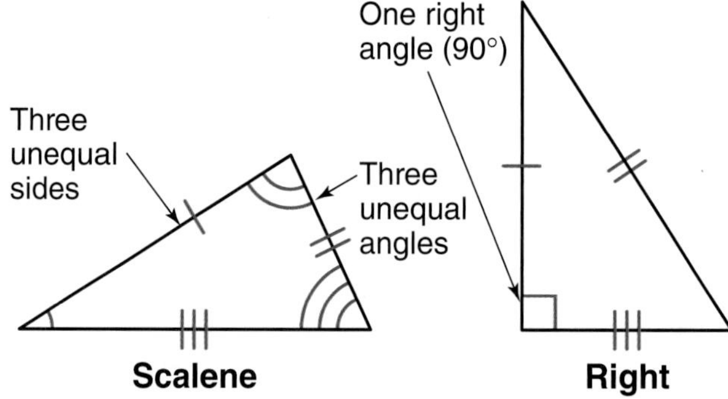

Example

Real-life examples of equilateral triangles are the sides of a classical Egyptian pyramid.

Perimeter

A *perimeter* is a measure of length around a figure. Add the length of each side to measure the perimeter of any figure whose sides are all line segments, such as a parallelogram or triangle.

The perimeter of a circle is called the *circumference*. To measure the perimeter, multiply the diameter by pi (π). Pi is approximately equal to 3.14. The following formulas can be used to calculate the perimeters of various figures.

Figure	Perimeter
parallelogram	2 × width + 2 × length
square	4 × side
rectangle	2 × width + 2 × length
triangle	side + side + side
circle	π × diameter

Example

A professional basketball court is a rectangle 94 feet long and 50 feet wide. The perimeter of the court is calculated as follows.

2 × 94 feet + 2 × 50 feet = 288 feet

Example

A tractor tire has a 43 inch diameter. The circumference of the tire is calculated as follows.

43 inches × 3.14 = 135 inches

Area

Area is a measure of the amount of surface within the perimeter of a flat figure. Area is measured in square units, such as square inches, square feet, or square miles. The areas of the following figures are calculated using the corresponding formulas.

Figure	Area
parallelogram	base × height
square	side × side
rectangle	length × width
triangle	1/2 × base × height
circle	π × radius² = π × radius × radius

Example

An interior designer needs to order decorative tiles to fill the following spaces. Measure the area of each space in square feet.

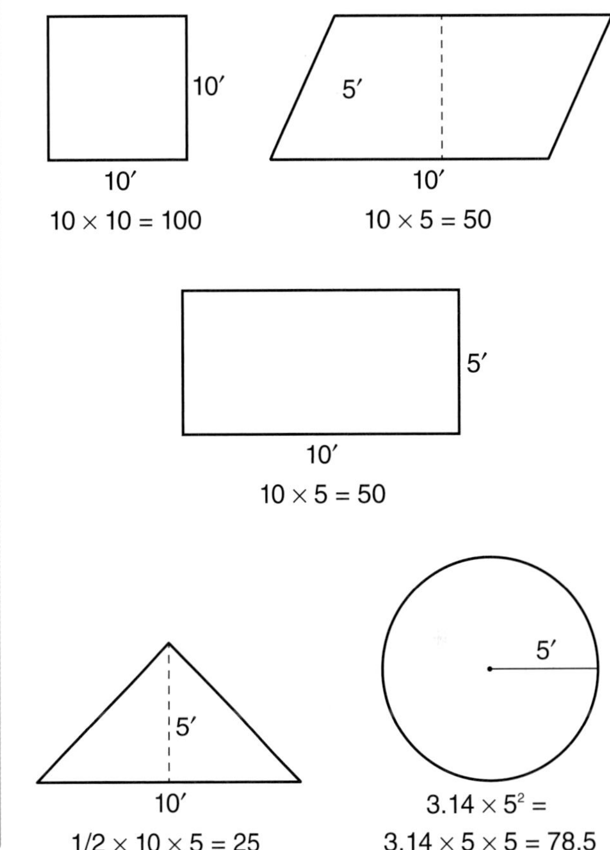

Surface Area

Surface area is the total area of the surface of a figure occupying three-dimensional space, such as a cube or prism. A *cube* is a solid figure that has six identical square faces. A *prism* has bases or ends which have the same size and shape and are parallel to each other, and each of whose sides is a parallelogram. The following are the formulas to find the surface area of a cube and a prism.

Object	Surface Area
cube	6 × side × side
prism	2 × [(length × width) + (width × height) + (length × height)]

Example

A manufacturer of cardboard boxes wants to determine how much cardboard is needed to make the following size boxes. Calculate the surface area of each in square inches.

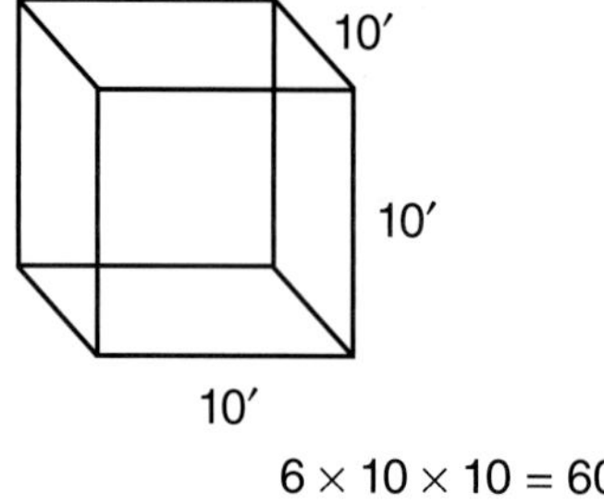

6 × 10 × 10 = 600

Cube

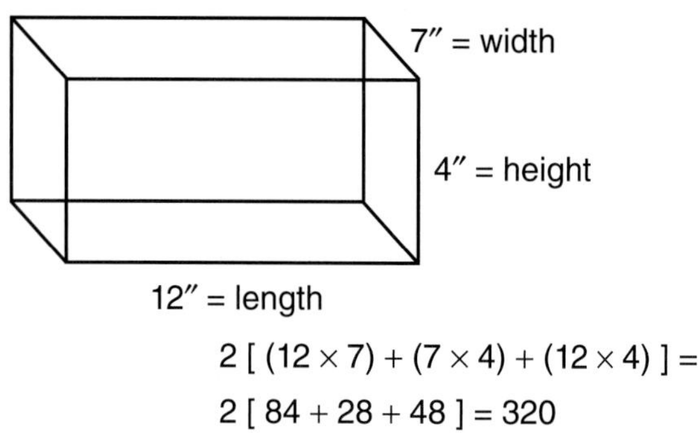

2 [(12 × 7) + (7 × 4) + (12 × 4)] =

2 [84 + 28 + 48] = 320

Prism

Volume

Volume is the three-dimensional space occupied by a figure and is measured in cubic units, such as cubic inches or cubic feet. The volumes of the following figures are calculated using the corresponding formulas.

Solid Figure	Volume
cube	side³ = side × side × side
prism	length × width × height
cylinder	π × radius² × height = π × radius × radius × height
sphere	4/3 × π × radius³ = 4/3 × π × radius × radius × radius

Example

Find the volume of packing material needed to fill the following boxes. Measure the volume of each in cubic inches.

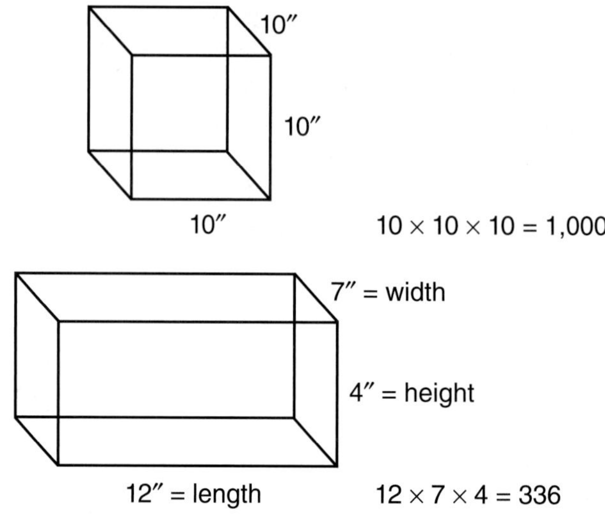

10 × 10 × 10 = 1,000

12 × 7 × 4 = 336

Example

Find the volume of grain that will fill the following cylindrical silo. Measure the volume in cubic feet.

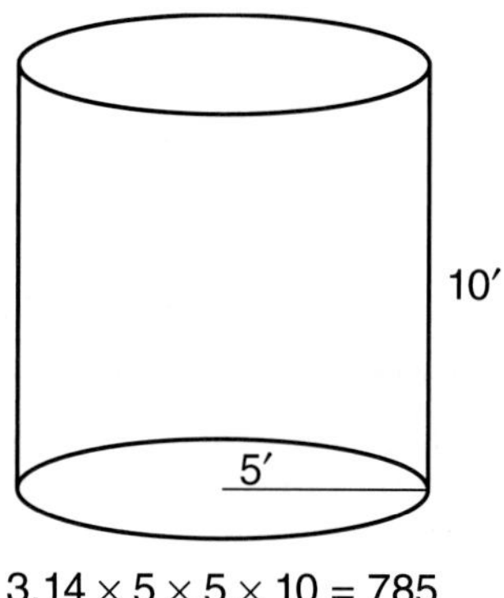

3.14 × 5 × 5 × 10 = 785

Example

A manufacturer of pool toys wants to stuff soft material into a ball with a 3 inch radius. Find the cubic inches of material that will fit into the ball.

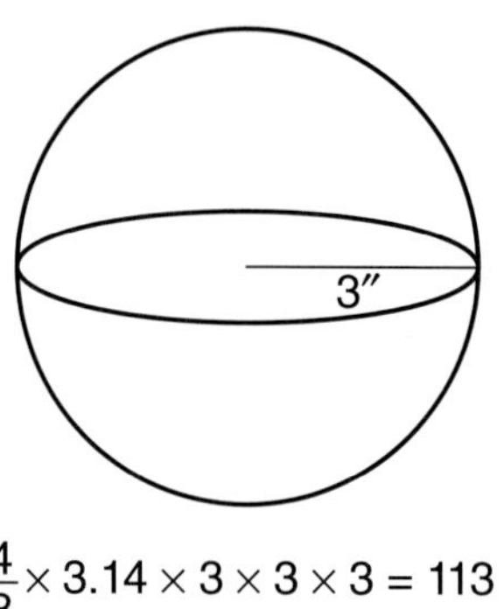

$\frac{4}{3}$ × 3.14 × 3 × 3 × 3 = 113

Data Analysis and Statistics

Graphs are used to illustrate data in a picture-like format. It is often easier to understand data when they are shown in a graphical form instead of a numerical form in a table. Common types of graphs are bar graphs, line graphs, and circle graphs.

A *bar graph* organizes information along a vertical axis and horizontal axis. The vertical axis runs up and down one side; the horizontal axis runs along the bottom.

A *line graph* also organizes information on vertical and horizontal axes; however, data are graphed as a continuous line rather than a set of bars. Line graphs are often used to show trends over a period of time.

A *circle graph* looks like a divided circle and shows how a whole object is cut up into parts. Circle graphs are also called *pie charts* and are often used to illustrate percentages.

Example

A business shows the following balances in its cash account for the months of March through July. These data are illustrated below in bar and line graphs.

Month	Account Balance	Month	Account Balance
March	$400	June	$800
April	$600	July	$900
May	$500		

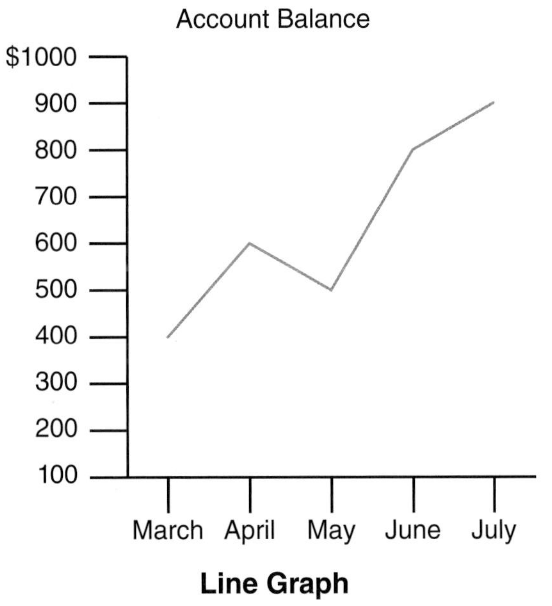

Line Graph

Example

A business lists the percentage of its expenses in the following categories. These data are displayed in the following circle graph.

Expenses	Percentage
Cost of goods	25
Salaries	25
Rent	21
Utilities	17
Advertising	12

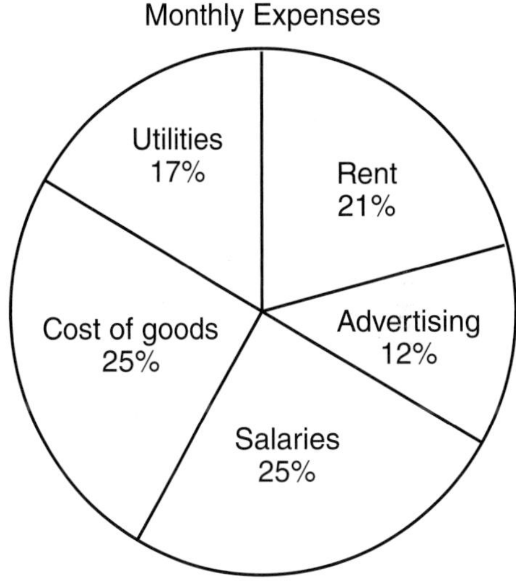

Circle Graph

Math Models for Business and Retail

Math skills used in business and retail are the same math skills required in everyday life. The ability to add, subtract, multiply, and divide different types of numbers is very important. However, this type of math is often focused on prices, taxes, profits, and losses.

Markup

Markup is a retailing term for the amount by which price exceeds the cost. One way to express markup is in dollars. Another way to express markup is percentage. The *markup percentage* is the amount of the markup as a percentage of the cost.

Example

A retailer pays $4 for a pair of athletic socks and prices them for sale at $7. The dollar markup is $3.

selling price – cost = dollar markup

$7 – $4 = $3

Example

A pair of athletic socks, which cost $4, is priced at $7. The dollar markup is $3 . To find the markup percentage, divide $3 by $4. The markup percentage is 75%.

markup dollars ÷ cost = markup percentage

$3 ÷ $4 = 0.75 = 75%

Percentage Markup to Determine Selling Price

The selling price of an item can be determined if you know the markup percentage and the cost. First, convert the markup percentage to a decimal. Next multiply the cost by the decimal. Then, add the markup dollars to the cost to determine the selling price. Another way to find the selling price is to convert the markup percentage to a decimal and add 1.0. Then multiply this amount by the cost.

Example

A pair of athletic socks costs $4, which the retailer marks up by 75%. Find the selling price.

1. Convert the markup percentage to a decimal.

   75% = 0.75

2. Multiply the cost by the markup.

   cost × markup = dollar markup

   $4 × 0.75 = $3

3. Add the $3 markup to the $4 cost to find the selling price. The selling price is $7.

   $4 + $3 = $7

Example

A pair of athletic socks costs $4, which the retailer marks up by 75%. Find the selling price.

1. Convert the 75% markup percentage to 0.75 and add 1.0.

   0.75 + 1.0 = 1.75

2. Multiply 1.75 by the $4 cost to find the selling price.

   $4 × 1.75 = $7

Markdown

A *markdown* is the amount by which the selling price of an item is reduced. Sometimes a markdown is also called a *discount.* To find the amount of a markdown, subtract the new or discounted price from the original price. A markdown can also be expressed as a percentage of the original price. Sometimes this is called a *percentage discount.*

Example

A package of meat at a supermarket is originally priced at $10. However, the meat has not sold and is nearing its expiration date. The supermarket wants to sell it quickly, so it reduces the price to $6. This is a markdown of $4.

selling price – discounted price = dollar markdown

$10 – $6 = $4

Example

A package of meat at a supermarket is originally priced at $10. However, the meat has not sold and is nearing its expiration date. The supermarket wants to sell it quickly, so it marks down the price by $4. The markdown percentage is determined by dividing the $4 markdown by the original $10 price.

markdown ÷ selling price = markdown percentage

$4 ÷ $10 = 40%

Gross Profit

Gross profit is a company's net sales minus the cost of goods sold. *Gross margin* is often expressed as a percentage of revenue.

Example

A wristband manufacturer generated net sales of $100,000 last year. The cost of goods sold for the wristbands was $30,000. The net sales of $100,000 minus the $30,000 cost of goods sold leaves a gross profit of $70,000.

net sales – cost of goods sold = gross profit

$100,000 – $30,000 = $70,000

Example

The gross profit of $70,000 divided by the net sales of $100,000 is 0.70, or 70%.

gross profit ÷ net sales = gross margin percentage

$70,000 ÷ $100,000 = 0.70 = 70%

Net Income or Loss

Net income or loss is a company's revenue after total expenses are deducted from gross profit. Total expenses include marketing, administration, interest, and taxes. A company earns a *net income* when gross profit exceeds expenses. A *net loss* is incurred when expenses exceed gross profit.

Example

A wristband manufacturer had a gross profit of $70,000. In addition, expenses for marketing, administration, interest, and taxes were $50,000. Net profit is calculated by subtracting the total expenses of $50,000 from the gross profit of $70,000. The net profit was $20,000.

gross profit on sales – total expenses = net income or loss

$70,000 – $50,000 = $20,000

Break-Even Point

A *break-even point* is the number of units a company must sell to cover its costs and expenses and earn a zero profit. Use the following formula to find a company's break-even point.

total costs ÷ selling price = break-even point

Sales Tax

Sales tax is a tax collected on the selling price of a good or service. The sales tax rate is usually expressed as a percentage of the selling price. Sales tax is calculated by multiplying the sale price by the tax rate.

Example

Suppose you buy a T-shirt for $10.00. How much is the sales tax if the tax rate is 5%? Convert 5% to a decimal (.05) and multiply it by the sale price.

sale price × sales tax rate percentage = sales tax

$10 × 0.05 = $0.50

Return on Investment

Return on investment (ROI) is a calculation of a company's net profit as a percentage of the owner's investment. One way to determine ROI is to divide net profit by the owner's investment.

Example

Suppose you start a dry-cleaning business with a $100,000 investment, and you earn a $20,000 net profit during the first year. Divide $20,000 by $100,000, which equals a 20% return on your investment.

net income ÷ owner's investment = return on investment (ROI)

$20,000 ÷ $100,000 = 0.20 = 20%

Glossary

529 plan. Savings plan for education operated by a state or educational institution. (19)

A

ability. Mastery of a skill or the capacity to do something. (19)

absolute advantage. Exists when a country or business can produce goods more efficiently, using the same amount of resources, and at a lower cost than the other country or business. (15)

acceptable use policy. Set of rules that explains what is and is not acceptable use of company-owned and company-operated equipment and networks. (21)

acceptance. All parties involved must agree to the terms of the contract. (13)

accountability. Accepting responsibility for one's actions. (8)

accounting. System of recording business transactions and analyzing, verifying, and reporting results. (4)

acquisition. Outright purchase of one business by another business. (16)

action plan. List of the marketing tactics with details about how to execute each tactic. (18)

active listening. Fully processing what a person says and interacting with the person who is speaking. (10)

adaptive organization. Organization that has the ability to adjust to events in the internal and external environment that affect operation of a business. (7)

administrative management. Classical management theory that focuses on the organization as a whole and identifies effective ways to organize and manage a business. (2)

adverse impact. Employment decisions, practices, or policies that appear neutral but have a discriminatory effect on a protected group. (7)

angel investor. Private investor who provides funding for a new business in exchange for an ownership interest. (16)

apprenticeship. Combination of on-the-job training, work experience, and classroom instruction. (19)

aptitude. Characteristic that an individual has developed naturally; also called talents. (19)

attitude. How personal thoughts or feelings affect a person's outward behavior. (10)

attrition. Reduction in staff as a result of employees retiring or resigning from an organization without plans to backfill those positions. (6)

authority. Power to carry out a task and make decisions. (1)

B

background check. Evaluation of personal data that is publicly available. (6)

barrier. Anything that prevents clear, effective communication. (9)

behavioral management. Theory that focuses on improving the organization through understanding employee motivation and behavior; also called *human relations management*. (2)

behavioral question. Questions that draw on a person's previous experiences and decisions. (20)

benefit. Form of noncash compensation received in addition to a wage or salary. (6)

bonus. Money added to an employee's base wage or salary. (6)

breach of contract. When one or more parties do not follow the agreed terms of a contract without having a legitimate reason. (13)

break-even point. Point at which revenue from sales is equal to the cost of manufacturing, transporting, and selling products. (18)

budget. Financial plan that reflects anticipated revenue in numerical terms and shows how it will be allocated in the operation of the business. (3)

bureaucratic management. Classical management theory that is an approach based on precisely defined procedures and a clearly defined order of command. (2)

business. All the activities involved in developing and exchanging goods and services. (13)

Note: The number in parentheses following each definition indicates the chapter in which the term can be found.

business cycle. Alternating periods of economic expansion and contraction. (14)

business environment. Internal and external factors that affect an organization. (13)

business ethics. Rules for professional conduct and integrity in all areas of business. (5)

business plan. Written document that describes a business, how it operates, and how it makes a profit. (3)

business risk. Possibility of loss or injury that might occur in an organization. (17)

C

capacity. Person is legally able to enter into a binding agreement. (13)

capitalism. Economic system in which resources are privately owned by individuals rather than the government; also known as a *free-enterprise system*. (14)

carbon footprint. Measurement of how much the everyday behaviors of an individual, company, or community impact the environment. (13)

career. Series of related jobs in the same profession. (19)

career and technical student organization (CTSO). National student organizations with local school chapters that are related to career and technical education (CTE) courses. (19)

career cluster. Sixteen groups of occupational and career specialties that share common knowledge and skills. (19)

career ladder. Series of jobs organized in order of education and experience requirements. (19)

career objective. Summary of the type of job for which the applicant is looking. (20)

career pathway. Subgroup within a career cluster that reflects occupations requiring similar knowledge and skills. (19)

career plan. List of steps on a timeline to reach a career goal; also known as a *postsecondary plan*. (19)

certification. Professional status earned by an individual after passing an exam focused on a specific body of knowledge. (19)

chain of command. Authority structure in a company from the highest to the lowest levels; also known as *line of authority*. (5)

change management. Applying processes and techniques to help employees adjust to organizational changes. (7)

channel. How the message is transmitted, such as face-to-face conversation, telephone, or any other vehicle that is appropriate for the situation. (9)

channel of distribution. Path goods take through the supply chain. (18)

chart. Shows a process or hierarchy. (4)

chronological résumé. Résumé that lists information in reverse chronological order, with the most recent information listed first. (20)

claim. Formal request to an insurance company for compensation related to a covered loss or event. (17)

classical management. Theory that focuses on organizing work with the goal of increasing worker productivity; also called *classical perspective of management* and *classical approach to management*. (2)

cloud computing. Using Internet-based resources to store and access data rather than on a personal computer or local server. (21)

code of conduct. Document that identifies the manner in which employees should behave while at work or when representing the company. (5)

code of ethics. Document that dictates how business is conducted within the organization; also called a *statement of ethics*. (5)

collaboration skills. Skills that enable individuals to work with others to achieve a common goal. (8)

collection agency. Company that collects past-due bills for a fee or a percentage of the amount collected. (17)

college access. Building awareness about college opportunities, providing guidance regarding college admissions, and identifying ways to pay for college. (19)

command economy. Economic system in which the government makes all economic decisions for its citizens and answers the three economic questions; also called a *centrally planned economy*. (14)

commission. Income paid as a percentage of sales made by a salesperson. (6)

communication. Sending and receiving of messages that convey information, ideas, feelings, and beliefs. (1)

communication competence. Individual's ability to understand basic principles of communication and apply them when interacting with others. (9)

communication management. Planning and execution of communication from an organization to its external and internal customers. (9)
communication plan. Road map that includes objectives and goals that clearly outline the way in which communication takes place. (7)
communication process. Series of actions on the part of the sender and receiver of a message and path the message follows. (9)
communication skills. Skills that affect a person's ability to understand others, establish positive relationships, and perform in most situations. (9)
communism. System in which the government's goal is to distribute the country's wealth among all its citizens equally or according to need. (14)
comparative advantage. Exists when a country or business specializes in products that it can produce efficiently. (15)
compensation. Payment to an employee for work performed including wages or salaries, incentives, and benefits. (6)
compensation and benefits laws. Laws that cover fair wages and benefits for all employees. (7)
competition. Two or more businesses attempting to attract the same customers. (3)
competitive analysis. Tool used to compare the strengths and weaknesses of a business with those of competing businesses. (3)
conceptual skills. Ability to formulate new ideas and think in abstract terms. (1)
concurrent control. Management technique that focuses on identifying and correcting problems that may occur while an activity is in progress. (11)
confidence. Being certain and secure about one's own abilities and judgment. (10)
confidentiality. Specific information about a company or its employees is not shared except with those who have clearance to receive it. (5)
conflict. Strong disagreement between two or more people or a difference that prevents agreement. (8)
conflict of interest. Exists when an employee has competing interests or loyalties. (5)
conflict resolution. Process of recognizing and resolving disputes. (8)
conflict-resolution skills. Skills required to resolve a situation that could lead to hostile behavior, such as shouting or fighting. (8)
consideration. Something of value is promised in return for something of value received. (13)
contract manufacturing. Transferring production work to another company; also known as *outsourcing.* (15)
contingency approach. Contemporary management theory that suggests the appropriate style of management depends on the situation. (2)
contingency plan. Backup plan that outlines alternative courses of action to take if other plans prove unproductive or circumstances beyond control change. (3)
continuous improvement plan. Set of activities designed to enhance the production process through constant review and product testing. (12)
contract. Legally binding agreement between two or more people or businesses. (13)
contract law. Regulates how contracts are written, executed, and enforced. (13)
controllable risk. Situation that can be minimized by actions or avoidance. (17)
controlling. Continuous process of comparing actual outcomes with planned outcomes and taking corrective action when goals are not met. (1)
cookies. Bits of data stored on a computer that record information about the websites the user has visited. (21)
corporate culture. Describes how the owners and employees of a company think, feel, and act as a business; also known as *organizational culture.* (5)
corporate social responsibility (CSR). All the actions taken by a business to promote social good. (5)
corporation. Business that is legally separate from its owners and has most of the legal rights of an actual person. (13)
cost-benefit analysis. Method of weighing the costs against the benefits of an action, a purchase, or a financial decision. (4)
cost standard. Estimated or predetermined cost to produce a good or deliver a service. (11)
cover message. Letter or e-mail sent with a résumé to introduce the applicant and summarize his or her reasons for applying for a job; also called a *cover letter* or *letter of application.* (20)

credit. Agreement or contract to receive goods or services before actually paying for them. (17)

credit bureau. Private firm that maintains consumer-credit data and provides credit information to businesses for a fee. (17)

credit report. Record of a business or person's credit history and financial behavior. (17)

credit risk. Potential of credit to the business not being repaid. (17)

critical thinking. Ability to analyze and interpret a situation and make reasonable judgments and decisions. (9)

cultural competency. Acknowledgement of cultural differences and the ability to adapt one's communication style to successfully send and receive messages despite those differences. (15)

cultural sensitivity. Acting with respect and awareness toward cultures different from one's own. (9)

culture. Shared beliefs, customs, practices, and social behavior of a particular group or nation. (5, 15)

current ratio. Shows the relationship of current assets to current liabilities. (11)

customer service. Way in which a business provides services before, during, and after a sale. (5)

customer-focused mindset. Attitude that customer satisfaction always comes first. (5)

cyberattack. Attempt to steal, damage, or destroy data or a computer system. (11)

cyberbullying. Using the Internet to harass or threaten an individual. (21)

cyberloafing. Occurs when an employee uses the Internet at work for personal use instead of performing required work tasks. (11)

cybersecurity. Protecting an information system against unintended or malicious changes or use. (11)

cybersecurity risk management. Process of evaluating risk and taking steps to avoid or minimize loss to the information technology system of an organization. (17)

D

data mining. Searching through large amounts of digital data to find useful patterns or trends. (4)

data processing. Process of transforming information into usable form. (4)

data security. Measures used to protect the privacy and prevent unauthorized access to the computers, databases, and websites of a business. (11)

debt financing. Borrowing money that is repaid in the future. (16)

debt ratio. Shows the percentage of dollars owed as compared to assets owned. (11)

decision-making. Process of choosing a course of action after evaluating available information and weighing the costs and benefits of alternative actions and their consequences. (4)

decline stage. Stage in which product sales begin to decrease. (18)

decoding. Translation of a message into terms the receiver can understand. (9)

deductible. Amount the insured is responsible for paying before the insurance pays a claim. (17)

deflation. General decline in prices throughout an economy. (14)

delegate. To assign authority to someone else to carry out a task. (1)

Deming Prize. Japanese award given to organizations that make the greatest strides in TQM. (12)

departmentalization. Process of creating groups whose members work together to accomplish the goals of an organization. (5)

digital citizenship. Standard of appropriate behavior when using technology to communicate. (21)

digital communication. Exchange of information through electronic means. (21)

digital footprint. Data history of all an individual's online activities. (21)

digital literacy. Ability to use technology to locate, evaluate, communicate, and create information. (21)

direct report. Employee who reports directly to one manager. (1)

directing. Process of influencing employees by supervising and overseeing them as they perform their job duties, providing motivation for them to be successful, and encouraging open communication. (8)

discrimination. Occurs when an individual is treated unfairly because of his or her race, gender, religion, national origin, disability, or age. (7)

distribution. Refers to the activities involved in getting a good or service to the end user; also known as *place*. (12)

diversification. Way to reduce risk that involves adding different goods, services, locations, or markets. (16)

diversity. Having representatives from different backgrounds, cultures, or demographics in a group. (1)

division of labor. Specialization of individuals who perform specific tasks; also called *job-specialization.* (2)

downsizing. General reduction in the number of employees within an organization. (6)

E

economic and political risk. Situation that occurs when the economy suffers due to negative business conditions in the United States or the world. (17)

economic environment. Consists of external factors outside the organization that directly influence its success. (14)

economic indicator. Statistic used to measure certain types of economic activities. (14)

economic problem. Concept that resources are limited and needs and wants are unlimited. (14)

economic system. Structure in which resources are used to create goods and services. (14)

economics. Science that examines how goods and services are produced, sold, and used. (14)

education. General process of acquiring knowledge and skills. (19)

effectiveness. Intended goals or objectives are achieved. (1)

efficiency. To use resources to get a job done with minimal waste of time and effort. (1)

embargo. Governmental order that prohibits trade with a foreign country. (15)

emotional control. Each person directs his or her feelings and reactions toward a desirable result that is socially acceptable. (8)

empathy. Having the ability to share someone else's emotions and showing understanding of how the other person is feeling. (10)

employability skill. Applicable skill used to help an individual find a job, perform in the workplace, and gain success in a job or career. (19)

employee handbook. Translates the policies of the business into day-to-day information that the employees need to know. (7)

employee perception. Employee's view of the organization and its impact on an individual. (5)

employee relations. Organization's efforts to manage communication and cooperation between employees. (7)

employer identification number (EIN). Number assigned by the IRS for businesses to use when preparing federal tax returns and forms. (13)

employment contract. Describes the terms of employment between a business and an employee. (13)

employment verification. Process through which the information provided on an applicant's résumé is verified that previous employment information is correct. (6)

empowerment. Management practice of giving decision-making authority to employees. (8)

encoding. Process of turning the ideas for a message into symbols that can be communicated. (9)

English as a second language (ESL). Field of education concerned with teaching English to those whose native language is not English. (9)

entrepreneur. Person who risks his or her own resources to start and operate a business. (16)

entrepreneurship. Capacity to take the risks and responsibilities of starting a new business. (16)

equal employment opportunity (EEO) laws. Laws that ensure that all workers have an equal opportunity for employment. (7)

equity financing. Capital brought into the business in exchange for a percentage of ownership in the business. (16)

ergonomics. Science concerned with designing and arranging things people use so that they can interact efficiently and safely. (7)

ethics. Rules of behavior based on a group's ideas about what is right and wrong. (5)

etiquette. Art of using good manners in any situation. (9)

evidence-based management. Emerging management theory in which decisions are based on a combination of critical thinking and the best-available evidence. (2)

exit interview. Formal interview with a departing employee during which he or she is asked to provide information about his or her reasons for leaving and his or her experience with the organization. (6)

expansion. Period of growth when GDP is rising. (14)

extractor. Business or person that takes natural resources from the land. (13)

extrinsic motivation. Engaging in activity in which an individual receives a reward from someone else. (8)

for-profit school. School that is set up to earn money for investors. (19)

franchise. License to sell a company's goods or services within a certain territory or location. (13)

F

factors of production. Economic resources used to make goods and services for a population. (14)

family leave. Time off work for certain life events. (6)

feedback. Receiver's response to the sender and concludes the communication process. (9)

feedback control. Management technique in which control happens after the activity is completed; also called *post-action control.* (11)

feedforward control. Management technique that involves anticipating potential problems before an activity starts; also called *preventative control.* (11)

financial control. Policies and procedures used by an organization to manage its finances. (11)

financial ratio. Evaluates the overall financial condition of the business by showing the relationships between selected figures on financial statements. (11)

financial statement analysis. Process of reviewing information provided in financial statements to analyze the performance of the business. (11)

finished goods inventory. Assortment or selection of finished products for sale that a business has in stock. (12)

firewall. Program that monitors information coming into a computer. (21)

fiscal policy. Taxation and spending decisions made by the president and Congress. (14)

flextime. Policy allowing employees to adjust work schedules to match personal schedules better. (6)

flowchart. Type of chart that depicts steps in a process. (4)

foreign exchange rate. Cost to convert one currency into another. (15)

formal communication. Sharing of information that conforms to specific protocol. (9)

formal education. Education received in a school, college, or university. (19)

for-profit business. Organization that generates revenue with the objective of earning a profit for its owners. (1)

G

glass ceiling. Invisible barrier that prevents a group of people from job advancement. (1)

global management. How an organization manages and directs its businesses internationally; also known as *international management.* (15)

global manager. Person who manages a business across country borders. (15)

globalization. Connection made among nations worldwide when economies freely move goods, labor, and money across borders. (15)

goal. Something to be achieved in a specified timeframe. (3)

graduate education. Education received after an individual has earned a bachelor degree. (19)

grant. Financial award that does not have to be repaid and is typically provided by a nonprofit organization. (19)

graph. Depicts information using lines, bars, or other symbols. (4)

grievance. Written claim by an employee stating that he or she was adversely affected by the application of a written company policy. (7)

gross domestic product (GDP). Measure of the value of all goods and services produced by a nation during a specific timeframe, usually one year. (14)

growth stage. Period in which product sales increase rapidly. (18)

H

hacking. Illegally accessing or altering digital devices, software, or networks. (21)

harassment. Uninvited conduct toward a person based on his or her race, color, religion, sex, national origin, age, or disability. (7)

hard skills. Critical skills necessary to perform the required work-related tasks of a position; also called *job-specific skills.* (1)

harvest strategy. Plan for extracting the cash from a business, brand, or product line. (16)

health and safety laws. Laws that establish regulations to eliminate illness and injury in the workplace. (7)
hierarchy. System in which people, items, or issues are ranked in order of importance. (2)
hierarchy of needs. Order in which certain needs are satisfied before others. (8)
human capital. Knowledge and skills that contribute to an individual's ability to produce economic benefit. (6)
human resources (HR) department. Division that oversees the human resources within an organization. (6)
human resources management (HRM). All the activities that lead to attracting, recruiting, hiring, training, evaluating, and compensating employees. (6)
human resources planning. Process of creating a strategy to meet the employment needs of an organization. (6)
human risk. Situation caused by human actions. (17)
hypothetical question. Questions that require a candidate to imagine a situation and describe how he or she would act. (20)

I

identity theft. Illegal act that involves stealing someone's personal information and using it to commit theft or fraud. (21)
illustration. Type of visual that includes maps, drawings, and photographs. (4)
incentive. Type of compensation based on performance; also known as *pay for performance*. (6)
inclusion. Practice of recognizing, accepting, valuing, and respecting diversity. (6)
income statement. Financial statement that reports the revenue and expenses of a business for a specific timeframe and shows a net income or net loss. (4)
Industrial Revolution. Time in history when machines replaced human and animal power. (2)
inflation. General rise in prices throughout an economy. (14)
inflation rate. Rate of change in prices calculated on a monthly or yearly basis. (14)
informal communication. Casual sharing of information without customs or rules of etiquette involved. (9)
information technology (IT). Use of computers for storing, sending, and retrieving information. (4)
information technology (IT) control. Procedures an organization follows to ensure information technology is used as intended, data is accurate, and information is in legal compliance. (4)
informational interviewing. Strategy used to interview a professional to ask for advice and direction, rather than asking for a job opportunity. (19)
infringement. Any use of copyrighted material without permission. (21)
inorganic growth. Occurs when a company buys a new product line, buys another business, or merges with another company. (16)
insider trading. When an employee uses private company information to purchase company stock or other securities for personal gain. (5)
insurable risk. Risk that insurance will cover in the event of loss. (17)
insurance. Financial service used to protect against loss. (17)
insurance policy. Contract that defines the types of losses covered, amount of coverage in dollars, and other conditions to which the parties agree. (17)
integrity. Honesty of a person's actions. (5)
intellectual property. Something that comes from a person's mind, such as an idea, invention, or process. (21)
intercultural communication. Process of sending and receiving messages between people of various cultures. (9)
interest. Amount a borrower pays to a lender for a loan. (14); Feeling of wanting to learn more about a topic or to be involved in an activity. (19)
interest rate. Cost of a loan. (14)
intermediary. Business that purchases goods from producers and resells them to individuals or businesses. (13)
International Organization for Standardization (ISO). Worldwide network composed of members from 162 countries that develops and publishes international standards. (12)
international trade. Buying and selling of goods and services between two or more countries. (15)
Internet protocol address. Unique number used to identify an electronic device connected to the Internet; also known as an *IP address*. (21)

internship. Short-term position with a sponsoring organization that gives the intern an opportunity to gain on-the-job experience in a certain field of study or occupation. (19)

interpersonal communication. Communication that occurs between two people. (9)

interpersonal skills. Skills that enable a person to work effectively with others; also called *human skills*. (1)

intrapersonal communication. Conversation a person has with himself or herself; also known as *self-talk*. (9)

intrinsic motivation. Engaging in an activity that is personally rewarding. (8)

introduction. Making a person known to someone else by sharing the person's name and other relevant information. (10)

introduction stage. Time when a new product is first brought to the market. (18)

inventory. Assortment or selection of items a business has on hand at a particular point in time. (12)

inventory management. Area of management involved in ordering items, receiving them on arrival, and paying vendors. (12)

ISO 9000. Series, or group, of international quality standards that define, establish, and maintain an effective quality assurance system for manufacturing and service industries. (12)

ISO 14000. Series of international standards designed to promote effective environmental management systems in organizations, regardless of size or industry. (12)

J

jargon. Language specific to a line of work or area of expertise. (4)

job. Work a person does regularly in order to earn money. (19)

job analysis. Process that identifies the job requirements for a position, employee qualifications needed, and metrics used to evaluate performance. (6)

job application. Form with spaces for contact information, education, and work experience. (20)

job shadowing. Observing a certain type of work by accompanying an experienced worker as he or she performs the assigned job. (6)

job sharing. Arrangement in which two part-time employees handle the responsibilities of a single full-time position. (6)

job-specific skill. Critical skill necessary to perform the required work-related tasks of a position. (19)

joint venture. Partnership of two or more companies that work together for a specific business purpose. (15)

just-in-time (JIT) inventory-control system. Strategy of managing inventory that keeps a minimal amount of raw materials on hand to meet production needs. (12)

K

keyword. Word or term that specifically relates to the functions of the position for which the employer is hiring. (20)

L

labor force. All the people in a nation who are capable of working and want to work. (14)

labor relations laws. Laws that give employees the right to organize and collectively bargain for rights. (7)

labor union. Group of workers united as a single body to protect and advance the rights and interests of its members; also called *organized labor*. (7)

language. System of symbols, signs, and gestures as a means of communication and the rules of using them. (9)

law of diminishing marginal utility. States that the marginal benefit of using each additional unit of an item tends to decrease as the quantity used increases. (4)

law of supply and demand. States that the price of a product is determined by the relationship of the supply of a product and the demand for a product. (14)

leadership. Ability to influence others to reach a goal. (8)

leading. Process of influencing others to work toward the attainment of common goals. (1)

lean manufacturing. Business practice that involves a continuous effort to reduce waste or any activity or practice that uses resources that do not add to the overall value of goods or services produced; also known as *lean production*. (12)

lease. Contract to rent an item or property. (13)

legal environment. Laws and regulations of a country that can affect business operations. (15)

letters of credit. Documents used to guarantee payment in other countries. (15)

libel. Publishing a false statement about someone that causes others to have a bad or untrue opinion of him or her. (21)

licensing. Occurs when a business sells the right to manufacture its products or use its trademark. (15)

lifelong learning. Voluntary attainment of knowledge throughout life. (19)

limited liability company (LLC). Form of business ownership that combines features of a corporation with those of a sole proprietorship and partnership. (13)

liquidation. Refers to the sale of all assets of a business, including inventory, equipment, and buildings. (16)

listening. Intellectual process that combines hearing with evaluating. (9)

logistics. Planning and managing the flow of goods, services, and people to a destination. (15)

M

Malcolm Baldrige National Quality Award (MBNQA). Award that raises awareness of quality management and recognizes US organizations that have implemented successful quality-management systems. (12)

malware. Term given to software programs that are intended to damage, destroy, or steal data; short for *malicious software*. (21)

management. Process of controlling and making decisions about an organization, as well as overseeing others to ensure activities are performed efficiently and effectively. (1)

management information. Data used for strategic purposes. (4)

Management Information System (MIS). Integrated system of computer hardware and software that gathers information and presents it in a manner to be used in the decision-making process. (3)

management theory. Idea or collection of ideas used as a set of guidelines for managing an organization. (2)

manager. Person who directs and oversees the work of others in order to achieve the goals of an organization. (1)

managerial role. Actions and behaviors that managers are expected to perform in an organization. (1)

manufacturer. Business that uses raw materials from other producers to convert them into finished products that can be sold to customers. (13)

manufacturing operations. All the activities involved in operating a manufacturing facility, often a factory. (12)

marginal benefit. Change in total benefit of using one additional unit. (4)

marginal cost. Change in total cost of using one additional unit. (4)

market. Anywhere buyers and sellers meet to buy and sell goods and services. (13)

market development. Expanding existing products to new physical locations or target markets. (16)

market economy. Economic system in which individuals and businesses are free to make their own economic decisions. (14)

market penetration. Involves increasing sales in the existing target market. (16)

market research. Gathering and analyzing information to help make sound marketing decisions. (3)

market risk. Potential that the target market for new goods or services is much less than originally thought. (17)

market segmentation. Process of dividing a large market into smaller groups. (18)

market structure. How a market is organized based on the number of businesses competing for sales in an industry. (14)

marketing. Consists of dynamic activities that identify, anticipate, and satisfy customer demand while making a profit. (18)

marketing concept. Approach to business that focuses on satisfying customers as the means of achieving profit goals for the company. (18)

marketing mix. Strategy for using the elements of product, price, place, and promotion. (18)

marketing plan. Document that describes business and marketing objectives and the strategies and tactics used to achieve them. (18)

marketing strategy. Decision made about how to execute the marketing plan and meet the goals of the business. (18)

marketing tactic. Specific activity implemented to carry out a marketing strategy. (18)
markup. Amount added to the cost to determine the selling price. (18)
maturity stage. Occurs when product sales are stable. (18)
mediation. Inclusion of a neutral person to help the conflicting parties resolve their dispute and reach an agreement. (8)
merger. Combining two companies into one new company. (16)
metrics. Standards of measurement. (18)
micromanagement. Management style that occurs when a manager closely controls or monitors the work of his or her employees. (1)
middle management. Level of management between the senior level and the supervisory level. (1)
mission statement. Organization's message to customers about why the business exists. (3)
mixed economy. Both the government and individuals make decisions about economic resources. (14)
mock interview. Practice interview conducted with another person. (20)
monetary policy. Actions taken by a central bank to regulate the money supply and interest rates. (14)
morals. Individual's ideas of what is right and wrong. (5)
motivation. Force that inspires employees to want to perform their best and achieve results. (8)
multinational corporation. Business that operates in more than one country. (15)

N

natural risk. Situation caused by acts of nature. (17)
nature of business. Industry in which a business is categorized. (13)
need-based award. Financial-aid awards available for students and families who meet certain economic requirements. (19)
negotiate. To have a formal discussion between two or more people in an attempt to reach an agreement. (6)
negotiation. Occurs when individuals involved in a conflict come together to discuss a compromise. (8)
net profit ratio. Illustrates profits generated per dollar of sales. (11)
netiquette. Etiquette used when communicating electronically; also known as *digital etiquette.* (21)
networking. Talking with others and establishing relationships with people who can help you achieve career, education, or personal goals. (19)
new product. Product that is different in some way from existing products. (18)
noise. Anything that interferes with clear, effective communication. (9)
nonverbal communication. Actions or behaviors, as opposed to words, that send messages. (9)
not-for-profit organization. Organization that exists to serve some public purpose; also known as *nonprofit organization* or *nonprofit.* (1)
not-for-profit school. School that returns the money it earns back into the school. (19)

O

occupational training. Education that prepares a person for a specific type of work. (19)
offer. Proposal to provide a good or service. (13)
office politics. Behaviors that individuals practice to gain advantages over others in the workplace. (10)
onboarding. System or process of integrating a new employee into the organization. (6)
open source. Software that makes its source code available to the public at no charge. (21)
operating budget. Projection of the sales revenue that will be earned and the expenses that will be incurred during a future period of time. (4)
operating ratio. Shows the relationship of expenses to sales. (11)
operational plan. Plan that defines the day-to-day tasks and activities that employees must perform to meet company goals. (3)
operations management. Area of management that focuses on the production of goods and services. (12)
operations manager. Person who is responsible for overseeing the production of goods and services for an organization. (12)
opportunity cost. Value of the option that was given up. (4)
oral language. System in which words are spoken to express ideas or emotions. (9)
organic growth. Occurs by expanding the current business. (16)

organization. Body of people that come together for a specific purpose. (1)
organization chart. Diagram that shows the structure of an organization. (5)
organizational change. Any modification to the structure of an organization, its people, or technology. (7)
organizational design. Identifies the hierarchy of employees within the business. (5)
organizational structure. Identifies the hierarchy of employees and determines their roles, authority, and communication flow within an organization. (5)
organizing. Coordination of activities and resources needed to accomplish a plan. (1)
orientation. Welcoming of a new person to a company. (6)

P

parliamentary procedure. Process for holding meetings so they are orderly and democratic. (8)
partnership. Association of two or more people who own a business with the objective of earning a profit. (13)
passive listening. Casually listening to someone talk and is appropriate when interaction is not required with the person speaking. (10)
peak. Highest point in the business cycle and occurs at the end of an economic expansion. (14)
peer. Person of equal standing or work position. (9)
peer-to-peer lending. Borrowing money from investors via a website; also known as *social lending*. (16)
performance evaluation. Formal assessment of an employee's job performance and progress made toward achieving set goals; also known as an *appraisal*. (6)
performance management. Manner in which a human resources department can measure the effectiveness of each employee. (6)
perpetual inventory system. Method of tracking inventory that shows the quantity on hand at all times. (12)
personal development. Education that provides opportunities for an individual to develop talents and skills to become more confident and self-aware. (6)
personal leave. Few days each year employees can use for personal reasons. (6)
PEST analysis. Evaluation of the political, economic, social, and technological factors in a certain market or geographic region that may affect the success of a business. (3)
philanthropy. Promoting the welfare of others. (13)
phishing. Use of fraudulent e-mails and copies of valid websites to trick people into providing private and confidential data. (21)
piecework. Wage based on a rate per unit of work completed. (6)
piracy. Unethical and illegal copying or downloading of software, files, and other protected material. (21)
place. Activities involved in getting products to end users. (18)
plagiarism. Claiming another person's material as your own, which is both unethical and illegal. (21)
plan. Outline of the actions needed to accomplish a goal. (1)
planning. Process of setting goals and objectives and deciding how to accomplish them. (1)
planning tool. Instrument or document that guides a plan into action. (3)
policy. Set of rules and regulations that guide the decision-making process. (3)
political environment. Refers to the economic and governmental actions that affect the operations of business. (15)
portfolio. Selection of related materials that an individual collects and organizes to show his or her qualifications, skills, and talents that support an individual's career or personal goals. (20)
postgraduate education. Education beyond a master degree. (19)
postsecondary education. Any education achieved after high school. (19)
premium. Amount the insured pays for insurance coverage. (17)
price. Amount of money requested or exchanged for a good or service. (18)
primary research. First-hand research conducted by a researcher. (3)
pro forma statement. Financial statement based on estimates of future business performance, sales, and expenses. (16)
procedure. Description of how to complete a task and how a policy will be applied. (3)

producer. Business that creates goods and services used by individuals, other businesses, and the government. (13)
product. Any good or service that can be bought or sold. (18)
product life cycle. Stages a product goes through from its beginning to end. (18)
product manager. Person responsible for evaluating and managing all aspects of a product from its inception and through the entire product life cycle. (18)
product mix. All the goods and services a business sells. (18)
production process. All the activities required to create a product. (12)
productivity. Measure of output accomplished by an employee in a specific amount of time. (1)
professional development. Education for people who have already completed their formal schooling and training to gain new skills and knowledge needed for growth and career development. (6)
professionalism. Act of exhibiting appropriate character, judgment, and behavior by a person trained to perform a job. (10)
profit. Difference between the income earned and expenses incurred by a business during a specified time. (13)
project manager. Person assigned to develop and execute a project plan. (5)
promotion. Process of communicating with potential customers in an effort to influence their buying behavior. (18)
promotional mix. Combination of the elements used to market products. (18)
proprietary information. Information a company wishes to keep private; also known as *trade secrets*. (5)
protectionism. Policy of protecting a country's domestic industries by enforcing trade regulations on foreign competitors. (15)
protocol. Set of customs that define how certain levels of employees interact with each other. (9)
public domain. Material not owned by a specific person and can be used without permission. (21)
pure risk. Risk with a possibility of loss but no possibility of gain. (17)

Q

qualitative. Data based on judgment. (4)
quality. Indicator of a product's excellence. (11)
quality characteristic. Something that makes an item distinctive. (12)
quality control. Activity of checking raw materials received or products produced to ensure the quality meets expectations. (12)
quality management. Formal system that documents each step of processes and procedures to achieve company goals and standards. (12)
quality standard. Established level of acceptability for the production of goods and services. (11)
quantitative. Data based on facts and figures. (4)
quantitative approach. Management theory that uses measurable techniques to improve decision-making in an organization; sometimes referred to as *management science*. (2)
quantity standard. Estimated or predetermined quantity of work to be completed in a specified amount of time. (11)
quota. Limit on the amount of a product imported into a country during a specific timeframe. (15)

R

ransomware. Type of malware that seizes control of a computer and demands payment from the owner to unlock it. (21)
ratio. Comparison of one figure to another. (11)
ratio analysis. Process of using ratios to compare the relationship between financial statement items. (11)
raw materials inventory. Selection of raw materials needed to produce a finished product. (12)
recession. Period of slow or no economic growth. (14)
recruiting. Process of finding people who are qualified for a position. (6)
reference. Person who can comment on the qualifications, work ethic, personal qualities, and work-related aspects of another person. (20)
relationship management. Processes that HR facilitates to ensure that employee relationships in an organization are productive and meet company goals. (7)

resilience. Person's ability to cope with and recover from change or adversity. (10)
resource. Supply of money, labor, materials, and other items that a person or organization can draw from in order to meet needs. (1)
résumé. Document that profiles a person's career goals, education, and work history. (20)
retailer. Business that buys products from wholesalers or directly from producers and sells them to consumers to make a profit. (13)
revenue. Money that a business makes from the goods and services it sells; also called *income* or *sales*. (3)
risk. Possibility of suffering loss or harm. (17)
risk management. Process of evaluating risks and taking steps to avoid or minimize loss should it occur. (17)

S

S corporation. Form of business ownership that is organized as a corporation but is taxed as a partnership. (13)
salary. Fixed payment for work and expressed as an annual figure. (6)
sales and service contracts. List the goods or services provided by a business and the price the customer pays in exchange. (13)
sales budget. Projection of sales in both units and dollars. (4)
sales forecast. Prediction of future sales based on past sales and a market analysis for a specific time period; also known as *projection*. (3)
saturated market. Market in which most of the potential customers who need, want, and can afford a product have bought it. (18)
scarcity. Situation that develops when there are not enough resources to meet needs and wants which, in turn, creates an economic problem. (14)
schedule. Plan that identifies the time and resources needed to complete tasks and activities. (3)
scholarship. Financial aid that may be based on financial need or some type of merit or accomplishment. (19)
scientific management. Classical management theory that uses science to study worker productivity and workflow. (2)
secondary research. Data already collected and recorded by someone else. (3)
selection process. Act of reviewing job applications and résumés and choosing candidates for potential interviews. (6)
self-funding. Owner uses his or her own money to start a business; also known as *bootstrapping*. (16)
senior management. Highest level of management in an organization; also called *top management*. (1)
service operations. All the activities involved in delivering a service to a customer. (12)
sexual harassment. Unwelcome sexual advances, requests for sexual favors, and other verbal or physical conduct of a sexual nature when either the conduct is made as a term or condition of an individual's employment, education, living environment, or participation in a University community. (7)
Six Sigma. Trademarked quality-improvement program that uses a set of tools designed to improve business processes by finding and eliminating errors that lead to defects in a product. (12)
skill. Something an individual does well. (19)
slander. Speaking a false statement about someone that causes others to have a bad opinion of him or her. (21)
small-group communication. Communication that occurs with 3 to 20 people. (9)
SMART goal. Goal that is specific, measurable, attainable, realistic, and timely. (3)
social audit. Review of a company's involvement in socially responsible activities. (13)
social responsibility. Behaving with sensitivity to social, environmental, and economic issues. (5)
socialism. System in which the government owns and controls most of the factors of production but allows more ownership of personal property. (14)
sociocultural environment. Refers to the external environment that focuses on the society and culture of a country. (15)
soft skills. Skills used to help an individual find a job, perform in the workplace, and gain success in a job or career. (1)
software virus. Computer program designed to negatively impact a computer system by infecting other files. (21)
sole proprietorship. Business owned by one person. (13)

sourcing. Finding suppliers of materials needed for production. (12)

span of control. Number of employees who report to a manager; also called *span of management*. (5)

specialization. Focus on the production of specific products so that a greater degree of efficiency is gained. (5)

speculative risk. Risk that can result in financial gain, financial loss, or nothing. (17)

spyware. Software that spies on a computer. (21)

staffing. Process of recruiting, hiring, training, evaluating, and compensating employees. (1)

standard. Established measure against which performance can be compared; also called a *control*. (11)

Standard English. Refers to English language usage that follows accepted rules for spelling, grammar, and punctuation. (9)

standard of living. Level of material comfort measured by the goods, services, and luxuries available. (13)

startup. Entrepreneurial venture of creating a new business. (16)

stereotyping. Belief or generalization about a group of people with a given set of characteristics. (5)

strategic plan. Plan designed to achieve the long-term goals of an organization as a whole. (3)

strategic planning process. Involves setting goals and allocating the resources necessary to achieve them. (3)

stress. Body's reaction to increased demands or dangerous situations. (7)

stress management. Variety of strategies used to cope with stress and limit its effects. (7)

stress-management skills. Skills that enable an individual to identify and control stress. (7)

succession plan. Details who will operate the company in the event the owner leaves the company, retires, or passes away. (16)

succession planning. Continuous process of identifying and developing new employees to replace employees in leadership positions who leave. (6)

supervisory management. Management level of individuals who coordinate and supervise the activities and duties of employees; also known as *first-line management*. (1)

supply chain. Businesses, people, and activities involved in turning raw materials into products and delivering them to end users. (12)

sustainability. Creating and maintaining conditions under which humans and nature can coexist both now and in the future. (13)

SWOT analysis. Identification of an organization's strengths, weaknesses, opportunities, and threats. (3)

T

table. Visual that displays information in columns and rows and often used to compare data. (4)

tactic. Strategy or action planned to reach the end goal. (3)

tactical plan. Plan that involves activities that are needed to implement strategic plans defined by senior management. (3)

talent management. Anticipation of employees needed in an organization and planning required to meet those needs. (6)

target market. Specific group of customers whose needs and wants a company will focus on satisfying. (18)

tariff. Governmental tax on imported goods. (15)

teamwork. Cooperative efforts by individual members to achieve a goal. (5)

technical skills. Specific skills managers need to perform duties related to their area of management. (1)

technological environment. External factors in technology that affect the way business is conducted. (15)

technology infrastructure. Hardware, software, and related equipment used to support IT. (4)

telecommuting. Arrangement in which employees work away from the business site. (6)

termination. Process of ending the relationship between an employer and an employee. (6)

time management. Practice of organizing time and work assignments to increase personal efficiency. (10)

time standard. Estimated or predetermined amount of time necessary to complete a single task or activity. (11)

total quality management (TQM). Management philosophy in which the success of an organization is directly related to customer satisfaction. (2)

trade agreement. Document listing the conditions and terms for importing and exporting products between countries. (15)
trade barrier. Any governmental action taken to control or limit the amount of imports. (15)
trade credit. Credit offered by a business to its customers that enables customers to buy now and pay later. (17)
trade policy. Body of laws related to the exchange of goods and services for international trade. (15)
trade-off. Choice that is given up when the business makes one choice over another. (4)
trade sanction. Embargo that affects only certain goods. (15)
trading bloc. Group of countries joined together to trade as if they were a single country. (15)
trait. Characteristic that a person portrays. (8)
transmission. Act of sending a message. (9)
trough. Lowest stage of a business cycle and occurs at the end of a recession. (14)
turnover. When an employee leaves the organization because he or she chooses to do so or is terminated by the employer. (6)
turnover rate. Percentage of employees leaving a company within a certain period of time, typically a year. (6)

U

ultimatum. Final proposal or statement of conditions. (8)
uncontrollable risk. Situation that cannot be predicted or covered by purchasing insurance. (17)
unemployment rate. Percentage of the civilian labor force that is unemployed. (14)
uninsurable risk. Loss that insurance will not cover. (17)
unity of command. States that each employee reports to one manager. (5)

V

value. Relative worth of something. (4)
value proposition. Explanation of the value of a certain product over others that are similar. (18)
values. Principles and beliefs that a person considers important. (19)
variance. Difference between the standard and the actual performance. (11)
venture capital. Investment from others who are willing to help fund a business in exchange for an ownership share and an active role in the company. (16)
vision statement. Organization's statement of what the business aspires to accomplish. (3)

W

wage. Payment for work and usually calculated on an hourly, daily, or weekly basis. (6)
wholesaler. Business that purchases large quantities of products directly from producers and sells the products in smaller quantities to retailers; also known as *distributor*. (13)
work in process inventory. Consists of products that are partially completed. (12)
work-life balance. Amount of time an individual spends working compared to the amount of time spent in a personal life. (6)
workplace bullying. Intentional or repeated mistreatment, verbal abuse, threatening, or any action that prevents a person from doing his or her job without fear. (7)
workplace rules. Established guidelines for behavior in the workplace. (7)
work-study program. Part-time job on a college campus that is subsidized by the government. (19)

Index

D

E

F

G

H

I

J

K

L

M

N

O

P

T

U

V

W

Z